12th Workshop on Computational Approaches to Subjectivity, Sentiment and Social Media Analysis (WASSA 2022)

Dublin, Ireland
26 May 2022

ISBN: 978-1-7138-6754-8

Printed from e-media with permission by:

Curran Associates, Inc.
57 Morehouse Lane
Red Hook, NY 12571

Some format issues inherent in the e-media version may also appear in this print version.

Printed with permission by Curran Associates, Inc. (2023)

Association for Computational Linguistics
209 N. Eighth Street
Stroudsburg, Pennsylvania 18360

Phone: 1-570-476-8006
Fax: 1-570-476-0860

acl@aclweb.org

Additional copies of this publication are available from:

Curran Associates, Inc.
57 Morehouse Lane
Red Hook, NY 12571 USA
Phone: 845-758-0400
Fax: 845-758-2633
Email: curran@proceedings.com
Web: www.proceedings.com

WASSA 2022

The 12th Workshop on Computational Approaches to Subjectivity, Sentiment & Social Media Analysis

Proceedings of the Workshop

May 26, 2022

The WASSA organizers gratefully acknowledge the support from the following sponsors.

Gold

Google

Introduction

The automatic analysis of Sentiment, Subjectivity, and Emotion (SSE) is once again the focus of WASSA. However, the breadth of each of these areas has expanded, both in the complexity of the tasks, as well as the number of applications where these techniques are applied.

On the one hand, more and more submissions approach more complex tasks in a large number of languages which were previously absent. On the other hand, many of the techniques developed in SSE have been applied to new tasks, such as hate speech, fake news detection, or narrative analysis.

This year we reran and expanded the Shared Task on Empathy and Personality Detection and Emotion Classification. The shared task aimed at developing models which can predict empathy and emotion based on essays written in reaction to news articles where there is harm to a person, group, or other.

For the main workshop, we accepted 14 papers as long, another 4 as short, and accepted 4 papers committed through the ACL Rolling Review system (2 long and 2 short), giving a total of 23/37 papers accepted (62%). For the Empathy and Personality Detection and Emotion Classification Shared Task, we received 10 system description paper submissions, out of which we accepted 10. 33 papers in total will be presented at the workshop.

In addition to the regular papers, we are glad that Professor Dirk Hovy from Bocconi University and Professor Rada Mihalcea from the University of Michigan accepted our invitation to give the keynote at the WASSA workshop.

The program is both well-connected to previous topics of the workshop and advances the current state-of-the-art in the field. It includes such diverse topics as multilingual sentiment and emotion analysis, stance detection or irony detection. Others include new tasks building upon this previous knowledge, e.g., politeness generation, personality profiling, ingroup vs. onlooker detection, or narrative analysis. This year we additionally give a best paper award to the paper "Distinguishing In-Groups and Onlookers by Language Use" by Joshua R. Minot, Milo Z. Trujillo, Samuel F. Rosenblatt, Guillermo de Anda Jáuregui, Emily Moog, Briane Paul V. Samson, Laurent Hébert-Dufresne, and Allison M. Roth.

We would like to thank the ACL Organizers and Workshop chairs for their help and support during the preparation. We thank Google for their gold sponsorship. We also thank the OpenReview support team for their technical support. Finally, we especially thank the program committee for the time and effort they spent on reviewing.

Jeremy Barnes, Orphée De Clercq, Valentin Barriere, Shabnam Tafreshi, Sawsan Alqahtani, João Sedoc, Roman Klinger, Alexandra Balahur

WASSA 2022 Chairs

Organizing Committee

Program Chairs

Jeremy Barnes, University of the Basque Country UPV/EHU, Spain
Orphée De Clercq, Ghent University, Belgium
Valentin Barriere, European Commission's Joint Research Center of Ispra, Italy
Shabnam Tafreshi, University of Maryland, U.S.A.
Sawsan Alqahtani, Princess Nourah bint Abdulrahman University, Saudi Arabia
João Sedoc, New York University, U.S.A.
Roman Klinger, University of Stuttgart, Germany
Alexandra Balahur, European Commission's Joint Research Center of Ispra, Italy

Program Committee

Program Committee

Wazir Ali, ILMA University Karachi, Pakistan
Kaveri Anuranjana, Saarland University, Germany
Cristina Bosco, University of Torino, Italy
Sven Buechel, Friedrich-Schiller Universität Jena, Germany
Luna Debruyne, Ghent University, Belgium
Lingjia Deng, Bloomberg, U.S.A.
Tommaso Fornaciari, Bocconi University, Italy
Michael Gamon, Microsoft Research, U.S.A.
Elma Kerz, Rheinisch Westfälische Technische Hochschule Aachen, Germany
Mayank Kulkarni, Bloomberg, U.S.A.
Sotiris Lamprinidis, Corti, Denmark
Els Lefever, Ghent University, Belgium
Nikola Ljubešić, Jožef Stefan Institute, Slovenia
Edison Marrese-Taylor, National Institute of Advanced Industrial Science and Technology, Japan
Ashutosh Modi, IIT Kanpur, India
Günter Neumann, German Research Center for AI, Germany
Laura Ana Maria Oberlaender, University of Stuttgart, Germany
Constantin Orasan, University of Surrey, United Kingdom
Jessica Ouyang, University of Texas at Dallas, U.S.A.
Sean Papay, University of Stuttgart, Germany
Daniel Preotiuc-Pietro, Bloomberg, U.S.A.
Paolo Rosso, Universitat Politècnica de València, Spain
Salim Sazzed, Old Dominion University, U.S.A.
Pranaydeep Singh, Ghent University, Belgium
Enrica Troiano, University of Stuttgart, Germany
Saif Tumrani, The University of Lahore, Pakistan
Piek Vossen, Vrije Universiteit Amsterdam, The Netherlands
Michael Wiegand, Alpen-Adria Universität Klagenfurt, Germany
Eugene Yang, Johns Hopkins University, U.S.A.
Taras Zagibalov, University of Sussex, United Kingdom
David Samuel, University of Oslo, Norway
Rodrigo Agerri, University of the Basque Country UPV/EHU, Spain
Soumya Vadlamannati, Bloomberg, U.S.A.
Jenny Chen, Bloomberg, U.S.A.
Silvio Amir, Northeastern University, U.S.A.
Somnath Banerjee, Università Milano Bicocca, Italy
Maaz Amjad, Instituto Politécnico Nacional, Mexico

Invited Speakers

Dirk Hovy, Bocconi University, Italy
Rada Mihalcea, University of Michigan, U.S.A.

Table of Contents

Program

Thursday, May 26, 2022

09:00 - 09:10	*Opening Remarks*
09:10 - 10:30	*Session 1*
	Assessment of Massively Multilingual Sentiment Classifiers Krzysztof Rajda, Lukasz Augustyniak, Piotr Gramacki, Marcin Gruza, Szymon Woźniak and Tomasz Jan Kajdanowicz
	English-Malay Word Embeddings Alignment for Cross-lingual Emotion Classification with Hierarchical Attention Network Ying Hao Lim and Jasy Suet Yan Liew
	Uncertainty Regularized Multi-Task Learning Kourosh Meshgi, Maryam Sadat Mirzaei and Satoshi Sekine
	Improving Social Meaning Detection with Pragmatic Masking and Surrogate Fine-Tuning Chiyu Zhang and Muhammad Abdul-Mageed
10:30 - 11:00	*Coffee Break*
11:00 - 12:00	*Shared Task*
	WASSA 2022 Shared Task: Predicting Empathy, Emotion and Personality in Reaction to News Stories Valentin Barriere, Shabnam Tafreshi, João Sedoc and Sawsan Alqahtani
	IUCL at WASSA 2022 Shared Task: A Text-only Approach to Empathy and Emotion Detection Yue Chen, Yingnan Ju and Sandra Kübler
	Continuing Pre-trained Model with Multiple Training Strategies for Emotional Classification Bin Li, Yixuan Weng, Qiya Song, Bin Sun and Shutao Li
12:00 - 13:00	*Invited Talk 1 - Dirk Hovy*
13:00 - 14:00	*Lunch Break*
14:00 - 15:00	*Invited Talk 2 - Rada Mihalcea*

Thursday, May 26, 2022 (continued)

15:00 - 15:30 *Break*

15:30 - 16:15 *In-Person Poster Session*

On the Complementarity of Images and Text for the Expression of Emotions in Social Media
Anna Khlyzova, Carina Silberer and Roman Klinger

Multiplex Anti-Asian Sentiment before and during the Pandemic: Introducing New Datasets from Twitter Mining
Hao Lin, Pradeep Kumar Nalluri, Lantian Li, Yifan Sun and Yongjun Zhang

"splink" is happy and "phrouth" is scary: Emotion Intensity Analysis for Nonsense Words
Valentino Sabbatino, Enrica Troiano, Antje Schweitzer and Roman Klinger

Irony Detection for Dutch: a Venture into the Implicit
Aaron Maladry, Els Lefever, Cynthia Van Hee and Veronique Hoste

Items from Psychometric Tests as Training Data for Personality Profiling Models of Twitter Users
Anne Kreuter, Kai Sassenberg and Roman Klinger

16:15 - 17:15 *Session 2*

Distinguishing In-Groups and Onlookers by Language Use
Joshua R Minot, Milo Z Trujillo, Samuel F Rosenblatt, Guillermo De Anda-Jáuregui, Emily Moog, Allison M. Roth, Briane Paul Samson and Laurent Hébert-Dufresne

"splink" is happy and "phrouth" is scary: Emotion Intensity Analysis for Nonsense Words
Valentino Sabbatino, Enrica Troiano, Antje Schweitzer and Roman Klinger

Can Emotion Carriers Explain Automatic Sentiment Prediction? A Study on Personal Narratives
Seyed Mahed Mousavi, Gabriel Roccabruna, Aniruddha Tammewar, Steve Azzolin and Giuseppe Riccardi

17:15 - 18:00 *Virtual Poster Session*

On the Complementarity of Images and Text for the Expression of Emotions in Social Media
Anna Khlyzova, Carina Silberer and Roman Klinger

On the Complementarity of Images and Text for the Expression of Emotions in Social Media

Anna Khlyzova[1,2], **Carina Silberer**[2] and **Roman Klinger**[2]
[1]Computer Science and Engineering, University of South Florida, USA
[2]Institut für Maschinelle Sprachverarbeitung, University of Stuttgart, Germany
{anna.khlyzova,carina.silberer,roman.klinger}
@ims.uni-stuttgart.de

Abstract

Authors of posts in social media communicate their emotions and what causes them with text and images. While there is work on emotion and stimulus detection for each modality separately, it is yet unknown if the modalities contain complementary emotion information in social media. We aim at filling this research gap and contribute a novel, annotated corpus of English multimodal Reddit posts. On this resource, we develop models to automatically detect the relation between image and text, an emotion stimulus category and the emotion class. We evaluate if these tasks require both modalities and find for the image–text relations, that text alone is sufficient for most categories (complementary, illustrative, opposing): the information in the text allows to predict if an image is required for emotion understanding. The emotions of anger and sadness are best predicted with a multimodal model, while text alone is sufficient for disgust, joy, and surprise. Stimuli depicted by objects, animals, food, or a person are best predicted by image-only models, while multimodal models are most effective on art, events, memes, places, or screenshots.

1 Introduction

The main task in emotion analysis in natural language processing is emotion classification into predefined sets of emotion categories, for instance, corresponding to basic emotions (fear, anger, joy, sadness, surprise, disgust, anticipation, and trust, Ekman, 1992; Plutchik, 1980). In psychology, emotions are commonly considered a reaction to an event which consists of a synchronized change of organismic subsystems, namely neurophysiological changes, reactions, action tendencies, the subjective feeling, and a cognitive appraisal (Scherer et al., 2001). These theories recently received increasing attention, for instance, by comparing the way how emotions are expressed, based on these components (Casel et al., 2021), and by modelling emotions in dimensional models of affect (Buechel and Hahn, 2017) or appraisal (Hofmann et al., 2020). Further, the acknowledgment of emotions as a reaction to some relevant event (Scherer, 2005) leads to the development of stimulus detection systems. This task is formulated in a token-labeling setup (Song and Meng, 2015; Bostan et al., 2020; Kim and Klinger, 2018; Ghazi et al., 2015; Oberländer and Klinger, 2020, i.a.), as clause classification (Gui et al., 2017, 2016; Gao et al., 2017; Xia and Ding, 2019; Oberländer and Klinger, 2020, i.a.), or as a classification task into a predefined inventory of relevant stimuli (Mohammad et al., 2014).

In social media, users express emotions including text and images. Most attention has been devoted to Twitter, due to its easy-to-use API and popularity (Mohammad, 2012; Schuff et al., 2017; Wang et al., 2012). However, this platform has a tendency to be text-focused, and has therefore not triggered too much attention towards other modalities. Although text may be informative enough to recognize an emotion in many cases, images may modulate the meaning, or sometimes solely convey the emotion itself (see examples in Figure 1). The growing popularity of vision-centered platforms like TikTok or Instagram, and lack of research on multimodal social media constitute a research gap.

With this paper, we study how users on social media make use of images and text jointly to communicate their emotion and the stimulus of that emotion. We assume that linking depictions of stimuli to the text supports emotion recognition across modalities. We study multimodal posts on the social media platform Reddit[1], given its wide adoption, the frequently found use of images and text, and the available programming interfaces to access the data (Baumgartner et al., 2020a). Our goal is to understand how users choose to use an image

[1]https://www.reddit.com/

Proceedings of the 12th Workshop on Computational Approaches to Subjectivity, Sentiment & Social Media Analysis, pages 1 - 15
May 26, 2022

(a) joy/complementary/animal. https://www.reddit.com/r/happy/comments/j76dog/my_everyday_joy_is_to_see_my_adorable_cat_smiles/

(b) fear/complementary/animal. https://www.reddit.com/r/WTF/comments/k2es5l/dont_move_to_australia_unless_you_can_handle/

(c) surprise/complementary/object. https://www.reddit.com/r/What/comments/exh0ms/why_didnt_it_fall/

Figure 1: Example of posts from Reddit (annotation are emotion/relation/stimulus category).

in addition to text, and the role of the relation, the emotion, and the stimulus for this decision. Further we analyze if the classification performance benefits from a joint model across modalities. Figure 1 shows examples for Reddit posts. In Figure 1a, both image and text would presumably allow to infer the correct emotion even when considered in isolation. In Figure 1b, additional knowledge of the complementary role of the picture depicting an animal can inform an emotion recognition model. In Figure 1c the image alone would not be sufficient to infer the emotion, but the text alone is.

We therefore contribute (1) a new corpus of multimodal emotional posts from Reddit, which is annotated for authors' emotions, image–text relations, and emotion stimuli. We (2) analyze the relations of the annotated classes and find that certain emotions are likely to appear with certain relations and emotion stimuli. Further, we (3) use a transformer-based language model (pretrained RoBERTa model, Liu et al., 2019) and a residual neural network (Resnet50, He et al., 2016) to create classification models for the prediction of each of the three classes mentioned above. We analyze for which classification tasks multimodal models show an improvement over unimodal models. Our corpus is publicly available at https://www.ims.uni-stuttgart.de/data/mmemo.

2 Related Work

Emotion Analysis. Emotion analysis has a rich history in various domains, such as fairy tales (Alm et al., 2005), email writing (Liu et al., 2003), news headlines (Strapparava and Mihalcea, 2007), or blog posts (Mihalcea and Liu, 2006; Aman and Szpakowicz, 2008; Neviarouskaya et al., 2010). The focus of our study is on emotion analysis in social media, which has also received considerable attention (Purver and Battersby, 2012; Wang et al., 2012; Colnerič and Demšar, 2018; Mohammad, 2012; Schuff et al., 2017, i.a.). Twitter[2] is a popular social media platform for emotion analysis, in both natural language processing (NLP) and computer vision. We point the reader to recent shared tasks for an overview of the methods that lead to the current state-of-the-art performance (Klinger et al., 2018; Mohammad et al., 2018).

One of the questions that needs to be answered when developing an emotion classification system is that of the appropriate set of emotions. There are two main theories regarding emotion models in psychology that found application in NLP: discrete sets of emotions and dimensional models. Psychological models that provide discrete sets of emotions include Ekman's model of basic emotions (anger, disgust, surprise, joy, sadness, and fear, Ekman, 1992) and Plutchik's wheel of emotions (adding trust and anticipation, Plutchik, 1980, 2001). Dimensional models define where emotions lie in a vector space in which the dimensions have another meaning, including affect (Russell, 1980; Bradley et al., 1992) and cognitive event appraisal (Scherer, 2005; Hofmann et al., 2020; Shaikh et al., 2009). In our study, we use the eight emotions from the Plutchik's wheel of emotions.

Multimodal Analyses. The area of emotion analysis also received attention from the computer vi-

[2] https://www.twitter.com/

sion community. A common approach is to use transfer learning from general image classifiers (He and Ding, 2019) or the analysis of facial emotion expressions, with features of muscle movement (De Silva et al., 1997) or deep learning (Li and Deng, 2020). Dellagiacoma et al. (2011) use texture and color features to analyze social media content. Other useful properties of images for emotion analysis include the occurrence of people, faces, shapes of objects, and color distributions (Zhao et al., 2018; Lu et al., 2012).

Such in-depth analyses are related to stimulus detection. Peng et al. (2016) detect emotion-eliciting image regions. They show, on a Flickr image dataset, that not only objects (Wu et al., 2020) and salient regions (Zheng et al., 2017) have an impact on elicited emotions, but also contextual background. Yang et al. (2018), inter alia, show that it is beneficial for emotion classification to explicitly integrate visual information from emotion-eliciting regions. Similarly, Fan et al. (2018) study the relationship between emotion-eliciting image content and human visual attention.

Image–Text Relation. A set of work aimed at understanding the relation between images and text. Marsh and White (2003) establish a taxonomy of 49 functions of illustrations relative to text in US government publications. The relations contain categories like "elicit emotion", "motivate", "explains", or "compares" and "contrasts". Martinec and Salway (2005) aim at understanding both the role of an image and of text.

In contrast to these studies which did not develop machine learning approaches, Zhang et al. (2018) develop automatic classification methods for detection of relations between the image and a slogan in advertisments. They detect if the image and the text make the same point, if one modality is unclear without the other, if the modalities, when considered separately, imply opposing ideas, and if one of the modalities is sufficient to convey the message. Weiland et al. (2018) focus on detecting if captions of images contain complementary information. Vempala and Preoţiuc-Pietro (2019) infer relationship categories between the text and image of Twitter posts to see how the meaning of the entire tweet is composed. Kruk et al. (2019) focus on understanding the intent of the author of an Instagram post and develop a hierarchy of classes, namely *advocative, promotive, exhibitionist, expressive, informative, entertainment, provocative/discrimination*, and *provocative/controversial*. They also analyze the relation between the modalities with the classes *divergent, additive*, or *parallel*. Our work is similar to the two previously mentioned papers, as the detection which emotion is expressed with a post is related to intent understanding.

3 Corpus Creation

To study the roles of images in social media posts, we create an annotated Reddit dataset with labels of emotions, text–image relations, and emotion stimuli. We first discuss our label sets and then explain the data collection and annotation procedures.

3.1 Taxonomies

We define taxonomies for the emotion, relation, and stimulus tasks.

Emotion Classification. To classify social media posts in terms of what emotion the author likely felt when creating the post, we use the Plutchik's wheel of emotions as the eight labels in our annotation scheme, namely *anger, anticipation, joy, sadness, trust, surprise, fear*, and *disgust*.

Relation Classification. To develop a classification scheme of relations of emotion-eliciting image–text pairs, we randomly sampled 200 posts, and created a simple annotation environment for preliminary annotation that displayed an image–text pair next to questions to be answered (see Figure 6 in the Appendix). Based on the preliminary annotation, we propose the following set of relation categories. 1. *complementary*: the image is necessary to understand the author's emotion; the text alone is not sufficient but when coupled with the image, the emotion is clear; 2. *illustrative*: the image illustrates the text but the text alone is enough to understand the emotion; the image does not communicate the emotion on its own; 3. *opposite*: the image and the text pull in different directions; they are contradicting when taken separately, but when together, the emotion is clear; 4. *decorative*: the image is used for aesthetic purposes; the emotion is primarily communicated with the text while the image may seem unrelated; 5. *emotion is communicated with image only*: the text is redundant for emotion communication.

We show examples for the *complementary* and *illustrative* relations in Figure 2. An example for the *opposite* relation could be an image with an ugly creature with a text "isn't he the prettiest thing

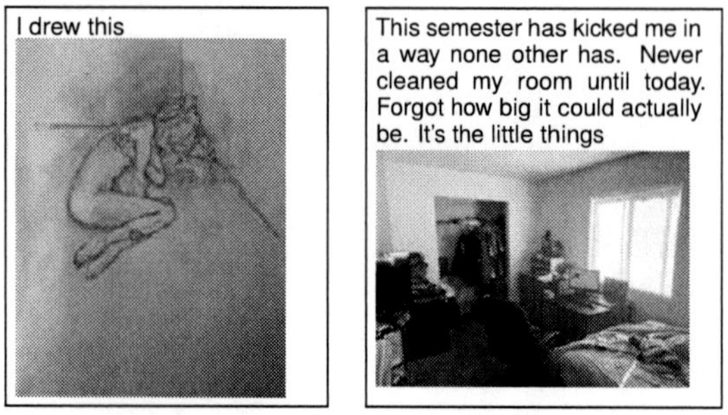

(a) Relation: complementary. https://www.reddit.com/r/sad/comments/jxgoxj/i_drew_this/

(b) Relation: illustrative. https://www.reddit.com/r/happy/comments/jwje64/this_semester_has_kicked_me_in_a_way_none_other/

Figure 2: Example of image–text relationships in posts.

in the world". Posts in which the text and the image are essentially unrelated fall into the *decorative* category. Posts where images have inspirational texts like "No Happiness is Ever Wasted" and the text contains the same words would fall into the last category (*image-only*).

Stimulus Classification. Based on the preliminary annotation procedure described for the relation taxonomy, we further obtain the following categories for emotion stimuli in images of multimodal posts: *person/people*, *animal*, *object*, *food*, *meme*, *screenshot/text in image*, *art/drawing*, *advertisement*, *event/situation*, and *place*. We provide examples of all stimuli in the Appendix in Figure 5.

3.2 Data Collection

We collect our multimodal data from Reddit, where posts are published under specific subreddits, user-created areas of interest, and are usually related to the topic of the group. Our data comes from 15 subreddits which we found by searching for emotion names. These subreddits are "happy", "happiness", "sad", "sadness", "anger", "angry", "fear", "disgusting", "surprise", "what", "WTF", "Cringetopia", "MadeMeSmile", "woahdude", which we complement by "r/all".

We collect the data from the Pushshift Reddit Dataset, a collection of posts and comments from Reddit from 2015 (Baumgartner et al., 2020b), with the help of the Pushshift-API[3]. We only consider posts which have both text and an image. From the initial set of instances that we collected (5,363) we manually removed those with images of low quality, pornographic and sexually inappropriate content, spam, or in a language other than English.

3.3 Data Annotation

We developed the annotation task with a subsample of 400 posts in a preliminary experiment. It was performed by two groups of three students and with a direct interaction with the authors of this paper, to obtain an understandable and unambiguous formulation of the questions that we used for the actual crowdsourcing annotation. The actual annotation of 1,380 randomly sampled posts was then performed with Amazon Mechanical Turk (AMT[4]) in two phases. In the first phase, we identify posts which likely contain an emotion by asking

1. Does the author want to express an emotion with the post?

In the second phase, we collect annotations for posts which contain an emotion (we accept a post if 1/3 of the annotators marked it as emotional) and ask

2. What emotion did the author likely feel when writing this post?
3. What is the relation between the image and the text regarding emotion communication?
4. What is it in the image that triggers the emotion?

For both phases/experiments, we gather annotations by three annotators. All questions allow one single answer. We show the annotation interface on Amazon Mechanical Turk for the second phase in the Appendix in Figure 7.

For the modelling which we describe in Section 4, we use a union of all labels from all annotators, acknowledging the subjective nature of the annotation task. This leads to multi-label classification, despite the annotation being a single-label annotation task.

Quality Assurance and Annotator Prescreening. Each potential annotator must reside in a predominantly English-speaking country (Australia, Canada, Ireland, New Zealand, United Kingdom, United States), and have an AMT approval rate of at least 90 %. Further, before admitting annotators to each annotation phase, we showed them five manually selected posts that we considered to be straightforward to annotate. For each phase, annotators needed to correctly answer 80 % of the questions associated with those posts. Phase 1 had a 100 % acceptance rate; in Phase 2 this qualifica-

[3] https://www.github.com/pushshift/api

[4] https://www.mturk.com/

	Label	≥ 1	≥ 2	$= 3$	κ
Emo.	Yes	1,061	670	333	0.3
	No	1,047	710	319	0.3
Which emotion?	Anger	138	41	8	.26
	Anticipation	85	12	1	.11
	Disgust	268	127	57	.45
	Fear	64	15	5	.28
	Joy	585	444	329	.67
	Sadness	103	52	27	.56
	Surprise	435	221	84	.38
	Trust	54	6	1	.11
	Overall	*1732*	*918*	*512*	*.47*
Relation?	Complementary	1042	773	388	.02
	Decorative	124	6	0	.01
	Illustrative	476	152	4	.07
	Image only	142	27	0	.11
	Opposite	28	0	0	−.01
	Overall	*1812*	*958*	*392*	*.04*
Stimulus?	Advertisement	23	4	0	.14
	Animal	146	112	83	.79
	Art/drawing	157	58	33	.46
	Event/situation	132	27	2	.15
	Food	78	56	36	.74
	Meme	129	58	8	.34
	Object	211	102	51	.50
	Person	260	168	91	.61
	Place	46	12	5	.34
	Screenshot	528	351	195	.53
	Overall	*1710*	*948*	*504*	*.53*

Table 1: Corpus statistics for emotions, relations, and stimuli. "≥ 1", "≥ 2", "$= 3$" means that at least one, at least two, and all three annotators labeled the post with the respective emotion respectively. The overall number of posts that were annotated in Phase 1 is 1,380, and 1,054 for Phase 2. κ refers to Fleiss' kappa.

tion test had a 55 % acceptance rate. We summarize participation and qualification statistics in Tables 4 and 5 in the Appendix.

Annotators and Payment. Altogether, 75 distinct annotators participated in Phase 1, and 38 annotators worked in Phase 2. We paid \$0.02 for each post in Phase 1, and \$0.08 for each post in Phase 2. The average time to annotate one post was 16 and 38 seconds in Phase 1 and 2, respectively. This leads to an average overall hourly wage of \$7. Overall, we paid \$337.44 to annotators and \$105.06 for platform fees and taxes.

3.4 Statistics of Annotated Dataset

In total, 1,380 posts were annotated via AMT (we do not discuss the preliminary annotations here). All results are summarized in Table 1.

Did the author want to express an emotion with the post? The total agreement of all three annotators (=3) was achieved in 47 % of the time (652 posts out of 1380). The overall inter-annotator agreement for this question is fair, with Fleiss κ=.3. We consider this value to be acceptable for a pre-filtering step to remove clearly non-emotional posts for the actual annotation in the next phase.

Of the 1,380 posts in Phase 1, 1,061 were labeled as "emotion", of which seven were flagged as being problematic by annotators (see Figure 7 in Appendix). Therefore, in total, 1,054 posts are considered for Phase 2.

What emotion did the author likely feel when writing this post? Table 1 gives the individual counts of instances that received a particular emotion label by at least one, two, or all three annotators. Note that the overall number of instances can be greater than the number of instances in the case that annotators disagree. *Joy*, *surprise* and *disgust* are the more frequent classes, with 585, 435, and 268 posts that received this label by at least one annotator. The number of posts in which at least two annotators agreed is considerably higher for *joy* than for the other emotions, which is also reflected in the moderate overall inter-annotator agreement with Fleiss κ=.47. For most classes, the agreement is moderate, with some exceptions (*anger* is often conflated with *disgust* as we will see below, and *anticipation*, and *trust*).

The agreement, however, can be considered to be similar to what has been achieved in other (crowdsourcing-based) annotation studies. As examples, Purver and Battersby (2012) report an agreement accuracy of 47 %. Schuff et al. (2017) report an agreement of less than 10 % when a set of 6 annotators needed to label an instance with the same emotion (but higher agreements for subsets of annotators).

What is the relation between the image and the text regarding emotion communication? The most dominant relations in our dataset are *complementary* (1,042 instances in which one annotator decided for this label) and *illustrative* (476). There are fewer instances in which annotators marked the relation *opposite* (28), *decorative* (124) and that the text is not required to infer the emotion (142).

The inter-annotator agreement is low, due to the skewness of the dataset and a therefore high expected agreement: overall, we only achieve κ=.04. Note that this inbalanced corpus poses a challenge in the results described in Section 5.

What is it in the image that triggers the emotion? The emotion stimuli categories are more balanced: Most frequently, people comment on what we classify as screenshots (528 out of 1054 received this label by at least one annotator), followed by depictions of people (260), objects (211), pieces of art (157), and depictions of animals (146). The agreement is moderate with an overall κ=.53. The labels *place* and *advertisement* are underrepresented in the dataset.

Cooccurrences. We now turn to the question which of the variables of the emotion category, the relation, and the stimulus category cooccur. Figure 3 shows the results with absolute counts above the diagonal, and odds-ratio values for the cooccurrence of multiple emotions annotated by different annotators below the diagonal (details regarding the calculation can be found in Schuff et al., 2017). The emotion combinations of *joy–surprise* (150 times), *surprise–disgust* (126), *surprise–anger* (63), and *disgust–anger* (62 times) are most often used. This is presumably an effect of the fact that people share information on social media that they find newsworthy. Further, this shows the role of *surprise* in combination with both positive and negative emotions—as common in emotion annotations to limit ambiguity, we modelled the task in a single-label annotation setup. Therefore, this shows that different interpretations of the same post are possible.

The odds-ratio values point out the specificity of the combination of *disgust–anger*. This could be explained with the difference of these emotions regarding their motivational component, namely to tackle a particular stimulus or to avoid it (known as the fight-or-flight response). The combination of *sadness–fear* can be explained with the importance of the confirmation status of a stimulus (future or past) which distinguishes these two emotions. This property might be ambiguous in depictions in social media. The combinations of *fear–anticipation* and *fear–trust* might be considered surprising. Such combinations of positive and negative emotions frequently occur in motivational text depictions, for instance "don't be afraid of your fears".

We show the cooccurrence counts and odds ratios for the stimulus and the emotion in Figure 4. For the emotions *anger*, the stimuli of *advertisments* and *screenshots* are outstanding. *Anticipation* has the highest value for art. *Disgust* is particularly specific for *food* and *advertisement*. This shows the metaphoric use of the term (in the sense of repugnance) and a more concrete use (in the sense of revulsion). Interestingly, *fear* is specific for stimuli of *animals*, *art*, and *memes*. *Joy* is the only emotion that has a high odds ratio with *places*, and *persons*, but also with *animals*. *Sadness* and *trust* have the highest value for *memes*.

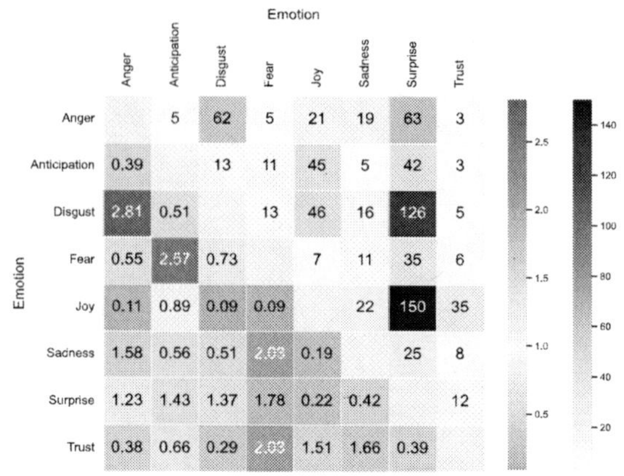

Figure 3: Emotion-Emotion cooccurrences. The values above the diagonal are absolute counts, while the numbers below the diagonal are odds ratios. I higher value denotes that the combination is particular specific.

We do not discuss the *relation* category further, given the predominance of the *complementary* class and its limited inter-annotator agreement.

4 Methods

In the following, we present the models that we used to predict (1) each variable (emotion, stimulus, relation) separately in each modality, and (2) across modalities with joint models.

4.1 Text

For the text-based model, we fine-tune the pretrained RoBERTa model[5] (Liu et al., 2019). We perform multi-task learning for emotion, stimulus and relation by adding a fully connected layer (for each set of labels), on top of the last hidden layer. The model combines the loss for all three sets of labels and updates the weights accordingly during the training phase.[6] We use a learning rate of $3 \cdot 10^{-5}$ for all layers, except for the top three fully connected ones ($3 \cdot 10^{-3}$). We use the learning rate scheduler with a step size of 5 and train for maximally 20 epochs, but perform early stopping if the validation loss does not improve by more than 0.005%.

[5] https://huggingface.co/transformers/model_doc/roberta.html

[6] Our first choice of only one layer performed en par to multiple stacked layers.

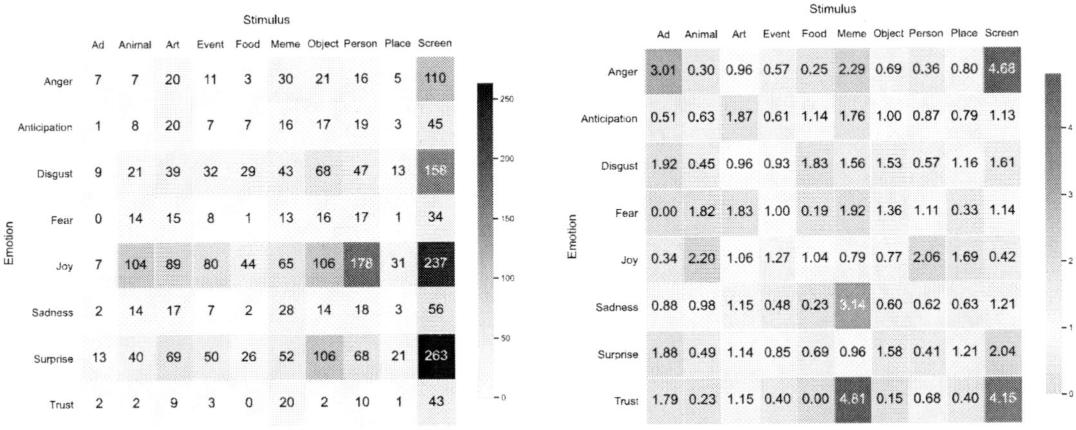

(a) Counts (b) Odds Ratio

Figure 4: Emotion-Stimulus Cooccurrences.

4.2 Images

We built the image-based model on top of a pre-trained deep residual network model with 48 convolutional layers and 2 pooling layers (ResNet, He et al., 2016). We use the ResNet50 that is provided by PyTorch[7] and was pretrained on 1,000 ImageNet categories (Russakovsky et al., 2015; Deng et al., 2009). As with the text-based model, we add three fully connected layers on top of the fully connected layer of the ResNet50 model, with the sigmoid activation function. Unlike RoBERTa, we do not fine-tune the convolutional layers to prevent the pre-trained weights to change.[8]

4.3 Joint Models

We evaluate three simple multimodal methods which combine the information from the text and the image modality on the traditional three different stages: early, late, and model-based fusion (Snoek et al., 2005).

In early (feature-based) fusion, the features extracted from both modalities are fused at an early stage and passed through a classifier. As the input, our early-fusion model takes the tokenized text and preprocessed image (images are resized, converted to tensors, and normalized by the mean and standard deviation[9]), and concatenates them into one vector to pass through the final classifier, that consists of several layers (three linear, dropout, and three fully connected layers) with the input size depending on the longest text in the training set and output size depending on the task. The activation function is, as in all our models, a sigmoid function.

In late (decision-based) fusion, classification scores are obtained for each modality separately. These scores are then fed into the joint model. In our late-fusion model, we pass the text and image through the text-based and image-based models respectively, and concatenate the output probabilities of these models.[10] We then pass this vector through a fully connected layer with twice the number of classes from the two models as input and output, and apply sigmoid for prediction. That is, for the emotion classification, the vectors of eight labels from RoBERTa and ResNet50, summing up to 16, are passed to the fully connected layer.

For model-based fusion, we extract text and image features from our unimodal text and image-based classifiers, respectively (from the last hidden layers before the fully conntected ones), and feed these to a final classifier.[11]

5 Results

We evaluate our models on predicting emotions, text–image relations, and emotion stimuli using unimodal and multimodal models, based on the F_1 measure. We use the dataset of 1054 instances in which we aggregate the labels from the three annotators by accepting a label if one annotator assigned

[7] https://pytorch.org/hub/pytorch_vision_resnet/

[8] We performed experiments with unfreezing several top convolutional layers, however, it did not lead to better results.

[9] https://pytorch.org/vision/stable/transforms.html

[10] Experiments with summed vectors did not improve results.

[11] Experiments with more complex models with multiple top layers did not improve results, thus, we chose a single-layer-on-top model for the experiments.

	Model	Emo.	Rel.	Stim.
	Majority Baseline	.22	.56	.21
uni-modal	Text	**.53**	**.77**	.45
	Image	.41	.67	.59
multi-modal	Early fusion	.40	.72	.33
	Late fusion	.47	.72	.41
	Model-based fusion	**.53**	.76	**.63**

Table 2: Experimental results in predicting emotions, relations, and stimuli using unimodal and multimodal models. The results are presented in weighted F_1 score. Bold face indicates the highest value in each column/task.

		Unimodal		Multimodal		
	Label	Txt	Img	Early	Late	Mb.
Emotions	Anger	.08	.04	.03	0	**.14**
	Anticipation	0	0	**.12**	0	0
	Disgust	**.47**	.23	.26	.27	.39
	Fear	0	0	**.04**	0	0
	Joy	**.84**	.66	.64	.85	.78
	Sadness	.28	0	.09	0	**.37**
	Surprise	.61	.57	.52	.57	**.70**
	Trust	**.04**	0	0	0	0
Relations	Compl.	**.99**	**.99**	.98	**.99**	**.99**
	Decorative	.05	0	.11	0	**.20**
	Illustrative	.65	.46	.50	**.66**	.61
	Image-only	**.38**	0	.24	0	.34
	Opposite	0	0	0	0	0
Stimuli	Advert.	0	0	0	0	0
	Animal	.60	**.78**	.28	.52	.74
	Art/drawing	.02	.27	.26	0	**.45**
	Event/sit.	.20	.16	.13	0	**.29**
	Food	.22	**.63**	.19	0	.62
	Meme	.40	.35	.17	0	**.57**
	Object	.32	**.68**	.17	.25	.65
	Person	.43	**.59**	.21	.52	**.59**
	Place	0	.06	.04	0	.19
	Screenshot	.72	.78	.63	.78	**.79**

Table 3: Experimental results for all labels in predicting emotions, relations, and stimuli using the text-based and image-based unimodal models, and fusion models. The results are presented in F1 score.

it (this approach might be considered a "high-recall" aggregation of the labels, similar to Schuff et al. (2017)). Despite being a single-label annotation task, this leads to a multi-label classification setup. In other words, the annotation process requires annotators to select a single label (for each set of labels), e.g. one emotion per post; however, the experiments are conducted using multiple labels per set, depending on how many labels are given by three annotators for each set of labels. The data is randomly split into 853 instances for training, 95 instances for validation, and 106 test instances.

Table 2 summarizes the results, averaging across the values for each class variable. We observe that the emotions and the relations can be predicted with the highest F_1 with the text-based unimodal model. The discrepancy to the image-based model is substantial, with .53 to .41 for the emotions and .77 to .67 for the relations. The stimulus detection benefits from the multimodal information from both the image and the text—the highest performance, .63, is achieved with the model-based fusion approach. From the unimodal models, the image-based model is performing better than the text-based model. This is not surprising—in multimodal social media posts that express an emotion, the depictions predominantly correspond to a stimulus, or their identification is at least important. The corpus statistics show that: posts in which the image is purely used decoratively are the minority.

Table 3 shows detailed per-label results. For the **emotion classification** task, we see that for three emotions, the text-only model leads to the best performance (*disgust, joy, trust,* while the latter is too low to draw a conclusion regarding the importance of the modalities). The other emotions benefit from a multimodal approach. Overall, still, the text-based model shows highest average performance, given the dominance of the emotion *joy*.

For most **stimulus** categories, either the image or a multimodal model performs best. This is not surprising, given that the stimulus is often depicted in the visual part of a multimodal post. More complex depictions that could receive various evaluations, like *art, events/situations,* and *memes* require multimodal information. In those, the image information alone is not sufficient—the performance difference is between 22pp and 13pp in F_1. For those stimuli, in which the text-based model outperforms the multimodal models, the difference is lower. The text-based model is never performing best, but shows acceptable performance for *animals, memes, screenshots* and *person* depictions.

Regarding the **relations**, the *complementary* class is predicted with the best performance; which is due to the frequency of this class. The label *decorative* can only be predicted with a (slightly) acceptable performance with the multimodal approach, while *illustrative* predictions based on text-only are nearly en par with a multimodal model.

From the three multimodal fusion approaches,

early fusion performs the worst, followed by late fusion. Model-based fusion most often leads to the best result. We show examples for instances in which the multimodal model performs better than unimodal models in Table 6 in the Appendix.

6 Conclusion and Future Work

With this paper, we presented the first study on how users in social media make use of text and images to communicate their emotions. We have seen that the number of multimodal posts in which the image does not contribute additional information over the text is in the minority, and, hence, interpretation of images in addition to the text is important. While the inter-annotator agreement for relation was not reliable enough to draw this conclusion, prediction of stimulus correlates with prediction of emotion due to the information that is present in the image but missing in the text, and thus makes images play a significant role in analysis of social media posts. This is also the first study on stimulus detection in multimodal posts, and we have seen that for the majority of stimulus categories, the information in the text is not sufficient.

In contrast to most work on emotion stimulus and cause detection in NLP, we treated this task as a discrete classification task, similar to early work in targeted sentiment analysis. An interesting step in the future will be to join segment-based open domain stimulus detection, as it is common in text analysis, with region-based image analysis, and ground the textual references in the image. This will allow to go beyond predefined categories.

Acknowledgements

This work was supported by Deutsche Forschungsgemeinschaft (project CEAT, KL 2869/1-2).

References

Cecilia Ovesdotter Alm, Dan Roth, and Richard Sproat. 2005. Emotions from text: Machine learning for text-based emotion prediction. In *Proceedings of Human Language Technology Conference and Conference on Empirical Methods in Natural Language Processing*, pages 579–586, Vancouver, British Columbia, Canada. Association for Computational Linguistics.

Saima Aman and Stan Szpakowicz. 2008. Using Roget's thesaurus for fine-grained emotion recognition. In *Proceedings of the Third International Joint Conference on Natural Language Processing: Volume-I.*

Jason Baumgartner, Savvas Zannettou, Brian Keegan, Megan Squire, and Jeremy Blackburn. 2020a. The pushshift reddit dataset. In *Proceedings of the International AAAI Conference on Web and Social Media*, volume 14, pages 830–839.

Jason Baumgartner, Savvas Zannettou, Brian Keegan, Megan Squire, and Jeremy Blackburn. 2020b. The pushshift reddit dataset. In *Proceedings of the international AAAI conference on web and social media*, volume 14, pages 830–839.

Laura Ana Maria Bostan, Evgeny Kim, and Roman Klinger. 2020. GoodNewsEveryone: A corpus of news headlines annotated with emotions, semantic roles, and reader perception. In *Proceedings of The 12th Language Resources and Evaluation Conference*, pages 1554–1566, Marseille, France. European Language Resources Association.

Margaret M Bradley, Mark K Greenwald, Margaret C Petry, and Peter J Lang. 1992. Remembering pictures: pleasure and arousal in memory. *Journal of experimental psychology: Learning, Memory, and Cognition*, 18(2):379.

Sven Buechel and Udo Hahn. 2017. EmoBank: Studying the impact of annotation perspective and representation format on dimensional emotion analysis. In *Proceedings of the 15th Conference of the European Chapter of the Association for Computational Linguistics: Volume 2, Short Papers*, pages 578–585, Valencia, Spain. Association for Computational Linguistics.

Felix Casel, Amelie Heindl, and Roman Klinger. 2021. Emotion recognition under consideration of the emotion component process model. In *Proceedings of the 17th Conference on Natural Language Processing (KONVENS 2021)*, pages 49–61, Düsseldorf, Germany. KONVENS 2021 Organizers.

Niko Colnerič and Janez Demšar. 2018. Emotion recognition on twitter: Comparative study and training a unison model. *IEEE transactions on affective computing*, 11(3):433–446.

Liyanage C. De Silva, Tsutomu Miyasato, and Ryohei Nakatsu. 1997. Facial emotion recognition using multi-modal information. In *Proceedings of ICICS, 1997 International Conference on Information, Communications and Signal Processing. Theme: Trends in Information Systems Engineering and Wireless Multimedia Communications (Cat.*, volume 1, pages 397–401 vol.1.

Michela Dellagiacoma, Pamela Zontone, Giulia Boato, and Liliana Albertazzi. 2011. Emotion based classification of natural images. In *Proceedings of the 2011 international workshop on DETecting and Exploiting Cultural diversiTy on the social web*, DETECT '11, page 17–22, New York, NY, USA. Association for Computing Machinery.

Jia Deng, Wei Dong, Richard Socher, Li-Jia Li, Kai Li, and Li Fei-Fei. 2009. Imagenet: A large-scale hierarchical image database. In *2009 IEEE Conference on Computer Vision and Pattern Recognition*, pages 248–255.

Paul Ekman. 1992. An argument for basic emotions. *Cognition & emotion*, 6(3-4):169–200.

Shaojing Fan, Zhiqi Shen, Ming Jiang, Bryan L. Koenig, Juan Xu, Mohan S. Kankanhalli, and Qi Zhao. 2018. Emotional attention: A study of image sentiment and visual attention. In *2018 IEEE/CVF Conference on Computer Vision and Pattern Recognition*, pages 7521–7531.

Qinghong Gao, Jiannan Hu, Ruifeng Xu, Gui Lin, Yulan He, Qin Lu, and Kam-Fai Wong. 2017. Overview of NTCIR-13 ECA task. In *Proceedings of the 13th NTCIR Conference on Evaluation of Information Access Technologies*, pages 361–366, Tokyo, Japan.

Diman Ghazi, Diana Inkpen, and Stan Szpakowicz. 2015. Detecting emotion stimuli in emotion-bearing sentences. In *International Conference on Intelligent Text Processing and Computational Linguistics*, pages 152–165. Springer.

Lin Gui, Jiannan Hu, Yulan He, Ruifeng Xu, Qin Lu, and Jiachen Du. 2017. A question answering approach for emotion cause extraction. In *Proceedings of the 2017 Conference on Empirical Methods in Natural Language Processing*, pages 1593–1602, Copenhagen, Denmark. Association for Computational Linguistics.

Lin Gui, Dongyin Wu, Ruifeng Xu, Qin Lu, and Yu Zhou. 2016. Event-driven emotion cause extraction with corpus construction. In *Proceedings of the 2016 Conference on Empirical Methods in Natural Language Processing*, pages 1639–1649, Austin, Texas. Association for Computational Linguistics.

Kaiming He, Xiangyu Zhang, Shaoqing Ren, and Jian Sun. 2016. Deep residual learning for image recognition. In *Proceedings of the IEEE conference on computer vision and pattern recognition*, pages 770–778.

Yuwei He and Guiguang Ding. 2019. Deep transfer learning for image emotion analysis: Reducing marginal and joint distribution discrepancies together. *Neural Processing Letters*, 3:2077–2086.

Jan Hofmann, Enrica Troiano, Kai Sassenberg, and Roman Klinger. 2020. Appraisal theories for emotion classification in text. In *Proceedings of the 28th International Conference on Computational Linguistics*, pages 125–138, Barcelona, Spain (Online). International Committee on Computational Linguistics.

Evgeny Kim and Roman Klinger. 2018. Who feels what and why? Annotation of a literature corpus with semantic roles of emotions. In *Proceedings of the 27th International Conference on Computational Linguistics*, pages 1345–1359. Association for Computational Linguistics.

Roman Klinger, Orphée De Clercq, Saif Mohammad, and Alexandra Balahur. 2018. IEST: WASSA-2018 implicit emotions shared task. In *Proceedings of the 9th Workshop on Computational Approaches to Subjectivity, Sentiment and Social Media Analysis*, pages 31–42, Brussels, Belgium. Association for Computational Linguistics.

Julia Kruk, Jonah Lubin, Karan Sikka, Xiao Lin, Dan Jurafsky, and Ajay Divakaran. 2019. Integrating text and image: Determining multimodal document intent in Instagram posts. In *Proceedings of the 2019 Conference on Empirical Methods in Natural Language Processing and the 9th International Joint Conference on Natural Language Processing (EMNLP-IJCNLP)*, pages 4622–4632, Hong Kong, China. Association for Computational Linguistics.

Shan Li and Weihong Deng. 2020. Deep facial expression recognition: A survey. *IEEE Transactions on Affective Computing*.

Hugo Liu, Henry Lieberman, and Ted Selker. 2003. A model of textual affect sensing using real-world knowledge. In *Proceedings of the 8th International Conference on Intelligent User Interfaces*, IUI '03, page 125–132, New York, NY, USA. Association for Computing Machinery.

Yinhan Liu, Myle Ott, Naman Goyal, Jingfei Du, Mandar Joshi, Danqi Chen, Omer Levy, Mike Lewis, Luke Zettlemoyer, and Veselin Stoyanov. 2019. Roberta: A robustly optimized bert pretraining approach. *arXiv preprint arXiv:1907.11692*.

Xin Lu, Poonam Suryanarayan, Reginald B Adams, Jia Li, Michelle G Newman, and James Z Wang. 2012. On shape and the computability of emotions. In *ACM International Multimedia Conference*, volume 2012, pages 229–238.

Emily E Marsh and Marilyn Domas White. 2003. A taxonomy of relationships between images and text. *Journal of Documentation*, 59(6):647–672.

Radan Martinec and Andrew Salway. 2005. A system for image–text relations in new (and old) media. *Visual communication*, 4(3):337–371.

Rada Mihalcea and Hugo Liu. 2006. A corpus-based approach to finding happiness. In *AAAI Spring Symposium: Computational Approaches to Analyzing Weblogs*, pages 139–144.

Saif Mohammad. 2012. #Emotional Tweets. In **SEM 2012: The First Joint Conference on Lexical and Computational Semantics – Volume 1: Proceedings of the main conference and the shared task, and Volume 2: Proceedings of the Sixth International Workshop on Semantic Evaluation (SemEval 2012)*, pages 246–255, Montréal, Canada. Association for Computational Linguistics.

Saif Mohammad, Felipe Bravo-Marquez, Mohammad Salameh, and Svetlana Kiritchenko. 2018. SemEval-2018 task 1: Affect in tweets. In *Proceedings of The 12th International Workshop on Semantic Evaluation*, pages 1–17, New Orleans, Louisiana. Association for Computational Linguistics.

Saif Mohammad, Xiaodan Zhu, and Joel Martin. 2014. Semantic role labeling of emotions in tweets. In *Proceedings of the 5th Workshop on Computational Approaches to Subjectivity, Sentiment and Social Media Analysis*, pages 32–41, Baltimore, Maryland. Association for Computational Linguistics.

Alena Neviarouskaya, Helmut Prendinger, and Mitsuru Ishizuka. 2010. *Recognition of Fine-Grained Emotions from Text: An Approach Based on the Compositionality Principle*, pages 179–207. Springer Berlin Heidelberg, Berlin, Heidelberg.

Laura Ana Maria Oberländer and Roman Klinger. 2020. Token sequence labeling vs. clause classification for English emotion stimulus detection. In *Proceedings of the Ninth Joint Conference on Lexical and Computational Semantics*, pages 58–70, Barcelona, Spain (Online). Association for Computational Linguistics.

Kuan-Chuan Peng, Amir Sadovnik, Andrew Gallagher, and Tsuhan Chen. 2016. Where do emotions come from? Predicting the emotion stimuli map. In *2016 IEEE International Conference on Image Processing (ICIP)*, pages 614–618.

Robert Plutchik. 1980. A general psychoevolutionary theory of emotion. In *Theories of emotion*, pages 3–33. Elsevier.

Robert Plutchik. 2001. The nature of emotions: Human emotions have deep evolutionary roots, a fact that may explain their complexity and provide tools for clinical practice. *American scientist*, 89(4):344–350.

Matthew Purver and Stuart Battersby. 2012. Experimenting with distant supervision for emotion classification. In *Proceedings of the 13th Conference of the European Chapter of the Association for Computational Linguistics*, pages 482–491, Avignon, France. Association for Computational Linguistics.

Olga Russakovsky, Jia Deng, Hao Su, Jonathan Krause, Sanjeev Satheesh, Sean Ma, Zhiheng Huang, Andrej Karpathy, Aditya Khosla, Michael Bernstein, Alexander C. Berg, and Li Fei-Fei. 2015. ImageNet Large Scale Visual Recognition Challenge. *International Journal of Computer Vision (IJCV)*, 115(3):211–252.

James A Russell. 1980. A circumplex model of affect. *Journal of personality and social psychology*, 39(6):1161.

Klaus R. Scherer. 2005. What are emotions? And how can they be measured? *Social Science Information*, 44(4):695–729.

Klaus R. Scherer, Angela Schorr, and Tom Johnstone. 2001. *Appraisal processes in emotion: Theory, methods, research.* Oxford University Press.

Hendrik Schuff, Jeremy Barnes, Julian Mohme, Sebastian Padó, and Roman Klinger. 2017. Annotation, modelling and analysis of fine-grained emotions on a stance and sentiment detection corpus. In *Proceedings of the 8th Workshop on Computational Approaches to Subjectivity, Sentiment and Social Media Analysis*, pages 13–23, Copenhagen, Denmark. Association for Computational Linguistics.

Mostafa Al Masum Shaikh, Helmut Prendinger, and Mitsuru Ishizuka. 2009. A linguistic interpretation of the occ emotion model for affect sensing from text. *Affective Information Processing*, pages 45–73.

Cees GM Snoek, Marcel Worring, and Arnold WM Smeulders. 2005. Early versus late fusion in semantic video analysis. In *Proceedings of the 13th annual ACM international conference on Multimedia*, pages 399–402.

Shuangyong Song and Yao Meng. 2015. Detecting concept-level emotion cause in microblogging. In *Proceedings of the 24th International Conference on World Wide Web*, WWW '15 Companion, page 119–120, New York, NY, USA. Association for Computing Machinery.

Carlo Strapparava and Rada Mihalcea. 2007. SemEval-2007 task 14: Affective text. In *Proceedings of the Fourth International Workshop on Semantic Evaluations (SemEval-2007)*, pages 70–74, Prague, Czech Republic. Association for Computational Linguistics.

Alakananda Vempala and Daniel Preoţiuc-Pietro. 2019. Categorizing and inferring the relationship between the text and image of Twitter posts. In *Proceedings of the 57th Annual Meeting of the Association for Computational Linguistics*, pages 2830–2840, Florence, Italy. Association for Computational Linguistics.

Wenbo Wang, Lu Chen, Krishnaprasad Thirunarayan, and Amit P. Sheth. 2012. Harnessing Twitter "Big Data" for automatic emotion identification. In *2012 International Conference on Privacy, Security, Risk and Trust and 2012 International Confernece on Social Computing*, pages 587–592. IEEE.

Lydia Weiland, Ioana Hulpuş, Simone Paolo Ponzetto, Wolfgang Effelsberg, and Laura Dietz. 2018. Knowledge-rich image gist understanding beyond literal meaning. *Data & Knowledge Engineering*, 117:114–132.

Lifang Wu, Mingchao Qi, Meng Jian, and Heng Zhang. 2020. Visual sentiment analysis by combining global and local information. *Neural Process. Lett.*, 51(3):2063–2075.

Rui Xia and Zixiang Ding. 2019. Emotion-cause pair extraction: A new task to emotion analysis in texts. In *Proceedings of the 57th Annual Meeting of the Association for Computational Linguistics*, pages 1003–1012, Florence, Italy. Association for Computational Linguistics.

Jufeng Yang, Dongyu She, Yu-Kun Lai, Paul L. Rosin, and Ming-Hsuan Yang. 2018. Weakly supervised coupled networks for visual sentiment analysis. In *2018 IEEE/CVF Conference on Computer Vision and Pattern Recognition*, pages 7584–7592.

Mingda Zhang, Rebecca Hwa, and Adriana Kovashka. 2018. Equal but not the same: Understanding the implicit relationship between persuasive images and text. In *Proceedings of the British Machine Vision Conference*.

Sicheng Zhao, Guiguang Ding, Qingming Huang, Tat-Seng Chua, Björn W Schuller, and Kurt Keutzer. 2018. Affective image content analysis: a comprehensive survey. In *Proceedings of the Twenty-Seventh International Joint Conference on Artificial Intelligence Survey track*, pages 5534–5541.

Honglin Zheng, Tianlang Chen, Quanzeng You, and Jiebo Luo. 2017. When saliency meets sentiment: Understanding how image content invokes emotion and sentiment. In *2017 IEEE International Conference on Image Processing (ICIP)*, pages 630–634.

A Appendix

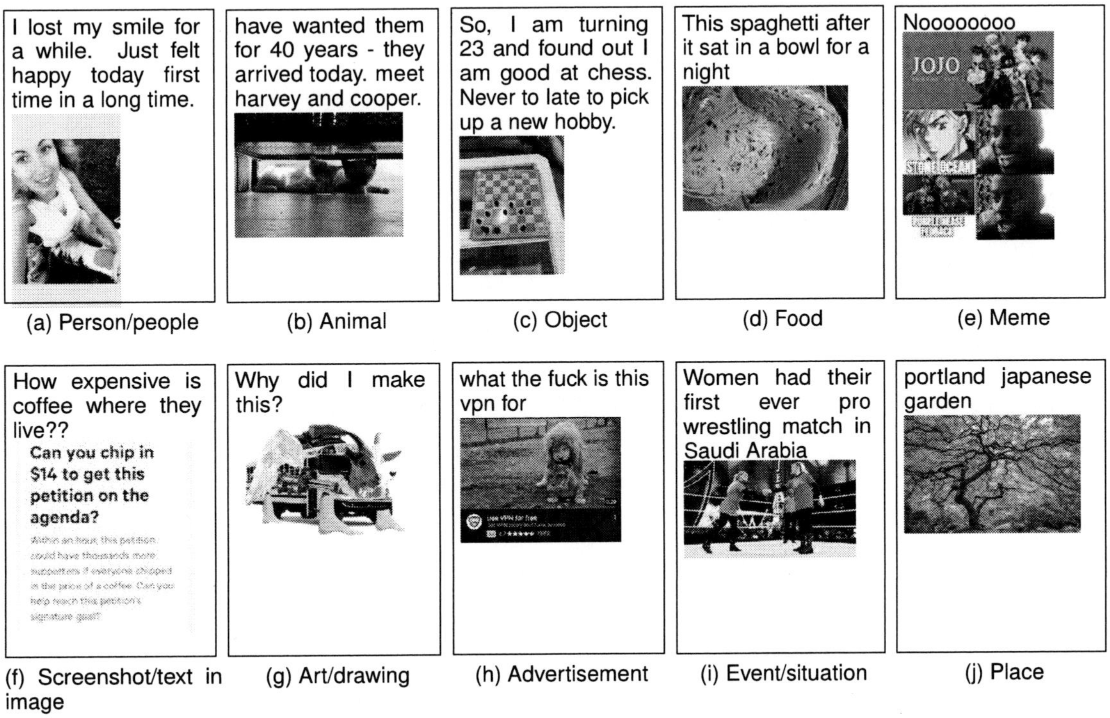

Figure 5: Examples of emotion stimuli in post images.

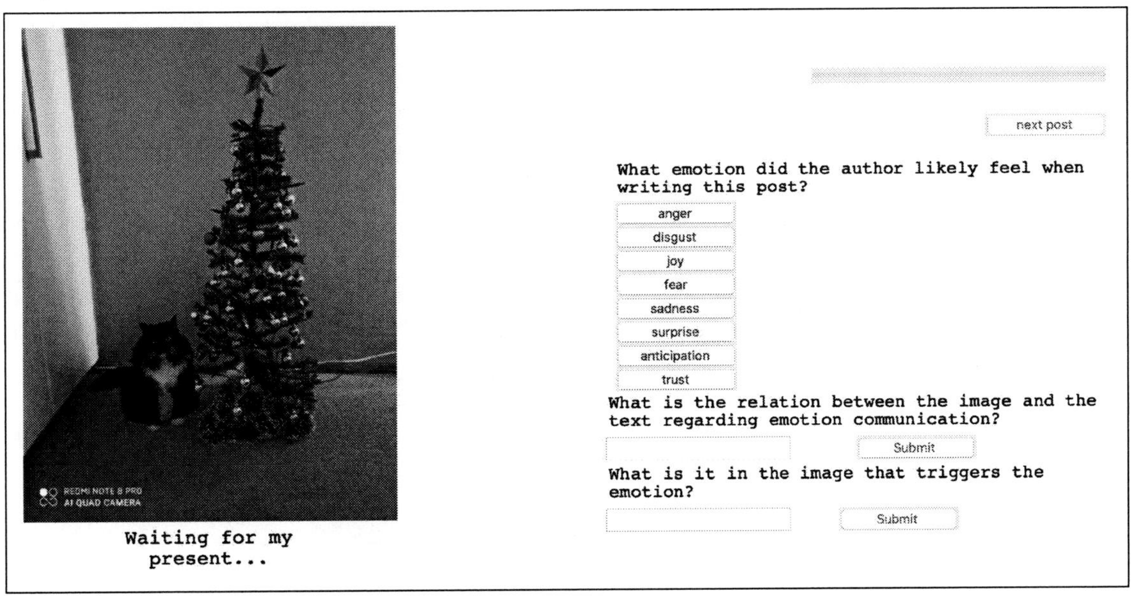

Figure 6: Annotation tool to define taxonomies.

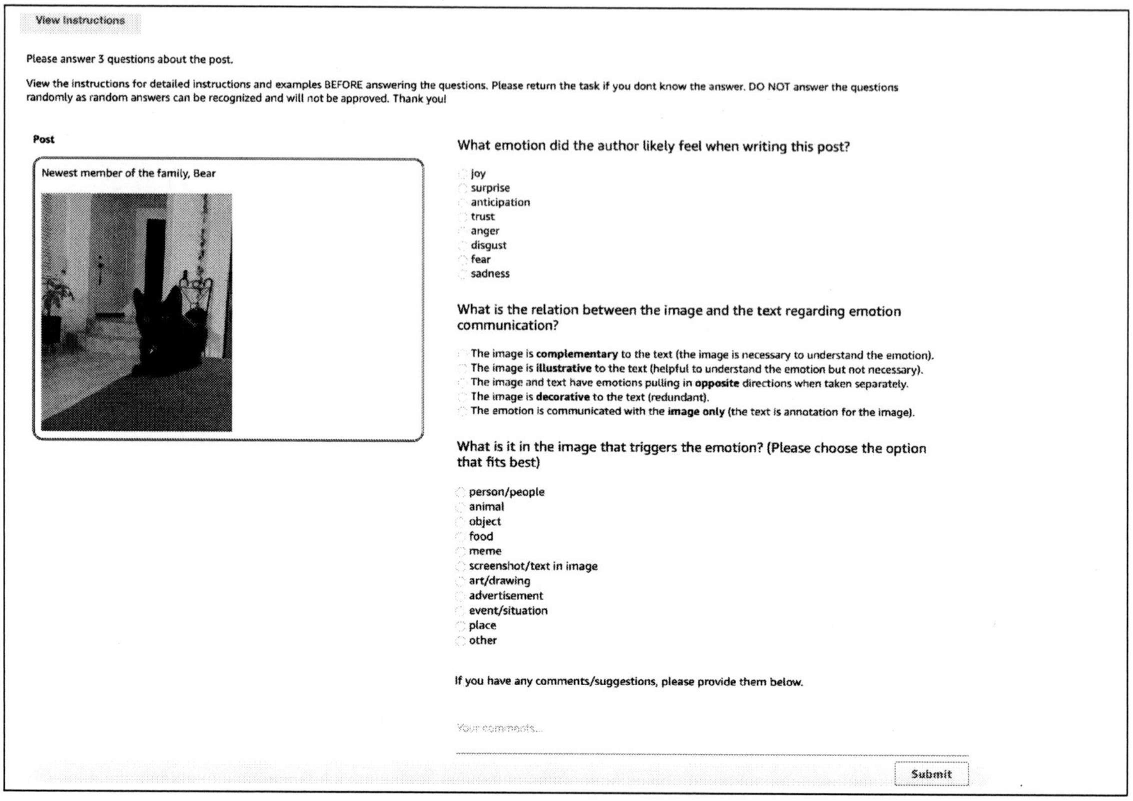

Figure 7: Annotation Environment on Amazon Mechanical Turk

Qualification	**Description**
Qualification test 1: emotional/non-emotional posts	5 posts presented to annotators to label the post emotional or non-emotional; passing score of 80%
Qualification test 2: emotion, relation, stimulus identification	5 posts presented to annotators to label the post for emotions, relations, and stimuli; passing score of 80%
Region	Annotators must reside in either of the six English-speaking countries (Australia, Canada, Ireland, New Zealand, United Kingdom, United States) to force the task to be done by native speakers.
Human Intelligence Task (HIT) approval rate	The HIT approval rate represents the proportion of completed tasks that are approved by Requesters and ensures the quality of the job workers do on the platform.

Table 4: Qualifications used on AMT for data annotation.

	Qualification		Participation	
	Attempted	Passed	From previous task	New
Task 1	75	75	-	75
Task 2	69	38	17	21

Table 5: Statistics on participation for the two tasks. All numbers are the counts of workers. Qualification tests are described in Table 4. *Attempted* are the number of workers that took the qualification test, while *passed* is the number of workers that answered at least 80% of the questions correctly. *From previous task* refers to the number of workers that participated in Phase 1 as well as Phase 2, while *new* are the participants that have not participated in the previous phase.

	Text	Image	Gold	Predictions (Emotions/Stimulus)		
				Image-only	Text-Only	Multimodal
Emotion	Found a fly in my tea halfway through it	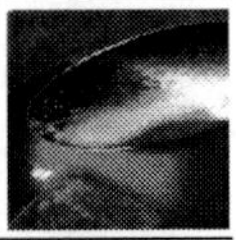	Disgust	Joy	Disgust/Surprise	Disgust
	Dont know if it has been posted before but here u go		Joy	Joy	Disgust	Joy
	I find a monster under my bed		Sadness	Joy	Fear/Surprise	Surprise
	Definitely stoked with how much weight I've lost since overcoming my alcoholism!		Joy	Fear	Joy	Joy
Stimulus	It causes unnatural amounts of pain to just look at it	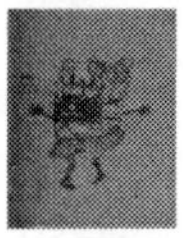	Art/Drawing	Art/Drawing	Person	Art/Drawing
	I have no idea the context of this picture from Steam Powered Giraffe but the sheer happiness in it makes me happy. Hope it does for you, too! You see, he never smiles that big!		Person	—	Person	Person
	After multiple tries, my sunflower finally bloomed! What a beauty.		Object	—	—	Object

Table 6: Examples in which the multimodal model-based model returns the correct result, but at least one unimodal model does not. "—" means that the model was not confident enough to predict any of the labels from the set.

Multiplex Anti-Asian Sentiment before and during the Pandemic: Introducing New Datasets from Twitter Mining

Hao Lin[1], Pradeep Nalluri[1], Lantian Li[2], Yifan Sun[1], Yongjun Zhang[1]
[1]Stony Brook University
[2] Northwestern University
[1]{hao.lin, pradeepkumar.nalluri}@stonybrook.edu
[1]{yifan.sun,yongjun.zhang}@stonybrook.edu
[2]lantianli2014@u.northwestern.edu

Abstract

COVID-19 has disproportionately threatened minority communities in the U.S, not only in health but also in societal impact. However, social scientists and policymakers lack critical data to capture the dynamics of the anti-Asian hate trend and to evaluate its scale and scope. We introduce new datasets from Twitter related to anti-Asian hate sentiment before and during the pandemic. Relying on Twitter's academic API, we retrieve hateful and counter-hate tweets from the Twitter Historical Database. To build contextual understanding and collect related racial cues, we also collect instances of heated arguments, often political, but not necessarily hateful, discussing Chinese issues. We then use the state-of-the-art hate speech classifiers to discern whether these tweets express hatred. These datasets can be used to study hate speech, general anti-Asian or Chinese sentiment, and hate linguistics by social scientists as well as to evaluate and build hate speech or sentiment analysis classifiers by computational scholars.

Keywords: Hate speech, Sinophobia, COVID19, Anti-Asian, Anti-China, Twitter mining

1 Introduction

The COVID-19 pandemic has disproportionately threatened minority communities in the U.S. In particular, COVID-19 has brought sinophobia to the surface (Croucher et al., 2020; Zhang, 2021; Horton, 2020). Since the outbreak of COVID-19, there were over 4,000 hate incidents such as harassment and physical attacks reported to stopaapihate.org. The growing anti-Asian attacks have led to the recent passage of the anti-Asian Hate Crimes Bill by the U.S. House after the mass shootings in Atlanta. Despite the problematic surge in COVID-hate incidents and crimes targeting Asian American and Pacific Islander (AAPI) communities, social scientists and policymakers lack critical data and quantitative measures to capture the evolution of anti-AAPI trends in the U.S., and cannot evaluate the scale and scope of anti-AAPI hate incidents in the pandemic.

Recent scholars have used social media data with machine learning techniques to track online anti-Asian hate speech (Vidgen et al., 2020; Ziems et al., 2020; Jiang et al., 2020). For instance, Ziems et al. (2020) examined the evolution and spread of anti-Asian hate speech from 30 million tweets collected between January 15 and April 17, 2020. Cook et al. (2021) classified over 297 million tweets about China or COVID-19 between January 2017 and June 2020 by using a BERT model trained on 5000 labeled tweets and found that the awareness of COVID-19 has led to a sharp rise in anti-China sentiments in the U.S. Although these studies provide training datasets to build hate speech classifiers and have insights about the spread of anti-Asian hate at the early stage of the outbreak, little is known about the enduring evolution of anti-Asian hate or counter hate before and during the continuing pandemic.

In this paper, we report trends and patterns of anti-Asian sentiments and hate speech on Twitter by introducing new datasets. Twitter has been one of the most salient battlegrounds of both propagating and fighting against misinformation, fake news, hatred, and xenophobia during the COVID-19 pandemic. We use computational tools with natural language processing and machine learning methods to detect hate speech on Twitter before and during the pandemic. Our datasets contain 68.38 million tweets, and they fall in four categories:

- COVID-related anti-AAPI tweets, which are collected by using Covid-related keywords such as *'chinavirus'* and *'kung-flu'*
- Non-COVID-related hateful tweets, which are collected by using general Anti-AAPI key-

Proceedings of the 12th Workshop on Computational Approaches to Subjectivity, Sentiment & Social Media Analysis, pages 16 - 24
May 26, 2022

words such as *'ching chong'* and *'chink'*

- Discussions that concern Chinese politics; The topics per se may not be hateful, but they often provoke hateful tweets such as discussions about Uyghers, Hong Kong protests, and Xi Jinping

- Counter-hate tweets, including keywords such as *'stopasianhate'* and *'racismisvirus'*

These datasets provide a comprehensive portrait of the dynamics of anti-Asian hate sentiments spanning from 2007 to 2021. Thus, we are able to address important questions related to the evolution of anti-Asian hate sentiments over time.

2 Background

In the past decade, computational scholars have made great efforts to detect hate speech on social media platforms (Davidson et al., 2017; Warner and Hirschberg, 2012; Del Vigna12 et al., 2017). Although there is no clear and formal definition of hate speech, scholars tend to define hate speech as language or speech "used to express hatred towards a targeted group or is intended to be derogatory, to humiliate, or to insult the members of the group" (Davidson et al., 2017). Anti-Asian hate speech, especially Sinophobia, has attracted numerous attention from both computer scientists and social scientists (Vidgen et al., 2020; Cook et al., 2021; Lee, 2021; Ziems et al., 2020). Anti-Asian hate speech could be understood as any speech that targets Asians and people of Asian descendants in a way that elevates hatred, violence, or social disorder.

Scapegoating immigrants in public crises is not unique to Asians during the COVID-19 pandemic, but has a long tradition in American history (Daniels et al., 2021; Reny and Barreto, 2020; Zhang, 2021). For instance, tuberculosis was called "the Jewish disease" in the 1890s and Italian immigrants were blamed for the 1916 polio epidemic. Chinese immigrants were blamed for the spread of smallpox in San Francisco in the later 1870s and the spread of SARS in 2003 (Daniels et al., 2021). Now Asian immigrants, specifically Chinese immigrants, are scapegoated for the origin and spread of COVID-19. Since the pandemic, around 2 million Asian American adults have experienced various forms of anti-Asian hate incident such as being beaten, spit on, and harassed based on AAPI Data reports (Lee, 2021). Federal-level hate crime data also shows that anti-Asian hate crimes increased by 149% in 16 major cities while hate crimes, in general, decreased by 7%. When former President Trump singled out China as the origin of the pandemic and publicly used derogatory terms such as "Chinese Virus" and "Kung Flu," Asian Americans, particularly immigrants of Chinese descendent, became the primary target of anti-Asian hate crimes (Lee, 2021; Horton, 2020).

Anti-Asian bigotry, violence, and misogyny were ingrained in American history following the passage of the Page Act of 1875 and the 1882 Chinese Exclusion Act which prohibited the importation of Chinese laborers and women(Kim, 1999; Zhang, 2021). Asian Americans were often perceived as "disease, unassimilable aliens, and economic, cultural, and moral threats to a free White republic"(Lee, 2021). Even today, Asian Americans, particularly women of Asian descendants, are still the victims of anti-Asian misogyny and hatred (e.g., the Atlanta mass shooting in March 2021). [1] Even before the COVID-19 outbreak, hate crimes against Asians increased by 31% in 2016-2018 under the Trump administration (Lee, 2021).

3 Data

To understand the anti-Asian hate sentiments before and in the pandemic, we use COVID specific hate terms, general anti-Asian hate terms, anti-Chinese politics terms, and counter-hate terms to extract all relevant tweets from Twitter's historical database. This allows us to obtain a holistic view of multiplex anti-China or Asian hate sentiment. Here we briefly describe how we built our datasets and more information can be found in the Appendix. Since online hate speech mainly targets China, we focus on these anti-China related keywords in the present study. In future works, we wish to extend this study to other Asian countries.

COVID-Specific Hate Data First, we use keywords, such as *'chinese virus'*, *'china virus'*, *'wuhan virus'*, *'kungflu'*, and their variants, to extract all relevant tweets that target AAPI communities. Next, we use Ziems et al.'s classifier to identify and exclude all these counter-hate tweets.

General Anti-AAPI Hate Data We use keywords, such as *'bamboo coon'*, *'chigger'*, *'chinese*

[1] see NPR article: For Asian American Women, Misogyny And Racism Are Inseparable, Sociologist Says

wetback', *'ching chong'*, *'chonky'*, *'chunky'*, *'slant eye'*, *'slopehead'*, *'bat eater'*, *'chink'*, *'ling ling'*, and *'commies'* to extract all non-COVID19 related but also hateful tweets that target AAPI communities. Some of the keywords can be used in a multitude of scenarios, in such cases we removed those keywords using a few filters to only collect tweets that target the AAPI community.

Anti-Chinese Politics Data We use keywords and hashtags, such as *'BoycottChina'*, *'MakeChinaPay'*, *'StandWithHongKong'*, *'FreeTibet'*, *'FuckChina'*, *'CCP_is_terrorist'*, and *'Chinazi'* to extract all tweets that target china politically.

Counter-Hate Data We collect counter-hate data from two sources. First, we use counter hate terms askeywords, such as *'Racisimisvirus'*, *'StopAsianHate'*, and *'StopAAPIHate'*. We then use Ziems et al's (2020) classifier to extract those counter-hate tweets from the datasets collected with hateful terms.

Table 1 shows basic statistics for our four main datasets collected using the Twitter academic API. Note that these datasets span across different time periods. Researchers can use these datasets for different purposes. For instance, we can use these datasets to test the following hypotheses related to the overall anti-Asian or Chinese hate sentiments in the COVID-19 pandemic or the persistence of anti-Asian sentiment.

Hypothesis 1. The overall anti-Asian hate sentiments should be consistent before and after the outbreak of the COVID-19 pandemic.

Hypothesis 2. The pandemic threat has engendered the rise of COVID-19 specific hate sentiments on Twitter.

4 Results

In this section, we report the major trends and patterns from our four main datasets. We start with COVID19-Specific hate data.

4.1 COVID-Specific Hate Data

In the early stage of the COVID-19 pandemic, Twitter users used COVID-19 specific terms such as *'chinese virus'*, *'china virus'*, *'wuhan virus'*, and *'kungflu'* to describe the novel coronavirus. In February 2020, WHO named the disease caused by the novel coronavirus as COVID-19, but still these racial slurs remained popular on Twitter, especially after U.S. President Trump tweeted Chinese Virus multiple times in three consecutive days in mid March, 2020:

> *The United States will be powerfully supporting those industries, like Airlines and others, that are particularly affected by the Chinese Virus. We will be stronger than ever before!* Mar 16, 2020

> *Cuomo wants "all states to be treated the same." But all states aren't the same. Some are being hit hard by the Chinese Virus, some are being hit practically not at all. New York is a very big "hotspot", West Virginia has, thus far, zero cases. Andrew, keep politics out of it....* Mar 17, 2020

> *I always treated the Chinese Virus very seriously, and have done a very good job from the beginning, including my very early decision to close the "borders" from China-against the wishes of almost all. Many lives were saved. The Fake News new narrative is disgraceful & false!* Mar 18, 2020

In Figure 1, the blue line shows the overall trend of tweets mentioning any COVID-19 related racial slurs, peaking around mid-March when Trump tweeted Chinese Virus. Note that Figure 7 is presented to normalize these patterns based on the estimated total number of tweets.

We also used state-of-the-art hate speech detection algorithms to classify whether these racial slurs count as hate speech. In general, all hate speech detectors have some degree of noise and subjectivity. For this reason, we provide our potential users with three sets of labels classified by algorithms of Ziems et al. (2020), Davidson et al. (2017), and Vidgen et al. (2020), whose aggregated counts are shown in Figure 1. Note that you can find more details regarding these classifiers in the appendix. The strong consistency between Ziems classifier and Vidgen classifier suggests that classification noise does not overwhelm the observed signal. We also notice that the Davidson classifier is less likely to classify tweets as hate speech, partly because it was initially trained on non-group-specific hate tweets.

4.2 General Anti-AAPI Hate Data

While Figure 1 clearly shows an increase in the volume of COVID-19 related hate tweets during

Table 1: **Summary of Twitter Data (in millions)**

	COVID-Hate	AAPI-Hate	Anti-Chinese Politics	Counter-Hate
# of tweets	12.93	12.92	32.6	9.93
# of unique tweets	3.29	7.24	6.36	2.14
# of retweets	9.64	5.68	26.29	7.79
# of Twitter users	3.15	4.58	2.85	3.39
Time range	2019.12-2021.3	2008.1-2021.3	2019.12-2020.12	2018.1-2021.12

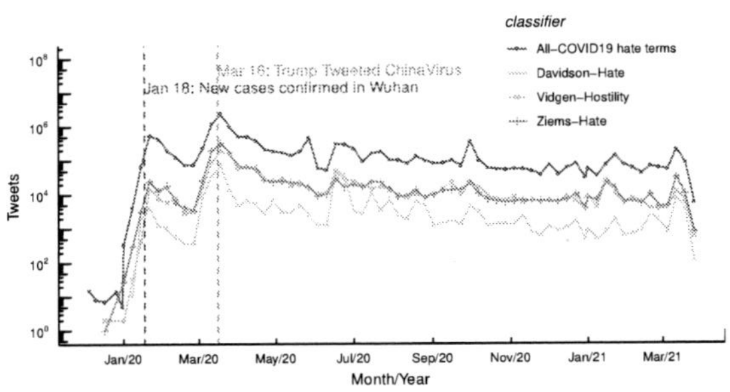

Figure 1: Weekly Trend of COVID-19 Hate Terms, as classified by three different hate-speech detectors.

the pandemic, it is unclear if this corresponds to an increase in hate or an increase in tweets about COVID-19. To provide a baseline, and to investigate anti-China or Asian hate sentiment *before* the COVID-19 outbreak, for comparison, we built the general anti-AAPI hate data using these anti-Chinese or Asian hate terms.

Figure 2 shows the monthly trends of different anti-AAPI hate terms in our database. We believe that these numbers significantly underestimate the true number of abusive tweets, since such slurs are easily identifiable and verifiable after reporting, and thus a large portion of them were removed by Twitter long ago.

The top blue line in Figure 2 shows the number of tweets containing any of the general hate terms between Jan 2008 and March 2021. We see a rapid increase in the number of tweets using anti-AAPI racial slurs from the founding of Twitter in 2007 to early 2013, and this growth may be attributed to the exponential growth of Twitter users at the same time. But after that, we see a decline pattern in the Obama administration before 2017. After Trump took over the Oval office, we see a clear increase in these hateful tweets. This could be attributed to a worsening of the US-China relations due to a growing trade war, or sentiments against the Chinese government due to its role in Taiwan and Hong Kong issues. We also present isolated counts of the major general hate terms used by Twitter users, including *'chink', 'coolie', 'sideways vagina', 'chinaman', 'chonk', etc.* One interesting pattern is that we see a huge increase in using *'Chunk' or 'chonk'* after 2018.

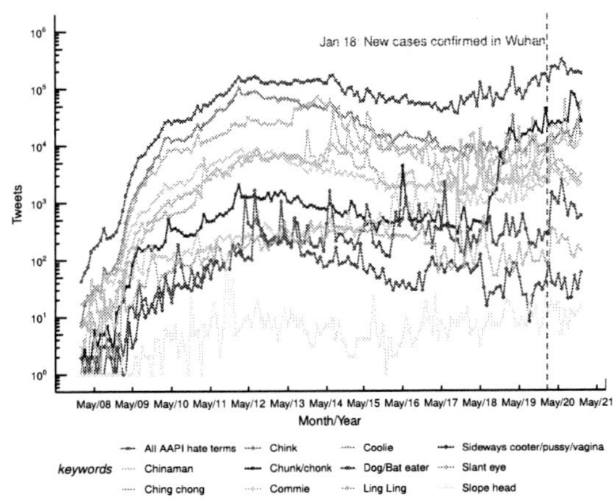

Figure 2: Monthly Trend for Anti-AAPI Hate Terms, as classified by three different hate-speech detectors.

4.3 Anti-Chinese Politics Data

While the general anti-AAPi dataset establishes a much clearer and COVID-agnostic metric of Asian hate, it also has faults as 1) these tweets include many outdated slurs that may not dominate the hateful users' vocabulary anymore, and 2) they are easy to detect by Twitter's own anti-hate software, and easily verified and removed and are thus likely undercounted. We therefore investigate a third AAPI hate dataset which covers a much grayer area, targeting subject matter that attracts hate speech: controversial Chinese politics. Here, our goal is not so much to argue that discussing Chinese politics in a negative way is in itself hateful, but that hateful users tend to use these subjects as an outlet to propagate anti-Asian sentiments. This can be measured, for example, by establishing significant overlap between users who post with obvious anti-Asian slurs and users who post in this dataset.

Figure 3 shows the weekly trend of these anti-Chinese politics terms on Twitter from Jan 2019 to December 2020. We observe an increase in the number of Tweets mentioning any anti-Chinese politics such as *'BoycottChina', 'MakeChinaPay'*, and *'Uyghur'* before the outbreak of COVID-19. But since then, the total number of anti-Chinese politics tweets bounced back and fluctuated in the early stage of the pandemic. We suspect Twitter users' attention has shifted from anti-Chinese politics to these COVID-19 specific issues.

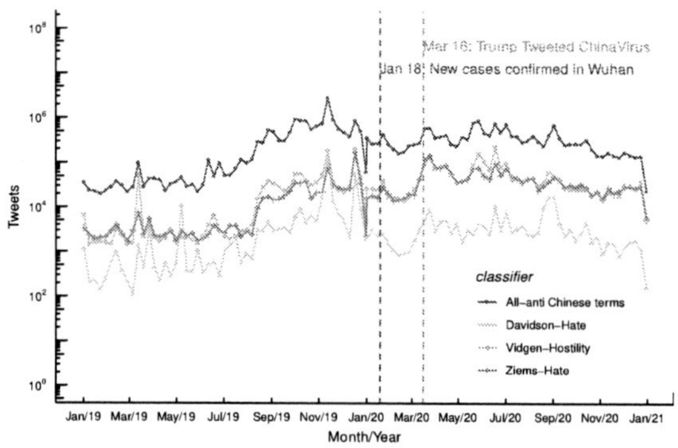

Figure 3: Weekly Trend of Anti-Chinese Politics tweets, as classified by three different hate-speech detectors.

4.4 COVID Counter-Hate Data

In addition to hate datasets, we also built a counter-hate dataset to assess the dynamics between pro- and anti-Chinese or Asian groups. Figure 4 shows the overall counter-hate weekly tweets after the outbreak of COVID-19.

Since the pandemic, we have seen a troublesome surge of anti-Asian attacks. This raises substantial concerns within the AAPI communities. We see a rapid increase in tweets that counter anti-AAPI hate speech such as *'RacismIsVirus'* and *'StopAAPIHate'*. The counter-hate tweets peaked after Trump tweets Chinese Virus on March and then declined. The StopAAPIHate movement took off after the early 2021 and peaked after the tragedy of Atlanta Spa mass shootings on March 16, 2021. Our dataset provides unique de-identified author IDs and conservation IDs which allow researchers to assess the interaction among Twitter users.

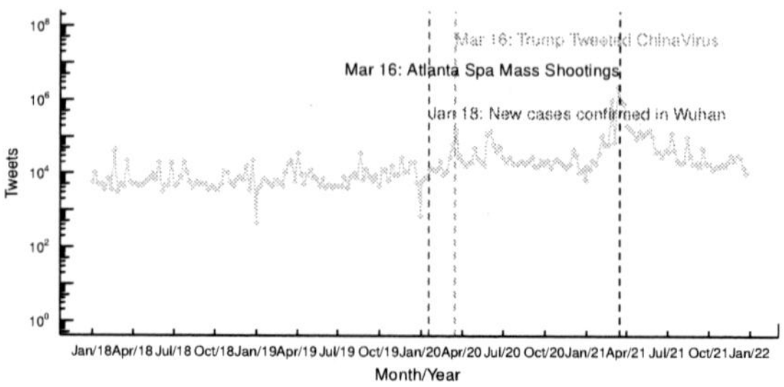

Figure 4: Weekly Trend of Counter-Hate Tweets

4.5 Hashtag Analysis

Here we provide some basic hashtag analysis in our four main datasets. What are the most popular hashtags in our datasets?

Figure 5 shows the hashtags used by Twitter users co-occurring with other keywords. Panel A shows that the most popular hashtags in anti-Chinese politics dataset are *#StandwithHongKong* and *#HongKong*. Panel B shows that the most popular hashtags used by counter hate users are related to *#StopAsianHate* and *#AsiansAreHuman*. Panel C shows that the most popular hashtags in COVID19-specific hate dataset are *#ChineseVirus*, *#CoronaVirus*, and *#WuhanVirus*. Panel D shows that the most popular hashtags used in general anti-AAPI hate dataset are *#boycottChina*, *#China*, and *#CCP*.

4.6 Overlapping Analysis

We conduct an extra analysis to examine the overlapping between COVID-Hate and AAPI-Hate data as well as between COVID-Hate and anti-Chinese politics data. We suspect that Twitter users who expressed general anti-AAPI hate and anti-Chinese politics were also more likely to show COVID-specific hatred in the pandemic. For those who posted COVID-19 specific hate terms in the pandemic, there are 741,802 Twitter users from the general anti-AAPI hate dataset and contributed 7.2 million tweets. These twitter users accounted for 23.57% of total users and 55.71% of total tweets in COVID-Hate dataset. There are also 864,287 Twitter users from anti-Chinese politics dataset overlapping with COVID specific hate data and contributed 7.86 million tweets. These twitter users accounted for 27.46% of total users and 60.77% of total tweets in COVID-Hate dataset. Figure 6 shows the monthly or weekly trends of these overlapping Twitter users.

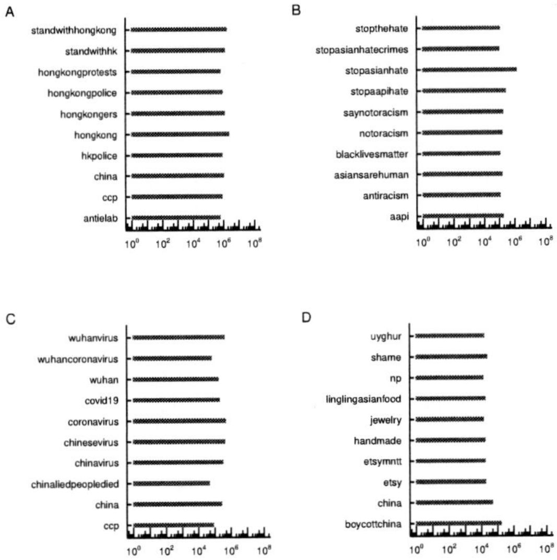

Figure 5: Top Hashtags in Four Main Datasets. Panel A: anti-Chinese politics; Panel B: Counter hate; Panel C: COVID-specific hate; Panel D: General Anti-AAPI Hate.

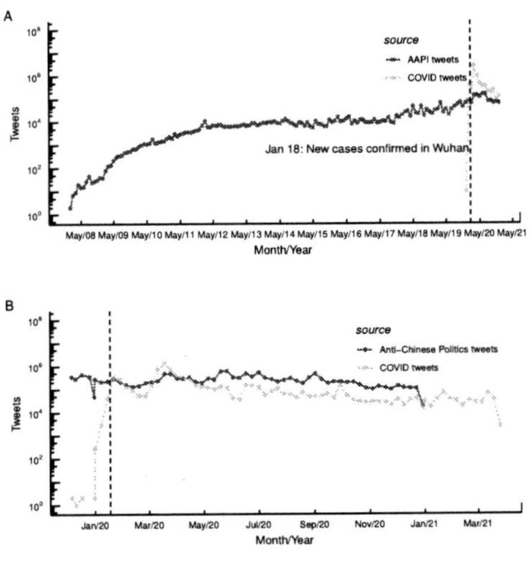

Figure 6: Monthly or Weekly Trend of Overlapping Twitter Users. Panel A: between COVID-Hate and AAPI-Hate; Panel B: between COVID-Hate and Anti-Chinese Politics

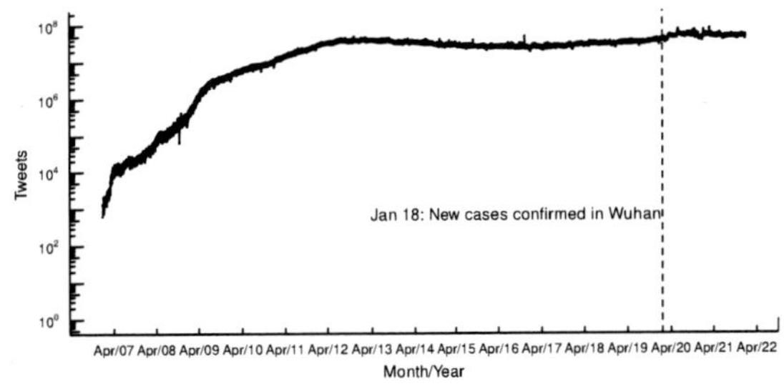

Figure 7: The Baseline Tweets for Normalizing Our Datasets Calculated by Counting the Number of Tweets including Common Words. (See appendix.)

5 Conclusion

This paper introduces new datasets to study anti-Asian hate speech and sentiment on Twitter before and during the pandemic. We show that the overall anti-Chinese/Asian hate sentiments were consistent before and after the outbreak of the COVID-19 pandemic, but the pandemic threat has engendered the rise of COVID-19 specific hate sentiments on Twitter.

Hate speech online is a multiplex phenomenon. We built our datasets using keywords related to COVID-19 specific hate terms, general anti-AAPI hate terms, and anti-Chinese politics terms as well as counter hate terms. As shown in our main analysis, we demonstrate that we can use these datasets to illustrate the overall trends and patterns of anti-Asian hate speech online, and use aggregate statistics to demonstrate and describe the rise in anti-AAPI hate speech during the COVID era.

Researchers can also use these datasets to study how Twitter users are radicalized by engaging into controversial conversations or what the linguistic features of hate speech on Twitter are. We also provide the baseline tweets for researchers to normalize the trend of our datasets as shown in Figure 7. Researchers can also use the de-identified author IDs and conversation IDs (which is unique IDs for all Tweets within the same reply thread and reply threads that are created from earlier reply threads) to conduct conversation network analysis. Future users should be aware of possible underreporting due to many blatantly abusive tweets already being removed. Still, our novel datasets can contribute to research in the areas of computational social science, machine learning, and hate speech detection.

Acknowledgements

We wish to thank the Institute for Advanced Computational Science at Stony Brook University for the access to high performance computing systems and its generous seed grant support for Yongjun Zhang and Yifan Sun.

References

Gavin Cook, Junming Huang, and Yu Xie. 2021. How COVID-19 has impacted american attitudes toward china: A study on twitter. *CoRR*, abs/2108.11040.

Stephen M. Croucher, Thao Nguyen, and Diyako Rahmani. 2020. Prejudice toward asian americans in the covid-19 pandemic: The effects of social media use in the united states. *Frontiers in Communication*, 5.

Chelsea Daniels, Paul DiMaggio, G. Cristina Mora, and Hana Shepherd. 2021. Has pandemic threat stoked xenophobia? how covid-19 influences california voters' attitudes toward diversity and immigration*. volume 36, pages 889–915.

Thomas Davidson, Dana Warmsley, Michael Macy, and Ingmar Weber. 2017. Automated hate speech detection and the problem of offensive language. In *Proceedings of the International AAAI Conference on Web and Social Media*, volume 11.

Fabio Del Vigna12, Andrea Cimino23, Felice Dell'Orletta, Marinella Petrocchi, and Maurizio Tesconi. 2017. Hate me, hate me not: Hate speech detection on facebook. In *Proceedings of the First Italian Conference on Cybersecurity (ITASEC17)*, pages 86–95.

Richard Horton. 2020. Offline: Covid-19 and the dangers of sinophobia. *Lancet (London, England)*, 396(10245):154.

Julie Jiang, Emily Chen, Shen Yan, Kristina Lerman, and Emilio Ferrara. 2020. Political polarization drives online conversations about covid-19 in the united states. *Human Behavior and Emerging Technologies*, 2(3):200–211.

Claire Jean Kim. 1999. The racial triangulation of asian americans. *Politics & society*, 27(1):105–138.

Jennifer Lee. 2021. Reckoning with asian america and the new culture war on affirmative action. In *Sociological Forum*. Wiley Online Library.

Tyler T Reny and Matt A Barreto. 2020. Xenophobia in the time of pandemic: othering, anti-asian attitudes, and covid-19. *Politics, Groups, and Identities*, pages 1–24.

Bertie Vidgen, Scott Hale, Ella Guest, Helen Margetts, David Broniatowski, Zeerak Waseem, Austin Botelho, Matthew Hall, and Rebekah Tromble. 2020. Detecting East Asian prejudice on social media. In *Proceedings of the Fourth Workshop on Online Abuse and Harms*, pages 162–172, Online. Association for Computational Linguistics.

William Warner and Julia Hirschberg. 2012. Detecting hate speech on the world wide web. In *Proceedings of the second workshop on language in social media*, pages 19–26.

Dennis Zhang. 2021. Sinophobic epidemics in america: Historical discontinuity in disease-related yellow peril imaginaries of the past and present. *Journal of Medical Humanities*, 42(1):63–80.

Caleb Ziems, Bing He, Sandeep Soni, and Srijan Kumar. 2020. Racism is a virus: Anti-asian hate and counterhate in social media during the covid-19 crisis. *arXiv preprint arXiv:2005.12423*.

A Appendix

A.1 Code and Data Availability

Codes and aggregated data used to replicate main figures are available via `https://osf.io/xtw4c/`. Dis-aggregated and de-identified data are available for academic use upon request. You can email the corresponding author for the data sharing agreement form.

A.2 Key words

Here we provide a detailed list of keywords and hashtags we used to extract all tweets.

COVID-Specific Hate Data. We use keywords, including *'chinese virus', 'china virus', 'wuhan virus', 'wuhan coronavirus', 'kungflu', 'china coronavirus', 'chinese coronavirus', 'chinavirus', 'chinesevirus', 'wuhanvirus', 'Kung flu'*.

General Anti-AAPI Hate Data. *'bamboo coon', 'bamboo coons', 'celestial', 'celestials', 'chigger', 'chiggers', 'chinese wetback', 'chinese wetbacks', 'ching chong', 'ching chongs', 'chinig', 'chinigs', 'chink a billies', 'chink a billy', 'chonkies', 'chonky', 'chunkies', 'chunky', 'coolie', 'coolies', 'sideways cooter', 'sideways cooters', 'sideways pussies', 'sideways pussy', 'sideways vagina', 'sideways vaginas', 'slant eye', 'slant eyes', 'slopehead', 'slopeheads', 'aseng', 'bat eater', 'boycottchina', 'chinadidthis', 'chinaman', 'chinamen', 'chink', 'chinky', 'cokin', 'dog eater', 'fuckchina', 'ling ling', 'makechinapay', 'niakoué', 'pastel de flango', 'slant-eye', 'ting tong', 'idiot chink', 'chinky bat', 'commie', 'commies'*.

Anti-Chinese Politics Data. *'BoycottChina', 'MakeChinaPay', 'BoycottChineseProducts', 'boycottchina', 'StandWithHongKong', 'BoyCottChina', 'Uyghur', 'ReplaceIT', 'BoycottMadeInChina', 'FreeUyghur', 'boycottChina', 'antichinazi', 'CCPChina', 'BoycottChineseProduct', 'FreeTibet', 'FuckChina', 'CCP_is_terrorist', 'FreeHongKong', 'StopChina', 'BOYCOTTChina', 'StandwithHK', 'fuckchina', 'Chinazi', 'Tibet', 'Genocide', 'AnywherebutChina', 'ABC_challenge', 'Uyghurs', 'China_is_terrorist', 'HongKongers', 'BOYCOTTCHINA', 'XiJinping', 'MadeInChina', 'Boycottchina', 'TakeDownTheCCP', 'AntiChinazi', 'FreeHK', 'ChineseProductsInDustbin', 'SOSHK', 'BoycottChineseApp', 'FUCKCHINA', 'SanctionChina', 'RemoveChinaApps', 'chinazism', 'fuckchina', 'SaveUygur', 'Chinamustfall', 'HKPoliceState', 'HoldChinaAccountable', 'StandWithHK', 'Xitler', 'CCPChina', 'HongKongPolice', 'Communist', 'BoycottCh', 'antitotalitarianism', 'ChinaBacksTerror', 'antiELAB', 'FreedomHK', 'TaiwanIsNotChina', 'Hongkongprotest', 'boycottchinaproducts', 'fuckChina'.*

Counter Hate Data. *'StopAsianHate', 'AsiansAreHuman', 'StopAAPIHate', 'stopasianhate', 'NOtoracistMedia', 'RacismIsNotComedy', 'NOSilence', 'StopAsianHateCrimes', 'AsianAmericans', 'PROTECTASIANLIVES', 'AsianLivesMatter', 'RacismIsAVirus', 'RacismIsNotAnOpinion', 'AAPI', 'RacismIsntComedy', 'StopAsianHa', 'STOPASIANHATE', 'NoRacismInMedia', 'SayNOtoRacism', 'STOPASIANRACISM', 'AsiansAreHu', 'IamNotAVirus', 'racismisavirus', 'stopaapihate', 'HATEISAVIRUS', 'ProtectOurElders', 'StopRacism', 'EndAntiAsianViolence', 'StopWhiteTerrorism', 'StopWhiteSupremacy', 'AsianAreHuman', 'stopracism', 'RacismInAmerica', 'RacismIsNotJoke', 'StandForAsians', 'StopTheHate', 'StopTheAttacks', 'stopasianhatecrimes', 'AAPIFightBack', 'FightRacism', 'NoToRacism', 'ProtectAsianWomen', 'AAPIHate', 'WorldAgainstRacism', 'WeCantBeSilenced', 'EndWhiteSupremacy', 'StandWithAsians', 'NoChanceForRacism', 'ProtectAsianLives', 'antiracism', 'EndViolenceAgainstWomen', 'IAmNotAVirus', 'WashTheHate', 'RacismIsAVirus', 'IAmNotCovid19', 'BeCool2Asians', 'StopAAPIHate', 'ActToChange', 'HateIsAVirus'.*

Common (Non-stopwords) Words for Normalization Plot. Note that Twitter API does not accept stop words in the query string to get an estimate of total number of tweets containg the word.

'ask', 'be', 'become', 'begin', 'call', 'can', 'come', 'could', 'do', 'feel', 'find', 'get', 'give', 'go', 'have', 'hear', 'help', 'keep', 'know', 'leave', 'let', 'like', 'live', 'look','make', 'may', 'mean', 'might', 'move', 'need', 'play', 'put', 'run', 'say', 'see', 'seem', 'should', 'show', 'start', 'take', 'talk', 'tell', 'think', 'try', 'turn', 'use', 'want', 'will', 'work', 'would'.

A.3 Information on Classifiers

Davidson et al. (2017)'s Model: The dataset used in constructing the model was scraped from Twitter with the help of hate speech lexicon available on hatespeech.org. The total dataset size is around 25k which were manually labeled into one of the following classes Hate (5.7%), Offensive (77.4%), and Neither (16.7%).

After text-preprocessing like lowercase and stemming, uni-gram, bi-gram and tri-grams were constructed and weighted by their TF-IDF scores. Along with this the authors included binary and count indicators for hashtags, mentions, retweets, and URLs, as well as features for the number of characters, words, and syllables in each tweet.

The authors experimented with different models and finally chose to use Logistic Regression with L2 regularization. They claim that the best performing model has an overall precision of 0.91, recall of 0.90, and F1 score of 0.90. The caveat they mention regarding this classifier is that it tends to classify tweets as less hateful or offensive than the human coders.

Ziems et al. (2020)'s Model: The training data used to build the classifier was a sampled version of a large text corpus scraped from Twitter. The authors manually labeled a set of 3,255 tweets. They then considered a set of 2,290 where all the annotators agreed with the same tag. The dataset is categorized into Hate Speech (18.7%), Counter hate speech (22.5%) and Neutral (58.6%).

The authors constructed three sets of features for classification: Linguistic, Hashtag, and BERT embeddings. Linguistic features are a set of 90 features which span across stylistic, metadata, and psycholinguistic categories. Hashtag feature is a vector representation of the number of occurrences of a hashtag or a keyword from the list the authors had compiled. BERT Embeddings are the embeddings constructed using a BERT model with a classification head that was fine tuned to label the tweets into one of the above mentioned classes.

Along with the BERT classification model authors also, separately trained two feed forward neural networks to classify the tweets using Linguistic and Hashtag features. They concluded that the BERT classification model outperformed these feed forward neural networks with better F1, recall, and precision metrics.

Vidgen et al. (2020)'s Model: A dataset of 20k is scrapped from Twitter using hashtags that relate to East Asian Hate and Virus, some of which express anti-East Asian sentiments. The data is segregated into 6 categories and the distribution is as follows: Hostility (19.5%), Criticism (7.2%), Counter Speech (0.6%), Discussion on East Asian Prejudice (5.1%), and Neutral (67.6%).

The authors combined Counter Speech and Discussion on East Asian Prejudice due to low prevalence and conceptual similarity. They replaced all the hashtags present in the data with suitable thematic words which they constructed during annotation setup or a generic hashtag token. Post this a large language model RoBERTa with a classification head is fine tuned for the task of this classification and they claim that they observed best results with this setup with an F1 score of 0.83 as opposed to their LSTM baseline with F1 score of 0.76.

Domain-Aware Contrastive Knowledge Transfer for Multi-domain Imbalanced Data

Zixuan Ke*
UIC Computer Science
Chicago, IL
zke4@uic.edu

Mohammad Kachuee
Amazon Alexa AI
Seattle, WA

Sungjin Lee
Amazon Alexa AI
Seattle, WA

{kachum, sungjinl}@amazon.com

Abstract

In many real-world machine learning applications, samples belong to a set of domains e.g., for product reviews each review belongs to a product category. In this paper, we study multi-domain imbalanced learning (MIL), the scenario that there is imbalance not only in classes but also in domains. In the MIL setting, different domains exhibit different patterns and there is a varying degree of similarity and divergence among domains posing opportunities and challenges for transfer learning especially when faced with limited or insufficient training data. We propose a novel domain-aware contrastive knowledge transfer method called DCMI to (1) identify the shared domain knowledge to encourage positive transfer among similar domains (in particular from head domains to tail domains); (2) isolate the domain-specific knowledge to minimize the negative transfer from dissimilar domains. We evaluated the performance of DCMI on three different datasets showing significant improvements in different MIL scenarios.

1 Introduction

The majority of existing works in imbalanced learning focus on the *class imbalance setting* where classes are presented in a long-tailed distribution: a subset of classes (head classes) have sufficient samples, while other uncommon or rare classes (tail classes) are underrepresented by limited samples. This setting is challenging because the model naturally focuses largely on the majority classes and there may be no sufficient data for tail classes to recover their underlying distribution (Liu et al., 2019).

Even though extensive work has been done on the class imbalance problem, the consideration of *domains*[1] is often missed. In many real-world scenarios, data naturally belongs to a set of domains e.g., for an online store, a potential domain assignment for each customer review can be defined based on the corresponding store departments.

A simplistic solution is to ignore domain assignments and train a classifier for all domains, which we refer to as *domain agnostic learning (D-AL)*. D-AL entirely ignores domains and assumes that the model can "automatically" discover the data distribution for domains and learn them equally well. The drawbacks of such an approach are obvious: if the training data is sourced from many domains, updating all parameters may lead the model to focus on the subsets of the data in proportion to their ease of access or frequency. Moreover, if the data from different domains are dissimilar, agnostic learning may cause undesirable convergence dynamics i.e., negative transfer. We, therefore, argue that in the *multi-domain imbalanced learning (MIL)* scenarios, a learning algorithm should consider domain information and leverage them to achieve effective knowledge transfer.

The MIL is a challenging problem. First, different domains may have very different number of samples and show a long-tailed distribution. For example, an intelligent assistant (e.g. Amazon Alexa) may provide a wide variety of skills and different skills may vary largely in number of examples. It is possible that some internal developed skills (e.g. music or whether) have hundreds of thousands of samples while many third-party developed skills may have only less than 10 samples in the same dataset (Kachuee et al., 2021). Second, domains may exhibit different semantic similarities and disparities with each other. For instance, a feature may show positive correlation with a label for cer-

*Work done as an intern at Amazon Alexa AI.

[1]In this paper, the term *domain* is used to refer to a segmentation of samples, and it should not be confused with the same term also used in the domain adaptation literature studying the distribution shift problem.

Proceedings of the 12th Workshop on Computational Approaches to Subjectivity, Sentiment & Social Media Analysis, pages 25 - 36
May 26, 2022 ©2022 Association for Computational Linguistics

tain domains while it is negatively correlated for others. Third, the data-provided domain annotation may not be completely accurate or sufficiently fine-grained. For example, a sentence *"Due to software or hardware issues, my computer cannot open my favorite text book, One hundred Years of Solitude"* may belong to both *computer* and *books* domains while it may have only one domain assignment in the dataset.

Perhaps the most intuitive approach for MIL is *multi-task learning (MTL)*, where separate heads are used for different domains. While MTL considers domains, we will show it performs poorly in our experiments due to the lack of knowledge transfer between the classifiers. We believe that the key to successful MIL is to not only enable but encourage positive transfer learning across domains.

In this paper, we propose Domain-aware Contrastive Knowledge Transfer for Muti-domain Imbalance learning (DCMI). DCMI introduces a novel *domain-aware representation layer* based on domain embeddings which enables fine-grained and scalable representation sharing or separation. Complementary to the data provided domain assignments, we use an auxiliary domain classification task to help determine the relevance of a *sample* to each domain i.e., *soft domain assignments*. DCMI uses a novel contrastive knowledge transfer objective to move the representation from similar domains closer and representation from dissimilar domains further apart. We conduct extensive experiments on three different multi-domain imbalanced datasets to demonstrate the effectiveness of DCMI.

2 Related Work

The recent imbalance learning literature can be organized into the following categories:

Data Resampling. This is one of the most widely used practices to artificially balance the distribution. Two popular options are under-sampling (Buda et al., 2018; More, 2016) and over-sampling (Buda et al., 2018; Sarafianos et al., 2018; Shen et al., 2016). Under-sampling removes data from the head (dominant classes) while over-sampling repeats the data from the tail (minority classes). These approaches can be problematic as discarding tends to remove important samples and duplicating tends to introduce bias or overfitting.

Data Augmentation. Data augmentation has been used to enrich the tail classes. A popular approach is to leverage the Mixup (Zhang et al., 2018) technique to augment the minority classes. Remix (Chou et al., 2020) assigns the label in favor of minority classes to the mixup samples, Liu et al. (2020) prepares a "feature cloud" for mixing up that has a larger distribution range for tail classes. Kim et al. (2020) adds noise to head classes to generate tail classes. Chu et al. (2020) decomposes the feature spaces and generate tail classes samples by combining class-shared feature from head classes and class-specific features from tail classes. However, this is usually a non-trivial work to generate meaningful samples that can help tail classes.

Loss Reweighting. The basic idea of reweighting is to allocate larger weight for loss terms corresponding to tail classes while less weight for head classes. In class-sensitive cross-entropy loss (Japkowicz and Stephen, 2002), the weight for each class is inversely proportional to the number of samples. Ren et al. (2018) leverages a hold-out evaluation set to minimize the balanced loss.

Regularization. This approach adds an additional regularization term to improve the training for the tail samples. Lin et al. (2017) adds a factor to the standard cross-entropy loss to put more focus on hard, misclassified samples (usually attributed to the minority classes). Cao et al. (2019) proposed to regularize the minority classes strongly so that the generalization error of minority classes can be improved. While regularization is simple and effective, the soft penalty can be insufficient to make the model focus on the tail classes and a large penalty may negatively affect the learning itself.

Parameter isolation. It has been shown that decoupling the learning into representation learning and classifier learning can be quite effective. BBN Zhou et al. (2020) proposed a two-branch approach where the representation learning branch is trained as there is no class imbalance (input random sampling data) while the classifier learning branch applies the reverse sampling technique. The two branches are then combined by a curriculum learning strategy. Wang et al. (2021) further improves BBN by replacing the cross-entropy loss in representation learning branch into a prototypical supervised contrastive loss. This approach offers the opportunity to optimize each part separately but also make it hard to transfer knowledge from head to tail classes

Domain Imbalanced Learning. The above approaches mostly consider the class imbalance but ignore the imbalance across domains. Cheng et al.

(2020) proposed a doubly balancing technique for both class imbalance and cross-domain imbalance, which only limited to two domains, without any explicit mechanism to encourage the positive transfer and avoid the negative transfer.

3 Problem Definition

In this paper, we assume access to a set of samples $(\boldsymbol{x}_i, y_i, j)$ for $i = \{1 \dots N\}$, $y_i \in \{1 \dots C\}$, and $j \in \{1 \dots M\}$. Here, N is the number of samples, C is the number of classes, and M is number of domains, i.e., shared feature space and label set across domains. We assume the scenario where exists (a) *class imbalance*: classes are not evenly distributed in each domain; (b) *domain imbalance*: domains are not evenly distributed, i.e., some domains may have much more or less number of examples than other domains; and (c) *domain divergence*: while some domains are naturally similar to others and thus positively correlated, some domains are naturally dissimilar to others and negatively correlated. Given these assumptions, in *multi-domain imbalanced learning* (MIL) we seek a model to minimize the expected loss for all domains (i.e., macro average).

4 Proposed Method

Fig. 1 presents an overview of the proposed method. In the MIL problem, it is crucial to identify the *shared knowledge* that can be transferred across similar domains to improve the tail domain performance and the *domain-specific knowledge* that needs to be handled carefully to avoid a negative transfer. To obtain domain-aware representations, we leverage domain embeddings to adaptively select the useful representation for each specific domain (Sec. 4.1). Additionally, regardless of the dataset provided domain assignment, in reality, a sample can belong to multiple domains to different degrees. To address this, we propose a *domain classification* task to obtain the relevance of a sample to each domain and transfer the related domain knowledge using a *contrastive* method (Sec. 4.2).

4.1 Domain-Aware Representation

We suggest a domain-aware representation layer to adaptively select the appropriate representation (neurons) for each domain. For a domain j, the corresponding embedding $\boldsymbol{v}^j$ consists of differentiable parameters that can be learned in an end-to-end fashion. Based on this, the sigmoid function is

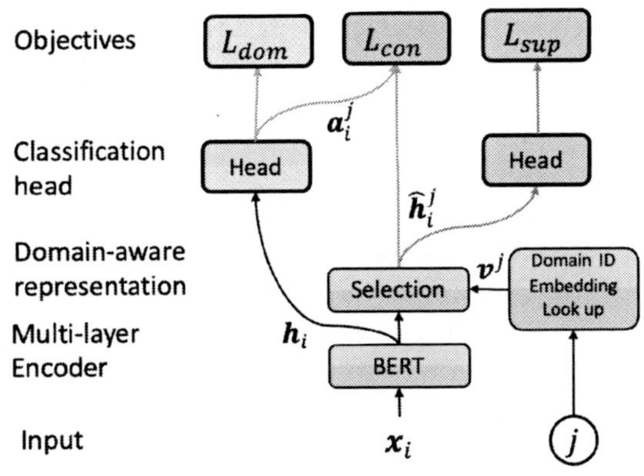

Figure 1: An overview of the DCMI training process. (i) DCMI takes as input a sample $x^{(i)}$ from domain j. (ii) The encoded feature vector $\boldsymbol{h}_i$ is computed using a shared body network (e.g., BERT). (iii) The domain index is used to get the corresponding domain embedding used to compute the domain mask $\boldsymbol{m}_j$ and domain-aware representation $\hat{\boldsymbol{h}}_i^j$. (iv) The supervised classification ($\mathcal{L}_{\text{sup}}$), contrastive ($\mathcal{L}_{\text{con}}$), and domain classification ($\mathcal{L}_{\text{dom}}$) loss terms are computed (see Section 4.2). (v) The flow of gradients from each loss term is controlled such that each term is only used to optimize a subset of trainable parameters as indicated by green, blue, and orange colors in the drawing.

used to find the corresponding domain mask $\boldsymbol{m}^j$:

$$\boldsymbol{m}^j = \sigma(\boldsymbol{v}^j / \tau) \; . \tag{1}$$

Where τ is a temperature variable, linearly annealed from 1 to τ_{min} (a small positive value).

To obtain the *domain-aware representation*, we use element-wise multiplication of the output of the body network (i.e., BERT in this paper) $\boldsymbol{h}$ and the mask $\boldsymbol{m}^j$:

$$\hat{\boldsymbol{h}}_i^j = \boldsymbol{h}_i \odot \boldsymbol{m}^j \; . \tag{2}$$

Note that the neurons in $\boldsymbol{m}^j$ may overlap with those in other domain masks to enable knowledge sharing.

To make sure the $\boldsymbol{v}^j$ to have a wide range and its gradient to have a large magnitude, a gradient compensation technique is employed to the original gradient $\boldsymbol{g}$ (Serrà et al., 2018). Specifically,

$$\boldsymbol{g}' = \frac{\tau[\cosh(\boldsymbol{v}^j/\tau) + 1]}{\tau_{\text{min}}[\cosh(\boldsymbol{v}^j) + 1]} \odot \boldsymbol{g} \; . \tag{3}$$

The embedding matrix is trained jointly with the supervised classification objective using a typical cross-entropy loss, denoted by $\mathcal{L}_{\text{sup}}$.

4.2 Contrastive Knowledge Transfer

Even though we obtain the domain-aware representation using the suggested domain embedding, there are two limitations: (a) apart from supporting shared features, there is no explicit mechanism to actively encourage knowledge transfer; (b) the dataset provided domains are not necessarily accurate and fine-grained in the real world. Certain examples can be attributed to multiple domains with different degrees of relevance. For example, a review written on a product is usually considered in the general domain of that product (e.g., computers); however, semantically, it may involve discussion of other domains (e.g., the music playback quality of a laptop).

To address the above issues, we employ a domain classification task to estimate the relevance of each sample to different domains. We leverage these relevance/confidence scores as soft labels to conduct contrastive learning, allowing knowledge transfer from similar domains at the instance level.

Domain Classification. To estimate the relevance of different domains for a given sample, we leverage a sigmoid classification head with M output neurons. For training, we employ binary cross-entropy (BCE) loss $\mathcal{L}_{\text{dom}}$ using the dataset provided domain assignments as labels. Using the trained domain classifier, assuming it can generalize and capture domain similarities, we estimate the relevance of sample i to each domain using its sigmoid output score for domain j, denoted by $\boldsymbol{a}_i^j$.

Note that the domain classification task is only an auxiliary task to be used in the contrastive learning objective explained next. Therefore, we block gradients from this objective to flow outside the domain classifier head.

Contrastive Learning. Fig. 2 shows an illustration of the proposed contrastive objective. Here, for a certain sample, regardless of the dataset provided domain, we compute its domain-aware representations for all domains: $\hat{\boldsymbol{h}}_i^1 \ldots \hat{\boldsymbol{h}}_i^M$. Then, we compute an augmented view of the sample by simply computing a weighted average of domain-aware representations and their normalized relevance:

$$\overline{\boldsymbol{h}}_i = \sum_{j=1}^{M} \frac{\boldsymbol{a}_i^j}{\sum_{j=1}^{M} \boldsymbol{a}_i^j} \hat{\boldsymbol{h}}^j \ . \quad (4)$$

Based on this, we define the contrastive objective

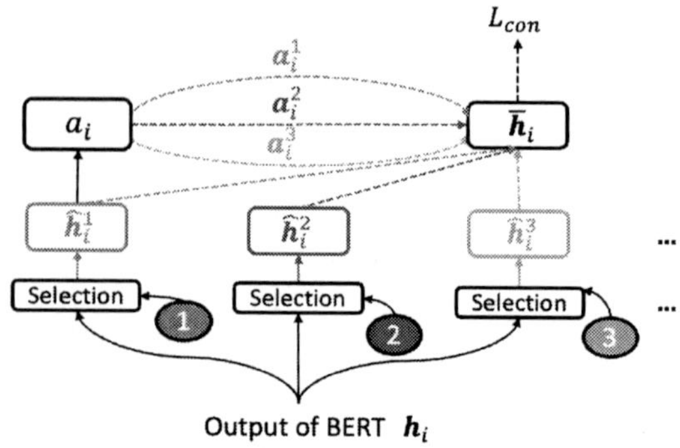

Figure 2: An illustration of the contrastive learning objective: (i) Domain-aware representations $\hat{\boldsymbol{h}}_i^j$ are computed for sample i and all domains indexed by j. (ii) Sigmoid outputs of the domain classifier head $\boldsymbol{a}_i^j$ are used to compute a weighted average of domain-aware representations resulting in an augmented view $\overline{\boldsymbol{h}}_i$. (iii) A soft cross-entropy loss based on the augmented view and domain certainties is used as the contrastive objective function.

as:

$$\mathcal{L}_{\text{con}} = -\frac{1}{N} \sum_{i=1}^{N} \sum_{j=1}^{M} \boldsymbol{a}_i^j \log(\sigma(\overline{\boldsymbol{h}}_i \cdot \hat{\boldsymbol{h}}_i^j)) + (1 - \boldsymbol{a}_i^j) \log(1 - \sigma(\overline{\boldsymbol{h}}_i \cdot \hat{\boldsymbol{h}}_i^j))) \ , \quad (5)$$

which is essentially a soft cross-entropy loss. Intuitively, the contrastive objective of (5) encourages learning representations that capture the attribution of the augmented view to each domain. Through this objective, similar domains are represented with closer representations and dissimilar domains are moved further apart such that they are easily distinguishable from the augmented view. Note that $\mathcal{L}_{\text{con}}$ is different from the typical contrastive objectives usually used in the literature as it relies on soft domain assignments for the augmented view rather than distinguishing augmented and real data.

As an example, assume that the domain-aware representation $\hat{\boldsymbol{h}}_i^j$ is not a good representation for sample i and lacks knowledge that is potentially transferable from other domains (indicating by a single color in their representation boxes), we can see how $\mathcal{L}_{\text{con}}$ helps (see Fig. 3):

- *Sample i semantically relevant to multiple domains* (domain 1 and domain 3). In this case, $\boldsymbol{a}_i^1$ and $\boldsymbol{a}_i^3$ have a large value while $\boldsymbol{a}_i^2$ has a smaller value. Consequently, $\overline{\boldsymbol{h}}_i$ is mostly the average of $\hat{\boldsymbol{h}}_i^1$ and $\hat{\boldsymbol{h}}_i^3$ (half orange and half

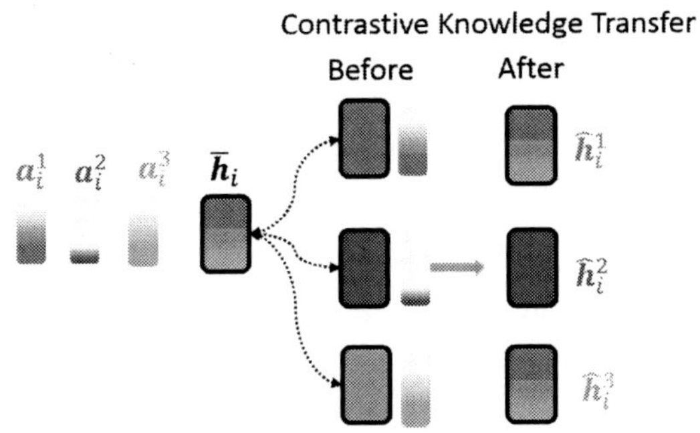

Figure 3: A simple example to show the effectiveness of the contrastive knowledge transfer. Orange, red, and green bars show the degrees of relevance to domains 1,2, and 3, respectively. Here, the contrastive objective encourages similar domains (domain 1 and 3) to have similar representations, while the sample belonging to a dissimilar domain (domain 2) is pushed apart in the representation space.

green). Here, updating based on $\mathcal{L}_{\text{con}}$ moves $\hat{\boldsymbol{h}}_i^1$ and $\hat{\boldsymbol{h}}_i^3$ closer to $\overline{\boldsymbol{h}}$. In other words, the knowledge transfer is encouraged between the first and third representations for that sample.

- *Sample i is not semantically relevant to a domain* (domain 2). Updating based on $\mathcal{L}_{\text{con}}$, $\hat{\boldsymbol{h}}_i^2$ moves further from $\overline{\boldsymbol{h}}_i$ to reflect the difference between them. Consequently, $\hat{\boldsymbol{h}}_i^2$ is discouraged from a negative knowledge transfer. This is expected as $\hat{\boldsymbol{h}}_i^2$ is not relevant to sample i.

4.3 Implementation Details

Final Objective. The final joint training objective is a combination of the supervised classification, domain classification and sample level contrastive loss terms:

$$\mathcal{L} = \mathcal{L}_{\text{sup}} + \lambda_1 \mathcal{L}_{\text{dom}} + \lambda_2 \mathcal{L}_{\text{con}}, \tag{6}$$

where, λ_1 and λ_2 are hyperparameters to adjust the impact of each term. Note that gradients computed from each objective update different parts of the network as shown in Fig. 1 via different colors. For example, $\mathcal{L}_{\text{dom}}$ only updates the domain classifier head, and $\mathcal{L}_{\text{con}}$ updates all parameters except those in the supervised classification head.

Architecture. A fully connected layer with softmax output is used as the classification head in the last layer of BERT. We use the embedding of `[CLS]` as the output of BERT. The training of BERT, follows that of (Xu et al., 2019). We adopt $\text{BERT}_{\textbf{BASE}}$ (uncased).

Hyperparameters. Unless otherwise stated, the domain id embeddings have 768 dimensions. We use 0.0025 for τ_{min} in Eq. 3. A dropout layer with the rate of 0.5 is placed between fully connected layers. To find the λ_1 and λ_2 hyperparameters in Eq. 6, we conducted a grid search in the $[0, 5000]$ range using about 200 logarithmic increments. We provide the selected λ_1 and λ_2 for each dataset in Section 5.1.3. For the contrastive objective, an l_2 normalization is applied before computing the contrastive loss. The max length of the number of input tokens is set to 128. We use Adam optimizer and set the learning rate to 3×10^{-5}. For all experiments, we train for 5 epochs using a mini-batch size of 64.

5 Experiments

5.1 Experimental Setup

5.1.1 Datasets

We conduct experiments using three datasets: *Document Sentiment Classification (DSC)* (Ni et al., 2019), *Aspect Sentiment Classification (ASC)* (Ke et al., 2021) and *Rumour and Fake News Detection (RFD)* (Zubiaga et al., 2016; Wang, 2017). These datasets have natural class and domain imbalance. For all datasets, we use a random data split of 10% for test, 10% for validation, and the rest for training. To better evaluate the performance of each method in efficient knowledge transfer, we down-sample the training and validation sets of the DSC, ASC, and RFD with a factor of 1000, 10, and 10, respectively. We provide the exact domain and class statistics in the appendix. In addition to these datasets, we conduct additional experiments using an altered version of the ASC dataset with artificially dissimilar domains (Sec. 5.2.2).

DSC. For this dataset, the task is to classify each full product review into one of the two opinion classes (*positive* and *negative*). The training data provides the particular type of product being reviewed as domain information. We adopt the text classification formulation in (Devlin et al., 2019), where the `[CLS]` token is used to predict the opinion polarity.

To build the DSC dataset, we use 29 domains from the Amazon Review Datasets (Ni et al., 2019) [2], then binarize the ratings by converting 1-2 stars to negative and 4-5 stars to positive.

[2] `https://nijianmo.github.io/amazon/index.html`

ASC. This dataset provides a classification of review sentences on their aspect-level sentiment (one of *positive* and *negative*). For example, the sentence "*The picture is great but the sound is lousy*" about a TV expresses a *positive* opinion about the aspect "picture" and a *negative* opinion about the aspect "sound." We adopt the ASC implementation by Xu et al. (2019), where the aspect term and sentence are concatenated via `[SEP]` in BERT. The opinion is predicted using the `[CLS]` token.

The ASC dataset (Ke et al., 2021) consists of 19 domains from 4 sources: (*a*) *HL5Domains* (Hu and Liu, 2004) with reviews of 5 products; (*b*) *Liu3Domains* (Liu et al., 2015) with reviews of 3 products; (*c*) *Ding9Domains* (Ding et al., 2008) with reviews of 9 products; and (*d*) *SemEval14* with reviews of 2 products - SemEval 2014 Task 4 for laptop and restaurant.

RFD. This dataset is compose of PHEME rumor detection (Zubiaga et al., 2016) and LIAR fake news detection (Wang, 2017) datasets. For rumor detection, the task is to identify whether a piece of given news is a rumor or not, while for the fake news detection, it is to identify fake or real news pieces. We follow Devlin et al. (2019) where the `[CLS]` token is used for the classification.

The RFD dataset consists of 6 domains from the PHEME dataset (5 domains) of rumor tweets (Zubiaga et al., 2016)[3] and the fake news detection LIAR (Wang, 2017) (1 domain). Note that domains in PHEME defined by different news events (e.g. a specific shooting incident), while the domain in LIAR is defined by news genres (e.g. politics). We intentionally selected this dataset to evaluate the performance of different methods when domains are merely a segmentation of samples rather than following a consistent definition.

5.1.2 Metrics

For each experiment, we report Area Under the ROC Curve (AUC) as the performance measure. Two types of results are reported: *macro* and *micro*. Macro is computed by macro averaging results computed for individual domains. Micro is computed from averaging the performance of all test samples regardless of their domain assignments. Note that there is an imbalance in the frequency of class labels (positive and negative in ASC, DSC; fake and real in RFD) in addition to the imbalance in the domains for each dataset. To ensure the statistical significance of the results, each experiment is repeated 5 times using random seed and random initialization, reporting the mean and standard deviation of each result.

5.1.3 Comparison Baselines

As the main focus of this study is the domain imbalance, to address class imbalance existing in our benchmarks, we adopt the existing DRS method (Cao et al., 2019) for all experiments. In our comparisons, we use multi-task learning (MTL) and domain-agnostic learning (D-AL) as intuitive and straightforward baselines. Additionally, since little work has been done in MIL, we adapt the recent class imbalance systems to MIL by re-sampling or re-weighting based on the domain statistics. For each case, we follow similar architectures as DCMI to ensure fair comparisons. The compared methods cover various approaches including: loss re-weighting (D-DRW (Cao et al., 2019)), regularization (D-Focal (Lin et al., 2017)), re-sampling (D-DRS (Cao et al., 2019)), parameter isolation (D-BBN (Zhou et al., 2020) and D-HybridSC (Wang et al., 2021)), and mixture-of-experts (D-MDFEND (Nan et al., 2021)). Note that the prefix "D-" in the model name is to indicate that we adapt them to the domain imbalance model.

Among these approaches, D-DRW and D-DRS are re-sampling and re-weighting methods with a deferred training scheduler. As suggested by Cao et al. (2019) the re-sampling or re-weighting are only effective after 80% of epochs have been trained. D-focal is a regularization-based method that uses an carefully designed loss function tailored for imbalanced data. D-BBN and D-HybridSC are two recent parameter isolation approaches that have shown state-of-the-art performance. D-MDFEND is used for multi-domain fake news detection which applies mixture-of-experts to deal with multi-domain transfer and isolation.

Regarding the DCMI hyperparameters i.e. (λ_1, λ_2), we used $(50, 6)$, $(30, 15)$, and $(4, 3)$ for the ASC, DSC, and RFD datasets, respectively. Refer to Section 4.3 for the hyperparameter search space and other implementation details.

5.2 Quantitative Results

5.2.1 Comparison with Other Work

Table 1 presents a comparison of DCMI with other baselines. From this table, DCMI consistently outperforms other competitors for both metrics.

[3] `https://figshare.com/articles/dataset/PHEME_dataset_of_rumours_and_non-rumours/4010619`

Model	DSC		ASC		RFD		Altered ASC	
	Macro	Micro	Macro	Micro	Macro	Micro	Macro	Micro
MTL (multitask learning)	74.1±3.1	77.3±3.8	80.0±1.8	84.1±0.7	57.4*	59.1*	76.3±2.9	84.9±2.4
D-AL (domain agnostic)	80.6±3.0	81.3±3.0	82.5±2.3	84.8±1.7	68.8±2.9	70.2±2.6	51.9±1.0	61.1*
D-DRS (Cao et al., 2019)	76.3*	76.6*	84.3±2.7	86.0±2.3	71.4±1.2	72.6±0.9	51.4±0.9	58.3*
D-DRW (Cao et al., 2019)	80.6±3.4	80.9±3.2	76.7*	78.0*	72.6±0.8	74.0±0.6	51.6±1.2	59.1*
D-Focal (Lin et al., 2017)	74.84*	74.97*	75.2*	77.1*	71.4±3.2	72.0±3.4	50.8±0.5	56.7*
D-BBN (Zhou et al., 2020)	79.2±3.7	79.8±3.8	75.6*	77.6*	64.3*	66.1*	49.9±1.4	54.5±3.9
D-HybridSC (Wang et al., 2021)	82.4*	82.4±3.9	83.5±2.2	84.9±2.2	71.2±1.4	72.3±1.2	50.7±1.0	56.7*
D-MDFEND (Nan et al., 2021)	80.5±3.5	80.8*	81.0±3.6	82.8±3.4	69.5±2.0	72.0±2.5	73.8*	83.4*
DCMI (this work)	**83.7**±1.3	**83.8**±1.3	**85.0**±0.7	**87.2**±0.4	**74.2**±1.2	**74.1**±1.0	**77.8**±1.9	**85.2**±1.4

* indicates that we only report the average results and there is a convergence issue due to the small training set or extreme imbalance

Table 1: Comparison of macro and micro averaged AUC results for DCMI (this work) and other baselines.

Specifically, DCMI is much more data-efficient compared to other baselines, as it effectively encourages positive knowledge transfer across domains. Among the three datasets, DCMI has the largest improvement margin for RFD. This can be attributed to the fact that domains in RFD are more diverse than those in ASC and DSC. The sentiment classification domains as in ASC and DSC have similarities as in these tasks positive or negative sentiments are usually expressed with similar words/phrases. For example, wonderful and terrible have similar interpretation for different tasks/domains to express positive or negative sentiment. However, expressions in fake news or rumors are far more diversified, follow more complex semantics, and even contradicting at times. For example, “guns” and “shooting” appear many times in “Charlie Hebdo” domain while they almost never appear in other domains like “Germanwings Flight”. Even more interestingly, “Trump” appears frequently in both the fake news of “COVID-19” domains and the real news of “government”, therefore it is a significant keyword with different domain interpretation. Under such domain disparities, selectively transferring common knowledge while preventing negative transfer becomes crucial which we believe is addressed by this work.

For the most recent state-of-the-art methods presented in Table 1, we can observe mixed MIL performance results for different datasets indicating less adaptability compared to DCMI. This is perhaps because they do not employ any viable mechanism to explicitly encourage positive transfer.

5.2.2 Extremely Dissimilar Data

We claim that DCMI is capable of adaptively selecting the useful knowledge (neurons) for a given domain and thus robust to extremely dissimilar domains. To demonstrate this, we create an artificial case where domains are extremely dissimilar in the dataset by design. Specifically, we divide the ASC dataset into two parts. The first part contains first 10 domains and the second part contains the other 9 domains. We keep the first part as is, while inverting the labels for the second part (i.e., flipping positive to negative and vice versa). Note that in a sentiment classification task such as ASC, domains are highly correlated so inverting labels for half of domains creates a drastic domain disparity.

Model	DSC		ASC		RFD	
	Macro	Micro	Macro	Micro	Macro	Micro
DCMI	**83.7**±1.3	**83.8**±1.3	**85.0**±0.7	**87.2**±0.4	**74.2**±1.2	74.1±1.0
-$\mathcal{L}_{\text{dom}}$	81.9±3.0	82.3±2.7	84.5±1.3	86.7±0.9	73.1±1.7	**74.3**±0.8
-$\mathcal{L}_{\text{dom}}, \mathcal{L}_{\text{con}}$	80.2±3.4	81.0±3.2	82.8±1.6	85.3±1.4	69.5±1.3	69.2±0.9

Table 2: Ablation study of DCMI. "-$\mathcal{L}_{\text{dom}}$" and "$-\mathcal{L}_{\text{con}}$" indicate omitting the domain classification and contrastive loss terms, respectively.

Table 1 shows the results of using the altered ASC data. We can see all baselines except MTL and D-MDFEND reach on only around 50% AUC. This is because the extremely high domain divergence is causing a severe negative transfer and making it difficult for the majority of baselines to learn a good predictor. However, MTL and D-MDFEND perform better than other baselines, perhaps since negative transfer is reduced due to the use of separate heads for different domains in MTL and mixture-of-experts in D-MDFEND. Nevertheless, DCMI still outperforms MTL and D-MDFEND, confirming that DCMI is not only capable of isolating domain-specific knowledge but also is able to encourage positive transfer among similar domains, which is here for domains within each data part of the altered dataset.

Domains	Review	Label	D-AL	DCMI $-\mathcal{L}_{\text{dom}}, \mathcal{L}_{\text{con}}$	DCMI
Laptop	The nicest part is the low heat output and ultra quiet *operation*.	P.	N.	P.	P.
MicroMP3	The flaw is inside the *Zen*.	N.	P.	N.	N.
Laptop	It feels cheap, the *keyboard* is not very sensitive.	N.	P.	P.	N.
Restaurant	The downstairs bar scene is very cool and chill...	P.	N.	N.	P.
Restaurant	The *sushi* is cut in blocks bigger than my cell phone.	N.	P.	P.	N.

Table 3: Qualitative comparison of predictions for different methods on a set of selected test samples from the ASC dataset (Ke et al., 2021). *Italic* text indicates the aspect in the review. "P." indicates positive and "N." indicates negative assignments.

5.2.3 Ablation Study

We conduct an ablation study to analyze the impact of each objective term. The results of this experiment are presented in Table 2. Here, "$-\mathcal{L}_{\text{dom}}$" indicates DCMI without the domain classification. "$-\mathcal{L}_{\text{dom}}, \mathcal{L}_{\text{con}}$" indicates DCMI without the domain classification and contrastive loss. Note that if we remove the domain-aware representation layer in addition to $\mathcal{L}_{\text{dom}}$ and $\mathcal{L}_{\text{con}}$, DCMI becomes D-AL. Based on the results provided in Table 2 the full DCMI system gives the best results, showing that every suggested component is crucial to the final model performance.

5.3 Qualitative Results

Table 3 shows several examples from ASC test set. For each example, we show the ground truth label (the third column), predictions of D-AL, DCMI and DCMI-[$\mathcal{L}_{\text{dom}}, \mathcal{L}_{\text{con}}$]. By comparing D-AL and DCMI-[$\mathcal{L}_{\text{dom}}, \mathcal{L}_{\text{con}}$], we can see the effectiveness of the domain-aware representation layer. By comparing DCMI and DCMI-[$\mathcal{L}_{\text{dom}}, \mathcal{L}_{\text{con}}$], we can see whether the contrastive knowledge transfer is successful.

In the first row, "quiet" is a positive sentiment word in the "laptop" domain. However, "quite" can indicate negative in other domains (e.g., a "quite" earbud in "MP3" domain indicates negative sentiment). We can see DCMI and DCMI -[$\mathcal{L}_{\text{dom}}, \mathcal{L}_{\text{con}}$] are able to separate the different polarity of the same sentiment word from different domains, while D-AL fails, suggesting that the knowledge selection in DCMI is capable of learning discriminative domain-aware representation.

In the second row, we can see D-AL mistakenly takes the review as positive due to the small amount of training data in the "MP3" domain. DCMI and DCMI -[$\mathcal{L}_{\text{dom}}, \mathcal{L}_{\text{con}}$] can make the correct prediction because of their ability to transfer knowledge from similar domains.

The last three rows of Table 3 showcase where only DCMI is correct. In the "laptop" domain (the third row), "cheap" conveys a negative sentiment in the example. However, "cheap" can indicate positive sentiment in the "laptop" domain if it is talking about the software domain. Therefore, an MIL model that only considers the annotated domain (e.g., DCMI-[$\mathcal{L}_{\text{dom}}, \mathcal{L}_{\text{con}}$]) fails.Similarly, the polarities of "cool" and "chill" depend not only on the dataset provided domain but also on the degrees of domain relevance for a given sample. The last case is an ironic expression, indicating DCMI provides a deeper understanding of the review.

In addition to the presented results, we provide a visual analysis of the domain-aware representation layer using t-SNE in the appendix.

6 Conclusion

In this work, we studied the problem of learning from multi-domain imbalanced data, where not only there is class imbalance but also there is an imbalance among domains with varying degrees of similarity. We proposed a novel technique called DCMI that is capable of identifying the *shared knowledge* that can be transferred to improve the tail domain performance and the *domain-specific knowledge* that needs to be handled carefully to avoid negative transfer. DCMI employs a domain-aware representation layer to adaptively select the relevant knowledge for each domain and leverages a novel contrastive learning objective to encourage knowledge transfer for relevant domains. Based on the experiments using three challenging multi-domain imbalanced datasets, DCMI shows improvements over the current state-of-the-art and demonstrates applicability to different scenarios.

References

Mateusz Buda, Atsuto Maki, and Maciej A Mazurowski. 2018. A systematic study of the class imbalance problem in convolutional neural networks. *Neural Networks*, 106:249–259.

Kaidi Cao, Colin Wei, Adrien Gaidon, Nikos Arechiga, and Tengyu Ma. 2019. Learning imbalanced datasets with label-distribution-aware margin loss. In *NeurIPS*, pages 1567–1578.

Lu Cheng, Ruocheng Guo, K Selçuk Candan, and Huan Liu. 2020. Representation learning for imbalanced cross-domain classification. In *Proceedings of the 2020 SIAM international conference on data mining*, pages 478–486. SIAM.

Hsin-Ping Chou, Shih-Chieh Chang, Jia-Yu Pan, Wei Wei, and Da-Cheng Juan. 2020. Remix: Rebalanced mixup. In *European Conference on Computer Vision*, pages 95–110. Springer.

Peng Chu, Xiao Bian, Shaopeng Liu, and Haibin Ling. 2020. Feature space augmentation for long-tailed data. In *Computer Vision–ECCV 2020: 16th European Conference, Glasgow, UK, August 23–28, 2020, Proceedings, Part XXIX 16*, pages 694–710. Springer.

Jacob Devlin, Ming-Wei Chang, Kenton Lee, and Kristina Toutanova. 2019. BERT: pre-training of deep bidirectional transformers for language understanding. In *NAACL-HLT*, pages 4171–4186. Association for Computational Linguistics.

Xiaowen Ding, Bing Liu, and Philip S Yu. 2008. A holistic lexicon-based approach to opinion mining. In *Proceedings of the 2008 international conference on web search and data mining*, pages 231–240.

Minqing Hu and Bing Liu. 2004. Mining and summarizing customer reviews. In *Proceedings of ACM SIGKDD*, pages 168–177.

Nathalie Japkowicz and Shaju Stephen. 2002. The class imbalance problem: A systematic study. *Intelligent data analysis*, 6(5):429–449.

Mohammad Kachuee, Hao Yuan, Young-Bum Kim, and Sungjin Lee. 2021. Self-supervised contrastive learning for efficient user satisfaction prediction in conversational agents. In *Proceedings of the 2021 Conference of the North American Chapter of the Association for Computational Linguistics: Human Language Technologies*, pages 4053–4064.

Zixuan Ke, Hu Xu, and Bing Liu. 2021. Adapting BERT for continual learning of a sequence of aspect sentiment classification tasks. In *NAACL-HLT*, pages 4746–4755. Association for Computational Linguistics.

Jaehyung Kim, Jongheon Jeong, and Jinwoo Shin. 2020. M2m: Imbalanced classification via major-to-minor translation. In *Proceedings of the IEEE/CVF Conference on Computer Vision and Pattern Recognition*, pages 13896–13905.

Tsung-Yi Lin, Priya Goyal, Ross Girshick, Kaiming He, and Piotr Dollár. 2017. Focal loss for dense object detection. In *Proceedings of the IEEE international conference on computer vision*, pages 2980–2988.

Jialun Liu, Yifan Sun, Chuchu Han, Zhaopeng Dou, and Wenhui Li. 2020. Deep representation learning on long-tailed data: A learnable embedding augmentation perspective. In *CVPR*, pages 2970–2979.

Qian Liu, Zhiqiang Gao, Bing Liu, and Yuanlin Zhang. 2015. Automated rule selection for aspect extraction in opinion mining. In *IJCAI*.

Ziwei Liu, Zhongqi Miao, Xiaohang Zhan, Jiayun Wang, Boqing Gong, and Stella X Yu. 2019. Large-scale long-tailed recognition in an open world. In *Proceedings of the IEEE/CVF Conference on Computer Vision and Pattern Recognition*, pages 2537–2546.

Ajinkya More. 2016. Survey of resampling techniques for improving classification performance in unbalanced datasets. *arXiv preprint arXiv:1608.06048*.

Qiong Nan, Juan Cao, Yongchun Zhu, Yanyan Wang, and Jintao Li. 2021. Mdfend: Multi-domain fake news detection. In *Proceedings of the 30th ACM International Conference on Information & Knowledge Management*, pages 3343–3347.

Jianmo Ni, Jiacheng Li, and Julian McAuley. 2019. Justifying recommendations using distantly-labeled reviews and fine-grained aspects. In *EMNLP*, pages 188–197.

Mengye Ren, Wenyuan Zeng, Bin Yang, and Raquel Urtasun. 2018. Learning to reweight examples for robust deep learning. In *International Conference on Machine Learning*, pages 4334–4343. PMLR.

Nikolaos Sarafianos, Xiang Xu, and Ioannis A Kakadiaris. 2018. Deep imbalanced attribute classification using visual attention aggregation. In *ECCV*, pages 680–697.

Joan Serrà, Didac Suris, Marius Miron, and Alexandros Karatzoglou. 2018. Overcoming catastrophic forgetting with hard attention to the task. In *ICML*, pages 4555–4564.

Li Shen, Zhouchen Lin, and Qingming Huang. 2016. Relay backpropagation for effective learning of deep convolutional neural networks. In *European conference on computer vision*, pages 467–482. Springer.

Peng Wang, Kai Han, Xiu-Shen Wei, Lei Zhang, and Lei Wang. 2021. Contrastive learning based hybrid networks for long-tailed image classification. In *CVPR*, pages 943–952.

William Yang Wang. 2017. "liar, liar pants on fire": A new benchmark dataset for fake news detection. In *ACL*, pages 422–426. Association for Computational Linguistics.

Hu Xu, Bing Liu, Lei Shu, and Philip S. Yu. 2019. BERT post-training for review reading comprehension and aspect-based sentiment analysis. In *NAACL-HLT*, pages 2324–2335. Association for Computational Linguistics.

Hongyi Zhang, Moustapha Cisse, Yann N Dauphin, and David Lopez-Paz. 2018. mixup: Beyond empirical risk minimization. In *International Conference on Learning Representations*.

Boyan Zhou, Quan Cui, Xiu-Shen Wei, and Zhao-Min Chen. 2020. Bbn: Bilateral-branch network with cumulative learning for long-tailed visual recognition. In *CVPR*, pages 9719–9728.

Arkaitz Zubiaga, Maria Liakata, and Rob Procter. 2016. Learning reporting dynamics during breaking news for rumour detection in social media. *CoRR*, abs/1610.07363.

A Detailed Datasets Statistics

In Table 4, 6, and 5, we provide the frequency of samples corresponding to each domain for the ASC, DSC, and RFD datasets.

Domains	Train N.	Train P.	Validation N.	Validation P.	Test N.	Test P.
Luxury Beauty	1	2	1	1	260	2780
Electronics	61	436	7	54	773	5459
CDs Vinyl	7	99	1	12	89	1243
Appliances	1	1	1	1	3	184
Digital Music	1	12	1	1	401	15883
AMAZON FASHION	1	1	1	1	21	262
Office Products	4	55	1	6	55	693
Books	146	1835	18	229	1834	22946
Gift Cards	1	1	1	1	4	290
Grocery Gourmet Food	7	77	1	9	91	970
Cell Phones Accessories	11	71	1	8	138	890
Prime Pantry	1	9	1	1	692	12160
Home Kitchen	53	457	6	57	663	5719
Magazine Subscriptions	1	1	1	1	22	192
Pet Supplies	19	133	2	16	244	1673
Software	1	1	1	1	222	899
Sports Outdoors	17	193	2	24	212	2415
All Beauty	1	1	1	1	18	498
Automotive	10	118	1	14	132	1475
Musical Instruments	1	16	1	2	1475	20058
Movies TV	29	215	3	26	365	2693
Video Games	4	31	1	3	5502	39327
Tools Home Improvement	13	140	1	17	170	1760
Toys Games	9	126	1	15	121	1575
Patio Lawn Garden	6	52	1	6	83	656
Arts Crafts Sewing	2	35	1	4	2714	43844
Clothing Shoes Jewelry	89	726	11	90	1120	9075
Kindle Store	9	152	1	19	115	1909
Industrial Scientific	1	5	1	1	442	6821

Table 4: The number of samples in each domain and data split for the DSC dataset. "N." indicates negative labels and "P." indicates positive labels.

Dataset	Domains	Train Fake/Rumour	Train Real	Validation Fake/Rumour	Validation Real	Test Fake/Rumour	Test Real
PHEME	Ferguson	51	17	8	2	258	86
	Charlie Hebdo	97	27	16	4	487	138
	Germanwings Crash	13	14	2	2	70	72
	Sydney Siege	41	31	7	5	210	157
	Ottawa Shooting	25	28	4	4	126	141
LIAR	Politic	199	168	26	16	250	211

Table 5: The number of samples in each domain and data split for the RFD dataset. RFD is composed of PHEME and LIAR data. "N." indicates negative labels and "P." indicates positive labels.

Dataset	Domains	Train N.	Train P.	Validation N.	Validation P.	Test N.	Test P.
SemEval14	laptop	80	93	66	57	128	341
	restaurant	77	209	26	70	196	728
Ding9Domains	HitachiRouter	3	9	9	18	32	74
	CanonS100	4	6	2	20	11	77
	ipod	3	6	6	13	20	57
	Nokia6600	8	14	15	30	48	134
	DiaperChamp	2	9	5	19	26	70
	CanonD500	1	5	1	13	8	52
	Norton	2	9	8	16	38	60
	MicroMP3	21	9	45	15	170	73
	LinksysRouter	7	3	20	2	59	30
HL5Domains	Creative40G	14	28	35	50	155	184
	ApexAD2600	12	9	26	17	87	85
	Nokia6610	11	5	28	6	114	22
	Nikon4300	8	1	16	4	74	8
	CanonG3	11	2	21	7	89	26
Liu3Domains	Computer	13	4	34	1	101	41
	Router	9	6	19	12	73	50
	Speaker	19	2	31	13	140	36

Table 6: The number of samples in each domain and data split for the ASC dataset. ASC is composed of four datasets. "N." indicates negative labels and "P." indicates positive labels.

B Visual Analysis of the Domain-aware Representation Layer

We visualize sample representations before and after the domain-aware representation layer using for ASC dataset. See Figure 4 for t-SNE visualizations. Here, we color the samples according to their domain assignments.

Before the domain-aware representation layer, we can see the points related to different domains are mixed and hard to differentiate. However, after the domain-aware representation layer, samples with similar colors form clusters, indicating a higher embedding distance for different domains. From this visualization, we can infer that the suggested method is able to learn discriminative domain-aware representations.

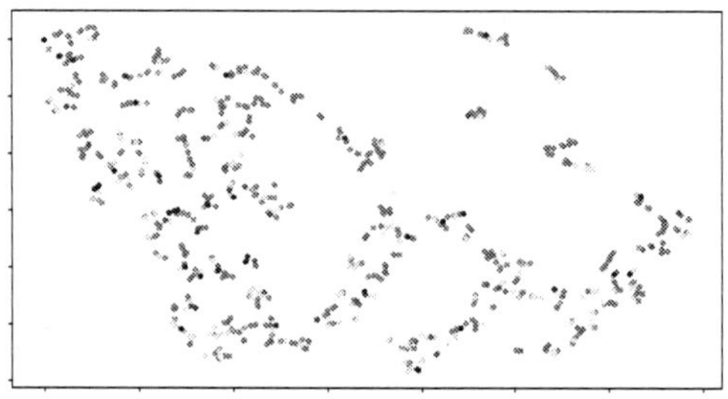

(a) Before domain-aware representation layer

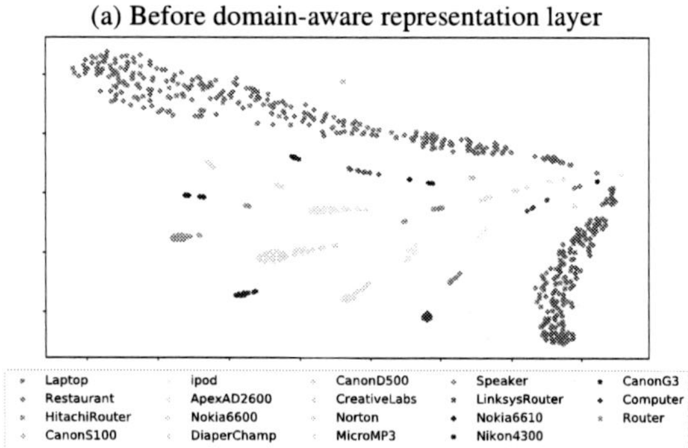

(b) After domain-aware representation layer

Figure 4: t-SNE visualization of sample representation for different domains, (a) before and (b) after the domain-aware representation layer for the ASC dataset (Ke et al., 2021). Figure best viewed in color.

"splink" is happy and "phrouth" is scary: Emotion Intensity Analysis for Nonsense Words

Valentino Sabbatino, Enrica Troiano, Antje Schweitzer, and **Roman Klinger**
Institut fur Maschinelle Sprachverarbeitung, University of Stuttgart, Germany
`{firstname.lastname}@ims.uni-stuttgart.de`

Abstract

People associate affective meanings to words – "death" is scary and sad while "party" is connotated with surprise and joy. This raises the question if the association is purely a product of the learned affective imports inherent to semantic meanings, or is also an effect of other features of words, e.g., morphological and phonological patterns. We approach this question with an annotation-based analysis leveraging nonsense words. Specifically, we conduct a best-worst scaling crowdsourcing study in which participants assign intensity scores for joy, sadness, anger, disgust, fear, and surprise to 272 nonsense words and, for comparison of the results to previous work, to 68 real words. Based on this resource, we develop character-level and phonology-based intensity regressors. We evaluate them on both nonsense words and real words (making use of the NRC emotion intensity lexicon of 7493 words), across six emotion categories. The analysis of our data reveals that some phonetic patterns show clear differences between emotion intensities. For instance, *s* as a first phoneme contributes to joy, *sh* to surprise, *p* as last phoneme more to disgust than to anger and fear. In the modelling experiments, a regressor trained on real words from the NRC emotion intensity lexicon shows a higher performance ($r = 0.17$) than regressors that aim at learning the emotion connotation purely from nonsense words. We conclude that humans do associate affective meaning to words based on surface patterns, but also based on similarities to existing words ("juy" to "joy", or "flike" to "like").

1 Introduction

With words come meanings, as well as a variety of associations such as emotional nuances. Emotions, feelings, and attitudes, which can be summarized under the umbrella term of "affect", are in fact a core component for the meaning of large portions of a language vocabulary (Mohammad, 2018). In English, they encompass nouns, verbs, adjectives, and adverbs (Mohammad and Turney, 2013). For instance, *dejected* and *wistful* can be said to directly express an emotion, but there are also terms that do not describe a state of emotion and are still associated to one (e.g., *failure* and *death*[1]), given an interpretation of an associated event.

Most computational studies of emotions in text deal with words in context, for instance in news headlines (Strapparava and Mihalcea, 2007; Bostan et al., 2020) or in Tweets (Schuff et al., 2017; Mohammad, 2012; Köper et al., 2017; Goel et al., 2017). Analyzing words in isolation, however, is equally important, as it can help to create lexical resources for use in applications (Mohammad and Turney, 2013; Mohammad, 2018; Warriner et al., 2013), to investigate how words are processed in general (Traxler and Gernsbacher, 2006, Part 2), and more specifically, to obtain a better understanding of first language acquisition processes (Bakhtiar et al., 2007).

When considering words in isolation, their meaning cannot be disambiguated by the surrounding text. This raises the question: can readers interpret an emotional load from unknown words, which are judged out of their context? We address this question by analyzing emotion associations of "nonsense" words – or nonwords, or pseudowords, i.e., terms which resemble real entries in the English vocabulary, but are actually not part of it (Keuleers and Brysbaert, 2010; Chuang et al., 2021). Our aim is to understand the degree to which nonsense words like *fonk*, *knunk*, or *snusp* can be associated to particular emotions. We model the problem as an emotion intensity analysis task with a set of basic emotions, namely *fear*, *anger*, *joy*, *disgust*, *surprise*, and *sadness*.

Other fields have provided evidence that some phonemes can be related to the affective dimension of valence (Myers-Schulz et al., 2013; Adelman

[1]Examples from Mohammad (2018).

Proceedings of the 12th Workshop on Computational Approaches to Subjectivity, Sentiment & Social Media Analysis, pages 37 - 50
May 26, 2022 ©2022 Association for Computational Linguistics

et al., 2018), but emotion analysis, and in particular word-based research, has not yet ventured this direction. Gaining insight on the emotional tone of non-existing expressions could be relevant for current computational emotion classification and intensity regression efforts, which have manifold applications across social media mining or digital humanities. As an example, when new product names are coined which do not have an established semantics, designers and marketing experts might want to be aware of the potential affective connections that these evoke, and avoid those with a negative impact.

Therefore, our main contributions are: (1) the creation of an emotion intensity lexicon of 272 nonsense words (with in addition 68 real words, for comparison to previous work), (2) the analysis of the phonemes present in them (if pronounced as English words) that aligns with emotion intensity studies across the Ekman (1999) basic emotions, and (3) experiments in which we develop intensity regressors on a large resource of real words, as well as on our nonsense words. Both regressors are evaluated on real and nonsense words.

2 Related Work

2.1 Emotion Analysis

Emotion analysis in text deals with the task of assigning (a set of) emotions to words, sentences, or documents (Bostan and Klinger, 2018; Schuff et al., 2017), and is conducted with various textual domains, including product reviews, tales, news, and (micro)blogs (Aman and Szpakowicz, 2007; Schuff et al., 2017). This task plays an important role in applications like dialog systems (e.g., chatbots), intelligent agents (Bostan and Klinger, 2018) and for identifying authors' opinions, affective intentions, attitudes, evaluations, and inclinations (Aman and Szpakowicz, 2007). Its scope extends beyond computer science and is of great interest for many fields, like psychology, health care, and communication (Chaffar and Inkpen, 2011).

Computational studies build on top of emotion theories in psychology (Ekman, 1999; Plutchik, 2001; Scherer, 2005; Russell, 1980). While these theories by and large agree that emotions encompass expressive, behavioral, physiological, and phenomenological features, in emotion analysis they mainly serve as a reference system consisting of basic emotions (Ekman, 1999; Plutchik, 2001) or of a vector space within which emotions can be represented (Russell, 1980; Scherer, 2005).

With respect to basic emotion approaches, dimensional ones explain relations between emotions. The task of emotion intensity regression can be thought of as a combination of these two. There, the goal is not only to detect a categorical label, but also to recognize the strength with which such emotion is expressed. This idea motivated a set of shared tasks (Mohammad and Bravo-Marquez, 2017b; Mohammad et al., 2018), some lexical resources which assign emotion intensities to words (Mohammad, 2018) or to longer textual instances (Mohammad and Bravo-Marquez, 2017a), and automatic systems relying on deep learning and said resources (Goel et al., 2017; Köper et al., 2017; Duppada and Hiray, 2017, i.a.).

2.2 Nonsense Words and Emotional Sound Symbolism

Meaning in a language is conveyed in many different ways. At a phonetic level, for example, languages systematically use consonant voicing (/b/ vs. /p/, /d/ vs. /t/) to signal differences in mass, vowel quality to signal size, vowel lengthening to signal duration and intensity, reduplication to signal repetition, and in some languages vowel height or frontality to mark diminutives (Davis et al., 2019).

Semantics has also been studied with respect to non-existing words (i.e., terms without an established meaning). By investigating their lexical category, Cassani et al. (2020) explored the hypothesis that there is "(at least partially) a systematic relationship between word forms and their meanings, such that children can infer" the core semantics of a word from its sound alone. Also Chuang et al. (2019) found that nonwords are semantically loaded, and that their meanings co-determine lexical processing. Their results indicate that "nonword processing is influenced not only by form similarity [..] but also by nonword semantics".

These "nonsense meanings" go beyond onomatopoeic connections: Cassani et al. (2020) showed that high vowels tend to evoke small forms, while low vowels tend to be associated with larger forms. As a matter of facts, research has unvealed many other links between visual and audio features of stimuli, besides the correspondences between verbal material and the size of non-speech percepts. The loudness of sounds and brightness of light have been shown to be perceived similarly, at various degrees of intensity (Bond and

Stevens, 1969), and so are pitch and visual brightness – with higher pitched sounds being matched to bright stimuli both by adults (Marks, 1987) and children (Mondloch and Maurer, 2004). These findings are related to the so-called Bouba-Kiki effect (Köhler, 1970, p. 224) which describes a non-arbitrary mapping between speech sounds and the visual shape of objects: speakers in several languages pair nonsense words such as *maluma* or *bouba* with round shapes, and *takete* or *kiki* with spiky ones (D'Onofrio, 2014).

Previous work exists also on the emotional connotation of word sounds. Majid (2012) provide an extensive overview of how emotions saturate language at all levels, from prosody and the use of interjections, to morphology and metaphoric expressions. In phonetics, the relationship between acoustic and affective phenomena is based on the concept of sound symbolism. Adelman et al. (2018) hypothesized that individual phonemes are associated with negative and positive emotions and showed that both phonemes at the beginning of a word and phonemes that are pronounced fast convey negativity. They demonstrated that emotional sound symbolism is front-loaded, i.e., the first phoneme contributes the most to decide the valence of a word. Similarly, Myers-Schulz et al. (2013) showed that certain strings of English phonemes have an inherent valence that can be predicted based on dynamic changes in acoustic features.

In contrast to past research on emotional sound symbolism, ours focuses on written material. In particular, we address nonsense words, which are sequences of letters composing terms that do not exist in a language (Keuleers and Brysbaert, 2010; Chuang et al., 2021), but conform to its typical orthographic and phonological patterns (Keuleers and Brysbaert, 2010). For this reason, they are of particular interest in the psycholinguistics of language comprehension (Bakhtiar et al., 2007; Keuleers and Brysbaert, 2010; Chuang et al., 2021, 2019).

3 Data Acquisition and Annotation

We now describe the creation of our corpus of nonsense and real words, with their respective emotion intensity scores for the six emotions of *joy*, *sadness*, *anger*, *fear*, *disgust*, and *surprise*.[2] We show an excerpt of our data in Appendix B.

[2]Our corpus is available base64 encoded in Appendix C, and at https://www.ims.uni-stuttgart.de/data/emotion

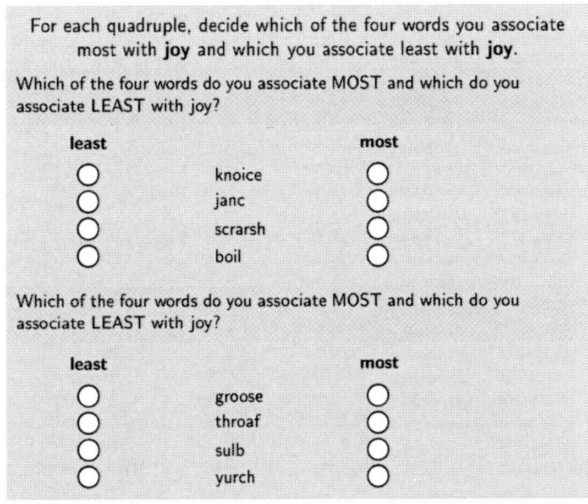

Figure 1: BWS Annotation Question example.

3.1 Term Selection

Our corpus consists of 272 nonsense words and 68 real words. The nonsense words are taken from the ARC Nonword Database[3] (Rastle et al., 2002), which consists of 358,534 monosyllabic nonwords, 48,534 pseudohomophones, and 310,000 non-pseudohomophonic nonwords. We randomly select nonsense words that have only orthographically existing onsets and bodies and only monomorphemic syllables, such as *bleve*, *foathe*, *phlerm*, and *snusp*.

In addition, for comparison to previous emotion intensity studies, we sample a small number of words that are only linked to one emotion from the NRC Emotion Lexicon (EmoLex, Mohammad and Turney, 2010). This resource contains a list of more than ≈10k English words and their associations with eight emotions: *anger*, *fear*, *anticipation*, *trust*, *surprise*, *sadness*, *joy*, and *disgust*. Its creators outlined some best practices to adopt in a crowdsourcing setup. They suggested to collect judgments by asking workers if a term is *associated* to an emotion, as to obtain more consistent judgments than could be collected by asking whether the term *evokes* an emotion. We hence align with such strategy in the design of our guidelines.

3.2 Annotation

To obtain continuous intensity scores for each of the six emotions for each word, we perform a best-worst scaling annotation (BWS, Louviere et al., 2015; Mohammad, 2018) via crowdsourcing.

[3]http://www.cogsci.mq.edu.au/research/resources/nwdb/nwdb.html

	Round 1	Round 2	Total
# Participants	33	87	120
male	11	19	30
female	22	66	88
other		2	2
Age	31	32	31.5
min	18	18	18
max	61	65	65
# Words	55	290	340
non-words	44	232	272
real words	11	58	68
Avg. duration	15 min	25 min	20 min
Overall cost	£90.09	£395.85	£485.94

Table 1: Summary of the annotation study. The total number of words is 340 instead of 345, due to an overlap in 5 selected words for Round 2.

	Nonsense		Real		NRC AIL	
Emotion	ρ	r	ρ	r	ρ	r
joy	.68	.72	.87	.87	.93	.92
sadness	.62	.68	.87	.88	.90	.91
anger	.69	.71	.81	.82	.91	.91
disgust	.68	.72	.83	.85	—	—
fear	.65	.70	.82	.85	.91	.91
surprise	.58	.60	.66	.71	—	—

Table 2: Split-half reliability for our nonsense word annotation in comparison to our real-word annotations and the scores obtained by Mohammad (2018) (whose lexicon contains four out of our six emotions). ρ: Spearman correlation, r: Pearson correlation.

Study Setup. We follow the experimental setup described by Kiritchenko and Mohammad (2016). For each experiment (i.e., an annotation task performed by three different annotators), we select N words out of the pool of 340 collected items. With these N words, we randomly generate 2N distinct 4-tuples that comply with the constraints of a word appearing in eight different tuples and no word appearing in one tuple more than once. We do this for all six emotions. Therefore, each word occurs in 24 best-worst judgements (8×4×3). Figure 1 exemplifies the annotation task.

To aggregate the annotations to score(w) for word w, we take the normalized difference between the frequency with which the word was labeled as best and as worst, i.e., score$(w) = \frac{\#\text{best}(w)-\#\text{worst}(w)}{\#\text{annotations}(w)}$ (Kiritchenko and Mohammad, 2016). We linearly transform the score to $[0;1]$[4].

Attention Checks. To ensure annotation quality, we include attention checks. Each check consists of an additional 4-tuple of only real, manually selected words for the emotion in question. Two of the words are neutral with respect to such emotion, and two are, respectively, strongly related and opposite to it. For instance, we check attendance for *joy* with the words *door*, *elbow*, *happiness*, and *depression*. Annotations by participants who fail any attention check are discarded from our data.

3.2.1 Study Details

Table 1 summarizes the study details. We hosted it on the platform SoSci-Survey[5] and recruited participants via Prolific[6], rewarding them with an hourly wage of £7.80. We performed the annotations in two iterations, the first of which was a small pretest to ensure the feasibility of the task. In the second round, we increased the amount of quadruples that one participant saw in one batch in each experiment, i.e. from five words (four nonsensical ones) to 10 (eight of which are nonsense).

Altogether, 120 participants worked on our 40 experiments, leading to a total of 340 annotated words[7]. We prescreened participants to be native English speakers and British citizens. Nevertheless, 19 participants indicated in the study that they have a language proficiency below a native speaker. All participants stated that they prefer British spelling over other variants. 58 participants have a high school degree or equivalent, 49 have a bachelor's degree, 11 have a master's degree and 2 have no formal qualification.

When asked for feedback regarding the study, participants remarked that words with k's or v's sounded harsher and unfriendlier than others, and expressed concern that assumptions about the pronunciation of the judged terms might vary from person to person. One participant noticed that some nonsense words included familiar and existing words, e.g., *nice* in *snice*, and this may have had an impact on their choices.

4 Corpus Analysis

We now discuss the reliability of the annotation process and then analyze the resulting resource.

[4]We use an adaptation of the scripts from `http://saifmohammad.com/WebPages/BestWorst.html`

[5]`https://www.soscisurvey.de/`

[6]`https://www.prolific.co/`

[7]A mistake in the word selection process led to an overlap of words, therefore we did not achieve 345 words but 340 words. We ignore the annotations of the affected tuples.

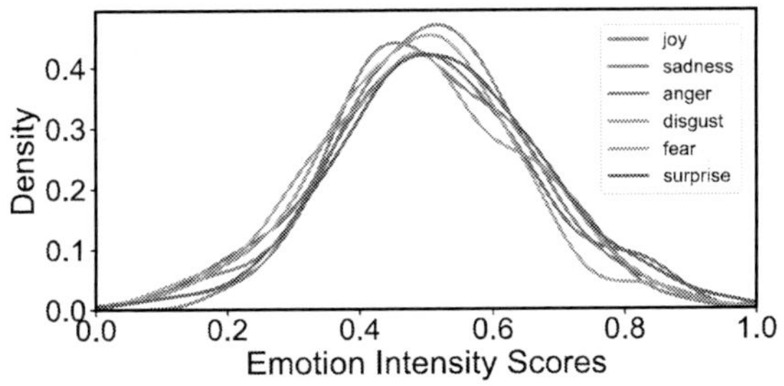

Figure 2: Density curves of nonsense word emotion intensities for our six emotions.

4.1 Reliability and Distribution

To assess the quality and reproducibility of our best-worst-scaling annotations, we calculate split-half reliability[8] (SHR) for each emotion and summarize the results in Table 2. We observe that Spearman's ρ correlation values for the nonsense words are consistently below our real word annotations, with differences between .08 and .25 points. Still, numbers indicate that annotations are strongly correlated.

Similar patterns hold for Pearson's r. *Sadness* shows the highest r variation between the annotation of real and nonsense words (r=.88 vs .68); the emotion *surprise* shows the smallest difference (r=.71 vs .60), but the absolute values of such correlations also lower than those obtained for other emotions.

To compare these results to past research, we observe our real word reliability scores to those found in work describing the NRC lexicon (column NRC AIL in Table 2). Similar to such work, we also obtained highest results for *joy* than for emotions like *anger* and *fear*. However, their results are generally higher, which might be an effect of dataset size, and accordingly, a potentially better familiarization of their annotators with the task. Figure 2 shows the distribution of the emotion intensity values. The plots for all emotions are similar and follow a Gaussian distribution.

In Table 3, we report the top ten nonsense words with the highest emotion intensity values for each emotion. These suggest some hypotheses relative to how annotators decide on the emotion intensity. Orthographical similarity to words with a clear emotional connotation might have led to the emotion association to the nonsense words. For instance, *juy* and *flike* resemble the words *joy* and *like*. Other nonwords might be interpreted by means of onomatopoeic associations that arguably evoke events, like *throoch* or *shrizz* for *surprise* and *snulge* or *druss* in *disgust*.

Some of these items exemplify the importance of the first phonemes, in agreement with earlier work (see Section 2.2). *Surprise*-bearing nonwords, for instance, tend to start with /s/ or /sh/, while the second or third phoneme is often an /r/ sound[9]. Examples for this pattern are *shrizz*, *shrier*, *spreil*, and *strem*.

In addition, we observe that there is a relationship between the words for the emotions *sadness*, *anger*, *disgust*, and *fear*. For the emotion pairs *sadness–disgust*, *anger–fear*, and *disgust–fear* we have Pearson correlation values ranging from 0.57 to 0.60. For all the other different pairings of emotions the Pearson correlation value is in $[0; 0.5]$. Furthermore, we can observe that for these four emotions we have negative Pearson correlation values when comparing them with joy. The Pearson correlation values here lie between -0.49 and -0.68, where the correlation is lowest for *joy–sadness* with a value of -0.68.

Details on BWS Reliability Calculation. Our study has 2N (for N nonwords) BWS questions, that is, 4-tuples per emotion. Since each nonword occurs on average in eight 4-tuples, and three different annotators evaluate the same words, each word is involved in $8 \times 3 = 24$ best-worst judgments. In contrast to the study design of Kiritchenko and Mohammad (2016), who ensure that the same tuple is evaluated by multiple annotators, in our setup the nonword are the unit being evaluated by the three annotators (but the tuples may differ for each of them). For us, one particular tuple might be annotated by less than three annotators.

Therefore, we compute the SHR by randomly placing one or two annotations per tuple in one bin and the remaining ones, if any exists, for the tuple in another bin. Then, two sets of intensity values (and rankings) are computed from the annotations in each of the two bins. This process is repeated 100 times, and the correlations between the two sets of rankings and intensity values are averaged per emotion (Mohammad and Bravo-Marquez, 2017b).

[8] We use available implementations from Kiritchenko and Mohammad (2016): `http://saifmohammad.com/WebPages/BestWorst.html`.

[9] We use ARPAbet for indicating phonemes.

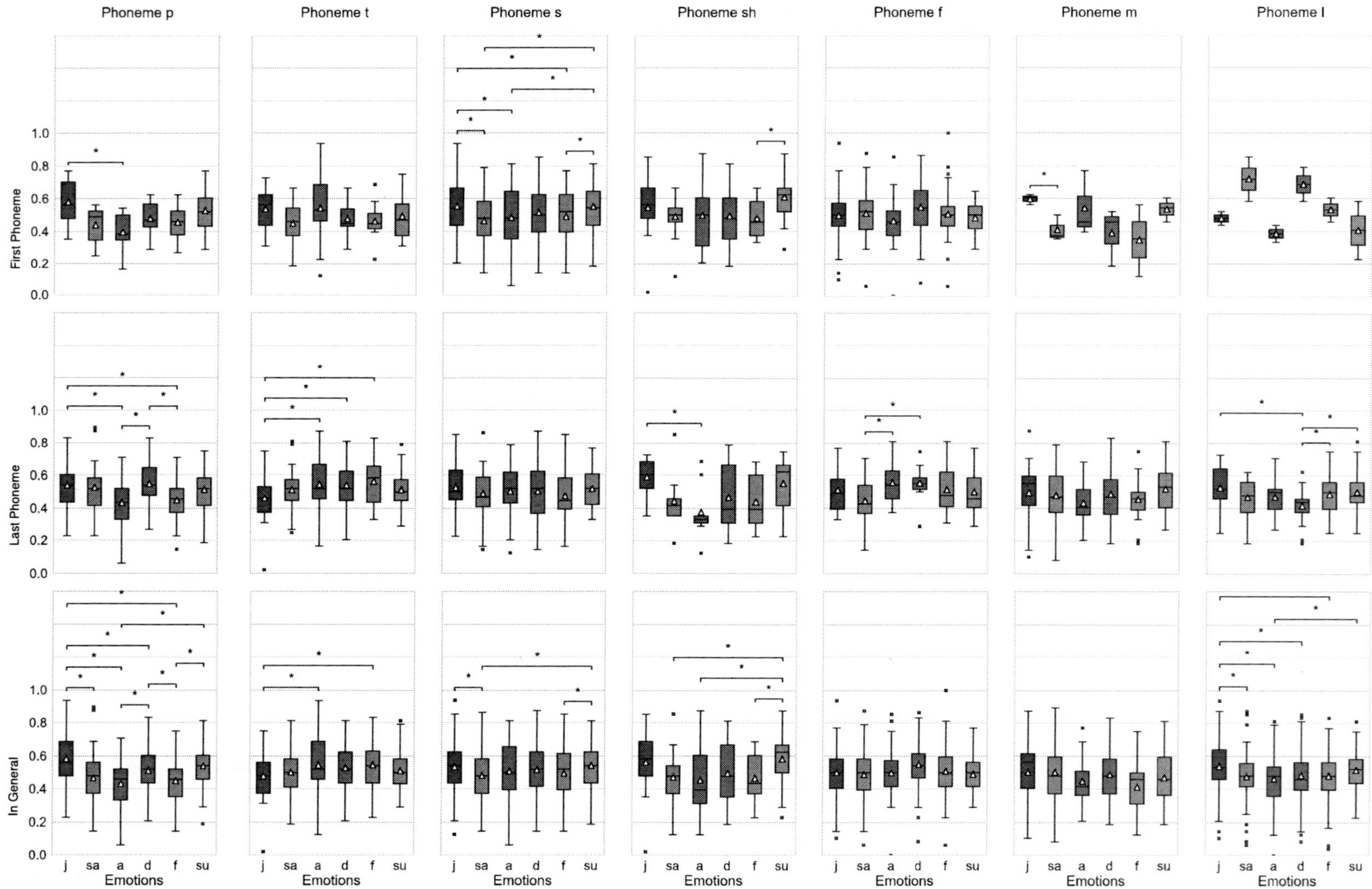

Figure 3: Comparison of the emotion intensity distributions of phonemes /p/, /t/, /s/, /sh/, /f/, /m/, and /l/ occurring as first or last phoneme in a word (rows one and two), or anywhere in a word (last row). The labels on the x-axis represent the emotions joy (j), sadness (sa), anger (a), disgust (d), fear (f), and surprise (su). The asterisk (*) indicates p$\leq$ .05, calculated with Welch's t-test between the intensity scores of the two emotions indicated by the bracket.

Joy		Sadness		Anger		Disgust		Fear		Surprise	
Word	Int.	Word	Int.	Word	Int.	Word	Int.	Word	Int.	Word	Int.
juy	.958	vomp	.896	terve	.938	druss	.875	phrouth	1.0	throoch	.896
flike	.938	phlump	.875	shait	.875	pheague	.865	ghoothe	.875	shrizz	.875
splink	.938	dis	.865	phrouth	.854	boarse	.854	boarse	.854	shrier	.833
glaim	.875	losh	.854	broin	.813	snulge	.854	wrorgue	.854	spreil	.813
roice	.854	drasque	.833	psench	.813	foathe	.833	drasque	.833	strem	.813
shrizz	.854	weathe	.833	slanc	.813	gneave	.833	dwalt	.833	swunt	.792
spreece	.854	dwaunt	.813	straif	.813	gream	.833	keff	.813	kease	.771
snusp	.833	phlerm	.792	thwealt	.792	phlerm	.833	bange	.792	purf	.771
spirp	.833	phreum	.792	zorce	.792	phlonch	.833	frete	.792	bange	.750
drean	.813	sout	.792	boarse	.771	vomp	.833	psoathe	.771	droosh	.750

Table 3: Top ten nonsense words, ordered by decreasing emotion intensity.

4.2 Relation Between Phonemes and Emotion Intensities

Motivated by previous work on the emotional import of word sounds (e.g., Adelman et al., 2018), we now analyse the relation between specific phonemes and emotion intensities across our set of emotions in our 272 annotated nonsense words.

4.2.1 Experimental Setting

For the phoneme analysis, we consider pronunciation, as it is provided in the ARC Nonword Database. Pronounciation follows the DISC character set of 42 symbols to represent 42 phonemes.[10] We convert such representation to ARPAbet for consistency with real word representations that are required for computational modelling (see Section 5).

We focus on the three most frequent phonemes from each of the top 10 nonword lists in Table 3. The selection results in the eight phonemes /p/, /t/, /s/, /sh/, /f/, /m/, /l/, and /r/.[11] Next, we separate the words that have such phonemes in the first or last position, or contain them in any position, and we compare the distributions of their respective intensities for each emotion. We calculate the p-values for the differences between the distributions with Welch's t-test. We perform the t-test on sets of emotion intensity scores that correspond to pairs of emotions, for the same phoneme and the same position.

4.2.2 Results

Figure 3 illustrates the distributions of emotion intensities for the chosen phonemes. The first row of plots corresponds to the distribution for the subset of words in which the phoneme appears in the first position of the nonword, the second row to the appearance as a last phoneme, and the third row relates to nonwords containing that phoneme at any possible position. Differences between emotions that have a p-value below 0.05 are denoted with a $*$. We limit our discussion to these cases.

1st Phoneme. For the phonemes /p/, /s/, /sh/, and /m/, certain emotion pairs show a p-value below 5%. For /p/ and /s/, *joy* has the highest median intensity (as in *splink*, *spreece*, *snusp*), and *anger* the lowest. Examples for low *joy* intensities which still have an /s/ at the beginning are *slanc* or *scunch* – but other parts of the nonword also seem to play an important role here. *Surprise* has a stronger intensity than all other emotions for items with /sh/ in first position, particularly in comparison to *fear* ($p<.05$ only for *joy/fear*). Examples for strongly *surprise*-loaded words are *shrizz*, *shrier*, and *shoach*. Counterexamples are *shogue* and *shuilt*.

Another noteworthy pattern is observable with the phoneme /m/, for which *joy* is substantially higher than *sadness*. It should be noted, however, that there are only three instances in our dataset starting with /m/ (i.e., *maut, marve, mauge*).

An interesting case is the occurrence of /t/ and its relation to *anger* intensities. These values cover a wide interval: examples for high *anger* degrees are *terve*, *trasque*, and *tource*, low intensity ones are *tish* and *twauve*. We hypothesize that the combination of /t/ with /r/ might be relevant.

[10] `https://www.cogsci.mq.edu.au/research/resources/nwdb/phonemes.html`

[11] Examples for these phonemes are /p/ as in *pie*, /t/ as in *tie*, /s/ as in *sigh*, /sh/ as in *shy*, /f/ as in *fight*, /m/ as in *my*, /l/ as in *lie*, and /r/ as in *rye* (`https://en.wikipedia.org/w/index.php?title=ARPABET&oldid=1062602312`).

Last Phoneme. Interestingly, and in contradiction to our expectations based on previous work, the occurrences of last phonemes of nonwords are related to a set of differences in emotion intensities. For /p/, *disgust* nonwords have the highest intensity, being clearly different from *anger* as well as *fear*, which are associated with comparably low values. /sh/, which showed interesting patterns in the first phoneme relative to *surprise*, contributes most to *joy* when found in the last position (as in *tish*), in contrast to instances that evoke negative emotions like *anger*.

General. The analysis of phonemes independent of their positions leads more often to comparably low p-values due to larger numbers of words in each set. The patterns, however, by and large resemble the observations for the first and the last phonemes.

5 Modeling

Our analysis has revealed that particular phonemes are indeed related to high intensities for some emotions. In the following section, we aim at understanding if these findings are exploited by computational models that perform emotion intensity regression (i.e., if these models perform better when they observe specific character sequences or phoneme sequences), and if a model that is trained on real words can generalize the learned emotion associations to nonsense words (or the other way around).

5.1 Experimental Setting

As for our architecture, we build on top of the model proposed by Köper et al. (2017) for Tweets. This model is a combination of a convolutional neural network with a bidirectional long short-term memory model. We opt against using a pre-trained transfomer approach like BERT (Devlin et al., 2019), to have full control over input sequences – we use character or phoneme sequences as input. These are represented as 300 dimensional embeddings, with the maximal sequence length being 16, which corresponds to the longest input sequence in our corpus (including real words from NRC-EIL, see below). We apply a dropout rate of 0.25, convolutions with window size of 3, followed by a max pooling layer of size 2 and a BiLSTM.

Train/Test Split. We divide the 272 data points into a train set of 204 nonsense words and a test set of 68 nonsense words. We further use the NRC-EIL lexicon (Mohammad, 2018) with 1268 words for *joy*, 1298 for *sadness*, 1483 for *anger*, 1094 for *disgust*, 1765 for *fear*, and 585 for *surprise*. We also split this corpus into train/test set, with 75 % of the data for training.

Phoneme Representation. We represent both nonsense words and real words as phoneme sequences following the ARPAbet representation. For the words from the NRC-EIL, we obtain the ARPAbet pronunciation from the Carnegie Mellon University (CMU) Pronouncing Dictionary (CMUdict). For words that are not included in CMUdict, we use the LOGIOS Lexicon Tool, which adds normalization heuristics on top of CMUdict.[12]

Input Embeddings. We compare two input representations, character embeddings and phoneme embeddings. For the character representations, we use pretrained FastText embeddings, which provide character-level information. These embeddings are trained on 400 million Tweets (Godin, 2019). We train the phoneme embeddings on the established corpus of 7392 sentences by Synnaeve (2015) which is based on the DARPA TIMIT Acoustic-Phonetic Continuous Speech Corpus (Garofolo et al., 1993).

Model Variants. We compare models that differ in the following parameters: (1) input representation (characters/phonemes), (2) n-grams length over characters/phonemes (1/2/3 grams), (3) input training data (real words from NRC-EIL, our nonsense words). The reason for considering different n-grams is that, in addition to the standard use of unigrams, we also want to investigate 2- and 3-grams under the assumption that the inter-word relationship can be better captured with n-grams. The FastText embeddings provide the capability to work with n-grams out-of-the-box. We do not fine-tune the pre-trained embeddings for the respective prediction task.

For each of the 12 models, we train a separate regressor per emotion, as an alternative to multi-task models. This choice prevents the output emotion

[12]CMUdict: http://www.speech.cs.cmu.edu/cgi-bin/cmudict, LOGIOS: http://www.speech.cs.cmu.edu/tools/lextool.html. Both URLs are not available as of April 2022. The websites can be accessed via the Wayback Machine at https://web.archive.org/web/20211109084743/http://www.speech.cs.cmu.edu/tools/lextool.html and https://web.archive.org/web/20210815020323/http://www.speech.cs.cmu.edu/tools/lextool.html.

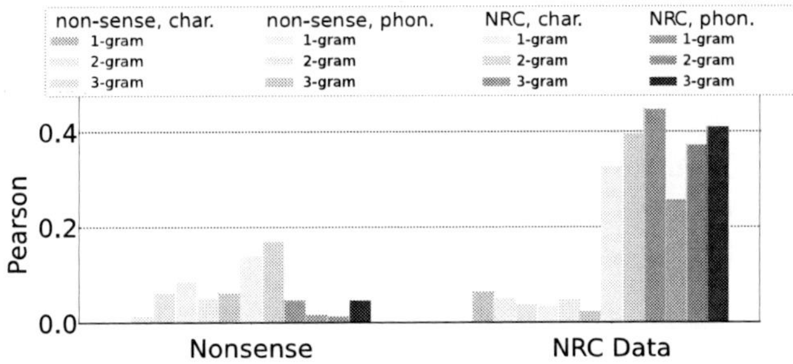

Figure 4: Barplot for Pearson correlation (averaged over all emotions). Each bar corresponds to one model configuration, either trained on nonsense words or on real words (NRC), with character embedding input or phoneme embedding input.

labels from interacting in the intensity predictions. Furthermore, preliminary experiments helped us establish that joint multi-task models are inferior to single regressors for our task.

5.2 Results

Figure 4 summarizes the results of our 12 emotion intensity prediction models and presents the performance using Pearson correlation (r). Numbers are average values over the results per emotion.

We first consider the models when tested on nonsense words (the left 12 bars in the figure). The phoneme-based models trained on nonsense words show slightly higher performance than the character-based models, but all these models are clearly outperformed by character-based models trained on real words. Therefore, we conclude that a model trained on real words does enable emotion intensity prediction on nonsense words, though to a limited degree (r=0.17). This is in accordance with the fact that human annotators declared to relate some of their judgments to existing English terms.

On the other side, testing on real words reveals a low performance of the models that were trained on nonsense words: the meaning of real words seems to dominate over phonetic patterns to take emotion decisions, which is a type of information that cannot be relied upon when training on nonwords. We should acknowledge, however, that this setup provided the models with an exceptionally limited amount of data, thus making it difficult to conclude that phonetic patterns do not play any role in automatic emotion inferences.

6 Conclusion & Future Work

We addressed the question of whether humans associate emotion intensities with nonsense words and tested if machine learning-based regressors pick up phonetic patterns to make emotion intensity predictions. Our annotation study revealed that humans do indeed make such associations. Especially the first phoneme of a word influences the resulting emotion intensity judgement: /p/ and /s/ seem to increase the perception of *joy*, /sh/ of *surprise*, and /m/ is more likely related to *sadness*. Contrary to our assumptions, phonemes placed at the last position of a nonword also play an important role. The phoneme /p/, for instance, points towards an increased degree of *disgust*.

We found that our emotion intensity regressors do predict emotion intensity based on word form and pronunciation, although only to a limited degree for nonsense words. Training on nonsense items and testing on real vocabulary entries results in a low performance, thus indicating that the meaning of known words overrules patterns that can be deduced from nonsense ones. When learned the other way around, our computational models make use of patterns found in real words that, to some degree, allow the emotion intensity prediction on nonsense counterparts.

One limitation of this first study of written nonsense words and their emotion association is the comparably limited size of the corpus we compiled. Future work could perform the annotation study with more items and across more diverse sets of annotators. Furthermore, our analysis focused on single phonemes that we selected based on their frequency in the data. This way of selecting the phonemes under investigation neglects the dependence between their frequencies and their positions. It also disregards potential interactions between different phonemes, as well as the role of less frequent phonemes in emotion intensity decisions. Future work should take into account these types of considerations.

Acknowledgements

We thank Sebastian Padó for helpful discussions. This research is funded by the German Research Council (DFG), project "Computational Event Analysis based on Appraisal Theories for Emotion Analysis" (CEAT, project number KL 2869/1-2).

References

James S. Adelman, Zachary Estes, and Martina Cossu. 2018. Emotional sound symbolism: Languages rapidly signal valence via phonemes. *Cognition*, 175:122–130.

Saima Aman and Stan Szpakowicz. 2007. Identifying expressions of emotion in text. In *Text, Speech and Dialogue*, pages 196–205, Berlin, Heidelberg. Springer Berlin Heidelberg.

Mehdi Bakhtiar, Dehqan Abad Ali, and Seif Sadegh. 2007. Nonword repetition ability of children who do and do not stutter and covert repair hypothesis. *Indian Journal of Medical Sciences*, 61(8):462–470.

Barbara Bond and Stanley S Stevens. 1969. Cross-modality matching of brightness to loudness by 5-year-olds. *Perception & Psychophysics*, 6(6):337–339.

Laura Ana Maria Bostan, Evgeny Kim, and Roman Klinger. 2020. GoodNewsEveryone: A corpus of news headlines annotated with emotions, semantic roles, and reader perception. In *Proceedings of the 12th Language Resources and Evaluation Conference*, pages 1554–1566, Marseille, France. European Language Resources Association.

Laura-Ana-Maria Bostan and Roman Klinger. 2018. An analysis of annotated corpora for emotion classification in text. In *Proceedings of the 27th International Conference on Computational Linguistics*, pages 2104–2119, Santa Fe, New Mexico, USA. Association for Computational Linguistics.

Giovanni Cassani, Yu-Ying Chuang, and R Harald Baayen. 2020. On the Semantics of Nonwords and Their Lexical Category. *Journal of Experimental Psychology: Learning, Memory, and Cognition*, 46(4):621–637.

Soumaya Chaffar and Diana Inkpen. 2011. Using a heterogeneous dataset for emotion analysis in text. In *Advances in Artificial Intelligence*, pages 62–67, Berlin, Heidelberg. Springer Berlin Heidelberg.

Yu-Ying Chuang, Marie-lenka Vollmer, Elnaz Shafaei-Bajestan, Susanne Gahl, Peter Hendrix, and R Harald Baayen. 2019. On the processing of nonwords in word naming and auditory lexical decision. In *Proceedings of the 19th International Congress of Phonetic Sciences, Melbourne, Australia 2019*, pages 1233–1237. Australasian Speech Science and Technology Association Inc.

Yu-Ying Chuang, Marie Lenka Vollmer, Elnaz Shafaei-Bajestan, Susanne Gahl, Peter Hendrix, and R Harald Baayen. 2021. The processing of pseudoword form and meaning in production and comprehension: A computational modeling approach using linear discriminative learning. *Behavior research methods*, 53(3):945–976.

Charles P. Davis, Hannah M. Morrow, and Gary Lupyan. 2019. What Does a Horgous Look Like? Nonsense Words Elicit Meaningful Drawings. *Cognitive Science*, 43(10):e12791.

Jacob Devlin, Ming-Wei Chang, Kenton Lee, and Kristina Toutanova. 2019. BERT: Pre-training of Deep Bidirectional Transformers for Language Understanding. In *Proceedings of the 2019 Conference of the North American Chapter of the Association for Computational Linguistics: Human Language Technologies, Volume 1 (Long and Short Papers)*, pages 4171–4186, Minneapolis, Minnesota. Association for Computational Linguistics.

Venkatesh Duppada and Sushant Hiray. 2017. Seernet at EmoInt-2017: Tweet emotion intensity estimator. In *Proceedings of the 8th Workshop on Computational Approaches to Subjectivity, Sentiment and Social Media Analysis*, pages 205–211, Copenhagen, Denmark. Association for Computational Linguistics.

Annette D'Onofrio. 2014. Phonetic Detail and Dimensionality in Sound-shape Correspondences: Refining the Bouba-Kiki Paradigm. *Language and Speech*, 57(3):367–393.

Paul Ekman. 1999. *Basic Emotions*, chapter 3. John Wiley & Sons, Ltd.

John S. Garofolo, Lori F. Lamel, William M. Fisher, Jonathan G. Fiscus, David S. Pallett, Nancy L. Dahlgren, and Victor Zue. 1993. TIMIT acoustic-phonetic continuous speech corpus. Linguistic Data Consortium.

Fréderic Godin. 2019. *Improving and Interpreting Neural Networks for Word-Level Prediction Tasks in Natural Language Processing*. Ph.D. thesis, Ghent University, Belgium.

Pranav Goel, Devang Kulshreshtha, Prayas Jain, and Kaushal Kumar Shukla. 2017. Prayas at EmoInt 2017: An Ensemble of Deep Neural Architectures for Emotion Intensity Prediction in Tweets. In *Proceedings of the 8th Workshop on Computational Approaches to Subjectivity, Sentiment and Social Media Analysis*, pages 58–65, Copenhagen, Denmark. Association for Computational Linguistics.

Emmanuel Keuleers and Marc Brysbaert. 2010. Wuggy: A multilingual pseudoword generator. *Behavior Research Methods*, 42(3):627–633.

Svetlana Kiritchenko and Saif M. Mohammad. 2016. Capturing reliable fine-grained sentiment associations by crowdsourcing and best–worst scaling. In *Proceedings of the 2016 Conference of the North*

American Chapter of the Association for Computational Linguistics: Human Language Technologies, pages 811–817, San Diego, California. Association for Computational Linguistics.

Wolfgang Köhler. 1970. *Gestalt Psychology*. Liveright, New York.

Maximilian Köper, Evgeny Kim, and Roman Klinger. 2017. IMS at EmoInt-2017: Emotion Intensity Prediction with Affective Norms, Automatically Extended Resources and Deep Learning. In *Proceedings of the 8th Workshop on Computational Approaches to Subjectivity, Sentiment and Social Media Analysis*, Copenhagen, Denmark. Workshop at Conference on Empirical Methods in Natural Language Processing, Association for Computational Linguistics.

Jordan J. Louviere, Terry N. Flynn, and A. A. J. Marley. 2015. *Best-Worst Scaling: Theory, Methods and Applications*. Cambridge University Press.

Asifa Majid. 2012. Current emotion research in the language sciences. *Emotion Review*, 4(4):432–443.

Lawrence E. Marks. 1987. On cross-modal similarity: Auditory–visual interactions in speeded discrimination. *Journal of Experimental Psychology: Human Perception and Performance*, 13(3):384.

Saif Mohammad. 2012. #emotional tweets. In **SEM 2012: The First Joint Conference on Lexical and Computational Semantics – Volume 1: Proceedings of the main conference and the shared task, and Volume 2: Proceedings of the Sixth International Workshop on Semantic Evaluation (SemEval 2012)*, pages 246–255, Montréal, Canada. Association for Computational Linguistics.

Saif Mohammad. 2018. Word affect intensities. In *Proceedings of the Eleventh International Conference on Language Resources and Evaluation (LREC 2018)*, Miyazaki, Japan. European Language Resources Association (ELRA).

Saif Mohammad and Felipe Bravo-Marquez. 2017a. Emotion intensities in tweets. In *Proceedings of the 6th Joint Conference on Lexical and Computational Semantics (*SEM 2017)*, pages 65–77, Vancouver, Canada. Association for Computational Linguistics.

Saif Mohammad and Felipe Bravo-Marquez. 2017b. WASSA-2017 shared task on emotion intensity. In *Proceedings of the 8th Workshop on Computational Approaches to Subjectivity, Sentiment and Social Media Analysis*, pages 34–49, Copenhagen, Denmark. Association for Computational Linguistics.

Saif Mohammad, Felipe Bravo-Marquez, Mohammad Salameh, and Svetlana Kiritchenko. 2018. SemEval-2018 task 1: Affect in tweets. In *Proceedings of The 12th International Workshop on Semantic Evaluation*, pages 1–17, New Orleans, Louisiana. Association for Computational Linguistics.

Saif Mohammad and Peter Turney. 2010. Emotions Evoked by Common Words and Phrases: Using Mechanical Turk to Create an Emotion Lexicon. In *Proceedings of the NAACL HLT 2010 Workshop on Computational Approaches to Analysis and Generation of Emotion in Text*, pages 26–34, Los Angeles, CA. Association for Computational Linguistics.

Saif M. Mohammad and Peter D. Turney. 2013. Crowdsourcing a Word-Emotion Association Lexicon. *Computational Intelligence*, 29(3):436–465.

Catherine J. Mondloch and Daphne Maurer. 2004. Do small white balls squeak? Pitch-object correspondences in young children. *Cognitive, Affective, & Behavioral Neuroscience*, 4(2):133–136.

Blake Myers-Schulz, Maia Pujara, Richard C Wolf, and Michael Koenigs. 2013. Inherent emotional quality of human speech sounds. *Cognition and Emotion*, 27(6):1105–1113.

Robert Plutchik. 2001. The nature of emotions: Human emotions have deep evolutionary roots, a fact that may explain their complexity and provide tools for clinical practice. *American Scientist*, 89(4):344–350.

Kathleen Rastle, Jonathan Harrington, and Max Coltheart. 2002. 358,534 nonwords: The ARC nonword database. *The Quarterly Journal of Experimental Psychology Section A*, 55(4):1339–1362.

James A. Russell. 1980. A Circumplex Model of Affect. *Journal of Personality and Social Psychology*, 39(6):1161–1178.

Klaus R Scherer. 2005. What are emotions? And how can they be measured? *Social Science Information*, 44(4):695–729.

Hendrik Schuff, Jeremy Barnes, Julian Mohme, Sebastian Padó, and Roman Klinger. 2017. Annotation, Modelling and Analysis of Fine-Grained Emotions on a Stance and Sentiment Detection Corpus. In *Proceedings of the 8th Workshop on Computational Approaches to Subjectivity, Sentiment and Social Media Analysis*, pages 13–23, Copenhagen, Denmark. Association for Computational Linguistics.

Carlo Strapparava and Rada Mihalcea. 2007. SemEval-2007 task 14: Affective text. In *Proceedings of the Fourth International Workshop on Semantic Evaluations (SemEval-2007)*, pages 70–74, Prague, Czech Republic. Association for Computational Linguistics.

Gabriel Synnaeve. 2015. Speech Embeddings. Github Repository at `https://github.com/syhw/speech_embeddings`.

Matthew J. Traxler and Morton A. Gernsbacher, editors. 2006. *Handbook of Psycholinguistics*. Elsevier.

Amy Beth Warriner, Victor Kuperman, and Marc Brysbaert. 2013. Norms of valence, arousal, and dominance for 13,915 English lemmas. *Behavior Research Methods*, 45(4):1191–1207.

Appendix

A Best and Worst Predictions of Models on Nonwords

	joy	sadness	anger	disgust	fear	surprise
Best Predictions	bange	gnirl	zunch	plert	phlump	scrare
	groose	drusp	sout	twauve	cruck	twale
	cisp	shuilt	swetch	framn	cliege	gnewn
	gnirl	scrare	wholk	sout	purf	psoathe
	broin	throoch	chuile	gnirl	snoob	phreum
	chuile	prote	cisp	throoch	scrol	theight
	swetch	phrouth	framn	theph	chuwk	grulch
	shuilt	zunch	preak	purf	grulch	cliege
	kass	theight	yirp	cisp	twale	thwick
	throoch	flalf	dwull	zorce	ghuge	plert
Worst Predictions	purf	hupe	snusp	ghuge	bange	blidge
	snoob	snoob	broin	grulch	phreum	zel
	cruck	phype	shrote	slanc	gnirl	cheff
	plert	broin	blidge	shrote	snusp	dwull
	snusp	dwear	slanc	groose	psoathe	purf
	skief	wholk	phrouth	thwick	phrouth	ghuge
	yirp	skief	plert	hupe	broin	throoch
	slanc	slanc	scrol	cruck	pseach	snoob
	choff	sout	skief	fonk	slanc	cisp
	yourse	preak	shuilt	theight	chuile	pseach

(a) Trained on nonsense words, phoneme 1-gram model

	joy	sadness	anger	disgust	fear	surprise
Best Predictions	blidge	slanc	blour	phype	tource	sloarse
	wholk	theph	drusp	twauve	twarp	preak
	yirp	zel	plert	twale	grulch	phrouth
	cheff	twauve	ghuge	phreum	yirp	gnewn
	hupe	bange	zant	fonk	sout	choff
	shrote	valf	wholk	yourse	swetch	phreum
	dwull	cliege	rhulch	zerge	cliege	glelve
	gnewn	grulch	cruck	scrare	scrol	cruck
	framn	phrouth	snoob	gnewn	sloarse	grulch
	yealt	gnirl	gnirl	scrush	dwull	psoathe
Worst Predictions	snoob	ghuge	blidge	valf	phrouth	zel
	theph	phlump	broin	shrote	prote	throoch
	thwick	chuick	valf	scrol	snusp	twale
	chymn	prote	chuile	phrouth	chuile	chymn
	snusp	chuile	swetch	skief	psoathe	scrare
	preak	zunch	snusp	dwull	cheff	purf
	swetch	purf	phrouth	zunch	shuilt	kass
	twale	yealt	zorce	prote	chymn	twauve
	yourse	swetch	sout	chymn	bange	bange
	cisp	choff	tource	ghuge	broin	snusp

(b) Trained on real words, character 2-gram model

Table 4: The top 10 best and worst predictions for nonsense words by the best model trained on nonsense words and the best model trained on real words.

B Excerpt from our lexicon of nonsense words with emotion intensity annotations

IDs	Word	ARPA Pron	Real	Joy	Sadness	Anger	Disgust	Fear	Surprise
0	afraid	ah f r ey d	1	0.3125	0.8333	0.3333	0.1875	0.6875	0.3333
1	alse	ae l s	0	0.6875	0.4375	0.5625	0.4792	0.4375	0.5625
2	apache	ah p ae ch iy	1	0.2917	0.6458	0.7708	0.4792	0.5	0.5833
3	aphid	ae f ih d	1	0.3333	0.625	0.4792	0.5625	0.6042	0.3125
4	bale	b ey l	1	0.5	0.5208	0.4167	0.3542	0.4583	0.0833
5	bange	b ae n jh	0	0.375	0.4375	0.6458	0.6042	0.7917	0.75
6	battle	b ae t ah l	1	0.1667	1.0	0.9583	0.7083	0.7292	0.5417
7	bias	b ay ah s	1	0.2292	0.5625	0.5625	0.4167	0.5417	0.4375
8	bizarre	b ah z aa r	1	0.4583	0.625	0.6042	0.5417	0.4792	0.5833
9	bleve	b l iy v	0	0.4792	0.4167	0.3125	0.375	0.4167	0.5417
10	blidge	b l ih jh	0	0.6042	0.4375	0.7083	0.4583	0.6042	0.7292
11	blister	b l ih s t er	1	0.4375	0.625	0.4375	0.625	0.7083	0.4583
12	blour	b l aw r	0	0.4583	0.5833	0.4375	0.4167	0.3125	0.6042
13	blurnt	b l er n t	0	0.5	0.4375	0.3542	0.3958	0.3958	0.5
14	blusp	b l ah s p	0	0.5417	0.5417	0.6458	0.5208	0.4583	0.4792
15	boarse	b ow r s	0	0.2708	0.6875	0.7708	0.8542	0.8542	0.5417
16	boil	b oy l	1	0.2708	0.75	0.75	0.3958	0.3958	0.3333
17	bowels	b aw ah l z	1	0.0833	0.5208	0.4792	0.8333	0.5	0.4583
18	break	b r ey k	1	0.6875	0.7917	0.6458	0.3125	0.2917	0.4792
19	broil	b r oy l	1	0.25	0.7083	0.875	0.75	0.7917	0.3333
20	broin	b r oy n	0	0.375	0.6458	0.8125	0.5833	0.6875	0.5208
...									
319	whalk	w ae l k	0	0.6458	0.3333	0.2708	0.3125	0.5417	0.5625
320	wheuth	w uw th	0	0.6875	0.4375	0.5	0.5417	0.5208	0.625
321	whoal	w ow l	0	0.6458	0.4375	0.3333	0.375	0.3542	0.7292
322	wholk	w aa l k	0	0.3958	0.625	0.5	0.5417	0.5208	0.5833
323	wrause	r ao s	0	0.4792	0.4375	0.6875	0.625	0.5833	0.5208
324	wrelt	r eh l t	0	0.5833	0.5208	0.5	0.4375	0.4375	0.3125
325	wrilge	r ih l jh	0	0.625	0.5208	0.4792	0.5833	0.625	0.5
326	wrorgue	r ao r g	0	0.3125	0.5417	0.7083	0.625	0.8542	0.4375
327	wruse	r uw s	0	0.4792	0.6042	0.5417	0.5417	0.6042	0.625
328	yage	y ey jh	0	0.3542	0.625	0.625	0.5833	0.6667	0.4583
329	yealt	y iy l t	0	0.3542	0.5208	0.4583	0.4167	0.6458	0.4375
330	yirp	y er p	0	0.4375	0.5625	0.4167	0.5417	0.4167	0.5417
331	yourse	y uw r s	0	0.6458	0.3542	0.25	0.3333	0.5208	0.5208
332	yurch	y er ch	0	0.5625	0.5	0.4792	0.5208	0.4583	0.5625
333	zant	z ae n t	0	0.5417	0.3542	0.4375	0.4792	0.4792	0.5
334	zany	z ey n iy	1	0.7708	0.0625	0.2708	0.3542	0.125	0.5417
335	zel	z eh l	0	0.6667	0.375	0.5417	0.2083	0.3958	0.75
336	zerge	z er jh	0	0.6667	0.3333	0.4375	0.4167	0.4375	0.5625
337	zorce	z ao r s	0	0.4583	0.5833	0.7917	0.6667	0.625	0.625
338	zourse	z ow r s	0	0.5625	0.3958	0.5833	0.5208	0.375	0.6458
339	zunch	z ah n ch	0	0.4583	0.6667	0.625	0.7292	0.7083	0.4375

C Complete Nonsense Word Emotion Intensity Lexicon

Copy-paste the following character sequence into a plain text file with the name `data.txt` and execute `base64 -d < data.txt | bzcat > nonsense-words-emotion-intensities.csv`

QlpoOTFBWSZTWdlU38YAIfpfgEAQQAF/6CUwWIA///+wYB3wPY1UFBfefHdly7Z2WwdmpRkdpzhgF2zo63GoO7KoaN
ngAAAAAAgAAfRuwRvttc4gPumOpUnGGmhB6iBMgmhU09TKNmpMnkGmCRRBNEmnqeUMgAABJlSKSfooADIaAAABJ6pU
JMSgAMgAAABo0KTRoGgAyB6jQNNASahETRJkamTRoAAAOZgzP2ec8BzlcRKPswRYFaYoY0bIsJSKNlLgbQSQD9NZOx
XQgJaC2o7QVhjaqjBkScQOGKwSyq2o2RRJFNQohe5ocTsDEZEhiRbYYZabmu4CJEkii8bIsITyAiNZCC4zEiFIwERG
gjigibYSPG6YTcbgYSEhZJCJQljM7qoYlYEKxLO7EqXaqmV3LtbL3BN17zZPNbN3/L5Ir/X+75pf//StJTrV50QeC7
/nR9BmjY1sZkPojGpFA7yDpvX+sacZ20nNtp4NNXOuloNNLTvpWs0zqXjekbOKYpFTvauaZMGp3NzBsZtvKVuGOdbe
vnq9z6rtc+44sO3/EM4+UNRh6pVw/8qwwA44gbUc3NCooX7OLZrzKe0YMbzZGxjB4V8S3Hp8xx3eeeYiFPp49b6PXo
T58/pWjruopCGq/KzxYVk9uwR3rmUHMDa2VY0qVKl97QLmj1t2mb0j21DyfUj4MPjnnhb6tr0kfSTYvjoFIAY+CF7h
cvOnfHNBbPOObE17fBBPCPbbbRWpnVpFuPfTJDfddHsdIJ7zEwcPkryX7Xm0BatKxeuJF4gcKOIevsfNEHere3u01Q
hTo+SQmdT4p6W+DqubA/CiJTIKTp1IgivW99ab6512gXvvzN7dqsjZ3xLvsetwGBaRix4p2aEdWqA+o7+CPwfj5JQQ
QKxp0wfP2/ALRu/NcBrN0ib10TxJO77d84RtOjyKNGlBJBBAy7zx4nSOlHpGv4DCICM9UQfkeJpxBw/AI1KKYN+ZUH
SHqWfHSANlVXeipeGyJNcfgzZYG9Z73PNK6dO9HgoEnqvEfXnauEeLCmxg4kDBrBkW1pqZrQVOXW2pk6kSYjRVZjlL
dU1XjTk8PPWPs+4hPqFSEhJJ+OMbbbX1fTV9+5zlXA/HbdONhcC4d11V0BznKn7BBcZBcr0AkguViUiqTYKEgSJiRl
KGijbBkoizNGo0GjYBsnnvPnx48e3lo2LRABmYlgD/ilKft/dL8frokkkkkkkkkjXRu4eIMm9buQu7LgwztKhTRV
UMSqWRiymazFRLla0IqzScxx71dyF3dw1AEmZlyF3dkyQfBCB0wHV7e3t6r1ExizN6tN0GCiGksloMaSxFWSJSIoii
xFGta1cmyAhmZchd3yEAJmZrppnOdEkkkkkkkkklKYkEkEkjz1whESjKQRTT5q+SB4hDmiLIEFJc3zzmSGZ1wNhBM
zLkLu7kLu67mmotNEUFRigsEezFPKJXTVIsCKUoxbKJN3XbGZbhVxMYNGqIxGKjbu4rJyk3SJd3SJpLI4aImBEQR49
982Oc52AGdkhrWrkLu++bkAamMiCKoixJNCnavXj1876YkxoiQSZeVw0oZKAsIJPft2TQMADMoFApSFJgUYKEowZNM
mikMhsSJlEZHt59vbz8fT3+vxlJJJJJJJJJJMGZqEgliWYsSSQQsVEFVHqQzLs7d4BGoGtauQu7CSbgoBkqQkrchI
kC5EtiqoqrRSYo1GZsaiN3r159Xnz5zISBmZmZmZ3DTFBRioip2Kpipmd3RDuuSaBEEySDBgyJC51Gw7ulIApFUUFi
xTe973t2b3ve5IQ61rWp74wZhZgxCozI0RgTTDIElCWIlopZKNJGkxEliSgwIJBYkEkEsCxBIBBmZmyze+MpJJJJJ
JJJJLERlmAYYAYVBZgSAwJYMGpSnjyzIWRsL11ySwmQDIIaRKEzQiBMwiaZEwpppmaHr169atb2vPnqrzA72wbmnLk
FFxsuByI7qmGiIlgzBoiHd3d7REVzS2c5ykkkkkkkl48ePHjx48izkF9KBWJoEalzK7UOkVyqNWqFq0U6EclXprKqs
gEnWZmF3dgQm4B2USCgCwFiyCwFSa1rV3dkhDrMzLu+/dEiAxptvW2tObWi2oqJLKDDEpSKilQjGZkiEwRhiRjKJlG
evXrl48eL5kZISwWRgHnqqnKKlEoiyEiZcM1KoLOVcuYYUqXZBWgtEELmoVUGrNK2mpnKWpqqSZs0FpJGlnJVlRFUY
qFiVYdRIlmGFs4ZdDpGmaYQZGpBiaWBElrKDJLWmmIqGhiXOGrILWZpUUctRNmRWnTKCIgxM2GMd3GUnd1BDs5xZ3J
dnImXVsK2MZSSSSSSSSSSWQwYPTrqrz6BFEHCuRfIc1WnUENirjuSWFkaTAkMJKaZGJAc4YyRRRda1VVkhJvk1rWr
u7JAOpC0IqyEWMUaMk8vLeKEiaJCTRmYymwoaQjSyxDCg1LIaMbERt47x5tTREO75GDMzeVfOFlJJJJJJJJJWgFp
YZoEhSjKZ9PJ9dtXcRiRQisGCoLDvqyqrrRCZmXd3VXqx5jjtlSahSRSHLOQQVkjKNEio4ETIiJUaQsgzLpxCBILss
gLMi7TtCmC5O7RCZy7MsmC5cVOci0laoF3ffdXYG5zlXAD01r6q1itS9evTXzNIooiElkILTBgikFIxslGImjMwRpp
JjYTIzCgpNMxIGGSJQGAE0mSjx3j39vj2+fn4+vx8JJJJJJJJJJK5MsSCCCQQCCQWJBgiqLDrWu8hLu6qsk0qqDBiA
IvW1dXa1G2yZGjQZtCJgJNAUVk0UWTUxFIsVRFUXWtVVaJN5mYXd9VjU7jckRy5znNgLlYiNzFWjHKqsC7vfAxRgoo
qKxUBJRJiEohMvp2uYlQhkh3boUmNJGTBREUEQgY0SJMUAmSc4DJFFANhACCSQQQSxBIIpSlM0vnOcJJJJJJJfHx8
fHx8fD58d9Zr3VERsSNKYbz57eEiA2ZFhmQIjEUEViixlSEaNUkKiRFLusJvrWtVVcQOyBxEJKQFgDEsBSlIiIoBEQ
7u7u7vObZws5SSSSSSSSSSVRMVFyTRi9IehFQWNYdnr+tKyz1Gxw8Ka4K2FtkioQE1oihHBy4hpukNpFomHi5WRNH
Dk0c1MPTQkCeBuQ6DogpNHOPOc27bNZa0h18Tg0aEyG0RAXGYGUbuaA+XjCI4XYkG2UiiF5nLLIERGp0NUWwOcKQ7F
DAN1R1CpFwUHgRLILMYUqdFGx4QkCQxxwTUUGCxSgbaCyFHq0KOMIOpw2LkuOt3SIy25WLMRA40HSWQxqc2kqkSxgH
h1kzTsCCBNoVbwogkAluMMMqKPDKnGGExVZDu2QguTeXZoVYQTILgsd402K0xrjNctYoOIgI0hVGYoWa0HEQZpg5WN
0Uw8NLIpCAMXLbqb2bHHJApbu21G7FJIShII0KzWUoK4I6nvHIt1i8R3aggntBIaRBd4EEbayQWKbENqEk0QrG1alU
TIqIVSZZI6lELyqzSSzDE3skUMnFA0qXRrG7Xk3SqVVzQFpr3UKcOmvEt0icQQvKnrVhZiSChupwg7hQIreMMU43bS
JkShKQRXNFTBocuAk1ThrhSjClhgcvNGu6iSiGNIZogYYQIIQaBlaFVrrIooKQEKaJLohxRcL0RFpvWnAdeWpFmEa6
1pWs0MMmA1Fmya0LlaxxsEiNDTu6cSdTpZEAJO16RBAW0jUKDUWVMJpNOApBQ1hWSOJESSQMV2BJERCKy7c3GktQ0z
NVYIqbtZ1CHnG0eHzGTyDuaTGbEIpSgYX1LY0rtFEBFYQZlPXle6goHoWwIbpQRxnKkmztsJqgxBOxxIOV5DSC3XYE
bkhTbTbKRUYjcCqyViuMx6WFFKtFqLa7bvGuZAdlpj4pprw4UWXG8JLm94gXNDUBRWwN1MPjDJGxyLNQvYxEghV3Q5
3sIOxgwJoIcLrDeVimxlmEkkklnWZDo2aHgfEN2WYcfEiIaykci0yBGA6Ai9cVSqFIIkSHEnCNRjRO8GrUCFuuHYVE
ncUo1OkTQi0VdArBu7A+uWijSQ0+hBjdFfRwkIzRQzrEQNI3TLkMKDHGpiHKiEIuGGmWiloSFCiLEzx59fz/R9kfsP
y+rpn79n36hfsuwfmXXsClNizUTfJjvl3xzvKIc7954/d4308bD+YNaQ5zXPK/I95pffTs96tnlLTaQV72Dr9KLel3
NYEbP/iyxZYxOmudUtnFiSFbIrM6i6vYGtI0mRXSRCkK85pSJu4N1WLqLEvYg20zF8a7a0WXsdVEuopqbTYRoIwhML
8Y2GrjS4478+LU540ONunzPINLReavDVt1R6gmhsAcIO7xzKzxdG2lqzaytY5RdaYU0r+PLv5PPw7VB2vpDkb8bvt9
d/rx8/fXPPKSSSS+hzrqNuN9999999990kln3pzx37yIj466cVhPYRd6ddddddddJJJJJJJLON+eJ8D6fj169Xu
lYqXE+ZtL+HFfHjx48ePHjx4SSWunvtzPP4MCvYitfiZES8nnnnnnnnnnnlJJJJJJJJJJJLA3IznOc1Gc/7U/T7bbR
9e/v5n7IBI8Vfv379+/fv344SS0611222222+LAfGM8ccccbbbL7+e/O+/kOA/XXbt2r9HXy7gjXR+uuuut99990kk
kkkkkkkkktfvw+oILdjtttttttt4XGmo5n6hyYmkeKN4j6IvLuCLJ7zz1IsKO5/tppSaKmPs5/tP3dVUB/fv379+/
fv37SXW3vXfcc/H1DU5555555555SSSSSSSSSSSSSSSSSSSSSSSSSSSSXGnBbv67R5LcGvb26uKKTXxaHrNeuuuuuuuu
uySSSSSSSSSSS539a66668Deo457du3bt22222Sx212Ouuuutb22Pwd99999tvz+rfwf8/s/+o/dkKyAAFPxwABX0f
jo8Cp7Z0oUIFVEAiTRZzo3/tMAXIDMSzAasv3P6KwHY7bfvS38X/fI1rgWBmH/mfAwtfyOA2SABu9zpkXfTUuV5Xj+
HqlednzagtWzUIO9Jt+T6mY8W5YADrkM5AYsBbF/ffXit2xFaTmZ5CTcAuw3B5OEDB9eHvj+iSnTeyDXX5zfYDy86w
xlHOB4q7RFvK7ZPCIqqkAQA8tY+DaowdZm4Y4pJVnRAYYgMAD5076XL/FYZF+J8084FBe1r9RXatdL5VLseopOtLw4
75nD0F0VtKFnE4mHOYoVjFFWuYFxhKJNoyaQ75KrR3ES32fPy4/5HPDm3le6fXrHiflZpQfLACxZhQScc/U96ZxIVH
xvbHT6BmZ/Ntrvr5yK59Vn4n3t2FW8+M35wh6QRFJBYwD5jTx5+9+Tfy1rfNcJxvAFIcodkSIUhGUyytZK9evdWr3n
WVWYPHCaO1QtmrokrXRZ4YfL2W/Gn5k8uyEeUcXLecn4lXedwO86pdBCSAIBCBQQXJLFiRJpwiXl6jvrrrt7RBVrHB
qlGMEppQzWmsGTjRd55rzXFUshGBZC2goo8jCLLMckQighCU1Hrx3dFMrqsSsCXyxxOfIkcyonQSPv7Wa8GurSANmu
Qvf00rQNEOIEoKAVkw9qVhmpEd+1/PUV6D95b077c9+dsRbayideO2Bp43z5AYDECdCa743IjGuu+JyFmX9adhhfKF
tc/88+nfj028fC6909WQnw9cwDABgiiIrFYosWMZCa6zn23HM69+ZqtVo5PoQ4ZF47UkigsiyCwgGTrdPO09+X31d7
vy9fl8+5nzsMNnq2nmaHEqaqhnHVBa09qcxFmmuL3HEw7nbTRMcA4gXRuS5dw6gTUWsL2GLU5LEksQzDtB500m9LBp
vC4tTZA3Dib0kDLEglgSQCxIDEkszRHpVfJ0fwDaF6uLtSuRiL/FjN40ACH6LGdrY0rlVpV50qK2mZea1FiIADcixH
PPxPi33rt61gW9T8awc0fVx5OPO9W1ppI3wO1LFj6qR9H+RpXqo26302HRrry/jIwQavW1e81iI3+e1J3LUtx8sAWr
z+Z9PG3/fXaCKSIiI1b3oPR+pca+TVRhvPX7PvfvohGDTgjSzqRJInnuEe7k2JvnXKLJZNX0lc2jo7rFrsyy13XJtB
QHIJZyASWBBBNk5dwod+3vvz6MY71l49RTvnQ5BLb+YkeNgtsw2wzTQw+z43LHbdpvLq2I1udmtiJcUvfGwf9qbxpr
xxi1DxL2NH4105d2Yg7xxBZedtnHPkeh6ee/YePL2e3mLFgoRBhFkAsCxLAlmLBgOf0827SOV4gQgwpbvc0MRE3t3N
64rVYnr2EeUk8EOeHfG9knG6JKHDrVXwkDMd6pdU5oDbJzFVERUZEAbHvjRydO+cHXS9lR5uyESdcVgYrLvYzTDXNX
iHt4hDwQvttfdR4txDcIe3kpGKrdQp/qlgTT7nyxJPE1au5lFqmtZpMcW1o9bRudVft9fjCpm2k98x4xMXTv29frLY
w5qbH+/QmtWHL+mZm7aeRaMJ8dXvmd8qvjvp4nKgpnFBbNYOUUotzGF3KhaZmIrVLQxpozCrBUYFiBxIJBEkIuRn6+
PqPn78/GKYmmhzkgE1pTmqwi7grvjwPQHwgSOBlIMJpANLEs4EmUQ20SmyES2UGSRcqDBuHLnPazYy5k6xksxDd2cY
IgFnWX/6LuSKcKEhsqm/jA==

SentEMO: A Multilingual Adaptive Platform for Aspect-based Sentiment and Emotion Analysis

Ellen De Geyndt, Orphée De Clercq, Cynthia Van Hee, Els Lefever, Pranaydeep Singh, Veronique Hoste
LT3, Language and Translation Technology Team, Ghent University, Belgium

Olivier Parent
Artevelde University College, Ghent, Belgium

Abstract

In this paper, we present the SentEMO platform, a tool that provides aspect-based sentiment analysis and emotion detection of unstructured text data such as reviews, emails and customer care conversations. Currently, models have been trained for five domains and one general domain and are implemented in a pipeline approach, where the output of one model serves as the input for the next. The results are presented in three interactive dashboards, allowing companies to gain more insights into what stakeholders think of their products and services. The SentEMO platform is available at https://sentemo.ugent.be/ [1].

1 Introduction

In the SentEMO project, we aim to develop a fine-grained sentiment analysis and emotion detection system for four languages (Dutch, English, French and German). Fine-grained sentiment and emotion detection is very interesting for every company or non-profit organization having user data at its disposal. The results of such a system not only provide insights into what the various stakeholders think of specific products or services, but can also be used to analyse sentiment at the company level and thus provide input for employer branding. We aim to meet companies' needs for automation when sentiment analysis is done manually or by using lexicons. With the dashboard, we furthermore want to offer an insightful alternative to black-box sentiment approaches by visualizing results at the aspect level.

The aim is to design a fully data-based and adaptable system: companies will be able to improve and fine-tune the output on their own data, and then retrain the system based on that corrected data. Thanks to this feedback loop, the system will be continuously customized to company-specific data and the quality will keep on improving. On the one hand, the user interface has an intuitive dashboard that provides a clear representation of the sentiment and emotion detection results, on the other hand, it will also have the functionality to label or correct data and easily retrain the system.

In this paper, we present the first prototype of our system, that includes an Aspect-based Sentiment Analysis (ABSA) and Aspect-based Emotion Analysis (ABEA) module for Dutch. First, we briefly introduce the task of aspect-based sentiment analysis and emotion detection. Next, we elaborate on the data we used and the annotation process. In section 4, the experimental set-up and results of the models are discussed. Section 5 and 6 cover details of the user interface. Finally, we give an outlook of the next steps of the project in section 7.

2 Aspect-Based Sentiment and Emotion Analysis

Aspect-based sentiment analysis or ABSA (Pontiki et al., 2016) not only aims at the detection of all sentiment expressions within a given document, but also detects the concepts and aspects (or features) to which they refer. ABSA is generally decomposed into three subtasks: (1) Aspect Term Extraction, (2) Aspect Category Classification, and (3) Aspect Polarity Classification. We provide more insights into each step in section 4.

Sometimes it does not suffice to report on a polarity level and it could be useful to know what specific emotions stakeholders experience (e.g. anger, sadness, joy,...) (Mohammad et al., 2018). Especially within customer relation management, it is valuable to detect strong emotions timely to provide an appropriate response. In order to predict emotions on a fine-grained level, we build on the results from the aspect-based sentiment analysis component and provide an additional emotion layer to the predicted positive or negative sentiment.

[1]The platform is presented in a demo video at https://youtu.be/HJoMpTOAz9E

Proceedings of the 12th Workshop on Computational Approaches to Subjectivity, Sentiment & Social Media Analysis, pages 51 - 61
May 26, 2022 ©2022 Association for Computational Linguistics

3 Data and Annotation

Since the SentEMO project is a collaboration with eight Belgian companies, we envisaged to collect both in-house data and proprietary user data coming from those project partners. In total, these efforts resulted in data sets covering six different domains: FMCG[2] (non-durable products which are often bought by consumers, e.g. cleaning products, food and self-care products), Airline, Hotel, Product Retail, Hospital and Telecom. Regarding the in-house Dutch data, 1,000 reviews were each time scraped from bol.com, Trustpilot and Tripadvisor for the domains FMCG, Airline and Hotel, respectively. For the other domains, data was received from the project partners. After some basic data cleaning where duplicates and instances written in languages other than Dutch were removed, we ended up with data sets consisting of at least 900 instances per domain.

In a next step, the data had to be manually enriched or annotated with ABSA and ABEA information in order to be able to train and evaluate machine learning systems. Annotation consisted of four steps (see Figure 1 for an illustration). First, the **aspect terms** had to be identified in the sentences (e.g. *kamer* (English: *room*) in Figure 1). Next, an **aspect category** corresponding to an entity-attribute pair[3] (e.g. *ROOM_style* in Figure 1) was selected. Subsequently, the annotator selected the sentiment words (e.g. *prachtige* (English: *beautiful*)) and assigned a corresponding sentiment or **polarity** (*positive*). We annotated five possible polarities: very positive, positive, neutral, negative and very negative. The sentiments very positive and very negative are only chosen when an intensifier is explicitly present in the text (e.g. *very* friendly). In a second annotation round, an emotion was added to the aspect term. The annotators could choose from a list of 12 emotions: anger, anticipation, disgust, dissatisfaction, distrust, fear, joy, neutral, sadness, satisfaction, surprise and trust. Neutral was only to be used when the sentiment was also tagged as neutral. For the selection of the emotion labels, we based ourselves on Plutchik's wheel of emotions (Plutchik, 1980). We started with anger, anticipation, disgust, fear, joy, sadness, surprise and trust and added satisfaction and dissatisfaction for statements with a softer emotion. After testing these emotions on 10 sentences per domain, we also added distrust as a negative opposite for trust.

[2] Fast-moving consumer goods

[3] See Section 3.1 for more information.

When the writer voiced an opinion about an aspect without explicitly mentioning it, a NULL annotation was created, which, as illustrated by Figure 2, included the appropriate aspect category (e.g. *PERSONNEL_friendliness*), polarity (e.g. *very positive*) and emotion (e.g. *satisfaction*).

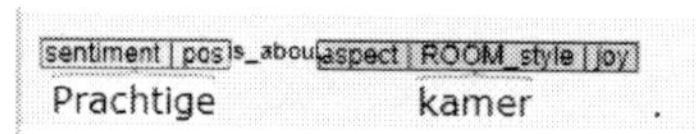

Figure 1: Example of an explicit annotation. Translation: Beautiful Room.

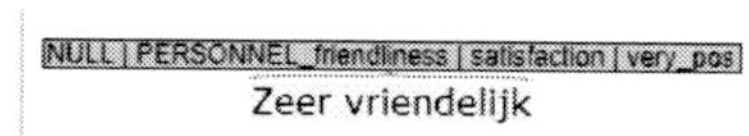

Figure 2: Example of an implicit aspect annotation. Translation: Very friendly.

3.1 Categorization Frameworks

For each domain, a framework of entity and attribute pairs was compiled representing the possible aspect categories (which can also be referred to as main categories and subcategories). An entity refers to a more general aspect category, e.g. personnel, store, hotel; whereas an attribute adds information and specifies what is said about the aspect category, e.g. friendliness, cleanliness, price. In Figure 1 the entity is *Room* and the attribute *style*. For each entity, a *general* and *misc* attribute were created to cover those cases in which the writer expressed a sentiment about the aspect category in general or when the writer discussed an attribute of the entity for which no label was created.

After closely inspecting the data of FMCG and Product Retail, we decided to merge both data sets since the entity-attribute labels were already very similar and the feedback was also very alike. This way, we created a larger data set for the domain **FCMG-Retail**. In a last phase, we also decided to create a **General** domain categorization in order to be able to train a more generic model. For this, we only use entity-attribute pairs that are highly likely to be useful for any company in any domain, i.e. Product, Personnel and Company. The final number of Entity-Attribute pairs per domain ranged between 44 for the **Hotel** domain and 11 for the **General** domain. In Appendix A, a complete overview can be found of the aspect categories per domain. After the creation of the frameworks, job students were hired to annotate the data using the INCEpTION annotation tool.[4]

4 Model Development

Once all data were annotated, they were pre-processed and experimental data splits were created in order to experiment with a variety of machine learning algorithms including both feature-based and deep learning approaches. In this section we report on the best approach for each ABSA and ABEA sub-task. Much work has already been carried out for each task separately, e.g. Poria et al. (2016) for aspect term extraction, Toh and Su (2015) for aspect category classification, Kiritchenko et al. (2014) for sentiment classification and Padme and Kulkarni (2018) for emotion classification. Approaches with multi-task learning usually only cover two of the tasks, very often aspect term extraction and sentiment classification (Akhtar et al., 2020) or aspect term extraction and aspect category classification (Xue et al., 2017). We opted for a pipeline approach in which we combine a feature-based approach for the first two ABSA sub-tasks (aspect term extraction and aspect category classification) with a transformer-based architecture for the polarity classification and emotion detection. While we also used transformer-based approaches to tackle the first two sub-tasks, we observed better results using a feature-engineered approach with CRF and SVM classifiers. Note that for each sub-task, results are reported with the gold standard input from the previous task, meaning that potential error percolation from previous steps is not yet taken into account.

4.1 Aspect Term Extraction

The first ABSA sub-task is Aspect Term Extraction, where a model is trained to recognize and extract explicit aspect terms. For this step, we based ourselves on previous work done by De Clercq et al. (2017) and applied a sequential IOB labeling supervised machine learning approach[5]. The algorithm used to this purpose is a Conditional Random Field (CRF) as implemented in CRFSuite (Okazaki, 2007).

For this feature-based approach, we used a combination of token-shape features, linguistic information extracted via the LeTs pre-processing toolkit (Van de Kauter et al., 2013) and dependency parsing information obtained from the Dutch dependency parser implemented within the open-source Spacy toolkit[6].

For the experiments, a model was trained for each domain separately on the training data splits, leading to six trained CRF models. All models were trained using the LBFGS (Nocedal, 1980) optimization function and all hyper-parameters were optimized using randomized search with 500 iterations in a 5-fold cross-validation setup. To evaluate, model accuracy was determined by calculating precision, recall and its harmonious set mean flat F1-score, all based on micro-averaging. The winning models were subsequently applied to the held-out test set. The results of these CRF models for the task of aspect term extraction per domain are presented in Table 1. As can be observed from these results for all domains a very good performance has been achieved.

Domain	Precision	Recall	F1
FMCG-Retail	90.9	92.3	91.4
Airline	92.2	92.8	92.4
Hotel	92.3	93.0	92.6
Hospital	93.0	93.8	93.4
Telecom	92.5	93.5	92.5
General	94.0	95.0	94.3

Table 1: Micro-averaged precision, recall and F1-scores for ATE on the held-out test sets in all domains.

4.2 Aspect Category Classification

For the Aspect Category Classification sub-task, a classifier was required that was capable of labeling a large number of classes (cfr. Appendix A). To this purpose we again relied on a supervised machine learning model, namely a Support Vector Machine, using the algorithm as implemented in Scikit Learn's C-Support Vector Classification[7], which is based on LibSVM (Chang and Lin, 2011). We implemented a combination of lexico-semantic features and Word2Vec embeddings on the training data using Gensim (Řehůřek and Sojka, 2010).

To evaluate, precision and recall were calculated, as well as micro F1-score on the entities. Given the

[4]https://inception-project.github.io/

[5]IOB labeling means that the data was transformed into the Inside Outside Begin format. For example, the sentence "The pizza margherita tastes good" becomes "The-O pizza-B margherita-I tastes-O good-O"

[6]https://spacy.io/models/nl

[7]https://scikit-learn.org/stable/modules/generated/sklearn.svm.SVC.html

large imbalance of the data sets - with a few classes with a very high representation in the training set and some classes with a very low representation - we decided to only report the accuracy of the model to predict the correct entity (main category) instead of all entity-attribute pairs (main + subcategories), e.g. for the domain FMCG-Retail the accuracy is reported on the 7 main categories instead of all 32 entity-attribute pairs. Table 2 presents the classification accuracy of the top-performing models of each domain on the held-out test set. The actual number of classes to predict per domain are listed in between brackets.

Domain	Precision	Recall	F1
FMCG-Retail (7)	81.5	79.2	79.8
Airline (7)	66.3	64.8	64.8
Hotel (7)	77.7	77.1	77.0
Hospital (5)	73.3	72.3	72.2
Telecom (7)	78.9	76.7	76.9
General (3)	87.1	86.3	86.6

Table 2: Micro-averaged precision, recall and F1-scores of the Main Aspect Category Classification experiments on the held-out test sets in all domains.

4.3 Aspect Polarity Classification

The final ABSA task consisted in predicting five different polarity labels: very positive, positive, neutral, negative and very negative. To this purpose a pre-trained version of RobBERT[8] was employed, which is the state-of-the-art in various downstream Dutch tasks. We use 768-dimensional token embeddings from RobBERT as features for a linear SVM[9]. The features in case of multiple aspect tokens are constructed by averaging the embeddings of all the sub-tokens involved and an additional context window of 3, i.e. 3 additional tokens before the first aspect token and after the last aspect token. To evaluate, again precision, recall and F1 are reported (Table 4), showing polarity classification F-scores up to 89.5% on the held-out test set. With an F1-score of 75 or more for each domain, performance is not perfect, but satisfying given the limited number of training data available and the five-way classification task.

[8]https://github.com/iPieter/RobBERT

[9]https://scikit-learn.org/stable/modules/generated/sklearn.svm.LinearSVC.html

Domain	Precision	Recall	F1
FMCG-Retail	82.0	81.7	80.9
Airline	84.3	84.7	82.8
Hotel	85.4	86.1	85.1
Hospital	91.0	90.2	89.5
Telecom	77.8	77.5	75.7
General	85.8	85.4	84.7

Table 3: Micro-averaged precision, recall and F1-scores of the Aspect Polarity Classification on the held-out test sets in all domains.

4.4 Emotion Classification

For the emotion analysis, we decided to build on the results of sentiment analysis, by dividing our emotions into two groups: positive emotions (anticipation, joy, satisfaction, surprise and trust) and negative emotions (anger, disgust, dissatisfaction, distrust, fear, sadness and surprise). The frequency for anticipation and fear were very low, so we merged the instances in which they were tagged with joy and distrust respectively. Since surprise could be either positive or negative, it occurs for both sentiments. Using the same approach as for polarity classification, we built an SVM classifier for each group using the same RobBERT-based features, this time using a context window of 5 words instead of 3 based on our cross-validation experiments. The predicted sentiment will decide whether a sentence is classified by the model for positive emotions or the one for negative emotions. This way, we avoid sentences where the sentiment prediction is positive, but the emotion is negative (e.g. very positive and anger) and vice versa.

To evaluate, precision, recall and F1 are reported. Moreover, we also calculated cost-corrected accuracy, which takes the severity of an error into account (De Bruyne et al., 2022). Since we make a distinction between strong (anger, disgust, distrust, joy, sadness, surprise, trust) and weak emotions (dissatisfaction, satisfaction) on the one hand and polarity (positive and negative) on the other, there are 5 values on the ordinal scale as can be seen in Figure 3. Based on this scale, we created our own cost matrix (Figure 4). When a prediction belongs to the same ordinal point of the scale, we apply a cost of 0.25 (e.g. gold label *anger* and predicted label *disgust*). When the gold label is a strong emotion, such as joy or anger, but the prediction is satisfaction or dissatisfaction respectively, the cost is 0.5. An incorrect neutral prediction is repre-

Domain	Prec.	Rec.	F1	CC Acc
FMCG-Ret.	65.3	68.6	61.2	84.8
Airline	65.7	67.9	62.6	85.0
Hotel	70.8	76.1	71.5	88.3
Hospital	79.1	88.8	83.6	94.4
Telecom	67.7	75.4	69.2	73.6
General	70.2	69.9	63.7	85.4

Table 4: Micro-averaged precision, recall and F1-scores of the Emotion Classification on the held-out test sets in all domains

sented by a cost of 0.75. As soon as an emotion of the opposite polarity is predicted, the cost is 1. In Table 4, the results for emotion classification are presented.

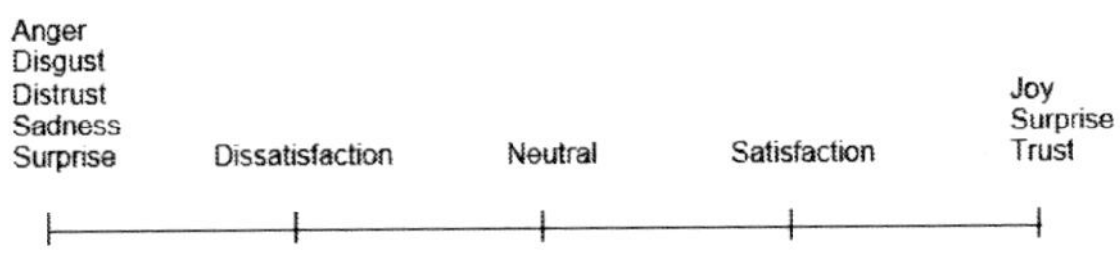

Figure 3: Placement of the emotional labels on an ordinal scale, according to sentiment.

	Anger	Disgust	Dissatisfaction	Distrust	Joy	Neutral	Sadness	Satisfaction	Trust
Anger	0	1/4	2/4	1/4	1	3/4	1/4	1	1
Disgust	1/4	0	2/4	1/4	1	3/4	1/4	1	1
Dissatisfaction	2/4	2/4	0	2/4	1	3/4	2/4	1	1
Distrust	1/4	1/4	2/4	0	1	3/4	1/4	1	1
Joy	1	1	1	1	0	3/4	1	2/4	1/4
Neutral	3/4	3/4	3/4	3/4	3/4	0	3/4	3/4	3/4
Sadness	1/4	1/4	2/4	1/4	1	3/4	0	1	1
Satisfaction	1	1	1	1	2/4	3/4	1	0	2/4
Trust	1	1	1	1	1/4	3/4	1	2/4	0

Figure 4: Emotion Label Cost matrix.

As can be observed from Table ??, the cost-corrected accuracy for the *Hospital* domain is high. This could be explained by the large representation of positive emotions in the data set.

5 Demonstration of the Interactive Dashboard

Users can access the SentEMO dashboard with their login details via the URL sentemo.ugent.be[10]. After logging in, users can upload data to be analysed or look at the analysis of previously uploaded data. **Manage Documents** gives an overview of the files that have been uploaded. The status indicates whether a file is being processed, is ready or failed. Users can drag and drop CSV files, which contain the domain in the first column and text in the second column. As soon as the status is set to *Ready*, the results are available in the dashboard.

On the **Analyse Texts** page, a distinction is made between the results for Sentiment and Emotion Analysis. On the sentiment analysis page, users can see details about the aspect category and polarity classification. The emotion dashboard focuses on emotion classification, but the aspect categories can be used as filters.

5.1 Aspect Category Dashboard

After selecting ABSA, users first land on the Aspect Category page. The dashboard presents the aspect categories ordered according to their frequency (Figure 5). Next to the aspect categories, a word cloud displays all the aspect terms the model extracted (Figure 6). *Impl* in the word cloud refers to implicit aspects. This means that the categorisation model was able to extract a category from a sentence, even when no explicit aspect term was found. Selecting a specific aspect category filters the word cloud to aspect terms for that specific category. Clicking on an aspect term lists all the sentences in which it occurs. This allows the user to have more insights into the context in which terms are used. The aspect term is highlighted in the sentence either in green, red or grey, depending on the predicted sentiment (positive, negative or neutral, respectively).

5.2 Polarity Dashboard

The polarity dashboard (Figure 7) shows a number of different graphs. First, the user can analyse the distribution of the polarities for each aspect main category on the one hand and for each complete aspect category (main and subcategory) on the other hand. Below, the distribution of the aspect categories is plotted for each polarity. An overview of the polarities in the entire data set can be observed in the doughnut chart on the right. Underneath, users can find the top five aspect terms and polarity terms for either polarity (Figure 8). Clicking on these terms once again displays the sentences in which they occur. The doughnut chart and top five terms can be filtered by aspect category, using the list in the middle.

[10]At this moment, a login can only be obtained through one of the members of the SentEMO research team

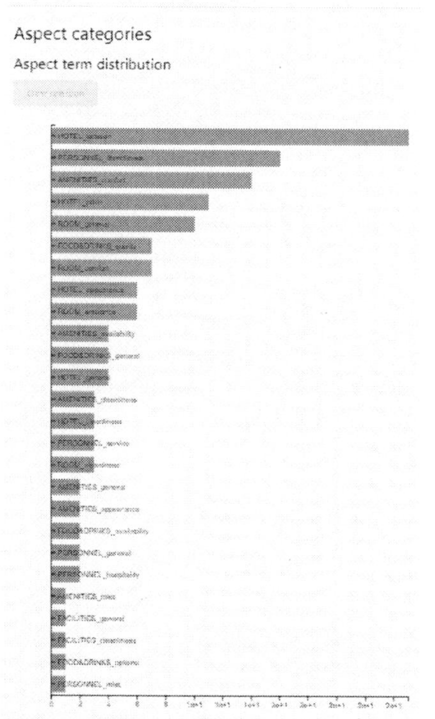

Figure 5: Visualisation of the Aspect Categories.

Figure 6: The aspect term cloud and corresponding instances for the aspect term 'kamers' (rooms).

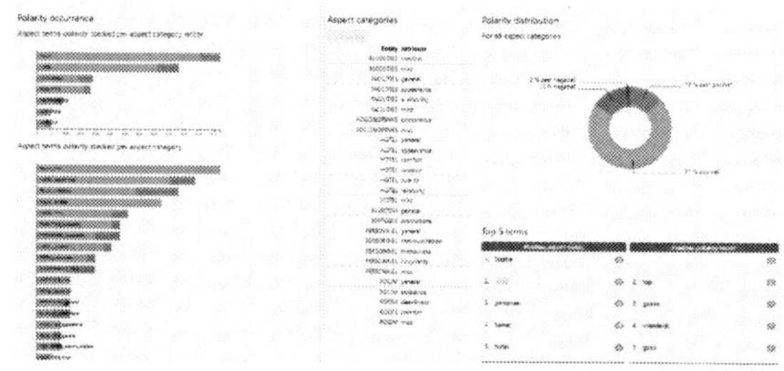

Figure 7: The polarity analysis dashboard.

5.3 Emotion Dashboard

The ABEA component of the analysis only consists of one dashboard. On the right hand side, next to the word cloud, a list of emotions and their corresponding counts is displayed. Below, a bar plot provides a clear visualisation of their distribution. Both the list of aspect categories and the word cloud can be used to filter the data. By selecting one of the aspect terms, the user can once more read the corresponding sentences. The aspect term is highlighted in a specific colour, depending on the predicted emotion.

6 Technical Implementation

The SentEMO platform consists of two separate applications: a front-end and a back-end. The front office is a full-stack web application for both users and administrators and is responsible for user management, document management and data visualisation. The back-end, on the other hand, is responsible for text processing and machine learning. Both applications are self-contained and hosted on different servers within the same local network. Each application can be replicated and/or customised independently as per use case requirements.

The data processing workflow is as follows: first, the user uploads a CSV file with texts.The CSV file is parsed, and the extracted data is stored into a relational database (PostgreSQL[11]). Next, a JSON object with the data is generated and sent to a message queue (RabbitMQ[12]). This message queue is read out by the SentEMO back-end at predefined intervals. The data is processed by the SentEMO bac-kend, and a response with the results is sent as a JSON object to a second message queue. The SentEMO Front Office reads this response and stores the data in the relational database. Finally, the user is notified that the document has been processed and that data visualisation is now available for the uploaded document.

The SentEMO Front Office is built with Docker containers[13] (as shown by Figure 10): a custom Node.js[14] application container, a PostgreSQL relational database container, and a RabbitMQ message queue container. This setup is hardware and operating system agnostic, making it easy to deploy on Windows, macOS, or Linux (Ubuntu Server), regardless of CPU architecture. It can even be run

[11] https://www.postgresql.org/
[12] https://www.rabbitmq.com/
[13] https://www.docker.com/
[14] https://nodejs.org/

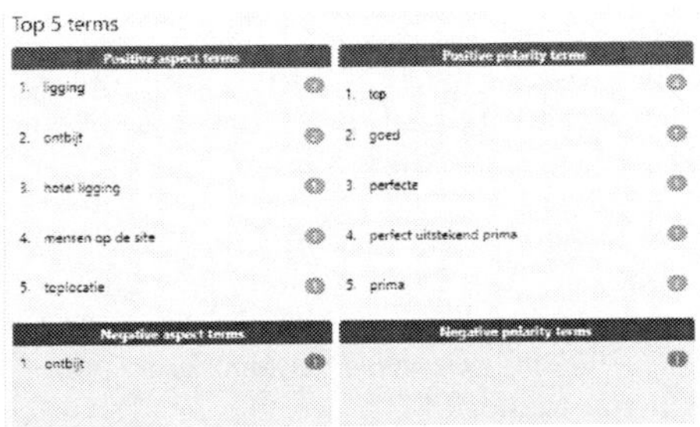

Figure 8: Positive and negative aspect and polarity terms.

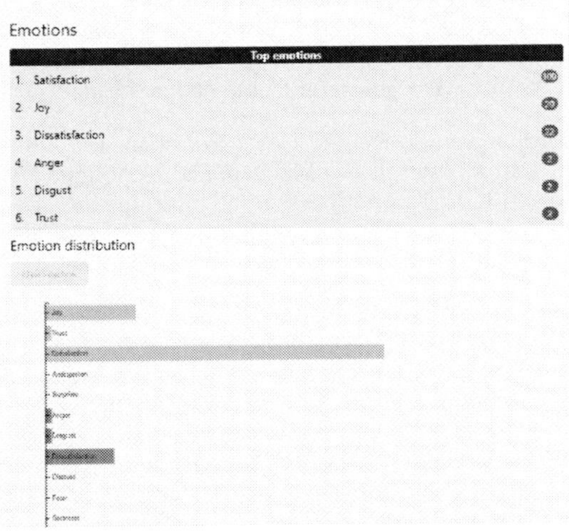

Figure 9: Emotion classification visualisations.

on a Raspberry Pi 4 Model B if needed. A reverse proxy (Apache HTTP Server) is used to connect the application to the internet.

The technology stack of the SentEMO consists of a Node.js application written in TypeScript and built with the React[15] framework Next.js[16] extended with Blitz[17] for session management, security and communication between client-side and server-side. Blitz uses a 'zero API' approach that takes care of API calls without a developer needing to explicitly program an API. This approach speeds up the development greatly but requires developers to be aware of where the code needs to be executed, as both client-side and server-side code can live within the same file and will work regardless. Prisma[18] is used for object-relational mapping. Data visualisation is done with D3[19] to generate interactive SVG based charts. Tailwind CSS[20] is used as a utility-first CSS framework and used in conjunction with the BEM methodology[21]. Atomic Design[22] is used to organise React components. A page is made up using layouts, organisms, molecules and atoms. Atoms are the most basic components and organisms are the most complex components, defining major parts of a page.

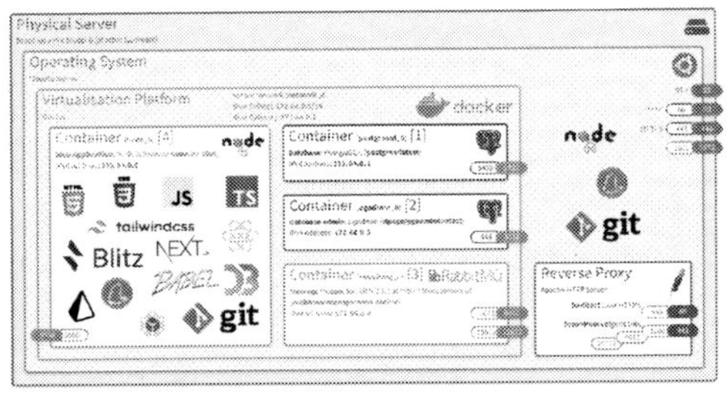

Figure 10: Overview of the front office architecture.

7 Future Work

Next steps of the project include adding extra languages to the platform. In the end, models should be available to analyse English, French and German data. For each language, similar data sets will be annotated. The methodologies used are language-independent, as the features used for aspect term extraction and aspect category classification can be applied to other languages. Finally, BERT-models are available for English, French and German, which allows us to adapt the third and fourth sub-task to these languages as well. On top of that, we want to allow users to indicate what predictions are wrong via an easy-to-use annotation interface, suggest corrections and eventually retrain the models.

Acknowledgements

We thank Gilles Floréal and Juliet van Rosendaal for their help in developing the pre-processing pipeline and models, and job students Wout, Febe, Marie, Linde and Hanne for their annotation efforts. Finally, we thank the partners of the SentEMO project for providing data and valuable feedback. This research has been funded by the Flemish funding agency VLAIO under project code HBC.2020.2095.

[15]https://reactjs.org/
[16]https://nextjs.org/
[17]https://blitzjs.com/
[18]https://www.prisma.io/
[19]https://d3js.org/
[20]https://tailwindcss.com/
[21]http://getbem.com/introduction/
[22]https://bradfrost.com/blog/post/atomic-web-design/

References

Md Shad Akhtar, Tarun Garg, and Asif Ekbal. 2020. Multi-task learning for aspect term extraction and aspect sentiment classification. *Neurocomputing*, 398:247–256.

Chih-Chung Chang and Chih-Jen Lin. 2011. LIBSVM: A library for support vector machines. *ACM Transactions on Intelligent Systems and Technology*, 2(3):1–27.

Luna De Bruyne, Orphée De Clercq, and Véronique Hoste. 2022. Prospects for dutch emotion detection: Insights from the new emotionl dataset. Manuscript under review.

De Clercq, Orphée and Lefever, Els and Jacobs, Gilles and Carpels, Tijl and Hoste, Veronique. 2017. Towards an integrated pipeline for aspect-based sentiment analysis in various domains. In *Proceedings of the 8th Workshop on Computational Approaches to Subjectivity, Sentiment and Social Media Analysis*, pages 136–142. Association for Computational Linguistics.

Svetlana Kiritchenko, Xiaodan Zhu, Colin Cherry, and Saif Mohammad. 2014. Nrc-canada-2014: Detecting aspects and sentiment in customer reviews. In *Proceedings of the 8th international workshop on semantic evaluation (SemEval 2014)*, pages 437–442.

Saif Mohammad, Felipe Bravo-Marquez, Mohammad Salameh, and Svetlana Kiritchenko. 2018. Semeval-2018 task 1: Affect in tweets. In *Proceedings of the 12th international workshop on semantic evaluation*, pages 1–17.

J. Nocedal. 1980. Updating Quasi-Newton Matrices with Limited Storage. *Mathematics of Computation*, 35(151):773–782.

Naoaki Okazaki. 2007. Crfsuite: a fast implementation of conditional random fields (crfs).

Swapnil Bhagaji Padme and Pallavi V Kulkarni. 2018. Aspect based emotion analysis on online user-generated reviews. In *2018 9th International Conference on Computing, Communication and Networking Technologies (ICCCNT)*, pages 1–5. IEEE.

Robert Plutchik. 1980. A general psychoevolutionary theory of emotion. In *Theories of emotion*, pages 3–33. Elsevier.

Maria Pontiki, Dimitris Galanis, Haris Papageorgiou, Ion Androutsopoulos, Suresh Manandhar, Mohammad AL-Smadi, Mahmoud Al-Ayyoub, Yanyan Zhao, Bing Qin, Orphée De Clercq, Véronique Hoste, Marianna Apidianaki, Xavier Tannier, Natalia Loukachevitch, Evgeniy Kotelnikov, Núria Bel, Salud María Jiménez-Zafra, and Gülşen Eryiğit. 2016. Semeval-2016 task 5: Aspect based sentiment analysis. In *Proceedings of the 10th International Workshop on Semantic Evaluation (SemEval-2016)*, pages 19–30.

Soujanya Poria, Erik Cambria, and Alexander Gelbukh. 2016. Aspect extraction for opinion mining with a deep convolutional neural network. *Knowledge-Based Systems*, 108:42–49.

Radim Řehůřek and Petr Sojka. 2010. Software Framework for Topic Modelling with Large Corpora. In *Proceedings of the LREC 2010 Workshop on New Challenges for NLP Frameworks*, pages 45–50, Valletta, Malta. ELRA. `http://is.muni.cz/publication/884893/en`.

Zhiqiang Toh and Jian Su. 2015. NLANGP: Supervised machine learning system for aspect category classification and opinion target extraction. In *Proceedings of the 9th International Workshop on Semantic Evaluation (SemEval 2015)*, pages 496–501, Denver, Colorado. Association for Computational Linguistics.

Marjan Van de Kauter, Geert Coorman, Els Lefever, Bart Desmet, Lieve Macken, and Véronique Hoste. 2013. LeTs Preprocess: The multilingual LT3 linguistic preprocessing toolkit. *Computational Linguistics in the Netherlands Journal*, 3:103–120.

Wei Xue, Wubai Zhou, Tao Li, and Qing Wang. 2017. MTNA: A neural multi-task model for aspect category classification and aspect term extraction on restaurant reviews. In *Proceedings of the Eighth International Joint Conference on Natural Language Processing (Volume 2: Short Papers)*, pages 151–156, Taipei, Taiwan. Asian Federation of Natural Language Processing.

A Aspect Category Overview

Airline	
Entity	**Attribute**
Airport	general information misc service speed
Booking	general misc price service
Company	general misc reliability service
Flight	comfort general misc price punctuality
Food & Drinks	availability general misc options price quality
Marcom	availability general misc speed
Personnel	communication friendliness general hospitality misc service

FMCG - Retail	
Entity	**Attribute**
Company	general misc price reliability service
Delivery	general information misc price service speed
Marcom	general misc promotions
Packaging	general misc style
Personnel	communication expertise friendliness general misc service speed
Product	appearance general misc options price quality usability
Store	general misc

Hospital	
Entity	**Attribute**
Hospital	comfort general information misc
Personnel	communication expertise friendliness general misc service speed
Procedure	comfort general information misc speed
Reception	friendliness general information misc speed
Visit	general misc options

Hotel	
Entity	**Attribute**
Amenities	appearance availability cleanliness comfort general misc
Facilities	appearance availability cleanliness comfort general misc price
Food & Drinks	appearance availability general misc options price quality
Hotel	appearance cleanliness comfort general location misc price quality reliability
Marcom	general misc promotions
Personnel	communication friendliness general hospitality misc service
Room	ambiance cleanliness comfort general misc price

Telecom	
Entity	**Attribute**
Company	general misc price reliability service
Internet	general misc
Marcom	general misc promotions
Mobile	general misc
Packages	general misc
Support	availability communication friendliness general misc service speed
Television	general misc

General	
Entity	**Attribute**
Company	general misc reliability
Personnel	friendliness general misc service
Product	general misc price quality

Can Emotion Carriers Explain Automatic Sentiment Prediction? A Study on Personal Narratives

Seyed Mahed Mousavi, Gabriel Roccabruna, Aniruddha Tammewar, Steve Azzolin, Giuseppe Riccardi
Signals and Interactive Systems Lab, University of Trento, Italy
{mahed.mousavi,gabriel.roccabruna,giuseppe.riccardi}@unitn.it

Abstract

Deep Neural Networks (DNN) models have achieved acceptable performance in sentiment prediction of written text. However, the output of these machine learning (ML) models cannot be natively interpreted. In this paper, we study how the sentiment polarity predictions by DNNs can be explained and compare them to humans' explanations. We crowdsource a corpus of Personal Narratives and ask human judges to annotate them with polarity and select the corresponding token chunks - the Emotion Carriers (EC) - that convey narrators' emotions in the text. The interpretations of ML neural models are carried out through Integrated Gradients method and we compare them with human annotators' interpretations. The results of our comparative analysis indicate that while the ML model mostly focuses on the explicit appearance of emotions-laden words (e.g. happy, frustrated), the human annotator predominantly focuses the attention on the manifestation of emotions through ECs that denote events, persons, and objects which activate narrator's emotional state.

1 Introduction

Neural data-driven models have managed to perform comparably well in various tasks related to natural language processing (Eberts and Ulges, 2020; Adoma et al., 2020). Nevertheless, the definition and the training processes of such models have made their decision non-natively interpretable. Several studies and experiments have been conducted to address this issue and explain the decision outputs of such models in various tasks such as emotion prediction (Yang et al., 2019), question answering (Ramnath et al., 2020), the classification of linguistic styles (Hayati et al., 2021), and lexicon-based sentiment prediction (Hwang and Lee, 2021).

Sentiment analysis is a well-established field of research that aims to extract sentiment and its aspects in a written text. Its performances have reached acceptable levels in different domains such as product reviews (Xie et al., 2020), movie reviews (Thongtan and Phienthrakul, 2019), social media (Tam et al., 2021), financial news (Takala et al., 2014), and Personal Narratives (PN) which are recollections of real-life events that are experienced by the narrator (Tammewar et al., 2019).

FU1: I experienced a bit of **distress** [Emotion-laden word] **in the office** [Emotion Carrier]

FU2: because **talking with colleagues** [Emotion Carrier] *makes me* **anxious** [Emotion-laden word]!

Figure 1: Example of a sentence consisting of two Functional Units (FU1, FU2), the basic units of annotation. Emotion-laden words in each Functional Unit manifest a sentiment explicitly while Emotion Carriers describe the events, persons or objects conveying emotions.

Recently, a deeper understanding of the expressed sentiment and emotion has gained growing research interest (Tammewar et al., 2020, 2021; Bayerl et al., 2021; Ding et al., 2020). These works focus on a more fine-grained analysis on the expressed sentiment/emotion by identifying the Emotion Carriers (entities or actions that explain, cause or carry the emotion). The concept of Emotion Carriers (EC) was first introduced by Tammewar et al. (2020) for German PNs. In this genre of text, the identification of ECs may help in better understanding the emotional state of the narrator and what has caused distress (Tammewar et al., 2021; Bayerl et al., 2021).

In this work, we address the problem of analyzing and comparing the text chunks used by machines and humans when predicting the sentiment polarity of text documents. For this study we have selected the Personal Narrative genre since it is rich with entities and relations which are sparsely distributed. We identify the tokens that contribute to the model's prediction according to their attributions given by Integrated Gradients (Sundarara-

Proceedings of the 12th Workshop on Computational Approaches to Subjectivity, Sentiment & Social Media Analysis, pages 62 - 70
May 26, 2022 ©2022 Association for Computational Linguistics

jan et al., 2017), an Explainable-AI technique, and compare them with the tokens tagged as ECs by the human annotator. Our comparative analysis shows the human annotator identifies the tokens that explain an event or its participants as the carrier of emotions and sentiments, which clearly convey the activation of the emotional state in the narrator, even though they are not explicitly manifesting a sentiment. Meanwhile, the DNN model bases its decision mostly on a limited set of tokens which belong to the category of emotion-laden words (see Figure 1 for an example).

We summarize our contribution as follows:

- The annotation of a dataset of Personal Narratives to obtain the sentiment polarity, and the Emotion Carriers at the Functional Unit (Bunt et al., 2010) level to take into account the communicative functions. This is in contrast with traditional annotation at the document or sentence level.
- The evaluation of the annotation results and training a sentiment prediction model based on the AlBERTo architecture (Polignano et al., 2019) using the annotated data, as well as a baseline architecture for the task of Emotion Carrier Detection.
- The study of the tokens contributing to the model's prediction of sentiment and comparing them with the Emotion Carriers identified by the human annotator, and the contribution of the Emotion Carriers in the prediction of the model by their influence on the output confidence score.

2 Literature Review

AI Explainability There have been several interesting works to address the unexplainability of neural architectures. Danilevsky et al. (2020) conducted a survey study on explainable AI (XAI) in natural language processing, summarizing the various XAI methods used by researchers. Bodria et al. (2020) proposed an attention model to investigate the words that contribute to the sentiment prediction, by adding an additional attention layer on top of the BERT architecture to fuse the token embeddings in one vector used to compute the prediction. Bacco et al. (2021) used the attention weights technique to extract summaries of reviews to explain the sentiment prediction of a Transformer-based model, by using a simplified model with 2 layers and one attention head per layer. Torres et al. (2021) designed a deep neural network with an interpretable decision process to recognize emotions from the Electroencephalography (EEG) signals.

While the approaches based on attention weights require a change in the architecture of the model, LIME (Local Model-Agnostic Explanations) (Ribeiro et al., 2016) and the Integrated Gradients technique (Sundararajan et al., 2017) can be applied to any model without changing the architecture. Using LIME, Hwang and Lee (2021) extracted a sentiment lexicon used as a weak classifier to categorize unseen examples to augment the initial training set. Similarly, Carton et al. (2018) used LIME and hard-attention to extract spans of text that convey personal attacks. Furthermore, Hayati et al. (2021) used the Integrated Gradients to compare most relevant tokens for the human and the machine in predicting the linguistic style of a text.

Emotion & Sentiment Analysis An approach to perform fine-grained analysis on the expressed emotion in the text is the task of emotion cause extraction (Chen et al., 2018; Xia and Ding, 2019; Ding et al., 2020; Gui et al., 2016). The aim of this task is to identify the explicit or implicit expressions of emotions in the text, as well as the corresponding causes or triggers of the emotion as a span in the text (Turcan et al., 2021; Li et al., 2021a,b). However, most of the works on this task have focused on datasets of news (Bostan et al., 2020; Gui et al., 2016) and microblogs (Oberländer and Klinger, 2020), which are very different from Personal Narratives.

Understanding of Personal Narratives (PN) is a comparatively new domain and is gaining growing attention in the research community (Stappen et al., 2019; Tammewar et al., 2019; Schuller et al., 2018; Rathner et al., 2018; Ong et al., 2021). Compared to the mentioned genres of text, PNs have a different and more complex structure as they are personal recollection of real-life events and may involve multiple characters, and several sub-events (Mousavi et al., 2021; Tammewar et al., 2019). A stream of works has been carried out on the fine-grained emotion analysis of PNs that tries to capture the semantics of the emotions through Emotion Carriers (EC), including the annotation of ECs (Tammewar et al., 2020) as well as the automatic recognition of the ECs (Tammewar et al., 2021; Bayerl et al.,

2021). In these works, every PN is associated with a positive or negative emotion and the ECs are defined as the persons, objects or actions that explain the emotion felt by the narrator, after recollecting the event.

3 Data Collection & Annotation

We used an extended version of the dataset of PNs from users receiving Cognitive Behavioural Therapy to handle their distress more effectively, introduced previously by Mousavi et al. (2021). Each PN encompasses a real-life personal event that has activated the narrator's emotional state, the participants of the event as well as the details about the user's thought and emotions. During two periods of 3 months, we collected 481 personal narratives written by 45 Italian speaker users, with the average length of 51 tokens per narrative and overall dictionary size of 5875 tokens.

3.1 Annotation of Sentiment & Emotion Carriers

We annotate the obtained dataset of PNs, with the sentiment and the Emotion Carrier tokens for each narrative[1]. The mentioned studies on identifying ECs (Tammewar et al., 2020; Bayerl et al., 2021) focus on the identification of emotion and the corresponding ECs at the narrative level. However, in this work we conduct a deeper analysis and identify the emotion and the corresponding ECs for each Functional Unit of the PN, making it possible to capture the emotion changes of the narrator throughout the narrative. A Functional Unit (FU) is defined as a minimal contiguous span in the text that represents coherent communicative intention (Bunt et al., 2010). We segment each PN to its FUs, using a RoBERTa-based model[2] (Liu et al., 2019), fine-tuned on ISO standard Dialogue Act tagging in Italian (Roccabruna et al., 2020) to jointly perform FU segmentation and Dialogue Act tagging. As the result, we obtained 4273 FUs to be annotated (approximately equal to 9 FUs for each narrative on average).

We recruited 3 Italian native speaker annotators from a pool of graduate students based on their research interests and previous experience with data annotation. The annotators were asked to annotate the sentiment polarity of the FU using a 5-point bipolar scale from -2 ($unpleasant$) to 2 ($pleasant$) with 0 representing $neutral$. The annotators were asked to adopt the point of view of the narrator. In the cases where the sentiment of the FU was not clear by its content, the annotators were asked to consider the adjacent FUs as context for better understanding.

For the FUs with an assigned sentiment polarity of positive or negative, the annotators were further asked to select the ECs that convey and carry the annotated sentiment of the narrator in the corresponding FU. Considering the characteristics of PNs as the recollection of real-life events, we focused on the manifestations of the sentiment in terms of persons, objects, places, organizations or actions that affected the narrator's emotional state. Therefore, we provided the annotators with a list of noun-chunks and verb-chunks in the FU as EC-candidate spans to select from, and excluded the explicit emotion-laden words such as *happy, sad, enjoyed, and overwhelmed*, since they directly express certain sentiment polarity. Besides, this approach helped to reduce the cognitive load of the subtask.

Prior to the annotation, we carried out a training session for the annotators administered by a psychotherapist, followed by two training batches by which a satisfactory Inter-Annotator Agreement (IAA) was achieved (the results of the training batches were manually controlled and few adjustments were made with the annotators and to the guidelines). We then distributed the samples in 10 batches with 20% overlap in each batch annotated by all 3 annotators (to monitor the IAA and ensure the annotation quality) and the remaining 80% annotated by a single annotator.

3.2 Annotation Results Analysis

Using the 481 Personal Narratives, we annotated 4273 functional units[3]. As the results, the majority of the FUs, 60%, were annotated as neutral, while 13% and 27% of them were labeled as positive and negative respectively. The Inter-Annotator Agreement (IAA), computed with the Fleiss' κ coefficient (Fleiss, 1971), on the sentiment annotation is 0.67 (Substantial) on the 5-point scale results, and 0.73 (Substantial) on the 3-point scale (obtained by regrouping the values into three groups of *positive*

[1]We are currently applying for further funds to anonymize the corpus and publish a version of the corpus that respects users' privacy and deontological requirements.

[2]`https://github.com/musixmatchresearch/umberto`

[3]As example of valence and ECs annotation on a PN at the level of Functional Units: `https://gitlab.com/sislab/PNs_Val-EC_annotation`

Polarity	Freq.	EC	non-EC
Positive	13%	566 (28%)	736 (30%)
Negative	27%	1425 (72%)	1725 (70%)
Neutral	60%	-	-

Table 1: The distribution of polarity and Emotion Carriers (EC) in the annotated dataset of Personal Narrative at functional unit level.

Model	F1	Prec.	Rec.
bi-LSTM + attn.	0.66	0.70	0.66
AlBERTo Emb.	0.69	0.69	0.69
AlBERTo Emb.+$[CLS]$	**0.70**	**0.70**	**0.70**

Table 2: Results of EC Detection experiments on the test set. All scores are measured with the "macro" average strategy. The AlBERTo-based architecture with the concatenation of $[CLS]$ token achieves the best performance.

{1,2}, *negative {-2,-1}* and *neutral {0}*). Furthermore, the IAA on the examples that were labelled with a non-neutral polarity by all annotators is 0.98 (Almost Perfect).

Regarding the EC selection, out of 4452 EC-candidate spans in the FUs that were labeled with a non-neutral sentiment polarity, 1991 spans (45%) were chosen as EC by the annotators, resulting in 2551 EC tokens (tokens in the EC-span) and the EC dictionary size of 962. The IAA on the EC annotation is 0.4 (Fair), computed by considering each EC-candidate as an example to annotate where the labels are *yes* if it is an EC, and *no* otherwise.

The statistics regarding the labelled ECs and the sentiment distribution are presented in Table 1. For our experiments, we split the obtained annotated dataset into training (80%), validation (10%) and test (10%) sets, stratified on the polarity distribution and on the lengths of the PN.

3.3 Emotion Carrier Detection Baseline

We trained a baseline model to assess the EC annotation on the PN dataset for the task of EC detection. The approaches used in previous works (Tammewar et al., 2021; Bayerl et al., 2021) do not fit with our case, since the annotators were asked to select the EC from a predefined set of candidates, rather than selecting any token in the text. Thus, in our case the model is tasked to classify each EC-candidate span as EC or non-EC.

The first part of the architecture computes the tokens embedding of each FU. Afterwards, we extract the encoded representation of the EC-candidate tokens and perform max-pooling, which takes the maximum value for every dimension of the vector encoding, producing the vector representation of the EC-candidate. The vector representation is then given as input to the classification layer (dense layer + softmax) yielding the probability distribution over the EC and non-EC classes. To compute the embeddings, we experimented with bi-LSTM with attention and AlBERTo, a pre-trained BERT-based model for the Italian language (Polignano et al., 2019). In the experiments with the AlBERTo model, we experimented concatenating the representation of the $[CLS]$ token with the EC-candidate representation, to better consider the context during the classification.

The results of these experiments, summarized in Table 2, indicate that the outperforming baseline combination is obtained by using the AlBERTo model for the input representation with the concatenation of the $[CLS]$ token.

3.4 Sentiment Prediction Model

We trained a sentiment prediction model to predict the polarity at the level of functional units. Our model is based on the AlBERTo architecture (Polignano et al., 2019) with a three-heads output layer, instead of the original two-heads fully connected layers, to predict the sentiment polarity of each FU over the 3-label output space of *negative, positive* and *neutral*. We split the training set of the SENTIPOLC16 dataset (Barbieri et al., 2016)[4] into training and validation sets of 90% and 10%, in a stratified manner. We then used the training set to fine-tune the model in the first step, and the validation set in the next step for hyper-parameter optimization and selecting the best model using the Optuna framework (Akiba et al., 2019). Using the obtained hyper-parameters[5], the model was then further fine-tuned on our own collected dataset of annotated functional units extracted from PNs. The results of these experiments are presented in Table 3.

[4]SENTIPOLC16 is a dataset of tweets in the Italian language

[5]`learning_rate=6.599e-05, weight_decay=0.0215, warmup_steps=0.899, num_epochs=11`

Model	F1	Prec.	Rec.
AlBERTo_SP16	0.64	0.63	0.70
AlBERTo_opt_SP16	0.63	0.62	0.71
AlBERTo_opt_SP16+PN	**0.76**	**0.76**	**0.76**

Table 3: Macro F1, Precision, and Recall of the sentiment prediction models optimized in different settings. *AlBERTo_SP16* is the vanilla AlBERTo model fine-tuned on SENTIPOLC16; *AlBERTo_opt_SP16* is the model optimized utilizing validation split; and *AlBERTo_opt_SP16+PN* is the *AlBERTo_opt_SP16* further fine-tuned on the training set of our Personal Narratives dataset. All evaluation results are obtained using the test split of the Personal Narratives dataset.

4 Prediction Decision Explainability

We investigate the explainability of the automatic sentiment prediction by comparing the tokens influencing the prediction with those selected by the human judge as ECs. In order to detect the tokens crucial to the model's prediction, we use the attribution assigned to each token by the Integrated Gradients (Sundararajan et al., 2017) technique. Integrated Gradients (IntGrad) is an attribution method for Explainable AI which builds on top of the classic backward gradient analysis. Given our sentiment prediction model $f(FU)$, where FU is the functional unit $FU = \{w_1, w_2, .., w_n\}$ and $w_i \in R^d$ are the token embeddings , the backward gradient is given by:

$$BackwardGrad_j(w_i) = \frac{\partial f}{\partial w_{ij}} \tag{1}$$

measuring how much perturbing the input token w_i by an infinitesimal amount along dimension j affects the output of function f. The IntGrad method extends this by computing the integral of the derivative along the path connecting a baseline token w', which is a neutral element, to the input point w:

$$\textit{IntGrad}_j(w_i) = (w_{ij} - w') \int_{\alpha=0}^{1} \frac{\partial f(w' + \alpha(w_{ij} - w'))}{\partial w_{ij}} \, d\alpha \tag{2}$$

where $\alpha \in [0, 1]$ draws a linear path, from the baseline token to the input token, along which the gradients are integrated. In our studies, we used a zero vector for the baseline token w', and the open-source library Captum (Kokhlikyan et al., 2020) for efficient IntGrad computation. In cases that a token is split into several subtokens by the tokenizer of our model (Kudo and Richardson, 2018), we average the Integrated Gradients attributions of the subtokens, to get the attribution of the whole token.

4.1 Token Analysis based on IntGrad Attributions

Using the test set samples for which the model predicts the sentiment polarity correctly, we employ two approaches regarding the explainability analysis. In the first approach, we extract the tokens influential or crucial to the prediction process of the model based on their Integrated Gradients (IntGrad) attributions, and study whether or not they belong to the spans annotated as EC by the human annotator.

In order to identify tokens crucial to the model's prediction we experimented with two different thresholds for the IntGrad attribution:

- **Greater than 0 (G0)**: This baseline is based on the fact that each token with a positive IntGrad attribution value has a positive influence on the prediction. Nevertheless, tokens with small IntGrad attributions have a marginal contribution and thus they are noisy for our analysis;

- **Lower Bound (LB)**: This threshold is obtained uniquely for each FU and is measured by consecutively masking each token in the FU, with a zero-vector embedding, in a descending order of IntGrad attributions until a change in the polarity prediction is observed. The IntGrad attribution of the last masked out token is then selected as the LB threshold.

The results of this analysis using the two mentioned threshold policies are presented in Table 4 and Figure 2. The analysis indicates that although 67.9% of the EC tokens (tokens in ECs selected by human annotators) have a positive contribution to the model's prediction, more than 60% of the tokens with an attribution above the thresholds do not overlap with the EC tokens. Nevertheless, the majority of EC tokens with an attribution higher than the thresholds are EC-heads, regardless of the threshold policy. Furthermore, the distributions of the Content Words (CW), i.e. nouns, verbs and adjectives, confirm our previous assumption that **G0** threshold is noisy since 54% of tokens above this threshold are non-CWs, while this number is smaller than 20% for the tokens with an IntGrad attribution higher than the **LB**. The CWs in LB and G0 groups are distributed as 52% nouns, 27%

Threshold (Thr.)	G0	LB
Tokens with IntGrad A.>Thr.	482 (46% CW)	109 (81% CW)
Tokens w. IntGrad A.>Thr. in EC-span	141 29.3%	43 39.5%
Tokens w. IntGrad A.>Thr. that are EC-heads	82 18.1%	32 29.3%

Table 4: The analysis of tokens influencing the model's prediction based on two different policies for the IntGrad attribution (IntGrad A.), namely Greater than 0 (G0) and Lower Bound (LB). Regardless of the threshold policy, the tokens inside the EC-span that contribute to the model's prediction are less than 40%.

Token set	Positive	Negative	Neutral
CW in G0	3.9%	13.6%	82.5%
CW in LB	10.3%	29.9%	59.8%
CW EC tokens	0.7%	4.0%	95.3%

Table 5: The polarity distribution of the Content Words (CW) with IntGrad attribution higher than the different thresholds. The results indicate that the majority of CWs in EC tokens are neutral and they do not represent any emotions explicitly. The polarity was retrieved using the OpeNER sentiment lexicon for the Italian language.

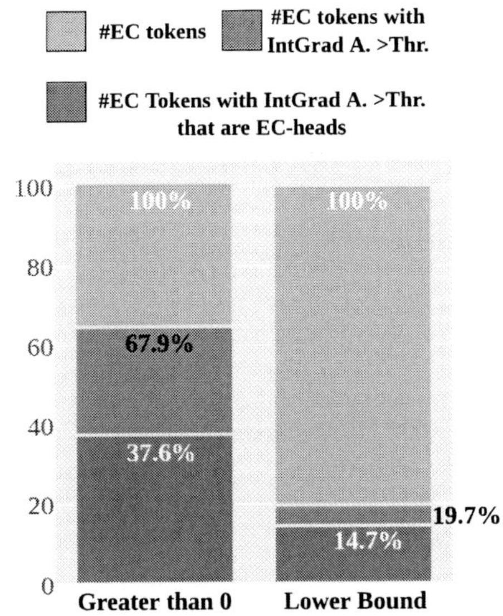

Figure 2: The percentage of the tokens in EC-spans with an Integrated Gradient attribution (IntGrad A.) higher than the threshold (Thr.). The majority of EC tokens with an attribution higher than the Lower Bound are EC-heads.

verbs, 21% adjectives, and 47% nouns, 40% verbs and 13% adjectives, respectively.

In the next step, we further analyzed the polarity distribution of CWs by using the OpeNER[6] lexicon-based sentiment model. The results, presented in Table 5, show that the percentage of non-neutral CWs in the ECs is less than 5%, while more than 40% of the influential tokens, i.e. tokens with attributions over the **LB** threshold, represent a positive or negative polarity. This remarks the importance of emotion-laden words, such as *anxiety*, *fear* and *worry*, for the model in predicting the sentiment, and suggests that the model mostly focuses on the tokens that explicitly convey emotions, and the ECs (as the implicit manifestations of emotions) are less significant in its decision process.

4.2 Contribution of ECs to the Model's Decision

For the second approach, we evaluate the influence of the ECs selected by the human annotators in the decision process of the model. For this purpose, we mask out the EC-span in the Functional Unit with the highest IntGrad attribution, and measure the drop in the confidence score for the initially predicted polarity. The confidence score represents the probability assigned by the model to a given class, which in our case the classes can be either *positive* or *negative*. In the next step, we extend this analysis to the token level and measure the drop in the confidence score caused by masking out the EC-head with the highest IntGrad attribution, as well as all EC-heads present in the corresponding FU.

The results, shown in Table 6, present the strong contribution of emotion-laden words that explicitly manifest the sentiment on the model's decision. Furthermore, the confidence drop caused by masking the EC-span is higher than masking only the head of the corresponding EC, suggesting that all the tokens in the EC-span contribute to the prediction confidence. However, the highest drop is achieved by masking the most influential token (the token with the highest IntGrad attribution) and emotion-laden words, respectively. These results once again support the findings of the previous analysis, suggesting the importance of tokens that explicitly manifest a sentiment in the decision process of the model.

[6]`https://www.opener-project.eu/`, This publicly available lexicon was semi-automatically created starting from 1,000 manually controlled keywords

Masked Content in FU	Conf. Score Drop
EC-Span w. highest IntGrad A.	0.15
EC-Head w. highest IntGrad A.	0.09
EC-Heads in FU	0.14
Token w. highest IntGrad A.	0.55
Emotion-laden Words	0.36

Table 6: The drop in the confidence score of the predicted polarity caused by masking out selected contents in Functional Units. The results show that the Emotion-laden words have a stronger influence than the tokens selected as ECs by the human annotator.

5 Conclusion

In this work we studied whether the sentiment prediction decision of DNN models can be explained by Emotion Carriers, spans of text that convey and carry emotions. We have focused our study on Personal Narratives which encompass real-life events and experiences that activate the emotional state of the narrator. We have collected a dataset of Personal Narratives and conducted an annotation task for sentiment polarity and Emotion Carrier selection at the Functional Unit for each narrative. We have then developed a sentiment prediction model based on AlBERTo architecture (Polignano et al., 2019). We have investigated whether the decision of the model is based on the Emotion Carriers that the human annotator selected to explain the sentiment of the text. Furthermore, we have studied the impact of the Emotion Carriers on the confidence score of the polarity prediction model. Our analysis has shown that the human annotators tend to focus on manifestation of emotions through words describing actions and events that have activated the emotional state of the narrator. However, the model bases its decision on explicit representations of sentiment such as emotion-laden words.

Acknowledgements

The research leading to these results has received funding from the European Union – H2020 Programme under grant agreement 826266: COADAPT.

References

Acheampong Francisca Adoma, Nunoo-Mensah Henry, and Wenyu Chen. 2020. Comparative analyses of bert, roberta, distilbert, and xlnet for text-based emotion recognition. In *2020 17th International Computer Conference on Wavelet Active Media Technology and Information Processing (ICCWAMTIP)*, pages 117–121. IEEE.

Takuya Akiba, Shotaro Sano, Toshihiko Yanase, Takeru Ohta, and Masanori Koyama. 2019. Optuna: A next-generation hyperparameter optimization framework. In *Proceedings of the 25rd ACM SIGKDD International Conference on Knowledge Discovery and Data Mining*.

Luca Bacco, Andrea Cimino, Felice Dell'Orletta, and Mario Merone. 2021. Extractive summarization for explainable sentiment analysis using transformers. In *DeepOntoNLP/X-SENTIMENT@ESWC*.

Francesco Barbieri, Valerio Basile, Danilo Croce, Malvina Nissim, Nicole Novielli, and Viviana Patti. 2016. Overview of the evalita 2016 sentiment polarity classification task. In *Proceedings of third Italian conference on computational linguistics (CLiC-it 2016) & fifth evaluation campaign of natural language processing and speech tools for Italian. Final Workshop (EVALITA 2016)*.

Sebastian P. Bayerl, Aniruddha Tammewar, Korbinian Riedhammer, and Giuseppe Riccardi. 2021. Detecting emotion carriers by combining acoustic and lexical representations. In *IEEE Automatic Speech Recognition and Understanding Workshop, ASRU 2021, Cartagena, Colombia, December 13-17, 2021*, pages 31–38. IEEE.

Francesco Bodria, André Panisson, Alan Perotti, and Simone Piaggesi. 2020. Explainability methods for natural language processing: Applications to sentiment analysis. In *SEBD*.

Laura Ana Maria Bostan, Evgeny Kim, and Roman Klinger. 2020. GoodNewsEveryone: A corpus of news headlines annotated with emotions, semantic roles, and reader perception. In *Proceedings of the 12th Language Resources and Evaluation Conference*, pages 1554–1566, Marseille, France. European Language Resources Association.

Harry Bunt, Jan Alexandersson, Jean Carletta, Jae-Woong Choe, Alex Chengyu Fang, Koiti Hasida, Kiyong Lee, Volha Petukhova, Andrei Popescu-Belis, Laurent Romary, et al. 2010. Towards an iso standard for dialogue act annotation. In *Seventh conference on International Language Resources and Evaluation (LREC'10)*.

Samuel Carton, Qiaozhu Mei, and Paul Resnick. 2018. Extractive adversarial networks: High-recall explanations for identifying personal attacks in social media posts. In *EMNLP*.

Ying Chen, Wenjun Hou, Xiyao Cheng, and Shoushan Li. 2018. Joint learning for emotion classification and emotion cause detection. In *Proceedings of the 2018 Conference on Empirical Methods in Natural Language Processing*, pages 646–651.

Marina Danilevsky, Kun Qian, Ranit Aharonov, Yannis Katsis, Ban Kawas, and Prithviraj Sen. 2020. A survey of the state of explainable ai for natural language processing. In *Proceedings of the 1st Conference of the Asia-Pacific Chapter of the Association for Computational Linguistics and the 10th International Joint Conference on Natural Language Processing*, pages 447–459.

Zixiang Ding, Rui Xia, and Jianfei Yu. 2020. Ecpe-2d: emotion-cause pair extraction based on joint two-dimensional representation, interaction and prediction. In *Proceedings of the 58th Annual Meeting of the Association for Computational Linguistics*, pages 3161–3170.

Markus Eberts and Adrian Ulges. 2020. Span-based joint entity and relation extraction with transformer pre-training. In *ECAI 2020*, pages 2006–2013. IOS Press.

Joseph L Fleiss. 1971. Measuring nominal scale agreement among many raters. *Psychological bulletin*, 76(5):378.

Lin Gui, Dongyin Wu, Ruifeng Xu, Qin Lu, and Yu Zhou. 2016. Event-driven emotion cause extraction with corpus construction. In *EMNLP*.

Shirley Hayati, Dongyeop Kang, and Lyle Ungar. 2021. Does bert learn as humans perceive? understanding linguistic styles through lexica. pages 6323–6331.

Hohyun Hwang and Younghoon Lee. 2021. Semi-supervised learning based on auto-generated lexicon using xai in sentiment analysis. In *RANLP*.

Narine Kokhlikyan, Vivek Miglani, Miguel Martin, Edward Wang, Bilal Alsallakh, Jonathan Reynolds, Alexander Melnikov, Natalia Kliushkina, Carlos Araya, Siqi Yan, and Orion Reblitz-Richardson. 2020. Captum: A unified and generic model interpretability library for pytorch.

Taku Kudo and John Richardson. 2018. Sentencepiece: A simple and language independent subword tokenizer and detokenizer for neural text processing. In *Proceedings of the 2018 Conference on Empirical Methods in Natural Language Processing: System Demonstrations*, pages 66–71.

Xiangju Li, Wei Gao, Shi Feng, Daling Wang, and Shafiq Joty. 2021a. Span-level emotion cause analysis by bert-based graph attention network. In *Proceedings of the 30th ACM International Conference on Information & Knowledge Management*, pages 3221–3226.

Xiangju Li, Wei Gao, Shi Feng, Yifei Zhang, and Daling Wang. 2021b. Boundary detection with bert for span-level emotion cause analysis. In *Findings of the Association for Computational Linguistics: ACL-IJCNLP 2021*, pages 676–682.

Yinhan Liu, Myle Ott, Naman Goyal, Jingfei Du, Mandar Joshi, Danqi Chen, Omer Levy, Mike Lewis, Luke Zettlemoyer, and Veselin Stoyanov. 2019. Roberta: A robustly optimized bert pretraining approach.

Seyed Mahed Mousavi, Alessandra Cervone, Morena Danieli, and Giuseppe Riccardi. 2021. Would you like to tell me more? generating a corpus of psychotherapy dialogues. In *Proceedings of the Second Workshop on Natural Language Processing for Medical Conversations*, pages 1–9, Online. Association for Computational Linguistics.

Laura Ana Maria Oberländer and Roman Klinger. 2020. Token sequence labeling vs. clause classification for english emotion stimulus detection. In *Proceedings of the Ninth Joint Conference on Lexical and Computational Semantics*, pages 58–70.

Desmond C. Ong, Zhengxuan Wu, Zhi-Xuan Tan, Marianne Reddan, Isabella Kahhale, Alison Mattek, and Jamil Zaki. 2021. Modeling emotion in complex stories: The stanford emotional narratives dataset. *IEEE Transactions on Affective Computing*, 12(3):579–594.

Marco Polignano, Pierpaolo Basile, Marco de Gemmis, Giovanni Semeraro, and Valerio Basile. 2019. AlBERTo: Italian BERT Language Understanding Model for NLP Challenging Tasks Based on Tweets. In *Proceedings of the Sixth Italian Conference on Computational Linguistics (CLiC-it 2019)*, volume 2481. CEUR.

Sahana Ramnath, Preksha Nema, Deep Sahni, and Mitesh M. Khapra. 2020. Towards interpreting BERT for reading comprehension based QA. In *Proceedings of the 2020 Conference on Empirical Methods in Natural Language Processing (EMNLP)*, pages 3236–3242, Online. Association for Computational Linguistics.

Eva-Maria Rathner, Yannik Terhorst, Nicholas Cummins, Björn Schuller, and Harald Baumeister. 2018. State of mind: Classification through self-reported affect and word use in speech. *Proc. Interspeech 2018*, pages 267–271.

Marco Tulio Ribeiro, Sameer Singh, and Carlos Guestrin. 2016. Model-agnostic interpretability of machine learning. *arXiv preprint arXiv:1606.05386*.

Gabriel Roccabruna, Alessandra Cervone, and Giuseppe Riccardi. 2020. Multifunctional iso standard dialogue act tagging in italian. *Seventh Italian Conference on Computational Linguistics (CLiC-it)*.

Björn Schuller, Stefan Steidl, Anton Batliner, Peter B. Marschik, Harald Baumeister, Fengquan Dong, Simone Hantke, Florian B. Pokorny, Eva-Maria Rathner, Katrin D. Bartl-Pokorny, Christa Einspieler, Dajie Zhang, Alice Baird, Shahin Amiriparian, Kun Qian, Zhao Ren, Maximilian Schmitt, Panagiotis Tzirakis, and Stefanos Zafeiriou. 2018. The interspeech

2018 computational paralinguistics challenge: Atypical self-assessed affect, crying heart beats. In *Proc. Interspeech 2018*, pages 122–126.

Lukas Stappen, Nicholas Cummins, Eva-Maria Meßner, Harald Baumeister, Judith Dineley, and Björn Schuller. 2019. Context modelling using hierarchical attention networks for sentiment and self-assessed emotion detection in spoken narratives. In *ICASSP 2019 - 2019 IEEE International Conference on Acoustics, Speech and Signal Processing (ICASSP)*, pages 6680–6684.

Mukund Sundararajan, Ankur Taly, and Qiqi Yan. 2017. Axiomatic attribution for deep networks.

Pyry Takala, Pekka Malo, Ankur Sinha, and Oskar Ahlgren. 2014. Gold-standard for topic-specific sentiment analysis of economic texts. In *LREC*.

Sakirin Tam, Rachid Ben Said, and Ö Özgür Tanriöver. 2021. A convbilstm deep learning model-based approach for twitter sentiment classification. *IEEE Access*, 9:41283–41293.

Aniruddha Tammewar, Alessandra Cervone, Eva-Maria Messner, and Giuseppe Riccardi. 2019. Modeling User Context for Valence Prediction from Narratives. In *Proc. Interspeech 2019*, pages 3252–3256.

Aniruddha Tammewar, Alessandra Cervone, Eva-Maria Messner, and Giuseppe Riccardi. 2020. Annotation of emotion carriers in personal narratives. In *Proceedings of the 12th Language Resources and Evaluation Conference*, pages 1517–1525.

Aniruddha Tammewar, Alessandra Cervone, and Giuseppe Riccardi. 2021. Emotion Carrier Recognition from Personal Narratives. In *Proc. Interspeech 2021*, pages 2501–2505.

Tan Thongtan and Tanasanee Phienthrakul. 2019. Sentiment classification using document embeddings trained with cosine similarity. In *ACL*.

Juan Manuel Mayor Torres, Mirco Ravanelli, Sara E. Medina-DeVilliers, Matthew Daniel Lerner, and Giuseppe Riccardi. 2021. Interpretable sincnet-based deep learning for emotion recognition from eeg brain activity. *2021 43rd Annual International Conference of the IEEE Engineering in Medicine & Biology Society (EMBC)*, pages 412–415.

Elsbeth Turcan, Shuai Wang, Rishita Anubhai, Kasturi Bhattacharjee, Yaser Al-Onaizan, and Smaranda Muresan. 2021. Multi-task learning and adapted knowledge models for emotion-cause extraction. *arXiv e-prints*, pages arXiv–2106.

Rui Xia and Zixiang Ding. 2019. Emotion-cause pair extraction: A new task to emotion analysis in texts. In *Proceedings of the 57th Annual Meeting of the Association for Computational Linguistics*, pages 1003–1012.

Qizhe Xie, Zihang Dai, Eduard Hovy, Thang Luong, and Quoc Le. 2020. Unsupervised data augmentation for consistency training. *Advances in Neural Information Processing Systems*, 33:6256–6268.

Yang Yang, Deyu Zhou, Yulan He, and Meng Zhang. 2019. Interpretable relevant emotion ranking with event-driven attention. In *EMNLP*.

Infusing Knowledge from Wikipedia to Enhance Stance Detection

Zihao He[1,2] **Negar Mokhberian**[1,2] **Kristina Lerman**[1]
[1]Information Sciences Institute, University of Southern California
[2]Department of Computer Science, University of Southern California
{zihaoh,nmokhber}@usc.edu lerman@isi.edu

Abstract

Stance detection infers a text author's attitude towards a target. This is challenging when the model lacks background knowledge about the target. Here, we show how background knowledge from Wikipedia can help enhance the performance on stance detection. We introduce **W**ikipedia **S**tance Detection BERT (WS-BERT) that infuses the knowledge into stance encoding. Extensive results on three benchmark datasets covering social media discussions and online debates indicate that our model significantly outperforms the state-of-the-art methods on target-specific stance detection, cross-target stance detection, and zero/few-shot stance detection.[1]

Target: Donald Trump **Stance:** Favor
Document: All Republican presidents are better!
Background knowledge required: Donald Trump was a Republican president.

Target: LeBron **Stance:** Favor
Document: James is a successful basketball player.
Background knowledge required: "LeBron" and "James" refer to the same person.

Figure 1: Two examples of stance detection where background knowledge is required.

1 Introduction

Stance detection aims to automatically identify author's attitude or standpoint (favor, neutral, against) towards a specific target or topic using text as evidence (Mohammad et al., 2016; Augenstein et al., 2016; Jang and Allan, 2018; Somasundaran and Wiebe, 2010; Stefanov et al., 2020). To precisely capture the stance towards a target, background knowledge about the target is often necessary, especially in cases where the text does not explicitly mention the target, as shown in Figure 1. People have wide-ranging background knowledge regarding various targets and use it to infer the implicit stance in a statement. However, machines by default do not have such knowledge and previous works on stance detection (Allaway and McKeown, 2020; Allaway et al., 2021; Liang et al., 2021; Augenstein et al., 2016; Siddiqua et al., 2019; Sun et al., 2018; Li et al., 2021b; Hardalov et al., 2021) fail to incorporate such knowledge in modeling stances.

In this paper, we propose to utilize background knowledge from Wikipedia about the target as a bridge to enable the model's deeper understanding of the target, thus improving its performance on stance detection. We crawl the Wikipedia pages for the targets and use them as external textual information. To infuse this information into stance detection, we propose **W**ikipedia **S**tance Detection BERT (WS-BERT), which integrates the representation of Wikipedia knowledge into that of documents and targets. Depending on the textual style of the documents, we introduce two variants of WS-BERT. We conduct a comprehensive set of experiments on three recently published benchmark datasets for stance detection that include social media discussions and online debates, covering three sub-tasks of stance detection: target-specific stance detection, cross-target stance detection, and zero/few-shot stance detection. Significant improvements over the state-of-the-art methods on all datasets and sub-tasks demonstrate the superiority of our model in terms of effectiveness and broad applicability.

Related Work. Baly et al. (2018, 2020) use Wikipedia pages of a news medium as an additional source of information to predict the factuality and bias of the medium. However, they use static pretrained BERT (Devlin et al., 2019) embeddings of the Wikipedia pages without finetuning, failing to align the pretrained embeddings to the domain of the target task. Hanawa et al. (2019) first propose to make use of the external knowledge from Wikipedia for stance detection; however,

[1]Code and data are publicly available at https://github.com/zihaohe123/wiki-enhanced-stance-detection.

Proceedings of the 12th Workshop on Computational Approaches to Subjectivity, Sentiment & Social Media Analysis, pages 71 - 77
May 26, 2022 ©2022 Association for Computational Linguistics

the authors only consider the promote/suppress relations between the texts and Wikipedia, which require a large amount of manual annotations to extract; in addition, a substantial amount of knowledge that is not captured by such relations is ignored; in contrast, WS-BERT utilizes the original Wikipedia textual knowledge and does not proactively exclude any information. Zhang et al. (2020) propose SEKT to extract external word-level semantic and emotion knowledge, which fails to capture the global relationship between the document and the target; moreover, such a model is designed for cross-target stance detection and is hardly applicable to target-specific and zero/few-shot stance detection. Liu et al. (2021) utilize commonsense knowledge from a knowledge graph by extracting the two-hop paths between entities in the targets and in the documents; however, the existence of such paths do not always hold true and we found that a well-finetuned BERT without external knowledge can achieve performance comparable with it, as shown in Section 3.6.

2 Methodology

2.1 Problem Definition

Let $D = \{(x_i = (d_i, t_i, w_i), y_i)\}_{i=1}^{N}$ denote N examples, with input x_i consisting of a document d_i, target t_i, and Wikipedia text w_i about the target, and a stance label $y_i \in \{\text{favor}, \text{against}, \text{neutral}\}$ as output. The goal is to infer y_i given x_i.

2.2 Encoding Wikipedia Knowledge

For the background knowledge, we use the raw text of Wikipedia pages instead of a Wikipedia knowledge graph because 1) a knowledge graph is more structured but inevitably suffers information loss when being constructed; Liu et al. (2021) uses a commonsense knowledge graph to enhance stance detection, which is outperformed by our method that simply uses raw texts, as shown in Section 3.6; 2) in addition, raw text is much more readily accessible and needs less preprocessing, especially for newly emerging targets.

To incorporate background knowledge about targets from Wikipedia, we propose **W**ikipedia **S**tance Detection BERT (WS-BERT). Depending on the textual style (formal vs. informal) of the documents, we introduce two variants of WS-BERT, namely WS-BERT-Single, for dealing with formal documents, and WS-BERT-Dual, for dealing with informal documents. Below we elaborate on the architectures of these models.

Infusing Wikipedia knowledge with formal documents. When documents are written in a formal style as Wikipedia articles, we use BERT that is also pretrained on Wikipedia articles to collectively encode the document d, the target t, and the Wikipedia knowledge w. Previous works (Allaway et al., 2021; Liang et al., 2021; Li et al., 2021a; Glandt et al., 2021; Allaway and McKeown, 2020; Liu et al., 2021) treat the document d and the target t as a sequence pair and use BERT to encode it, with the input format as "[CLS] d [SEP] t [SEP]". Since BERT was originally designed to deal with at most two sequences[2], to encode the Wikipedia knowledge in addition to the document-target pair, we merge the document and the target into a single sequence and redesign the input format as "[CLS] Text: d Target: t [SEP] w [SEP]" as shown in Figure 2(a). Such an input format enables d, t, and w to attend to each other during the encoding process. The pooled output of the final layer [CLS] embedding is used as the final representation of the input x. Since one BERT is used, we call the model WS-BERT-Single.

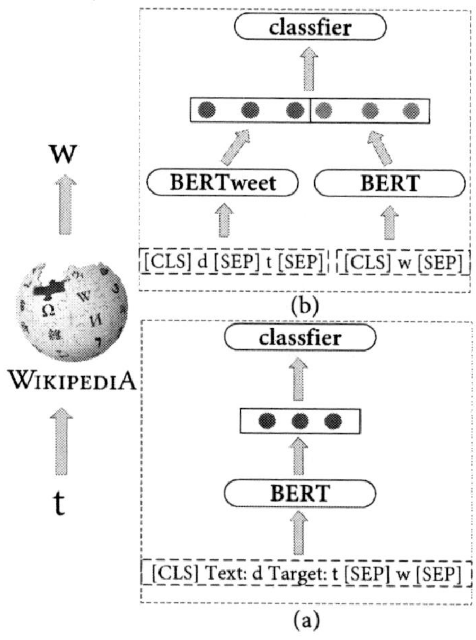

Figure 2: Architecture of (a) WS-BERT-Single and (b) WS-BERT-Dual.

Infusing Wikipedia knowledge with informal documents. Social media has become a popular platform for people to express their views on

[2]There do exist some works that have tried to make it encode three sequences simultaneously by using three [SEP] tokens (Xu et al., 2021).

public figures or political events. The opinions of online users are documented by noisy and casual user-generated texts. Such texts have a different distribution than the Wikipedia corpus that BERT is pretrained on. In this case, we use BERTweet (Nguyen et al., 2020) or COVID-Twitter-BERT (Müller et al., 2020) that is pretrained on social media texts to encode the document-target pair, and use the vanilla BERT to encode Wikipedia knowledge, as shown in Figure 2(b). We encode the document-target pair and the Wikipedia knowledge separately with two language models so as to minimize domain shift between the training examples used in this paper and the original pretraining corpora of the language models. We concatenate the two pooled outputs of the final layer [CLS] embeddings from two language models as the final representation of the input x.[3] We call this model WS-BERT-Dual since we use two BERT-based language models.

2.3 Stance Prediction

The final representation from WS-BERT is fed into a single fully-connected layer and softmax layer to predict the stance label $\hat{y} \in \{\text{favor, against, neutral}\}$, which is optimized by a cross-entropy loss.

3 Experiments

3.1 Datasets

We evaluate the proposed WS-BERT model on three newly published datasets since 2020. For the targets in the three datasets, we use summaries of the fetched Wikipedia pages as the textual background knowledge.

P-Stance (Li et al., 2021a) is for target-specific and cross-target stance detection and it consists of tweets related to three politicians "Biden", "Sanders" and "Trump". We manually fetched the individual Wikipedia pages of the three politicians.

COVID-19-Stance (Glandt et al., 2021) is a dataset of pandemic-related tweets for target-specific stance detection and contains four targets: "Anthony Fauci", "stay-at-home orders", "wear a face mask", and "keeping school closed". The titles of the Wikipedia pages used are "Anthony Fauci", "COVID-19 lockdowns", "Face masks during the COVID-19 pandemic in the United States", and "Impact of the COVID-19 pandemic on education". Locating these Wikipedia pages is also a manual process.

Varied Stance Topics (VAST) (Allaway and McKeown, 2020) is for zero/few-shot stance detection and comprises comments from *The New York Times* "Room for Debate" section on a large range of topics covering broad themes. It has ~6000 targets. We use an API[4] to crawl the Wikipedia pages of them. For the targets that have multiple related Wikipedia pages, we choose the first one recommended by the API. For the targets that do not have any Wikipedia pages (~200, e.g., "salt preference" and "tennis fans"), we use the targets themselves as background knowledge, with no additional information introduced.

3.2 Evaluation Metric

Following previous works (Mohammad et al., 2016, 2017), we adopt macro-average of F1-score as the evaluation metric. For P-Stance where the examples only have two stance labels, $F_{\text{avg}} = (F_{\text{favor}} + F_{\text{against}})/2$. For COVID-19-Stance and VAST that have three stance labels, $F_{\text{avg}} = (F_{\text{favor}} + F_{\text{against}} + F_{\text{neutral}})/3$.

3.3 Experimental Setup

We use WS-BERT-Dual in experiments on P-Stance and COVID-19-Stance, both of which consist of tweets. Following the setup in their original papers (Li et al., 2021a; Glandt et al., 2021), for P-Stance, we use BERTweet as the document-target encoder, and for COVID-19 Stance, we use COVID-Twitter-BERT as the the document-target encoder; for both datasets, BERT-base is used to encode Wikipedia knowledge. On VAST that comprises online debates, we use BERT-base to jointly encode the document-target-knowledge tuple.

All models are implemented using PyTorch. The Wikipedia summaries are truncated to a maximum of 512 tokens. We train the models using Adam optimizer with a batch size of 32 for a maximum of 100 epochs with patience of 10 epochs. The weight decay is set to $5e-5$. To speed up the training process we only finetune the top layers of the Wikipedia encoder in WS-BERT-Dual. We search the learning rate in $\{1e-5, 2e-5\}$ and the number of Wikipedia encoder layers to finetune in $\{1, 2\}$.

[3] Admittedly, concatenation of the two vectors seems naive, but it achieves satisfactory performance as shown in Section 3.4 and 3.5; more sophisticated ways to fuse them like cross-attention count towards our future work.

[4] https://pypi.org/project/wikipedia/

On target-specific and zero/few-shot stance detection, we follow the standard train/validation/test splits of the three datasets. On cross-target stance detection, the model is trained on the train set of the source target, evaluated on the validation set of the source target, and tested on the combination of train, validation, and test set of the destination target, following the setup in P-Stance. The results are reported from the model with the best performance on the validation set.

3.4 Target-specific Stance Detection

For target-specific stance detection on P-Stance and COVID-19-Stance, we train a model separately for each target and test it on the same target.

Baselines. On P-Stance we compare to the baselines TAN (Du et al., 2017), BiCE (Augenstein et al., 2016), PGNN (Huang and Carley, 2018), BERT, and BERTweet. On COVID-19-Stance we compare to TAN, ATGRU (Zhou et al., 2017), GCAE (Xue and Li, 2018), COVID-Twitter-BERT, COVID-Twitter-BERT-NS (Xie et al., 2020), and COVID-Twitter-BERT-DAN (Xu et al., 2020).

Method	Trump	Biden	Sanders	Avg.
TAN	77.1	77.6	71.6	75.1
BiCE	77.2	77.7	71.2	75.4
PGCNN	76.9	76.6	72.1	75.2
GCAE	79.0	78.0	71.8	76.3
BERT	78.3	78.7	72.5	76.5
BERTweet	82.5	81.0	78.1	80.5
BERTweet†	85.2	82.5	78.5	82.1
WS-BERT-Dual	**85.8**	**83.5**	**79.0**	**82.8**

Table 1: Macro-average F1 scores of target-specific stance detection on P-Stance. BERTweet is implemented in (Li et al., 2021a) and BERTweet† is implemented in this paper.

Method	Fauci	Home	Mask	School	Avg.
TAN	54.7	53.6	54.6	53.4	54.1
ATRGU	61.2	52.1	59.9	52.7	56.5
GCAE	64.0	64.5	63.3	49.0	60.2
CT-BERT	81.8	80.0	80.3	75.5	79.4
CT-BERT-NS	82.1	78.4	83.3	75.3	79.8
CT-BERT-DAN	83.2	78.7	82.5	71.7	79.0
CT-BERT†	83.0	83.6	83.8	81.7	83.0
WS-BERT-Dual	**83.6**	**85.0**	**86.6**	**82.2**	**84.4**

Table 2: Macro-average F1 scores of target-specific stance detection on COVID-19-Stance. CT-BERT (short for COVID-Twitter-**BERT**) represents COVID-Twitter-BERT implemented in (Glandt et al., 2021) and CT-BERT† represents the model implemented in this paper.

Results and Analysis. Results for P-Stance and COVID-19-Stance are shown in Table 1 and Table 2. On P-Stance, BERTweet† outperforms the baselines on all targets, and WS-BERT-Dual further improves the performance and achieves the new state-of-the-art. On COVID-19-Stance, COVID-Twitter-BERT† outperforms all the baselines on targets except "Fauci", including the self-training baseline COVID-Twitter-BERT-NS and the domain adaptation baseline COVID-Twitter-BERT-DAN, both of which are trained using some additional external data. However, WS-BERT-Dual augmented with background knowledge outperforms state-of-the-art on all targets. Therefore, even on target-specific stance detection, where the models are fed sufficient data to learn the target, background knowledge about the target still helps improve performance.

3.5 Cross-target Stance Detection

We use P-Stance for cross-target stance detection, where the model is trained on one target, e.g., "Trump'," and tested on another, e.g., "Biden."

Baselines. We use BERTweet as a strong baseline, which is the most performant method reported in (Li et al., 2021a).

Target	BERTw	BERTw†	WS-BERT-D
Trump→Biden	58.9	52.2	**68.3**
Trump→Sanders	56.5	53.0	**64.4**
Biden→Trump	63.6	66.8	**67.7**
Biden→Sanders	67.0	68.5	**69.0**
Sanders→Trump	58.7	60.0	**63.6**
Sanders→Biden	73.0	74.6	**76.8**
Avg.	63.0	62.5	**68.3**

Table 3: Macro-average F1 scores of cross-target stance detection on P-Stance. Trump→Biden indicates that the model is trained on "Donald Trump" and tested on "Joe Biden". BERTweet is implemented in (Li et al., 2021a) and BERTweet† is implemented in this paper.

Results and Analysis. Results are shown in Table 3. We see that our implementation of BERTweet† outperforms BERTweet when the model is trained on "Biden" and "Sanders". After infusing Wikipedia knowledge, WS-BERT-Dual enhances the performance on all six target pairs compared to BERTweet† and achieves the new state-of-the-art. Notably, the performance gains on "Trump"→"Biden" and "Trump"→"Sanders" are the biggest, which we argue is because the tweets about "Trump" mention the other two targets less, so that the model trained on "Trump" learns little knowledge transferable to the other two targets. In this case, background knowledge about "Biden" or "Sanders" brings huge information gains, leading to substantial performance improvement. In addition, compared to performance gain on target-specific stance detection, the gains in performance are more noticeable on this cross-target task, which signifies that background knowledge from Wikipedia is more important when the test target is outside of the training set.

3.6 Zero-shot and Few-shot Stance Detection

Finally, we evaluate our model on zero-shot and few-shot stance detection using VAST, where the model is trained on thousands of targets and evaluated on targets that are not seen in the training data (zero-shot learning) and are seen just a few times in the training data (few-shot learning).

Baselines. We compare our model to BERT, TGA-Net (Allaway and McKeown, 2020), BERT-GCN (Lin et al., 2021), and CKE-Net (Liu et al., 2021).

Method	Zero-shot	Few-shot	Overall
TGA-Net	66.6	66.3	66.5
BERT	68.5	68.4	68.4
BERT-GCN	68.6	69.7	69.2
CKE-Net	70.2	70.1	70.1
BERT†	70.1	70.0	70.0
WS-BERT-Single	**75.3**	**73.6**	**74.5**

Table 4: Macro-average F1 scores of zero-shot and few-shot stance detection on VAST. BERT is implemented in (Liu et al., 2021) and BERT† is implemented in this paper.

Results and Analysis. Results are shown in Table 4. CKE-Net extracts the links between entities in targets and documents from a knowledge graph so as to make use of the commonsense knowledge. However, a well-finetuned BERT† implemented in this paper achieves performance on par with it, putting the effectiveness of CKE-Net into question. WS-BERT-Single significantly improves the performance on both zero-shot and few-shot learning by a huge margin, thus creating new state-of-the-art. We argue that such nontrivial performance gain is due to the presence of many targets in VAST that are difficult for the model to understand without background knowledge, such as "b-12" (a vitamin) and "2big2fail".

As mentioned in Section 3.1, the Wikipedia pages of the thousands of targets in VAST are retrieved by an API. Admittedly, such an automated process might incur noisy information because the retrieved pages are not guaranteed to be the most relevant ones, and the summaries might miss useful content. However, even with the noise, our method manages to outperform the state-of-the-art baselines significantly, with an improvement in F1 of 4.5%. Such a huge improvement demonstrates the robustness of our method in handling the noisy external knowledge: when the model is trained with noisy Wikipedia summaries, it learns to deal with such perturbations; as a result, during inference, with noisy external knowledge, it is still able to infer the correct stance.

Moreover, the improvement on zero-shot learning is more observable compared to that on few-shot learning, because in few-shot learning the model is able to attend to some examples in the training data to understand the targets, while in zero-shot learning the model is not exposed to the targets at all, in which case background knowledge is of more importance.

4 Conclusion

In this paper we propose to utilize background knowledge about targets from Wikipedia to enhance stance detection. We propose WS-BERT with two variants to encode such knowledge. Such a simple yet effective method achieves state-of-the-art performance on three benchmark datasets and on three sub-tasks: in-target stance detection, cross-target stance detection, and zero/few-shot stance detection. The comprehensive and growing list of topics covered by Wikipedia ensures that our method will adapt to newly emerging targets.

In the future, we plan to investigate incorporating knowledge about entities in the input documents, in addition to knowledge about the targets. Since Wikipedia pages may contain subjective opinions towards the targets, how to prevent the model from being negatively impacted by such bias when modeling the knowledge remains a promising research direction. Moreover, background knowledge from relevant news articles might also be helpful for inferring stances.

Acknowledgements

We sincerely thank the reviewers for their insightful and constructive comments and suggestions that helped improve the paper. This research was supported in part by DARPA under contract HR001121C0168.

References

Emily Allaway and Kathleen McKeown. 2020. Zero-Shot Stance Detection: A Dataset and Model using Generalized Topic Representations. In *Proceedings of the 2020 Conference on Empirical Methods in Natural Language Processing (EMNLP)*, pages 8913–8931, Online. Association for Computational Linguistics.

Emily Allaway, Malavika Srikanth, and Kathleen McKeown. 2021. Adversarial learning for zero-shot stance detection on social media. In *Proceedings of the 2021 Conference of the North American Chapter of the Association for Computational Linguistics: Human Language Technologies*, pages 4756–4767, Online. Association for Computational Linguistics.

Isabelle Augenstein, Tim Rocktäschel, Andreas Vlachos, and Kalina Bontcheva. 2016. Stance detection with bidirectional conditional encoding. In *Proceedings of the 2016 Conference on Empirical Methods in Natural Language Processing*, pages 876–885, Austin, Texas. Association for Computational Linguistics.

Ramy Baly, Georgi Karadzhov, Dimitar Alexandrov, James Glass, and Preslav Nakov. 2018. Predicting factuality of reporting and bias of news media sources. In *Proceedings of the 2018 Conference on Empirical Methods in Natural Language Processing*, pages 3528–3539, Brussels, Belgium. Association for Computational Linguistics.

Ramy Baly, Georgi Karadzhov, Jisun An, Haewoon Kwak, Yoan Dinkov, Ahmed Ali, James Glass, and Preslav Nakov. 2020. What was written vs. who read it: News media profiling using text analysis and social media context. In *Proceedings of the 58th Annual Meeting of the Association for Computational Linguistics*, pages 3364–3374, Online. Association for Computational Linguistics.

Jacob Devlin, Ming-Wei Chang, Kenton Lee, and Kristina Toutanova. 2019. BERT: Pre-training of deep bidirectional transformers for language understanding. In *Proceedings of the 2019 Conference of the North American Chapter of the Association for Computational Linguistics: Human Language Technologies, Volume 1 (Long and Short Papers)*, pages 4171–4186, Minneapolis, Minnesota. Association for Computational Linguistics.

Jiachen Du, Ruifeng Xu, Yulan He, and Lin Gui. 2017. Stance classification with target-specific neural attention networks. In *Proceedings of the 26th International Joint Conference on Artificial Intelligence*, pages 3988–3994.

Kyle Glandt, Sarthak Khanal, Yingjie Li, Doina Caragea, and Cornelia Caragea. 2021. Stance detection in COVID-19 tweets. In *Proceedings of the 59th Annual Meeting of the Association for Computational Linguistics and the 11th International Joint Conference on Natural Language Processing (Volume 1: Long Papers)*, pages 1596–1611, Online. Association for Computational Linguistics.

Kazuaki Hanawa, Akira Sasaki, Naoaki Okazaki, and Kentaro Inui. 2019. Stance detection attending external knowledge from wikipedia. *Journal of Information Processing*, 27:499–506.

Momchil Hardalov, Arnav Arora, Preslav Nakov, and Isabelle Augenstein. 2021. Cross-domain label-adaptive stance detection. In *Proceedings of the 2021 Conference on Empirical Methods in Natural Language Processing*, pages 9011–9028, Online and Punta Cana, Dominican Republic. Association for Computational Linguistics.

Binxuan Huang and Kathleen Carley. 2018. Parameterized convolutional neural networks for aspect level sentiment classification. In *Proceedings of the 2018 Conference on Empirical Methods in Natural Language Processing*, pages 1091–1096, Brussels, Belgium. Association for Computational Linguistics.

Myungha Jang and James Allan. 2018. Explaining controversy on social media via stance summarization. In *The 41st International ACM SIGIR Conference on Research & Development in Information Retrieval*, pages 1221–1224.

Yingjie Li, Tiberiu Sosea, Aditya Sawant, Ajith Jayaraman Nair, Diana Inkpen, and Cornelia Caragea. 2021a. P-stance: A large dataset for stance detection in political domain. In *Findings of the Association for Computational Linguistics: ACL-IJCNLP 2021*, pages 2355–2365, Online. Association for Computational Linguistics.

Yingjie Li, Chenye Zhao, and Cornelia Caragea. 2021b. Improving stance detection with multi-dataset learning and knowledge distillation. In *Proceedings of the 2021 Conference on Empirical Methods in Natural Language Processing*, pages 6332–6345, Online and Punta Cana, Dominican Republic. Association for Computational Linguistics.

Bin Liang, Yonghao Fu, Lin Gui, Min Yang, Jiachen Du, Yulan He, and Ruifeng Xu. 2021. Target-adaptive graph for cross-target stance detection. In *Proceedings of the Web Conference 2021*, pages 3453–3464.

Yuxiao Lin, Yuxian Meng, Xiaofei Sun, Qinghong Han, Kun Kuang, Jiwei Li, and Fei Wu. 2021. BertGCN: Transductive text classification by combining GNN and BERT. In *Findings of the Association for Computational Linguistics: ACL-IJCNLP 2021*, pages 1456–1462, Online. Association for Computational Linguistics.

Rui Liu, Zheng Lin, Yutong Tan, and Weiping Wang. 2021. Enhancing zero-shot and few-shot stance detection with commonsense knowledge graph. In *Findings of the Association for Computational Linguistics: ACL-IJCNLP 2021*, pages 3152–3157.

Saif Mohammad, Svetlana Kiritchenko, Parinaz Sobhani, Xiaodan Zhu, and Colin Cherry. 2016. SemEval-2016 task 6: Detecting stance in tweets. In *Proceedings of the 10th International Workshop on Semantic Evaluation (SemEval-2016)*, pages 31–41, San Diego, California. Association for Computational Linguistics.

Saif M Mohammad, Parinaz Sobhani, and Svetlana Kiritchenko. 2017. Stance and sentiment in tweets. *ACM Transactions on Internet Technology (TOIT)*, 17(3):1–23.

Martin Müller, Marcel Salathé, and Per E Kummervold. 2020. Covid-twitter-bert: A natural language processing model to analyse covid-19 content on twitter. *arXiv preprint arXiv:2005.07503*.

Dat Quoc Nguyen, Thanh Vu, and Anh Tuan Nguyen. 2020. BERTweet: A pre-trained language model for English tweets. In *Proceedings of the 2020 Conference on Empirical Methods in Natural Language Processing: System Demonstrations*, pages 9–14, Online. Association for Computational Linguistics.

Umme Aymun Siddiqua, Abu Nowshed Chy, and Masaki Aono. 2019. Tweet stance detection using an attention based neural ensemble model. In *Proceedings of the 2019 Conference of the North American Chapter of the Association for Computational Linguistics: Human Language Technologies, Volume 1 (Long and Short Papers)*, pages 1868–1873, Minneapolis, Minnesota. Association for Computational Linguistics.

Swapna Somasundaran and Janyce Wiebe. 2010. Recognizing stances in ideological on-line debates. In *Proceedings of the NAACL HLT 2010 Workshop on Computational Approaches to Analysis and Generation of Emotion in Text*, pages 116–124, Los Angeles, CA. Association for Computational Linguistics.

Peter Stefanov, Kareem Darwish, Atanas Atanasov, and Preslav Nakov. 2020. Predicting the topical stance and political leaning of media using tweets. In *Proceedings of the 58th Annual Meeting of the Association for Computational Linguistics*, pages 527–537, Online. Association for Computational Linguistics.

Qingying Sun, Zhongqing Wang, Qiaoming Zhu, and Guodong Zhou. 2018. Stance detection with hierarchical attention network. In *Proceedings of the 27th International Conference on Computational Linguistics*, pages 2399–2409, Santa Fe, New Mexico, USA. Association for Computational Linguistics.

Qizhe Xie, Minh-Thang Luong, Eduard Hovy, and Quoc V Le. 2020. Self-training with noisy student improves imagenet classification. In *Proceedings of the IEEE/CVF Conference on Computer Vision and Pattern Recognition*, pages 10687–10698.

Chang Xu, Cécile Paris, Surya Nepal, Ross Sparks, Chong Long, and Yafang Wang. 2020. Dan: Dual-view representation learning for adapting stance classifiers to new domains. In *ECAI 2020*, pages 2260–2267. IOS Press.

Yichong Xu, Chenguang Zhu, Ruochen Xu, Yang Liu, Michael Zeng, and Xuedong Huang. 2021. Fusing context into knowledge graph for commonsense question answering. In *Workshop on Commonsense Reasoning and Knowledge Bases*.

Wei Xue and Tao Li. 2018. Aspect based sentiment analysis with gated convolutional networks. In *Proceedings of the 56th Annual Meeting of the Association for Computational Linguistics (Volume 1: Long Papers)*, pages 2514–2523, Melbourne, Australia. Association for Computational Linguistics.

Bowen Zhang, Min Yang, Xutao Li, Yunming Ye, Xiaofei Xu, and Kuai Dai. 2020. Enhancing cross-target stance detection with transferable semantic-emotion knowledge. In *Proceedings of the 58th Annual Meeting of the Association for Computational Linguistics*, pages 3188–3197, Online. Association for Computational Linguistics.

Yiwei Zhou, Alexandra I Cristea, and Lei Shi. 2017. Connecting targets to tweets: Semantic attention-based model for target-specific stance detection. In *International Conference on Web Information Systems Engineering*, pages 18–32. Springer.

Uncertainty Regularized Multi-Task Learning

Kourosh Meshgi and **Maryam Sadat Mirzaei** and **Satoshi Sekine**
RIKEN Center for Advanced Intelligence Project (AIP)
Tokyo, Japan
{kourosh.meshgi, maryam.mirzaei, satoshi.sekine}@riken.jp

Abstract

By sharing parameters and providing task-independent shared features, multi-task deep neural networks are considered one of the most interesting ways for parallel learning from different tasks and domains. However, fine-tuning on one task may compromise the performance of other tasks or restrict the generalization of the shared learned features. To address this issue, we propose to use task uncertainty to gauge the effect of the shared feature changes on other tasks and prevent the model from overfitting or over-generalizing. We conducted an experiment on 16 text classification tasks, and findings showed that the proposed method consistently improves the performance of the baseline, facilitates the knowledge transfer of learned features to unseen data, and provides explicit control over the generalization of the shared model.

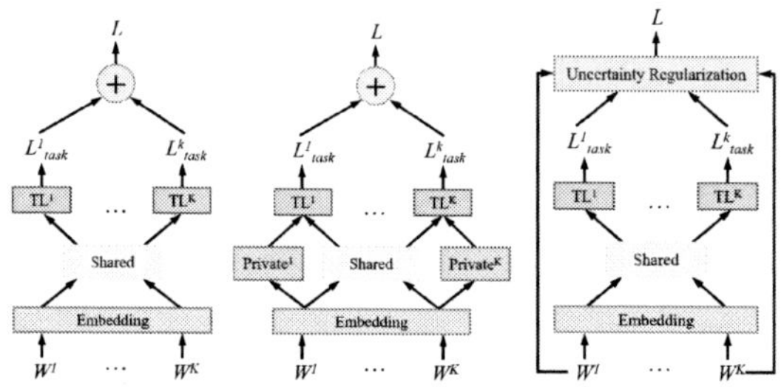

(a) FS-MTL (b) SP-MTL (c) UFS-MTL

Figure 1: Different architectures for multi-task learning (MTL) for text classification with the LSTM baseline. (a) Fully-Shared MTL in which the shared layer provides a shared feature space and task-layers (TLs) convert them into final task outputs, (b) Shared-Private MTL, where tasks jointly learn a shared feature set while having their own (private) features, (c) Uncertainty-regularized FS-MTL (proposed) in which the uncertainty of all tasks are measured while fine-tuning for each task to grant more generalization to the learned shared features.

1 Introduction

Multi-task learning (MTL) is a branch of supervised learning that strives to improve the generalization of the regression or classification task by leveraging the domain-specific information contained in the training signals of related tasks (Caruana, 1993). MTL has been investigated in various applications of machine learning, from natural language processing (Collobert and Weston, 2008; Clark et al., 2019) and speech recognition (Deng et al., 2013; Suthokumar et al., 2020) to computer vision (Girshick, 2015; Zamir et al., 2018). The tasks can be defined as applying the same model on different data (also known as multi-domain learning) (Nam and Han, 2016; Liu et al., 2017a), or on various problems (e.g., named entity recognition, entity mention detection and relation extraction in HMTL (Sanh et al., 2019)).

When training a multi-task learner, training each task normally increases its accuracy (fine-tuning) and, at the same time, provides more information for the shared representation that affects the accuracy of the rest of the tasks (generalization). Balancing the finetuning-generalization trade-off has been the subject of several studies. Kendall et al. (2018) adjusts tasks' relative weights in the loss function in proportion to the task uncertainty. Liu et al. (2016) divides the feature space into task-specific and shared spaces and later employs adversarial learning to encourage shared feature space to contain more common information and no task-specific information (Liu et al., 2017a). Bousmalis et al. (2016) proposed orthogonality constraints to punish redundancy between shared and task-specific layers. In line with this direction, learning through hints (Abu-Mostafa, 1990) directly trains a network to predict the most important features. Yet, none of those methods explicitly balances the fine-tuning of the under-training task with its effect on the other tasks.

Here, we propose a method that considers the

Proceedings of the 12th Workshop on Computational Approaches to Subjectivity, Sentiment & Social Media Analysis, pages 78 - 88

generalization of all tasks along with the task-specific loss function. As a good indicator of how other tasks are affected by the change of the shared feature space, we proposed measuring the learner's uncertainty on each task. Task uncertainty captures the relative confidence between tasks and reflects the inherent uncertainty in each task (Kendall et al., 2018). Therefore, the objective of the proposed MTL would be to maximally fine-tune each task on its corresponding training data while keeping the uncertainty of other tasks to the minimum. In other words, the MTL is expected to maintain a low level of the overall uncertainty and disentangle the training on the shared layers and task-specific layers. Our main contributions are

- Exploring task uncertainty to elicit more generalizable features in the shared layers,
- Conducting extensive ablation experiments to investigate the effects of different uncertainty metrics, pre-training, fine-tuning, using auxiliary tasks, and semi-supervised learning on the performance of this method,
- Experimenting on multi-domain and multi-task learning problems with homogeneous and heterogeneous tasks.

2 Related Works

Multi-Task Learning: MTL exchanges information learned by different tasks to improve overall performance. Such information may be obtained by jointly working with adversarial tasks (Ganin and Lempitsky, 2015), tasks working on different subsets of a common data pool (Meyerson and Miikkulainen, 2018), or tasks in a hierarchy (Sanh et al., 2019). Additionally, some tasks are serving as facilitators for harder or more complicated ones in various ways, such as providing hints/attention map (Yu and Jiang, 2016; Caruana, 1997), learning base representations (Rei, 2017; Subramanian et al., 2018) and preventing quick-plateaus during training (Bingel and Søgaard, 2017). Discovering the relationship between tasks or dynamically grouping them are other ways that MTL promotes the information transfer between tasks (Ruder et al., 2017; Zamir et al., 2018; Standley et al., 2019).

When used with deep learning, MTL models tend to share learned parameters across different tasks through *(i)* hard parameter sharing (Caruana, 1993; Kokkinos, 2017) in which the hidden layers are shared between all tasks, while several task-specific output layers are fine-tuned for each task, *(ii)* soft parameter sharing, in which each task has its model, and the distance between the parameters of the models for different tasks are regularized to encourage the parameters to be similar using, e.g., ℓ_1 norm (Duong et al., 2015) or trace norm (Yang and Hospedales, 2017), or *(iii)* partial parameter sharing, to avoid task interference and leverage task commonalities among a subset of the tasks (Zaremoodi et al., 2018; Rosenbaum et al., 2018).

In the hard parameter sharing architectures, shared parameters provide a global feature representation, while task-specific layers further process these features or provide a complementary set of features suitable for a specific task. Some MTL approaches are based on the intuition that learning easy tasks is the prerequisite for learning more complex ones (Ruder, 2017), hence put tasks in hierarchies (Søgaard and Goldberg, 2016; Hashimoto et al., 2017; Sanh et al., 2019) or try to automatically group similar tasks to dynamically form shared layers (Liu et al., 2017b).

Task Uncertainty: In an MTL setting, multiple tasks are intermittently trained and modify the shared parameters to minimize their loss (the losses can be back-propagated at once as well). This change affects how other tasks behave in various ways, one of which is the amount of uncertainty that each task bears. Uncertainty signals the information that the model lacks, or the sort of information that cannot be inferred from data (Kendall and Gal, 2017). There are various ways to measure uncertainty. Kendall et al. (2015) measures uncertainty via drop-out sampling. Later, Kendall et al. (2018) proposed Homoscedastic uncertainty to measure the uncertainty of entire tasks independent of the data. In another attempt, Kampffmeyer et al. (2016) computes the standard deviation of softmax outputs and average them to quantify the uncertainty of all tasks in MTL. Other approaches that leverage uncertainty to reduce the overfitting in MTL framework are presented in (Uma et al., 2020; Fornaciari et al., 2021).

3 Multi-task Classification

Neural text classification has been studied as one of the fundamental NLP problems. Some researchers replace hand-crafted features with with word-level and character-level representations obtained by CNNs (Kim, 2014; Zhang et al., 2015), others use RNNs, Convolutional RNNs and Self-attentive LSTMs for sequence modeling (Liu et al., 2016;

Lai et al., 2015; Liu and Guo, 2019). To highlight the effect of the proposed uncertainty regularization, here we use a simple LSTM-based text classifier as in (Jozefowicz et al., 2015).

3.1 Baseline Classifier

The text sequence $\mathbf{w} = \{w_1, w_2, \ldots, w_T\}$ is converted to a sequence of word embeddings $\mathbf{x}_i$ and is given to an LSTM layer. Each unit of LSTM layer at time t, includes an input gate $\mathbf{i}_t$, a forget gate $\mathbf{f}_t$, an output gate $\mathbf{o}_t$, a memory cell $\mathbf{c}_t$ and a hidden state $\mathbf{h}_t$. The LSTM implements

$$\begin{bmatrix} \tilde{\mathbf{c}}_t \\ \mathbf{o}_t \\ \mathbf{i}_t \\ \mathbf{f}_t \end{bmatrix} = \begin{bmatrix} \tanh \\ \sigma \\ \sigma \\ \sigma \end{bmatrix} \left(\mathbf{W}_p \begin{bmatrix} \mathbf{x}_t \\ \mathbf{h}_{t-1} \end{bmatrix} + \mathbf{b}_p \right) \tag{1}$$
$$\mathbf{c}_t = \tilde{\mathbf{c}}_t \odot \mathbf{i}_t + \mathbf{c}_{t-1} \odot \mathbf{f}_t$$
$$\mathbf{h}_t = \mathbf{o}_t \odot \tanh(\mathbf{c}_t)$$

in which $\sigma(.)$ and $\tanh(.)$ are logistic sigmoid and hyperbolic tangent functions, $\mathbf{W}_p$ and $\mathbf{b}_p$ are the weights and biases of LSTM (summarized in θ_p), and $\odot$ represents element-wise multiplication. The LSTM is then updated as

$$\mathbf{h}_t = \mathrm{LSTM}(\mathbf{h}_{t-1}, \mathbf{x}_t, \theta_p) \tag{2}$$

where the output of the last unit $\mathbf{h}_T$ represents the whole sequence. This is then fed to the task-specific output layers. The network is then trained on a training corpus with N samples $(\mathbf{w}_i, y_i)$ using cross-entropy loss function

$$L(\hat{y}, y) = -\sum_{i=1}^{N}\sum_{j=1}^{C} y_i^j \log\left(\hat{y}_i^j\right) \tag{3}$$

where y_i^j is the groundtruth inside $\{1..C\}$ and $\hat{y}_i^j$ is the predicted probability of label j for document i.

3.2 Multi-Task Learning Formalization

MTL aims to promote learning efficiency and overall task performances by exploiting commonalities and shared structures among tasks. In a neural net MTL, each task shares a portion of its parameters with a few or all other tasks to benefit from extra training they might get from those parallel tasks.

In an MTL text classification, the tasks may share all parameters of certain layers. In this fully-shared setting (Figure 1(a)), the shared LSTM layers are shared between all tasks to extract similar features. MTL training in this setting optimizes these features such that they are useful for all tasks. We used this approach in this study. Another way of parameter sharing is to share a common feature extractor (shared LSTM), but on top of that, each task has its own private feature extractor to complement the shared features (Figure 1(b)) as proposed in (Liu et al., 2017a).

4 Proposed Method

Let's assume an MTL with K tasks, in which each task k has a dataset D_k with N_k samples, where $D_k = \{(w_i^k, y_i^k)\}_{i=1}^{N_k}$. To obtain a probability distribution $\hat{y}^{(k)}$ for labels of task k, the shared feature $\mathbf{h}_T^{(k)}$ are fed to the final task-specific softmax layer. We train the network by minimizing the cross entropy loss between predicted and true label distributions ($\hat{y}^{(k)}$ and $y^{(k)}$) as follows:

$$L_{task} = \sum_{k=1}^{K} \alpha_k L\left(\hat{y}^{\langle k\rangle}, y^{\langle k\rangle}\right) \tag{4}$$

where α_k is the task importance coefficient and $L(\hat{y}, y)$ is defined in eq(3).

4.1 Proposed Uncertainty Regularization

Learning model uncertainty can be attributed to the uncertainty of the model due to the lack of training data and the information that the data cannot explain. The latter can be either *(i)* data-dependent that is reflected by observing the model output and *(ii)* data-independent that varies between different tasks (Kendall et al., 2018). MTL improves the learning over single-task learning by drawing on commonalities between inputs for different tasks to learn a shared representation, averaging on different task noises (Ruder, 2017), and exploiting the relations between tasks.

In a fully-shared MTL setting, each task contributes to the loss function based on errors it made, and since one task is being trained at a time, minimizing this error may negatively change the shared parameters for other tasks. This is usually alleviated by separating task-specific features from shared features using adversarial training and orthogonality constraints, yet the effect of the change in the shared layers on the performance of other tasks, while they are not being trained, is ignored.

A good MTL training procedure should be able to punish the changes in the shared feature space that increases the uncertainty of the task classifiers while only a single task is being fine-tuned to have better accuracy. Using uncertainty instead of task accuracy provides an additional signal to train the model. This helps by reflecting the internal state of the classifiers rather than their performance on a specific type of data, as the uncertainty signal includes both data- and task-dependent components. Using uncertainty regularization promotes the emergence of features that are more decisive to label the samples, and increases the overall performance of the classification. Coupled with overall task accuracy, the summation of uncertainty and task accuracy brings up features that are more independent and decisive, leading to the improvement of the MTL performance.

To calculate the uncertainty of a multi-class classifier, uncertainty sampling methods could be used. Thus, we proposed the uncertainty loss term as

$$L_{unc} = \frac{1}{K}\sum_{k=1}^{K}\frac{1}{N_k}\sum_{i=1}^{N_k}\zeta(x_i), \tag{5}$$

where the uncertainty of all label predictions are averaged for each task, and $\zeta(.)$ can be calculated using least confidence (Settles and Craven, 2008)

$$\zeta_{LC} = 1 - P_k\left(\hat{y}^{(1)}|x\right), \tag{6}$$

or margin (Scheffer et al., 2001)

$$\zeta_M = 1 - P_k\left(\hat{y}^{(1)}|x\right) + P_k\left(\hat{y}^{(2)}|x\right), \tag{7}$$

or Shanon's entropy

$$\zeta_H = -2\sum_j P_k\left(\hat{y}^{(j)}|x\right) logP_k\left(\hat{y}^{(j)}|x\right); \tag{8}$$

where $\hat{y}^{(j)}$ is the label with jth largest predicted probability. The final loss function of the model can be written as

$$L = L_{task} + \lambda L_{unc} \tag{9}$$

in which λ is the regularization parameter.

4.2 Semi-Supervised Learning

As seen in eq(5), calculating the proposed uncertainty term L_{unc} is label-agnostic. This allows for using unlabeled data along with labeled ones during training. Therefore, the training data for each task can be augmented with synthetic data as well as data from other datasets (with matching statistics, context, and distribution).

4.3 Implementation Details

In our implementation we used 300D GloVe word embedding (Pennington et al., 2014) and a 128D LSTM with temporal dropout (0.5). The network weights are initialized with Xavier initialization, and the learning rate and regularization coefficients are selected by a grid search in the range $[0.001, 0.1]$ on the dev set (initial LR=0.01, λ =0.025). The tasks are trained in a round-robin order with mini-batches of size 16. For the rest of the procedure, we followed Søgaard and Goldberg (2016). We report the average of three independent runs of our method in experiment sections, and we used margin uncertainty (ζ_M) unless stated otherwise in all of our experiments.

5 Experiment

To evaluate our system, we considered two different settings to investigate the performance of our proposed system in multi-domain and multi-task settings. In the former case, a similar task is done on different datasets, while on the latter, several heterogeneous but related tasks are performed. The first experiment comes with extensive analysis on performance, generalization, uncertainty regularization, measuring uncertainty, convergence speed, internal dynamics, and system errors, as well as leveraging auxiliary tasks, unlabeled data, pre-training, and task fine-tuning.

5.1 Multiple Domains

In this experiment, we consider a homogeneous multi-task learning scenario in which 16 text classification tasks on various datasets are considered. Each dataset contains several reviews on the different products and movies with binary labels. After joint training on all domains (obtaining vanilla version which is the LSTM regularized by uncertainty loss), to conduct a fair comparison, we incorporated the additional modules that are also used in competitive models.Thus, we included fine-tuning, pre-training, and training on unlabeled data to obtain the final UFS-MTL. It has the state-of-the-art performance among MTL methods with the same LSTM baseline (Table 2), while the vanilla version itself leads to significant improvement in the performance as compared to LSTM which indicates the effectiveness of uncertainty regularization. Here, we used LSTM as a simple model to demonstrate the effectiveness of uncertainty, while other architectures such as RNN, CNN, and transformers can also use the benefits of this regularization. However, for the sake of simplicity we used LSTM to convey that using uncertainty improves the overall performance of the architecture.

Dataset: We took 14 product review datasets for different products, each serving as an individual domain from (Blitzer et al., 2007), and converted the labels to positive ($> 3\star$) or negative ($< 3\star$). We also take two movie review datasets, IMDB and

Datasets	Train	Dev	Test	Un.	Avg.Len	Vocab
Books	1400	200	400	2000	159	62K
Electronics	1398	200	400	2000	101	30K
DVD	1400	200	400	2000	173	69K
Kitchen	1400	200	400	2000	89	28K
Apparel	1400	200	400	2000	57	21K
Camera	1397	200	400	2000	130	26K
Health	1400	200	400	2000	81	26K
Music	1400	200	400	2000	136	60K
Toys	1400	200	400	2000	90	28K
Video	1400	200	400	2000	156	57K
Baby	1300	200	400	2000	104	26K
Magazines	1370	200	400	2000	117	30K
Software	1315	200	400	475	129	26K
Sports	1400	200	400	2000	94	30K
IMDB	1400	200	400	2000	269	44K
MR	1400	200	400	2000	21	12K

Table 1: Statistics of 16 datasets for multi-domain text classification experiment.

MR, with binary labels from (Maas et al., 2011), and (Pang and Lee, 2005) respectively. Each domain has approximately 2000 labeled comments with 70-10-20 split for train-dev-test dataset and 2000 unlabeled data (Table 1).

Competitor Models: We compared our algorithm with the vanilla LSTM baseline, MT-DNN (Liu et al., 2015) with bag-of-word representation and multi-layer perceptrons in which a hidden fully-connected layer is shared. We also compared it with MT-CNN (Collobert and Weston, 2008) with partially shared convolutional layers for different tasks, FS-MTL with word embedding and shared LSTM layers, as well as SP-MTL (Liu et al., 2016) in which a shared LSTM provides a part of feature representation for all tasks while each task has its private LSTM. Other comparisons include SSP-MTL (Chen et al., 2018) that stacks layers of SP-MTL, ASP-MTL (Liu et al., 2017a) that uses adversarial learning and orthogonality constraints to prevent the cross-interference of shared and private latent feature spaces in SP-MTL, and Meta-MTL (Chen et al., 2018) that uses a shared meta-network to capture the meta knowledge of semantic composition and generates the parameters of task-specific semantic composition models in SP-MTL.

Task-Specific Output Layer: The obtained shared representation is fed to the task-specific output classifiers composed of a fully connected layer followed by a softmax layer to predict the label

$$\hat{\mathbf{y}}^{\langle k \rangle} = \mathrm{softmax}\left(\mathbf{W}^{\langle \mathbf{k} \rangle}\mathbf{h}_T + \mathbf{b}^{\langle k \rangle}\right) \quad (10)$$

where $\mathbf{W}^{\langle k \rangle}$ and $\mathbf{b}^{\langle k \rangle}$ are the weights and biases of the task layer k and $\hat{\mathbf{y}}^{\langle k \rangle}$ is prediction probabilities.

Task Fine-Tuning: The training procedure selects mini-batches of all tasks intermittently. We can further optimize each task by freezing the shared layer and fine-tune each task individually. The results of this fine-tuning procedure are denoted by "+Fine" in Table 2.

Pre-Training: Initializing the shared layers with an unsupervised pre-training phase is a common practice. Thus, we initialize it by a language model (Bengio et al., 2007) which we trained on all of our dataset. Table 2 shows improvement in "+Pre".

Adding Auxiliary Task: One of the main challenges of sequence modeling is to capture semantic composition functions. Composition models can be sequential (Sutskever et al., 2014; Chung et al., 2014), convolutional (Collobert et al., 2011; Kalchbrenner et al., 2014), syntactic (Socher et al., 2013; Tai et al., 2015), and functional (Chen et al., 2018; Singh et al., 2021). Different compositional functions are learned from scratch in different tasks, while some tasks are more suitable in capturing them. Additionally, it should be noted that composition functions are mainly similar in different tasks. Therefore, at the end of each training epoch, we fine-tune our shared layer on the Part-of-speech Tagging task (a task that explicitly considers compositional functions) to enrich our feature space with potentially missed compositional properties of the language model. The model is trained on WSJ dataset with a learning rate of 0.001 and a CRF as output layer (*r.f.* experiment 2). The benefits of this compared to the vanilla version is clear under "+Aux" in Table 2.

Using Unlabeled Data: For each mini-batch, the uncertainty regularizer calculates the uncertainty to guide the backpropagation toward features that reduce task uncertainty. Since the regularization term does not rely on data labels, we include the unlabeled data in task uncertainty calculation for each mini-batch. The positive effects are clear in "+Semi" in Table 2 compared to vanilla version.

Performance Evaluation: We perform the multi-task learning on all 16 tasks to compare the task-specific and overall performance of the proposed method. All of the extensions are added to the vanilla version of UFS-MTL, and the final version

Task	LSTM	MT-DNN	MT-CNN	FS-MTL	SP-MTL	SSP-MTL	ASP-MTL	Meta-MTL	UFS-MTL Vanilla	+Fine	+Pre	+Aux	+Semi	All
Books	79.5	82.2	84.5	82.5	81.2	85.3	84.0	87.5	86.9	85.7	85.9	85.5	85.9	87.9
Electronics	80.5	81.7	83.2	85.7	84.7	87.5	86.8	89.5	87.8	89.0	88.0	88.0	87.9	89.8
DVD	81.7	84.2	84.0	83.5	84.0	86.5	85.5	88.0	86.3	87.2	87.1	86.4	86.5	88.4
Kitchen	78.0	80.7	83.2	86.0	85.2	86.5	86.2	91.3	87.8	90.2	89.6	87.9	88.3	91.7
Apparel	83.2	85.0	83.7	84.5	86.5	86.0	87.0	87.0	87.0	89.0	87.2	87.5	86.8	89.0
Camera	85.2	86.2	86.0	86.5	88.0	87.5	89.2	89.7	88.9	89.7	89.0	89.8	89.0	90.0
Health	84.5	85.7	87.2	88.0	87.2	87.5	88.2	90.3	89.3	89.8	89.4	90.0	91.3	90.5
Music	76.7	84.7	83.7	81.2	83.0	85.8	82.5	86.3	83.2	83.9	83.5	84.7	84.1	86.7
Toys	83.2	87.7	89.2	84.5	85.2	87.0	88.0	88.5	87.7	87.9	88.5	87.9	88.1	88.8
Video	81.5	85.0	81.5	83.7	83.2	85.5	84.5	88.3	85.5	87.8	87.7	85.8	86.2	88.7
Baby	84.7	88.0	87.7	88.0	86.7	87.0	88.2	88.0	90.0	90.7	90.3	90.5	91.2	91.2
Magazines	89.2	89.5	87.7	92.5	92.0	88.0	92.2	91.0	92.6	92.7	92.7	92.7	92.8	92.9
Software	84.7	85.7	86.5	86.2	87.0	86.0	87.2	88.5	86.3	86.5	87.4	88.1	88.1	88.7
Sports	81.7	83.2	84.0	85.5	87.2	85.0	85.7	86.7	86.0	86.2	86.3	86.5	86.0	86.8
IMDB	81.7	83.2	86.2	82.5	84.7	84.5	85.5	88.0	84.1	86.8	85.3	84.4	85.4	88.4
MR	72.7	75.5	74.5	74.7	76.0	75.8	76.7	77.0	75.0	75.3	76.9	76.9	77.8	77.9
AVG	81.8	84.3	84.5	84.7	85.1	85.7	86.1	87.9	86.5	87.4	87.2	87.0	87.2	88.6

Table 2: The accuracy of the model on 16 tasks in the dataset (%), compared to its LSTM baseline, and other MTL text classifiers. First, second, and third rankings are denoted in color. Our method (UFS-MTL) performs best in most of the tasks.

("+All") involves all of these improvements on top of the vanilla version.

As can be seen from Table 1, except for two marginal cases, the proposed regularization improves the performance of the FS-MTL up to 5.7% (for Kitchen domain), and 3.5% on average. Besides, this method outperforms other classifiers in most of the tasks and, on average, performs the best. Interestingly, for some of these tasks (such as `Music`, `Toys`, and `Baby`), the LSTM baseline does not perform well, and bag-of-word representation and MLP structure seem more promising. Another interesting pattern is observed when comparing the effect of pre-training and the auxiliary classifier. While both extensions improve the baseline performance, their improvements do not completely stack as they have many commonalities.

Shared Knowledge Transfer: In this study, we strive to provide a better-shared representation between tasks that reduces the uncertainty of all tasks when trained on the data of each of the tasks. We assume that such representation generalizes better on other tasks, and this trained shared layer can be used for other unseen tasks.

To test this hypothesis, we perform a leave-one-out experiment on all of the tasks in which the proposed classifier is trained on the remaining 15 tasks. To test the trained model on the left-out task, we freeze the weights of the shared model, perform 5-fold cross-validation on the target task, and report the result in Table 3. Since only the task-layer of the network for the new task may affect the results, we provide an over parameterized version of our model (UFS-MTL+OP) to ensure that the network can learn the task at hand, given the shared representation. As the table shows, UFS-MTL has a better performance than the FS-MTL, thanks to the uncertainty regularization of the tasks. Also, the effect of over parameterization on the task layer was not considerable on the result, indicating that transferring the trained shared features was the main contributor to the good results of UFS-MTL.

Task	LSTM	SP-MTL	ASP-MTL	Meta-MTL	UFS-MTL	UFS-MTL +OP
ϕ (Books)	79.5	82.2	83.2	86.3	86.4	86.7
ϕ (Electronics)	80.5	84.7	82.2	86.0	86.3	86.6
ϕ (DVD)	81.7	85.2	85.5	86.5	86.4	86.2
ϕ (Kitchen)	78.0	85.0	83.7	86.3	86.7	86.9
ϕ (Apparel)	83.2	85.2	87.5	86.0	88.0	88.2
ϕ (Camera)	85.2	86.7	88.2	87.0	88.2	88.5
ϕ (Health)	84.5	85.5	87.7	88.7	88.9	89.2
ϕ (Music)	76.7	80.0	82.5	85.7	86.7	86.8
ϕ (Toys)	83.2	86.2	87.0	85.3	87.0	87.7
ϕ (Video)	81.5	85.7	85.2	85.5	87.1	87.4
ϕ (Baby)	84.7	83.5	86.5	86.0	86.5	86.7
ϕ (Magazines)	89.2	89.5	91.2	90.3	91.2	91.7
ϕ (Software)	84.7	87.0	85.5	86.5	87.7	87.8
ϕ (Sports)	81.7	83.7	86.7	85.7	86.8	87.4
ϕ (IMDB)	81.7	87.2	87.5	87.3	87.6	88.0
ϕ (MR)	72.7	74.0	75.2	75.5	75.3	75.4
ϕ (AVG)	81.8	84.4	85.3	85.9	85.9	86.0

Table 3: Performance of our model tested on unseen tasks. ϕ(`TASK`) means that we transfer the knowledge of the other 15 tasks to the target `TASK`. Colors show first, second, and third rankings. By learning a shared representation that lowers uncertainty of all tasks while learning from each, we enhanced the overall accuracy of the MTL classifier by 4.1% compared to the baseline.

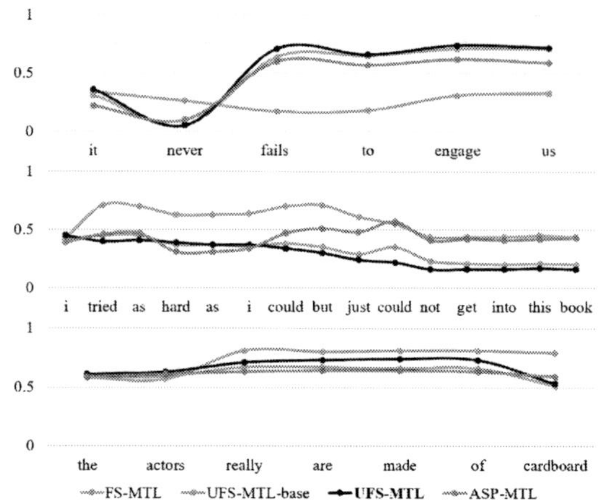

Figure 2: Predicted sentiment score by observing next word. We depict a true positive (top), a true negative (middle) and a false positive case (bottom) of our proposed method (UFS-MTL) compared with FS-MTL, ASP-MTL, and the vanilla version of proposed network, UFS-MTL-base.

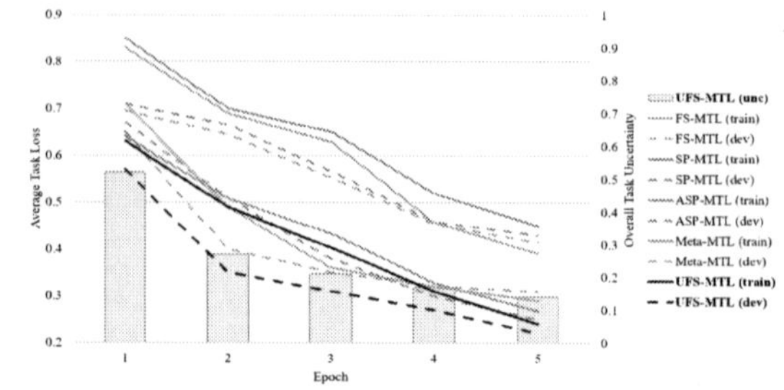

Figure 3: The train and dev loss of several MTL schemes. The overall task uncertainty of UFS-MTL measure by eq(5) on dev data is also shown here.

Error Analysis: We found two major groups of mistakes made by our model: *(i)* sentences with complicated structures such as complicated forms of negation and *(ii)* sentences that require reasoning or external references (e.g., to pop culture) that conveys a particular sentiment, analogies (e.g., Figure 2 (bottom)) or other types of inferences reaching out of the dataset's scope. In the former case, the use of auxiliary task helps significantly with capturing the essence of the sentences, while the networks that solely focus on sentiment analysis task faced difficulty in capturing the overall sentiment of a complex sentence. In this view, having an auxiliary task to assist the main task such as framework that models definitions of emotions as an auxiliary task while being trained on the primary task of emotion prediction (Singh et al., 2021)) could benefit the model to compensate these errors.

To visualize our model, we picked two successful cases and a failed case of sentiment classification from our model. We depict the sentiment score changes when traversing through words of the sentence by our model and three competing models. It is evident that the uncertainty regularization term guides the network to react to particular words, phrases, and structures considerably. It is also evident that adding auxiliary task (UFS-MTL vs. UFS-MTL-base) boosts the confidence of the method to capture essential structures for the task.

Speed of Convergence: We compared the average loss of the proposed method with Meta-MTL, SP-MTL, and ASP-MTL on train and dev sets of all tasks. We also calculated the total uncertainty of each model on dev. set using (5), for each epoch. As illustrated in Figure 3, our method is more efficient, performs better on dev splits, and reduces the overall task uncertainties more effectively.

Effect of Regularization: In this section, we investigate the effect of regularization on the performance of the system. While smaller λ derives the system toward the vanilla FS-MTL, larger λ emphasizes more on the ability of all classifiers to have less uncertain decision criteria. Such a decrease in uncertainty is directly attributed to the shared features since only one of the tasks is trained at a time. Overemphasizing the regularization, on the other hand, pushes the task-specific features in the shared space, as the effect of individual task-specific layers is diminished by increasing the λ. Figure 4 shows the effect of changing λ on the system performance. As larger values of λ prevent the MTL classifier from fine-tuning for each task, the system is prone to catastrophic forgetting resulting from over-generalization of the shared layer in MTL (Subramanian et al., 2018).

Comparing Uncertainty Measures: The choice of uncertainty measure is important to capture the source of uncertainty in the classifier. Table 4 shows the effect of different uncertainty measures on the vanilla UFS-MTL. We denote the average of the softmax outputs of each task used in (Kampffmeyer et al., 2016) by ζ_σ.

While the least confident measure (ζ_{LC}) considers only the most probable class label and tries to maximize it, it effectively throws away information about the remaining label distribution. Entropy in ζ_H considers the full distributions of the posteriors. However, task-specific features in the shared feature space may reduce the entropy for some tasks

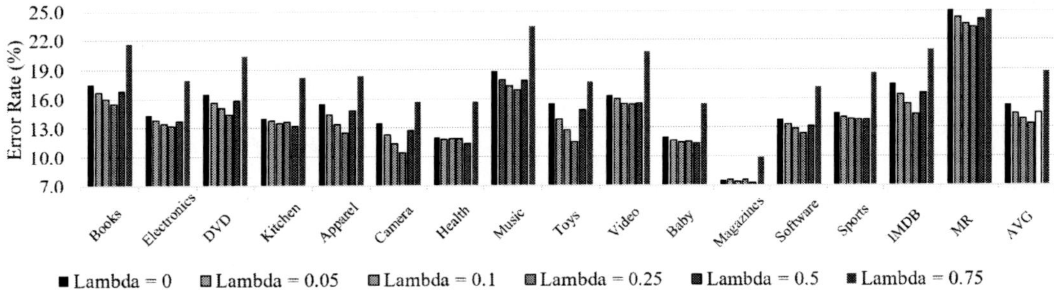

Figure 4: The effect of uncertainty regularization on the UFS-MTL. Small λ reduces the classifier to the FS-MTL, whereas excessively large values of λ prevent fine-tuning for each task in the multi-task learning framework.

	ζ_{LC}	ζ_M	ζ_H	ζ_σ
AVG	85.9	86.5	85.3	85.6

Table 4: Comparing average effect of uncertainty measures on vanilla UFS-MTL performance on all tasks. ζ_{LC} denotes the least confidence uncertainty, ζ_M refers to margin uncertainty, ζ_H indicates the Shanon's entropy, and ζ_σ calculates the average of softmax outputs.

while increasing it for others. Margin uncertainty ζ_M strives to address the shortcoming in the least confident strategy by incorporating the posterior of the second most likely label. Intuitively, instances with large margins have less uncertainty since the second best option is not very competitive.

Discussion on Disentanglement: To obtain an effective shared feature space, while the task-specific features should be pushed out, task-independent features should be pulled in, and redundant features should be punished. PS-MTL explicitly separates the private and shared features, and ASP-MTL tries to push out private features from shared space and omit redundancy by using adversarial training and orthogonality constraint. Yet, there is no encouragement except the training loss to have good shared features in this method. Here, we took an opposite approach and pulled good shared features in shared space (that promote the decisiveness of the MTL) while implicitly pushing away task-specific and redundant features that don't contribute much to overall certainty of MTL.

5.2 Multiple Tasks

In this experiment, we consider a heterogeneous multi-task learning scenario in which three different tasks (part-of-speech tagging, chunking, and named entity recognition) on various datasets are considered. After joint training on all domains (obtaining vanilla version), we include fine-tuning and training on unlabeled data to obtain the final UFS-MTL that has the state-of-the-art performance among MTL methods with the same LSTM baseline (Table 6). We excluded pre-training from our model to provide a fair comparison.

Datasets	Task	Train	Dev	Test
WSJ	POS Tagging	912,344	131,768	129,654
CoNLL 2000	Chunking	211,727	-	47,377
CoNLL 2003	NER	204,567	51,578	46,666

Table 5: Statistics of 3 datasets for multi-task sequence tagging experiment.

	Chunking (CoNLL2000)	NER (CoNLL2003)	POS Tagging (WSJ)
Single Task Models:			
BiLSTM+CRF	93.67	89.91	97.25
Meta-BiLSTM+CRF	93.71	90.08	97.30
(Collobert et al., 2011)	94.32	89.59	97.29
Multi-Task Models:			
SSP-MTL + CRF	94.32	90.38	97.23
Meta-MTL + CRF	95.11	90.72	97.45
UFS-MTL + CRF **(ours)**	96.11	91.12	97.37

Table 6: Accuracy rates of the models for chunking and NER tasks using F1-score (%) and for POS tagging using Accuracy (%). First, second, and third rankings of each task are denoted in color. Our method (UFS-MTL) outperforms the others in most of the tasks.

Task-Specific Output Layer: Inspired by (Ma and Hovy, 2016), the obtained shared representation is fed to a conditional random field (Lafferty et al., 2001) to perform sequence tagging.

Dataset: For sequence tagging tasks, we use Wall Street Journal (WSJ) subset of Penn Treebank (Marcus et al., 1993), CoNLL 2000 chunking, and CoNLL 2003 English NER datasets (Table 5).

Competitor Models: We compare our method with (Huang et al., 2015) which uses a BiLSTM encoding and CRF output layer. We also compared it with stacked SP-MTL, a bidirectional version of Meta-LSTM (single task), and a Meta-LSTM on top of an SP-MTL, all proposed in (Chen et al., 2018), followed by a CRF output layer. We also compared it with (Collobert et al., 2011).

Results: As shown in Table 6, with the help of uncertainty regularization, we observe that our model is consistently outperforming the competitor models, which shows that our model is very robust and our shared learned features can generalize well among related tasks.

6 Conclusion

In this study, we augment the fully-shared multi-task learning framework with a regularization term to improve the shared representation by lowering the classification uncertainty for all tasks while fine-tuning for each task. The learned representation increased the overall accuracy of the multi-task classifier, achieved competitive results compared to state-of-the-art MTL algorithms, and successfully transferred the knowledge to the unseen tasks.

References

Yaser S Abu-Mostafa. 1990. Learning from hints in neural networks. *Journal of Complexity*, 6(2):192–198.

Yoshua Bengio, Pascal Lamblin, Dan Popovici, and Hugo Larochelle. 2007. Greedy layer-wise training of deep networks. In *Advances in neural information processing systems*, pages 153–160.

Joachim Bingel and Anders Søgaard. 2017. Identifying beneficial task relations for multi-task learning in deep neural networks. In *ACL'15*, pages 164–169.

John Blitzer, Mark Dredze, and Fernando Pereira. 2007. Biographies, bollywood, boom-boxes and blenders: Domain adaptation for sentiment classification. In *Proceedings of the 45th annual meeting of the association of computational linguistics*, pages 440–447.

Konstantinos Bousmalis, George Trigeorgis, Nathan Silberman, Dilip Krishnan, and Dumitru Erhan. 2016. Domain separation networks. In *NIPS'16*, pages 343–351.

R Caruana. 1993. Multitask learning: A knowledge-based source of inductive bias.

Rich Caruana. 1997. Multitask learning. *Machine learning*, 28(1):41–75.

Junkun Chen, Xipeng Qiu, Pengfei Liu, and Xuanjing Huang. 2018. Meta multi-task learning for sequence modeling. In *Thirty-Second AAAI Conference on Artificial Intelligence*.

Junyoung Chung, Caglar Gulcehre, KyungHyun Cho, and Yoshua Bengio. 2014. Empirical evaluation of gated recurrent neural networks on sequence modeling. *arXiv preprint arXiv:1412.3555*.

Kevin Clark, Minh-Thang Luong, Urvashi Khandelwal, Christopher D Manning, and Quoc V Le. 2019. Bam! born-again multi-task networks for natural language understanding. *arXiv preprint arXiv:1907.04829*.

Ronan Collobert and Jason Weston. 2008. A unified architecture for natural language processing: Deep neural networks with multitask learning. In *ICML'08*, pages 160–167. ACM.

Ronan Collobert, Jason Weston, Léon Bottou, Michael Karlen, Koray Kavukcuoglu, and Pavel Kuksa. 2011. Natural language processing (almost) from scratch. *Journal of machine learning research*, 12(Aug):2493–2537.

Li Deng, Geoffrey Hinton, and Brian Kingsbury. 2013. New types of deep neural network learning for speech recognition and related applications: An overview. In *ICASSP'13*, pages 8599–8603. IEEE.

Long Duong, Trevor Cohn, Steven Bird, and Paul Cook. 2015. Low resource dependency parsing: Cross-lingual parameter sharing in a neural network parser. In *ACL-IJCNLP'15*, pages 845–850.

Tommaso Fornaciari, Alexandra Uma, Silviu Paun, Barbara Plank, Dirk Hovy, and Massimo Poesio. 2021. Beyond black & white: Leveraging annotator disagreement via soft-label multi-task learning. In *Proceedings of the 2021 Conference of the North American Chapter of the Association for Computational Linguistics: Human Language Technologies*, pages 2591–2597.

Yaroslav Ganin and Victor Lempitsky. 2015. Unsupervised domain adaptation by backpropagation. In *ICML'15*, pages 1180–1189.

Ross Girshick. 2015. Fast r-cnn. In *ICCV'15*, pages 1440–1448.

Kazuma Hashimoto, Yoshimasa Tsuruoka, Richard Socher, et al. 2017. A joint many-task model: Growing a neural network for multiple nlp tasks. In *EMNLP'17*, pages 1923–1933.

Zhiheng Huang, Wei Xu, and Kai Yu. 2015. Bidirectional LSTM-CRF models for sequence tagging. *arXiv preprint arXiv:1508.01991*.

Rafal Jozefowicz, Wojciech Zaremba, and Ilya Sutskever. 2015. An empirical exploration of recurrent network architectures. In *ICML'15*, pages 2342–2350.

Nal Kalchbrenner, Edward Grefenstette, and Phil Blunsom. 2014. A convolutional neural network for modelling sentences. *arXiv preprint arXiv:1404.2188*.

Michael Kampffmeyer, Arnt-Borre Salberg, and Robert Jenssen. 2016. Semantic segmentation of small objects and modeling of uncertainty in urban remote sensing images using deep convolutional neural networks. In *Proceedings of the IEEE conference on computer vision and pattern recognition workshops*, pages 1–9.

Alex Kendall, Vijay Badrinarayanan, and Roberto Cipolla. 2015. Bayesian segnet: Model uncertainty in deep convolutional encoder-decoder architectures for scene understanding. *arXiv preprint arXiv:1511.02680*.

Alex Kendall and Yarin Gal. 2017. What uncertainties do we need in bayesian deep learning for computer vision? In *Advances in neural information processing systems*, pages 5574–5584.

Alex Kendall, Yarin Gal, and Roberto Cipolla. 2018. Multi-task learning using uncertainty to weigh losses for scene geometry and semantics. In *CVPR'18*, pages 7482–7491.

Yoon Kim. 2014. Convolutional neural networks for sentence classification. In *EMNLP'14*, pages 1746–1751.

Iasonas Kokkinos. 2017. Ubernet: Training a universal convolutional neural network for low-, mid-, and high-level vision using diverse datasets and limited memory. In *Proceedings of the IEEE Conference on Computer Vision and Pattern Recognition*, pages 6129–6138.

John Lafferty, Andrew McCallum, and Fernando CN Pereira. 2001. Conditional random fields: Probabilistic models for segmenting and labeling sequence data.

Siwei Lai, Liheng Xu, Kang Liu, and Jun Zhao. 2015. Recurrent convolutional neural networks for text classification. In *AAAI'15*.

Gang Liu and Jiabao Guo. 2019. Bidirectional lstm with attention mechanism and convolutional layer for text classification. *Neurocomputing*, 337:325–338.

Pengfei Liu, Xipeng Qiu, and Xuanjing Huang. 2016. Recurrent neural network for text classification with multi-task learning. *arXiv preprint arXiv:1605.05101*.

Pengfei Liu, Xipeng Qiu, and Xuanjing Huang. 2017a. Adversarial multi-task learning for text classification. In *ACL'17*, pages 1–10.

Sulin Liu, Sinno Jialin Pan, and Qirong Ho. 2017b. Distributed multi-task relationship learning. In *ACM SIGKDD'17*, pages 937–946. ACM.

Xiaodong Liu, Jianfeng Gao, Xiaodong He, Li Deng, Kevin Duh, and Ye-Yi Wang. 2015. Representation learning using multi-task deep neural networks for semantic classification and information retrieval. In *Proceedings of the 2015 Conference of the North American Chapter of the Association for Computational Linguistics: Human Language Technologies*, pages 912–921.

Xuezhe Ma and Eduard Hovy. 2016. End-to-end sequence labeling via bi-directional LSTM-CNNs-CRF. *arXiv preprint arXiv:1603.01354*.

Andrew L Maas, Raymond E Daly, Peter T Pham, Dan Huang, Andrew Y Ng, and Christopher Potts. 2011. Learning word vectors for sentiment analysis. In *Proceedings of the 49th annual meeting of the association for computational linguistics: Human language technologies-volume 1*, pages 142–150. Association for Computational Linguistics.

Mitchell Marcus, Beatrice Santorini, and Mary Ann Marcinkiewicz. 1993. Building a large annotated corpus of english: The penn treebank.

Elliot Meyerson and Risto Miikkulainen. 2018. Pseudo-task augmentation: From deep multitask learning to intratask sharing—and back. *ICML'18*.

Hyeonseob Nam and Bohyung Han. 2016. Learning multi-domain convolutional neural networks for visual tracking. In *ICPR'16*, pages 4293–4302.

Bo Pang and Lillian Lee. 2005. Seeing stars: Exploiting class relationships for sentiment categorization with respect to rating scales. In *Proceedings of the 43rd annual meeting on association for computational linguistics*, pages 115–124. Association for Computational Linguistics.

Jeffrey Pennington, Richard Socher, and Christopher Manning. 2014. Glove: Global vectors for word representation. In *EMNLP'14*, pages 1532–1543.

Marek Rei. 2017. Semi-supervised multitask learning for sequence labeling. In *ACL'17*, pages 2121–2130.

Clemens Rosenbaum, Tim Klinger, and Matthew Riemer. 2018. Routing networks: Adaptive selection of non-linear functions for multi-task learning. *ICML'18*.

Sebastian Ruder. 2017. An overview of multi-task learning in deep neural networks. *arXiv preprint arXiv:1706.05098*.

Sebastian Ruder, Joachim Bingel, Isabelle Augenstein, and Anders Søgaard. 2017. Sluice networks: Learning what to share between loosely related tasks. *stat*, 1050:23.

Victor Sanh, Thomas Wolf, and Sebastian Ruder. 2019. A hierarchical multi-task approach for learning embeddings from semantic tasks. In *AAAI'19*, volume 33, pages 6949–6956.

Tobias Scheffer, Christian Decomain, and Stefan Wrobel. 2001. Active hidden markov models for information extraction. In *Advances in Intelligent Data Analysis*, pages 309–318, Berlin, Heidelberg. Springer Berlin Heidelberg.

Burr Settles and Mark Craven. 2008. An analysis of active learning strategies for sequence labeling tasks. In *EMNLP'08*, pages 1070–1079. Association for Computational Linguistics.

Gargi Singh, Dhanajit Brahma, Piyush Rai, and Ashutosh Modi. 2021. Fine-grained emotion prediction by modeling emotion definitions. In *2021 9th International Conference on Affective Computing and Intelligent Interaction (ACII)*, pages 1–8. IEEE.

Richard Socher, Alex Perelygin, Jean Wu, Jason Chuang, Christopher D Manning, Andrew Y Ng, and Christopher Potts. 2013. Recursive deep models for semantic compositionality over a sentiment treebank. In *Proceedings of the 2013 conference on empirical methods in natural language processing*, pages 1631–1642.

Anders Søgaard and Yoav Goldberg. 2016. Deep multi-task learning with low level tasks supervised at lower layers. In *ACL'16*, pages 231–235.

Trevor Standley, Amir R Zamir, Dawn Chen, Leonidas Guibas, Jitendra Malik, and Silvio Savarese. 2019. Which tasks should be learned together in multi-task learning? *arXiv preprint arXiv:1905.07553*.

Sandeep Subramanian, Adam Trischler, Yoshua Bengio, and Christopher J Pal. 2018. Learning general purpose distributed sentence representations via large scale multi-task learning. *arXiv preprint arXiv:1804.00079*.

Gajan Suthokumar, Vidhyasaharan Sethu, Kaavya Sriskandaraja, and Eliathamby Ambikairajah. 2020. Adversarial multi-task learning for speaker normalization in replay detection. In *ICASSP 2020-2020 IEEE International Conference on Acoustics, Speech and Signal Processing (ICASSP)*, pages 6609–6613. IEEE.

Ilya Sutskever, Oriol Vinyals, and Quoc V Le. 2014. Sequence to sequence learning with neural networks. In *Advances in neural information processing systems*, pages 3104–3112.

Kai Sheng Tai, Richard Socher, and Christopher D Manning. 2015. Improved semantic representations from tree-structured long short-term memory networks. *arXiv preprint arXiv:1503.00075*.

Alexandra Uma, Tommaso Fornaciari, Dirk Hovy, Silviu Paun, Barbara Plank, and Massimo Poesio. 2020. A case for soft loss functions. In *Proceedings of the AAAI Conference on Human Computation and Crowdsourcing*, volume 8, pages 173–177.

Yongxin Yang and Timothy M Hospedales. 2017. Trace norm regularised deep multi-task learning. *ICLR'2017*.

Jianfei Yu and Jing Jiang. 2016. Learning sentence embeddings with auxiliary tasks for cross-domain sentiment classification. In *EMNLP'16*, pages 236–246.

Amir R. Zamir, Alexander Sax, William Shen, Leonidas J Guibas, Jitendra Malik, and Silvio Savarese. 2018. Taskonomy: Disentangling task transfer learning. In *CVPR'18*, pages 3712–3722.

Poorya Zaremoodi, Wray Buntine, and Gholamreza Haffari. 2018. Adaptive knowledge sharing in multi-task learning: Improving low-resource neural machine translation. In *Proceedings of the 56th Annual Meeting of the Association for Computational Linguistics (Volume 2: Short Papers)*, pages 656–661.

Xiang Zhang, Junbo Zhao, and Yann LeCun. 2015. Character-level convolutional networks for text classification. In *NIPS'15*, pages 649–657.

Evaluating Contextual Embeddings and their Extraction Layers for Depression Assessment

Matthew Matero **Albert Hung** **H. Andrew Schwartz**
Department of Computer Science
Stony Brook University
{mmatero, has}@cs.stonybrook.edu

Abstract

Recent works have demonstrated ability to assess aspects of mental health from personal discourse. At the same time, pre-trained contextual word embedding models have grown to dominate much of NLP but little is known empirically on how to best apply them for mental health assessment. Using degree of depression as a case study, we do an empirical analysis on which off-the-shelf language model, individual layers, and combinations of layers seem most promising when applied to human-level NLP tasks. Notably, we find RoBERTa most effective and, despite the standard in past work suggesting the second-to-last or concatenation of the last 4 layers, we find layer 19 (sixth-to last) is at least as good as layer 23 when using 1 layer. Further, when using multiple layers, distributing them across the second half (i.e. Layers 12+), rather than last 4, of the 24 layers yielded the most accurate results.

1 Introduction

Over the past decade natural language processing (NLP) has increasingly set its sights on interdisciplinary tasks, notably those within the computational social sciences (Sap et al., 2014; Preoţiuc-Pietro et al., 2016; Zamani et al., 2018). As more and more language has been generated on social media sites such as Facebook, Twitter, and Reddit, researchers have had a wealth of personal discourse available to them that spans across thousands of users.

Many researchers focus on applying these social media datasets to predict user demographics, personality, or mental health (Matero et al., 2019; Iyyer et al., 2014; Lynn et al., 2020). Those predicting facets of mental health, such as depression and suicide risk, can help an over-burdened mental health industry by using automated screening (Coppersmith et al., 2018). Often these automated tools can be applied to forums where a user is an active member and their account could be flagged to be brought to the attention of a moderator. Thus, a personalized and potentially early intervention could be provided to the user in question.

Here, we investigate one prominent aspect of mental health: *degree of depression* (DDep) as measured by answers to an online questionnaire administered to Facebook users. Depression assessment of social media users is of interest for the following reasons: (1) Depression is often highly correlated with suicidal tendencies (Leonard, 1974) with deaths by suicide on the rise (Curtin et al., 2016) and (2) Automated assessment of depression is of high importance as it is often an under-diagnosed ailment, where such predictions could be useful to screen individuals who are at risk (Eichstaedt et al., 2018).

While many recent NLP pipelines have moved onto leveraging large pre-trained language models based on the transformer architecture (Vaswani et al., 2017), applying these models to human-level analysis, such as predicting a person's states or traits, has received little attention. Even the use of extracted embeddings, often called contextual embeddings, has yet to be fully explored in this level of analysis (V Ganesan et al., 2021). We expand this area of research by investigating how best to leverage the individual layers of off-the-shelf transformer models for depression assessment. Notably, we are interested in going beyond just a single layer and propose a greedy algorithm for selecting layers to extract contextual embeddings and aggregate them for large user-level embeddings.

Our contributions include: (1) A predictive model for depression assessment that out-performs the current state-of-the-art, (2) Evaluation of standard extraction techniques on contextual embeddings and their ability to detect depression levels and (3) Analysis on the effectiveness of layer selection to generate large contextual embedding representations of users.

Proceedings of the 12th Workshop on Computational Approaches to Subjectivity, Sentiment & Social Media Analysis, pages 89 - 94
May 26, 2022 ©2022 Association for Computational Linguistics

2 Related Works

One of the downsides when modeling mental health data is often that it is very small, with only a few hundred participants per study (Guntuku et al., 2017). However, it is sometimes possible to get around this by using data from Social Media websites where participants can choose to opt in to share past language data and take a small survey or questionnaire (Coppersmith et al., 2014). Schwartz et al. (2014) applies this technique to Facebook users and evaluates their DDep over a continuous scale (1-5) rather than bucketing users into classes such as mild/moderate/severe.

Even somewhat recent human-level models in NLP have used bag-of-words style approaches for prediction (Lynn et al., 2019; Andy et al., 2021), while other areas such as word or document-level tasks have adopted contextual embedding representations (Bao and Qiao, 2019; Babanejad et al., 2020; Matero et al., 2021). As these are often output from very large models, with hundreds of millions or more parameters, they are able to encode syntactic and semantic information that transfer to downstream tasks either through word or sentence embeddings (Guu et al., 2020).

While there has been some work applying contextual embeddings and transformer language models to human-level predictions, the most in depth has been V Ganesan et al. (2021) who investigated the use of contextual embeddings in low-data scenarios across various areas including mental health, demographics, and personality assessment. However, they only focus on using the base-size variants with an emphasis on dimensionality reduction techniques to apply contextual embeddings to small datasets (N <= 1000). Here, we work with a medium size dataset of 3 million Facebook posts across 25 thousand users and apply both base and large sized language models, as well as investigate layer selection beyond using just the second to last layer of the model.

3 Methods

Task: A person's degree of depression score is estimated by their response to a subset of neuroticism questions on a personality assessment through Facebook's MyPersonality app (Schwartz et al., 2013). The responses were on a scale of 1 to 5 and averaged together to represent a person's overall degree of depression. Here, we formulate the task of depression assessment as building a single user representation where each status is processed through a language model as a sentence and then all words from a user are avg-pooled. We evaluate our models using mean squared error(MSE) and disattenuated pearson r(r_{dis}) to account for questionnaire reliability (Lynn et al., 2018). We perform all experiments using the DLATK (Schwartz et al., 2017) library.

Model	r_{dis}	MSE
Baselines		
Open-Ridge	.507	.7696
Schwartz et al.	.526	N/A
AvgPool-XLNet	.499	.7728
AvgPool-BERT	.528	.7575
AvgPool-ALBERT	.508	.7675
AvgPool-RoBERTa	**.542***	**.7497***

Table 1: Performance of extracting embeddings from second to last layer (11) from *base* sized variants of each language model on the held-out test set. Each model is used to encode a 768 dimensional vector for all words that are then averaged to a user representation. **Bold** indicates best in column and * indicates statistical significance $p < .05$ w.r.t AvgPool-BERT via paired t-test.

Transformer Language Models: From the wide selection of general purpose language models, we select the following: XLNet, RoBERTa, ALBERT and BERT (Yang et al., 2019; Liu et al., 2019; Lan et al., 2019; Devlin et al., 2019). These models are chosen as they cover common language model types (e.g. autoregressor vs autoencoder), have been pre-trained on various corpus sizes, and in the case of ALBERT offer a more lightweight footprint in terms of total model parameters.

When comparing which language model to perform our layer analysis on, we first evaluate performance using only the second to last layer on our held-out test set. This allows us to deduce which model may lead to better application to aggregate human-level predictions.

Layer Selection: To decide on which layers to extract for our final model, we perform a 10-fold cross-fold validation, for each individual layer or combination of layers. First we select the best performing layer, once found, we then concatenate all other layers to find the best 2-layer combination. This process is iterated on until we reach a number of layers where we cease to see a performance increase via the cross-folds. Once the best

Model	Hid. Size	r_{dis}	MSE
RoBERTa-B L11	768	.542	.7497
RoBERTa-L L23	1024	**.543**	**.7476**
DistilRoBERTa L5	768	.533	.7545

Table 2: Performance of extracting embeddings from second to last layer of RoBERTa variants, which was found to be the best performing among base models, on the held-out test set. DistilRoBERTa is also considered as a small sized alternative. **Bold** indicates best in column.

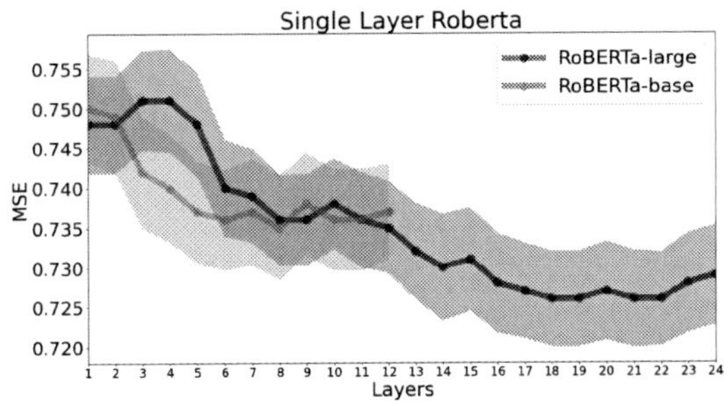

Figure 1: Layer-wise mean squared error performance across the 10-fold validation set with standard error shown by the shaded region for both RoBERTa-base and large. At lower layers (3-6), RoBERTa-base shows a much lower error rate. However at layer 13 and higher of RoBERTa-large there is lower error beyond any available base layer.

performing layers are found via cross-folds, we extract a final test set representation and run the final selection on our held-out test set. When comparing within cross-folds we only compare the MSE, rather than correlation, as that is the metric being optimized as well as being a less noisy evaluation of each model.

As well as our best performing layer combinations, for a final comparison on the test set, we also evaluate performance of standard layer extraction techniques. This includes the second-to-last layer and the concatenation of the top-4 layers enabling us to validate that our layer selection method and suggested layers are worthwhile.

Regression: Our model of choice is a regularized linear regression (ridge) with input being the mean aggregate of extracted contextual embeddings. To find the regularization parameter α, we use a 10-fold cross-validation technique searching between 10 and 1 million, increasing by powers of 10 each time, then selecting the α that gave the lowest mean squared error. A simple predictive model is chosen to highlight the improvements from the features themselves rather than any specific network architecture.

4 Dataset & Baseline

Dataset: The dataset is comprised of Facebook users who opted in to share their status updates between 2009 and 2011 and completed a personality questionnaire (Schwartz et al., 2014). There are 25,000 train users and 1,000 test users which are then filtered down to those who wrote at least 1,000 words across all of their status updates. The final result is a training set of 17,599 and test set of 986 users.

Baseline: We compare to the proposed model of Schwartz et al. (2014) which leverages both open-vocab and count based lexicons. Notably, the model is trained on 1 - 3 grams, a 2000 dimensional social media LDA topic vector, Lexical Inquiry and Word Count (LIWC) lexicon, and NRC sentiment lexicon (Pennebaker et al., 2001; Mohammad et al., 2013). We compare our models both to the reported scores in the original publication and to a version we recreated, referred to as Open-Ridge.

5 Evaluation

Our recreated Open-Ridge came within .019 r_{dis} of the original work, however, both the recreated and original model are outperformed by both BERT and RoBERTa base variants, as shown in table 1. Interestingly ALBERT, while being 10x smaller than the other language models, performs quite well; outperforming XLNET and baseline models. We also see that all models based on the autoencoder style architecture (BERT variant) perform better than autoregressors (XLNet). This suggests that for human-level analysis the autoencoder style models are better than autoregressors, agreeing with the findings of V Ganesan et al. (2021).

We also compare against possible variants of RoBERTa, which offer a computation versus performance trade-off, RoBERTa-large (24 layers) and DistilRoBERTa (6 layers) in table 2. Ultimately, RoBERTa-large performs only slightly better than the base model. While this small difference is found to not be statistically significant, due to the number of available layers of RoBERTa-large this gives more options for layer selection without a loss in performance and move forward with RoBERTa-large as our selected model.

Rank	*1 Layer*		*2 Layers*		*3 Layers*		*4 Layers*		*5 Layers*		*6 Layers*	
1	**19**	**0.7257**	**16**	**0.7234**	**24**	**0.7215**	**22**	**0.7208**	**18**	**0.7206**	**14**	**0.7207**
2	18	0.7264	15	0.7241$\downarrow$	22	0.7216	21	0.7210	17	0.7206	15	0.7207
3	22	0.7263	17	0.7241$\downarrow$	23	0.7218	18	0.7210	15	0.7207	12	0.7207
4	21	0.7265	22	0.7242$\downarrow$	21	0.7220	14	0.7211	14	0.7207	17	0.7207
5	17	0.7272	14	0.7242$\downarrow$	20	0.7225$\downarrow$	17	0.7211	21	0.7208	21	0.7208
6	20	0.7275	23	0.7246$\downarrow$	18	0.7225$\downarrow$	15	0.7211	12	0.7208	23	0.7208
7	23	0.7282$\downarrow$	18	0.7246$\downarrow$	14	0.7226$\downarrow$	23	0.7211$\downarrow$	13	0.7209	9	0.7211
8	16	0.7284$\downarrow$	21	0.7247$\downarrow$	17	0.7226$\downarrow$	12	0.7212	23	0.7210$\downarrow$	7	0.7211
9	24	0.7286$\downarrow$	13	0.7247$\downarrow$	15	0.7226$\downarrow$	13	0.7213$\downarrow$	20	0.7210$\downarrow$	6	0.7213
10	15	0.7305$\downarrow$	24	0.7248$\downarrow$	12	0.7227$\downarrow$	20	0.7213$\downarrow$	10	0.7211	4	0.7215
Layers Included	–		*19*		*19;16*		*19;16;24*		*19;16;24;22*		*19;16;24;22;18*	

Table 3: Comparison of performance between the top 10 best individual layers and additional layers on the 10-fold cross validation data, ordered by mean squared error. **Bold** indicates best in column and $\downarrow$ indicates significantly lower performing models $p < .05$ via paired t-test compared to best in column (rank 1). The best performing of the previous column is used to find the next best layer to add on (via concatenation indicated by ;). During cross-folds training N=16,694 and validation N=905.

Layer Combo	r_{dis}	MSE
Standard		
L23	.542	.7476
L21+22+23+24	.546	.7479
Optimized		
L19	.553	.7439
L16+19+22+24	.552*	.7208*
Other Sizes		
L16+18+19+22+24	**.554***	**.7206***
L14+16+18+19+22+24	.553*	.7433*

Table 4: Performance of extracting embeddings using standard techniques and from the optimized layers we find to be most promising via cross-fold selection. **Bold** indicates best in column and * indicates statistical significance $p < .05$ w.r.t standard top-4 (21-24) layer extraction via paired t-test.

As mentioned in section 3, for investigating layer selection we only evaluate on cross-fold validation results to avoid any overfitting to the test set. First, we look at all individual layers of RoBERTa, as shown in in figure 1, and the standard errors associated with each layer's performance across the 10 cross-folds. We find that performance slowly improves as you move up the model but begins to slow down around the middle layers and peaks at layer 19.

Next, we explore the question of how many layers should be used as well as which layers to extract in order to build a user representation. For this, we apply our layer selection technique based on empirical results of the cross-folds. We show results for the top 10 best combinations per layer amount in table 3. We find 3 interesting outcomes from our experiments: (1) When using only a single layer the second-to-last is not the best and is not even in the top 5, (2) We do not see a drop in performance from using more than 4 layers, in fact, we do not see a plateau until we try 6 total layers thus suggesting that for human-level predictions large representations are ideal and (3) The layers that boost performance all come from the top half of RoBERTa-large likely due to them including more semantic information than syntactic (Rogers et al., 2020), which could be more informative for modeling at the human-level.

Lastly, we compare our optimized extraction models to the standard approaches on the held-out test set; shown in table 4. We find that our layer 19 model performs quite well but is not a statistically significant finding (p=.08) when compared against layer 23. Our 4-layer model continues to give a boost in performance and is found to be statistically significant compared to standard top-4 extraction. The 5-layer version has a small improvement in both metrics and is found to be significant(p=.02) compared to our optimized 4-layer model. For the 6-layer model we see an expected drop in performance, based on cross-fold analysis, suggesting that the additional layer has hurt the model's ability to generalize.

6 Conclusion

With many tasks in NLP focused around human-level prediction, methods that can use state-of-the-art, off-the-shelf models in the best way are of interest to the community at large. In this work, we found that applying pre-trained transformer language models to depression assessment benefited from non-standard extraction techniques. Further, applying a straight forward empirical analysis of layer performance could lead to noticeable boosts in downstream applications. Ultimately, we achieved sate-of-the-art performance of $r_{dis} = .554$ and $MSE = .7206$ using a 5-layer user representation from RoBERTa-large.

Ethics Statement: Our work is part of a growing body of interdisciplinary research that aims to improve the automatic assessment of a person's mental health. However, at this time we do not suggest our model(s) be used in practice to label mental health states. Instead, this should be viewed as a step toward a clinical tool that would be used with professional oversight. This research has been approved (deemed exempt status) by an academic institutional review board.

References

Anietie U Andy, Sharath C Guntuku, Srinath Adusumalli, David A Asch, Peter W Groeneveld, Lyle H Ungar, and Raina M Merchant. 2021. Predicting cardiovascular risk using social media data: performance evaluation of machine-learning models. *JMIR cardio*, 5(1):e24473.

Nastaran Babanejad, Heidar Davoudi, Aijun An, and Manos Papagelis. 2020. Affective and contextual embedding for sarcasm detection. In *Proceedings of the 28th International Conference on Computational Linguistics*, pages 225–243.

Xingce Bao and Qianqian Qiao. 2019. Transfer learning from pre-trained BERT for pronoun resolution. In *Proceedings of the First Workshop on Gender Bias in Natural Language Processing*, pages 82–88, Florence, Italy. Association for Computational Linguistics.

Glen Coppersmith, Craig Harman, and Mark Dredze. 2014. Measuring post traumatic stress disorder in twitter. In *Eighth international AAAI conference on weblogs and social media*.

Glen Coppersmith, Ryan Leary, Patrick Crutchley, and Alex Fine. 2018. Natural language processing of social media as screening for suicide risk. *Biomedical informatics insights*, 10:1178222618792860.

Sally C Curtin, Margaret Warner, and Holly Hedegaard. 2016. Increase in suicide in the united states, 1999–2014.

Jacob Devlin, Ming-Wei Chang, Kenton Lee, and Kristina Toutanova. 2019. Bert: Pre-training of deep bidirectional transformers for language understanding. In *Proceedings of NAACL-HLT 2019: The Annual Meeting of the North American Association for Computational Linguistics*.

Johannes C Eichstaedt, Robert J Smith, Raina M Merchant, Lyle H Ungar, Patrick Crutchley, Daniel Preoţiuc-Pietro, David A Asch, and H Andrew Schwartz. 2018. Facebook language predicts depression in medical records. *Proceedings of the National Academy of Sciences*, 115(44):11203–11208.

Sharath Chandra Guntuku, David B Yaden, Margaret L Kern, Lyle H Ungar, and Johannes C Eichstaedt. 2017. Detecting depression and mental illness on social media: an integrative review. *Current Opinion in Behavioral Sciences*, 18:43–49.

Kelvin Guu, Kenton Lee, Zora Tung, Panupong Pasupat, and Ming-Wei Chang. 2020. Realm: Retrieval-augmented language model pre-training. *arXiv preprint arXiv:2002.08909*.

Mohit Iyyer, Peter Enns, Jordan Boyd-Graber, and Philip Resnik. 2014. Political ideology detection using recursive neural networks. In *Proceedings of the 52nd Annual Meeting of the Association for Computational Linguistics (Volume 1: Long Papers)*, volume 1, pages 1113–1122.

Zhenzhong Lan, Mingda Chen, Sebastian Goodman, Kevin Gimpel, Piyush Sharma, and Radu Soricut. 2019. Albert: A lite bert for self-supervised learning of language representations. *arXiv preprint arXiv:1909.11942*.

CV Leonard. 1974. Depression and suicidality. *Journal of consulting and clinical psychology*, 42(1):98.

Yinhan Liu, Myle Ott, Naman Goyal, Jingfei Du, Mandar Joshi, Danqi Chen, Omer Levy, Mike Lewis, Luke Zettlemoyer, and Veselin Stoyanov. 2019. Roberta: A robustly optimized bert pretraining approach. *arXiv preprint arXiv:1907.11692*.

Veronica Lynn, Niranjan Balasubramanian, and H Andrew Schwartz. 2020. Hierarchical modeling for user personality prediction: The role of message-level attention. In *Proceedings of the 58th Annual Meeting of the Association for Computational Linguistics*, pages 5306–5316.

Veronica Lynn, Salvatore Giorgi, Niranjan Balasubramanian, and H Andrew Schwartz. 2019. Tweet classification without the tweet: An empirical examination of user versus document attributes. In *Proceedings of the Third Workshop on Natural Language Processing and Computational Social Science*, pages 18–28.

Veronica Lynn, Alissa Goodman, Kate Niederhoffer, Kate Loveys, Philip Resnik, and H. Andrew Schwartz. 2018. CLPsych 2018 shared task: Predicting current and future psychological health from childhood essays. In *Proceedings of the Fifth Workshop on Computational Linguistics and Clinical Psychology: From Keyboard to Clinic*, pages 37–46, New Orleans, LA. Association for Computational Linguistics.

Matthew Matero, Akash Idnani, Youngseo Son, Salvatore Giorgi, Huy Vu, Mohammadzaman Zamani, Parth Limbachiya, Sharath Chandra Guntuku, and H Andrew Schwartz. 2019. Suicide risk assessment with multi-level dual-context language and bert.

Matthew Matero, Nikita Soni, Niranjan Balasubramanian, and H. Andrew Schwartz. 2021. MeLT: Message-level transformer with masked document representations as pre-training for stance detection. In *Findings of the Association for Computational Linguistics: EMNLP 2021*, pages 2959–2966, Punta Cana, Dominican Republic. Association for Computational Linguistics.

Saif M Mohammad, Svetlana Kiritchenko, and Xiaodan Zhu. 2013. Nrc-canada: Building the state-of-the-art in sentiment analysis of tweets. *arXiv preprint arXiv:1308.6242*.

James W Pennebaker, Martha E Francis, and Roger J Booth. 2001. Linguistic inquiry and word count: Liwc 2001. *Mahway: Lawrence Erlbaum Associates*, 71(2001):2001.

Daniel Preoţiuc-Pietro, H Andrew Schwartz, Gregory Park, Johannes Eichstaedt, Margaret Kern, Lyle Ungar, and Elisabeth Shulman. 2016. Modelling valence and arousal in facebook posts. In *Proceedings of the 7th Workshop on Computational Approaches to Subjectivity, Sentiment and Social Media Analysis*, pages 9–15.

Anna Rogers, Olga Kovaleva, and Anna Rumshisky. 2020. A primer in bertology: What we know about how bert works. *Transactions of the Association for Computational Linguistics*, 8:842–866.

Maarten Sap, Gregory Park, Johannes Eichstaedt, Margaret Kern, David Stillwell, Michal Kosinski, Lyle Ungar, and Hansen Andrew Schwartz. 2014. Developing age and gender predictive lexica over social media. In *Proceedings of the 2014 Conference on Empirical Methods in Natural Language Processing (EMNLP)*, pages 1146–1151.

H Andrew Schwartz, Johannes Eichstaedt, Margaret Kern, Gregory Park, Maarten Sap, David Stillwell, Michal Kosinski, and Lyle Ungar. 2014. Towards assessing changes in degree of depression through facebook. In *Proceedings of the workshop on computational linguistics and clinical psychology: from linguistic signal to clinical reality*, pages 118–125.

H Andrew Schwartz, Johannes C Eichstaedt, Margaret L Kern, Lukasz Dziurzynski, Stephanie M Ramones, Megha Agrawal, Achal Shah, Michal Kosinski, David Stillwell, Martin EP Seligman, et al. 2013. Personality, gender, and age in the language of social media: The open-vocabulary approach. *PloS one*, 8(9):e73791.

H Andrew Schwartz, Salvatore Giorgi, Maarten Sap, Patrick Crutchley, Lyle Ungar, and Johannes Eichstaedt. 2017. Dlatk: Differential language analysis toolkit. In *Proceedings of the 2017 Conference on Empirical Methods in Natural Language Processing: System Demonstrations*, pages 55–60.

Adithya V Ganesan, Matthew Matero, Aravind Reddy Ravula, Huy Vu, and H. Andrew Schwartz. 2021. Empirical evaluation of pre-trained transformers for human-level NLP: The role of sample size and dimensionality. In *Proceedings of the 2021 Conference of the North American Chapter of the Association for Computational Linguistics: Human Language Technologies*, pages 4515–4532, Online. Association for Computational Linguistics.

Ashish Vaswani, Noam Shazeer, Niki Parmar, Jakob Uszkoreit, Llion Jones, Aidan N Gomez, Łukasz Kaiser, and Illia Polosukhin. 2017. Attention is all you need. In *Advances in neural information processing systems*, pages 5998–6008.

Zhilin Yang, Zihang Dai, Yiming Yang, Jaime Carbonell, Russ R Salakhutdinov, and Quoc V Le. 2019. Xlnet: Generalized autoregressive pretraining for language understanding. In *Advances in neural information processing systems*, pages 5753–5763.

Mohammadzaman Zamani, H Andrew Schwartz, Veronica E Lynn, Salvatore Giorgi, and Niranjan Balasubramanian. 2018. Residualized factor adaptation for community social media prediction tasks. *arXiv preprint arXiv:1808.09479*.

Emotion Analysis of Writers and Readers of Japanese Tweets on Vaccinations

Patrick Ramos
Ateneo de Manila University, Philippines
patrick.john.ramos@obf.ateneo.edu

Kiki Ferawati and **Kongmeng Liew** and **Eiji Aramaki** and **Shoko Wakamiya**
Nara Institute of Science and Technology, Japan
{kiki.ferawati.kb6, liew.kongmeng, aramaki, wakamiya}@is.naist.jp

Abstract

Public opinion in social media is increasingly becoming a critical factor in pandemic control. Understanding the emotions of a population towards vaccinations and COVID-19 may be valuable in convincing members to become vaccinated. We investigated the emotions of Japanese Twitter users towards Tweets related to COVID-19 vaccination. Using the WRIME dataset, which provides emotion ratings for Japanese Tweets sourced from writers (Tweet posters) and readers, we fine-tuned a BERT model to predict levels of emotional intensity. This model achieved a training accuracy of MSE = 0.356. A separate dataset of 20,254 Japanese Tweets containing COVID-19 vaccine-related keywords was also collected, on which the fine-tuned BERT was used to perform emotion analysis. Afterwards, a correlation analysis between the extracted emotions and a set of vaccination measures in Japan was conducted. The results revealed that surprise and fear were the most intense emotions predicted by the model for writers and readers, respectively, on the vaccine-related Tweet dataset. The correlation analysis also showed that vaccinations were weakly positively correlated with predicted levels of writer joy, writer/reader anticipation, and writer/reader trust. Code will be made available at https://github.com/PatrickJohnRamos/BERT-Japan-vaccination.

1 Introduction

Vaccination against COVID-19 has been demonstrated to reduce the spread of the virus (Jones et al., 2021; Hall et al., 2021; Voysey et al., 2021). However, vaccine hesitancy can prevent vaccine uptake, increasing risk of infection. Searching for and understanding causes of vaccine hesitancy can lead to more effective methodologies in convincing community members to become vaccinated. One possible area of understanding vaccine hesitancy is the emotions felt towards vaccines and the COVID-19 pandemic. For example, fear felt towards vaccination might discourage one from receiving the vaccine. Meanwhile, fear felt towards contracting COVID-19 could encourage one to become vaccinated against it. Leveraging emotions has also been proposed in communication to reduce COVID-19 vaccine hesitancy (Chou and Budenz, 2020).

There have been several attempts at extracting emotions regarding COVID-19 vaccines, particularly from social media. The wealth of information available on social networking services such as Twitter already makes them a popular source for mining sentiment and emotions in other areas such as politics (Bose et al., 2019) and consumerism (Rathan et al., 2018). Social media information extraction has seen continued research during the COVID-19 pandemic, with multiple works specifically seeking to mine sentiments and emotions surrounding the pandemic and vaccination (Boon-Itt and Skunkan, 2020; Sakti et al., 2021; Aygün et al., 2021; Niu et al., 2022).

Existing emotion analysis studies on COVID-19-related Japanese Twitter corpora only focus on the emotions of writers, or those who post Tweets (Lee et al., 2020; Bashar, 2021). However, the emotions of readers, or those who read Tweets, are not necessarily the same as those of writers. For instance, if a writer expresses disgust towards vaccination, a reader might express anger out of disagreement in response. These reader emotions may also contain useful information in understanding vaccine hesitancy. We contribute to this research area by using a BERT to extract emotions of both writers and readers towards Tweets related to COVID-19 vaccines and comparing the predicted emotions to vaccination uptake. We do this by fine-tuning a BERT (Devlin et al., 2019) to predict intensity scores for Plutchik's eight emotions (Plutchik, 1980) for writers and readers from Tweets containing keywords related to COVID-19 vaccination, and performing a correlation analysis between the mined emotions

Proceedings of the 12th Workshop on Computational Approaches to Subjectivity, Sentiment & Social Media Analysis, pages 95 - 103

and a set of vaccination measures in Japan. Note that one limitation of our study is that the dataset of COVID-19 vaccine-related Tweets does not guarantee that COVID-19 or vaccination are the topics of the texts, or are necessarily the object of any inferred emotion.

We find that the emotion most prominently predicted by the model for writers on the vaccine-related Tweet dataset is surprise, with fear being the most intensely predicted emotion for readers. Additionally, writer joy, writer/reader anticipation, and writer/reader trust are weakly positively correlated with vaccinations.

2 Related Work

Prior to the adoption of deep learning, emotion analysis of Tweets was performed with a combination of feature engineering, lexicon-based approach, and traditional off-the-shelf classifiers. Balabantaray et al. (2012) and Wang et al. (2012) engineered overlapping sets of features from Tweets, with shared features including n-grams, POS, adjectives, and lexicon-based sentiment polarity scores. Balabantaray et al. (2012) fed the features to an SVM while Wang et al. (2012) used linear and Naive Bayes classifiers. EmpaTweet (2012) used a similar set of features and also an SVM, but exchanged sentiment polarity scores for synonym rings, hypernyms, and LDA topic scores.

However, these classical methods have been outperformed by more contemporary and dedicated sequence modelling techniques such as RNNs and LSTMs. Vateekul and Koomsubha (2016) demonstrated the superiority of LSTMs in emotion analysis over SVMs and Naive Bayes on Thai Twitter text, while Colnerič and Demšar (2018) showed the effectiveness of character-based RNNs.

The introduction of Transformers (Vaswani et al., 2017) as the new state-of-the-art sequence modelling architecture and their increasing ubiquity has also lead to their application in social media emotion analysis for a variety of languages. BERT models can outperform CNNs and BiLSTMs on English Twitter (Harb et al., 2020); Naive Bayes, logistic regression, and SVMs on Romanian Twitter (Ciobotaru and Dinu, 2021); and TF-IDF and word2vec on Arabic Twitter (Al-Twairesh, 2021). During the COVID-19 pandemic, a RoBERTa (Liu et al., 2019) was fine-tuned on emotion analysis to classify the emotions of Tweets containing hashtags related to the pandemic (Choudrie et al., 2021).

Meanwhile, emotion analyses of Japanese Tweets related to COVID-19 have been conducted using traditional techniques such as lexicon-based methods (Bashar, 2021) and frequency analysis (Lee et al., 2020).

The work most similar to ours is that of Niu et al. (2022), who perform sentiment analysis of COVID-19-related Japanese Tweets; investigate the correlation of the mined sentiments with infections, deaths, and vaccinations; and conduct additional analyses comparing multiple vaccine brands. Our study differs from this by extracting emotions rather than sentiments from both writers and readers, and comparing these mined features to vaccinations, vaccinated people, and fully vaccinated people.

3 Method

3.1 Dataset

To gauge the emotions of the Japanese public towards COVID-19 vaccines and related topics, a dataset of 20,254 vaccine-related Tweets from December 2021 containing any of the keywords"ワクチン" ("vaccine"), "モデルナ" ("Moderna"), "ファイザー" ("Pfizer"), or "オミクロン" ("Omicron") was constructed. "Moderna" and "Pfizer" were specifically selected as keywords as these are brands of COVID-19 vaccines commonly administered in Japan. The dataset was created by sampling 15 random minutes from each day of December 2021 for each keyword, and scraping all Tweets containing the assigned keyword for each sampled minute. A distribution of the dataset according to keyword is shown in Table 1.

Table 2 compares our constructed dataset against WRIME (Kajiwara et al., 2021), the fine-tuning dataset we discuss in Section 3.2. Our dataset contains longer texts on average. Postpositional particles, nouns, punctuation marks, and verbs are among the most common parts of speech in both datasets. However, auxiliary verbs are more common in the vaccine-related Tweet dataset while non-punctuation symbols are more common in WRIME.

3.2 Fine-tuning BERT for Emotion Analysis

We used BERT to perform emotion analysis by fine-tuning it to extract writer and reader emotional intensity scores from text, with higher scores indicating higher intensities. Writer emotions refer to emotions felt by the writers of a Tweet as they

Keyword	Number of Tweets
vaccine	13,664
Moderna	349
Pfizer	1,352
Omicron	7,761

Table 1: Number of Tweets per keyword in the vaccine Tweet dataset. Keywords are translated from Japanese. Some Tweets contain multiple keywords.

	Vaccine-related Tweets	WRIME
Average # of tokens per text	51	23
Five most common POS (descending)	ADP, AUX, NOUN, PUNCT, VERB	ADP, NOUN, PUNCT, SYM, VERB

Table 2: Average number of tokens and the five most common parts of speech using UniDic.[1]

write the post, while reader emotions refer to the emotions felt by the readers of a Tweet as they read it. We followed Plutchik's (1980) framework and fine-tuned BERT to extract intensity scores for eight emotions: joy, sadness, anticipation, surprise, anger, fear, disgust, and trust.

Using BERT for emotion analysis was straightforward and required only a simple modification to the head of the BERT model. First, input texts were tokenized using MeCab (Kudo et al., 2004) and WordPiece (Wu et al., 2016). The tokenized inputs were then each prepended with `[CLS]` classification tokens and fed through the BERT model. After the last layer, each `[CLS]` token was linearly projected into 16 class scores, representing the 8 emotions of writers and readers.

A PyTorch (Paszke et al., 2019) implementation of $\text{BERT}_{\text{BASE}}$ (110M parameters) pre-trained on Japanese Wikipedia from HuggingFace (Wolf et al., 2020)[2] was fine-tuned on WRIME (Kajiwara et al., 2021). WRIME is a dataset for emotional intensity estimation comprised of 43,200 Japanese Tweets annotated with Plutchik's 8 emotions by the posts' writers and 3 "reader" annotators hired by the dataset authors to read the posts.[3] Each emotion is annotated across 4 levels (0 to 3) of increasing intensity, with 0 referring to no presence and 3 referring to strong intensity. To create only a single set of reader emotion scores per data point, we averaged the scores across the three readers. BERT was then trained with mean squared error loss to directly predict the emotional intensity scores of writers and readers for given Tweets. A sample data point can be seen in Table 3.

Our fine-tuning was inspired by common BERT fine-tuning procedures (Devlin et al., 2019). We fine-tuned BERT on WRIME for 3 epochs using the AdamW optimizer (Loshchilov and Hutter, 2017) with a learning rate of 2e-5, β_1=0.9, β_2=0.999, weight decay of 0.01, linear decay, a warmup ratio of 0.01, and a batch size of 32. Training was conducted with an NVIDIA Tesla K80 and finished in 3 hours. The fine-tuned BERT was dubbed "emotion analysis BERT."

We evaluated emotion analysis BERT by comparing its mean squared errors to those of two baselines based on Kajiwara et al. (2021). The first was a bag-of-words and linear regression model (BoW+LinReg). Each text was tokenized using MeCab, vectorized into a bag-of-words using the 2000 most common words in the vocabulary, and then fed into a linear regression model. While Kajiwara et al. (2021) used logistic regression, we used linear regression for a fairer comparison with emotion analysis BERT, which directly predicts intensity scores. The second model we compared to uses fastText (Bojanowski et al., 2017) and an SVM (fastText+SVM). Each word of was embedded using fastText, after which the average of all the embeddings in the sequence were used as input into an SVM that regresses the emotional intensity scores. We used a linear kernel and $C = 100$.

3.3 Inferring Emotions from Vaccine-related Tweets

Emotions from the vaccine-related Tweet dataset were extracted using emotion analysis BERT following the procedure described in Section 3.2. Tweets were tokenized, prepended with a `[CLS]` token, and processed through emotion analysis BERT, with the `[CLS]` token being projected into writer and reader emotion scores after the last layer. Note that this is purely inference and no training is done using the vaccine Tweet data.

[2] We use the `cl-tohoku/bert-base-japanse-v2` Japanese BERT checkpoint available at `https://huggingface.co/cl-tohoku/bert-base-japanese-v2`.

[3] As of February 2022, there are two versions of this dataset. We use Version 1. WRIME is available at `https://github.com/ids-cv/wrime`.

Tweet	車のタイヤがパンクしてた。。いたずらの可能性が高いんだって。。(The tire of my car was flat. I heard that it might be mischief.)							
Annotator	**Joy**	**Sadness**	**Anticipation**	**Surprise**	**Anger**	**Fear**	**Disgust**	**Trust**
Writer	0	3	0	1	3	0	0	0
Reader	0	2.33	0	2.33	0.33	1	0.67	0

Table 3: Sample training data point. While WRIME has annotations for three separate readers, we create only one set by averaging the reader scores per emotion.

Model	Joy	Sadness	Anticipation	Surprise	Anger	Fear	Disgust	Trust	Overall
				Writer Emotions					
BoW+LinReg	0.889	0.830	0.849	0.617	0.605	0.536	0.822	**0.399**	0.692
fastText+SVM	1.141	0.973	1.066	0.801	0.754	0.628	1.032	0.394	0.849
BERT (ours)	**0.658**	**0.688**	**0.746**	**0.542**	**0.486**	**0.462**	**0.664**	0.400	**0.581**
				Reader Emotions					
BoW+LinReg	0.351	0.270	0.344	0.172	0.049	0.201	0.175	0.037	0.200
fastText+SVM	0.374	0.297	0.422	0.177	0.047	0.269	0.221	0.090	0.237
BERT (ours)	**0.192**	**0.178**	**0.211**	**0.139**	**0.032**	**0.147**	**0.123**	**0.029**	**0.131**
				Both Emotions					
BoW+LinReg	0.615	0.550	0.597	0.394	0.327	0.368	0.499	0.218	0.446
fastText+SVM	0.758	0.635	0.744	0.489	0.400	0.449	0.626	0.242	0.543
BERT (ours)	**0.425**	**0.433**	**0.479**	**0.341**	**0.259**	**0.304**	**0.394**	**0.214**	**0.356**

Table 4: Mean squared errors for each emotion in the test split of WRIME.

4 Experimental Results and Discussion

4.1 Fine-tuning results

Results for emotional intensity prediction on WRIME are shown in Table 4. The only emotion for which we do not achieve the best mean squared error is writer trust, where we still remain competitive a difference of 0.001 MSE from the best performing model. For all other emotions for both writers and readers, emotion analysis BERT outperforms both of the other models. We achieve 0.111 MSE and 0.106 MSE improvements on writer and reader emotion prediction respectively. For overall emotional intensity prediction, we outperform the next best model by 0.090 MSE.

Table 5 presents inferred emotions for sample test entries from WRIME. We qualitatively examined these results, which showed that emotion analysis BERT is capable of detecting emotion even when emotions are not explicitly stated, like they would be in a sentence such as "I am joyful." The model was able to infer anger and disgust from texts including phrases like "I waited for an hour but no one came!!", and joy and anticipation from "Haven't had back-to-back holidays in a while. Tomorrow is a weekday break!!"

4.2 Emotion inference results

Figure 1 presents the distributions of emotions for both writers and readers predicted by emotion analysis BERT. The highest average predicted score was surprise for writers and fear for readers. With the exception of fear, inferred writer scores were more intense, especially in sadness, anger, and trust, where median inferred writer scores were greater than the third quartile of inferred reader scores. Why the emotion intensities predicted for writers differed from those assumed for readers could be of interest to future studies.

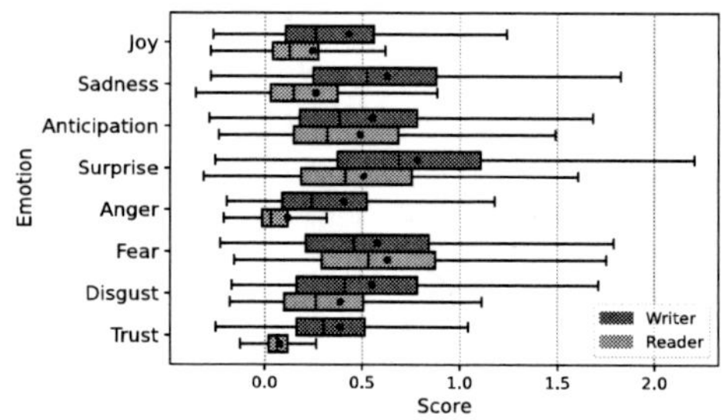

Figure 1: Box plots of distributions of predicted emotion scores for writers and readers. Whiskers are draw at 1.5 $\times$ inter-quartile range from the first and third quartiles. Mean predicted scores are indicated by black points.

The distributions of predicted writer and reader emotions are compared in a Q-Q plot in Figure 2. Anticipation and fear followed similar distributions for both writer and reader inferences, while other emotions showed lower values for readers, especially for trust.

Tweet	一時間待ってもこない！！ガス会社なんなの！！急いで帰ってきたのに?時間守らないひときらい！！！なんか食べ物でも持ってきたら許そう。(I waited for an hour but no one came!! What's up with this gas company!! Even though I hurried back? I hate people who can't keep track of time!!! Maybe I'll forgive them though if they bring me food.)

Annotator	Joy	Sadness	Anticipation	Surprise	Anger	Fear	Disgust	Trust
Writer	0.019	1.206	-0.069	0.785	**2.424**	0.070	**2.224**	-0.106
Reader	0.049	0.648	0.120	0.657	**1.573**	0.369	**2.139**	-0.060

Tweet	久しぶりの2連休。明日平日休み！！(Haven't had back-to-back holidays in a while. Tomorrow is a weekday break!!)

Annotator	Joy	Sadness	Anticipation	Surprise	Anger	Fear	Disgust	Trust
Writer	**2.989**	0.171	**2.111**	0.469	0.107	0.069	0.126	0.827
Reader	**2.396**	0.049	**1.567**	0.241	-0.011	0.022	-0.005	0.023

Table 5: Inferred emotion scores for data points from the WRIME test set. English translations are provided in parentheses after each Japanese Tweet. The two most intense emotions per annotator for each Tweet are in bold.

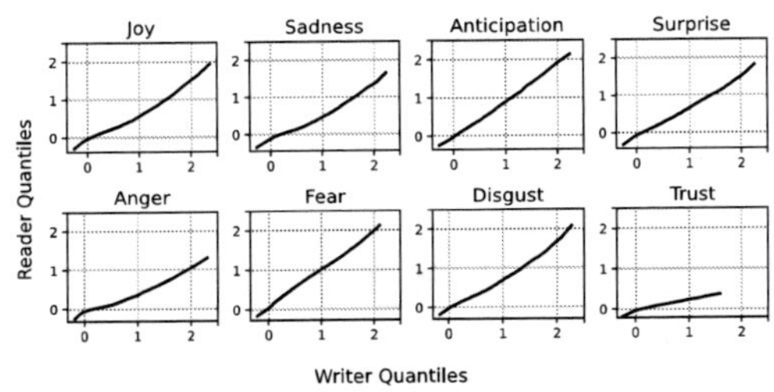

Figure 2: Q-Q plots of predicted writer and reader emotions.

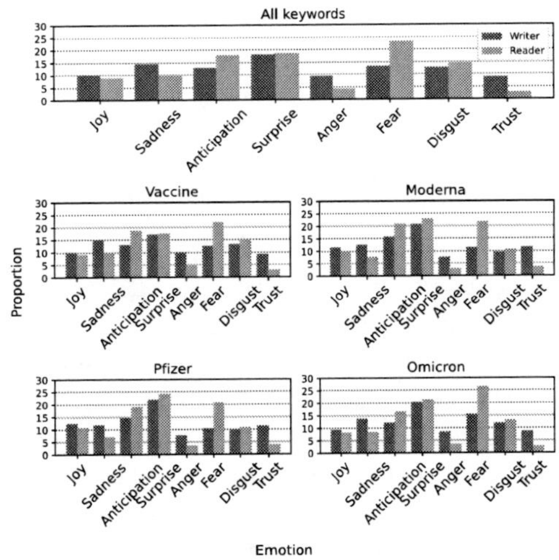

Figure 3: Distributions of predicted emotions for writers and readers for all keywords and for each keyword. Emotion proportions were calculated by dividing the total score of each emotion by the sum of all emotion scores for the emotion's assigned subject (writer or reader).

The percentage distributions of emotions for writers and readers inferred by the model for all keywords and per keyword are shown in Figure 3. While predicted writer emotion scores tended to be higher, this did not necessarily mean the same for the proportion each emotion constituted of the sum of all emotion scores. Although writers had higher predicted average anticipation, surprise, and disgust, these emotions comprised a larger percentage of inferred reader emotions than they did writer emotions. Fear, which was predicted at higher levels for readers, also constituted a larger proportion of total inferred reader emotion.

Predicted emotions of Tweets referencing Moderna were compared to those of Tweets referencing Pfizer to identify any differences in emotions towards the two brands of vaccines. The results of a Kolmogorov-Smirnov test for the intensities of emotions towards the two brands are presented in Table 6. Only differences in predictions for writer joy (Pfizer higher), writer sadness (Moderna higher), and reader sadness (Moderna higher) could be considered attributable to differences in underlying distributions.

Sample emotion inferences can be seen in Table 7. Like with the qualitative results from WRIME, emotion analysis BERT was capable of detecting emotion even in a lack of explicitly mentioned emotions. The model could identify anger and disgust from Tweets containing phrases such as "I can't call it anything other than foolish," and trust from "Today, I finally got vaccinated. My arm hurts a little bit, but other than that there are no problems."

Emotion	KS statistic	p-value
Writer Joy	**0.099**	**0.008**
Writer Sadness	**0.098**	**0.008**
Writer Anticipation	0.069	0.135
Writer Surprise	0.067	0.153
Writer Anger	0.054	0.379
Writer Fear	0.073	0.101
Writer Disgust	0.039	0.765
Writer Trust	0.065	0.188
Reader Joy	0.073	0.099
Reader Sadness	**0.124**	**0.0003**
Reader Anticipation	0.066	0.165
Reader Surprise	0.065	0.187
Reader Anger	0.063	0.207
Reader Fear	0.069	0.134
Reader Disgust	0.055	0.350
Reader Trust	0.066	0.163

Table 6: Kolmogorov-Smirnov test results for emotions between Tweets referencing Moderna and Pfizer. Significant KS statistics and p-values are in bold.

4.3 Comparison to vaccinations in Japan

Vaccination data was taken from Our World in Data (Mathieu et al., 2021)[4]. The vaccination data was comprised of a set of periodic vaccination measures for several countries. We filtered the dataset to only include entries from Japan in December 2021, matching the collection period of our vaccine-related Tweet dataset. For each date in the dataset, we focused on vaccinations, or the number of vaccinations administered on that date; new people vaccinated, or the number of people who received their first dose on said date; and new people fully vaccinated, or the number of people who received their second dose on that date. One thing to note is that vaccinations have plateaued starting November 2021, resulting from a lower number of vaccinations and a slower uptake of boosters (Mathieu et al., 2021).

Figure 4 compares the average predicted score for each emotion to the number of new vaccinations, people vaccinated, and people fully vaccinated across December 2021. No easily discernible trend common to both emotion scores and vaccination metrics was found.

For each writer and reader emotion, we performed a correlation analysis with each vaccination measure by taking the Pearson correlation coefficient between the sums of the particular emotion's predicted intensities and their corresponding vaccination metric for each date recorded in the vaccination dataset. The results are presented in Figure 5. The only results with satisfactory p-values were under vaccinations, which were positive correlated with writer joy ($r = 0.36$, $p = 0.047$), writer anticipation ($r = 0.40$, $p = 0.027$), writer trust ($r = 0.40$, $p = 0.025$), reader anticipation ($r = 0.44$, $p = 0.013$), and reader trust ($r = 0.39$, $p = 0.031$). We did not observe any significant correlations between the predicted emotion scores and people vaccinated or people fully vaccinated, as all p-values for these results were greater than or equal to 0.157, which is above the alpha of 0.05.

5 Broader Impact

Research into understanding the emotions of a population towards vaccines could hold both positive and negative societal impacts. Any relationship discovered between emotions and vaccinations could be leveraged in campaigns aimed at convincing citizens to receive vaccinations, reducing the spread of COVID-19. On the other hand, knowledge of what emotions could affect vaccine acceptance can be used in efforts to increase vaccination hesitancy and slow down vaccination rates, which could prolong risks of infection.

6 Conclusion

We fine-tuned a BERT on the task of emotion analysis, and used the emotion analysis BERT to infer emotion intensities of writers and readers from a corpus of Tweets containing keywords related to COVID-19 and COVID-19 vaccination. Our results revealed that surprise and fear were respectively the most intensely predicted emotions for writers and readers. Furthermore, vaccinations were weakly positively correlated with writer joy, writer anticipation, writer trust, reader anticipation, and reader trust.

Future works can extend this study by designing the emotion analysis to be aspect-based with respect to the keywords, as it is possible that the keywords are not the objects of the inferred emotions. Another possible area for further research could be correlation analyses with other COVID-19 metrics, such as infections and reproduction rate.

[4]Vaccination data is available at `https://github.com/owid/covid-19-data/tree/master/public/data/vaccinations`.

Tweet	バカとしか言いようがない。アメリカ帰りの女が自宅待機期間に男と会って、その男がサッカー場で撒き散らす。あああ、バカだなあ、オミクロン株接触者 天皇杯観戦 2021年12月16日 (I can't call it anything other than foolish. A woman who returned from the United States met with a man while she was still in quarantine, then that man went to a soccer game and infected others. Ah, it really is foolish. There are close contacts with the Omicron strain among spectators at the Emperor's Cup on December 16, 2021.)							
Annotator	**Joy**	**Sadness**	**Anticipation**	**Surprise**	**Anger**	**Fear**	**Disgust**	**Trust**
Writer	0.180	0.675	0.214	1.250	**2.138**	0448	**2.077**	0.259
Reader	-0.030	0.648	0.104	0.762	**1.147**	0.575	**1.848**	0.090
Tweet	皆様、お疲れ様です。今日はようやくワクチン接種しました。腕がちょっと痛いですが、それ以外に問題はありません。神宮球場にもちょこっと顔を出してノムさんを偲んできました。皆様、身の安全確保と体調管理に気をつけて、お過ごし下さい。今日も一日お疲れ様でした。(Thank you everyone for your hard work. Today, I finally got vaccinated. My arm hurts a little bit, but other than that there are no problems. I also swung by Jingū Stadium for a bit to think about Mr. Nomu. Everyone, please look after your safety and health. Thank you for working hard today.)							
Annotator	**Joy**	**Sadness**	**Anticipation**	**Surprise**	**Anger**	**Fear**	**Disgust**	**Trust**
Writer	**2.020**	0.428	1.321	0.594	0.075	0.145	0.014	**2.069**
Reader	**1.582**	0.100	**0.827**	-0.089	-0.038	0.239	0.046	0.419

Table 7: Inferred emotion scores for data points from the constructed vaccine-related Tweet dataset. English translations are provided in parentheses after each Japanese Tweet. Links are removed. The two most intense emotions per annotator for each Tweet are in bold.

Acknowledgements

This work was supported by JST SICORP Grant Number JPMJSC2107, Japan.

References

Nora Al-Twairesh. 2021. The evolution of language models applied to emotion analysis of arabic tweets. *Information*, 12(2):84.

İrfan Aygün, Buket Kaya, and Mehmet Kaya. 2021. Aspect based twitter sentiment analysis on vaccination and vaccine types in covid-19 pandemic with deep learning. *IEEE Journal of Biomedical and Health Informatics*.

Rakesh C Balabantaray, Mudasir Mohammad, and Nibha Sharma. 2012. Multi-class twitter emotion classification: A new approach. *International Journal of Applied Information Systems*, 4(1):48–53.

Md Khayrul Bashar. 2021. Exploration of public emotion dynamics in japan from twitter data during covid-19. In *2021 6th International Conference on Intelligent Informatics and Biomedical Sciences (ICIIBMS)*, volume 6, pages 310–315. IEEE.

Piotr Bojanowski, Edouard Grave, Armand Joulin, and Tomas Mikolov. 2017. Enriching word vectors with subword information. *Transactions of the Association for Computational Linguistics*, 5:135–146.

Sakun Boon-Itt and Yukolpat Skunkan. 2020. Public perception of the covid-19 pandemic on twitter: Sentiment analysis and topic modeling study. *JMIR Public Health and Surveillance*, 6(4):e21978.

Rajesh Bose, Raktim Kumar Dey, Sandip Roy, and Debabrata Sarddar. 2019. Analyzing political sentiment using twitter data. In *Information and communication technology for intelligent systems*, pages 427–436. Springer.

Wen-Ying Sylvia Chou and Alexandra Budenz. 2020. Considering emotion in covid-19 vaccine communication: addressing vaccine hesitancy and fostering vaccine confidence. *Health communication*, 35(14):1718–1722.

Jyoti Choudrie, Shruti Patil, Ketan Kotecha, Nikhil Matta, and Ilias Pappas. 2021. Applying and understanding an advanced, novel deep learning approach: A covid 19, text based, emotions analysis study. *Information Systems Frontiers*, 23(6):1431–1465.

Alexandra Ciobotaru and Liviu P. Dinu. 2021. RED: A novel dataset for Romanian emotion detection from tweets. In *Proceedings of the International Conference on Recent Advances in Natural Language Processing (RANLP 2021)*, pages 291–300, Held Online. INCOMA Ltd.

Niko Colnerič and Janez Demšar. 2018. Emotion recognition on twitter: Comparative study and training a

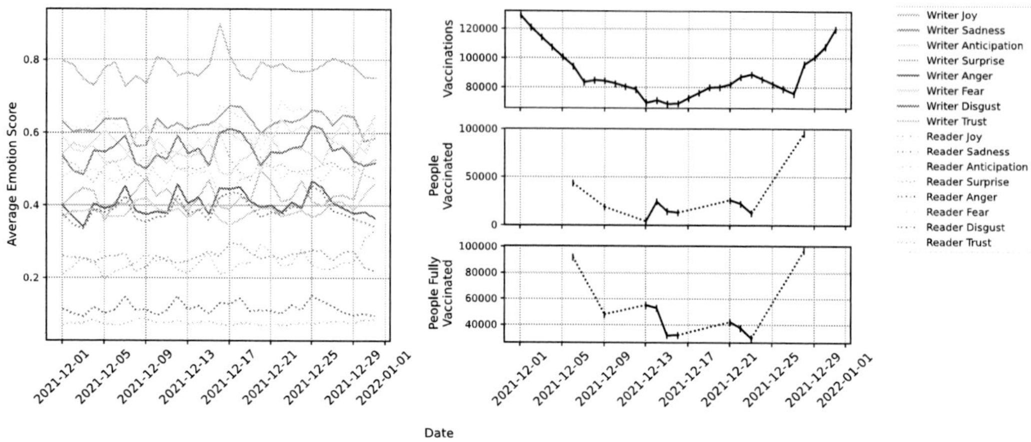

Figure 4: Average score for each emotion and the number of new vaccinations, people vaccinated, and people fully vaccinated for several days in December 2021. Vaccination data missing due to gaps in the dataset is represented with broken lines.

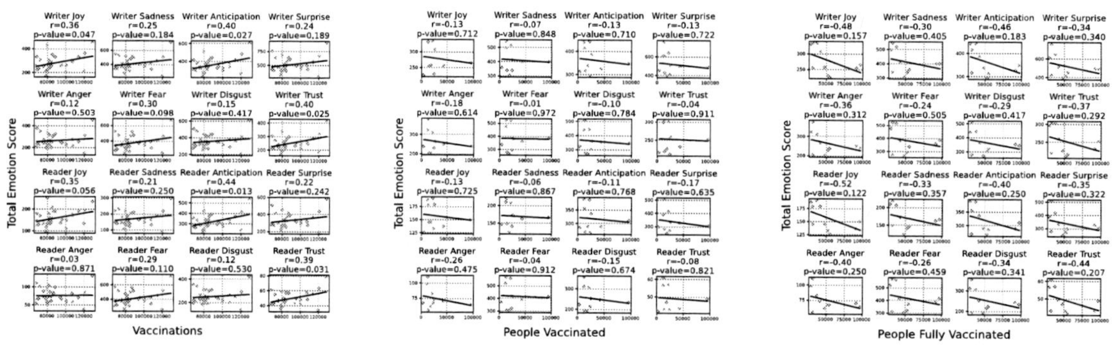

(a) With vaccinations. (b) With people vaccinated. (c) With people fully vaccinated.

Figure 5: Correlation analysis of emotion scores and vaccination statistics. Emotion scores are scatter plotted against vaccination numbers with best fit lines. No significant correlations are found for emotions with people vaccinated and people fully vaccinated.

unison model. *IEEE transactions on affective computing*, 11(3):433–446.

Jacob Devlin, Ming-Wei Chang, Kenton Lee, and Kristina Toutanova. 2019. BERT: Pre-training of deep bidirectional transformers for language understanding. In *Proceedings of the 2019 Conference of the North American Chapter of the Association for Computational Linguistics: Human Language Technologies, Volume 1 (Long and Short Papers)*, pages 4171–4186, Minneapolis, Minnesota. Association for Computational Linguistics.

Victoria Jane Hall, Sarah Foulkes, Ayoub Saei, Nick Andrews, Blanche Oguti, Andre Charlett, Edgar Wellington, Julia Stowe, Natalie Gillson, Ana Atti, et al. 2021. Covid-19 vaccine coverage in health-care workers in england and effectiveness of bnt162b2 mrna vaccine against infection (siren): a prospective, multicentre, cohort study. *The Lancet*, 397(10286):1725–1735.

Jonathas GD Harb, Régis Ebeling, and Karin Becker. 2020. A framework to analyze the emotional reactions to mass violent events on twitter and influential factors. *Information Processing & Management*, 57(6):102372.

Nick K Jones, Lucy Rivett, Shaun Seaman, Richard J Samworth, Ben Warne, Chris Workman, Mark Ferris, Jo Wright, Natalie Quinnell, Ashley Shaw, et al. 2021. Single-dose bnt162b2 vaccine protects against asymptomatic sars-cov-2 infection. *Elife*, 10:e68808.

Tomoyuki Kajiwara, Chenhui Chu, Noriko Takemura, Yuta Nakashima, and Hajime Nagahara. 2021. WRIME: A new dataset for emotional intensity estimation with subjective and objective annotations. In *Proceedings of the 2021 Conference of the North American Chapter of the Association for Computational Linguistics: Human Language Technologies*, pages 2095–2104, Online. Association for Computational Linguistics.

Taku Kudo, Kaoru Yamamoto, and Yuji Matsumoto. 2004. Applying conditional random fields to Japanese morphological analysis. In *Proceedings of the 2004 Conference on Empirical Methods in Natural Language Processing*, pages 230–237, Barcelona, Spain. Association for Computational Linguistics.

Hocheol Lee, Eun Bi Noh, Sea Hwan Choi, Bo Zhao, and Eun Woo Nam. 2020. Determining public opinion of the covid-19 pandemic in south korea and japan: social network mining on twitter. *Healthcare Informatics Research*, 26(4):335–343.

Yinhan Liu, Myle Ott, Naman Goyal, Jingfei Du, Mandar Joshi, Danqi Chen, Omer Levy, Mike Lewis, Luke Zettlemoyer, and Veselin Stoyanov. 2019. Roberta: A robustly optimized bert pretraining approach. *arXiv preprint arXiv:1907.11692*.

Ilya Loshchilov and Frank Hutter. 2017. Decoupled weight decay regularization. *arXiv preprint arXiv:1711.05101*.

Edouard Mathieu, Hannah Ritchie, Esteban Ortiz-Ospina, Max Roser, Joe Hasell, Cameron Appel, Charlie Giattino, and Lucas Rodés-Guirao. 2021. A global database of covid-19 vaccinations. *Nature human behaviour*, 5(7):947–953.

Qian Niu, Junyu Liu, Masaya Kato, Yuki Shinohara, Natsuki Matsumura, Tomoki Aoyama, and Momoko Nagai-Tanima. 2022. Public opinion and sentiment before and at the beginning of covid-19 vaccinations in japan: Twitter analysis. *medRxiv*.

Adam Paszke, Sam Gross, Francisco Massa, Adam Lerer, James Bradbury, Gregory Chanan, Trevor Killeen, Zeming Lin, Natalia Gimelshein, Luca Antiga, et al. 2019. Pytorch: An imperative style, high-performance deep learning library. *Advances in neural information processing systems*, 32.

Robert Plutchik. 1980. A general psychoevolutionary theory of emotion. In *Theories of emotion*, pages 3–33. Elsevier.

M Rathan, Vishwanath R Hulipalled, KR Venugopal, and LM Patnaik. 2018. Consumer insight mining: aspect based twitter opinion mining of mobile phone reviews. *Applied Soft Computing*, 68:765–773.

Kirk Roberts, Michael A. Roach, Joseph Johnson, Josh Guthrie, and Sanda M. Harabagiu. 2012. EmpaTweet: Annotating and detecting emotions on Twitter. In *Proceedings of the Eighth International Conference on Language Resources and Evaluation (LREC'12)*, pages 3806–3813, Istanbul, Turkey. European Language Resources Association (ELRA).

Andi Muhammad Tri Sakti, Emma Mohamad, and Arina Anis Azlan. 2021. Mining of opinions on covid-19 large-scale social restrictions in indonesia: public sentiment and emotion analysis on online media. *Journal of medical Internet research*, 23(8):e28249.

Ashish Vaswani, Noam Shazeer, Niki Parmar, Jakob Uszkoreit, Llion Jones, Aidan N Gomez, Łukasz Kaiser, and Illia Polosukhin. 2017. Attention is all you need. In *Advances in neural information processing systems*, pages 5998–6008.

Peerapon Vateekul and Thanabhat Koomsubha. 2016. A study of sentiment analysis using deep learning techniques on thai twitter data. In *2016 13th International joint conference on computer science and software engineering (JCSSE)*, pages 1–6. IEEE.

Merryn Voysey, Sue Ann Costa Clemens, Shabir A Madhi, Lily Y Weckx, Pedro M Folegatti, Parvinder K Aley, Brian Angus, Vicky L Baillie, Shaun L Barnabas, Qasim E Bhorat, et al. 2021. Single-dose administration and the influence of the timing of the booster dose on immunogenicity and efficacy of chadox1 ncov-19 (azd1222) vaccine: a pooled analysis of four randomised trials. *The Lancet*, 397(10277):881–891.

Wenbo Wang, Lu Chen, Krishnaprasad Thirunarayan, and Amit P Sheth. 2012. Harnessing twitter" big data" for automatic emotion identification. In *2012 International Conference on Privacy, Security, Risk and Trust and 2012 International Confernece on Social Computing*, pages 587–592. IEEE.

Thomas Wolf, Lysandre Debut, Victor Sanh, Julien Chaumond, Clement Delangue, Anthony Moi, Pierric Cistac, Tim Rault, Remi Louf, Morgan Funtowicz, Joe Davison, Sam Shleifer, Patrick von Platen, Clara Ma, Yacine Jernite, Julien Plu, Canwen Xu, Teven Le Scao, Sylvain Gugger, Mariama Drame, Quentin Lhoest, and Alexander Rush. 2020. Transformers: State-of-the-art natural language processing. In *Proceedings of the 2020 Conference on Empirical Methods in Natural Language Processing: System Demonstrations*, pages 38–45, Online. Association for Computational Linguistics.

Yonghui Wu, Mike Schuster, Zhifeng Chen, Quoc V Le, Mohammad Norouzi, Wolfgang Macherey, Maxim Krikun, Yuan Cao, Qin Gao, Klaus Macherey, et al. 2016. Google's neural machine translation system: Bridging the gap between human and machine translation. *arXiv preprint arXiv:1609.08144*.

Opinion-based Relational Pivoting for Cross-domain Aspect Term Extraction

Ayal Klein[1] Oren Pereg[2] Daniel Korat[2] Vasudev Lal[2]

Moshe Wasserblat[2] Ido Dagan[1]

[1]Computer Science Department, Bar Ilan University
[2]Emergent AI Lab, Intel Labs, Israel
ayal.s.klein@gmail.com
{oren.pereg,daniel.korat,vasudev.lal,moshe.wasserblat}@intel.com
dagan@cs.biu.ac.il

Abstract

Domain adaptation methods often exploit domain-transferable input features, a.k.a. pivots. The task of Aspect and Opinion Term Extraction presents a special challenge for domain transfer: while opinion terms largely transfer across domains, aspects change drastically from one domain to another (e.g. from *restaurants* to *laptops*). In this paper, we investigate and establish empirically a prior conjecture, which suggests that the linguistic relations connecting opinion terms to their aspects transfer well across domains and therefore can be leveraged for cross-domain aspect term extraction. We present several analyses supporting this conjecture, via experiments with four linguistic dependency formalisms to represent relation patterns. Subsequently, we present an aspect term extraction method that drives models to consider opinion–aspect relations via explicit multitask objectives. This method provides significant performance gains, even on top of a prior state-of-the-art linguistically-informed model, which are shown in analysis to stem from the relational pivoting signal.

1 Introduction

Sentiment Analysis is one of the most widely used applications of natural language processing. A common fine grained formulation of the task, termed Aspect Based Sentiment Analysis, matches the terms in the text expressing *opinions* to corresponding *aspects*. For example, in the restaurant review in Figure 1, *great*, *calm* and *quiet* are opinion terms (OTs) referring to the aspect term (AT) *ambience*.

Following the SemEval shared tasks (Pontiki et al., 2014, 2015), the preliminary task of AT and OT extraction has attracted significant research attention (Wang and Pan, 2020; Pereg et al., 2020, inter alia), especially for its domain adaptation setup,

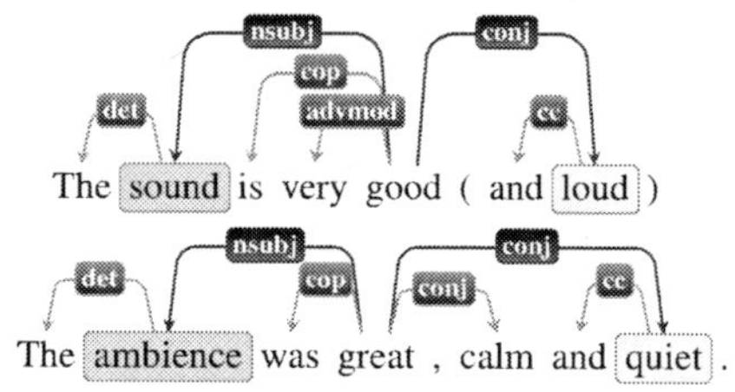

Figure 1: An OT (yellow) to AT (blue) path-pattern (green), defined on top of Universal Dependencies (UD), occurring in sentences from the *Devices* (top) and *Restaurants* (bottom) domains.

where a model trained on one domain is tested on another, unseen domain. Considering each product or service as a "domain", domain adaptation is crucial for making models of this task widely applicable. Yet performance on cross-domain aspect term extraction is still low, reflecting that it poses a special challenge to common domain adaptation paradigms.

In most domain adaptation settings, some features of the input are domain specific, while others — also known as *pivot features* (Blitzer et al., 2006) — do transfer into unseen domains. Hence, cross-domain generalization concerns focusing the model's learning on the latter. However, aspect terms across domains share little direct commonalities. Essentially, their common denominator is being the target topic referred to by opinion terms. For this reason, prior works suggested using handcrafted syntactic rules (Hu and Liu, 2004; Ding et al., 2017), or alternatively, injecting a full syntactic analysis into the model (Wang and Pan, 2018; Pereg et al., 2020), aiming to capture the transferable relation-based properties of aspects.

Our first contribution is establishing the *relational pivoting* approach for cross-domain AT extraction on quantitative, data driven analysis (§3). We utilize four different linguistic formalisms (i.e.,

Proceedings of the 12th Workshop on Computational Approaches to Subjectivity, Sentiment & Social Media Analysis, pages 104 - 112
May 26, 2022 ©2022 Association for Computational Linguistics

syntactic and semantic dependencies) to characterize OT–AT relations, and empirically confirm their domain transferability and importance for the task. Following, we propose an auxiliary multi-task learning method with specialized relation-focused tasks, designed to teach the model to focally capture these relations during OT and AT extraction training (§4). Our method improves cross-domain AT extraction performance when applied over both vanilla BERT (Devlin et al., 2019) and the state-of-the-art SA-EXAL (Pereg et al., 2020) models. We conclude with a quantitative analysis of model predictions, ascribing observed performance gains to enhanced relational pivoting.[1]

2 Background

Following the SemEval Aspect Based Sentiment Analysis shared tasks (Pontiki et al., 2014, 2015), recent works have formulated the *OT and AT extraction* task: given an opinionated text, identify the spans denoting OTs and ATs. We adopt the benchmark dataset that was used by recent works (Wang and Pan, 2020; Pereg et al., 2020), which consists of three customer-review domains — (R)estaurants, (L)aptops and digital (D)evices — and was aggregated from the SemEval tasks jointly with several published resources (Hu and Liu, 2004; Wang et al., 2016). While promising AT extraction performance has been demonstrated for in-domain settings (Li et al., 2018; Augustyniak et al., 2019), it does not scale to unseen domains, where state-of-the-art models exhibited small incremental improvements and struggle to surpass F1 scores of 40–55 (for the different domain pairs).

Previous works have conjectured that aspect and opinion terms maintain frequent syntactic relations between them. Subsequently, Hu and Liu (2004), followed by Qiu et al. (2011), crafted a handful of simple syntactic patterns for in-domain AT extraction based on OTs. Motivated by the hypothesized domain transferability of syntactic OT–AT relations, Ding et al. (2017) employed pseudo labeling of AT based on the aforementioned patterns, which was used as auxiliary supervision for domain adaptation setup. We, however, extract our patterns from the data rather than manually crafting them.

In a related line of work, syntax was leveraged more broadly for the same relational pivoting motivation. Wang and Pan (2018) and Wang and Pan (2020) encoded dependency relations with a recursive neural network using multitask learning, where the latter also applied domain-invariant adversarial learning. Most recently, the Syntactically Aware Extended Attention Layer model (SA-EXAL) (Pereg et al., 2020) improved cross-domain OT and AT extraction by augmenting BERT with an additional self-attention head that attends solely to the syntactic head of each token.

[1]Our code for all experiments and analyses can be found here: https://github.com/IntelLabs/nlp-architect/tree/libert-path-amtl/nlp_architect/models/libert

	Aspects	Opinions
D → R	7.3	78.6
D → L	42.3	83.2
R → D	12.2	59.1
R → L	11	61.4
L → D	41.3	65.4
L → R	9.1	68.3
Mean	**20.5**	**69.3**

Table 1: Cross-Domain lexical term overlap — how many term instances from target domain occur at least once in source domain (percentage).

3 Motivating Data Analysis

The *Relational Pivoting* hypothesis is jointly entailed from two observations: (1) Opinion terms are similar across domains. (2) The relationships between corresponding OT–AT pairs have common, domain transferable linguistic characteristics. Taken together, these suggest that OT–AT linguistic relations are informative pivot features for transferring aspect extraction across domains. In the following subsections, we show several analyses supporting the above observations and hypothesis.

3.1 Opinions vs. Aspects Domain Variability

We first measure the degree to which OTs and ATs are shared across domains, by computing cross-domain lexical overlap. Table 1 shows the percentage of term instances in the target domain occurring at least once in the source domain. Overall, unlike aspect terms, opinion terms have significant overlap across domains. For example, the terms *great*, *good*, *best*, *better* and *nice* all occur in the top-10 common OTs in each of the three domains, jointly covering 22%, 20% and 14% of OTs in the *Restaurants*, *Devices* and *Laptops* domains, respectively.

In sharp contrast, there is only one aspect (*price*) occurring in the top 50 common ATs at all three domains. This is in sync with model experiments — both in-house and as reported by Wang and Pan (2020) — showing a drastic performance drop for cross-domain AT extraction, from lower 70s in-domain to around 45 F1, while exhibiting a "reasonable" drop in OT extraction, from lower 80s to around 70 F1.

3.2 OT–AT Path Patterns

Next, we measure the degree to which linguistic relations connecting OT–AT pairs are shared across domains. To this end, we capture OT–AT linguistic relations using their *path pattern* in a dependency graph, i.e., the ordered list of the dependency relation labels occurring throughout the shortest (undirected) path between the terms (Figure 1).[2]

We investigate and compare four linguistic formalisms: **Spacy**'s syntactic dependencies[3], Universal Dependencies (**UD**), and two formalisms from Semantic Dependency Parsing (Oepen et al., 2015) — DELPH-IN MRS (**DM**) and Prague Semantic Dependencies (**PSD**).[4] We parsed all the sentences in the benchmark dataset with state-of-the-art parsers — SpaCy 2.0, UDPipe[5], and HIT-SCIR (Che et al., 2019) for DM and PSD. Importantly, since correspondences between ATs and OTs are not annotated in the benchmark dataset, we first heuristically define which (OT, AT) pairs would be considered related. Following a preliminary analysis, we selected for each formalism all pairs whose shortest path length is ≤ 2. This yields 9K–10K pairs which cover 60%–70% of the ATs across the different formalisms. These pairs and their path patterns constitute the data for the analyses below, as well as for training relation-focused auxiliary tasks (§4).

We find that between 94%–97% of the patterns in one domain are covered by another domain (More details in Appendix A). This confirm the prior presupposition that the linguistic structure of OT–AT relations is fairly domain invariant, and put forward path-patterns as promising features for domain transfer. In section 3.4 we further analyze the variability across different domain transfer settings.

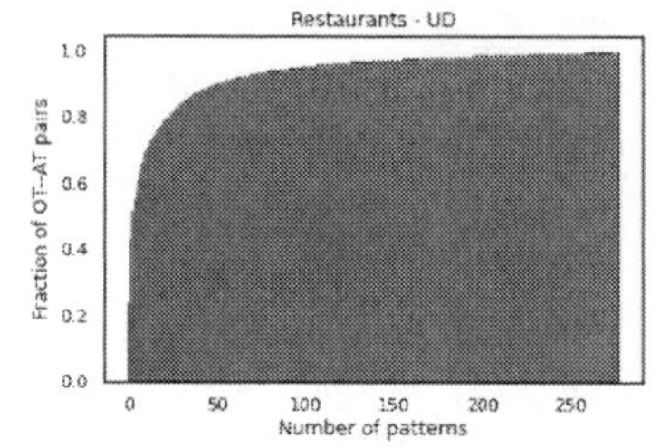

Figure 2: Relative cumulative frequency distribution of path patterns — *Restaurants* domain, **UD** formalism.

	In-Domain						Cross-Domain					
	$k=10$			All			$k=10$			All		
	P	R	F1	P	R	F1	P	R	F1	P	R	F1
UD	41	32	35	22	54	31	40	30	34	22	52	30
DM	46	34	39	31	46	37	46	34	38	31	45	36

Table 2: Results of deterministically applying the top k common path patterns (in source domain) on gold OTs for extracting ATs. Evaluation is macro-averaged over the 3 in-domain or 6 cross-domain settings.

3.3 Deterministic Relational Pivoting

To quantify the estimated potential of relation-based pivoting, we analyze a deterministic method for extracting ATs via gold OTs based on path patterns, similar to prior rule-based methods (Hu and Liu, 2004; Qiu et al., 2011), and assess how well such an approach transfer across domains. Given predicted linguistic parses, we select the top k common OT-to-AT path patterns and apply them on every OT, where traversal destination tokens are selected as ATs. To illustrate, given the UD pattern $\text{OT}\xleftarrow{\text{CONJ}} * \xrightarrow{\text{NSUBJ}}\text{AT}$, the OTs *quiet* and *calm* would both yield *ambience* as an AT (Figure 1, bottom). Notably, this analysis is only a rough upper-bound estimate; it is limited to identifying single-word ATs (70% of all ATs) which furthermore relates to an OT in a strictly known pattern, whereas models may generalize over some of these limitations.

Averaged results (across domain settings) are shown in Table 2 for varying k sizes (see Appendix B for a breakdown by domain pairs). Overall, pattern-based AT extraction can bring averaged F1 score up to **39** (DM), and recall up to **54** (UD). Crucially, there is hardly any drop in cross-domain settings relative to in-domain, affirming that patterns from a different source domain are as informative as in-domain patterns for opinion based AT extraction, consistent with observed pattern stability (§3.2). These findings suggest that driving a model to encode OT–AT relations should enhance domain adaptation.

[2] We maintain edge direction by appending a directionality marker to each edge label. In case of multi-word terms, we take the token pair across the terms having the shortest path.

[3] https://spacy.io/

[4] We also experimented with three application-oriented UD extensions: Enhanced UD, Enhanced UD++ (Schuster and Manning, 2016), and pyBART (Tiktinsky et al., 2020). These formalisms introduced more label variability compared with UD, but also shortened OT–AT paths and performed slightly better in the multitask experiments. However, we omit these for presentation convenience.

[5] https://ufal.mff.cuni.cz/udpipe

3.4 Analysis of Domain Differences

It is illuminating to examine the differences between domains with respect to the path-pattern variability and transferability. In order to assess the linguistic diversity of OT–AT relations within each domain, we plot the relative cumulative pattern distribution for each linguistic formalism, visualizing how many OT–AT pairs (%) are covered by how many different patterns (See Figure 2 for a representative, and Appendix Figure 3 for the complete set of figures). The general picture is that the vast majority of OT–AT pairs exhibit a few dozens of path patterns, albeit most pairs are covered by a few high-frequency patterns.

Specifically, we observe that the *Laptops* domain is the most diverse and slowly-accumulating, while the opposite is true for the *Restaurants* domain. We conjecture that the linguistic variability of OT–AT relations inside a domain affects its transferability. High variability makes the domain harder to transfer to, as many relation patterns were not seen during training on the source domain. At the same time, it might make it a good choice for the source domain, acquainting the model with a rich set of relational linguistic constructions to generalize from.

Obviously, the within-domain variability is not the most prominent factor affecting domain transfer; rather, it interacts with the similarity of the domain pairs, both on the pivot features (here: OT–AT relations) and on the non-pivot features (here: the lexical and semantic profile of ATs and OTs). To have a better handle on cross-domain similarity of OT–AT relations that accounts for pattern frequency in each domain, we compute the Jensen-Shannon Distance between path-pattern probability distributions (Table 6 in Appendix A), where smaller distance indicates greater similarity. While the *Devices* and *Laptops* domains are the most similar to each other, the *Restaurants* and *Laptops* domains are least similar.

By and large, this is inline both with results of the deterministic pivoting analysis (Section 3.3) broken down by domain pairs (Table 7 in Appendix B), and, to a smaller degree, with performance gains of our relation-focused multitask learning experiments (Section 5).

4 Multi-task Learning Method

To propagate the relational pivoting signal into an OT and AT extraction model, we apply auxiliary multitask learning (AMTL). We experimented with two auxiliary tasks for steering the model to encode OT–AT relationship information during training. Given an OT from an OT–AT pair of the collected auxiliary training data (§3.2), the model learns to: (1) predict its counterpart AT (ASP); and (2) predict the path-pattern connecting them on the dependency graph (PATT).[6] The ASP task should foreground the implicit representation of OT–AT relations, whereas PATT injects explicit, linguistically-oriented relation information.

	R ↔ L	R ↔ D	L ↔ D	Mean
Spacy	0.62	0.60	0.58	0.60
UD	0.60	0.59	0.56	0.58
DM	0.50	0.50	0.50	0.50
PSD	0.60	0.56	0.58	0.58
Mean	0.58	0.56	0.55	0.57

Table 3: Jensen-Shannon Distances between pattern probabilities in different domains. Lower distance indicates similarity between the frequency signature of patterns in a domain pair.

Prior multitask learning approaches for enriching models with syntax (Strubell et al., 2018; Wang and Pan, 2018, 2020) have pushed them to encode a full syntactic analysis, possibly including irrelevant information. In contrast, our auxiliary tasks form a "partial parsing" objective, specialized in the relevant terms and their multifarious relations. We use both vanilla BERT (Devlin et al., 2019) and state-of-the-art SA-EXAL (Pereg et al., 2020) as base models, where the latter may imply whether our relation-focused signal is subsumed by SA-EXAL's awareness to the full syntactic parse (§2).

Implementation details We follow the experimental setup of (Pereg et al., 2020) and formulate OT and AT extraction as a single BIO-tagging task. One-layer classifiers are applied on top of either `bert-base-uncased` or SA-EXAL encoders, both for the main task and for the auxiliary tasks. Let $Z = \{z_1, z_2, \ldots, z_n\}$ be the contextualized representations of the input sequence produced by the encoder, and *op* be the OT index from an extracted OT–AT pair. The auxiliary classifiers are defined as follows:

$$\text{PATT}(Z, op) = \text{softmax}(z_{op}W^P + U^P)$$
$$\text{ASP}(Z, op) = \text{softmax}(o_1, \ldots, o_n)$$
$$o_i = (z_{op}W^A + U^A) \cdot z_i$$

where $W^P \in \mathbb{R}^{d \times m}$, $U^P \in \mathbb{R}^m$, $W^A \in \mathbb{R}^{d \times d}$,

[6]The SA-EXAL model was amended to generalize over the graph structures (rather than trees) produced by semantic formalisms (Appendix E).

Model (+ AMTL task — Formalism)	L → R	D → R	R → L	D → L	R → D	L → D	Mean
BERT	47.2 (4.0)	51.6 (2.1)	44.5 (3.1)	**46.7 (1.7)**	38.3 (2.4)	42.6 (0.6)	45.16
BERT + ASP — DM	**53.5 (3.3)**	**52.0 (2.1)**	45.7 (2.4)	45.9 (2.3)	38.8 (1.5)	**42.8 (1.0)**	**46.45**
BERT + ASP — Spacy	49.8 (3.2)	51.6 (1.5)	**46.2 (2.5)**	45.2 (2.5)	**39.4 (1.6)**	42.5 (1.0)	45.77
BERT + PATT — DM	46.3 (4.7)	50.9 (2.6)	42.9 (3.4)	46.2 (2.4)	38.0 (1.9)	42.1 (1.0)	44.40
BERT + PATT — Spacy	50.1 (3.0)	51.6 (2.0)	43.1 (2.2)	46.6 (2.5)	37.8 (1.6)	42.0 (0.9)	45.20
SA-EXAL — DM	48.7 (5.8)	53.8 (2.8)	46.0 (3.1)	**47.7 (1.8)**	**40.7 (1.3)**	41.9 (0.6)	46.48
SA-EXAL — Spacy	47.9 (3.1)	54.1 (1.9)	45.4 (3.3)	47.1 (1.1)	**40.7 (1.7)**	42.1 (1.4)	46.24
SA-EXAL + ASP — DM	**54.1 (2.3)**	51.6 (2.0)	45.6 (2.9)	45.8 (4.1)	39.2 (1.9)	41.8 (0.9)	46.37
SA-EXAL + ASP — Spacy	54.0 (3.1)	52.6 (1.9)	47.1 (3.0)	46.9 (2.4)	39.1 (2.7)	**42.2 (0.6)**	47.00
SA-EXAL + PATT — DM	52.8 (4.3)	**54.3 (1.8)**	**47.5 (1.9)**	**47.7 (2.2)**	40.3 (1.5)	41.6 (0.8)	**47.37**
SA-EXAL + PATT — Spacy	51.2 (3.4)	53.3 (2.3)	46.5 (2.3)	46.6 (1.8)	39.5 (1.2)	41.5 (0.9)	46.42

Table 4: Cross-domain AT-extraction for different models and linguistic formalisms, evaluated by mean F1 score (and standard deviation). Each column (e.g. L → R) stands for a cross-domain transfer (e.g. *Laptops* to *Restaurants*), where the best BERT and SA-EXAL results are highlighted in bold.

$U^A \in \mathbb{R}^d$ are model parameters, $\cdot$ stands for dot product, d is the hidden vector size and m is the size of the output pattern vocabulary. m is set by taking all the patterns whose frequency in training data (i.e., source domain) is ≥ 3, while mapping other patterns to a fixed UNK symbol.

5 Results and Analysis

Following Pereg et al. (2020), we run each model on 3 random data splits and 3 different random seeds, presenting the mean F1 (and standard deviation) of the 9 runs. Detailed results are shown in Table 4,[7] omitting the UD and PSD formalisms — which perform virtually on par with the other formalisms — for space considerations.[8]

For BERT, training for ASP consistently improves the mean F1 score, by up to 1.3 points (DM), bringing BERT's performance to be on par with the state-of-the-art SA-EXAL model. Improvements over the SA-EXAL baseline is generally smaller, yet some settings improve by 0.5–1 mean F1 points. Best performance is attained using SA-EXAL + PATT with semantic formalisms, indicating that pattern-focused signal is complementary to generic syntax enrichment methods.

Performance Analysis The overlap between model predictions and the deterministic relational pivoting method (§3.3) indicates to what extent the model utilizes relational pivot features. Given model predictions, we define *pivot-*ΔR as the recall improvement a model gains by unifying its true predicted ATs with those of the deterministic method (at $k = 10$).[9] Greater *pivot-*ΔR indicates greater discrepancy from the potential scope of pattern-based coverage, hinting that the model incorporates less relational pivot features. Taking **DM** as the formalism, we find that for the vanilla **BERT** model, average *pivot-*ΔR across 6 domain transfers is **16.5** recall points, with **22.6** for the Laptops to Restaurants transfer (L → R). This implies that relational features have a significant potential for enhancing its cross-domain coverage, especially on L → R, where we indeed observe the most profound model improvements using our relation-focused tasks. In comparison, **BERT + ASP** (DM) has an averaged *pivot-*ΔR of **14**, with **15.7** on L → R (See Appendix E for more details). This drop confirms that the AMTL objective pushes the model to cover more OT-related ATs using relational pivoting.

6 Conclusion

We establish an opinion-based cross-domain AT extraction approach, by analyzing the domain invariance of linguistic OT–AT path pattern. We consequently propose a relation-focused multitask learning method, and demonstrate that it enhances models results by utilizing relational features.

Acknowledgments

The authors would like to thank Intel Emergent AI Lab members and the anonymous reviewers for their valuable comments and feedback.

[7] Our reported baseline figures are slightly different than those reported by Pereg et al. (2020), as we could not fully reproduce their hyperparameter settings, e.g. random seeds. Aiming for a controlled experiment concerning only the AMTL improvements over baselines, we have not optimized the random seeds for any condition.

[8] Results for models trained with both ASP and PATT were also omitted due to their lower performance.

[9] We average this measure as well over the 9 model runs.

References

Łukasz Augustyniak, Tomasz Kajdanowicz, and Przemysław Kazienko. 2019. Comprehensive analysis of aspect term extraction methods using various text embeddings. *arXiv preprint arXiv:1909.04917*.

John Blitzer, Ryan McDonald, and Fernando Pereira. 2006. Domain adaptation with structural correspondence learning. In *Proceedings of the 2006 conference on empirical methods in natural language processing*, pages 120–128.

Wanxiang Che, Longxu Dou, Yang Xu, Yuxuan Wang, Yijia Liu, and Ting Liu. 2019. Hit-scir at mrp 2019: A unified pipeline for meaning representation parsing via efficient training and effective encoding. In *Proceedings of the Shared Task on Cross-Framework Meaning Representation Parsing at the 2019 Conference on Natural Language Learning*, pages 76–85.

Jacob Devlin, Ming-Wei Chang, Kenton Lee, and Kristina Toutanova. 2019. Bert: Pre-training of deep bidirectional transformers for language understanding. In *Proceedings of the 2019 Conference of the North American Chapter of the Association for Computational Linguistics: Human Language Technologies, Volume 1 (Long and Short Papers)*, pages 4171–4186.

Ying Ding, Jianfei Yu, and Jing Jiang. 2017. Recurrent neural networks with auxiliary labels for crossdomain opinion target extraction. In *Association for the Advancement of Artificial Intelligence*, pages 3436––3442.

Minqing Hu and Bing Liu. 2004. Mining opinion features in customer reviews. In *American Association for Artificial Intelligence*.

Xin Li, Lidong Bing, Piji Li, Wai Lam, and Zhimou Yang. 2018. Aspect term extraction with history attention and selective transformation. *CoRR*, abs/1805.00760.

Stephan Oepen, Marco Kuhlmann, Yusuke Miyao, Daniel Zeman, Silvie Cinková, Dan Flickinger, Jan Hajic, and Zdenka Uresova. 2015. Semeval 2015 task 18: Broad-coverage semantic dependency parsing. In *Proceedings of the 9th International Workshop on Semantic Evaluation (SemEval 2015)*, pages 915–926.

Oren Pereg, Daniel Korat, and Moshe Wasserblat. 2020. Syntactically aware cross-domain aspect and opinion terms extraction. In *Proceedings of the 28th International Conference on Computational Linguistics*, pages 1772–1777.

Maria Pontiki, Dimitrios Galanis, Harris Papageorgiou, Ion Androutsopoulos, and Suresh Manandhar. 2014. Semeval-2014 task 4: Aspect based sentiment analysis. In *Proceedings of the 8th International Workshop on Semantic Evaluation (SemEval 2014) at (COLING 2014)*, pages 27–35.

Maria Pontiki, Dimitrios Galanis, Harris Papageorgiou, Suresh Manandhar, and Ion Androutsopoulos. 2015. Semeval-2015 task 12: Aspect based sentiment analysis. In *Proceedings of the 9th international workshop on semantic evaluation (SemEval 2015)*, pages 486–495.

Guang Qiu, Bing Liu, Jiajun Bu, and Chun Chen. 2011. Opinion word expansion and target extraction through double propagation. *Comput. Linguist.*, 37(1):9–27.

Sebastian Schuster and Christopher D Manning. 2016. Enhanced english universal dependencies: An improved representation for natural language understanding tasks. In *Proceedings of the Tenth International Conference on Language Resources and Evaluation (LREC'16)*, pages 2371–2378.

Emma Strubell, Patrick Verga, Daniel Andor, David Weiss, and Andrew McCallum. 2018. Linguistically-informed self-attention for semantic role labeling. In *Proceedings of the 2018 Conference on Empirical Methods in Natural Language Processing*, pages 5027–5038.

Aryeh Tiktinsky, Yoav Goldberg, and Reut Tsarfaty. 2020. pybart: Evidence-based syntactic transformations for ie. *arXiv preprint arXiv:2005.01306*.

Wenya Wang and Sinno Jialin Pan. 2018. Recursive neural structural correspondence network for cross-domain aspect and opinion co-extraction. In *Proceedings of the 56th Annual Meeting of the Association for Computational Linguistics*, pages 1—-11.

Wenya Wang and Sinno Jialin Pan. 2020. Syntactically meaningful and transferable recursive neural networks for aspect and opinion extraction. *Computational Linguistics*, 45(4):705–736.

Wenya Wang, Sinno Jialin Pan, Daniel Dahlmeier, and Xiaokui Xiao. 2016. Recursive neural conditional random fields for aspect-based sentiment analysis. In *Proceedings of the 2016 Conference on Empirical Methods in Natural Language Processing*, pages 616–626.

Appendices

A Cross-domain overlap in path patterns

In Table 5, we present the percentage of target domain path patterns occurring at least once in the source domain. To account for pattern frequency in each domain, we also compute the Jensen-Shannon Distance between pattern probability distributions (Table 6). Overall, DM has the best cross-domain pattern overlap, while the *Devices* and *Laptops* domains are slightly more similar to each other.

	R→L	R→D	L→R	L→D	D→R	D→L
Spacy	89.9	87.4	97.5	96.8	95.3	93
UD	93.4	94	96.7	95.9	95.7	93.1
DM	97.8	97.9	97.9	97	97.3	97.1
PSD	93.8	95.5	95.3	96.8	93.2	90.4

Table 5: Cross-domain pattern overlap — how many AT–OT paths in target domain share a pattern with paths in source domain (percentage).

	R↔L	R↔D	L↔D	Mean
Spacy	0.62	0.60	0.58	0.60
UD	0.60	0.59	0.56	0.58
DM	0.50	0.50	0.50	0.50
PSD	0.60	0.56	0.58	0.58
Mean	0.58	0.56	0.55	0.57

Table 6: Jensen-Shannon Distances between pattern probabilities in different domains. Lower distance indicates similarity between the frequency signature of patterns in a domain pair.

B Deterministic relation pivoting per domain pair

In Section 3.3 we describe a deterministic domain-transfer AT extraction method based on gold opinion terms and top k most frequent OT–AT path patterns in source domain. Results per domain pair are shown in Table 7 for $k = 10$, which approximately optimizes recall-precision trade-off.

Noticeably, the method is less effective for the *Laptops* target domain. This finding aligns with its wider pattern diversity, as mentioned in Section 3.4 and illustrated in Figure 3, but should also be attributed to it having relatively fewer OT–AT pairs that exceed our path-length ≤ 2 criterion. In **DM**, for example, the ratio of the number of selected OT–AT pairs to the total number of aspect terms is **0.93** for *Restaurants*, **0.77** for *Devices*, but only **0.67** for the *Laptops* domain. Altogether, our investigation suggests that the domains vary in linguistic complexity, reflected in richer and longer path patterns for truly corresponding OT–AT pairs in some domains (e.g. *Laptops*) compared to others (e.g. *Restaurants*). Relational pivoting might be more contributive to the latter, as also demonstrated by the multitask experiments (§5).

C Pattern distribution for different linguistic formalisms

As mentioned in Section 3.4, we plot the relative cumulative pattern distribution for each domain and formalism, visualizing the number of different patterns vs. OT–AT pairs coverage (%) (Figure 3).

Referring to differences between linguistic formalisms, we find the cumulative distributions of **DM** and **PSD** more "dense". In **DM**, for example, the most frequent common pattern (simply OT$\xrightarrow{\text{ARG1}}$AT) covers 55% of the paths. This implies that semantic formalisms, designed for abstracting out surface realization details, strengthen the commonalities across different sentences, thus might have greater potential for relational pivoting. This conjecture is also backed by the deterministic pivoting analysis (§3.3). However, we did not find a significant advantage for semantic vs. syntactic formalisms in model experiments (See §5).

D SA-EXAL for semantic graphs

As mentioned in Section 2, the SA-EXAL model augments BERT with a specialized, 13th attention head, incorporating the syntactic parse directly into the model attention mechanism. In the original paper, SA-EXAL was fed with syntactic dependency trees, where each token has a syntactic head token to which it should attend. The learned attention matrix $A \in \mathbb{R}^{n \times n}$ is multiplied element-wise by a matrix representation of the syntactic parse P, where each row is a one-hot vector stating the token to which to attend.

However, semantic dependency formalisms, such as PSD and DM, produce bi-lexical directed acyclic graphs, in which a word can have zero "heads" (for semantically vacuous words, e.g. copular verbs) or multiple "heads" (i.e. outgoing edges). We modify the SA-EXAL model such that instead of one-hot rows, P can have all-one rows (no heads) or multiple-ones rows (multiple heads). Consequently, for tokens with no heads the network is learning the attention without external interference, whereas for tokens with multiple heads, the attention mass is distributed between the heads.

E Correlating pivot-ΔR and model improvement

In Section 5 we define the *pivot-ΔR* measure for model predictions, which quantifies how much can model predictions be improved with pattern-based relational pivoting. We observe that *pivot-ΔR* is higher for the baseline models compared to the corresponding models enhanced by our AMTL objectives (specifically the **Asp** objective). Nonetheless, this reduction in *pivot-ΔR* seem to correlate with model's improvement along the transfer settings. In Figure 4 we illustrate this for the **BERT** and **BERT + ASP** (DM) models. Observed Spearman's ρ over

	R → L	R → D	L → R	L → D	D → R	D → L
Spacy	P: 0.32 R: 0.22 F1: 0.26	P: 0.61 R: 0.29 F1: 0.4	P: 0.49 R: 0.37 F1: 0.42	P: 0.58 R: 0.33 F1: 0.42	P: 0.54 R: 0.37 F1: 0.44	P: 0.3 R: 0.24 F1: 0.27
UD	P: 0.26 R: 0.23 F1: 0.24	P: 0.46 R: 0.29 F1: 0.36	P: 0.44 R: 0.39 F1: 0.41	P: 0.47 R: 0.3 F1: 0.36	P: 0.49 R: 0.37 F1: 0.43	P: 0.26 R: 0.23 F1: 0.24
DM	P: 0.29 R: 0.25 F1: 0.27	P: 0.6 R: 0.34 F1: 0.44	P: 0.52 R: 0.4 F1: 0.45	P: 0.6 R: 0.37 F1: 0.46	P: 0.47 R: 0.39 F1: 0.43	P: 0.26 R: 0.26 F1: 0.26
PSD	P: 0.22 R: 0.26 F1: 0.24	P: 0.41 R: 0.34 F1: 0.37	P: 0.35 R: 0.4 F1: 0.38	P: 0.41 R: 0.35 F1: 0.38	P: 0.3 R: 0.4 F1: 0.34	P: 0.19 R: 0.27 F1: 0.22

Table 7: Results of deterministic relational pivoting per DA settings (K=10).

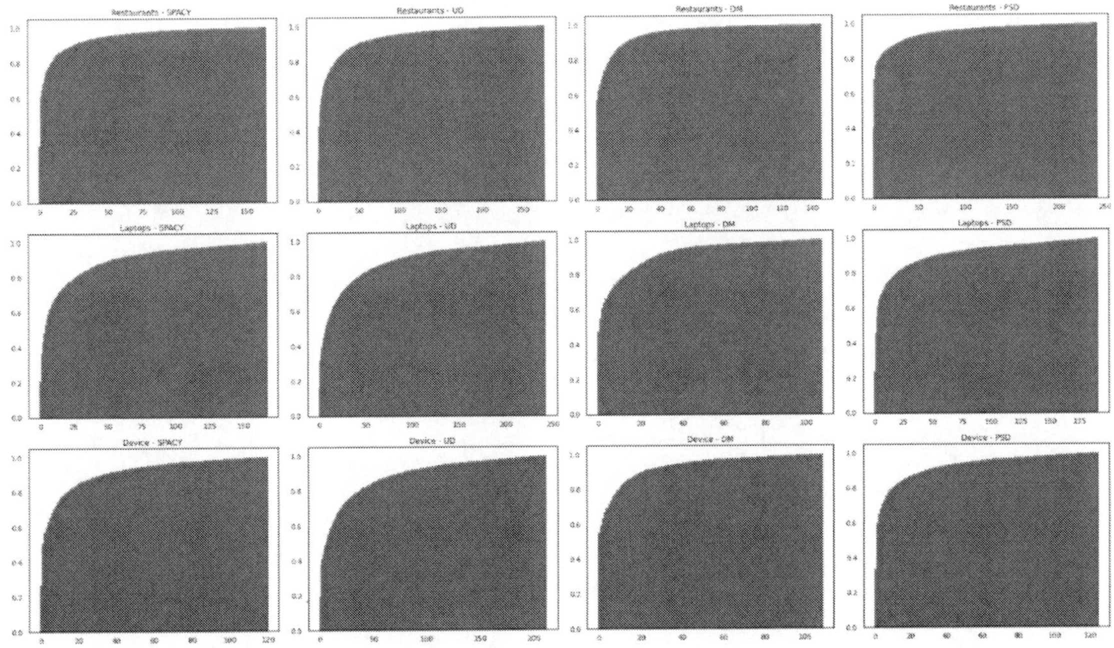

Figure 3: Relative cumulative frequency distributions of path patterns for each domain in all formalisms, showing how many different patterns (X axis) cover what percentage of OT–AT pairs (Y axis).

the 6 transfer settings is 0.83 (though obviously this small sample cannot be tested for statistical significance). This examination of model predictions entails that the improvement we observe in model performance is indeed attributed to instances that exhibit a relation pattern present in the source domain.

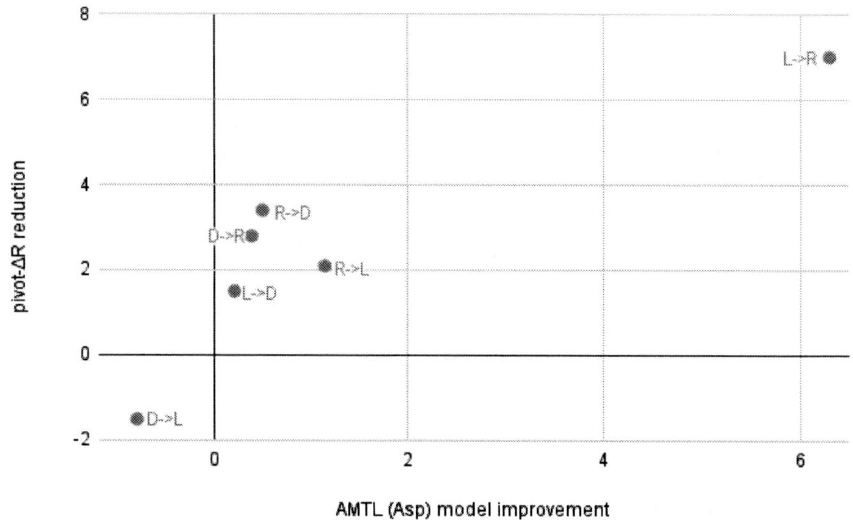

Figure 4: Relation between reduction in *pivot-*ΔR from **BERT** to **BERT + ASP** and the corresponding improvement in model performance. Results are provided for DM dependencies.

English-Malay Word Embeddings Alignment for Cross-lingual Emotion Classification with Hierarchical Attention Network

Lim Ying Hao, Jasy Liew Suet Yan
School of Computer Sciences, Universiti Sains Malaysia
11800 Penang, Malaysia
yinghaoly@student.usm.my, jasyliew@usm.my

Abstract

The main challenge in English-Malay cross-lingual emotion classification is that there are no Malay training emotion corpora. Given that machine translation could fall short in contextually complex tweets, we only limited machine translation to the word level. In this paper, we bridge the language gap between English and Malay through cross-lingual word embeddings constructed using singular value decomposition. We pre-trained our hierarchical attention model using English tweets and fine-tuned it using a set of gold standard Malay tweets. Our model uses significantly less computational resources compared to the language models. Experimental results show that the performance of our model is better than mBERT in zero-shot learning by 2.4% and Malay BERT by 0.8% when a limited number of Malay tweets is available. In exchange for 6 – 7 times less in computational time, our model only lags behind mBERT and XLM-RoBERTa by a margin of 0.9 – 4.3 % in few-shot learning. Also, the word-level attention could be transferred to the Malay tweets accurately using the cross-lingual word embeddings.

1 Introduction

Sentiment analysis and opinion mining are used interchangeably to represent the task of classifying the sentiment polarity of opinionated text (Meng et al., 2012). On a coarse-grained level, the task is often a binary classification problem (positive or negative) (Pang & Lee, 2005). The neutral sentiment in addition to positive and negative could also be taken into consideration, as demonstrated in Salameh et al. (2015). Beyond sentiment polarity, the text could be analysed at a finer-grained level to detect emotions, which is also known as emotion analysis. This could help narrow down the broad concepts of sentiment to better capture a person's emotional state (Ahmad et al., 2020). For instance, while anger and fear express negative sentiments, each semantically represents a different emotional state. Anger is perceived as the possible driving force of collective action, whereas fear is viewed as an action inhibitor (Miller et al., 2009).

Regardless of the level of sentiment analysis, it had only been the privilege of languages with rich resources like English. Most existing studies focusing on resource-rich languages have produced extensively annotated corpora and computational tools exclusive to these languages. However, the advent of cross-lingual sentiment analysis opens up the possibility of performing sentiment analysis on resource-poor languages by leveraging the resources from richer counterparts. With cross-lingual sentiment analysis, resource-poor languages can be endowed with comparable computational ability in identifying sentiments.

Among the seven thousand languages documented across the world, only approximately 30 languages have been equipped with linguistically annotated resources (Eberhard et al., 2021; Maxwell & Hughes, 2006). While Malaysian Malay is not the most spoken language globally, it is a language that is dominantly spoken in Malaysia. Nonetheless, Malay still lacks linguistic resources for sentiment analysis, which poses a challenge in automatically identifying sentiments expressed in Malay texts on a large scale, especially on social media platforms where almost everyone shares their personal and affective experiences. There is a need for sentiment analysis in Malay to more accurately assess individual or public emotions expressed in the local language, particularly during natural disasters, pandemics or political instability in Malaysia.

Proceedings of the 12th Workshop on Computational Approaches to Subjectivity, Sentiment & Social Media Analysis, pages 113 - 124
May 26, 2022 ©2022 Association for Computational Linguistics

To extend the application of sentiment analysis to the Malay language, we explore transfer learning through cross-lingual word embeddings. We also refine the cross-lingual word embeddings to capture the sentiment relationship between two languages. In this study, we use English as the source language and (Malaysian) Malay as the target language. We build a hierarchical attention model that is pre-trained using annotated English tweets and fine-tuned on a small number of Malay tweets using refined cross-lingual word embeddings. By employing such an approach, we show that the word-level attention on English tweets can be transferred to Malay tweets. In other words, if certain English words carry more weight in expressing the underlying emotions of the tweets, the corresponding Malay words sharing similar sentiment meaning would also carry the same amount of emotional weight in Malay tweets.

To the best of our knowledge, there is no gold-standard Malay emotion corpus available for our emotion classification task. The publicly available Malay tweet corpus (Husein, 2018) was previously annotated with emotions using a rule-based classifier. The rule-based classifier that relied on lexicon matching to assign emotions was not able to capture the overall context of the tweets and thus was likely to assign inaccurate emotions. We subset Husein (2018)'s corpus randomly and provide additional validation to create our gold standard Malay emotion corpus. Additionally, we also attempt to recover the truncated part of incomplete tweets to make them contextually complete.

The contributions of this study are three-fold: **a)** We demonstrate the feasibility of training the model using only English tweets to classify emotions from Malay tweets, unlike previous studies, which relied on machine translation to produce parallel training corpora to train hierarchical attention models. **b)** Our results can be used as the benchmark for any future studies as this is the first study to explore cross-lingual emotion classification in the Malay language. **c)** We validate and create a gold standard Malay emotion corpus that can be used to advance future research in the Malay language.

2 Related Work

The main challenge in cross-lingual sentiment analysis is how to bridge the language gap between the source (rich-resourced) and target (low-resourced) languages. The approaches adopted by prior studies had the element of machine translation of varying degrees.

One approach uses direct translation. Wan (2012) translated Chinese reviews into English and classified the translated English reviews using a rule-based classifier or support vector machine. Salameh et al. (2015) translated Arabic social media posts to English using their in-house machine translation system and manual translation. The Arabic-to-English translated posts were then classified automatically and manually.

Another approach tries to project annotations from the source language to the target language. Mihalcea et al. (2007) annotated the English side of the English-Romanian parallel corpus automatically using a rule-based classifier and a Naïve Bayes classifier from OpinionFinder before projecting the annotations to the Romanian-side corpus for training. Balahur and Turchi (2014) translated English sentences into French, German and Spanish, and the English-side annotations were then projected to their corresponding translated sentences to train a classifier respectively.

The third approach uses joint learning. Banea et al. (2010) translated the English corpus into five different languages. They then concatenated monolingual unigram from different languages as the features to train the model. Fuadvy and Ibrahim (2019) created a synthetic multilingual training corpus by combining English movie reviews and corresponding translated Malay movie reviews. They then trained multilingual word embeddings using a blended approach that made differentiating original English and Malay words impossible. Chen et al. (2019) first translated English documents into the target language to obtain paired training documents in the training phase. They embedded every sentence in the documents with trained monolingual sentence representations and concatenated the document representations in both languages to train a classifier subsequently.

The fourth approach uses alignment. Abdalla and Hirst (2017) adopted a simple vector space transformation for which the matrix was obtained using a closed-form solution to linearly map the Spanish/Chinese monolingual word embeddings to the English vector space. These word embeddings were later used to predict the Affective Norms for English Words (ANEW) values of the word and form the sentence arrays of the reviews for sentiment classification. Ahmad et al. (2020) adopted a similar approach but constrained the transformation matrix to be orthogonal. They then pre-trained a model using the English tweets and fine-tuned it using Hindi reviews. Hassan et al. (2021) adopted MUSE (Conneau et al., 2018) to construct English-Arabic and English-Spanish cross-lingual word embeddings. The transformation matrix was first learnt using adversarial training and subsequently refined using a synthetic parallel lexicon built from the shared embeddings space. Farra (2019) constructed cross-lingual word embeddings between English and each of the 17 low-resourced languages using VecMap (Artetxe et al., 2018). The initial bilingual word pairs were constructed without supervision by exploiting similarity matrices of each language. The transformation matrix was then iteratively refined using self-learning until the convergence criterion was met. Nasharuddin et al. (2017) exploited the structural similarity of Wordnet Bahasa and English Wordnet to map synonyms in Malay to the corresponding English counterparts using synset value and POS value. To classify documents, they aggregated the polarity scores of every word in the documents, but the classification was not satisfactory. Zabha et al. (2019) also used a similar approach by considering code-switched tweets containing both English and Malay words and classified the tweets by the sign of the total sentiment score.

The fifth approach uses co-training or its variants. Wan (2009) adopted a co-training approach by translating labelled English and unlabeled Chinese reviews into the other language. Two classifiers were trained on each view of the labelled reviews, and the classifiers were retrained iteratively by augmenting their training corpus with confidently predicted unlabeled reviews. Hajmohammadi (2014) combined self-training and active learning in their study. They first trained a base classifier on English reviews to predict the unlabeled Chinese/French reviews translated to English. The unlabeled reviews predicted with high confidence and human-annotated reviews were then selected to retrain the classifier.

Two studies on the Malay language relied on lexicon-based approaches and reported less than promising results, while the third one relying on bilingual word embeddings was ambiguous. There have also not been any studies on finer-grained sentiment analysis in the Malay language. This study aims to improve cross-lingual sentiment analysis in the Malay language using a better but also less computational expensive approach at a finer-grained level on informal corpora, and our approach is similar to that by Ahmad et al. (2020).

3 Data Sources

3.1 Corpora

English training tweets are a subset of the tweets from the EmoTweet-28 corpus curated by Liew et al. (2016). Only tweets labelled with 'anger', 'fear', 'happiness', 'love', 'none (no emotion)', 'sadness' and 'surprise' were selected to match with the emotion categories available in the Malay evaluation tweets. We included only single-label tweets as the downstream task was framed as a multiclass classification problem. Table 1 shows the emotion class distribution of the English tweets. We converted every word to lowercase, removed any mentions (@username), URLs, and tags (#hashtag), converted emojis to emoticons, expanded contractions, and removed stopwords and tweets with less than three words.

Emotion	Tweet Counts
Anger	944
Fear	178
Happiness	1299
Love	385
None	7562
Sadness	349
Surprise	178

Table 1: Emotion distribution of English training tweets

Malay evaluation tweets are a random subset of the tweets available on Malaya Documentation (Husein, 2018), previously labelled using a rule-based classifier. We hired and trained three native speakers to validate the emotions using majority voting. The Malaya Documentation corpus contains both Malaysian Malay and Indonesian Malay tweets. Therefore, we adopted a hybrid approach (Google's language detector followed by human detection) to remove the Indonesian Malay tweets from our corpus. Table 2 shows the class distribution of the Malay tweets.

Emotion	Tweet Counts
Anger	304
Fear	423
Happiness	117
Love	160
None	257
Sadness	279
Surprise	366

Table 2: Emotion distribution of Malay evaluation tweets

We performed similar pre-processing steps as in the English training tweets. Contractions in Malay were first normalised and then spell-checked according to the context. For example, *msg2*[1] were expanded to *masing-masing* (individually or respectively), and *x* was expanded to *tidak* (no).

We then performed stratified sampling to select 1000 Malay evaluation tweets as the test set (**Malay test set**) and the remaining 843 tweets (after removing tweets shorter than 3 words) as the fine-tuning set (**Malay fine-tuning set**) to fine-tune our model.

3.2 Word Embeddings

Our study used the **English monolingual word embeddings (EWE)** pre-trained on tweets by Godin (2019) using the Skip-gram architecture and contained approximately 3 million words. The words were represented by 400-dimensional vectors.

Malay monolingual word embeddings (MWE) were pre-trained on tweets and Instagram posts by Husein (2018) using Skip-gram architecture and contained approximately 1.3 million words. Normalisation and spell-check were performed to standardise non-standard Malay words in these embeddings. Normalisation ensured that contractions were expanded to the full form (e.g., *x* was expanded to *tidak*). In spell-check, abbreviated words like *nnt,* which remained unchanged after normalisation, would be augmented by adding vowels, producing a list of candidate words like *nenet*, *nanto* and *nanti*. The abbreviated word would be matched to the candidate closest to a legitimate Malay word. For example, *nnt* would be corrected to *nanti* (wait or later), a legitimate Malay word, after the augmentation. This step was essential as it would ensure more word pairs to be used in the subsequent mapping as our bilingual lexicon contained standard words.

We also selected the top 800,000 most frequent words from its training corpora and compared them against the words extracted from selected corpora by *Dewan Bahasa dan Pustaka Malaysia*[2] (DBP) written in standard Malay so that non-(standard) Malay words from the vocabulary could be removed (**F-MWE**). This step minimised concurrent standard and non-standard entries of a word that could create unnecessary noise.

3.3 Bilingual Lexicon

An **English-Malay bilingual lexicon** was obtained from Malaya Documentation (Husein, 2018). Invalid words, non-English words and non-Malay words were filtered out. We randomly selected 90% of these lexicon word pairs for mapping in the training phase (**T-BL**), while the remaining 10% were used to create a set of gold standard test English-Malay word pairs. For every word pair, we retained its English side, for which we then manually extracted its corresponding Malay translations from the English-Malay dictionary by DBP to create a gold standard bilingual lexicon (**G-BL**). G-BL contains 1273 entries of which one English word can have one or many Malay translations from G-BL. G-BL consists of 3675 unique Malay words.

4 Methodology

4.1 Cross-lingual Word Embeddings

To create cross-lingual word embeddings, we mapped the English embeddings, $\boldsymbol{E}$ to the Malay embeddings space using the orthogonal transformations approach proposed by Smith et al. (2017). Malay embeddings were first made to have the same dimensions as English embeddings by post-padding with arrays of zeros. We also normalised both embeddings to a unit length.

From the bilingual lexicons (T-BL) containing n word pairs, two ordered matrices $S_D \in \mathbb{R}^{n\times 400}$ and $T_D \in \mathbb{R}^{n\times 400}$ were formed where i^{th} row of the matrices corresponded to the English and Malay word vectors of the i^{th}word pairs. We then performed Singular Value Decomposition (SVD) operation on the matrix product $P = {S_D}^T T_D \in$

[1] It is common in non-standard Malay to form contraction indicating reduplication using a number suffix based on how many times the word is repeated.

[2] A government body that coordinates the use of the Malay language in Malaysia.

$\mathbb{R}^{400\times400}$ and subsequently, P was represented by $U\sum V^T$. English embeddings, $\boldsymbol{E}$ were then aligned to the Malay embeddings space by multiplying it with the transformation matrix $\boldsymbol{O} = UV^T$ that was subject to the orthogonal constraint:

$$\max_{O} \sum_{i=1}^{n} t_i{}^T \boldsymbol{O} s_i \text{, subject to } \boldsymbol{O}^T\boldsymbol{O} = \boldsymbol{I} \quad (1)$$

4.2 Embeddings Refinement

To refine the cross-lingual word embeddings in Section 4.1, we modified Yuan et al. (2020)'s method by eliminating human intervention in capturing sentiment information. The refinement pulled words similar to the keyword closer and pushed words dissimilar to the keyword apart. We used Extended Affective Norms for English Words (E-ANEW) (Warriner et al., 2013) to determine these sentiment keywords. Words with a valence score of more than 6 (positive sentiment words) or less than 4 (negative sentiment words) were chosen.

For each keyword κ, we collected ten nearest neighbours in English and Malay languages from the cross-lingual word embeddings using cosine similarity. These nearest neighbours were then categorised to either the positive set $\mathcal{P}_\kappa$, if they were part of the WordNet synsets of the keyword or otherwise negative set $\mathcal{N}_\kappa$. To refine the neighbourhood of the keywords, we increased the similarity between the keyword and each positive word in its positive set and decreased the similarity between the keyword and each negative word in its negative set. The embeddings would be updated by minimising the following cost function:

$$C_f(\mathbf{E}) = \sum_{\kappa\in\mathrm{K}}(\sum_{n\in\mathcal{N}_\kappa} \boldsymbol{E}_n^T\boldsymbol{E}_\kappa - \sum_{p\in\mathcal{P}_\kappa} \boldsymbol{E}_p^T\boldsymbol{E}_\kappa) \quad (2)$$

We also preserved the topology of the embeddings by retaining the regularisation term measuring the squared Euclidean distance between the original embeddings and the refined embeddings:

$$R(\mathbf{E}) = \sum_{w\in\mathcal{V}} \parallel \hat{\mathbf{E}}_w - \mathbf{E}_w \parallel_2^2 \quad (3)$$

The final cost function is the combination of $C_f(E)$ and $R(\mathbf{E})$:

$$C(\mathbf{E}) = C_f(\mathbf{E}) + \lambda R(\mathbf{E}) \quad (4)$$

where we set λ to 1 in our study. Without human intervention, the categorisation of the nearest neighbours was definite and entirely dependent on the lemmas in the synsets in which most of the nearest neighbours of the keywords were categorised to the negative set. This implies that lemmas in the synsets that were semantically close to the keywords were located far apart in the embeddings space. Thus, regardless of their distance, we added lemmas that were not part of the nearest neighbours into the positive set such that they would be closer to the keywords after the refinement.

4.3 Emotions Classification Model

To classify emotions, we developed a hierarchical attention model similar to Yang et al. (2016) in which only the attention at the sentence level was swapped with a multi-head self-attention mechanism. We also experimented with swapping the original attention with a multi-head self-attention mechanism at only the word level and both word level and sentence level, but both degraded the performance significantly. The model can be divided into four main layers: the input layer, the word-level layer, the sentence-level layer and the output layer.

Input layer: For each tweet, $\boldsymbol{x}$, it contains S sentences s_i and each sentence contains W words.

Word-level layers: i) **Word encoder**: We use a BiLSTM to get the contextual information of the words from both directions. We encode the word by concatenating the hidden states from both directions. ii) **Word hidden layer**: We apply another hidden layer to encode the word annotations further to capture any complex relationship between words. iii) **Word attention**: The attention mechanism introduced by Bahdanau et al. (2016) is used to capture the weights of the words in expressing the underlying emotion in a sentence. A detailed description of the attention mechanism and how it is used to form representations can be found in Yang et al. (2016).

Sentence-level layers: i) **Sentence encoder:** We also use a BiLSTM to obtain the sentence contextual information from both directions. Similarly, we encode the sentence by concatenating the hidden states from both directions. ii) **Sentence hidden layer**: We use another hidden layer of size (64×1), the multiplier of the number of heads, to encode the sentence annotations further to capture any complex relationship between sentences. iii) **Sentence attention:** We swapped Bahdanau (2016)'s attention mechanisms originally used in Yang et al. (2016) with a one-head scaled dot-product attention mechanism (Vaswani et al., 2017). We set the dimension of the queries, keys and values in the attention mechanism to have the same values in this study. The encoded sentence annotations are used as the query vectors, key vectors and value vectors. To obtain the tweet representation, we apply a global max-pooling operation on the output.

Output layer: The tweet representation with dropout is then sent to the output layer. We use a hidden layer of 7 neurons to match the number of emotion classes.

4.4 Model Implementation

We performed hyperparameter tuning, pre-training, fine-tuning and evaluation for our model on Google TPU using TensorFlow 2.5.0 with Python3.

Hyperparameter tuning: The hyperparameters of the model were tuned solely on English training tweets using grid search with 5-fold cross-validation. The hyperparameters and their search space are listed in Appendix A. The optimal values are as follows: the hidden unit in the word-level hidden layer = 200, the hidden unit in the sentence-level hidden layer = 64, alphas of all Leaky ReLU functions = 0.3, dropout rate = 0.2, initial learning rate = 7e-3, epoch = 30 and batch size = 500.

Pre-training: We set the dimension for a unidirectional LSTM at both word level and sentence level to 200 dimensions and the context vectors required in the word attention to 400 dimensions. All intermediate layers were activated using Leaky ReLU. We pre-trained our model on English training tweets with frozen refined cross-lingual English embeddings, AdamW optimiser with a warm-up proportion of 0.1 and sparse categorical cross-entropy as the loss function.

Fine-tuning: All layers in the model underwent the fine-tuning process. Using the Malay fine-tuning set with our refined cross-lingual Malay embeddings, we fine-tuned our model for another 30 epochs with a default batch size of 32. The other hyperparameters and loss function remained unchanged as they were in pre-training. The optimiser's step_per_epoch was also changed accordingly.

5 Experiment Results

5.1 Bilingual Lexicon Induction

We used bilingual lexicon induction to evaluate the quality of our embeddings mapping by finding the top-10 most semantically similar Malay words to the English words in G-BL using cosine similarity from the shared vector space (P@10). P@10 measures the proportion of English words in G-BL, obtaining at least one correct translation among the 10 induced Malay translations for each English word in the G-BL. We used a more lenient measure as, unlike other studies which had embeddings trained on formal corpora, our embeddings were trained on notoriously noisy corpora. We also used this method to justify selecting the most frequent words in the embeddings' vocabulary. The results of the induction are shown in Table 3.

Embeddings	P@10
MWE	22.2041% (274/1234)
F-MWE	24.9167% (299/1200)

Table 3: Mapping quality between MWE and F-MWE using T-BL

Although we fixed the number of word pairs in the G-BL, F-MWE has a smaller vocabulary size and hence a different number of effective word pairs for evaluation as reflected in the denominator in P@10. The improvement in the mapping quality when using F-MWE was attributed to the reduced noise in the cross-lingual embeddings space since we had removed numerous non-(standard) Malay words from F-MWE. In other words, the English words were not obscured by irrelevant 'Malay' neighbours and could induce the correct Malay translations more easily. Although using F-MWE would not directly affect the downstream classification performance, the loading of the word embeddings was more efficient in terms of time and computational power as a large number of non-(standard) Malay words have been discarded.

Embeddings	P@10
MWE	24.8784% (307/1234)
F-MWE	27.3333% (328/1200)

Table 4: Mapping quality between MWE and F-MWE using N-BL

We also investigated the quality of T-BL by translating the English-side words in T-BL to Malay using Google Cloud Translation API, resulting in a new set of bilingual word pairs (**N-BL**). The results are presented in Table 4. We observed that each embedding mapping was improved approximately by about 2.5%, and this suggests that there is still room for improvement for the quality of T-BL. It is possible that the words in T-BL were paired up imprecisely. F-MWE also achieved better mapping quality than MWE, even when using N-BL. This again emphasises the importance of our filter when the embeddings were pre-trained on tweets or noisy corpora. Essentially, the embedding vectors remain unchanged for the Malay words but are significantly smaller in size.

Next, we attempted to augment N-BL using the nearest neighbours (NN) of English words in N-BL by using cosine similarity. However, realising some of the English NN were noise, we filtered out those not in Words Corpus by Natural Language Processing Toolkit (NLTK). The remaining neighbours were then translated to Malay using Google Cloud Translation API. The results of the augmentation using F-MWE are given in Table 5.

Augmentation Strategy	P@10
N-BL	27.3333% (328/1200)
N-BL + 1NN	29.6667% (356/1200)
N-BL + 5NN	32.7500% (393/1200)
N-BL + 10NN	31.8333% (382/1200)

Table 5: Mapping quality when augmenting N-BL by 1NN, 5NN and 10NN

We observed that augmentation generally led to better mapping quality as the larger set of training bilingual word pairs could cover more English/Malay words in the induction of the transformation matrix. It increased P@10 by a minimum of 2%. However, we acknowledged that having an enormous training set was not desirable, such as in the case of N-BL+10NN. It took us significantly longer than N-BL+5NN to perform the embeddings mapping, yet the performance degraded. From the results in Table 5, we decided to proceed with augmentation using 5-nearest neighbours as it yielded the best balance between translation time, training time and mapping quality in our experiment. The cross-lingual English and Malay embeddings created using EWE and F-MWE and mapped on N-BL+5NN were then used for the downstream emotion classification task.

5.2 Emotion Classification Model

We compare the performance of our model with other baselines, including a multilayer perceptron (MLP), hierarchical attention model (HAN) proposed by Yang et al. (2016), mBERT by Pires et al. (2019) and XLM-R by Conneau et al. (2020) and Malay BERT by Husein (2018).

MLP: We use a neural network of two layers. The hidden layer of 200 hidden units is activated using the Leaky-ReLU function with a default alpha value. The output layer has a Softmax activation function. The tweet representation is obtained using global average pooling. We pre-train this network using Adam optimiser with its default learning rate for 30 epochs and batch size of 500 on English training tweets. Every layer is fined-tuned on Malay fine-tuning set for another 30 epochs of batch size 32 in few shot-learning.

HAN: We modify the hierarchical attention network proposed by Yang et al. (2016) but use BiLSTM instead of BiGRU to encode tweets. Unidirectional LSTM is set to 200 dimensions. The following intermediate layers of 200 hidden units and the output layer have Leaky ReLU and Softmax with default parameters as the activation functions, respectively. The pre-training of this model in zero-shot learning and fine-tuning in few-shot learning are identical to MLP.

mBERT: We adopt the pre-trained mBERT by Pires et al. (2019) and attach an additional output layer having a SoftMax of default parameters as the activation function. The 'pooled output' representation with a dropout rate of 0.2 is fed to the output layer for classification. This model is fine-tuned using an AdamW optimiser with an initial learning rate of 3e-5 and a warm-up proportion of 0.1 for 30 epochs and a batch size of 32 on English training tweets in zero-shot learning. It is further fine-tuned on the Malay fine-tuning set using the fine-tuning setting applied to our model in few-shot learning.

XLM-R: We adopt the pre-trained XLM-RoBERTa by Conneau et al. (2020) and attach an additional output layer having a SoftMax of default parameters as the activation function. The input to the output layer and the fine-tuning processes are identical to that of mBERT in both zero-shot and few-shot learning.

Malay BERT: We adopt the monolingual tiny-BERT pre-trained by Husein (2018) and attach an additional output layer having a Softmax of default parameters as the activation function. The input to the output layer is identical to mBERT but we fine-tune the model using the Malay fine-tuning set and the settings applied to our model.

HMAN: Hierarchical multi-head attention model described in Section 4.3. The architectural difference between HAN and HMAN is that we swapped the sentence-level attention with scaled dot-product attention.

Model	Macro F1-score
MLP	0.0469
HAN	0.2890
mBERT	0.2162
XLM-R-base	0.5193
HMAN	0.2403

Table 6: Cross-lingual emotion prediction of our model and the comparison with the baselines in zero-shot learning.

Table 6 shows the performance comparison of our methods with the four baselines on zero-shot learning on the Malay test set. Although XLM-R-base yielded the best performance in zero-shot learning, our HMAN model slightly outperforms mBERT by 2.4% even when it was not exposed to the Malay language during pre-training and is significantly less computationally expensive compared to the multilingual pre-trained language models. We also experimented with more heads for sentence attention, but the model did not have significant improvement. Even though our experiment is simpler and on a different task, the results agree with that by Michel et al. (2019), claiming that most of the heads in multi-head attention are redundant in machine translation.

Model	Macro F1-score
MLP	0.7277
HAN	0.8104
mBERT	0.8925
XLM-R-base	0.9262
Malay BERT	0.8760
HMAN	0.8836

Table 7: Cross-lingual emotion prediction of our model and the comparison with selected baselines in few-shot learning.

In Table 7, we demonstrate the capability of our model after fine-tuning the model. While HAN yielded better performance on zero-shot transfer, our HMAN model outperforms it by 7.3% and is more effective after both models underwent the same fine-tuning process. HMAN's performance is at par with mBERT and is better than the monolingual Malay BERT without using considerable computational power. It is also worth mentioning that our model only falls behind XLM-R-base by 4.3 % in exchange for 6 – 7 times[3] increase in the computational speed. In fact, our model remains feasible on the CPU and can run in approximately one hour, while fine-tuning the multilingual language model takes days using the current batch size (32) and is unachievable if using the batch size (500) in our model. The fine-tuning helps in this task because it exposes our model to how a complete Malay tweet can be formed from words and sentences.

Fine-tuning Layers	Macro F1-score
Only output	0.3648
Sentence-level + Output	0.5762
All layers	0.8836

Table 8: Performance of our model HMAN on different fine-tuning layers

The performance of only fine-tuning the output layer of our model aligns with our prior expectations. As seen in Table 8, the macro F1-score drops drastically as the model does not have knowledge of how Malay words and sentences can be joined to form tweets. We also attempted to freeze only the word-level layers during fine-tuning, but the performance of the model degraded by about 30.74%. We attribute this degradation to the inability of the model in learning how Malay words are used to form sentences.

Setting	Macro F1-score	
	Zero-shot	Few-shot
With alignment	0.2403	0.8836
Without alignment	0.1379	0.8693

Table 9: Performance of our model HMAN with and without alignment in zero and few-shot learning

Table 9 compares the performance of our model with and without the word alignment. In without alignment, the monolingual English and Malay embeddings were merely combined into a single vector space without performing any English-Malay word mapping. The model degraded in both zero-shot and few-shot scenarios as expected. While it is not significant in few-shot learning, the model did not perform satisfactorily in the zero-shot scenario. Therefore, the word alignment still plays a vital role.

5.3 Words Attention Visualisation

To inspect how our model captures the attention of Malay words, we select two Malay tweets from the test set and visualise their attention scores using heatmaps in Figure 1. A darker shade indicates the

[3] Comparison was made on TPU using the same batch size in our model.

words receive higher attention scores, while words with a lighter shade receive lower attention scores.

We show two tweets with emotions of opposite sentiments. The tweets appear to be incomplete as we had removed stopwords in pre-processing steps. Our model can accurately place attention on the important Malay sentiment words after fine-tuning using the cross-lingual Malay embeddings.

padan muka pemaju tamak! rumah mahal gila. tunjuk dah bunda rasa mustahil, mudah

(a)

alhamdulillah tahniah selamat pengantin baru sahabat, semoga berbahagia. tengkera

(b)

Figure 1: Malay tweet examples with correctly predicted anger (a) and happiness (b)

In Figure 1(a), the tweeter is expressing anger at the greedy (property) developer who sells crazily expensive houses. Our model successfully places more attention on the sentiment words, *padan muka* (serve you right), *tamak* (greedy) and *gila* (crazily). *Mudah* (easy) has a darker colour here because it is treated as a sentence of only one word in our sentence tokenisation process and thus, receives all the attention score.

In Figure 1(b), the tweeter is expressing happiness and congratulating someone for getting married. The words *tahniah* (congratulation), *semoga* (wish) and the phrase *selamat pengantin baru* (happy newlyweds) were given attention correctly in the context of this tweet.

6 Conclusion and Future Work

We evaluated the quality of the existing set of Malay-English bilingual word pairs as part of the experiments in this paper and discovered that its quality could be further improved. Apart from this, we demonstrated that Malay words could benefit from their semantically and sentimentally similar English counterparts through refined cross-lingual word embeddings that were mapped using our bilingual lexicon after fine-tuning. Most importantly, our model is better than monolingual Malay BERT and at par with mBERT but utilises significantly less computational power. Even though XLM-R-base shows slightly better performance than our model by 4.3% in few-shot learning, our model is still competitive as the amount of finetuning and computational time can be reduced by 6 – 7 times. This provides us with a more cost-effective alternative to predict emotions in Malay tweets on a large scale more efficiently and possibly generalise to other languages with limited training corpora.

Unlike English, Malay remains a low-resource language with no standard Malay emotion corpus. Thus, we could not evaluate our model on other test sets to obtain a more unbiased judgement. Our Malay emotion corpus may contain some bias as the emotion labels were verified from the Malaya Documentation corpus as part of our effort to build upon existing language resources, and not annotated from scratch. Nonetheless, we hope our study can serve as the benchmark for future research, especially in English-Malay cross-lingual emotion classification using a higher quality gold-standard Malay emotion corpus we have created. Our Malay emotion corpus can be expanded in the future to include more emotion annotations. As we only performed word-level mapping and refinement, we would like to explore sentence-level mapping and refinement in future work to investigate if this will lead to further improvement. Also, we would like to evaluate our model on standard Malay emotion corpora to compare the performance of our model in formal and informal use of the Malay language.

In the future, we also plan to explore semi-supervised and unsupervised approaches such as MUSE and VecMap in creating cross-lingual word embeddings. These approaches have shown to be promising for other language pairs. Therefore, it is a possible direction to explore in building more computationally efficient cross-lingual models particularly for English-Malay that can compete with or even outperform multilingual language models.

Acknowledgement

This study was funded by "Ministry of Higher Education Malaysia for Fundamental Research Grant Scheme with Project Code: FRGS/1/2020/ICT02/USM/02/3". We would also like to thank the annotators, Siti Sakinah Ahmad Sanusi, Aqilah Syahirah Shahabudin and Nur Alya Mazlan, native speakers who helped us with the Malay corpus annotation and verification.

References

Abdalla Mohamed, and Graeme Hirst. 2017. "Cross-Lingual Sentiment Analysis without (Good)

Translation." Pp. 506–15 in Proceedings of the Eighth International Joint Conference on Natural Language Processing (Volume 1: Long Papers). Taipei, Taiwan: Asian Federation of Natural Language Processing.

Ahmad Zishan, Raghav Jindal, Asif Ekbal and Pushpak Bhattachharyya. 2020. "Borrow from Rich Cousin: Transfer Learning for Emotion Detection Using Cross Lingual Embedding." Expert Systems with Applications 139:112851.

Artetxe, M., Labaka, G., & Agirre, E. (2018). A Robust Self-Learning Method For Fully Unsupervised Cross-Lingual Mappings Of Word Embeddings. Proceedings of the 56th Annual Meeting of the Association for Computational Linguistics (Volume 1: Long Papers), 789–798.

Bahdanau Dzmitry, Kyunghyun Cho, and Yoshua Bengio. 2016. "Neural Machine Translation by Jointly Learning to Align and Translate." ArXiv:1409.0473 [Cs, Stat].

Balahur Alexandra, and Marco Turchi. 2014. "Comparative Experiments Using Supervised Learning and Machine Translation for Multilingual Sentiment Analysis." Computer Speech & Language 28(1):56–75.

Banea Carmen, Rada Mihalcea, and Janyce Wiebe. 2010. "Multilingual Subjectivity: Are More Languages Better?" Pp. 28–36 in Proceedings of the 23rd International Conference on Computational Linguistics (Coling 2010). Beijing, China: Coling 2010 Organizing Committee.

Chen Zhenpeng, Sheng Shen, Ziniu Hu, Xuan Lu, Qiaozhu Mei, and Xuanzhe Liu. 2019. "Emoji-Powered Representation Learning for Cross-Lingual Sentiment Classification." Pp. 251–62 in The World Wide Web Conference on - WWW '19. San Francisco, CA, USA: ACM Press.

Conneau Alexis, Khandelwal Kartikay, Goyal Naman, Chaudhary Vishrav, Wenzek Guillaume, Guzmán Francisco, Grave Edouard, Ott Myle, Zettlemoyer Luke and Stoyanov Veselin. 2020. Unsupervised Cross-lingual Representation Learning at Scale. Proceedings of the 58th Annual Meeting of the Association for Computational Linguistics, 8440–8451.

Conneau, A., Lample, G., Ranzato, M., Denoyer, L., & Jégou, H. (2018). Word Translation Without Parallel Data. ArXiv:1710.04087 [Cs].

Eberhard, M. David, F. Simons Gary, and D. Fennig Charles. 2021. Ethnologue: Languages of the World. 24th ed. Dallas: SIL International.

Farra, N. (2019). Cross-Lingual And Low-Resource Sentiment Analysis. [Doctoral Dissertation]. Columbia University.

Fuadvy Muhammad Jauharul., and Roliana Ibrahim. 2019. "Multilingual Sentiment Analysis on Social Media Disaster Data." Pp. 269–72 in 2019 International Conference on Electrical, Electronics and Information Engineering (ICEEIE). Vol. 6.

Godin, Fréderic. 2019. "Improving and Interpreting Neural Networks for Word-Level Prediction Tasks in Natural Language Processing." Ghent University, Belgium.

Hajmohammadi Mohammad Sadegh, Roliana Ibrahim, and Ali Selamat. 2014. "Density Based Active Self-Training for Cross-Lingual Sentiment Classification." Pp. 1053–59 in Advances in Computer Science and its Applications. Vol. 279, Lecture Notes in Electrical Engineering, edited by H. Y. Jeong, M. S. Obaidat, N. Y. Yen, and J. J. Park. Berlin, Heidelberg: Springer Berlin Heidelberg.

Hassan, S., Shaar, S., & Darwish, K. (2021). Cross-Lingual Emotion Detection. ArXiv:2106.06017 [Cs].

Husein Zolkepli. 2018. "Malaya, Natural-Language-Toolkit Library for Bahasa Malaysia, Powered by Deep Learning Tensorflow." Malaya.

Liew Jasy Suet Yan, Howard R. Turtle and Elizabeth D. Liddy. 2016. "EmoTweet-28: A Fine-Grained Emotion Corpus for Sentiment Analysis." Pp. 1149–56 in Proceedings of the Tenth International Conference on Language Resources and Evaluation (LREC'16). Portorož, Slovenia: European Language Resources Association (ELRA).

Maxwell Mike and Baden Hughes. 2006. "Frontiers in Linguistic Annotation for Lower-Density Languages." Pp. 29–37 in Proceedings of the Workshop on Frontiers in Linguistically Annotated Corpora 2006 - LAC '06. Sydney, Australia: Association for Computational Linguistics.

Meng Xinfan, Furu Wei, Xiaohua Liu, Ming Zhou, Ge Xu and Houfeng Wang. 2012. "Cross-Lingual Mixture Model for Sentiment Classification." Pp. 572–81 in Proceedings of the 50th Annual Meeting of the Association for Computational Linguistics (Volume 1: Long Papers). Jeju Island, Korea: Association for Computational Linguistics.

Michel Paul, Omer Levy and Graham Neubig. 2019. "Are Sixteen Heads Really Better than One?" in Advances in Neural Information Processing Systems. Vol. 32. Curran Associates, Inc.

Mihalcea Rada, Carmen Banea, and Janyce Wiebe. 2007. "Learning Multilingual Subjective Language via Cross-Lingual Projections." Pp. 976–83 in Proceedings of the 45th Annual Meeting of the Association of Computational Linguistics. Prague, Czech Republic: Association for Computational Linguistics.

Miller Daniel A., Tracey Cronin, Amber L. Garcia and Nyla R. Branscombe. 2009. "The Relative Impact of Anger and Efficacy on Collective Action Is Affected by Feelings of Fear." Group Processes & Intergroup Relations 12(4):445–62.

Nasharuddin Nurul Amelina, Muhamad Taufik Abdullah, Azreen Azman and Rabiah Abdul Kadir. 2017. "English and Malay Cross-Lingual Sentiment Lexicon Acquisition and Analysis." Pp. 467–75 in Information Science and Applications 2017. Vol. 424, Lecture Notes in Electrical Engineering, edited by K. Kim and N. Joukov. Singapore: Springer Singapore.

Pang Bo and Lillian Lee. 2005. "Seeing Stars: Exploiting Class Relationships for Sentiment Categorization with Respect to Rating Scales." Pp. 115–24 in Proceedings of the 43rd Annual Meeting of the Association for Computational Linguistics (ACL'05). Ann Arbor, Michigan: Association for Computational Linguistics.

Pires Telmo, Schlinger Eva and Garrette, Dan. 2019. How Multilingual is Multilingual BERT? Proceedings of the 57th Annual Meeting of the Association for Computational Linguistics, 4996–5001.

Salameh Mohammad, Saif Mohammad and Svetlana Kiritchenko. 2015. "Sentiment after Translation: A Case-Study on Arabic Social Media Posts." Pp. 767–77 in Proceedings of the 2015 Conference of the North American Chapter of the Association for Computational Linguistics: Human Language Technologies. Denver, Colorado: Association for Computational Linguistics.

Smith Samuel L., David H. P. Turban, Steven Hamblin, and Nils Y. Hammerla. 2017. "Offline Bilingual Word Vectors, Orthogonal Transformations and the Inverted Softmax." ArXiv:1702.03859 [Cs].

Vaswani Ashish, Noam Shazeer, Niki Parmar, Jakob Uszkoreit, Llion Jones, Aidan N. Gomez, Lukasz Kaiser and Illia Polosukhin. 2017. "Attention Is All You Need." in Advances in Neural Information Processing Systems. Vol. 30. Curran Associates, Inc.

Wan Xiaojun. 2009. "Co-Training for Cross-Lingual Sentiment Classification." Pp. 235–43 in Proceedings of the Joint Conference of the 47th Annual Meeting of the ACL and the 4th International Joint Conference on Natural Language Processing of the AFNLP. Suntec, Singapore: Association for Computational Linguistics.

Wan Xiaojun. 2012. "A Comparative Study of Cross-Lingual Sentiment Classification." Pp. 24–31 in 2012 IEEE/WIC/ACM International Conferences on Web Intelligence and Intelligent Agent Technology. Vol. 1.

Warriner Amy Beth, Victor Kuperman and Marc Brysbaert. 2013. "Norms of Valence, Arousal, and Dominance for 13,915 English Lemmas." Behavior Research Methods 45(4):1191–1207.

Yang Zichao, Diyi Yang, Chris Dyer, Xiaodong He, Alex Smola, and Eduard Hovy. 2016. "Hierarchical Attention Networks for Document Classification." Pp. 1480–89 in Proceedings of the 2016 Conference of the North American Chapter of the Association for Computational Linguistics: Human Language Technologies. San Diego, California: Association for Computational Linguistics.

Yuan Michelle, Mozhi Zhang, Benjamin Van Durme, Leah Findlater and Jordan Boyd-Graber. 2020. "Interactive Refinement of Cross-Lingual Word Embeddings." Pp. 5984–96 in Proceedings of the 2020 Conference on Empirical Methods in Natural Language Processing (EMNLP). Online: Association for Computational Linguistics.

Zabha Nur Imanina, Zakiah Ayop, Syarulnaziah Anawar, Erman Hamid and Zaheera Zainal. 2019. "Developing Cross-Lingual Sentiment Analysis of Malay Twitter Data Using Lexicon-Based Approach." International Journal of Advanced Computer Science and Applications 10(1).

A. Appendix A: Hyperparameter Search Space

Some hyperparameters would be fixed throughout the experiments, such as the number of units in the unidirectional word-level/sentence-level LSTM layer and the number of heads in the sentence self-attention. The search space of the hyperparameters is as below:

Hyperparameters	**Search Space**
Number of Units in Word Hidden Layer	[100,200,300,400,500,600,700,800,900,1000]
Alpha for Word-level Leaky ReLU	[0.01,0.02,0.03,0.04,0.05, 0.3, 0.4, 0.5]
Number of Units in Sentence Hidden Layer	64
Alpha for Sentence-level Leaky ReLU	[0.01,0.02,0.03,0.04,0.05, 0.3, 0.4, 0.5]
Dropout Rate before Output Layer	[0.1,0.2,0.3,0.4,0.5]
Initial Learning Rate of AdamW Optimizer	[0.001,0.002,0.003,0.004,0.005,0.006,0.007,0.008,0.009]
Epoch	[10,20,30,40]
Batch Size	[500,600,700,800,900,1000]

Assessment of Massively Multilingual Sentiment Classifiers

Krzysztof Rajda[1,2], **Łukasz Augustyniak**[1,2],
Piotr Gramacki[2], **Marcin Gruza**[1,2], **Szymon Woźniak**[2]
Tomasz Kajdanowicz[1]
[1]Department of Artificial Intelligence,
Wrocław University of Science and Technology
[2]Brand24 AI
{krzysztof.rajda,lukasz.augustyniak}@pwr.edu.pl
{piotr.gramacki,marcin.gruza,szymon.wozniak}@brand24.com

Abstract

Models are increasing in size and complexity in the hunt for SOTA. But what if those 2% increase in performance does not make a difference in a production use case? Maybe benefits from a smaller, faster model outweigh those slight performance gains. Also, equally good performance across languages in multilingual tasks is more important than SOTA results on a single one. We present the biggest, unified, multilingual collection of sentiment analysis datasets. We use these to assess 11 models and 80 high-quality sentiment datasets (out of 342 raw datasets collected) in 27 languages and included results on the internally annotated datasets. We deeply evaluate multiple setups, including fine-tuning transformer-based models for measuring performance. We compare results in numerous dimensions addressing the imbalance in both languages coverage and dataset sizes. Finally, we present some best practices for working with such a massive collection of datasets and models from a multilingual perspective.

1 Introduction

Multilingual text representations are becoming increasingly important in science as well as the business community. However how universal and versatile they truly are? Can we use them to train one, multilingual, production-ready sentiment classifier? To verify this research question, we gathered a massive collection of sentiment analysis datasets and evaluated 11 different models on them. We want to assess the performance of fine-tuning languages models as well as language models as feature extractors for simpler, even linear models.

Sentiment analysis is subjective and both domain and language-dependent, hence there is an even greater need to understand the behaviour and performance of the multilingual setup. We focused on multilingual sentiment classification because our business use cases involve the analysis of texts in multiple languages across the world. Moreover, one universal model in a production environment is much easier to deploy, maintain, monitor, remove biases or improve the model's fairness - especially in cases when the load differs between languages and could change over time. We want to compare state-of-the-art multilingual embedding methods and select the ones with the best performance across languages.

The main objective of this article is to answer the following Research Questions: (RQ1) Are we able to create a single multilingual sentiment classifier, that performs equally well for each language? (RQ2) Does fine-tuning of transformer-based models significantly improve sentiment classification results? (RQ3) What is the relationship between model size and performance? Is bigger always better?

Our main contribution includes 3 main points. Firstly, we perform a large scoping review of published sentiment datasets. Using a set of rigid inclusion and exclusion criteria, we filter the initial pool of 342 datasets down to 80 high-quality datasets representing 27 languages. Secondly, we evaluated how universal and versatile multilingual text representations are for the sentiment classification problem. Finally, we compared many deep learning-based approaches with fine-tuning and without it for multilingual sentiment classification.

The remainder of this paper is organized as follows: Section 2 presents a literature review on the topic of multilingual sentiment analysis; Section 3 describes the language models, datasets, and our evaluation methodology; Section 4 describes the conducted experiments and summarizes the results; Section 5 discusses the results in terms of research questions; Section 6 presents conclusions and describes further works.

Proceedings of the 12th Workshop on Computational Approaches to Subjectivity, Sentiment & Social Media Analysis, pages 125 - 140
May 26, 2022 ©2022 Association for Computational Linguistics

2 Related Work

Multilingual Text Representations. Initially, multilingual text representations were obtained using multilingual word embeddings (Ruder et al., 2019). These were created using various training techniques, parallel corpora, and dictionaries, for example by aligning the monolingual Word2Vec (Mikolov et al., 2013a) vector spaces with linear transformations using small parallel dictionaries (Mikolov et al., 2013b). To better represent longer texts, modern approaches use more complex contextual language models like BiLSTM (Artetxe and Schwenk, 2019) and Transformers (Feng et al., 2020; Conneau et al., 2020; Devlin et al., 2019; Xue et al., 2021; Yang et al., 2020). Their multilingual capabilities result from pretraining on multilingual objective tasks like machine translation (Artetxe and Schwenk, 2019), translation language modelling (TLM) (Conneau et al., 2020; Conneau and Lample, 2019) or translation ranking (Feng et al., 2020; Yang et al., 2019). Details of the models used in our experiments are described in Section 3.1.

The quality of multilingual text representations is usually evaluated with cross- and multilingual tasks like cross-lingual natural language inference (Conneau et al., 2018), question answering (Lewis et al., 2020), named entity recognition (Tjong Kim Sang, 2002; Tjong Kim Sang and De Meulder, 2003) or parallel text extraction (Zweigenbaum et al., 2017; Ziemski et al., 2016). Another important benchmark is XTREME (Hu et al., 2020), which is designed for testing the abilities of cross-lingual transfer across 40 languages and 9 tasks. Despite its massive character, XTREME lacks benchmarking task of sentiment analysis, also only mBERT, XLM, XLM-R, and MMTE are used as baseline models. We try to fill this gap with our work.

K et al. (2020) performed extensive research on the cross-lingual ability of mBERT. Wu and Dredze (2020) compared mBERT with monolingual models and found that it under-performs on low-resource languages. Liu et al. (2020) analyzed a cross-lingual ability of mBERT considering a contextual aspect of mBERT and dataset size. There is a significant lack of detailed analysis of characteristics of other language models, despite mBERT.

Multilingual Sentiment Analysis. In literature, there are several examples of reviews, which focus on *traditional* sentiment analysis methods (e.g., lexicon-based, lexical features engineering, shallow models), while not mentioning any embedding-based methods (Dashtipour et al., 2016; Sagnika et al., 2020). They are a valuable source of information about sentiment datasets. However, modern NLP applications often utilize deep learning techniques, which were not covered there. An example of a deep learning-based approach was presented by Attia et al. (2018), who trained a convolutional neural network (CNN) on word-level embeddings of texts in English, German and Arabic, a separate model for each language. This approach requires many resources and computations as one has to create a separate embedding dictionary for each language. An alternative approach is to use character-level embeddings. Wehrmann et al. (2017) trained such a model to classify tweets written in English, German, Portuguese, and Spanish as either positive or negative. This approach requires fewer parameters than word embedding models.

Newer approaches to multilingual sentiment analysis use deep models and machine translation e.g. Can et al. (2018) trained a Recurrent Neural Network (RNN) on English reviews and evaluated it on machine-translated reviews in Russian, Spanish, Turkish and Dutch. They used the Google Translation API and pre-trained GloVe embeddings for English. Kanclerz et al. (2020) used LASER sentence embeddings to learn a sentiment classifier on Polish reviews and used this classifier to predict sentiment on reviews translated into other languages. As we can see most of the research covers only a couple of languages for sentiment analysis. Hence, we decided to gather a massive collection of 342 datasets in 27 languages.

3 Evaluation Methodology

We conducted several experiments to answer if there is a truly universal multilingual text representation model (Table 1). We tested their performance based on the largest sentiment analysis dataset in the literature.

3.1 Multilingual Language Models

We used multiple language models as text representation methods (Table 1). We aimed to select models varied in terms of architecture, size, and type of data used in pre-training. We selected two models which do not use transformer architecture (CNN and BiLSTM) as a baseline. We also used models, based on multiple different transformer architec-

Table 1: Models used in experiments - inference times, number of parameters, and languages used in pre-training, base model and data used in pre-training

Model	Inf. time [s]	#params	#langs	base[a]	data	reference
mT5	1.69	277M	101	T5	CC[b]	(Xue et al., 2021)
LASER	1.64	52M	93	BiLSTM	OPUS[c]	(Artetxe and Schwenk, 2019)
mBERT	1.49	177M	104	BERT	Wiki	(Devlin et al., 2019)
MPNet**	1.38	278M	53	XLM-R	OPUS[c], MUSE[d], Wikititles[e]	(Reimers and Gurevych, 2020)
XLM-R-dist**	1.37	278M	53	XLM-R	OPUS[c], MUSE[d], Wikititles[e]	(Reimers and Gurevych, 2020)
XLM-R	1.37	278M	100	XLM-R	CC	(Conneau et al., 2020)
LaBSE	1.36	470M	109	BERT	CC, Wiki + mined bitexts	(Feng et al., 2020)
DistilmBERT	0.79	134M	104	BERT	Wiki	(Sanh et al., 2020)
mUSE-dist**	0.79	134M	53	DistilmBERT	OPUS[c], MUSE[d], Wikititles[e]	(Reimers and Gurevych, 2020)
mUSE-transformer*	0.65	85M	16	transformer	mined QA + bitexts, SNLI	(Yang et al., 2020)
mUSE-cnn*	0.12	68M	16	CNN	mined QA + bitexts, SNLI	(Yang et al., 2020)

*mUSE models were used in TensorFlow implementation in contrast to others in torch [a] Base model is either monolingual version on which it was based or another multilingual model which was used and adopted [b] Colossal Clean Crawled Corpus in multilingual version (mC4) [c] multiple datasets from OPUS website (https://opus.nlpl.eu), [d] bilingual dictionaries from MUSE (https://github.com/facebookresearch/MUSE), [e] just titles from wiki articles in multiple languages

tures (T5, BERT, RoBERTa). We also included models' trained with multilingual knowledge distillation (Reimers and Gurevych, 2020) such as *paraphrase-xlm-r-multilingual-v1* (XLM-R-dist), *distiluse-base-multilingual-cased-v2* (mUSE-dist), *paraphrase-multilingual-mpnet-base-v2* (MPNet). We also included models trained on multilingual corpus like Wikipedia (Wiki) or Common Crawl (CC) as well as models trained with the use of parallel datasets. Selected models differ in size - from LASER with 52M parameters to LaBSE with 470M. They also differ regarding covered languages, from 16 up to more than a hundred. By a number of languages, we mean how many were used to create a specific model, not all languages supported by the model (an example is MPNet, trained using 53 languages, but as it is based on XLM-R, it supports 100). We also compared inference time which was calculated as a mean of inference times of 500 randomly selected texts samples from all datasets. The hardware used is described in Section A.1. We searched for models comparison in similar tasks in literature but failed to find any, which compares more than 2 or 3 models. All models used are characterized in Table 1.

3.2 Datasets

We gathered 342 sentiment analysis datasets containing texts from multiple languages, data sources and domains to check our research questions. We searched for datasets in various sources, like Google Scholar, GitHub repositories, and the HuggingFace datasets library. Such a large number of datasets allows us to estimate the quality of language models in various conditions with greater certainty. To the best of our knowledge, this is the largest sentiment analysis datasets collection currently gathered and researched in literature. After preliminary analysis, we selected 80 datasets of reasonable quality based on 5 criteria. (1) We rejected datasets containing weak annotations (e.g., datasets with labels based on emoji occurrence or generated automatically through classification by machine learning models), as our analysis showed that they may contain too much noise (Northcutt et al., 2021). (2) We reject datasets without sufficient information about the annotation procedure (e.g., whether annotation was manual or automatic, number of annotators) because it is always a questionable decision to merge datasets created with different annotation guidelines. (3) We accepted reviews datasets and mapped their rating labels to sentiment values. The mapping rules are described in section 3.2.1. (4) We rejected 2-class only datasets (positive/negative without neutral), as our analysis showed their low quality in terms of 3-class usage. (5) Some datasets contain samples in multiple languages - we split them and treated each language as a separate dataset.

3.2.1 Data Preprocessing

Working with many datasets means that they could contain different types of text, various artefacts such as URL or HTML tags, or just different sentiment classes mappings. We applied a couple of preprocessing steps to each dataset to unify all datasets. We dropped duplicated texts. We removed URLs, Twitter mentions, HTML tags, and emails. During

Table 2: Summary of 80 high-quality datasets selected. Categories: N - News, O - Other, R - Reviews, SM - Social Media

	Count	Category				Samples			Mean #	
		N	O	R	SM	NEG	NEU	POS	words	characters
English	17	3	4	4	6	305,782	289,847	1,734,857	42	233
Arabic	9	0	1	4	4	139,173	192,463	600,439	28	159
Spanish	5	0	1	3	2	110,156	120,668	188,068	145	864
Chinese	2	0	0	2	0	118,023	68,953	144,726	48	-
German	6	0	0	1	5	105,416	99,291	111,180	19	131
Polish	4	0	0	2	2	78,309	61,041	97,338	39	245
French	3	0	0	1	2	84,324	43,097	83,210	19	108
Japanese	1	0	0	1	0	83,985	41,976	83,819	60	-
Czech	4	0	0	2	2	39,687	59,181	97,419	29	168
Portuguese	4	0	0	0	4	57,737	54,145	45,952	12	73
Slovenian	2	1	0	0	1	34,178	50,055	29,310	161	1054
Russian	2	0	0	0	2	32,018	47,852	31,060	11	73
Croatian	2	1	0	0	1	19,907	19,298	38,389	86	556
Serbian	3	0	0	2	1	25,580	31,762	19,026	176	1094
Thai	2	0	0	1	1	9,327	28,615	34,377	18	317
Bulgarian	1	0	0	0	1	14,040	28,543	19,567	12	85
Hungarian	1	0	0	0	1	9,004	17,590	30,088	11	83
Slovak	1	0	0	0	1	14,518	12,735	29,370	13	97
Albanian	1	0	0	0	1	6,958	14,675	22,651	13	90
Swedish	1	0	0	0	1	16,664	12,912	11,770	14	94
Bosnian	1	0	0	0	1	12,078	11,039	13,066	12	75
Urdu	1	0	1	0	0	5,244	8,580	5,836	13	69
Hindi	1	0	0	0	1	4,992	6,392	5,615	27	128
Persian	1	0	0	1	0	1,619	5,074	6,832	21	104
Italian	2	0	0	0	2	4,043	4,193	3,829	16	104
Hebrew	1	0	0	0	1	2,283	238	6,098	22	110
Latvian	1	0	0	0	1	1,379	2,617	1,794	20	138

an exploratory analysis, we spotted that review-based datasets often contain many repeated texts with contradictory sentiment scores. We deduplicated such cases and applied a majority voting to choose a sentiment label. Finally, we unified labels from all datasets into 3-class (negative, neutral, positive). In the case of datasets containing user ratings (on a scale of 1-5) along with their review texts, we mapped the ratings to sentiment as follows: the middle value (3) of the rating scale was treated as a neutral sentiment, ratings below the middle as negative sentiment, and ratings above the middle as positive sentiment.

Presenting statistics of 80 datasets across 27 languages could be challenging. We checked different aggregating and sorting of datasets to make their statistics as readable as possible and easily usable for results discussion. We decided to group datasets by their language and next sorted them based on the number of examples in every aggregate - Table 2. In total, we selected 80 datasets containing 6,164,942 text samples. Most of the texts in the datasets are in English (2,330,486 samples across 17 datasets), Arabic (932,075 samples across 9 datasets), and Spanish (418,892 samples across 5 datasets). The datasets contain text from various categories: social media (44 datasets), reviews (24 datasets), news (5 datasets), and others (7 datasets). They also differ in the mean number of words and characters in examples. See the detailed information of datasets used is in Tables 5 and 6.

We also selected around 60k samples for training and validation and another 60k for testing. This is enough for training a small classifier on top of

Table 3: Statistics of the internal dataset

lang	samples	NEG	NEU	POS
pl	2968	14%	60%	26%
en	943	4%	74%	22%

a frozen embedding or fine-tuning a transformer-based model (see Section 3.3). This was also done due to computation resources limitations.

3.2.2 Internal Dataset

We have also used an internal dataset that was manually annotated. It is multi-domain and consists of texts from various Internet sources in Polish and English. It includes texts from social media, news sites, blogs and forums. We used this dataset as a gold standard. We need it because we do not know exact annotation guidelines from literature datasets and we assume that those guidelines differed between datasets. In our gold dataset, each text was annotated by 3 annotators with majority label selection. The annotators achieved a high agreement measured by Cohen's kappa: 0.665 and Krippendorff's alpha: 0.666. Statistics of this dataset are presented in Table 3. All samples were trimmed to the length of 350 chars (mean length of 145 chars).

3.3 Experimental Scenarios

We wanted to compare multilingual models in different use cases. Firstly, we wanted to see how much information is stored in pre-trained embedding. In this scenario, we used each of the text representations models listed in Section 3.1 as a feature extractor and coupled them with only a small linear classification head. We used an average from a final layer as a text representation. We will refer to this scenario **Just Head - Linear**. In the second scenario, we replaced a linear classifier with a BiLSTM classifier, still using the text representation model as a feature extractor. We fed BiLSTM layer with outputs from the last layer of the feature extractor (**Just Head - BiLSTM**). LASER and mUSE do not provide per-token embeddings and therefore, were not included in this scenario. Since most of our models are transformer-based, we decided to test them in a fine-tuning setup. This last scenario evaluated the fine-tuning of all transformer-based models (referred to as **fine-tuning**), with an exception made for mUSE-transformer because it was not possible to do with our implementation in PyTorch with Huggingface models.

For each scenario, we prepared 3 test metrics, which we refer to as a *whole test*, *average by dataset* and *internal*. Each of them separately measures model performance but all of them are based on a macro F1-score. The *whole test* is calculated on all samples from datasets described in 3.2 combined. It is meant to reflect the real-life performance of a model because our real-world applications often deal with an imbalance in languages distribution (with English being the most popular language used on the Internet). On *average by dataset*, we first calculate the macro F1-score on each dataset and then calculate the average of those scores. This is meant to show whether the model was not too over-fitted for the majority of languages or the biggest datasets. Finally, in the *internal* scenario, we assess them on our internal dataset (described in 3.2.2) to measure performance in our domain-specific examples.

3.4 Evaluation Procedure

To show how each model performs in a bird's eye view, we prepared Nemenyi diagrams (Nemenyi, 1963) for all three experimental setups. Nemeneyi post-hoc statistical test finds groups of models that differ. It was used on the top of multiple comparisons Friedman test (Demšar, 2006). The Nemeneyi test makes a pair-wise comparison of all model's ranks. We used alpha equal to 5%. The Nemeneyi test provides critical distance for compared groups that are not significantly different from each other.

3.5 Models Setup

For each scenario, we adjusted hyperparameters. The hidden size was set to LM's embedding size for linear and fine-tuning and 32 for BiLSTM. By hidden size, we mean middle linear layer size, or in the case of BiLSTM - its hidden size parameter. BiLSTM uses a smaller hidden size because our experiments showed that it does not hurt performance but increases efficiency. The learning rate was initially the same for all scenarios, at the well-established value of 1e-3. We then modified it for each version by decreasing it for fine-tuning (to 1e-5) and slightly increasing it for BiLSTM based model (5e-3). The batch size was determined by our GPU's memory size. We used 200 for linear and BiLSTM and 6 for fine-tuning. We used dropout in classification head - 0.5 for BiLSTM and 0.2 for other scenarios. We trained our models for 5 epochs in the fine-tuning scenario and 15 in two

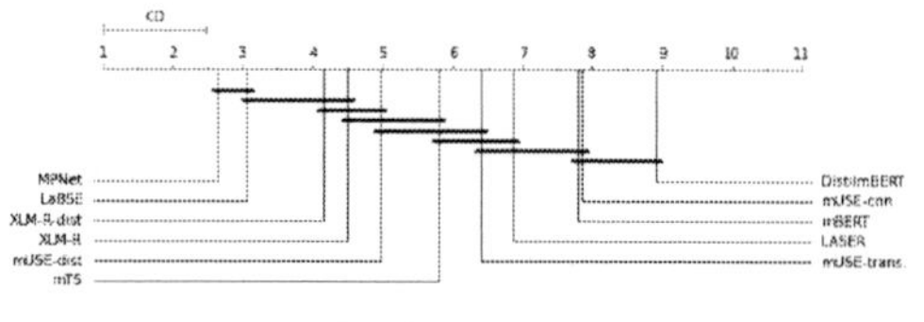

(a) Just head - Linear

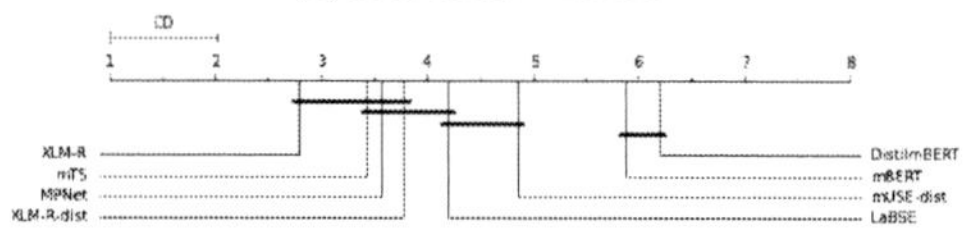

(b) Just head - BiLSTM

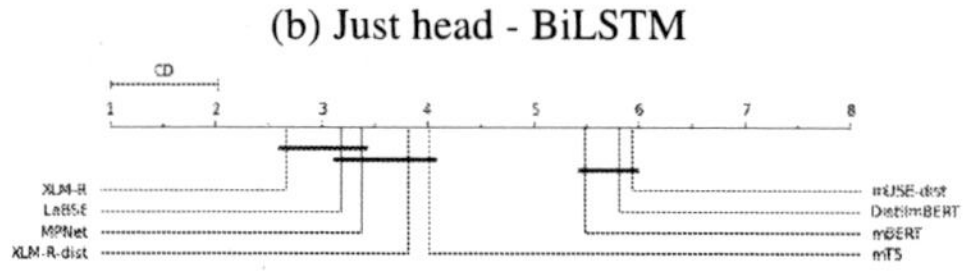

(c) Fine-tuning

Figure 1: Nemenyi diagrams based on the ranking of models according to the F1-score on each dataset

Table 4: Aggregated results of models (F1 score in %). The best results for each test set are highlighted. (W - whole test, A - avg. by dataset, I - internal)

	XLM-R	LaBSE	MPNet	XLM-R-dist	mT5	mBERT	DistilmBERT	mUSE-dist	LASER	mUSE-trans.	mUSE-cnn
	Just Head - Linear										
W	62	62	**63**	60	59	56	55	59	55	55	54
A	51	54	**55**	51	49	45	43	50	47	47	45
I	55	**61**	**61**	56	50	43	38	60	50	49	50
	Just Head - BiLSTM										
W	**66**	62	63	62	65	60	59	62	-	-	-
A	**57**	55	56	54	56	49	48	54	-	-	-
I	**64**	63	**64**	63	63	54	48	**64**	-	-	-
	Fine-tuning										
W	**68**	**68**	67	67	66	65	**64**	63	-	-	-
A	61	**62**	**62**	**62**	60	56	56	56	-	-	-
I	**70**	69	65	67	67	57	58	60	-	-	-

others, as those were the max number of epochs before the models started overfitting. We tested with the best F1-score on a validation dataset.

4 Results

We divided our results into three layers. Firstly, we show a general bird's eye view of all models - it helps to spot the best and the worst models. Then, we provide detailed results for each model aggregated per dataset. Finally, to dig deeper into the model's performance, we show numerical results for each model for each language.

4.1 Bird's Eye View

There is no significantly best embedding model in any of the tested scenarios based on the Nemenyi diagrams - Figure 1. However, we can see that the MPNet proved to be the best (for the linear scenario) and not significantly worse than the best - XLR-M model - in the other two scenarios. It is also worth mentioning that mBERT-based models (mBERT and DistillmBERT) proved to be the worst language models for our tasks.

4.2 Aggregated by Dataset

All models achieve better results with fine-tuning (up to 0.7 F1-score) than with extraction of vectors from text and then applying linear (up to 0.61) or BiLSTM (up to 0.64) layers, shows Table 4. The performance gains are higher when fine-tuning models pretrained on MLM and TLM tasks (like mBERT or XLM-R) compared to models, which were trained with sentence classification tasks, sentence similarity tasks or similar (like LaBSE). For example, mBERT had gains of 9, 11, and 14 percentage points (pp) on *whole test*, *average by dataset* and *internal* test cases, DistilmBERT - 9, 13 and 20pp, XLM-R - 6, 10, and 15pp. At the same time, LaBSE had only 6, 8, and 7pp and MPNet - 4, 7, 4pp. Still, those models achieve better overall performance. Fine-tuning reduces inequalities in the results between models (0.55 vs 0.43 for best and worst models in Just head - Linear setup, and 0.62 vs 0.56 after Fine-tuning for *average by dataset* metric). Those results were meant to show a general comparison between fine-tuned models against training just classification head.

The additional BiLSTM layer on top of transformer token embeddings improves the results of the model with only a linear layer in most cases. The differences are most clear in the case of the results for our internal dataset, where the result improved even by 13pp. (from 50% to 63%) for the mT5 model.

Those results show, that three models are the most promising choices: XLM-R, LaBSE and MPNet. They achieve comparable performance in all scenarios and test cases. Furthermore, they are better than other models in almost all test cases. XLM-R-dist was very close to those, but analysis with Nemenyi diagrams shows that it is slightly worse than those three.

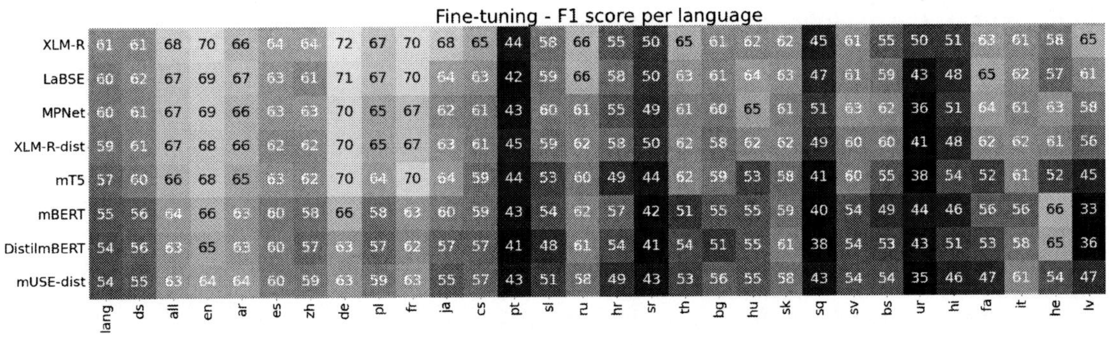

Figure 2: Detailed results of models' comparison.

Legend: **lang** - averaged by all languages, **ds** - averaged by dataset, **ar** - Arabic, **bg** - Bulgarian, **bs** - Bosnian, **cs** - Czech, **de** - German, **en** - English, **es** - Spanish, **fa** - Persian, **fr** - French, **he** - Hebrew, **hi** - Hindi, **hr** - Croatian, **hu** - Hungarian, **it** - Italian, **ja** - Japanese, **lv** - Latvian, **pl** - Polish, **pt** - Portuguese, **ru** - Russian, **sk** - Slovak, **sl** - Slovenian, **sq** - Albanian, **sr** - Serbian, **sv** - Swedish, **th** - Thai, **ur** - Urdu, **zh** - Chinese.

4.3 Every Model for Every Language

We assessed the performance of each model in each experimental scenario concerning the language. The texts were sub-sampled with stratification by language and class label so that language distribution in the test dataset reflects this in the whole dataset. It means that some languages are under-represented. We also include the total Macro F1 score value in column "all". Results are presented in Figure 2 for fine-tuning scenario and in Figure 5 for others. Those results confirm conclusions from the previous section about the advantage of XLM-R, LaBSE and MPNet. They have the best performance in most languages and together with XLM-R-dist, there are no big differences between them.

5 Discussion

RQ1: Are we able to create a single multilingual sentiment classifier, performing equally well for each language? When considering only the best models (XLM-R, LaBSE, MPNet) in the fine-tuning setup, we observed that they achieve best or close to best results in every language - Figure 5. In some languages, results are significantly worse than in others, but this is also true for other models evaluated as it may be caused by differences in the number of samples, quality, and difficulty of samples in those languages. Therefore, we can say that one model can work exceptionally well in all languages. On the other hand, statistical analysis which is presented in the form of Nemenyi diagrams in Figures 1a, 1b and 1c showed that there is no statistical difference between top models in fine-tuning setup, so it is not possible to state which of those is the best one. We can rather state which group of models proved to be significantly better than others.

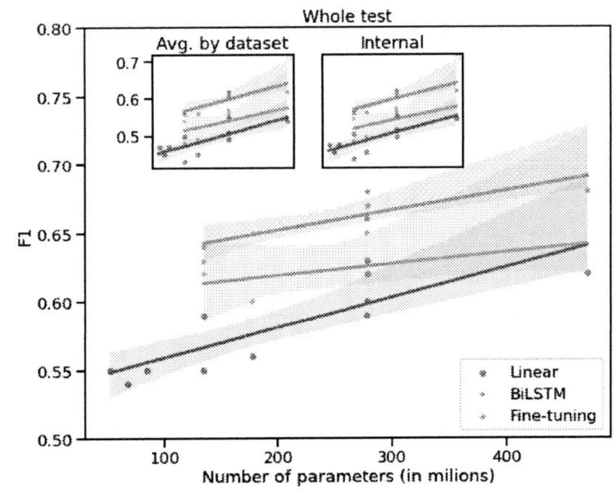

Figure 3: Results for models by their size and scenario.

RQ2: Does fine-tuning of transformer-based models significantly improve sentiment classification results? All models worked better when fine-tuned, but the performance gain varied from one to another. It was between 4 (mUSE-dist) and 9 (mBERT and DistilmBERT) pp. F1 on the benchmark test dataset, and between 0 (mUSE-dist) and 20 pp. (DistilmBERT) on our internal dataset. The 17, 15, and 14 pp. gain of mT5, XLM-R, and DistilmBERT on the internal dataset is also worth noting. In general, the most significant gain can be observed in models trained on language modelling only (MLM or TLM), such as XLM-R and mBERT.

RQ3: What is the relationship between model size and performance? Is bigger always better? The results of our experiments showed that there exists a correlation between the classification result of the language model with its number of parameters. Figure 3 shows that, for all scenarios and test dataset types, bigger models achieve better performance in most cases. However, there are some counterexamples, e.g., mUSE-dist is smaller than mBERT but achieves better performance in Just head - Linear setup, for all dataset types. This indicates that the size of the model is an important factor in its performance, but other factors, like the domain and the type of pretraining task, may also affect the results. Moreover, we observed that this correlation is weaker after fine-tuning. We can often find the model with similar performance to the best one but significantly smaller and faster for the production environment.

Your Dataset Splits Matter To determine which model works best, we repeated fine-tuning five times to remove a right/wrong random seed factor for each model and dataset subsampling. Due to computation resources limitations, we selected eight models available in Huggingface for fine-tuning. Interestingly, we can see that one of the samples looks like the outlier - Figure 4 for almost all the evaluated models. The F1-score for this sample is even 4 percentage points worse than other samples' scores. We investigated this anomaly and spotted that it is always the same sample (the same seed for sample generation). As a reminder, since we collected a massive dataset and had limited computational resources, we sub-sampled texts for each of the five runs. Sub-samples between different models stay the same. It looks like the mentioned sample was more difficult than others or had distinctive characteristics. It is hard to tell why without in-depth analysis, hence we intend to conduct further research on the topic of data quality in sentiment analysis tasks using techniques like noise ratio (Northcutt et al., 2021) or data cartography (Swayamdipta et al., 2020). Here, we see an outstanding example of how vital the dataset's preparation could be regarding split for train/dev/test sets.

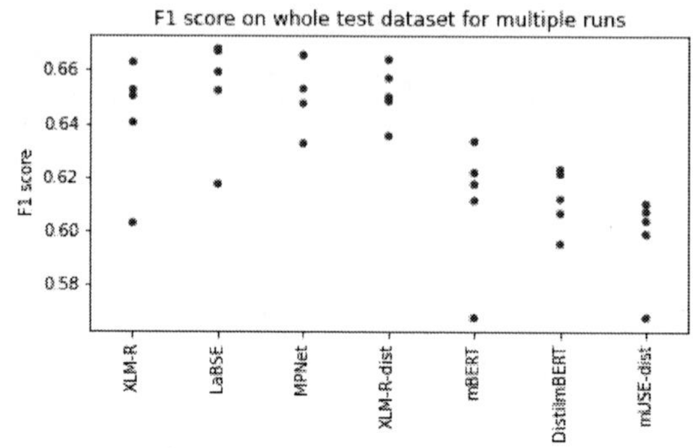

Figure 4: Results of multiple runs of fine-tuning experiments with different seeds.

6 Conclusions and Further Works

In this work we evaluated multilingual text representations for the task of sentiment classification by comparing multiple approaches, using different deep learning methods. In the process, we gathered the biggest collection of multi-lingual sentiment datasets - 80 datasets for 27 languages. We evaluated 11 models (language models and text vectorization techniques) in 3 different scenarios. We found out that it is possible to create one model which achieves the best or most competitive results in all languages in our collected dataset, but there is no statistical difference between top-performing models. We found out that there is a significant benefit from fine-tuning transformer-based language models and that a model size is correlated with performance.

While conducting experiments we identified further issues which we find worth addressing. Dataset quality assessment is in our opinion the most important one and we are planning to address it in further works. Meanwhile, we used datasets with a literature background and trust that they were carefully prepared and have decent quality annotations. We also found out that it is difficult to propose a coherent experiments methodology with such imbalance in languages and datasets sizes. Moreover, analyzing results is difficult, when one must address dimensions of datasets, languages, data sources, models, and experiments scenarios.

Finally, we found out that when sub-sampling a dataset for experiments, seeds play a significant role (see results in Figure 4). To analyze this phenomenon, we intend to launch further research and use noise ratio (Northcutt et al., 2021) and data cartography (Swayamdipta et al., 2020) to understand how this split differs from the others. This will be, in our opinion, a good start to a comprehensive analysis of datasets quality for the multi-lingual sentiment classification task which we intend to perform.

Acknowledgements

The work was partially supported by the Department of Artificial Intelligence at Wroclaw University of Science and Technology, and by European Regional Development Fund (ERDF) in RPO WD 2014-2020 (project no. RPDS.01.02.02-02-0065/20). We want to thank Mikołaj Morzy for an initial review and feedback. We want to thank our annotators team - Barbara Orłowska, Daria Szałamacha, Konrad Gajewski and Paweł Odrowąż-Sypniewski.

References

Marwan Al Omari, Moustafa Al-Hajj, Nacereddine Hammami, and Amani Sabra. 2019. Sentiment classifier: Logistic regression for arabic services' reviews in lebanon. In *2019 International Conference on Computer and Information Sciences (ICCIS)*, pages 1–5.

Mohamed Aly and Amir Atiya. 2013. LABR: A large scale Arabic book reviews dataset. In *Proceedings of the 51st Annual Meeting of the Association for Computational Linguistics (Volume 2: Short Papers)*, pages 494–498, Sofia, Bulgaria. Association for Computational Linguistics.

Adam Amram, Anat Ben David, and Reut Tsarfaty. 2018. Representations and architectures in neural sentiment analysis for morphologically rich languages: A case study from Modern Hebrew. In *Proceedings of the 27th International Conference on Computational Linguistics*, pages 2242–2252, Santa Fe, New Mexico, USA. Association for Computational Linguistics.

Mikel Artetxe and Holger Schwenk. 2019. Massively Multilingual Sentence Embeddings for Zero-Shot Cross-Lingual Transfer and Beyond. *Transactions of the Association for Computational Linguistics*, 7:597–610.

Mohammed Attia, Younes Samih, Ali Elkahky, and Laura Kallmeyer. 2018. Multilingual multi-class sentiment classification using convolutional neural networks. In *Proceedings of the Eleventh International Conference on Language Resources and Evaluation (LREC 2018)*, Miyazaki, Japan. European Language Resources Association (ELRA).

Ramy Baly, Alaa Khaddaj, Hazem M. Hajj, Wassim El-Hajj, and Khaled Bashir Shaban. 2018. ArSentD-LEV: A Multi-Topic Corpus for Target-based Sentiment Analysis in Arabic Levantine Tweets. In *Proceedings of the Eleventh International Conference on Language Resources and Evaluation (LREC 2018)*, Paris, France. European Language Resources Association (ELRA).

Francesco Barbieri, Valerio Basile, Danilo Croce, Malvina Nissim, Nicole Novielli, and Viviana Patti. 2016. Overview of the Evalita 2016 SENTIment POLarity Classification Task. In *Proceedings of Third Italian Conference on Computational Linguistics (CLiC-it 2016) & Fifth Evaluation Campaign of Natural Language Processing and Speech Tools for Italian. Final Workshop (EVALITA 2016)*, Naples, Italy.

Mohaddeseh Bastan, Mahnaz Koupaee, Youngseo Son, Richard Sicoli, and Niranjan Balasubramanian. 2020. Author's sentiment prediction. In *Proceedings of the 28th International Conference on Computational Linguistics*, pages 604–615, Barcelona, Spain (Online). International Committee on Computational Linguistics.

Vuk Batanović, Boško Nikolić, and Milan Milosavljević. 2016. Reliable baselines for sentiment analysis in resource-limited languages: The Serbian movie review dataset. In *Proceedings of the Tenth International Conference on Language Resources and Evaluation (LREC'16)*, pages 2688–2696, Portorož, Slovenia. European Language Resources Association (ELRA).

Vuk Batanović, Miloš Cvetanović, and Boško Nikolić. 2020. A versatile framework for resource-limited sentiment articulation, annotation, and analysis of short texts. *PLOS ONE*, 15(11):1–30.

Henrico Brum and Maria das Graças Volpe Nunes. 2018. Building a sentiment corpus of tweets in Brazilian Portuguese. In *Proceedings of the Eleventh International Conference on Language Resources and Evaluation (LREC 2018)*, Miyazaki, Japan. European Language Resources Association (ELRA).

Jože Bučar, Martin Žnidaršič, and Janez Povh. 2018. Annotated news corpora and a lexicon for sentiment analysis in slovene. *Language Resources and Evaluation*, 52(3):895–919.

Ethem F. Can, Aysu Ezen-Can, and Fazli Can. 2018. Multilingual sentiment analysis: An RNN-based framework for limited data. *Computing Research Repository*, arXiv:1806.04511. Version 1.

Emile Chapuis, Pierre Colombo, Matteo Manica, Matthieu Labeau, and Chloé Clavel. 2020. Hierarchical pre-training for sequence labelling in spoken dialog. In *Findings of the Association for Computational Linguistics: EMNLP 2020*, pages 2636–2648, Online. Association for Computational Linguistics.

Mark Cieliebak, Jan Milan Deriu, Dominic Egger, and Fatih Uzdilli. 2017. A Twitter corpus and benchmark resources for German sentiment analysis. In *Proceedings of the Fifth International Workshop on Natural Language Processing for Social Media*, pages 45–51, Valencia, Spain. Association for Computational Linguistics.

Alexis Conneau, Kartikay Khandelwal, Naman Goyal, Vishrav Chaudhary, Guillaume Wenzek, Francisco

Guzmán, Edouard Grave, Myle Ott, Luke Zettlemoyer, and Veselin Stoyanov. 2020. Unsupervised cross-lingual representation learning at scale. In *Proceedings of the 58th Annual Meeting of the Association for Computational Linguistics*, pages 8440–8451, Online. Association for Computational Linguistics.

Alexis Conneau and Guillaume Lample. 2019. Cross-lingual language model pretraining. In *Proceedings of the 33rd International Conference on Neural Information Processing Systems*, Red Hook, NY, USA. Curran Associates Inc.

Alexis Conneau, Ruty Rinott, Guillaume Lample, Adina Williams, Samuel Bowman, Holger Schwenk, and Veselin Stoyanov. 2018. XNLI: Evaluating cross-lingual sentence representations. In *Proceedings of the 2018 Conference on Empirical Methods in Natural Language Processing*, pages 2475–2485, Brussels, Belgium. Association for Computational Linguistics.

Fermin L Cruz, Jose A Troyano, Fernando Enriquez, and Javier Ortega. 2008. Experiments in sentiment classification of movie reviews in spanish. *Procesamiento del Lenguaje Natural*, 41:73–80.

Kia Dashtipour, Soujanya Poria, Amir Hussain, Erik Cambria, Ahmad YA Hawalah, Alexander Gelbukh, and Qiang Zhou. 2016. Multilingual sentiment analysis: state of the art and independent comparison of techniques. *Cognitive computation*, 8(4):757–771.

Janez Demšar. 2006. Statistical comparisons of classifiers over multiple data sets. *Journal of Machine Learning Research*, 7:1–30.

Jacob Devlin, Ming-Wei Chang, Kenton Lee, and Kristina Toutanova. 2019. BERT: Pre-training of deep bidirectional transformers for language understanding. In *Proceedings of the 2019 Conference of the North American Chapter of the Association for Computational Linguistics: Human Language Technologies, Volume 1 (Long and Short Papers)*, pages 4171–4186, Minneapolis, Minnesota. Association for Computational Linguistics.

Ashraf Elnagar and Omar Einea. 2016. BRAD 1.0: Book reviews in arabic dataset. In *2016 IEEE/ACS 13th International Conference of Computer Systems and Applications (AICCSA)*, pages 1–8.

Ashraf Elnagar, Yasmin S. Khalifa, and Anas Einea. 2018. *Hotel Arabic-Reviews Dataset Construction for Sentiment Analysis Applications*. Springer International Publishing, Cham.

Fangxiaoyu Feng, Yinfei Yang, Daniel Cer, Naveen Arivazhagan, and Wei Wang. 2020. Language-agnostic BERT Sentence Embedding. *Computing Research Repository*, arXiv:2007.01852. Version 2.

Ivan Habernal, Tomáš Ptáček, and Josef Steinberger. 2013. Sentiment analysis in Czech social media using supervised machine learning. In *Proceedings of the 4th Workshop on Computational Approaches to Subjectivity, Sentiment and Social Media Analysis*, pages 65–74, Atlanta, Georgia. Association for Computational Linguistics.

Pedram Hosseini, Ali Ahmadian Ramaki, Hassan Maleki, Mansoureh Anvari, and Seyed Abolghasem Mirroshandel. 2018. SentiPers: A sentiment analysis corpus for persian. *Computing Research Repository*, arXiv:1801.07737. Version 2.

Junjie Hu, Sebastian Ruder, Aditya Siddhant, Graham Neubig, Orhan Firat, and Melvin Johnson. 2020. XTREME: A massively multilingual multi-task benchmark for evaluating cross-lingual generalisation. In *Proceedings of the 37th International Conference on Machine Learning*, volume 119 of *Proceedings of Machine Learning Research*, pages 4411–4421. PMLR.

Clayton J. Hutto and Eric Gilbert. 2014. VADER: A parsimonious rule-based model for sentiment analysis of social media text. In *Proceedings of the International AAAI Conference on Web and Social Media*, volume 8, pages 216–225.

Crowdflower Inc. 2015. Twitter us airline sentiment.

Karthikeyan K, Zihan Wang, Stephen Mayhew, and Dan Roth. 2020. Cross-lingual ability of multilingual bert: An empirical study. In *International Conference on Learning Representations*.

Kamil Kanclerz, Piotr Miłkowski, and Jan Kocoń. 2020. Cross-lingual deep neural transfer learning in sentiment analysis. *Procedia Computer Science*, 176:128–137. Knowledge-Based and Intelligent Information & Engineering Systems: Proceedings of the 24th International Conference KES2020.

Brian Keith Norambuena, Exequiel Lettura, and Claudio Villegas. 2019. Sentiment analysis and opinion mining applied to scientific paper reviews. *Intelligent Data Analysis*, 23:191–214.

Phillip Keung, Yichao Lu, György Szarvas, and Noah A. Smith. 2020. The multilingual Amazon reviews corpus. In *Proceedings of the 2020 Conference on Empirical Methods in Natural Language Processing (EMNLP)*, pages 4563–4568, Online. Association for Computational Linguistics.

Jan Kocoń, Piotr Miłkowski, and Monika Zaśko-Zielińska. 2019. Multi-level sentiment analysis of PolEmo 2.0: Extended corpus of multi-domain consumer reviews. In *Proceedings of the 23rd Conference on Computational Natural Language Learning (CoNLL)*, pages 980–991, Hong Kong, China. Association for Computational Linguistics.

Patrick Lewis, Barlas Oguz, Ruty Rinott, Sebastian Riedel, and Holger Schwenk. 2020. MLQA: Evaluating cross-lingual extractive question answering. In *Proceedings of the 58th Annual Meeting of the Association for Computational Linguistics*, pages 7315–7330, Online. Association for Computational Linguistics.

Yiou Lin, Hang Lei, Jia Wu, and Xiaoyu Li. 2015. An empirical study on sentiment classification of Chinese review using word embedding. In *Proceedings of the 29th Pacific Asia Conference on Language, Information and Computation: Posters*, pages 258–266, Shanghai, China.

Chi-Liang Liu, Tsung-Yuan Hsu, Yung-Sung Chuang, and Hung yi Lee. 2020. What makes multilingual bert multilingual? *Computing Research Repository*, arXiv:2010.10938. Version 1.

Pekka Malo, Ankur Sinha, Pekka Korhonen, Jyrki Wallenius, and Pyry Takala. 2014. Good debt or bad debt: Detecting semantic orientations in economic texts. *Journal of the Association for Information Science and Technology*, 65(4):782–796.

Tomás Mikolov, Kai Chen, Greg Corrado, and Jeffrey Dean. 2013a. Efficient estimation of word representations in vector space. In *1st International Conference on Learning Representations, ICLR 2013, Scottsdale, Arizona, USA, May 2-4, 2013, Workshop Track Proceedings*.

Tomas Mikolov, Quoc V. Le, and Ilya Sutskever. 2013b. Exploiting similarities among languages for machine translation. *Computing Research Repository*, arXiv:1309.4168. Version 1.

Igor Mozetič, Miha Grčar, and Jasmina Smailović. 2016. Multilingual twitter sentiment classification: The role of human annotators. *PLOS ONE*, 11(5):1–26.

Mahmoud Nabil, Mohamed Aly, and Amir Atiya. 2015. ASTD: Arabic sentiment tweets dataset. In *Proceedings of the 2015 Conference on Empirical Methods in Natural Language Processing*, pages 2515–2519, Lisbon, Portugal. Association for Computational Linguistics.

Sascha Narr, Michael Hülfenhaus, and Sahin Albayrak. 2012. Language-independent twitter sentiment analysis. In *Workshop on Knowledge Discovery, Data Mining and Machine Learning (KDML-2012)*.

Peter Nemenyi. 1963. *Distribution-free Multiple Comparisons*. Princeton University.

Jianmo Ni, Jiacheng Li, and Julian McAuley. 2019. Justifying recommendations using distantly-labeled reviews and fine-grained aspects. In *Proceedings of the 2019 Conference on Empirical Methods in Natural Language Processing and the 9th International Joint Conference on Natural Language Processing (EMNLP-IJCNLP)*, pages 188–197, Hong Kong, China. Association for Computational Linguistics.

Curtis Northcutt, Lu Jiang, and Isaac Chuang. 2021. Confident learning: Estimating uncertainty in dataset labels. *Journal of Artificial Intelligence Research*, 70:1373–1411.

Parth Patwa, Gustavo Aguilar, Sudipta Kar, Suraj Pandey, Srinivas PYKL, Björn Gambäck, Tanmoy Chakraborty, Thamar Solorio, and Amitava Das. 2020. SemEval-2020 task 9: Overview of sentiment analysis of code-mixed tweets. In *Proceedings of the Fourteenth Workshop on Semantic Evaluation*, pages 774–790, Barcelona (online). International Committee for Computational Linguistics.

Andraž Pelicon, Marko Pranjić, Dragana Miljković, Blaž Škrlj, and Senja Pollak. 2020. Zero-shot learning for cross-lingual news sentiment classification. *Applied Sciences*, 10(17).

Nils Reimers and Iryna Gurevych. 2020. Making monolingual sentence embeddings multilingual using knowledge distillation. In *Proceedings of the 2020 Conference on Empirical Methods in Natural Language Processing (EMNLP)*, pages 4512–4525, Online. Association for Computational Linguistics.

Anna Rogers, Alexey Romanov, Anna Rumshisky, Svitlana Volkova, Mikhail Gronas, and Alex Gribov. 2018. RuSentiment: An enriched sentiment analysis dataset for social media in Russian. In *Proceedings of the 27th International Conference on Computational Linguistics*, pages 755–763, Santa Fe, New Mexico, USA. Association for Computational Linguistics.

Sara Rosenthal, Noura Farra, and Preslav Nakov. 2017. SemEval-2017 task 4: Sentiment analysis in Twitter. In *Proceedings of the 11th International Workshop on Semantic Evaluation (SemEval-2017)*, pages 502–518, Vancouver, Canada. Association for Computational Linguistics.

Sebastian Ruder, Ivan Vulić, and Anders Søgaard. 2019. A survey of cross-lingual word embedding models. *Journal of Artificial Intelligence Research*, 65:569–631.

Piotr Rybak, Robert Mroczkowski, Janusz Tracz, and Ireneusz Gawlik. 2020. KLEJ: Comprehensive benchmark for Polish language understanding. In *Proceedings of the 58th Annual Meeting of the Association for Computational Linguistics*, pages 1191–1201, Online. Association for Computational Linguistics.

Santwana Sagnika, Anshuman Pattanaik, Bhabani Shankar Prasad Mishra, and Saroj K Meher. 2020. A review on multi-lingual sentiment analysis by machine learning methods. *Journal of Engineering Science & Technology Review*, 13(2):154–166.

Mohammad Salameh, Saif Mohammad, and Svetlana Kiritchenko. 2015. Sentiment after translation: A case-study on Arabic social media posts. In *Proceedings of the 2015 Conference of the North American Chapter of the Association for Computational Linguistics: Human Language Technologies*, pages 767–777, Denver, Colorado. Association for Computational Linguistics.

Niek J Sanders. 2011. Sanders-Twitter Sentiment Corpus. *Sanders Analytics LLC*.

Victor Sanh, Lysandre Debut, Julien Chaumond, and Thomas Wolf. 2020. DistilBERT, a distilled version of BERT: smaller, faster, cheaper and lighter. *Computing Research Repository*, arXiv:1910.01108. Version 4.

Dietmar Schabus and Marcin Skowron. 2018. Academic-industrial perspective on the development and deployment of a moderation system for a newspaper website. In *Proceedings of the Eleventh International Conference on Language Resources and Evaluation (LREC 2018)*, Miyazaki, Japan. European Language Resources Association (ELRA).

Zareen Sharf and Saif Ur Rahman. 2018. Performing natural language processing on roman urdu datasets. In *International Journal of Computer Science and Network Security*, volume 18, pages 141–148.

Emily Sheng and David Uthus. 2020. Investigating societal biases in a poetry composition system. In *Proceedings of the Second Workshop on Gender Bias in Natural Language Processing*, pages 93–106, Barcelona, Spain (Online). Association for Computational Linguistics.

Pawel Sobkowicz and Antoni Sobkowicz. 2012. Two-year study of emotion and communication patterns in a highly polarized political discussion forum. *Social Science Computer Review*, 30(4):448–469.

Uga Sprogis and Matiss Rikters. 2020. What can we learn from almost a decade of food tweets. *Computing Research Repository*, arXiv:2007.05194. Version 2.

Rachele Sprugnoli. 2020. Multiemotions-it: a new dataset for opinion polarity and emotion analysis for italian. In *Proceedings of the Seventh Italian Conference on Computational Linguistics*.

Arthit Suriyawongkul, Ekapol Chuangsuwanich, Pattarawat Chormai, and Charin Polpanumas. 2019. Pythainlp/wisesight-sentiment: First release (v1.0). Zenodo.

Swabha Swayamdipta, Roy Schwartz, Nicholas Lourie, Yizhong Wang, Hannaneh Hajishirzi, Noah A. Smith, and Yejin Choi. 2020. Dataset cartography: Mapping and diagnosing datasets with training dynamics. In *Proceedings of the 2020 Conference on Empirical Methods in Natural Language Processing (EMNLP)*, pages 9275–9293, Online. Association for Computational Linguistics.

Mike Thelwall, Kevan Buckley, and Georgios Paltoglou. 2012. Sentiment strength detection for the social web. *J. Am. Soc. Inf. Sci. Technol.*, 63(1):163–173.

Ekkalak Thongthanomkul, Tanapol Nearunchorn, and Yuwat Chuesathuchon. 2019. wongnai-corpus. `https://github.com/wongnai/wongnai-corpus`.

Erik F. Tjong Kim Sang. 2002. Introduction to the CoNLL-2002 shared task: Language-independent named entity recognition. In *COLING-02: The 6th Conference on Natural Language Learning 2002 (CoNLL-2002)*.

Erik F. Tjong Kim Sang and Fien De Meulder. 2003. Introduction to the CoNLL-2003 shared task: Language-independent named entity recognition. In *Proceedings of the Seventh Conference on Natural Language Learning at HLT-NAACL 2003*, pages 142–147.

Joonatas Wehrmann, Willian Becker, Henry E. L. Cagnini, and Rodrigo C. Barros. 2017. A character-based convolutional neural network for language-agnostic twitter sentiment analysis. In *2017 International Joint Conference on Neural Networks (IJCNN)*, pages 2384–2391.

Shijie Wu and Mark Dredze. 2020. Are all languages created equal in multilingual BERT? In *Proceedings of the 5th Workshop on Representation Learning for NLP*, pages 120–130, Online. Association for Computational Linguistics.

Linting Xue, Noah Constant, Adam Roberts, Mihir Kale, Rami Al-Rfou, Aditya Siddhant, Aditya Barua, and Colin Raffel. 2021. mT5: A massively multilingual pre-trained text-to-text transformer. In *Proceedings of the 2021 Conference of the North American Chapter of the Association for Computational Linguistics: Human Language Technologies*, pages 483–498, Online. Association for Computational Linguistics.

Yinfei Yang, Daniel Cer, Amin Ahmad, Mandy Guo, Jax Law, Noah Constant, Gustavo Hernandez Abrego, Steve Yuan, Chris Tar, Yun-hsuan Sung, Brian Strope, and Ray Kurzweil. 2020. Multilingual universal sentence encoder for semantic retrieval. In *Proceedings of the 58th Annual Meeting of the Association for Computational Linguistics: System Demonstrations*, pages 87–94, Online. Association for Computational Linguistics.

Yinfei Yang, Gustavo Hernandez Abrego, Steve Yuan, Mandy Guo, Qinlan Shen, Daniel Cer, Yun-hsuan Sung, Brian Strope, and Ray Kurzweil. 2019. Improving multilingual sentence embedding using bi-directional dual encoder with additive margin softmax. In *Proceedings of the Twenty-Eighth International Joint Conference on Artificial Intelligence, IJCAI-19*, pages 5370–5378. International Joint Conferences on Artificial Intelligence Organization.

Michał Ziemski, Marcin Junczys-Dowmunt, and Bruno Pouliquen. 2016. The United Nations parallel corpus v1.0. In *Proceedings of the Tenth International Conference on Language Resources and Evaluation (LREC'16)*, pages 3530–3534, Portorož, Slovenia. European Language Resources Association (ELRA).

Pierre Zweigenbaum, Serge Sharoff, and Reinhard Rapp. 2017. Overview of the second BUCC shared task: Spotting parallel sentences in comparable corpora. In *Proceedings of the 10th Workshop on Building and Using Comparable Corpora*, pages 60–67, Vancouver, Canada. Association for Computational Linguistics.

A Appendices

A.1 Hardware and Software

We performed our experiments using Python 3.9 and PyTorch (1.8.1) (and Tensorflow (2.3.0) for original mUSE). Our experimental setup consists of Intel(R) Xeon(R) CPU E5-2630 v4 @ 2.20GHz and Nvidia Tesla V100 16GB.

A.2 Detailed Datasets Information

We present detailed lists of datasets included in our research in Tables 5 and 6. They include language, category, dataset size, class balance and basic texts characteristics.

A.3 Full Results for Languages

We include full results of our experiments with results for each language in Figure 5. Part with finetuning results was presented earlier in Figure 2.

Table 5: List of all monolingual datasets used in experiments. Category (Cat.): R - Reviews, SM - Social Media, C - Chats, N - News, P - Poems, M - Mixed. HL - human labeled, #Words and #Chars are mean values

Paper	Lang	Cat.	HL	Samples	NEG/NEU/POS	#Words	#Char.
(Al Omari et al., 2019)	ar	R	No	3096	13.0/10.2/76.8	9	51
(Elnagar et al., 2018)	ar	R	No	400101	13.0/19.9/67.1	22	127
(Aly and Atiya, 2013)	ar	R	No	6250	11.6/17.9/70.5	65	343
(Elnagar and Einea, 2016)	ar	R	No	504007	15.4/21.0/63.6	77	424
(Baly et al., 2018)	ar	SM	Yes	2809	47.2/23.9/29.0	22	130
(Nabil et al., 2015)	ar	SM	Yes	3224	50.9/25.0/24.1	16	94
(Salameh et al., 2015)	ar	SM	Yes	1199	48.0/10.5/41.5	11	51
(Salameh et al., 2015)	ar	SM	Yes	1998	67.5/10.1/22.4	20	107
(Habernal et al., 2013)	cs	R	No	91140	32.4/33.7/33.9	50	311
(Habernal et al., 2013)	cs	R	No	92758	7.9/23.4/68.7	20	131
(Habernal et al., 2013)	cs	SM	Yes	9752	20.4/53.1/26.5	10	59
(Habernal et al., 2013)	cs	SM	Yes	2637	30.8/60.6/8.6	33	170
(Cieliebak et al., 2017)	de	SM	Yes	9948	16.3/59.2/24.6	11	86
(Schabus and Skowron, 2018)	de	SM	Yes	3598	47.3/51.5/1.2	33	237
(Chapuis et al., 2020)	en	C	Yes	12138	31.8/46.5/21.7	12	48
(Chapuis et al., 2020)	en	C	Yes	4643	22.3/48.9/28.8	15	71
(Malo et al., 2014)	en	N	Yes	3448	12.2/62.1/25.7	22	124
(Bastan et al., 2020)	en	N	Yes	5333	11.6/37.3/51.0	388	2129
(Hutto and Gilbert, 2014)	en	N	No	5190	29.3/52.9/17.8	17	104
(Sheng and Uthus, 2020)	en	P	Yes	1052	18.3/15.8/65.9	7	37
(Hutto and Gilbert, 2014)	en	R	No	3708	34.2/19.5/46.3	16	87
(Hutto and Gilbert, 2014)	en	R	No	10605	49.6/1.5/48.9	19	111
(Ni et al., 2019)	en	R	No	1883238	8.3/8.0/83.7	70	382
(Sanders, 2011)	en	SM	Yes	3424	16.7/68.1/15.2	14	97
(Thelwall et al., 2012)	en	SM	Yes	11759	28.0/34.0/38.0	26	147
(Inc., 2015)	en	SM	Yes	14427	63.0/21.2/15.8	17	104
(Hutto and Gilbert, 2014)	en	SM	No	4200	26.9/17.0/56.1	13	79
(Keith Norambuena et al., 2019)	es	M	No	163	33.7/33.7/32.5	135	835
(Keith Norambuena et al., 2019)	es	R	Yes	399	44.4/27.8/27.8	167	1020
(Cruz et al., 2008)	es	R	No	3871	32.9/32.3/34.9	511	3000
(Hosseini et al., 2018)	fa	R	Yes	13525	12.0/37.5/50.5	21	104
(Amram et al., 2018)	he	SM	Yes	8619	26.5/2.8/70.8	22	110
(Pelicon et al., 2020)	hr	N	Yes	2025	22.5/61.4/16.0	161	1021
(Barbieri et al., 2016)	it	SM	Yes	8926	36.7/41.7/21.6	14	101
(Sprugnoli, 2020)	it	SM	Yes	3139	24.4/14.9/60.6	17	106
(Sprogis and Rikters, 2020)	lv	SM	Yes	5790	23.8/45.2/31.0	20	138
(Rybak et al., 2020)	pl	R	No	10074	30.8/13.2/56.0	80	494
(Kocoń et al., 2019)	pl	R	Yes	57038	42.4/26.8/30.8	30	175
(Sobkowicz and Sobkowicz, 2012)	pl	SM	Yes	645	50.7/47.3/2.0	33	230
(Brum and Volpe Nunes, 2018)	pt	SM	Yes	10109	28.8/25.1/46.1	12	74
(Rogers et al., 2018)	ru	SM	Yes	23226	16.8/54.6/28.6	12	79
(Bučar et al., 2018)	sl	N	Yes	10417	32.0/52.0/16.0	309	2017
(Batanović et al., 2016)	sr	R	No	4724	17.8/43.7/38.5	498	3097
(Batanović et al., 2020)	sr	R	Yes	3948	30.3/18.1/51.5	18	105
(Thongthanomkul et al., 2019)	th	R	No	46193	5.4/30.5/64.1	29	544
(Suriyawongkul et al., 2019)	th	SM	Yes	26126	26.1/55.6/18.3	6	90
(Sharf and Rahman, 2018)	ur	M	Yes	19660	26.7/43.6/29.7	13	69
(Lin et al., 2015)	zh	R	No	125725	28.6/21.9/49.5	51	128

Table 6: List of all multilingual datasets used in experiments. Category (Cat.): R - Reviews, SM - Social Media, C - Chats, N - News, P - Poems, M - Mixed. HL - human labeled

Paper	Cat.	Lang	HL	Samples	(NEG/NEU/POS)	#Words	#Char.
(Narr et al., 2012)	SM	de	Yes	953	10.0/75.1/14.9	12	80
		de	Yes	1781	16.9/63.3/19.8	13	81
		en	Yes	7073	17.4/60.0/22.6	14	78
		fr	Yes	685	23.4/53.4/23.2	14	82
		fr	Yes	1786	25.0/54.3/20.8	15	83
		pt	Yes	759	28.1/33.2/38.7	14	78
		pt	Yes	1769	30.7/33.9/35.4	14	78
(Keung et al., 2020)	R	de	No	209073	40.1/20.0/39.9	33	208
		en	No	209393	40.0/20.0/40.0	34	179
		es	No	208127	40.2/20.0/39.8	27	152
		fr	No	208160	40.2/20.1/39.7	28	160
		ja	No	209780	40.0/20.0/40.0	2	101
		zh	No	205977	39.8/20.1/40.1	1	50
(Rosenthal et al., 2017)	M	ar	Yes	9391	35.5/40.6/23.9	14	105
		en	Yes	65071	19.1/45.7/35.2	18	111
(Patwa et al., 2020)	SM	es	Yes	14920	16.8/33.1/50.0	16	86
		hi	Yes	16999	29.4/37.6/33.0	27	128
(Mozetič et al., 2016)	SM	bg	Yes	62150	22.6/45.9/31.5	12	85
		bs	Yes	36183	33.4/30.5/36.1	12	75
		de	Yes	90534	19.7/52.8/27.4	12	94
		en	Yes	85784	26.8/44.1/29.1	12	77
		es	Yes	191412	11.8/37.9/50.3	14	92
		hr	Yes	75569	25.7/23.9/50.4	12	91
		hu	Yes	56682	15.9/31.0/53.1	11	83
		pl	Yes	168931	30.0/26.1/43.9	11	82
		pt	Yes	145197	37.2/35.0/27.8	10	61
		ru	Yes	87704	32.0/40.1/27.8	10	67
		sk	Yes	56623	25.6/22.5/51.9	13	97
		sl	Yes	103126	29.9/43.3/26.8	13	91
		sq	Yes	44284	15.7/33.1/51.1	13	90
		sr	Yes	67696	34.8/42.8/22.4	13	81
		sv	Yes	41346	40.3/31.2/28.5	14	94

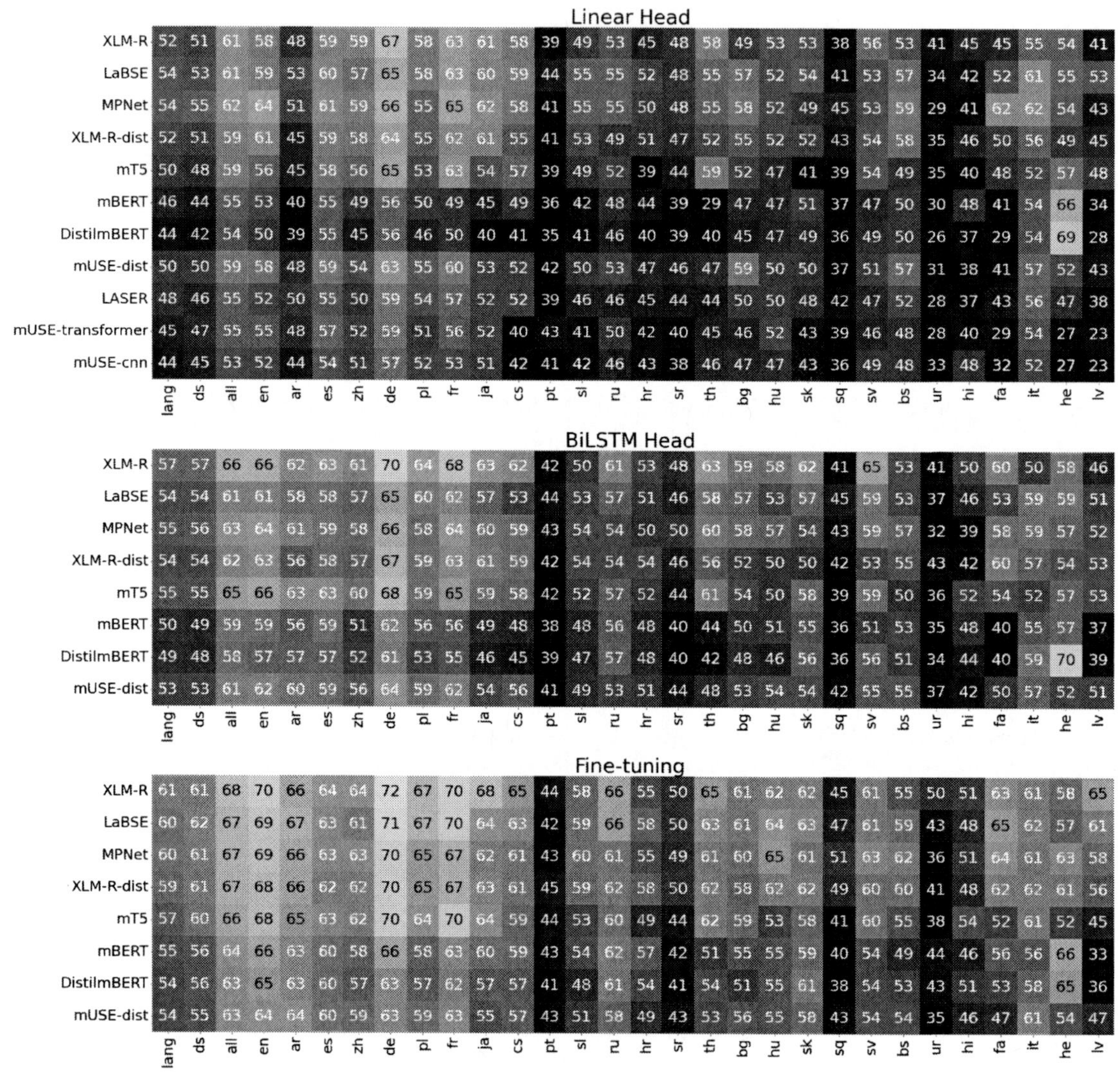

Figure 5: Detailed results of models' comparison. Legend: lang - averaged by all languages, ds - averaged by dataset, ar - Arabic, bg - Bulgarian, bs - Bosnian, cs - Czech, de - German, en - English, es - Spanish, fa - Persian, fr - French, he - Hebrew, hi - Hindi, hr - Croatian, hu - Hungarian, it - Italian, ja - Japanese, lv - Latvian, pl - Polish, pt - Portuguese, ru - Russian, sk - Slovak, sl - Slovenian, sq - Albanian, sr - Serbian, sv - Swedish, th - Thai, ur - Urdu, zh - Chinese.

Improving Social Meaning Detection with Pragmatic Masking and Surrogate Fine-Tuning

Chiyu Zhang   Muhammad Abdul-Mageed
Deep Learning & Natural Language Processing Group
The University of British Columbia
`chiyuzh@mail.ubc.ca, muhammad.mageed@ubc.ca`

Abstract

Masked language models (MLMs) are pre-trained with a denoising objective that is in a mismatch with the objective of downstream fine-tuning. We propose pragmatic masking and surrogate fine-tuning as two complementing strategies that exploit social cues to drive pre-trained representations toward a broad set of concepts useful for a wide class of social meaning tasks. We test our models on 15 different Twitter datasets for social meaning detection. Our methods achieve 2.34% F_1 over a competitive baseline, while outperforming domain-specific language models pre-trained on large datasets. Our methods also excel in few-shot learning: with only 5% of training data (severely few-shot), our methods enable an impressive 68.54% average F_1. The methods are also language agnostic, as we show in a zero-shot setting involving six datasets from three different languages.[1]

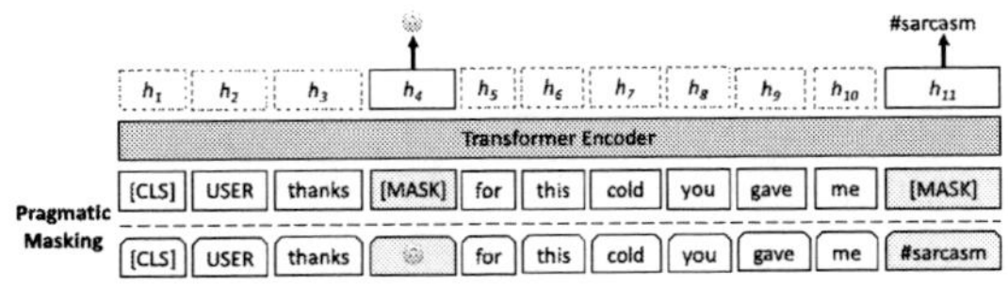

(a) Pragmatic masking

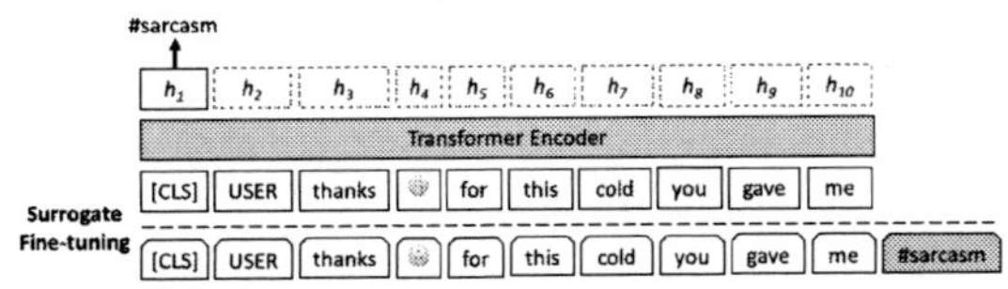

(b) Surrogate fine-tuning

Figure 1: Illustration of our proposed pragmatic masking and surrogate fine-tuning methods.

1 Introduction

Masked language models (MLMs) such as BERT (Devlin et al., 2019) have revolutionized natural language processing (NLP). These models exploit the idea of self-supervision where sequences of unlabeled text are masked and the model is tasked to reconstruct them. Knowledge acquired during this stage of denoising (called *pre-training*) can then be transferred to downstream tasks through a second stage (called *fine-tuning*). Although pre-training is general, does not require labeled data, and is task agnostic, fine-tuning is narrow, requires labeled data, and is task-specific. For a class of tasks $\mathcal{T}$, some of which we may not know in the present but which can become desirable in the future, it is unclear how we can bridge the learning objective mismatch between these two stages. In particular, how can we **(i)** make pre-training more tightly related to downstream task learning objective; and **(ii)** focus model pre-training representation on an all-encompassing range of concepts of general affinity to various downstream tasks?

We raise these questions in the context of learning a cluster of tasks to which we collectively refer as *social meaning*. We loosely define social meaning as meaning emerging through human interaction such as on social media. Example social meaning tasks include emotion, irony, and sentiment detection. We propose two main solutions that we hypothesize can bring pre-training and fine-tuning closer in the context of learning social meaning: First, we propose a particular type of guided masking that prioritizes learning contexts of tokens crucially relevant to social meaning in interactive discourse. Since the type of "meaning in interaction" we are interested in is the domain of linguistic pragmatics (Thomas, 2014), we will refer to our proposed masking mechanism as *pragmatic masking*. We explain pragmatic masking in Section 3.1.

Second, we propose an additional novel stage of fine-tuning that does not depend on gold labels but instead exploits general data cues possibly relevant to *all* social meaning tasks. More precisely, we

[1] Our code is available at: `https://github.com/chiyuzhang94/PMLM-SFT`.

Proceedings of the 12th Workshop on Computational Approaches to Subjectivity, Sentiment & Social Media Analysis, pages 141 - 156
May 26, 2022 ©2022 Association for Computational Linguistics

leverage proposition-level user assigned tags for *intermediate* fine-tuning of pre-trained language models. In the case of Twitter, for example, hashtags naturally assigned by users at the end of posts can carry discriminative power that is by and large relevant to a wide host of tasks. Although cues such as hashtags and emojis have been previously used as surrogate lables before for one task or another, we put them to a broader use that is not focused on a particular (usually narrow) task that learns from a handful of cues. In other words, our goal is to learn extensive concepts carried by tens of thousands of cues. A model endowed with such a knowledge-base of social concepts can then be further fine-tuned on any narrower task in the ordinary way. We refer to this method as *surrogate fine-tuning* (Section 3.2). Another migration from previous work is that our methods excel not only in the full-data setting but also for *few-shot learning*, as we will explain below.

In order to evaluate our methods, we present a social meaning benchmark composed of 15 different datasets crawled from previous research sources. We perform an extensive series of methodical experiments directly targeting our proposed methods. Our experiments set new state-of-the-art (SOTA) in the supervised setting across different datasets. Moreover, our experiments reveal a striking capacity of our models in improving downstream task performance in few-shot and severely few-shot settings (i.e., as low as 1% of gold data), and even the zero-shot setting on languages other than English (i.e., as evaluated on six different datasets from three languages in Section 6).

To summarize, we make the following **contributions**: **(1)** We propose a novel pragmatic masking strategy that makes use of social media cues akin to improving social meaning detection. **(2)** We introduce a new effective surrogate fine-tuning method suited to social meaning that exploits the same simple cues as our pragmatic masking strategy. **(3)** We report new SOTA on eight out of 15 supervised datasets in the full-data setting. **(4)** Our methods are remarkably effective for few-shot and zero- and learning. We now review related work.

2 Related works

Masked Language models. Devlin et al. (2019) introduced BERT, a language representation model pre-trained by joint conditioning on both left and right context in all layers with the Transformer encoder (Vaswani et al., 2017). BERT's pre-training introduces a self-supervised learning objective, i.e., masked language modeling (MLM), to train the Transformer encoder. MLM predicts masked tokens in input sequences exploiting bi-directional context. RoBERTa (Liu et al., 2019) optimizes BERT performance by removing the next sentence prediction objective and by pre-training on a larger corpus using a bigger batch size. In the last few years, several variants of LMs with different masking methods were proposed. Examples are XLNet (Yang et al., 2019) and MASS (Song et al., 2019). To incorporate more domain specific knowledge into LMs, some works introduce knowledge-enabled masking strategies. For example, Sun et al. (2019); Zhang et al. (2019); Lin et al. (2021) propose to mask tokens of named entities, while Tian et al. (2020) and Ke et al. (2020) select sentiment-related words to mask during pre-training. Gu et al. (2020) and Kawintiranon and Singh (2021) propose selective masking methods to mask the more important tokens for downstream tasks (e.g., sentiment analysis and stance detection). However, these masking strategies depend on external resources and/or annotations (e.g., a lexicon or labeled corpora). Corazza et al. (2020) investigate the utility of hybrid emoji-based masking for enhancing abusive language detection. Previous works, therefore, only focus on one or another particular task (e.g., sentiment, abusive language detection) rather than the type of broad representations we target.

Intermediate Fine-Tuning. Although pre-trained language models (PLM) have shown significant improvements on NLP tasks, intermediate training of the PLM on one or more data-rich tasks can further improve performance on a target downstream task. Most previous work (e.g., (Wang et al., 2019; Pruksachatkun et al., 2020; Phang et al., 2020; Chang and Lu, 2021; Poth et al., 2021)) focus on intermediate fine-tuning on a given gold-labeled dataset related to a downstream target task. Different to these works, our surrogate fine-tuning method is *agnostic* to narrow downstream tasks and fine-tunes an PLM on large-scale data with tens of thousands of *surrogate* labels that may be relevant to all social meaning. We now introduce our methods.

3 Proposed Methods

3.1 Pragmatic Masking

MLMs employ random masking, and so are not guided to learn any particular type of information during pre-training. Several attempts have been

(1) Just got chased through my house with a bowl of tuna fish. 😨 ing.	**[Disgust]**
(2) USER thanks 😒 for this cold you gave me #sarcasm	**[Sarcastic]**
(3) USER Awww 😢 😢 CUPCAKES SUCK IT UP. SHE LOST 😂 😂 GET OVER IT 😂 😂	**[Offensive]**

Table 1: Samples from our social meaning benchmark.

made to employ task-specific masking where the objective is to predict information relevant to a given downstream task. Task relevant information is usually identified based on world knowledge (e.g., a sentiment lexicon (Gu et al., 2020; Ke et al., 2020), part-of-speech (POS) tags (Zhou et al., 2020)) or based on some other type of modeling such as pointwise mutual information (Tian et al., 2020) with supervised data. Although task-specific masking is useful, it is desirable to identify a *more general* masking strategy that *does not depend on external information* that may not be available or hard to acquire (e.g., costly annotation). For example, there are no POS taggers for some languages and so methods based on POS tags would not be applicable. Motivated by the fact that random masking is intrinsically sub-optimal (Ke et al., 2020; Kawintiranon and Singh, 2021) and this particular need for a more general and dependency-free masking method, we introduce our novel pragmatic masking mechanism that is suited to a wide range of social meaning tasks.

To illustrate, consider the tweet samples in Table 1: In example (1), the emoji " 😨 " combined with the suffix "-ing" in " 😨 ing" is a clear signal indicating the *disgust* emotion. In example (2) the emoji " 😒 " and the hashtag "#sarcasm" communicate *sarcasm*. In example (3) the combination of the emojis " 😢 " and " 😂 " accompany 'hard' emotions characteristic of *offensive* language. We hypothesize that by simply masking cues such as emojis and hashtags, we can bias the model to learn about different shades of social meaning expression. This masking method can be performed in a *self-supervised* fashion since hashtags and emojis can be automatically identified. We call the resulting language model ***pragmatically masked language model (PMLM)***. Specifically, when we choose tokens for masking, we prioritize hashtags and emojis as Figure 1a shows. The pragmatic masking strategy follows several steps: **(1) Pragmatic token selection.** We randomly select up to 15% of input sequence, giving masking **priority** to hashtags or emojis. The tokens are selected by whole word masking (i.e., whole hashtag or emoji). **(2) Regular token selection.** If the pragmatic tokens are less than 15%, we then randomly select regular BPE tokens to complete the percentage of masking to the 15%. **(3) Masking.** This is the same as the RoBERTa MLM objective where we replace 80% of selected tokens with the [MASK] token, 10% with random tokens, and we keep 10% unchanged.

3.2 Surrogate Fine-tuning

The current transfer learning paradigm of first pre-training then fine-tuning on particular tasks is limited by how much labeled data is available for downstream tasks. In other words, this existing set up works only given large amounts of labeled data. We propose surrogate fine-tuning where we intermediate fine-tune PLMs to predict thousands of example-level cues (i.e., hashtags occurring at the end of tweets) as Figure 1b shows. This method is inspired by previous work that exploited hashtags (Riloff et al., 2013; Ptáček et al., 2014; Rajadesingan et al., 2015; Sintsova and Pu, 2016; Abdul-Mageed and Ungar, 2017; Barbieri et al., 2018) or emojis (Wood and Ruder, 2016; Felbo et al., 2017; Wiegand and Ruppenhofer, 2021) as proxy for labels in a number of social meaning tasks. However, instead of identifying a small *specific* set of hashtags or emojis for a *single* task and using them to collect a dataset of *distant* labels, we diverge from the literature in proposing to use data with *any* hashtag or emoji as a surrogate labeling approach suited for *any* (or at least most) social meaning task. As explained, we refer to our method as ***surrogate fine-tuning (SFT).***

4 Experiments

4.1 Pre-training Data

TweetEnglish Dataset. We extract 2.4B English tweets[2] from a larger in-house dataset collected between 2014 and 2020. We lightly normalize tweets by removing usernames and hyperlinks and add white space between emojis to help our model identify individual emojis. We keep all the tweets, retweets, and replies but remove the 'RT USER:' string in front of retweets. To ensure each tweet

[2]We select English tweets based on the Twitter language tag.

contains sufficient context for modeling, we filter out tweets shorter than 5 English words (not counting the special tokens hashtag, emoji, USER, URL, and RT). We call this dataset **TweetEng**. Exploring the distribution of hashtags and emojis within TweetEng, we find that 18.5% of the tweets include at least one hashtag but no emoji, 11.5% have at least one emoji but no hashtag, and 2.2% have both at least one hashtag and at least one emoji. Investigating the hashtag and emoji location, we observe that 7.1% of the tweets use a hashtag as the last term, and that the last term of 6.7% of tweets is an emoji. We will use TweetEng as a general pool of data from which we derive for both our PMLM and SFT methods.

PM Datasets. We extract five different subsets from TweetEng to explore the utility of our proposed PMLM method. Each of these five datasets comprises 150M tweets as follows: **Naive**. A randomly selected tweet set. Based on the distribution of hashtags and emojis in TweetEng, each sample in Naive still has some likelihood to include one or more hashtags and/or emojis. We are thus still able to perform our PM method on Naive. **Naive-Remove**. To isolate the utility of using pragmatic cues, we construct a dataset by removing all hashtags and emojis from Naive. **Hashtag_any**. Tweets with at least one hashtag anywhere but no emojis. **Emoji_any**. Tweets with at least one emoji anywhere but no hashtags. **Hashtag_end**. Tweets with a hashtag as the last term but no emojis. **Emoji_end**. Tweets with an emoji at the end of the tweet but no hashtags.[3]

SFT Datasets. We experiment with two SFT settings, one based on *hashtags* (*SFT-H*) and another based on *emojis* (*SFT-E*). For SFT-H, we utilize the Hashtag_end dataset mentioned above. The dataset includes 5M unique hashtags (all occurring at the end of tweets), but the majority of these are low frequency. We remove any hashtags occurring < 200 times, which gives us a set of $63K$ hashtags in $126M$ tweets. We split the tweets into Train (80%), Dev (10%), and Test (10%). For each sample, we use the end hashtag as the sample label.[4] We refer to this resulting dataset as **Hashtag_pred**. For emoji SFT, we work with the emoji_end dataset. Similar to SFT-H, we remove low-frequence emojis (< 200 times), extract the same number of tweets as Hashtag_pred, and follow the same data splitting method. We acquire a total of $1,650$ unique emojis in final positions, which we assign as class labels and remove them from the original tweet body. We refer to this dataset as **Emoji_pred**.

4.2 Evaluation Benchmark

We collect 15 datasets representing eight different social meaning tasks to evaluate our models, as follows: [5]

Crisis awareness. We use $\texttt{Crisis}_{\texttt{Oltea}}$ (Olteanu et al., 2014), a corpus for identifying whether a tweet is related to a given disaster or not.

Emotion. We utilize $\texttt{Emo}_{\texttt{Moham}}$, introduced by Mohammad et al. (2018), for emotion recognition. We use the version adapted in Barbieri et al. (2020).

Hateful and offensive language. We use $\texttt{Hate}_{\texttt{Waseem}}$ (Waseem and Hovy, 2016), $\texttt{Hate}_{\texttt{David}}$ (Davidson et al., 2017), and $\texttt{Offense}_{\texttt{Zamp}}$ (Zampieri et al., 2019a).

Humor. We use the humor detection datasets $\texttt{Humor}_{\texttt{Potash}}$ (Potash et al., 2017) and $\texttt{Humor}_{\texttt{Meaney}}$ (Meaney et al., 2021).

Irony. We utilize $\texttt{Irony}_{\texttt{Hee-A}}$ and $\texttt{Irony}_{\texttt{Hee-B}}$ from Van Hee et al. (2018).

Sarcasm. We use four sarcasm datasets from $\texttt{Sarc}_{\texttt{Riloff}}$ (Riloff et al., 2013), $\texttt{Sarc}_{\texttt{Ptacek}}$ (Ptáček et al., 2014), $\texttt{Sarc}_{\texttt{Rajad}}$ (Rajadesingan et al., 2015), and $\texttt{Sarc}_{\texttt{Bam}}$ (Bamman and Smith, 2015).

Sentiment. We employ the three-way sentiment analysis dataset from $\texttt{Senti}_{\texttt{Rosen}}$ (Rosenthal et al., 2017).

Stance. We use $\texttt{Stance}_{\texttt{Moham}}$, a stance detection dataset from Mohammad et al. (2016). The task is to identify the position of a given tweet towards a target of interest.

We use the Twitter API [6] to crawl datasets which are available only in tweet ID form. We note that we could not download all tweets since some tweets get deleted by users or become inaccessible for some other reason. Since some datasets are old (dating back to 2013), we are only able to retrieve 73% of the tweets on average (i.e., across the different datasets). We normalize each tweet by re-

[3]We perform an analysis based on two 10M random samples of tweets from Hashtag_any and Emoji_any, respectively. We find that on average there are 1.83 hashtags per tweet in Hashtag_any and 1.88 emojis per tweet in Emoji_any.

[4]We use the last hashtag as the label if there are more than one hashtag in the end of a tweet. Different from PMLM, SFT is a multi-class single-label classification task. We plan to explore the multi-class multi-label SFT in the future.

[5]To facilitate reference, we give each dataset a name.

[6]https://developer.twitter.com/

placing the user names and hyperlinks to the special tokens 'USER' and 'URL', respectively. For datasets collected based on hashtags by original authors (i.e., *distant supervision*), we also remove the seed hashtags from the original tweets. For datasets originally used in cross-validation, we acquire 80% Train, 10% Dev, and 10% Test via random splits. For datasets that had training and test splits but not development data, we split off 10% from training data into Dev. The data splits of each dataset are presented in Table 2.

Task	**Lg**	**Classes**	**Train**	**Dev**	**Test**
$\text{Crisis}_{\text{Oltea}}$	EN	{on-topic, off-topic,}	48.0K	6.0K	6.0K
$\text{Emo}_{\text{Moham}}$	EN	{anger, joy, opt., sad.}	3.3K	374	1.4K
$\text{Hate}_{\text{Waseem}}$	EN	{racism, sexism, none}	8.7K	1.1K	1.1K
$\text{Hate}_{\text{David}}$	EN	{hate, off., neither}	19.8K	2.5K	2.5K
$\text{Humor}_{\text{Potash}}$	EN	{humor, not humor}	11.3K	660	749
$\text{Humor}_{\text{Meaney}}$	EN	{humor, not humor}	8.0K	1.0K	1.0K
$\text{Irony}_{\text{Hee-A}}$	EN	{ironic, not ironic}	3.5K	384	784
$\text{Irony}_{\text{Hee-B}}$	EN	{IC, SI, OI, NI}	3.5K	384	784
$\text{Offense}_{\text{Zamp}}$	EN	{off., not off.}	11.9K	1.3K	860
$\text{Sarc}_{\text{Riloff}}$	EN	{sarc., non-sarc.}	1.4K	177	177
$\text{Sarc}_{\text{Ptacek}}$	EN	{sarc., non-sarc.}	71.4K	8.9K	8.9K
$\text{Sarc}_{\text{Rajad}}$	EN	{sarc., non-sarc.}	41.3K	5.2K	5.2K
Sarc_{Bam}	EN	{sarc., non-sarc.}	11.9K	1.5K	1.5K
$\text{Senti}_{\text{Rosen}}$	EN	{neg., neu., pos.}	42.8K	4.8K	12.3K
$\text{Stance}_{\text{Moham}}$	EN	{against, favor, none}	2.6K	292	1.3K
$\text{Emo}_{\text{Mageed}}$	AR	{anger, joy, sad.}	-	-	372
$\text{Irony}_{\text{Ghan}}$	AR	{ironic, not ironic}	-	-	805
Emo_{Bian}	IT	{anger, joy, sad.}	-	-	196
$\text{Hate}_{\text{Bosco}}$	IT	{hate, not hate}	-	-	1.0K
$\text{Emo}_{\text{Moham}}$	ES	{anger, joy, sad.}	-	-	2.0K
Hate_{Bas}	ES	{hate, not hate}	-	-	1.6K

Table 2: Social meaning data. **opt.:**: Optimism, **sad.:** Sadness, **off.:** offensive, **sarc.:** sarcastic, **IC:** Ironic by clash, **SI:** Situational irony, **OI:** Other irony, **NI:** Non-ironic, **neg.:** Negative, **neu.:** Neutral, **pos.:** Positive.

To test our models under the ***few-shot setting***, we conduct few-shot experiments on varying percentages of the Train set of each task (i.e., 1%, 5%, 10%, 20% ... 90%). For each of these sizes, we randomly sample three times with replacement (*as we report the average of three runs in our experiments*) and evaluate each model on the original Dev and Test sets. We also evaluate our models on the ***zero-shot setting*** utilizing data from Arabic: $\texttt{Emo}_{\texttt{Mageed}}$ (Abdul-Mageed et al., 2020), $\texttt{Irony}_{\texttt{Ghan}}$ (Ghanem et al., 2019); Italian: $\texttt{Emo}_{\texttt{Bian}}$ (Bianchi et al., 2021) and $\texttt{Hate}_{\texttt{Bosco}}$ (Bosco et al., 2018); and Spanish: $\texttt{Emo}_{\texttt{Moham}}$ (Mohammad et al., 2018) and $\texttt{Hate}_{\texttt{Bas}}$ (Basile et al., 2019).

4.3 Implementation and Baselines

For both our experiments on PMLM (Section 5.1) and SFT (Section 5.2), we use the pre-trained English $\text{RoBERTa}_{\text{Base}}$ (Liu et al., 2019) model as the initial checkpoint model. We use this model, rather than a larger language model, since we run a large number of experiments and needed to be efficient with GPUs. We use the RoBERTa [7] tokenizer to process each input sequence and pad or truncate the sequence to a maximal length of 64 BPE tokens. We continue training RoBERTa with our proposed methods for five epochs with a batch size of 8,192 and then fine-tune the further trained models on downstream datasets. We provide details about our hyper-parameters in AppendixA. Our **baseline (1)** fine-tunes original pre-trained RoBERTa on downstream datsets without any further training. Our **baseline (2)** fine-tunes a SOTA Transformer-based PLM for English tweets, i.e., BERTweet (Nguyen et al., 2020), on downstream datasets. For PMLM experiments, we provide **baseline (3)**, which further pre-trains RoBERTa on `Naive-Remove` dataset with the random masking strategy and MLM objectives. We refer to this model as RM-NR. We now present our results.

5 Results and Analysis

We report performance of our models trained with our PM strategy in Section 5.1, where we investigate two types of pragmatic signals (i.e., hashtag and emoji) and the effect of their locations (anywhere vs. at the end). Section 5.2 shows the results of our SFT method with hashtags and emojis. Moreover, we combine our two proposed methods and compare our models to the SOTA models in Sections 5.3 and 5.4, respectively.

5.1 PMLM Experiments

PM on Naive. We further pre-train RoBERTa on the `Naive` dataset with our pragmatic masking strategy (PM) and compare to a model trained on the same dataset with random masking (RM). As Table 3 shows, PM-N outperforms RM-N with an average improvement of 0.69 macro F_1 points across the 15 tasks. We also observe that PM-N improves over RM-N in 12 out of the 15 tasks, thus reflecting the effectiveness of our PM strategy even when working with a dataset such as `Naive` where it is not guaranteed (although likely) that a tweet has hashtags and/or emojis. Moreover, RM-N outperforms RM-NR on eight tasks with improvement of 0.12 average F_1. This indicates that pragmatic cues (i.e., emoji and hashtags) are essential for learning social media data.

PM of Hashtags. To study the effect of PM on the controlled setting where we guarantee each sam-

[7] For short, we refer to the official released English $\text{RoBERTa}_{\text{Base}}$ as RoBERTa in the rest of the paper.

Task	RB	RM-NR	RM-N	PM-N	RM-HA	PM-HA	RM-HE	PM-HE	RM-EA	PM-EA	RM-EE	PM-EE	BTw
$\text{Crisis}_{\text{Oltea}}$	95.95	95.78	95.78	+0.14	95.75	+0.10	95.85	+0.02	95.91	**+0.07**	95.95	-0.18	95.88
$\text{Emo}_{\text{Moham}}$	77.99	79.15	79.43	+1.30	80.31	-1.75	79.51	+0.64	80.03	+1.06	81.28	**+0.90**	80.14
$\text{Hate}_{\text{Waseem}}$	57.34	57.22	56.75	-0.41	57.16	**+0.35**	56.97	+0.16	57.00	+0.01	57.08	-0.39	57.47
$\text{Hate}_{\text{David}}$	77.71	77.54	77.47	**+0.81**	76.87	+0.59	77.55	-0.33	78.13	+0.13	78.16	-0.23	77.15
$\text{Humor}_{\text{Potash}}$	54.40	54.80	55.45	-0.19	55.32	-2.83	50.06	+4.54	**57.14**	-2.04	55.25	+0.32	52.77
$\text{Humor}_{\text{Meaney}}$	92.37	93.50	93.24	+0.45	93.58	-0.10	92.85	**+1.67**	93.55	+0.95	93.19	-0.50	94.46
$\text{Irony}_{\text{Hee-A}}$	73.93	74.46	74.52	+0.45	74.50	+0.66	73.97	+2.27	75.34	**+2.59**	74.40	+1.22	77.35
$\text{Irony}_{\text{Hee-B}}$	52.30	50.70	52.91	+0.88	51.43	-2.14	50.41	+4.35	54.94	**+1.15**	54.73	-2.26	58.67
$\text{Offense}_{\text{Zamp}}$	80.13	80.38	79.97	+0.27	79.74	-0.40	79.95	-1.08	80.18	**+0.96**	80.18	+0.47	78.49
$\text{Sarc}_{\text{Riloff}}$	73.85	73.90	72.02	+3.22	71.42	+3.30	74.16	+1.72	76.52	+1.41	76.30	**+3.80**	78.81
$\text{Sarc}_{\text{Ptacek}}$	95.09	96.15	95.81	-0.17	95.50	+0.12	95.24	+0.57	95.81	**+0.25**	95.67	+0.34	96.35
$\text{Sarc}_{\text{Rajad}}$	85.07	85.63	86.18	+0.05	85.04	+0.51	85.20	+0.73	86.14	+0.51	86.02	**+0.92**	87.58
Sarc_{Bam}	79.08	79.27	80.03	+0.10	80.22	-0.06	79.83	+0.48	80.73	+0.39	81.13	**+0.60**	82.08
$\text{Senti}_{\text{Rosen}}$	71.08	71.55	72.03	**+0.62**	72.10	-0.11	71.84	-0.02	72.24	-0.26	72.27	-0.71	71.83
$\text{Stance}_{\text{Moham}}$	**70.41**	67.00	67.14	+2.80	69.51	-1.38	69.23	+0.45	70.20	-1.58	70.04	-1.56	67.41
Average	75.78	75.80	75.92	+0.69	75.90	-0.21	75.51	+1.08	76.92	**+0.38**	76.78	+0.18	77.10

Table 3: Pragmatic masking results. **Baselines:** (1) RB: RoBERTa, (2) BTw: BERTweet, (3) RM-NR. Light green indicates our models outperforming the baseline (1). **Bold** font indicates best model across all *our* random and pragmatic masking methods. **Masking: RM:** Random masking, **PM:** Pragmatic masking. **Datasets: N:** `Naive`, **NR:** `Naive-Remove`, **HA:** `Hashtag_any`, **HE:** `Hashtag_end`, **EA:** `Emoji_any`, **EE:** `Emoji_end`.

ple has at least one hashtag *anywhere*, we further pre-train RoBERTa on the `Hashtag_any` dataset with PM (PM-HA in Table 3) and compare to a model further pre-trained on the same dataset with the RM (RM-HA). As Table 3 shows, PM-HA does not improve over RM-HA. Rather, PM-HA results are marginally lower than those of RM-HA. We suspect that the degradation is due to confusions when a hashtag is used as a word of a sentence. Thus, we investigate the effectiveness of hashtag location.

Effect of Hashtag Location. Previous studies (Ren et al., 2016; Abdul-Mageed and Ungar, 2017) use hashtags as a proxy to label data with social meaning concepts, indicating that hashtags occuring at the end of posts are reliable cues. Hence, we further pre-train RoBERTa on the `Hashtag_end` dataset with PM and RM, respectively. As Table 3 shows, PM exploiting hashtags in the end (PM-HE) outperforms random masking (RM-HE) with an average improvement of 1.08 F_1 across the 15 tasks. It is noteworthy that PM-HE shows improvements over RM-HE in the majority of tasks (12 tasks), and both of them outperform the baselines (1) and (3). Compared to RM-HA and PM-HA, the results demonstrate the utility of end-location hashtags on training a LM.

PM of Emojis. Again, in order to study the impact of PM of emojis under a controlled condition where we guarantee each sample has at least one emoji, we further pre-train RoBERTa on the `Emoji_any` dataset with PM and RM, respectively. As Table 3 shows, both methods result in sizable improvements on most of tasks. PM-EA outperforms the random masking method (RM-EA) (macro F_1 =0.38 improvement) and also exceeds the baseline (1), (2), and (3) with 1.52, 0.20, and 1.50 average F_1, respectively. PM-EA thus obtains the best overall performance (macro F_1 = 77.30) and also achieves the best performance on $\text{Crisis}_{\text{Oltea-14}}$, two irony detection tasks, $\text{Offense}_{\text{Zamp}}$, and $\text{Sarc}_{\text{Ptacek}}$ across all settings of our PM. This indicates that emojis carry important knowledge for social meaning tasks and demonstrates the effectiveness of our PM mechanism to distill and transfer this knowledge to diverse tasks.

Effect of Emoji Location. We analyze whether learning is sensitive to emoji location: we further pre-train RoBERTa on `Emoji_end` dataset with PM and RM and refer to these two models as PM-EE and RM-EE, respectively. Both models perform better than our baselines (1) and (3), and PM-EE achieves the best performance on four datasets across all settings of our PM. Unlike the case of hashtags, the location of the masked emoji is not sensitive for the learning.

Overall, results show the effectiveness of our PMLM method in improving the self-supervised LM. All models trained with PM on emoji data obtain better performance than those pre-trained on hashtag data. It suggests that emoji cues are somewhat more helpful than hashtag cues for this type of guided model pre-training in the context of social meaning tasks. This implies emojis are more relevant to many social meaning tasks than hashtags are. In other words, in addition to them being cues for social meaning, hashtags can also stand for general topical categories to which different social meaning concepts can apply (e.g., *#lunch* can be accompanied by both *happy* and *disgust* emotions).

5.2 SFT Experiments

We conduct SFT using hashtags and emojis. We continue training the original RoBERTa on the `Hashtag_pred` and `Emoji_pred` dataset for 35 epochs and refer to these trained models as **SFT-H** and **SFT-E**, respectively. To evaluate SFT-H and SFT-E, we further fine-tune the obtained models on 15 task-specific datasets. As Table 4 shows, SFT-E outperforms the first baseline (i.e., RoBERTa) with 1.16 F_1 scores. Comparing SFT-E and PMLM trained with the same dataset (PM-EE), we observe that the two models perform similarly (76.94 for SFT-E vs. 76.96 for PM-EE). Our proposed SFT-H method is also highly effective. On average, SFT-H achieves 2.19 and 0.87 F_1 improvement over our baseline (1) and (2), respectively. SFT-H also yields sizeable improvements on datasets with smaller training samples, such $Irony_{Hee\text{-}B}$ (improvement of 7.84 F_1) and $Sarc_{Riloff}$ (improvement of 6.65 F_1). Comparing SFT-H to the PMLM model trained with the same dataset (i.e., PM-HE), we observe that SFT-H also outperforms PM-H with 1.38 F_1. This result indicate that SFT can more effectively utilize the information from tweets with hashtags.

Task	RB	SFT-E	SFT-H	PragS1	PragS2	BTw
$Crisis_{Oltea}$	95.95	95.76	95.87	**96.02**	95.68	95.88
Emo_{Moham}	77.99	79.69	78.69	**82.04**	80.50	80.14
$Hate_{Waseem}$	57.34	56.47	**63.97**	60.92	60.25	57.47
$Hate_{David}$	**77.71**	76.45	77.29	77.00	76.93	77.15
$Humor_{Potash}$	54.40	54.75	**55.51**	54.93	53.83	52.77
$Humor_{Meaney}$	92.37	93.82	93.74	93.68	**94.49**	94.46
$Irony_{Hee\text{-}A}$	73.93	76.63	76.22	72.73	**79.89**	77.35
$Irony_{Hee\text{-}B}$	52.30	57.59	60.14	56.11	**61.67**	58.67
$Offense_{Zamp}$	80.13	80.18	79.82	**81.34**	79.50	78.49
$Sarc_{Riloff}$	73.85	78.34	**80.50**	78.74	80.49	78.81
$Sarc_{Ptacek}$	95.09	95.88	96.01	96.16	**96.24**	96.35
$Sarc_{Rajad}$	85.07	86.80	87.56	87.48	**88.92**	87.58
$Sarc_{Bam}$	79.08	81.48	81.19	**82.53**	81.53	82.08
$Senti_{Rosen}$	71.08	71.27	71.83	**72.07**	71.08	71.38
$Stance_{Moham}$	70.41	69.06	**71.27**	69.65	70.77	67.41
Average	75.78	76.94	77.97	77.43	**78.12**	77.10

Table 4: Surrogate fine-tuning (SFT). **Baselines:** RB (RoBERTa) and BTw (BERTweet). **SFT-H:** SFT with hashtags. **SFT-E:** SFT with emojis. **PragS1:** PMLM with `Hashtag_end` (best hashtag PM condition) followed by SFT-H. **PragS2:** PMLM with `Emoji_any` (best emoji PM condition) followed by SFT-E.

5.3 Combining PM and SFT

To further improve the PMLM with SFT, we take the best hashtag-based model (i.e., PM-HE in Table 3) and fine-tune on `Emoji_pred` (i.e., SFT-E) for 35 epochs. We refer to this last setting as PM-HE+SFT-E but use the easier alias **PragS1** in Table 4. We observe that PragS1 outperforms both, reaching an average F_1 of 77.43 vs. 75.78 for the baseline (1) and 76.94 for SFT-E. Similarly, we also take the best emoji-based PMLM (i.e., PM-EA in Table 3) and fine-tune on `Hashtag_pred` SFT (i.e., SFT-H) for 35 epochs. This last setting is referred to as PM-EA+SFT-H, but we again use the easier alias **PragS2**. Our best result is achieved with a combination of PM with emojis and SFT on hashtags (the PragS2 condition). This last model achieves an average F_1 of 78.12 and is 2.34 and 1.02 average points higher than baselines of RoBERTa and BERTweet, respectively.

5.4 Model Comparisons

The purpose of our work is to produce representations effective across all social meaning tasks, rather than a single given task. However, we still compare our best model (i.e., PragS2) on each dataset to the SOTA of that particular dataset and the published results on a Twitter evaluation benchmark (Barbieri et al., 2020). *All our reported results are an average of three runs*, and we report using the same respective metric adopted by original authors on each dataset. As Table 5 shows, our model achieves the best performance on eight out of 15 datasets. On average, our models are 0.97 points higher than the closest baseline, i.e., BERTweet. This shows the superiority of our methods, even when compared to models trained simply with MLM with $\sim 3\times$ more data (850M tweets for BERTweet vs. only 276M for our best method). We also note that some SOTA models adopt task-specific approaches and/or require task-specific resources. For example, Bamman and Smith (2015) utilize Stanford sentiment analyzer to identify the sentiment polarity of each word. In addition, task-specific methods can still be combined with our proposed approaches to improve performance on individual tasks.

6 Zero- and Few-Shot Learning

Since our methods exploit general cues in the data for pragmatic masking and learn a broad range of social meaning concepts, we hypothesize they should be particularly effective in ***few-shot learning***. To test this hypothesis, we fine-tune our best models (i.e., PragS1 and PragS2) on varying percentages of the Train set of each task as explained in Section 4.2. Figure 2 shows that our two mod-

Task	Metric	SOTA	TwE	BTw	Ours (PragS2)
$\text{Crisis}_{\text{Oltea}}$	M-F_1	95.60*	-	**95.88**	95.68
$\text{Emo}_{\text{Moham}}$	M-F_1	-	78.50	80.14	**80.50**
$\text{Hate}_{\text{Waseem}}$	W-F_1	73.62**	-	88.00	**88.36**
$\text{Hate}_{\text{David}}$	W-F_1	90.00†	-	**91.27**	91.01
$\text{Humor}_{\text{Potash}}$	M-F_1	-	-	52.77	**53.83**
$\text{Humor}_{\text{Meaney}}$	M-F_1	**98.54**=	-	94.46	94.49
$\text{Irony}_{\text{Hee-A}}$	$F^{(i)}$	70.50††	65.40	71.49	**76.47**
$\text{Irony}_{\text{Hee-B}}$	M-F_1	50.70††	-	58.67	**61.67**
$\text{Offense}_{\text{-Zamp}}$	M-F_1	**82.90**‡	80.50	78.49	79.50
$\text{Sarc}_{\text{Riloff}}$	$F^{(s)}$	51.00‡‡	-	66.35	**68.88**
$\text{Sarc}_{\text{Ptacek}}$	M-F_1	92.37§	-	**96.35**	96.24
$\text{Sarc}_{\text{Rajad}}$	Acc	92.94§§	-	95.29	**95.66**
Sarc_{Bam}	Acc	**85.10**‖	-	82.28	81.27
$\text{Senti}_{\text{Rosen}}$	M-Rec	68.50◇	72.60	**72.90**	71.76
$\text{Stance}_{\text{Moham}}$	Avg(a,f)	71.00⊚	69.30	69.79	**73.45**
Average	-	77.02	73.26	79.61	**80.58**

Table 5: Model comparisons. **SOTA:** Best performance on each respective dataset. **TwE:** TweetEval (Barbieri et al., 2020) is a benchmark for tweet classification evaluation. **BTw:** BERTweet (Nguyen et al., 2020). We compare using the same metrics employed on each dataset. **Metrics: M-F_1:** macro F_1, **W-F_1:** weighted F_1, $F_1^{(i)}$: F_1 irony class, $F_1^{(i)}$: F_1 irony class, $F_1^{(s)}$: F_1 sarcasm class, **M-Rec:** macro recall, **Avg(a,f)**: Average F_1 of the *against* and *in-favor* classes (three-way dataset). * Liu et al. (2021b), ** Waseem and Hovy (2016), † Davidson et al. (2017), = Meaney et al. (2021), †† Van Hee et al. (2018), ‡ Zampieri et al. (2019b), ‡‡ Riloff et al. (2013), § Ptáček et al. (2014), §§ Rajadesingan et al. (2015), ‖ Bamman and Smith (2015), ◇ Rosenthal et al. (2017), ⊚ Mohammad et al. (2016).

els *always* achieve better average macro F_1 scores than each of the RoBERTa and BERTweet baselines across *all* data size settings. Strikingly, our PragS1 and PragS2 outperform RoBERTa with an impressive 11.16 and 10.55 average macro F_1, respectively, when we fine-tune them on only 1% of the downstream gold data. If we use only 5% of gold data, our PragS1 and PragS2 improve over the RoBERTa baseline with 5.50% and 5.08 points, respectively. This demonstrates that our proposed methods most effectively alleviate the challenge of labeled data even under the *severely* few-shot setting. In addition, we observe that the domain-specific LM, BERTweet, is outperformed by RoBERTa when labeled training data is severely scarce ($\leq$ 20%) (although it achieves superior performance when it is fine-tuned on the full dataset). *These results suggest that, for the scarce data setting, it may be better to further pre-train and surrogate fine-tune an PLM than pre-train a domain-specific LM from scratch.* We provide model performance on each downstream task and various few-shot settings in Section B in Appendix.

Our proposed methods are language agnostic,

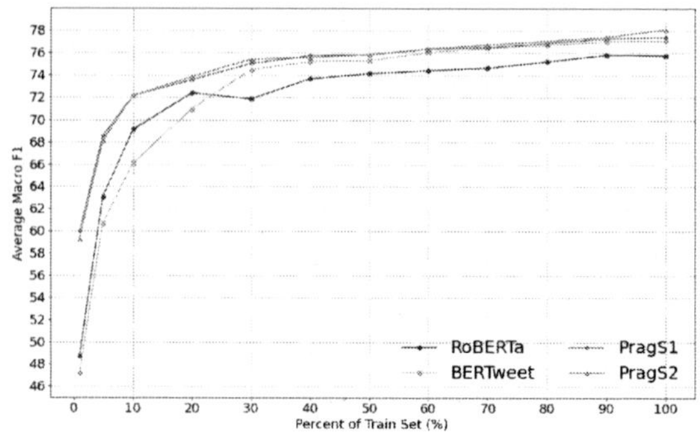

Figure 2: Few-shot learning on downstream with varying percentages of Train sets. The y-axis indicates the average Test macro F_1 across the 15 tasks. The x-axis indicates the percentage of Train set used to fine-tune the model.

	Task	RB	Prag2
Arabic	$\text{Emo}_{\text{Mageed}}$	29.81	**40.37**
	$\text{Irony}_{\text{Ghan}}$	31.53	**44.40**
Italian	Emo_{Bian}	**27.22**	26.40
	$\text{Hate}_{\text{Bosco}}$	40.59	**47.04**
Spanish	$\text{Emo}_{\text{Moham}}$	30.58	**35.09**
	Hate_{Bas}	41.43	**43.66**
Average		33.53	**39.49**

Table 6: Zero-shot performance. **RB:** RoBERTa.

and may fare well on languages other than English. Although we do not test this claim directly in this work, we do score our English-language best models on six datasets from three other languages (***zero-shot setting***). We fine-tune our best English model (i.e., PragS2 in Table 4) on the English dataset $\text{Emo}_{\text{Moham}}$, $\text{Irony}_{\text{Hee-A}}$, and $\text{Hate}_{\text{David}}$ and, then, evaluate on the Test set of emotion, irony, and hate speech datasets from other languages, respectively. We compare these models against the English RoBERTa baseline fine-tuned on the same English data. As Table 6 shows, our models outperform the baseline in the zero-shot setting on five out of six dataset with an average improvement of 5.96 F_1. These results emphasize the effectiveness of our methods even in the zero-shot setting across different languages and tasks, and motivate future work further extending our methods to other languages.

7 Model Analyses

To better understand model behavior, we carry out both a qualitative and a quantitative analysis. For the qualitative analysis, we encode all the Dev and Test samples from one emotion downstream task using two PLMs (RoBERTa and BERTweet) and our two best models (i.e., PragS1 and PragS2)[8]. We then use the hidden state of the [CLS] token from the last Transformer encoder layer as the representation of each input. We then map these tweet representation vectors (768 dimensions) to a 2-D space through t-SNE technique (Van der Maaten and Hinton, 2008) and visualize the results. Comparing our models to the original RoBERTa and BERTweet, we observe that the representations from our models give sensible clustering of emotions before fine-tuning on downstream dataset.

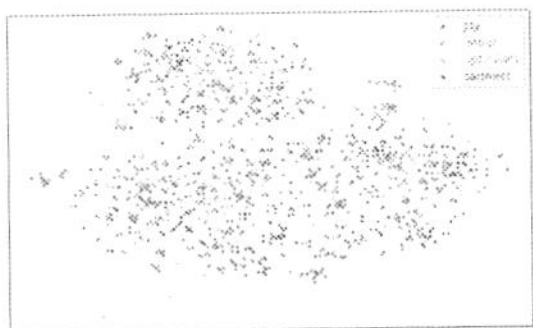

(a) RoBETa

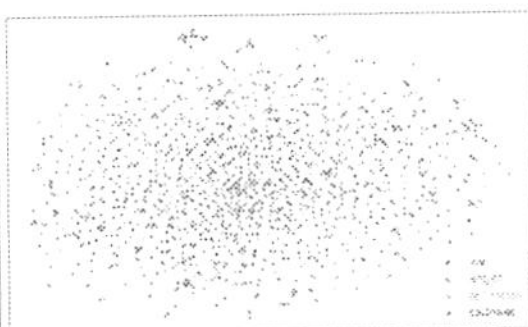

(b) BERTweet

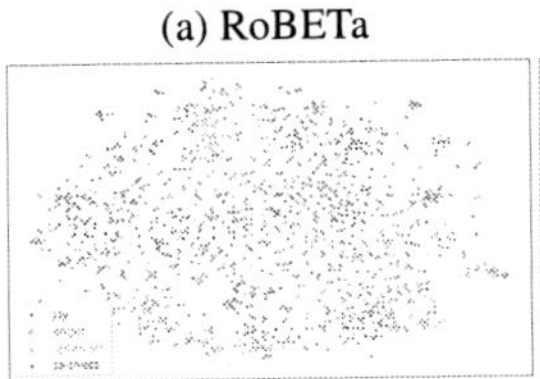

(c) PragS1

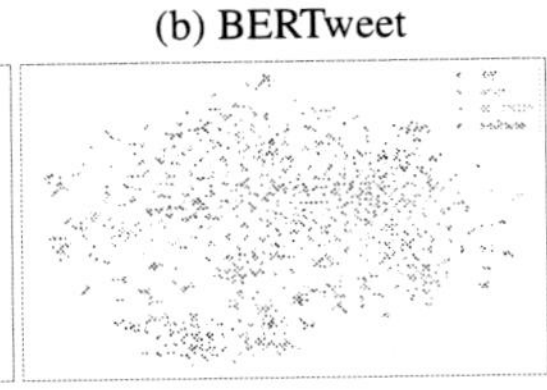

(d) PragS2

Figure 3: t-SNE plots of the learned embeddings on Dev and Test sets of $\text{Emo}_{\text{Moham}}$. Our learned representations clearly help tease apart the different classes.

Recent research (Ethayarajh, 2019; Li et al., 2020; Gao et al., 2021) has identified an anisotropy problem with the sentence embedding from PLMs, i.e., learned representations occupy a narrow cone, which significantly undermines their expressiveness. Hence, several concurrent studies (Gao et al., 2021; Liu et al., 2021a) seek to improve uniformity of PLMs. However, Wang and Liu (2021) reveal a uniformity-tolerance dilemma, where excessive uniformity makes a model intolerant to semantically similar samples, thereby breaking its underlying semantic structure. Following Wang and Liu (2021), we investigate the uniformity and tolerance of our models. The uniformity metric indicates the embedding distribution in a unit hypersphere, and the tolerance metric is the mean similarities of samples belonging to the same class. Formulas of uniformity and tolerance are defined in Section C in appendix. We calculate these two metrics for each model using development data from our 13 downstream datasets (excluding $\text{Crisis}_{\text{Oltea}}$ and $\text{Stance}_{\text{Moham}}$). As Table 7 shows, RoBERTa obtains a low uniformity and high tolerance score with its representations are located at a narrow cone where the cosine similarities of data points are extremely high. Results reveal that none of MLMs (i.e., pragmatic masking and random masking models) improves the spatial anisotropy. Nevertheless, surrogate fine-tuning is able to alleviate the anisotropy improving the uniformity. SFT-H achieves best uniformity (at 3.00). Our hypothesis is that fine-tuning on our extremely fine-grained hashtag prediction task forces the model to learn a more uniform representation where hashtag classes are separable. Finally, we observe that our best model, Prag2, makes a balance between uniformity and tolerance (uniformity= 2.36, tolerance= 0.35).

Model	Performance	Uniformity	Tolerance
RoBERTa	75.78	0.02	**1.00**
RM-NR	75.80	0.06	0.99
RM-N	75.92	0.06	0.99
PM-N	76.61	0.02	0.99
RM-HA	75.90	0.01	0.99
PM-HA	75.69	0.04	0.99
RM-HE	75.51	0.02	0.99
PM-HE	76.59	0.05	0.99
RM-EA	76.92	0.02	1.00
PM-EA	77.30	0.02	0.99
RM-EE	76.78	0.02	0.99
PM-EE	76.96	0.03	0.99
SFT-H	77.79	**3.00**	0.21
SFT-E	76.94	2.65	0.30
PragS1	77.43	2.98	0.21
PragS2	**78.12**	2.36	0.35

Table 7: Comparison of uniformity and tolerance. For both metrics, higher is better.

8 Conclusion

We proposed two novel methods for improving transfer learning with PLMs, pragmatic masking and surrogate fine-tuning, and demonstrated the effectiveness of these methods on a wide range of social meaning datasets. Our models exhibit remarkable performance in the few-shot setting and even the severely few-shot setting. Our models also establish new SOTA on eight out of fifteen datasets when compared to tailored, task-specific models with access to external resources. Our proposed methods are also language independent, and show promising performance when applied in zero-shot settings on six datasets from three different languages. In future research, we plan to further test this language independence claim. We hope our methods will inspire new work on improving language models without use of much labeled data.

[8]Note that we use these representation models *without* downstream fine-tuning.

Acknowledgements

We gratefully acknowledge support from the Natural Sciences and Engineering Research Council of Canada (NSERC; RGPIN-2018-04267), the Social Sciences and Humanities Research Council of Canada (SSHRC; 435-2018-0576; 895-2021-1008), Canadian Foundation for Innovation (CFI; 37771), Compute Canada (CC),[9], and UBC ARC-Sockeye.[10] Any opinions, conclusions or recommendations expressed in this material are those of the author(s) and do not necessarily reflect the views of NSERC, SSHRC, CFI, CC, or UBC ARC-Sockeye. We thank AbdelRahim ElMadany for help with data preparation.

References

Muhammad Abdul-Mageed and Lyle Ungar. 2017. EmoNet: Fine-grained emotion detection with gated recurrent neural networks. In *Proceedings of the 55th Annual Meeting of the Association for Computational Linguistics (Volume 1: Long Papers)*, pages 718–728, Vancouver, Canada. Association for Computational Linguistics.

Muhammad Abdul-Mageed, Chiyu Zhang, Azadeh Hashemi, and El Moatez Billah Nagoudi. 2020. AraNet: A deep learning toolkit for Arabic social media. In *Proceedings of the 4th Workshop on Open-Source Arabic Corpora and Processing Tools, with a Shared Task on Offensive Language Detection*, pages 16–23, Marseille, France. European Language Resource Association.

David Bamman and Noah A. Smith. 2015. Contextualized sarcasm detection on twitter. In *Proceedings of the Ninth International Conference on Web and Social Media, ICWSM 2015, University of Oxford, Oxford, UK, May 26-29, 2015*, pages 574–577. AAAI Press.

Francesco Barbieri, Jose Camacho-Collados, Luis Espinosa Anke, and Leonardo Neves. 2020. TweetEval: Unified benchmark and comparative evaluation for tweet classification. In *Findings of the Association for Computational Linguistics: EMNLP 2020*, pages 1644–1650, Online. Association for Computational Linguistics.

Francesco Barbieri, Jose Camacho-Collados, Francesco Ronzano, Luis Espinosa-Anke, Miguel Ballesteros, Valerio Basile, Viviana Patti, and Horacio Saggion. 2018. SemEval 2018 task 2: Multilingual emoji prediction. In *Proceedings of The 12th International Workshop on Semantic Evaluation*, pages 24–33, New Orleans, Louisiana. Association for Computational Linguistics.

[9]https://www.computecanada.ca

[10]https://arc.ubc.ca/ubc-arc-sockeye

Valerio Basile, Cristina Bosco, Elisabetta Fersini, Debora Nozza, Viviana Patti, Francisco Manuel Rangel Pardo, Paolo Rosso, and Manuela Sanguinetti. 2019. SemEval-2019 task 5: Multilingual detection of hate speech against immigrants and women in Twitter. In *Proceedings of the 13th International Workshop on Semantic Evaluation*, pages 54–63, Minneapolis, Minnesota, USA. Association for Computational Linguistics.

Federico Bianchi, Debora Nozza, and Dirk Hovy. 2021. FEEL-IT: emotion and sentiment classification for the italian language. In *Proceedings of the Eleventh Workshop on Computational Approaches to Subjectivity, Sentiment and Social Media Analysis, WASSA@EACL 2021, Online, April 19, 2021*, pages 76–83. Association for Computational Linguistics.

Cristina Bosco, Felice Dell'Orletta, Fabio Poletto, Manuela Sanguinetti, and Maurizio Tesconi. 2018. Overview of the EVALITA 2018 hate speech detection task. In *Proceedings of the Sixth Evaluation Campaign of Natural Language Processing and Speech Tools for Italian. Final Workshop (EVALITA 2018) co-located with the Fifth Italian Conference on Computational Linguistics (CLiC-it 2018), Turin, Italy, December 12-13, 2018*, volume 2263 of *CEUR Workshop Proceedings*. CEUR-WS.org.

Ting-Yun Chang and Chi-Jen Lu. 2021. Rethinking why intermediate-task fine-tuning works. In *Findings of the Association for Computational Linguistics: EMNLP 2021*, pages 706–713, Punta Cana, Dominican Republic. Association for Computational Linguistics.

Michele Corazza, Stefano Menini, Elena Cabrio, Sara Tonelli, and Serena Villata. 2020. Hybrid emoji-based masked language models for zero-shot abusive language detection. In *Findings of the Association for Computational Linguistics: EMNLP 2020*, pages 943–949, Online. Association for Computational Linguistics.

Thomas Davidson, Dana Warmsley, Michael W. Macy, and Ingmar Weber. 2017. Automated hate speech detection and the problem of offensive language. In *Proceedings of the Eleventh International Conference on Web and Social Media, ICWSM 2017, Montréal, Québec, Canada, May 15-18, 2017*, pages 512–515. AAAI Press.

Jacob Devlin, Ming-Wei Chang, Kenton Lee, and Kristina Toutanova. 2019. BERT: Pre-training of deep bidirectional transformers for language understanding. In *Proceedings of the 2019 Conference of the North American Chapter of the Association for Computational Linguistics: Human Language Technologies, Volume 1 (Long and Short Papers)*, pages 4171–4186, Minneapolis, Minnesota. Association for Computational Linguistics.

Kawin Ethayarajh. 2019. How contextual are contextualized word representations? Comparing the geometry of BERT, ELMo, and GPT-2 embeddings. In

Proceedings of the 2019 Conference on Empirical Methods in Natural Language Processing and the 9th International Joint Conference on Natural Language Processing (EMNLP-IJCNLP), pages 55–65, Hong Kong, China. Association for Computational Linguistics.

Bjarke Felbo, Alan Mislove, Anders Søgaard, Iyad Rahwan, and Sune Lehmann. 2017. Using millions of emoji occurrences to learn any-domain representations for detecting sentiment, emotion and sarcasm. In *Proceedings of the 2017 Conference on Empirical Methods in Natural Language Processing*, pages 1615–1625, Copenhagen, Denmark. Association for Computational Linguistics.

Tianyu Gao, Xingcheng Yao, and Danqi Chen. 2021. SimCSE: Simple contrastive learning of sentence embeddings. In *Proceedings of the 2021 Conference on Empirical Methods in Natural Language Processing*, pages 6894–6910, Online and Punta Cana, Dominican Republic. Association for Computational Linguistics.

Bilal Ghanem, Jihen Karoui, Farah Benamara, Véronique Moriceau, and Paolo Rosso. 2019. IDAT at FIRE2019: overview of the track on irony detection in arabic tweets. In *FIRE '19: Forum for Information Retrieval Evaluation, Kolkata, India, December, 2019*, pages 10–13. ACM.

Yuxian Gu, Zhengyan Zhang, Xiaozhi Wang, Zhiyuan Liu, and Maosong Sun. 2020. Train no evil: Selective masking for task-guided pre-training. In *Proceedings of the 2020 Conference on Empirical Methods in Natural Language Processing (EMNLP)*, pages 6966–6974, Online. Association for Computational Linguistics.

Kornraphop Kawintiranon and Lisa Singh. 2021. Knowledge enhanced masked language model for stance detection. In *Proceedings of the 2021 Conference of the North American Chapter of the Association for Computational Linguistics: Human Language Technologies*, pages 4725–4735, Online. Association for Computational Linguistics.

Pei Ke, Haozhe Ji, Siyang Liu, Xiaoyan Zhu, and Minlie Huang. 2020. SentiLARE: Sentiment-aware language representation learning with linguistic knowledge. In *Proceedings of the 2020 Conference on Empirical Methods in Natural Language Processing (EMNLP)*, pages 6975–6988, Online. Association for Computational Linguistics.

Bohan Li, Hao Zhou, Junxian He, Mingxuan Wang, Yiming Yang, and Lei Li. 2020. On the sentence embeddings from pre-trained language models. In *Proceedings of the 2020 Conference on Empirical Methods in Natural Language Processing (EMNLP)*, pages 9119–9130, Online. Association for Computational Linguistics.

Chen Lin, Timothy Miller, Dmitriy Dligach, Steven Bethard, and Guergana Savova. 2021. EntityBERT: Entity-centric masking strategy for model pretraining for the clinical domain. In *Proceedings of the 20th Workshop on Biomedical Language Processing*, pages 191–201, Online. Association for Computational Linguistics.

Fangyu Liu, Ivan Vulic, Anna Korhonen, and Nigel Collier. 2021a. Fast, effective, and self-supervised: Transforming masked language models into universal lexical and sentence encoders. In *Proceedings of the 2021 Conference on Empirical Methods in Natural Language Processing, EMNLP 2021, Virtual Event / Punta Cana, Dominican Republic, 7-11 November, 2021*, pages 1442–1459. Association for Computational Linguistics.

Junhua Liu, Trisha Singhal, Luciënne T. M. Blessing, Kristin L. Wood, and Kwan Hui Lim. 2021b. Crisisbert: A robust transformer for crisis classification and contextual crisis embedding. In *HT '21: 32nd ACM Conference on Hypertext and Social Media, Virtual Event, Ireland, 30 August 2021 - 2 September 2021*, pages 133–141. ACM.

Yinhan Liu, Myle Ott, Naman Goyal, Jingfei Du, Mandar Joshi, Danqi Chen, Omer Levy, Mike Lewis, Luke Zettlemoyer, and Veselin Stoyanov. 2019. Roberta: A robustly optimized BERT pretraining approach. *CoRR*, abs/1907.11692.

Ilya Loshchilov and Frank Hutter. 2019. Decoupled weight decay regularization. In *7th International Conference on Learning Representations, ICLR 2019, New Orleans, LA, USA, May 6-9, 2019*. OpenReview.net.

J. A. Meaney, Steven R. Wilson, Luis Chiruzzo, Adam Lopez, and Walid Magdy. 2021. Semeval 2021 task 7: Hahackathon, detecting and rating humor and offense. In *Proceedings of the 15th International Workshop on Semantic Evaluation, SemEval@ACL/IJCNLP 2021, Virtual Event / Bangkok, Thailand, August 5-6, 2021*, pages 105–119. Association for Computational Linguistics.

Saif Mohammad, Felipe Bravo-Marquez, Mohammad Salameh, and Svetlana Kiritchenko. 2018. SemEval-2018 task 1: Affect in tweets. In *Proceedings of The 12th International Workshop on Semantic Evaluation*, pages 1–17, New Orleans, Louisiana. Association for Computational Linguistics.

Saif Mohammad, Svetlana Kiritchenko, Parinaz Sobhani, Xiaodan Zhu, and Colin Cherry. 2016. SemEval-2016 task 6: Detecting stance in tweets. In *Proceedings of the 10th International Workshop on Semantic Evaluation (SemEval-2016)*, pages 31–41, San Diego, California. Association for Computational Linguistics.

Dat Quoc Nguyen, Thanh Vu, and Anh Tuan Nguyen. 2020. BERTweet: A pre-trained language model for English tweets. In *Proceedings of the 2020 Conference on Empirical Methods in Natural Language Processing: System Demonstrations*, pages 9–14, Online. Association for Computational Linguistics.

Alexandra Olteanu, Carlos Castillo, Fernando Diaz, and Sarah Vieweg. 2014. Crisislex: A lexicon for collecting and filtering microblogged communications in crises. In *Proceedings of the Eighth International Conference on Weblogs and Social Media, ICWSM 2014, Ann Arbor, Michigan, USA, June 1-4, 2014*. The AAAI Press.

Jason Phang, Iacer Calixto, Phu Mon Htut, Yada Pruksachatkun, Haokun Liu, Clara Vania, Katharina Kann, and Samuel R. Bowman. 2020. English intermediate-task training improves zero-shot cross-lingual transfer too. In *Proceedings of the 1st Conference of the Asia-Pacific Chapter of the Association for Computational Linguistics and the 10th International Joint Conference on Natural Language Processing*, pages 557–575, Suzhou, China. Association for Computational Linguistics.

Peter Potash, Alexey Romanov, and Anna Rumshisky. 2017. SemEval-2017 task 6: #HashtagWars: Learning a sense of humor. In *Proceedings of the 11th International Workshop on Semantic Evaluation (SemEval-2017)*, pages 49–57, Vancouver, Canada. Association for Computational Linguistics.

Clifton Poth, Jonas Pfeiffer, Andreas Rücklé, and Iryna Gurevych. 2021. What to pre-train on? Efficient intermediate task selection. In *Proceedings of the 2021 Conference on Empirical Methods in Natural Language Processing*, pages 10585–10605, Online and Punta Cana, Dominican Republic. Association for Computational Linguistics.

Yada Pruksachatkun, Jason Phang, Haokun Liu, Phu Mon Htut, Xiaoyi Zhang, Richard Yuanzhe Pang, Clara Vania, Katharina Kann, and Samuel R. Bowman. 2020. Intermediate-task transfer learning with pretrained language models: When and why does it work? In *Proceedings of the 58th Annual Meeting of the Association for Computational Linguistics*, pages 5231–5247, Online. Association for Computational Linguistics.

Tomáš Ptáček, Ivan Habernal, and Jun Hong. 2014. Sarcasm detection on Czech and English Twitter. In *Proceedings of COLING 2014, the 25th International Conference on Computational Linguistics: Technical Papers*, pages 213–223, Dublin, Ireland. Dublin City University and Association for Computational Linguistics.

Ashwin Rajadesingan, Reza Zafarani, and Huan Liu. 2015. Sarcasm detection on twitter: A behavioral modeling approach. In *Proceedings of the Eighth ACM International Conference on Web Search and Data Mining, WSDM 2015, Shanghai, China, February 2-6, 2015*, pages 97–106. ACM.

Yafeng Ren, Yue Zhang, Meishan Zhang, and Donghong Ji. 2016. Context-sensitive twitter sentiment classification using neural network. In *Proceedings of the Thirtieth AAAI Conference on Artificial Intelligence, February 12-17, 2016, Phoenix, Arizona, USA*, pages 215–221. AAAI Press.

Ellen Riloff, Ashequl Qadir, Prafulla Surve, Lalindra De Silva, Nathan Gilbert, and Ruihong Huang. 2013. Sarcasm as contrast between a positive sentiment and negative situation. In *Proceedings of the 2013 Conference on Empirical Methods in Natural Language Processing*, pages 704–714, Seattle, Washington, USA. Association for Computational Linguistics.

Sara Rosenthal, Noura Farra, and Preslav Nakov. 2017. SemEval-2017 task 4: Sentiment analysis in Twitter. In *Proceedings of the 11th International Workshop on Semantic Evaluation (SemEval-2017)*, pages 502–518, Vancouver, Canada. Association for Computational Linguistics.

Valentina Sintsova and Pearl Pu. 2016. Dystemo: Distant supervision method for multi-category emotion recognition in tweets. *ACM Trans. Intell. Syst. Technol.*, 8(1).

Kaitao Song, Xu Tan, Tao Qin, Jianfeng Lu, and Tie-Yan Liu. 2019. MASS: masked sequence to sequence pre-training for language generation. In *Proceedings of the 36th International Conference on Machine Learning, ICML 2019, 9-15 June 2019, Long Beach, California, USA*, volume 97 of *Proceedings of Machine Learning Research*, pages 5926–5936. PMLR.

Yu Sun, Shuohuan Wang, Yu-Kun Li, Shikun Feng, Xuyi Chen, Han Zhang, Xin Tian, Danxiang Zhu, Hao Tian, and Hua Wu. 2019. ERNIE: enhanced representation through knowledge integration. *CoRR*, abs/1904.09223.

Jenny A Thomas. 2014. *Meaning in interaction: An introduction to pragmatics*. Routledge.

Hao Tian, Can Gao, Xinyan Xiao, Hao Liu, Bolei He, Hua Wu, Haifeng Wang, and Feng Wu. 2020. SKEP: Sentiment knowledge enhanced pre-training for sentiment analysis. In *Proceedings of the 58th Annual Meeting of the Association for Computational Linguistics*, pages 4067–4076, Online. Association for Computational Linguistics.

Laurens Van der Maaten and Geoffrey Hinton. 2008. Visualizing data using t-sne. *Journal of machine learning research*, 9(11).

Cynthia Van Hee, Els Lefever, and Véronique Hoste. 2018. SemEval-2018 task 3: Irony detection in English tweets. In *Proceedings of The 12th International Workshop on Semantic Evaluation*, pages 39–50, New Orleans, Louisiana. Association for Computational Linguistics.

Ashish Vaswani, Noam Shazeer, Niki Parmar, Jakob Uszkoreit, Llion Jones, Aidan N. Gomez, Lukasz Kaiser, and Illia Polosukhin. 2017. Attention is all you need. In *Advances in Neural Information Processing Systems 30: Annual Conference on Neural Information Processing Systems 2017, December 4-9, 2017, Long Beach, CA, USA*, pages 5998–6008.

Alex Wang, Jan Hula, Patrick Xia, Raghavendra Pappagari, R. Thomas McCoy, Roma Patel, Najoung Kim, Ian Tenney, Yinghui Huang, Katherin Yu, Shuning Jin, Berlin Chen, Benjamin Van Durme, Edouard Grave, Ellie Pavlick, and Samuel R. Bowman. 2019. Can you tell me how to get past sesame street? sentence-level pretraining beyond language modeling. In *Proceedings of the 57th Annual Meeting of the Association for Computational Linguistics*, pages 4465–4476, Florence, Italy. Association for Computational Linguistics.

Feng Wang and Huaping Liu. 2021. Understanding the behaviour of contrastive loss. In *IEEE Conference on Computer Vision and Pattern Recognition, CVPR 2021, virtual, June 19-25, 2021*, pages 2495–2504. Computer Vision Foundation / IEEE.

Zeerak Waseem and Dirk Hovy. 2016. Hateful symbols or hateful people? predictive features for hate speech detection on Twitter. In *Proceedings of the NAACL Student Research Workshop*, pages 88–93, San Diego, California. Association for Computational Linguistics.

Michael Wiegand and Josef Ruppenhofer. 2021. Exploiting emojis for abusive language detection. In *Proceedings of the 16th Conference of the European Chapter of the Association for Computational Linguistics: Main Volume*, pages 369–380, Online. Association for Computational Linguistics.

Thomas Wolf, Lysandre Debut, Victor Sanh, Julien Chaumond, Clement Delangue, Anthony Moi, Pierric Cistac, Tim Rault, Remi Louf, Morgan Funtowicz, Joe Davison, Sam Shleifer, Patrick von Platen, Clara Ma, Yacine Jernite, Julien Plu, Canwen Xu, Teven Le Scao, Sylvain Gugger, Mariama Drame, Quentin Lhoest, and Alexander Rush. 2020. Transformers: State-of-the-art natural language processing. In *Proceedings of the 2020 Conference on Empirical Methods in Natural Language Processing: System Demonstrations*, pages 38–45, Online. Association for Computational Linguistics.

Ian Wood and Sebastian Ruder. 2016. Emoji as emotion tags for tweets. In *Proceedings of the Emotion and Sentiment Analysis Workshop LREC2016, Portorož, Slovenia*, pages 76–79.

Zhilin Yang, Zihang Dai, Yiming Yang, Jaime G. Carbonell, Ruslan Salakhutdinov, and Quoc V. Le. 2019. XLNet: Generalized autoregressive pretraining for language understanding. In *Advances in Neural Information Processing Systems 32: Annual Conference on Neural Information Processing Systems 2019, NeurIPS 2019, December 8-14, 2019, Vancouver, BC, Canada*, pages 5754–5764.

Marcos Zampieri, Shervin Malmasi, Preslav Nakov, Sara Rosenthal, Noura Farra, and Ritesh Kumar. 2019a. Predicting the type and target of offensive posts in social media. In *Proceedings of the 2019 Conference of the North American Chapter of the Association for Computational Linguistics: Human Language Technologies, Volume 1 (Long and Short Papers)*, pages 1415–1420, Minneapolis, Minnesota. Association for Computational Linguistics.

Marcos Zampieri, Shervin Malmasi, Preslav Nakov, Sara Rosenthal, Noura Farra, and Ritesh Kumar. 2019b. SemEval-2019 task 6: Identifying and categorizing offensive language in social media (OffensEval). In *Proceedings of the 13th International Workshop on Semantic Evaluation*, pages 75–86, Minneapolis, Minnesota, USA. Association for Computational Linguistics.

Zhengyan Zhang, Xu Han, Zhiyuan Liu, Xin Jiang, Maosong Sun, and Qun Liu. 2019. ERNIE: Enhanced language representation with informative entities. In *Proceedings of the 57th Annual Meeting of the Association for Computational Linguistics*, pages 1441–1451, Florence, Italy. Association for Computational Linguistics.

Junru Zhou, Zhuosheng Zhang, Hai Zhao, and Shuailiang Zhang. 2020. LIMIT-BERT : Linguistics informed multi-task BERT. In *Findings of the Association for Computational Linguistics: EMNLP 2020*, pages 4450–4461, Online. Association for Computational Linguistics.

Appendices

A Hyper-parameters and Procedure

Pragmatic Masking. For pragmatic masking, we use the Adam optimizer with a weight decay of 0.01 (Loshchilov and Hutter, 2019) and a peak learning rate of $5e-5$. The number of the epochs is five.

Surrogate Fine-Tuning. For surrogate fine-tuning, we fine-tune RoBERTa on surrogate classification tasks with the same Adam optimizer but use a peak learning rate of $2e-5$.

The pre-training and surrogate fine-tuning models are trained on eight Nvidia V100 GPUs (32G each). On average the running time is 24 hours per epoch for PMLMs, 2.5 hours per epoch for SFT models. All the models are implemented by Huggingface Transformers (Wolf et al., 2020).

Downstream Fine-Tuning. We evaluate the further pre-trained models with pragmatic masking and surrogate fine-tuned models on the 15 downstream tasks in Table 2. We set maximal sequence length as 60 for 13 text classification tasks. For $\text{Crisis}_{\text{Oltea}}$ and $\text{Stance}_{\text{Moham}}$, we append the topic term behind the post content, separate them by [SEP] token, and set maximal sequence length to 70, especially. For all the tasks, we pass the hidden state of [CLS] token from the last Transformer-encoder layer through a non-linear layer to predict. Cross-Entropy calculates the training loss. We then use Adam with a weight decay of 0.01 to optimize the model and fine-tune each task for 20 epochs with early stop ($patience = 5$ epochs). We fine-tune the peak learning rate in a set of $\{1e-5, 5e-6\}$ and batch size in a set of $\{8, 32, 64\}$. We find the learning rate of $5e-6$ performs best across all the tasks. For the downstream tasks whose Train set is smaller than $15,000$ samples, the best mini-batch size is eight. The best batch size of other larger downstream tasks is 64. For fine-tuning BERTweet, we use the hyperparameters identified in Nguyen et al. (2020), i.e., a fixed learning rate of $1e-5$ and a batch size of 32.

We use the same hyperparameters to run three times with random seeds for all downstream fine-tuning (unless otherwise indicated). All downstream task models are fine-tuned on four Nvidia V100 GPUs (32G each). At the end of each epoch, we evaluate the model on the Dev set and identify the model that achieved the highest performance on Dev as our best model. We then test the best model on the Test set. In order to compute the model's overall performance across 15 tasks, we use same evaluation metric (i.e., macro F_1) for all tasks. We report the average Test macro F_1 of the best model over three runs. We also average the macro F_1 scores across 15 tasks to present the model's overall performance.

B Few-Shot Experiment

Tables B.1, B.2, B.3, and B.4 respectively, present the performance of RoBERTa, BERTweet, PragS1, and PragS2 on all our 15 English downstream datasets and various few-shot settings.

C Uniformity and Tolerance

Wang and Liu (2021) investigate representation quality measuring the uniformity of an embedding distribution and the tolerance to semantically similar samples. Given a dataset D and an encoder Φ, the uniformity metric is based on a gaussian potential kernel and is formulated as:

$$Uniformity = log \mathop{\mathbb{E}}_{x_i, x_j \in D} [e^{t||\Phi(x_i) - \Phi(x_j)||_2^2}], \quad (1)$$

where $t = 2$.

The tolerance metric measures the mean of similarities of samples belonging to the same class, which defined as:

$$Tolerance = log \mathop{\mathbb{E}}_{x_i, x_j \in D} [(\Phi(x_i)^T \Phi(x_j)) \cdot I_{l(x_i)=l(x_j)}], \quad (2)$$

where $l(x_i)$ is the supervised label of sample x_i. $I_{l(x_i)=l(x_j)}$ is an indicator function, giving the value of 1 for $l(x_i) = l(x_j)$ and the value of 0 for $l(x_i) \neq l(x_j)$. In our experiments, we use gold development samples from 13 our social meaning datasets.

Task	1	5	10	20	30	40	50	60	70	80	90
Crisis$_{Oltea-14}$	94.67	95.36	95.55	95.74	95.90	95.81	95.89	95.84	95.99	96.03	96.11
Emo$_{Moham-18}$	14.10	30.36	71.76	73.62	76.26	77.02	77.59	77.19	77.38	77.84	78.86
Hate$_{Waseem-16}$	28.23	52.66	54.66	54.82	56.26	56.42	56.70	57.10	56.92	56.99	57.25
Hate$_{David-17}$	42.01	70.92	74.76	75.71	75.08	75.70	76.05	75.21	76.38	76.58	77.63
Humor$_{Potash-17}$	47.91	47.91	52.89	52.67	54.43	52.30	53.89	55.00	53.69	54.16	56.78
Humor$_{Meaney-21}$	53.44	89.50	89.47	90.12	91.95	91.65	92.33	91.96	92.65	91.78	92.27
Irony$_{Hee-18A}$	40.75	60.47	61.97	70.49	67.64	70.40	72.04	71.33	72.01	72.67	72.54
Irony$_{Hee-18B}$	19.41	26.27	43.61	46.47	44.78	48.41	50.40	51.65	51.80	53.15	53.17
Offense$_{-Zamp-19}$	41.89	76.87	74.44	76.53	79.75	79.29	78.95	78.13	79.01	79.42	79.90
Sarc$_{Riloff-13}$	44.41	44.80	43.99	70.49	51.10	70.70	67.72	72.46	67.98	72.88	73.75
Sarc$_{Ptacek-14}$	81.57	85.92	87.18	88.78	89.84	91.33	91.76	92.38	93.58	94.29	94.98
Sarc$_{Rajad-15}$	68.52	77.80	78.47	81.59	82.60	82.58	83.61	83.77	84.44	84.76	84.43
Sarc$_{Bam-15}$	64.17	74.01	75.95	76.18	77.00	78.07	78.43	78.68	79.35	79.08	79.40
Senti$_{Rosen-17}$	64.84	68.00	69.95	70.10	70.51	70.04	71.70	70.07	70.12	70.30	71.17
Stance$_{Moham-16}$	25.20	44.73	62.03	62.67	65.11	65.44	64.97	65.74	68.59	68.54	69.21
Average	48.74	63.04	69.11	72.40	71.88	73.68	74.14	74.43	74.66	75.23	75.83

Table B.1: Full result of few-shot learning on Baseline (1), fine-tuning RoBERTa.

Task	1	5	10	20	30	40	50	60	70	80	90
Crisis$_{Oltea-14}$	94.71	94.95	95.38	95.32	95.60	95.53	95.78	95.72	95.65	95.71	95.68
Emo$_{Moham-18}$	21.68	17.29	66.13	75.03	76.50	77.72	76.20	79.16	79.22	79.37	80.58
Hate$_{Waseem-16}$	30.92	52.27	53.70	55.05	55.18	55.80	56.48	56.44	56.46	57.10	56.66
Hate$_{David-17}$	29.21	69.18	74.17	76.58	77.95	76.97	77.19	77.43	77.29	77.72	78.30
Humor$_{Potash-17}$	47.90	47.91	48.24	51.68	51.25	53.37	54.80	54.39	54.91	52.31	55.83
Humor$_{Meaney-21}$	52.07	90.67	92.43	92.68	93.50	93.32	92.88	93.52	94.31	94.18	94.55
Irony$_{Hee-18A}$	44.88	57.78	67.90	71.87	74.40	75.42	75.15	75.94	75.42	76.80	76.82
Irony$_{Hee-18B}$	17.16	20.69	27.30	39.72	46.40	49.26	50.29	51.41	54.08	54.08	55.49
Offense$_{-Zamp-19}$	45.03	74.68	76.49	78.02	79.26	78.55	78.86	79.59	80.54	79.74	78.30
Sarc$_{Riloff-13}$	44.38	43.99	44.88	43.99	77.89	78.23	77.73	79.73	78.20	79.98	78.82
Sarc$_{Ptacek-14}$	85.36	88.06	89.18	90.58	91.44	92.60	93.44	93.64	94.40	95.30	95.77
Sarc$_{Rajad-15}$	47.01	81.87	83.24	84.22	85.31	85.38	85.73	85.86	86.11	86.77	86.76
Sarc$_{Bam-15}$	56.24	76.75	78.61	80.01	80.06	81.05	81.05	81.64	81.86	82.72	82.84
Senti$_{Rosen-17}$	65.42	67.96	69.85	70.38	71.24	71.49	71.76	71.29	71.49	72.29	71.63
Stance$_{Moham-16}$	25.69	25.36	24.27	59.25	61.58	63.45	62.31	65.08	66.64	66.54	67.63
Average	47.18	60.63	66.12	70.96	74.50	75.21	75.31	76.06	76.44	76.71	77.04

Table B.2: Full result of few-shot learning on BERTweet.

Task	1	5	10	20	30	40	50	60	70	80	90
Crisis$_{Oltea-14}$	94.35	95.34	95.37	95.74	95.85	95.83	95.92	95.92	95.91	95.98	95.86
Emo$_{Moham-18}$	36.95	64.31	74.68	77.94	79.79	80.19	80.23	80.19	80.30	80.78	81.27
Hate$_{Waseem-16}$	38.81	51.76	53.54	54.32	55.70	56.00	56.49	56.43	57.06	59.56	59.76
Hate$_{David-17}$	57.07	68.95	72.66	75.03	75.14	75.11	75.86	77.53	77.09	76.11	76.88
Humor$_{Potash-17}$	47.91	50.24	51.87	51.21	51.92	54.91	53.26	52.22	52.37	54.36	54.39
Humor$_{Meaney-21}$	87.10	91.79	92.16	92.42	92.80	93.01	93.05	93.53	93.64	93.86	93.70
Irony$_{Hee-18A}$	60.35	66.13	70.77	72.26	74.24	73.82	74.95	74.92	75.97	75.87	77.37
Irony$_{Hee-18B}$	29.82	36.42	41.72	46.50	50.14	53.57	52.63	55.80	54.23	55.92	56.62
Offense$_{-Zamp-19}$	61.17	74.22	77.05	77.63	79.22	80.62	79.09	80.77	81.27	79.85	79.68
Sarc$_{Riloff-13}$	52.83	63.39	73.40	74.34	77.10	78.01	77.87	77.53	77.32	77.32	78.72
Sarc$_{Ptacek-14}$	85.64	87.81	88.87	89.90	91.17	92.18	92.82	93.64	94.00	95.08	95.68
Sarc$_{Rajad-15}$	82.80	84.95	85.84	85.79	86.62	86.39	86.84	86.96	86.81	87.14	87.02
Sarc$_{Bam-15}$	72.44	77.74	78.97	80.27	81.08	81.74	81.56	81.62	81.98	81.53	82.29
Senti$_{Rosen-17}$	59.48	65.39	69.06	69.29	70.18	70.32	71.51	71.42	71.28	71.87	72.13
Stance$_{Moham-16}$	31.80	49.63	56.29	60.94	64.59	64.58	65.44	67.27	68.23	67.95	68.13
Average	59.90	68.54	72.15	73.57	75.04	75.75	75.83	76.38	76.50	76.88	77.30

Table B.3: Full result of few-shot learning on PragS1.

Task	1	5	10	20	30	40	50	60	70	80	90
$\text{Crisis}_{\text{Oltea-14}}$	93.92	95.07	95.50	95.30	95.60	95.50	95.73	95.66	95.52	95.70	95.96
$\text{Emo}_{\text{Moham-18}}$	35.90	58.23	71.27	75.36	77.71	78.80	79.25	78.99	79.74	80.06	81.28
$\text{Hate}_{\text{Waseem-16}}$	43.42	53.24	59.36	54.85	55.51	56.32	56.57	56.52	56.91	61.08	63.86
$\text{Hate}_{\text{David-17}}$	57.30	71.09	73.10	75.37	77.25	74.36	75.91	77.72	75.76	77.30	76.59
$\text{Humor}_{\text{Potash-17}}$	49.75	51.72	51.59	52.39	54.80	53.39	52.82	52.31	53.41	53.82	54.26
$\text{Humor}_{\text{Meaney-21}}$	84.95	92.09	92.73	93.16	94.17	94.07	93.54	93.57	93.81	93.52	93.89
$\text{Irony}_{\text{Hee-18A}}$	57.95	68.51	71.96	73.41	75.17	75.66	75.60	77.34	76.72	77.49	77.79
$\text{Irony}_{\text{Hee-18B}}$	29.69	35.93	41.51	48.44	52.77	52.71	55.87	56.07	58.13	55.63	55.43
$\text{Offense}_{\text{-Zamp-19}}$	52.61	70.40	74.09	76.45	78.80	78.02	76.90	79.53	79.35	79.73	79.42
$\text{Sarc}_{\text{Riloff-13}}$	49.57	64.07	75.80	75.46	78.28	78.93	78.89	78.31	79.71	78.86	79.04
$\text{Sarc}_{\text{Ptacek-14}}$	86.19	88.52	89.53	90.75	91.55	92.21	93.03	93.73	94.28	95.04	95.71
$\text{Sarc}_{\text{Rajad-15}}$	84.69	85.43	85.61	86.48	87.13	86.86	87.08	87.05	87.36	87.29	87.48
$\text{Sarc}_{\text{Bam-15}}$	73.40	77.28	77.88	79.84	79.40	80.29	80.31	80.32	80.60	80.95	80.39
$\text{Senti}_{\text{Rosen-17}}$	55.75	62.50	66.50	68.90	70.09	70.64	70.89	71.32	71.34	71.51	71.64
$\text{Stance}_{\text{Moham-16}}$	34.36	47.62	56.00	61.47	63.45	66.13	65.47	67.09	68.60	68.09	69.06
Average	59.30	68.11	72.16	73.84	75.44	75.59	75.86	76.37	76.75	77.07	77.45

Table B.4: Full result of few-shot learning on PragS2.

Distinguishing In-Groups and Onlookers by Language Use

Joshua R. Minot*
Vermont Complex Systems Center
University of Vermont
joshua.minot@uvm.edu

Milo Z. Trujillo*
Vermont Complex Systems Center
University of Vermont
milo.trujillo@uvm.edu

Samuel F. Rosenblatt
Department of Computer Science
Vermont Complex Systems Center
University of Vermont
samuel.f.rosenblatt@uvm.edu

Guillermo de Anda Jáuregui
National Institute of Genomic Medicine
(INMEGEN)
Universidad Nacional Autónoma de México
gdeanda@inmegen.edu.mx

Emily Moog
University of Illinois at Urbana-Champaign
Sandia National Laboratories
ermoog@sandia.gov

Briane Paul V. Samson
Center for Complexity
and Emerging Technologies
De La Salle University
briane.samson@dlsu.edu.ph

Laurent Hébert-Dufresne
University of Vermont
laurent.hebert-dufresne@uvm.edu

Allison M. Roth
University of Florida
amr2264@columbia.edu

Abstract

Inferring group membership of social media users is of high interest in many domains. Group membership is typically inferred via network interactions with other members, or by the usage of in-group language. However, network information is incomplete when users or groups move between platforms, and in-group keywords lose significance as public discussion *about* a group increases. Similarly, using keywords to filter content and users can fail to distinguish between the various groups that discuss a topic—perhaps confounding research on public opinion and narrative trends. We present a classifier intended to distinguish members of groups from users discussing a group based on contextual usage of keywords. We demonstrate the classifier on a sample of community pairs from Reddit and focus on results related to the COVID-19 pandemic.

1 Introduction

Online communities today have unprecedented power to impact the course of disease spread (Prandi and Primiero, 2020; Armitage, 2021), sway elections (Bovet and Makse, 2019; Persily, 2017), and manipulate global markets (Anand and Pathak, 2022). However, studies of online communities are often limited to single platforms due, in part, to the fact that the overlap in users across platforms is never explicitly known or because user networks and user behavior may differ across platforms (Hall et al., 2018; Trujillo et al., 2021; Grange, 2018). Nevertheless, there are some exceptions (*inter alia* (Yarchi et al., 2021; Alatawi et al., 2021; Horawalavithana et al., 2019)) and account mapping is an area of active research (*inter alia* (Chen et al., 2020)).

A powerful alternative to account mapping is to track language rather than users, which only requires data on the content of the platform and not necessarily their user base. There remain important caveats to this approach, however: 1) shifts in language can be hard to differentiate from shifts in user demographics and 2) language *about* a group of interest can look very similar to the language *of* the group itself. This is especially true if in-group vocabulary is used by outsiders when discussing the group, or if the in-group's vocabulary percolates into the general lexicon. An example of such language spread involves the word "incel", which was popularized in a specific online community before becoming more widely known.

Here, we address the second problem of distinguishing in-group members from onlookers engaged in discussion about the in-group, based on language alone. We introduce a group-classifier,

*These authors contributed equally to this work

Proceedings of the 12th Workshop on Computational Approaches to Subjectivity, Sentiment & Social Media Analysis, pages 157 - 171
May 26, 2022

which labels users as being in a group or discussing a group. We train our classifier on Reddit, an online forum broken into explicit sub-communities (i.e., "subreddits"). We identify pairs of subreddits, where one subreddit focuses on a particular topic (e.g., COVID conspiracies), and a second subreddit of "onlookers" discusses the first community or topic. Consistent user participation in a subreddit implies group membership, providing training labels; we filter outlier users who participate in or "troll" their chosen subreddit's counterpart. Our classifier attempts to distinguish users from each community based on their usage of topic words.

Our contributions in this piece are focused on two main points:

1. We propose a framing for in-group and onlooker discussion communities and discuss the value of differentiating between them in downstream analyses. This point is especially important for future work on cross-platform community activity.

2. We collect a novel data set of in-group and onlooker subreddit pairs and present a baseline classification pipeline to demonstrate the feasibility of separating groups of users accounts based on the content of their posts. We go on to present preliminary results on how this automatic labelling of user accounts may affect downstream analyses relative to the ground truth data.

The rest of this manuscript is organized as follows: in Section 2 we provide an overview of prior work, mainly in the complimentary spaces of stance detection and counter speech. In Section 3 we outline our methods, including the collection of a novel dataset of subreddit pairs. In Section 4 we present the results from our in-group and onlooker classifier along with the impact of automatic labelling on resulting language distributions. We discuss the implications of our work in Section 5 and concluding remarks in Section 6. Finally, in Section 7 we suggest areas for future work which could build upon our in-group and onlooker framing, improve our classification pipeline, and address broader research questions.

2 Previous work

We classify authors as being "in a group", or "discussing a group", not necessarily in an adversarial way. This closely resembles stance detection (Küçük and Can, 2020; Alkhalifa and Zubiaga, 2021). Research involving stance detection may be divided into two main categories (Alkhalifa and Zubiaga, 2021):

1. Predicting the likelihood of a rumor being true (i.e., rumor detection) by examining whether the stance of posts is supporting, refuting, commenting on, or questioning the rumor (Zubiaga et al., 2016, 2018; Hardalov et al., 2021).

2. Assessing whether the stance of a post is "pro", "against", or "neither" with respect to any given subject (Anand et al., 2011; Augenstein et al., 2016; Joshi et al., 2016; Abercrombie and Batista-Navarro, 2018; Alkhalifa and Zubiaga, 2021).

In some cases, manually labelled datasets are used to evaluate the quality of stance detection pipelines (Joseph et al., 2021) or train stance classifiers using supervised learning (Mønsted and Lehmann, 2022).

Similar to the latter category of stance detection, topic-dependent argument classification in argument mining also parallels our classification scheme, as it may work to evaluate whether a sentence argues for a topic, argues against a topic, or is not an argument (Mayer et al., 2018; Reimers et al., 2019; Lawrence and Reed, 2020).

"Perspective identification" works to assess an author's point of view, e.g., classifying individuals as "democrats" or "republicans" based the content of their post (Lin et al., 2006; Wong et al., 2016; Sobhani, 2017; Bhatia and Deepak, 2018). Our work also relates to the automated identification of "counter-speech", in which hateful or uncivil speech is countered in order to establish more civil discourse (Wright et al., 2017; He et al., 2021).

Our work is similar to the form of stance detection that evaluates "pro", "anti", or "neither" attitudes, but the problems of stance detection tend to assume that any discussion about a group are adversarial. However, the problem of distinguishing the language *about* a group from language *of* the group is much more general, as people discussing an emerging subculture do not necessarily oppose it. For example, onlookers may talk about non-political groups formed around new music scenes, small social movements or communities surrounding specific activities without holding opposing views to these groups. Political or not, identifying these onlookers can be of critical importance when studying a specific subculture.

3 Methods

3.1 Data Selection

Reddit partitions content into "subreddits": forums dedicated to a particular topic, with individual community guidelines and moderation policies. We identified seven (7) pairs of subreddits where one subreddit was focused on a highly-specific topic and another subreddit was dedicated to discussion about the first community. We selected clearly distinguishable communities that formed pairs of in-group and onlooking group subreddits. For example, r/NoNewNormal is a COVID-conspiracy and anti-vaccination group, while r/CovIdiots is dedicated to discussing anti-vaccination and COVID conspiracy theories (see Fig. 1 for an overview of 2-gram distributions for these subreddits). We selected this pair as our main case study because of the timeliness of the COVID-19 topic and the volume of conversation in each community. Partially owing to the contentious nature of the communities we were interested in, many of the subreddits we examined had previously been banned. Since data from banned subreddits remains available (Baumgartner et al., 2020), this did not inhibit our study or reproducibility.

Relationships between the primary community and the onlooking community were typically antagonistic. However, this does not mean that the results from standard sentiment analysis would have been able to correctly classify utterances from each group. For example, the r/NoNewNormal community may express negative opinions about vaccines or masking mandates, while r/CovIdiots may express positive sentiment about both topics, but negative sentiment about the opinions held by members of r/NoNewNormal.

For some of our subreddit pairs, the onlooker subreddit was created specifically to discuss the in-group subreddit. For example, r/TheBluePill was created in response to r/TheRedPill. For other pairs, both subreddits discussed the same topic from different viewpoints but were not directly connected. For example, r/ProtectAndServe is a subreddit populated by current and former law enforcement officers, while r/Bad_Cop_No_Donut is a subreddit dedicated to the criticism of law enforcement, but it is not specifically a criticism of r/ProtectAndServe itself. Including both types of subreddit pairs allowed us to measure the effectiveness of our classifier on communities with varying degrees of similarity.

3.2 Subreddits Chosen

The following are qualitative descriptions of each subreddit pair we examined. The size of each subreddit corpus, in terms of users and comments, as well as the mean comment score on each subreddit, can be found in the appendix (Table 4).

r/NoNewNormal and r/CovIdiots

r/NoNewNormal self-described as discussing "concerns regarding changes in society related to the coronavirus (COVID-19) pandemic, described by some as a 'new normal', and opposition to [those societal changes]." Most posts focused on perceived government overreach and fear-mongering. Reddit banned the subreddit on September 1st, 2021.

r/CovIdiots is dedicated to "social shaming" of covid conspiracy theorists, "anti-maskers," and "anti-vaxxers."

r/TheRedPill and r/TheBluePill

r/TheRedPill is a "male dating strategy" subreddit, commonly associated with extreme misogyny and a broader collection of "Manosphere" online communities including incels, men's rights activists, and pick up artists.

r/TheBluePill is a satirical subreddit targeting content from r/TheRedPill.

r/BigMouth and r/BanBigMouth

r/BigMouth is an online fan community that discusses the Netflix television series, "Big Mouth." The show often features coming of age topics, including puberty and teen sexuality.

r/BanBigMouth was a community focused on associating the TV show with pedophilia and child grooming, and petitioning for the show to be discontinued and removed. Reddit banned the subreddit in June, 2021 for promoting hate.

r/SuperStraight and r/SuperStraightPhobic

r/SuperStraight was an anti-trans subreddit that defined "Super Straight" as heterosexual individuals who were not attracted to trans people. Reddit banned the subreddit for promoting hate towards marginalized groups in March, 2021.

r/SuperStraightPhobic was an antagonistic subreddit critiquing the users, posts, and intentions of the r/SuperStraight subreddit. It was banned shortly after r/SuperStraight.

r/ProtectAndServe and r/Bad_Cop_No_Donut

r/ProtectAndServe is self-described as "a place where the law enforcement professionals of Reddit can communicate with each other and the general public." Users who submit documents proving their active law enforcement status have identifying labels next to their usernames.

Bad_Cop_No_Donut is a subreddit for documenting law enforcement abuse of power and misconduct. Most posts are links to news articles, while comments discuss article content and general police behavior.

r/LatterDaySaints and r/ExMormon

r/LatterDaySaints is an unofficial subreddit for members of the Church of Latter-Day Saints. While non-members of the church are permitted to ask questions and engage in conversation, criticizing church doctrine, policy, or leadership is forbidden, and the subreddit is heavily moderated.

r/ExMormon is a subreddit for former members of the Mormon church to discuss their experiences. Posts are typically highly critical of the church.

r/vegan and r/antivegan

r/vegan is a broad vegan community, with topics ranging from cooking tips, to animal cruelty, environmental impacts of meat consumption, and social challenges with veganism.

r/antivegan is ideologically opposed to veganism. Much of the subreddit's content is satirical, or critical discussion about the actions of perceived vegan activists.

3.3 Data Collection

For each pair of subreddits, we first chose an "ending date" for data collection: If either subreddit was banned prior to the start of our study, we used the earliest ban-date as our ending date. Otherwise, we used the date of our data download. We then downloaded all comments made in the subreddit for one year prior to the ending date, using pushshift.io, an archive of all public Reddit posts and comments which is frequently used by researchers (Baumgartner et al., 2020). We then filtered out comments made by bot users, using a bot list provided by (Trujillo et al., 2021).

We anecdotally observed users from some of our selected subreddits "raiding" other selected subreddits. For example, users from subreddits opposed to the r/NoNewNormal COVID-conspiracy group sometimes harassed users in r/NoNewNormal, and vice-versa. We did not want these harassment-comments to bias our text-analysis, so we filtered out all users who had an average comment-score less than unity for their comments in the subreddit. In other words, we only kept comments from users that the community did not strongly disagree with. This did not filter out coordinated attacks, where many members of one community raided another, upvoted their raiding comments, and downvoted the in-community comments. However, this type of attack (often referred to as "brigading") is a bannable offense on Reddit, and we did not observe it in our dataset.

3.4 Determining In-Group Vocabulary

To compare the n-gram distributions of pairs of subreddits we used rank-turbulence divergence (RTD) (Dodds et al., 2020). We used RTD to both summarize overall divergence and highlight specific n-grams that contributed most to this divergence value. We found RTD to be an effective choice when making more nuanced comparisons between the disjoint distributions of subreddit pairs. It avoids construction of the mixed-distribution found in other divergence measures—such as Jensen-Shannon divergence (JSD)—which may be less effective at highlighting salient terms with the subreddit-scale distributions.

The rank-turbulence divergence between two sets, Ω_1 and Ω_2, is calculated as follows,

$$D_\alpha^R(\Omega_1||\Omega_2) = \sum \delta D_{\alpha,\tau}^R = \frac{\alpha+1}{\alpha} \sum_\tau \left| \frac{1}{r_{\tau,1}^\alpha} - \frac{1}{r_{\tau,2}^\alpha} \right|^{1/(\alpha+1)},$$

where $r_{\tau,s}$ is the rank of element τ (n-grams in our case) in system s and α is a tunable parameter that affects the impact of starting and ending ranks.

We used a divergence-of-divergence metric (RTD^2) to identify n-grams that contributed to disagreement between base-divergence results derived from n-gram distributions. More specifically, we ranked the RTD values calculated from the ranks of the RTD contributions to divergence results for ground truth and predicted distributions (using our classifiers). Said another way, in cases where n-grams had high RTD^2 values, those n-grams would either be over- or under-emphasized in the data re-

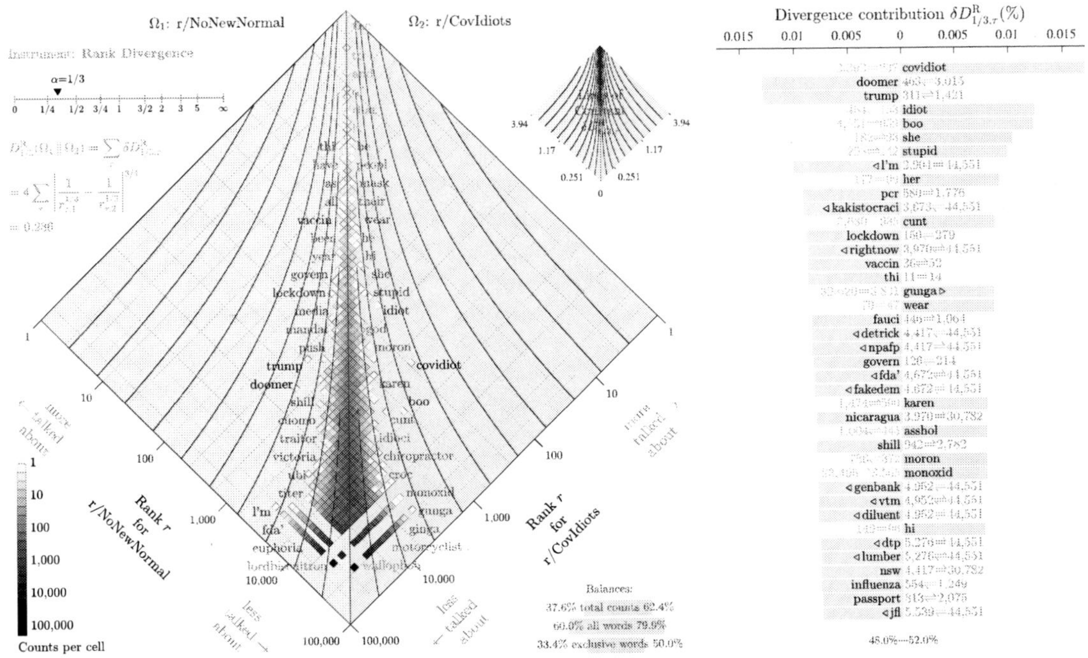

Figure 1: **An allotaxonograph (Dodds et al., 2020) showing the 1-gram rank distributions of `r/NoNewNormal` and `r/CovIdiots` along with rank-turbulence divergence results.** The central diamond shaped plot shows a rank-rank histogram for 1-grams appearing in each subreddit. The horizontal bar chart on the right shows the individual contribution of each 1-gram to the overall rank-turbulence divergence value ($D^{R}_{1/3}$). The 3 bars under "Balances" represent the total volume of 1-gram occurring in each subreddit, the percentage of all unique words we saw in each subreddit, and the percentage of words that we saw in a subreddit that were unique to that subreddit.

sulting from our classification pipeline when compared with the ground truth.

3.5 In-group and out-group prediction

We inferred membership of individual users in in-group or onlooker subreddits using two binary classification models. These models were applied to the entire concatenated comment history of users for a given subreddit. In addition to the data filtering described in Section 3.3, we removed users whose concatenated comment histories contained fewer than 10 1-grams. In order to investigate the effect of comment length on classification performance, we created a second training and evaluation data set—referred to as the "threshold" data set—with users whose comment histories contained at least 100 1-grams and who made at least 10 comments on their assigned subreddit. Due to the large class imbalance in most subreddit pairings, we under-sampled the majority class to rebalance the training and testing data sets.

To establish a baseline, we trained a logistic regression model on term frequency-inverse document frequency (TF-IDF) features. For the logistic regression model, we generated TF-IDF features by selecting 1-grams that appeared in at least 10 documents and at most 95% of total documents. We also removed English stopwords before feeding these features to a logistic regression model.

We compared the performance of the logistic regression model with a Longformer-based classifier (Beltagy et al., 2020). The Longformer model uses a sparse attention mechanism to address the quadratic memory scaling of the standard transformers (Vaswani et al., 2017)—in our cases allowing for the consideration of longer documents (comment histories). For the Longformer model, we used the default Transformers library (Wolf et al., 2020) implementation of a sequence classifier with a maximum sequence length of 2,048.

4 Results

4.1 Language classifier

For all subreddit pairs, we found that both language classifiers performed better than random, with some variation along subreddit size and community characteristics, as in Figs. 4 and 5. The Longformer model performed better in all cases (as indicated by the Matthews correlation coefficient (MCC) in Table 1). However, with sufficient data volume, the logistic regression classifier was able to achieve comparable results, especially notable given the reduced model complexity.

For the Longformer model trained and evaluated on r/NoNewNormal and r/CovIdiots, we achieved precision and recall values of approximately 0.75 for both classes Table 5. For the other subreddits, precision and recall values ranged between approximately 0.65 and 0.9 with near parity between the classes. See Fig. 2 for receiver operator characteristic (ROC) curves for the Longformer model.

The logistic regression classifier offered lower performance but relatively similar results with the added benefit of interpretable feature importance scores. In the case of r/NoNewNormal and r/CovIdiots, we report feature importance for the logistic regression model in Table 3. The feature importance results provide some insights on how bag-of-words models are capturing community-specific language. For instance, "media", "doomer", and "trump" are language features highly predictive of the r/NoNewNormal subreddit accounts. On the other hand, "idiots", "crocs", and "5g" are language features highly predictive of the r/CovIdiots accounts.

4.2 Divergence results

4.2.1 Initial observations

We found that RTD identified salient terms when comparing the 1-gram distributions of r/NoNewNormal and r/CovIdiots. As seen in Fig. 1, we found that terms relating to specific people and institutions such as "trump", "fda", and "fauci" drove RTD contributions from the r/NoNewNormal distribution. For the same subreddit, we found 1-grams related to vaccines—"vaccine[s]", "dtp" (Diphtheria-Tetanus-Pertussis), and "npafp" (Non-polio Acute Flaccid Paralysis)—which ranked higher than the opposing subreddit. Finally, some 1-grams related to non-pharmaceutical interventions ranked relatively higher in the r/NoNewNormal distribution, including "lockdown" and "passport". From the r/CovIdiots 1-gram distribution, we saw the eponymous term "covidiot" contributing the greatest to RTD followed by insults such as "stupid" and "karen"—illustrating the insulting critiques that many of the r/CovIdiots posts level at r/NoNewNormal.

The RTD results suggest a few characteristics of each subreddit. Both r/NoNewNormal and r/CovIdiots discussed prominent topics related to the pandemic—as seen by terms such as "mask", "vaccine", and "lockdown" ranking in the top 300 1-grams for each subreddit. The subreddits' focuses constrast each other with r/NoNewNormal appearing more focused on discussion that is critical of pandemic interventions and r/CovIdiots criticizing r/NoNewNormal (as evidenced by a higher degree of insulting language).

4.2.2 Effect of classifier on divergence results

Overall RTD values were similar for both the ground truth and predicted distributions ($D^{R}_{1/3}$ = 0.286 and 0.274, respectively). In Table 2 we present the top 20 1-grams as highlighted by RTD^2 . We saw fluctuations for terms related to internet memes (e.g., "gunga", "ginga", and "boo"). In other cases, function words like "he" and "be" are ranked as contributing notably to the RTD^2 results—this may be owing to nuanced differences in speech patterns between the two communities that are amplified by the classification and RTD^2 results. For some highly topical 1-grams, such "trump", "covidiot", and "influenza", we found shifts in rank limited to an order of magnitude—in these cases the salient 1-grams contributed more to RTD in the classifier-derived data set, likely owing to the bias of the model.

4.3 Accuracy versus user attributes

We expected our classifier to perform better on active users who received praise from a community (as indicated by the voting score on their comments). To confirm this hypothesis, we plotted the likelihood of correctly labeling users that post in r/NoNewNormal compared to their number of comments in the subreddit, total comment-score, and mean comment-score, shown in Fig. 3.

Our classifier performed most reliably on users with ten to three hundred comments in the subreddit, and ten to five hundred total karma. Performance decayed for users with over 400 comments, but there were only 520 users in this category out of about 58,000 r/NoNewNormal users. Anecdotally, this small subset of users engaged in longer

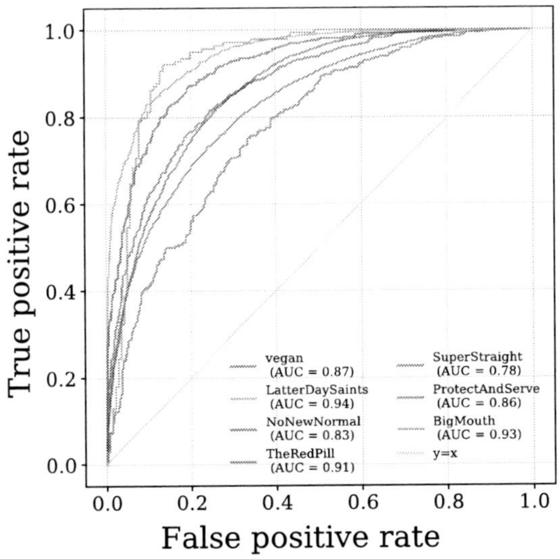

Figure 2: **Receiver operator characteristic curves for classification models evaluated on the subreddit pairs.** For each subreddit pair we trained a binary classifier based on the Longformer language model. The classifier trained on `r/BigMouth` and `r/BanBigMouth` showed the best performance (AUC = 0.93) while our primary case study—`r/NoNewNormal` and `r/CovIdiots`—had an AUC value of 0.83. It is worth noting the variation in sample sizes and as described in Table 1.

and more general discussions, and as a result, used language that is more common and more difficult to classify compared to their less active peers.

To filter out low-activity users, we re-ran our classifier after pruning accounts with less than under 100 one-grams in their comment history or less than 10 total comment in their associated subreddit. This filtering is discussed in Section 3.5 and labeled "Threshold" in Table 1 where we present the classification results. The threshold data generally improved the performance of both the logistic regression and Longformer models.

5 Discussion

The work outlined here is motivated by the challenge of accurately classifying communities that discuss the same topics but are distinct in their exact views. Further, we are motivated by the task of identifying these communities in the absence of interaction data that may allow for the construction of a social graph.

Our methodology addresses the challenge of analyzing online conversation around contentious topics where there may be polarized communities that share similar linguistic features. For instance, when studying online discourse around a specific topic one approach to collecting relevant content is anchor wording (selecting posts based on the presence of key words defined by a researcher). In the case of `r/NoNewNormal` and `r/CovIdiots`, "vaccine", "mask", and "covid" share similar rank values in the 1-gram distributions for each subreddit (55, 37; 24, 28; 51, 58; respectively). A naive anchor-word selection would capture much of the conversation in each of these communities. However, anchor word selection would fail to disambiguate the dramatically differing views held by the majority of users in each community. This has impacts on down stream analysis such as sentiment analysis, tracking narrative diffusion, and topic modelling.

Considering our main motivation was a problem description and initial demonstration of a classification pipeline, we did not extensively explore model architectures or hyperparameters. We included n-gram order in the initial hyperparameter sweep when developing the logistic-regression pipeline, and results suggested that 1-grams were most effective. However, including higher order n-grams is still worth exploring more in-depth, and may have benefits for model interpretabilility and down stream results (e.g., feature importance). Further, we selected the word-embedding model (the Longformer) based mainly on considerations related to maximum sequence length and preliminary performance observations. Additional word-embedding models could be considered—choosing models trained on more recent and/or domain specific data may be especially helpful.

As in stance detection (Alkhalifa and Zubiaga, 2021), there are several limitations to the methodology we present. First, our data set covers a limited time frame, and past work has demonstrated that models which are trained on old data sets may perform relatively poorly when fed new data (Alkhalifa et al., 2021; Alkhalifa and Zubiaga, 2021). Additionally, our methodology does not account for the fact that users may change opinions throughout time. For example, a user may initially be a member of a group, but a shift in opinion may cause the user to leave the group but still engage in discussion about said group. Lastly, our classifier is only trained on English posts, and we cannot guarantee the same level of performance across languages.

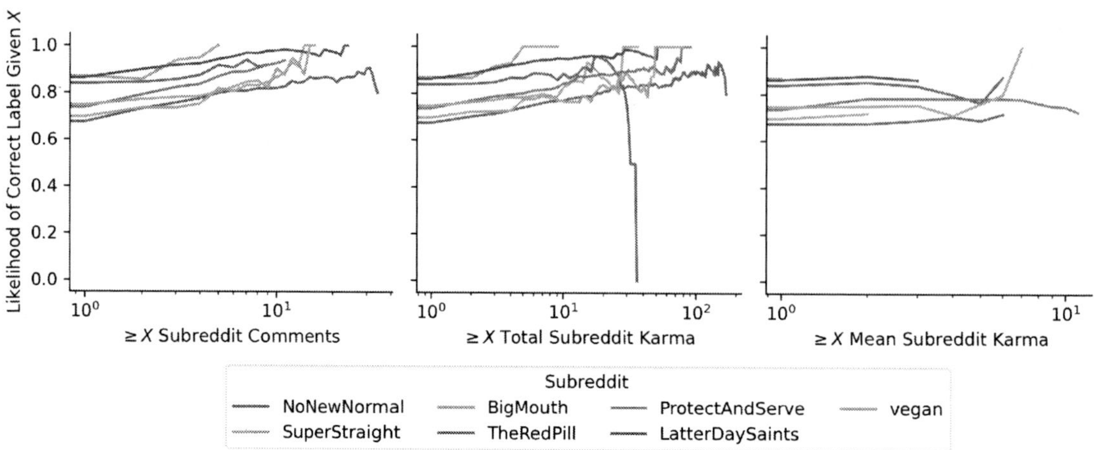

Figure 3: **Likelihood of correctly labeling users in in-group subreddits by user attributes.** From left to right, correct labeling versus user comments in the subreddit, correct labeling versus total karma in the subreddit, and correct labeling versus mean karma in the subreddit. In all cases, the classifier performed poorly with low-activity users, better with moderate activity. We have pruned the 10% of users with the highest attributes from this plot, to improve legibility. An unabridged version of the plot is in the appendix, with a more detailed explanation. Plots include only users that commented in the primary "of" subreddit. Results from base-LR classifier.

Table 1: **Data set size and classification performance for logistic regression (LR) and Longformer (LF) models.** Subreddit pairs, primary "of" community first, "onlooking" subreddit second. Matthews correlation coefficient (MCC) refers to performance on the test set. The threshold results refer models trained on a thresholded data set where user comment histories must contain at least 100 1-grams and at least 10 comments. Results excluded due to small sample size are represented with an "*".

Subreddits	**MCC**				**Data set size**	
	Base		**Threshold**		**Base**	**Threshold**
	LR	**LF**	**LR**	**LF**		
r/NoNewNormal v. r/Covidiots	0.41	0.48	0.57	0.60	44185	6778
r/TheRedPill v. r/TheBluePill	0.55	0.65	*	*	4680	402
r/BigMouth v. r/BanBigMouth	0.64	0.80	*	*	1394	140
r/SuperStraight v. r/SuperStraightPhobic	0.35	0.43	*	*	3310	584
r/ProtectAndServe v. r/BadCopNoDonut	0.50	0.55	0.65	0.76	41158	6930
r/LatterDaySaints v. r/ExMormon	0.65	0.72	0.80	0.83	15062	4122
r/vegan v. r/antivegan	0.49	0.56	0.65	0.72	6896	1692

6 Conclusion

In the present study, we frame the research challenge of classifying in-groups and onlookers based on the linguistic features of social media posts. The classification task is made difficult by the significant intersection of terms shared between the two communities, which may confound classification attempts. We collect a data set of seven (7) subreddit pairs that match the in-group and onlooker-group criteria, focusing our efforts on a case study of pro- and anti-COVID mitigation communities. These subreddits provide an appealing proving ground for group identification tasks, because subreddit participation acts as a noisy label in lieu of ground truth for group identity. We identify salient 1-grams that differentiate each communities' language distributions. Using the full collection of subreddit pairs, we train two classifiers to assign users to communities based on their posts. We demonstrate the feasibility of the classi-

1-gram	RTD^2 Rank	RTD rank (pred.)	RTD rank (actual)
he	1	11.0	446.0
be	2	4285.0	19.0
vaccin	3	7.0	104.0
thi	4	143.0	8.0
nyt	5	15.0	459.0
they	6	27.0	3414.5
diffrent	7	42.5	17076.0
ginga	8	73.5	9.0
gunga	9	24.0	5.0
shill	10	103.0	13.0
titer	11	11026.0	59.5
boo	12	2.0	1.0
covidiot	12	1.0	2.0
sham	14	52.0	4253.0
voluntari	15	53.0	4420.5
influenza	16	14.0	103.0
purg	17	1694.5	44.0
postul	18	16.0	123.0
trump	19	8.0	3.0
dui	20	51.0	1956.0

Table 2: **Rank-turbulence divergence (RTD) of divergence results from actual and predicted 1-gram distributions.** As a divergence-of-divergences measurement, RTD^2, shows disagreement between the divergence results derived from 1-gram distributions of generated with ground truth labels and the distribution generated with our classification pipeline. Highly ranked RTD^2 values highlight the 1-grams that have the greatest difference in rank of contribution to the divergence results for each pairing. For instance, "trump" is the 1-gram with the 3rd highest contribution in ground-truth data, whereas the 1-gram is ranked 8th in the classifier-generated data. We stemmed the 1-grams prior to calculation of divergence results.

fication scheme with these results. In most cases, our classifier recovers 70% or more of a community's users. From these results, we show how our initial language distribution divergence results may be affected by using data labelled by our classifier. In the case of the COVID subreddits, the true and classifier-generated distributions are qualitatively similar, identifying notable 1-grams in each case. We hope the research questions and combined set of results is motivating for future work that leverages training generalizable classifiers on labelled community data that can then be used in a variety of settings.

7 Future Work

We present a first attempt at in-group classification based on contextual language use, in a challenging environment where both the in-group and onlookers discuss many of the same topics. We believe that classifiers in this domain have important applications for cross-platform group detection, where more reliable labels like consistent usernames and network interactions are unavailable. More powerful classifiers may account for additional text features, including user sentiment, shared topics, stance towards those topics, and language style. Longer time-span studies should be wary of semantic drift over time (Schlechtweg et al., 2019), as well as more specific changes in group language and stance on topics. Models of community language style (Tran and Ostendorf, 2016) could also help identify communities across platforms, as long as platform-specific language style features are identified and controlled for.

References

Gavin Abercrombie and Riza Theresa Batista-Navarro. 2018. Identifying opinion-topics and polarity of parliamentary debate motions. In *Proceedings of the 9th workshop on computational approaches to subjectivity, sentiment and social media analysis*. Association for Computational Linguistics.

Hind S Alatawi, Areej M Alhothali, and Kawthar M Moria. 2021. Detecting white supremacist hate speech using domain specific word embedding with deep learning and bert. *IEEE Access*, 9:106363–106374.

Rabab Alkhalifa, Elena Kochkina, and Arkaitz Zubiaga. 2021. Opinions are made to be changed: Temporally adaptive stance classification. In *Proceedings of the 2021 Workshop on Open Challenges in Online Social Networks*, pages 27–32.

Rabab Alkhalifa and Arkaitz Zubiaga. 2021. Capturing stance dynamics in social media: Open challenges and research directions. *arXiv preprint arXiv:2109.00475*.

Abhinav Anand and Jalaj Pathak. 2022. The role of Reddit in the GameStop short squeeze. *Economics Letters*, 211:110249.

Pranav Anand, Marilyn Walker, Rob Abbott, Jean E Fox Tree, Robeson Bowmani, and Michael Minor. 2011. Cats rule and dogs drool!: Classifying stance in online debate. In *Proceedings of the 2nd Workshop on Computational Approaches to Subjectivity and Sentiment Analysis (WASSA 2.011)*, pages 1–9.

R. Armitage. 2021. Online 'anti-vax' campaigns and COVID-19: censorship is not the solution. *Public Health*, 190:e29–e30.

Isabelle Augenstein, Tim Rocktäschel, Andreas Vlachos, and Kalina Bontcheva. 2016. Stance detection with bidirectional conditional encoding. *arXiv preprint arXiv:1606.05464*.

Jason Baumgartner, Savvas Zannettou, Brian Keegan, Megan Squire, and Jeremy Blackburn. 2020. The pushshift Reddit dataset. In *Proceedings of the International AAAI Conference on Web and Social Media*, volume 14, pages 830–839.

Iz Beltagy, Matthew E Peters, and Arman Cohan. 2020. Longformer: The long-document transformer. *arXiv preprint arXiv:2004.05150*.

Sumit Bhatia and P Deepak. 2018. Topic-specific sentiment analysis can help identify political ideology. In *Proceedings of the 9th Workshop on Computational Approaches to Subjectivity, Sentiment and Social Media Analysis*, pages 79–84.

Alexandre Bovet and Hernán A. Makse. 2019. Influence of fake news in Twitter during the 2016 US presidential election. *Nature Communications*, 10(1):7.

Hongxu Chen, Hongzhi Yin, Xiangguo Sun, Tong Chen, Bogdan Gabrys, and Katarzyna Musial. 2020. Multi-level graph convolutional networks for cross-platform anchor link prediction. In *Proceedings of the 26th ACM SIGKDD International Conference on Knowledge Discovery & Data Mining*, page 1503–1511. ACM.

Peter Sheridan Dodds, Joshua R Minot, Michael V Arnold, Thayer Alshaabi, Jane Lydia Adams, David Rushing Dewhurst, Tyler J Gray, Morgan R Frank, Andrew J Reagan, and Christopher M Danforth. 2020. Allotaxonometry and rank-turbulence divergence: A universal instrument for comparing complex systems. *arXiv preprint arXiv:2002.09770*.

Camille Grange. 2018. The generativity of social media: Opportunities, challenges, and guidelines for conducting experimental research. *International Journal of Human–Computer Interaction*, 34(10):943–959.

Margeret Hall, Athanasios Mazarakis, Martin Chorley, and Simon Caton. 2018. Editorial of the special issue on following user pathways: Key contributions and future directions in cross-platform social media research. *International Journal of Human–Computer Interaction*, 34(10):895–912.

Momchil Hardalov, Arnav Arora, Preslav Nakov, and Isabelle Augenstein. 2021. A survey on stance detection for mis-and disinformation identification. *arXiv preprint arXiv:2103.00242*.

Bing He, Caleb Ziems, Sandeep Soni, Naren Ramakrishnan, Diyi Yang, and Srijan Kumar. 2021. Racism is a Virus: Anti-Asian Hate and Counterspeech in Social Media during the COVID-19 Crisis. In *Proceedings of the 2021 IEEE/ACM International Conference on Advances in Social Networks Analysis and Mining*, ASONAM '21, page 90–94, New York, NY, USA. Association for Computing Machinery.

Sameera Horawalavithana, Abhishek Bhattacharjee, Renhao Liu, Nazim Choudhury, Lawrence O. Hall, and Adriana Iamnitchi. 2019. Mentions of security vulnerabilities on reddit, twitter and github. In *IEEE/WIC/ACM International Conference on Web Intelligence*, page 200–207. ACM.

Kenneth Joseph, Sarah Shugars, Ryan Gallagher, Jon Green, Alexi Quintana Mathé, Zijian An, and David Lazer. 2021. (Mis) alignment Between Stance Expressed in Social Media Data and Public Opinion Surveys. In *Proceedings of the 2021 Conference on Empirical Methods in Natural Language Processing*, pages 312–324.

Aditya Joshi, Pushpak Bhattacharyya, and Mark Carman. 2016. Political issue extraction model: A novel hierarchical topic model that uses tweets by political and non-political authors. In *Proceedings of the 7th Workshop on Computational Approaches to Subjectivity, Sentiment and Social Media Analysis*, pages 82–90.

Dilek Küçük and Fazli Can. 2020. Stance detection: A survey. *ACM Computing Surveys (CSUR)*, 53(1):1–37.

John Lawrence and Chris Reed. 2020. Argument mining: A survey. *Computational Linguistics*, 45(4):765–818.

Wei-Hao Lin, Theresa Wilson, Janyce Wiebe, and Alexander G Hauptmann. 2006. Which side are you on? Identifying perspectives at the document and sentence levels. In *Proceedings of the Tenth Conference on Computational Natural Language Learning (CoNLL-X)*, pages 109–116.

Tobias Mayer, Elena Cabrio, Marco Lippi, Paolo Torroni, and Serena Villata. 2018. Argument mining on clinical trials. In *COMMA*, pages 137–148.

Bjarke Mønsted and Sune Lehmann. 2022. Characterizing polarization in online vaccine discourse—a large-scale study. *PloS one*, 17(2):e0263746.

Nathaniel Persily. 2017. The 2016 US Election: Can democracy survive the internet? *Journal of democracy*, 28(2):63–76.

Lorenzo Prandi and Giuseppe Primiero. 2020. Effects of misinformation diffusion during a pandemic. *Applied Network Science*, 5(1):82.

Nils Reimers, Benjamin Schiller, Tilman Beck, Johannes Daxenberger, Christian Stab, and Iryna Gurevych. 2019. Classification and clustering of arguments with contextualized word embeddings. *arXiv preprint arXiv:1906.09821*.

Dominik Schlechtweg, Anna Hätty, Marco Del Tredici, and Sabine Schulte im Walde. 2019. A wind of change: Detecting and evaluating lexical semantic change across times and domains. In *Proceedings of the 57th Annual Meeting of the Association for Computational Linguistics*, pages 732–746.

Parinaz Sobhani. 2017. *Stance detection and analysis in social media*. Ph.D. thesis, Universite d'Ottawa/University of Ottawa.

Trang Tran and Mari Ostendorf. 2016. Characterizing the language of online communities and its relation to community reception. In *Proceedings of the 2016 Conference on Empirical Methods in Natural Language Processing*, pages 1030–1035, Austin, Texas. Association for Computational Linguistics.

Milo Trujillo, Sam Rosenblatt, Guillermo de Anda Jáuregui, Emily Moog, Briane Paul V Samson, Laurent Hébert-Dufresne, and Allison M Roth. 2021. When the echo chamber shatters: Examining the use of community-specific language post-subreddit ban. In *Proceedings of the 5th Workshop on Online Abuse and Harms (WOAH 2021)*, pages 164–178.

Ashish Vaswani, Noam Shazeer, Niki Parmar, Jakob Uszkoreit, Llion Jones, Aidan N Gomez, Łukasz Kaiser, and Illia Polosukhin. 2017. Attention is all you need. *Advances in neural information processing systems*, 30.

Thomas Wolf, Lysandre Debut, Victor Sanh, Julien Chaumond, Clement Delangue, Anthony Moi, Pierric Cistac, Tim Rault, Rémi Louf, Morgan Funtowicz, Joe Davison, Sam Shleifer, Patrick von Platen, Clara Ma, Yacine Jernite, Julien Plu, Canwen Xu, Teven Le Scao, Sylvain Gugger, Mariama Drame, Quentin Lhoest, and Alexander M. Rush. 2020. Transformers: State-of-the-art natural language processing. In *Proceedings of the 2020 Conference on Empirical Methods in Natural Language Processing: System Demonstrations*, pages 38–45, Online. Association for Computational Linguistics.

Felix Ming Fai Wong, Chee Wei Tan, Soumya Sen, and Mung Chiang. 2016. Quantifying political leaning from tweets, retweets, and retweeters. *IEEE transactions on knowledge and data engineering*, 28(8):2158–2172.

Lucas Wright, Derek Ruths, Kelly P Dillon, Haji Mohammad Saleem, and Susan Benesch. 2017. Vectors for counterspeech on Twitter. In *Proceedings of the First Workshop on Abusive Language Online*, pages 57–62, Vancouver, BC, Canada. Association for Computational Linguistics.

Moran Yarchi, Christian Baden, and Neta Kligler-Vilenchik. 2021. Political polarization on the digital sphere: A cross-platform, over-time analysis of interactional, positional, and affective polarization on social media. *Political Communication*, 38(1–2):98–139.

Arkaitz Zubiaga, Elena Kochkina, Maria Liakata, Rob Procter, Michal Lukasik, Kalina Bontcheva, Trevor Cohn, and Isabelle Augenstein. 2018. Discourse-aware rumour stance classification in social media using sequential classifiers. *Information Processing & Management*, 54(2):273–290.

Arkaitz Zubiaga, Maria Liakata, Rob Procter, Geraldine Wong Sak Hoi, and Peter Tolmie. 2016. Analysing how people orient to and spread rumours in social media by looking at conversational threads. *PloS one*, 11(3):e0150989.

Appendix

Subreddit Corpus Sizes

Table 4 indicates the size of each subreddit, in terms of user count and comment count, after pruning bots and low-karma users as specified in our methodology. It also includes the mean karma (comment score) for remaining comments in each subreddit corpus.

Comparison of Subreddit Activity

If subreddits in a pair have dramatically different activity levels, such as much longer comments in one subreddit than another, these differences in writing style may correlate with classification difficulty. Figs. 4 and 5 show cumulative distributions of comment length and comment count per user, respectively, to illustrate which subreddits are closer in behavior than others.

Uniquely Identifying Words

Table 3 shows the words that most strongly correlate with membership in `r/NoNewNormal` and `r/CovIdiots`.

Labeled Language versus Predicted Language

Fig. 1 shows word use divergence between `r/NoNewNormal`and `r/CovIdiots`using all comments from users in each subreddit. For comparison, Fig. 7 shows the same word use divergence based only on users our classifier predicted as members of each subreddit.

Classifier performance metrics

Table 5 shows F1 scores and precision values for the logistic regression and longformer model.

Classifier Accuracy versus User Attributes

Our classifier performs best on accounts with above 10 comments and a minimum comment-karma threshold. However, the classifier cannot reliably label every user in the tail of the distribution. This leads to a misleading visualization, conflating the low-density of users that have high comment counts or karma scores with classifier performance. Therefore, we did not include the tail of each performance graph in Fig. 3. For posterity, we have included an unabridged version of the graph that includes these misleading tails, in Fig. 6.

`r/NowNewNormal`	`r/CovIdiots`
media	covidiots
emails	covidiot
questioning	retard
lockdown	cunt
jab	nnn
power	report
restrictions	idiot
narrative	deniers
woke	idiots
yall	idiocy
guys	crocs
passport	ugh
msm	5g
subreddit	selection
dystopian	wedding
sheep	frustrating
doomer	fox
doomers	hoax
sub	beard
trump	department

Table 3: **Feature importance for logistic regression classifier trained on `r/NowNewNormal` and `r/CovIdiots`**. The two columns correspond to the text features that are most strongly predictive of each subreddit.

Subreddit	Users	Comments	Mean Karma
r/NoNewNormal	57966	1245398	4.743
r/CovIdiots	28427	174056	4.119
r/TheRedPill	10149	59388	3.608
r/TheBluePill	2744	9616	4.716
r/BigMouth	6252	19904	1.895
r/BanBigMouth	981	3226	1.359
r/SuperStraight	5914	46491	2.686
r/SuperStraightPhobic	1897	11498	1.449
r/ProtectAndServe	25096	241328	7.484
r/Bad_Cop_No_Donut	77288	314933	5.898
r/LatterDaySaints	9130	131055	2.498
r/ExMormon	35672	852607	3.440
r/vegan	62544	622069	4.908
r/antivegan	4492	47738	3.878

Table 4: Users and comments in each subreddit, after filtering out bots and low-karma users

Subreddits	F1				Precision				Data set size	
	Base		Threshold		Base		Threshold		Base	Threshold
	LR	LF	LR	LF	LR	LF	LR	LF		
r/NoNewNormal v. r/Covidiots	0.71	0.74	0.83	0.80	0.71	0.74	0.83	0.80	44185	6778
r/TheRedPill v. r/TheBluePill	0.79	0.84	*	*	0.84		*	*	4680	402
r/BigMouth v. r/BanBigMouth	0.80	0.88	*	*	0.80	0.88	*	*	1394	140
r/SuperStraight v. r/SuperStraightPhobic	0.67	0.69	*	*	0.67	0.69	*	*	3310	584
r/ProtectAndServe v. r/BadCopNoDonut	0.75	0.78	0.90	0.88	0.75	0.78	0.90	0.88	41158	6930
r/LatterDaySaints v. r/ExMormon	0.83	0.86	0.95	0.91	0.83	0.86	0.95	0.91	15062	4122
r/vegan v. r/antivegan	0.75	0.78	0.88	0.86	0.75	0.78	0.88	0.86	6896	1692

Table 5: **Data set size and classification performance for logistic regression (LR) and Longformer (LF) models.** Subreddit pairs, primary "of" community first, "onlooking" subreddit second. F1 scores and precision values are calculated using weighted average for the balanced data sets. F1, precision, and recall (not shown) values were all approximately equal for specific models and subreddit pairs in our experiments—partially owing to the balanced datasets. The threshold results refer models trained on a thresholded data set where user comment histories must contain at least 100 1-grams and at least 10 comments. Results excluded due to small sample size are represented with an "*".

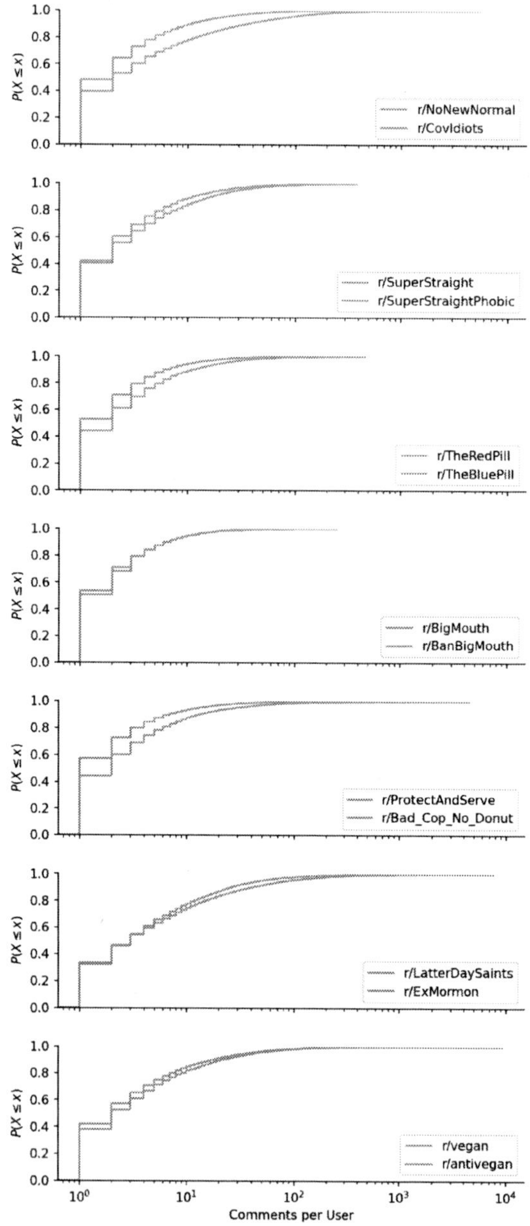

Figure 4: **Cumulative distribution of comments made by each user in each examined subreddit pair.** Distribution taken after filtering.

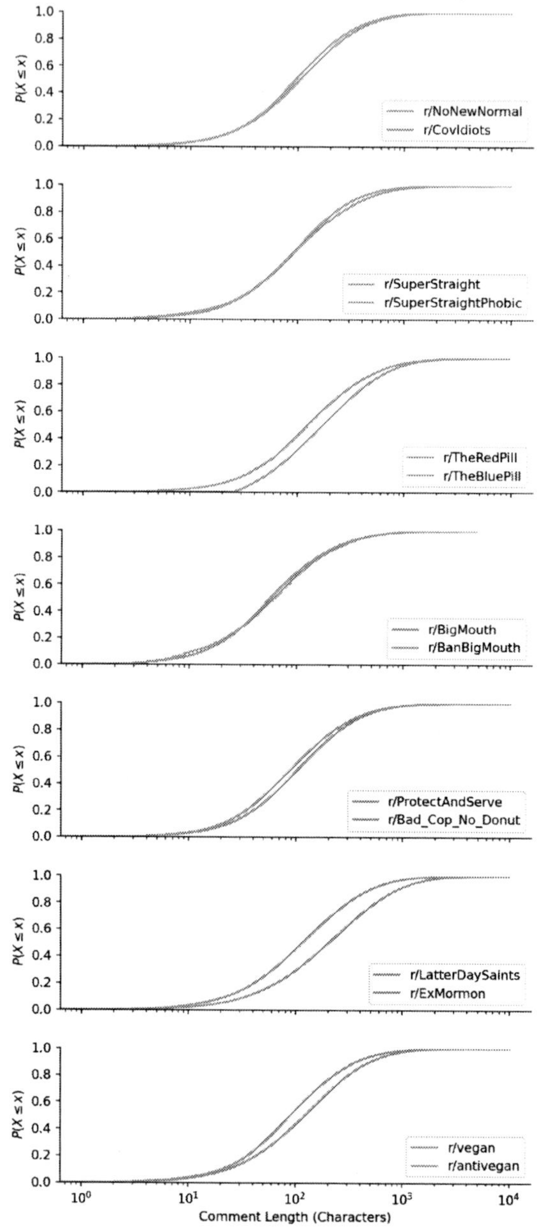

Figure 5: **Cumulative distribution of comment length in each examined subreddit pair.** Distribution taken after filtering.

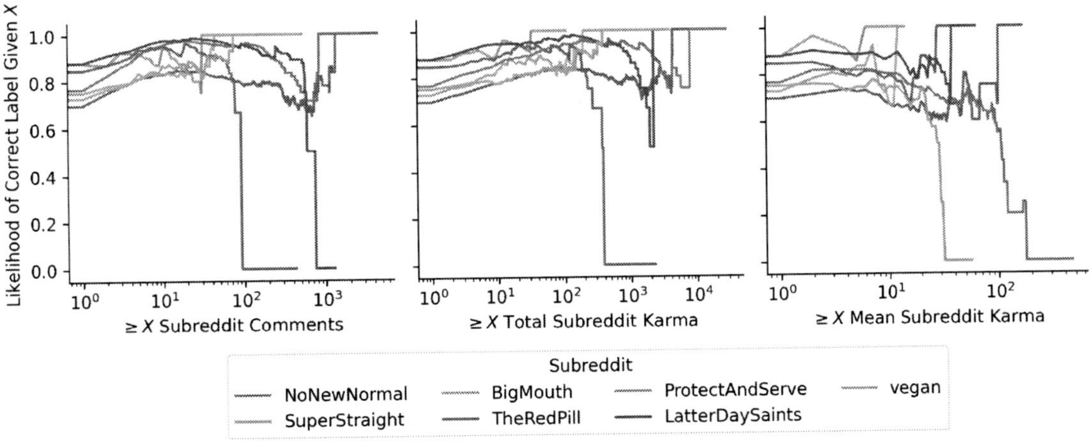

Figure 6: **Likelihood of correctly labeling users in in-group subreddits by user attributes.** This is the unabridged version of Fig. 3, including unstable long-tail behavior when classifying the small minority of high-activity accounts.

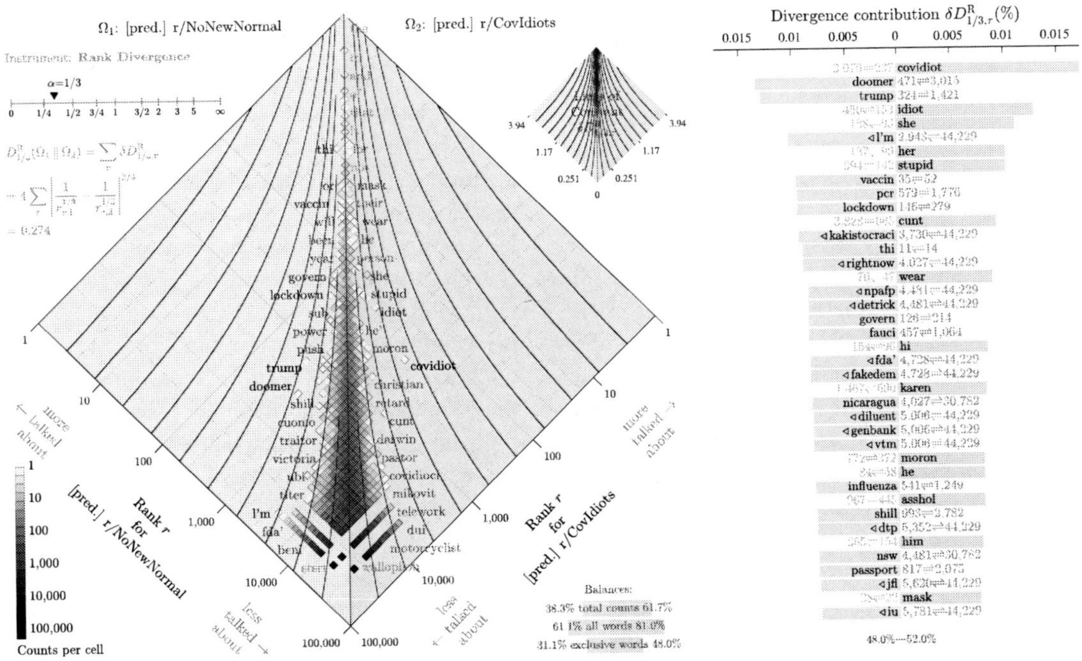

Figure 7: **An allotaxonograph (Dodds et al., 2020) showing the 1-gram rank distributions of predicted users of `r/NoNewNormal` and `r/CovIdiots` using our classifier to assign membership.** See Fig. 1 for allotaxonograph of actual users. The central diamond shaped plot shows a rank-rank histogram for 1-grams appearing in each subreddit. The horizontal bar chart on the right show the individual contribution of each 1-gram to the overall rank-turbulence divergence value ($D^R_{1/3}$). The 3 bars under "Balances" represent the total volume of 1-gram occurring in each subreddit, the percentage of all unique words we see in each subreddit, and the percentage of words that we see in a subreddit that are unique to that subreddit.

Irony Detection for Dutch: a Venture into the Implicit

Aaron Maladry, Els Lefever, Cynthia Van Hee, Veronique Hoste
LT3, Language and Translation Technology Team,
Ghent University, Belgium
firstname.lastname@ugent.be

Abstract

This paper presents the results of a replication experiment for automatic irony detection in Dutch social media text, investigating both a feature-based SVM classifier, as was done by Van Hee et al. (2017) and a transformer-based approach. In addition to building a baseline model, an important goal of this research is to explore the implementation of common-sense knowledge in the form of implicit sentiment, as we strongly believe that common-sense and connotative knowledge are essential to the identification of irony and implicit meaning in tweets. We show promising results and how the presented approach can provide a solid baseline and serve as a staging ground to build on in future experiments for irony detection in Dutch.

1 Introduction

Irony is traditionally defined as a rhetorical device where an evaluative utterance expresses the opposite of what is actually intended (Camp, 2012; Burgers, 2010; Grice, 1978b). In order to understand the intended implicit meaning of such an ironic utterance, the message often requires presupposed common-sense knowledge. We expect most people to know that 'walking in the rain' is not pleasant or that 'visiting the dentist' can result in a painful experience. In addition to such presupposed knowledge, a sarcastic or ironic utterance is often enriched with an explicit mention of the opposite sentiment [1]. When using sarcasm[2], we usually are not just 'fine' with walking in the rain but we say we 'love it'. People are able to recognize such figurative language because we possess both the common-sense knowledge and can catch explicit semantic or lexical cues. Previous research has proven the value of lexical and semantic features for irony detection and has shown that they already allow us to recognize some cases of irony (Cignarella et al., 2020; Van Hee, 2017).

Gathering and modeling the common-sense knowledge required for irony recognition is more problematic. How can we expect an automatic system to know that an implicit negative connotation is attached to an event expressed in a given utterance, if the exact opposite information is provided in a text like 'Oh god, I love it when I have to walk home in the rain!'. In our research, we aimed to identify the general implicit sentiment behind a concept or event by looking at the tweets other people have posted containing that very concept or event. If 9 out of 10 people complain about 'walking in the rain', people who say they 'love it' might very well say that ironically. The combination of lexical features and this kind of data-driven common sense are the foundation of our machine learning approach for irony detection, which has already been applied successfully to English data (Van Hee, 2017). Yet, transferring the methodology from a high-resource language (English) to a lesser-resourced language (Dutch) is not as straight-forward as it might seem. English language models and lexicons can generally rely on larger amounts of data, and not every previously-used resource for the task (e.g. SenticNet (Cambria et al., 2020)) includes Dutch data or has a Dutch counterpart. In addition, the concept of irony might be language-universal, but the realization of irony might employ different language-specific tools and structures. In the next Section, we will discuss related research and the most recent approaches applied to irony detection. Next, we give a short description of the experimental corpus.

[1] This kind of sentiment clash was first examined by Riloff et al. (2013).

[2] Technically, there is a small difference between the two. Sarcasm is regarded as more negative and suggests a harshly-intended form of irony used to mock or ridicule someone. However, not only in popular speech and social media, but also in academic literature, the term 'sarcasm' is often used interchangeably with 'irony'. Therefore, we take note of the negative connotation but use the terms as synonyms, as is done in the related research (Van Hee et al., 2016a; Filatova, 2012; Jijkoun and Hofmann, 2009)

Proceedings of the 12th Workshop on Computational Approaches to Subjectivity, Sentiment & Social Media Analysis, pages 172 - 181
May 26, 2022

Section 4 follows an elaborate description of the proposed systems and an explanation of the features we developed for our classifiers. Finally, we present the results of our experiments and we wrap up the paper with a conclusion and identify some avenues for future research.

2 Related Research

The detection of sarcasm and irony remains one of the primary hurdles for sentiment analysis and other natural language processing (NLP) tasks like detection of cyberbullying, humor and toxicity.

When it comes to methodology, the techniques applied to English irony detection range from feature-based classifiers to neural networks and transformers, including many combinations of (transformer-generated) embeddings with neural or traditional classifiers. Feature-based classifiers like Support Vector Machines or Classifiers (SVM or SVC) are flexible and can easily be equipped with new features, but they generally require a lot of manual work. Van Hee (2017) provides a successful example of an approach combining lexical, semantic and syntactic features for a strong baseline system. This kind of supervised classifier is advantageous when determining the informative value a specific linguistic feature (like part-of-speech tags) contributes to the decision-making process.

Transformer language models (Devlin et al., 2019) and bidirectional transformers (Vaswani et al., 2017) currently occupy the throne of the state-of-the-art in NLP. While these language models are remarkably adaptable and perform well for a variety of tasks (providing they have been fine-tuned for classification), they usually do not suffice on their own. Often the language models are used to generate word embeddings as a (partial) input for a traditional or neural classifier. Potamias et al. (2020) combine the embeddings from RoBERTa, a robust bi-directional transformer approach, with a recurrent convolutional neural network. Cignarella et al. (2020) use a Long Short-Term Memory (LSTM) neural network to exploit both transformer (BERT) word embeddings and syntactic dependency-based n-gram features (Sidorov et al., 2012).

In the SemEval 2018 shared task for irony detection (Van Hee et al., 2018b), the best-performing model (Wu et al., 2018) exploited word embeddings, syntactic and sentiment features using a Long Short-Term Memory neural network. Other participants made use of ensemble learning techniques with majority voting on neural network approaches. One example is presented by Baziotis et al. (2018), who used ensemble learning of two LSTM models, one exploiting character n-grams and the other word n-grams. The third ranking approach also used ensemble learning, but instead opted for traditional machine learning classifiers (Logistic Regression and Support Vector Machines) with word embeddings and manually extracted features (Rohanian et al., 2018).

While research into English sarcasm and irony detection is thriving and receives a lot of attention, other languages are lagging behind (Cakebread-Andrews, 2021). SemEval 2022 again includes a sub-task specifically for sarcasm detection in English and Arabic (iSarcasmEval), which aims to both improve the state-of-the-art methodology for English and expand the scope to less-researched languages. Irony detection for Dutch is still in its infancy. Ever since Kunneman et al. (2015) and Van Hee et al. (2016a) collected and analyzed Dutch irony corpora, and gathered some initial insights into irony detection for Dutch, no new research on the topic has been presented (to the best of our knowledge).

One way to overcome the lack of language-specific research is the use of multilingual language models, like multilingual BERT (Devlin et al., 2018), which makes sense as irony and sarcasm are assumed to be language-universal. Multilingual approaches that utilize the exact same feature set and language models, have shown promising results, but generally do not aim to outperform language-specific models and rather attempt to catch up to their performance levels. An example is the language-universal approach presented by Cignarella et al. (2020), who successfully created a syntactically informed BERT model for English, French, Italian and Spanish social media data. Dutch was not included in this research.

3 Experimental Corpus and Data Description

For this research, we made use of the Dutch data set for irony detection collected by Van Hee et al. (2016a). The balanced corpus consists of 5,566 annotated tweets and was gathered in two ways. One part (3,179 tweets) contains irony-related hashtags (i.e. *#sarcasme, #ironie, #not*) and was annotated with a fine-grained annotation scheme. The

	irony 3-way	irony binary	hashtag indication	polarity contrast
Dutch data set	0.77	0.84	0.60	0.63

Table 1: Cohen's kappa scores for all annotator pairs as presented in Van Hee et al. (2018a).

remaining tweets, which balance out the corpus, were posted by the same users as the ironic tweets and were confirmed to be non-ironic by annotators. Out of the 3,179 tweets with irony-related hashtags, 6% were found to be non-ironic. This is notably lower than in the English data set, which was collected and labeled for SemEval 2018 using the same annotation guidelines and methods (Van Hee et al., 2018b), where 19% of the hashtag-containing tweets are non-ironic. The inclusion of "#not" as an irony-related hashtag was found to make the ironic data set less noisy for Dutch compared to English, where 'not' had sometimes been used as a negating particle rather than an irony marker.

There are a couple of reasons why we selected this data set for our research. The first and most important reason is that the tweets containing irony-related hashtags were manually checked to confirm if they are actually ironic, and to define the type of irony being used. As noted by Van Hee et al. (2017) and Kunneman et al. (2015), tweets containing irony-related hashtags can still be non-ironic and introduce noise in the corpus. Having them checked by annotators ensures a better corpus quality compared to hashtag-based approaches that are common in this research field. The fine-grained annotation guidelines are another useful aspect of the data set, because they allow for more insight and understandability in how irony is linguistically realized. Each ironic tweet receives a label indicating the type of irony: ironic with sentiment clash, situational irony or other irony. A first traditional distinction is made between *verbal* and *situational* irony. Situational irony happens when a situation fails to meet our expectations (Lucariello, 1994; Shelley, 2001). A common example of this is when firefighters have a fire in their kitchen while they are out to answer a fire alarm (Shelley, 2001). Verbal irony, here represented by the labels *ironic by clash* and *other irony*, is defined as expressions that convey the opposite meaning of what is said (Grice, 1975) and implies the expression of a feeling, attitude or evaluation (Grice, 1978a; Van Hee et al., 2016b). *Ironic by clash* occurs when a text expresses an evaluation whose literal polarity is opposite to the intended polarity. Any other forms of verbal irony are categorized as *other irony*. The distribution of the data is as follows:

1. Ironic: 2,783 instances
    - ironic by clash: 2,201 (79%)
    - situational irony: 190 (7%)
    - other irony: 392 (14%)
2. Non-ironic: 2,783 instances

Besides the type of irony used, the annotators also indicated whether or not the irony-related hashtags (#sarcasme, #ironie, #not) were essential to recognize the irony. In fact, more than half of the data set (53%) of the ironic tweets required the irony hashtag to be recognized as ironic by human annotators, as illustrated by the following examples:

- @user een gezellige moskee met hele tolerante gematigde lieden. #not (English: @user a cozy mosque with very tolerant moderate people. #not)
- Ge moogt allemaal fier zijn op uzelf. #sarcasme (English: You should all be proud of yourselves. #sarcasm)
- @user maar vanavond zat er in Het Journaal toch maar mooi een Belgische opiniepeiling, die weer heel ernstig werd geduid. #ironie

  (English: @user but tonight there was a nice Belgian opinion poll in Het Journaal, which was again interpreted very seriously. #irony)

The English equivalent of this Dutch data set is the foundation of the irony detection shared task of SemEval2018 (Van Hee et al., 2018b) and often used as one of the go-to data sets for irony or sarcasm detection (included in Cignarella et al. (2020); Potamias et al. (2020); Ahuja and Sharma (2021); Chowdhury and Chaturvedi (2021)). As the Dutch counterpart is collected, annotated in the same manner by native speakers and shows an acceptable level of agreement between the annotators with scores ranging from moderate to substantial (see Table 1), the quality of the data set should be comparable. For binary irony classification, the inter-annotator agreement indicates almost perfect agreement, with a Cohen's kappa (Cohen, 1960) of 0.84. After removing the irony hashtags, the data set was randomly divided into a test and training split, respectively containing 20% and 80% of the total tweet count. This leaves 1113 tweets in the test set with a fairly balanced label distribution (52% ironic to 48% non-ironic).

4 System Setup and Features

The baseline Support Vector Classifier (SVC) system leverages a core set of lexical character and word n-gram features, which are augmented with more elaborate syntactic, semantic and sentiment lexicon features. Syntactic features include Part-of-Speech frequencies, temporal clash and named entity features. The temporal clash feature indicates whether two different verb tenses occur in the same tweet. Named entity features include both a binary feature (whether or not there is a named entity), and a frequency feature (counting the number of named entities in the tweet). Semantic features are binary features based on Word2Vec (Mikolov et al., 2013) clusters of semantically related words, generated from a large Twitter background corpus. Such a feature could, for example, check whether the tweet contains a word in the semantic cluster [school, dissertation, presentation, degree, classes, papers, etc.] (Van Hee et al., 2016a). Lastly, the sentiment lexicon features count the number of positive and negative token occurrences in each lexicon and take the sum of the sentiment values. We used a variety of sentiment lexicons, including the NRC Word-Emotion Lexicon (Mohammad and Turney, 2013), PATTERN (De Smedt and Daelemans, 2012), the Duoman Lexicon (Jijkoun and Hofmann, 2009), the Hogenboom Emoticon Lexicon (Hogenboom et al., 2013) and The Emoji Sentiment Ranking (Kralj Novak et al., 2015). All SVM models were trained using libsvm (Chang and Lin, 2011) to stick as closely as possible to the methodology of Van Hee (2017). In the same way, we optimized the hyperparameters of the SVM on the train set through grid search[3].

In addition to this baseline model, a Dutch transformer language model (de Vries et al., 2019), built from diverse corpora containing 2.4 billion tokens, was fine-tuned on the training data for irony detection. The methodology used for fine-tuning and deciding on the number of epochs is strongly based on the experiments of Van Hee et al. (2021), who adapted the same transformer (BERTje) for sentiment analysis on news data. The transformer model was thus trained to classify the tweets as ironic or not for 15 epochs with AdamW (Adam optimizer with weight decay) as the optimization algorithm and a learning rate of 5e-05 (Van Hee et al., 2021). The number of epochs was decided on by evaluating the F-score on a held-out validation set (10% of the train data), to keep adding epochs as the F-score improved.

Finally, we created an additional feature to add to our baseline SVC model: *implicit sentiment clash.* This feature captures a clash between the sentiment of an annotated *irony target* and an explicit mention of the opposite sentiment, which is extracted from the remainder of the tweet based on the aforementioned sentiment lexicons. The annotated *irony targets* denote the topic of the ironic utterance. In the annotation guidelines they are defined as "text spans whose implicit sentiment (i.e. connotation) contrasts with that of the literally expressed evaluation" (Van Hee, 2017). These strings can be of any length and syntactic structure, for example "group assignments" or "can't sleep".

We developed two versions of the implicit clash feature. One version utilizes the annotated sentiment of the irony target (considered the gold standard implicit sentiment) to determine the upper boundary for the integration of implicit sentiment. In other words, this scenario presumes perfectly inferred implicit sentiment for each annotated target. The other version of the feature deducts the implicit sentiment automatically with a data-driven approach. To this end, a new set of tweets was collected for each individual target string to function as a background corpus from which we derive implicit sentiment. We fine-tuned a transformer model for sentiment analysis, implementing the same methodology as was used for the inference of implicit sentiment in news data by Van Hee et al. (2021) but trained the model on our own sentiment data[4]. Automatic sentiment analysis thus determined the sentiment of each tweet in the background corpus and we then grouped the resulting sentiments per irony target. Based on

[3]For all SVM models, the optimal c and gamma values turned out to be 2 and 0.00195, respectively.

[4]This corpus contains review texts collected in the framework of a student assignment in a course on Digital Communication. The same data set was utilized for the creation of the LT3 demo for sentiment analysis (https://www.lt3.ugent.be/sentiment-demo/).

the number of positive, neutral and negative sentiments for each target, the most common of the three is assumed as the target's implicit sentiment. For the target "drilled awake", for example, 44% of the tweets were classified as negative, 22% as neutral and 33% as positive. Because the negative partition is the largest, we assign a negative polarity to that target. After determining the implicit sentiment of the target using the method described above, we looked for the presence of a sentiment clash by searching the remainder of each tweet (without the target string) for any positive or negative sentiment token in any of our sentiment lexicons (NRC, PATTERN (De Smedt and Daelemans, 2012), Duoman (Jijkoun and Hofmann, 2009), Hogenboom (Hogenboom et al., 2013) and Emoji (Kralj Novak et al., 2015)), considering it the tweet's explicit sentiment, and compared it to the implicit sentiment of the target. This method was able to cover 756 out of 939 (81%) of all annotated targets (in test and train set). In such manner, the correct implicit sentiment was predicted for 636 out of 756 targets (84%).

If the explicit sentiment in the tweet contradicts the implicit sentiment of the irony target, we call this an *implicit sentiment clash.* This feature only occurs when we were able to determine an implicit sentiment for the annotated target, meaning there are no targets for non-ironic tweets. Despite the high coverage and accurate analysis for implicit sentiment, only 16% of our ironic test tweets and 17% in the training set received the sentiment clash feature. This might seem surprisingly low considering 79% of all ironic tweets have been annotated with the label 'ironic by clash'. However, we should keep in mind that only about a third of the tweets with the label 'ironic by clash' received an annotated irony target. A closer look reveals that the use of lexicons as indicators for explicit sentiment works quite well[5].

We believe this could still be improved. In some cases, the explicit sentiment that causes the clash was annotated as part of the irony target[6].

Besides the clash between implicit and explicit sentiment, we implemented another feature to indicate a contrast among explicitly mentioned sentiments. This time, the explicit sentiments were gathered across all lexicons collectively instead of per lexicon as was done for the baseline SVM. An explicit clash occurs, for example, when a text contains a word like "lovely" and an angry emoji or other word like "disgusting". This *explicit clash* occurs in 22% of all test tweets and co-occurs with the irony label in 58% of the cases. Although this feature did not show a high information gain in the data set (0.005), we still considered it worthwhile to combine it with the implicit clash feature for our experiments.

For the evaluation of the features and SVM models, we developed separate SVM systems containing (1) the baseline feature set, (2) all mentioned features including the implicit and explicit sentiment clash and (3) the baseline feature set with the implicit sentiment clash, but without the explicit clash[7]. For each of the systems with implicit clash as a feature, we evaluated two versions of the feature: one with the automatically predicted implicit sentiment and one with the annotated implicit sentiment.

5 Experimental Results and Analysis

First of all, we noticed that all models reached F-scores above 70% (see Table 2), which was the top result for the English data set (Van Hee, 2017). The fine-tuned transformer model (BERTje) performed the worst out of all tested systems with an F-score of 73.08%. The baseline SVM system (without the implicit sentiment feature) clearly outperforms it with an F-score of 77.82%.

Our SVM system containing the automatically generated clash feature successfully leverages the implicit sentiment of irony target strings and is able to improve the baseline F-score with another percentage. This might seem a modest improvement, but we should stress that this feature was only one out of the 15,845 features and could have been 'undersnowed' by the many lexical features.

These results are further confirmed when comparing the performance of both implicit clash models. Our automatic implicit clash model without the explicit feature even slightly outperformed the model with manually annotated implicit sentiment. We hypothesize this is because of the nature of some of the annotated strings. The annotation guidelines did not include any length or format restrictions for the irony targets, which causes them

[5]In 86% of tweets with an automatic implicit sentiment, we also detected some form of explicit sentiment.

[6]The annotators were free to choose the formats of the irony targets, so the irony target strings vary in length and syntactic format.

[7]Since this feature could introduce more noise, we also develop a system without it.

	Accuracy	Precision	Recall	F-score
Baseline				
Baseline SVM	75.47	73.02	83.30	77.82
Transformer (Bertje)	72.33	73.46	72.70	73.08
SVM with clash features				
Implicit (auto)	**77.00**	74.81	**83.65**	**78.98**
Implicit (gold)	77.00	**75.20**	82.78	78.81
Implicit (auto) and explicit	76.91	74.77	83.48	78.88
Implicit (gold) and explicit	76.82	75.04	82.61	78.64

Table 2: Overview of all experimental results (metrics in %) for binary classification (irony or not). Accuracy was calculated for the full test set. F-score, recall and precision were calculated for the positive label. By *implicit clash* we mean a contrast between implicit and explicit sentiment. An *explicit clash* is a clash between two explicit sentiments.

sometimes to be exceedingly long and therefore noisy. Some of the targets already contain a sentiment clash. The most obvious explanation would be a mistake during annotation, which makes it impossible to detect a clash between the target and the remainder of the tweet. However, it could just as well be a nested clash. In that case there would be two clashes in the tweet, one inside the target and one between the target and the rest of the tweet. Others contain common sense that is strongly connected to the physical world and require the understanding of price values for certain goods or the duration of some activities, etc. Unreasonably large amounts should generally be considered negative, but there are no methods yet to explain a machine how many agents should man a station or what the appropriate price for a t-shirt is. Many of these kind of appreciations and opinions even depend on personal, geographical or cultural preferences and characteristics. Below we present some of the targets without an implicit sentiment prediction (original Dutch tweet with English translation):

- **long and noisy targets:**
  - *En als de batterij van je Random Reader op is, kan je gelijk een nieuwe halen bij jouw Rabobank*
    (English: *and if the battery of your Random Reader runs out, you can just go get a new one at Rabobank)*
- **implicit clash:**
  - *op een zonnige zondagmiddag aan je practicum werken*
    (English: *working on your practicum on a sunny afternoon*)
- **common sense clash:**
  - *Net m'n haar gestyled, zitten er nu door de regen alweer losse krullen in*
    (English: *just straightened my hair and the rain just put loose curls in it again*)
- **complex common sense:**
  - *Er vliegen 1700 privéjets met gasten naar #Davos om de #klimaatveranderingen te bespreken*
    (English:*1700 private jets with guests are flying to #Davos to talk about #climatechange*)
- **real-world common sense**
  - *€175 voor n fietsbroek en -shirt*
    (English: *€175 for cycling shorts and shirt*)

Evaluation on a subset containing only the tweets with an annotated target leads to some fascinating outcomes (see Table 3). It seems that the impact of the missing target coverage is canceled out by the fact that many of the missing targets were actually noisy and possibly reduced prediction accuracy or is caused by a minor annotation mistake. As it stands, the predictions for the implicit sentiment work out exceptionally well, which confirms our working hypothesis that we can reliably deduct implicit sentiment using a large background corpus. As we can tell by the last three rows in Table3, the addition of the explicit clash feature did not improve our results. Consequently, we deem this feature redundant and unnecessary.

A cursory manual analysis of the wrong predictions of our best system reveals that many contain a

	Accuracy	Recall	F-score
Baseline			
Baseline SVM	89.08	89.08	94.86
Transformer (BERTje)	78.74	78.74	88.10
SVM with clash features			
Implicit (auto)	90.80	90.80	95.18
Implicit (gold)	90.23	90.23	94.86
Implicit and explicit (auto)	90.23	90.23	94.86
Implicit and explicit (gold)	90.23	90.23	94.86

Table 3: Evaluation of **only** the tweets that contained an annotated irony target (metrics in %). These tweets have all been annotated as ironic by clash. F-score, recall and precision were calculated for the positive label. We do not report the precision scores as they are all 100% because targets are only present for the positive class.

more openly expressed positive sentiment. Van Hee et al. (2018a) and Kunneman et al. (2015) both noted the relevance of hyperboles and intensifiers as linguistic features for irony detection. While not all cases of very positive sentiments are sarcastic, they do seem to occur often, especially when an irony hashtag was required to identify the tweet as ironic, as illustrated by the following examples (we show the tweets without the hashtag, as they were available to our systems):

- *Gij geeft mij echt zo een goed gevoel*

  (English: *You really make me feel so good*)

- *Maar 't is echt een heel goed idee! #alzegikhetzelf :-)*

  (English: *Well it really is a very good idea! #ifidosaysomyself :-)*)

- *Wat een heerlijk weer!*

  (English: *What wonderful weather!*)

- *Het voelt zo bijzonder als mensen op je stemmen! Dank allen voor het vertrouwen. #trots #dankbaar*

  (English: *It feels so special when people vote for you! Thank you all for the trust. #proud #thankful*)

Not every hyperbole in the test set causes misclassification, though, as many examples in the test set have been classified correctly. We hypothesize this bias could be caused by the removal of irony hashtags for ironic tweets. Whilst annotators indicated that 53% of ironic tweets required an irony-related hashtag to be recognized as ironic, we deprived the tweets of that necessary hashtag but kept the irony label. By consequence, the system might have learned to conceive a very positive sentiment as a possible indicator of irony. However, further manual evaluation and further research are needed to confirm this presumption.

The SVM with automatic implicit sentiment still attains the best results when looking at the accuracy of each model per label, as shown in Table 4. Ironically, this model does not outperform the baseline SVM on the category *ironic by clash*, which was the purpose of the implicit sentiment feature. While our transformer model achieved the best results on *not ironic* tweets, the system does not attain a higher precision on the complete data set compared to the SVMs. The smallest classes in the data set reveal the Achilles heel of the transformer model: it could not detect situational and other irony very well. One could argue that these classes only represent a small portion of the irony class[8] and that neural models would be able to generalize those given a larger data set. The SVM models, on the contrary, did not need additional data and already perform well on the different types of irony. Despite the comparable precision scores, all SVM systems surpass the transformer's recall score by about 10%. This shows the value of efficient feature engineering. Thanks to our manually-selected features, the SVMs were able to capture sarcasm and irony significantly more often than the automatically derived features used by our transformer model.

[8]The *situational irony* and *other irony* classes only contribute to 6% and 15% of the irony label in the test data respectively.

	Ironic by clash (454)	Situational irony (36)	Other irony (85)	not ironic (538)
Baseline				
Baseline SVM	87.44	75.00	64.71	67.10
Transformer (BERTje)	77.75	54.12	52.78	**71.93**
SVM with clash features				
Implicit (auto)	**87.44**	**77.78**	**65.88**	69.89
Implicit (gold)	86.56	75.00	64.71	70.82
Implicit (auto) and explicit	87.22	77.78	65.88	69.89
Implicit (gold) and explicit	86.56	75.00	68.53	70.63

Table 4: Accuracy (in %) for each system per annotated label. Per class label, we also provide the frequency of the label (between brackets). The total number of test instances is 1,113.

6 Conclusion and Future Research

This paper presents a set of experiments for irony detection on Dutch tweets. The proposed SVM models obtained good classification scores, considerably outperformed our baseline transformer model (BERTje) and were able to exploit the sentiment clash feature to achieve more accurate results. For the task of irony detection, the results confirmed that feature-based approaches, although requiring a lot of effort, obtain good results and give more insight into feature relevance and possible future improvements. Although the Dutch data set has until now remained uncharted and has no comparable results yet, the applied methodology in this replication experiment has shown 7% to 9% higher F-scores compared to the English data set.

Implicit sentiment was successfully inferred for irony targets by running sentiment analysis on a large background corpus containing these targets. Our approach using sentiment lexicons for the detection of explicit sentiment to clash with our detected implicit seems to be efficient. Our feature indicating a clash between implicit and explicit sentiment has proven to be a valuable addition to the feature set, even when it can only be activated in a portion of the tweets identified as 'ironic by clash'. It is somewhat unusual that our automatic prediction for implicit sentiment achieved better results than the feature with manually annotated sentiment. Further manual analysis of the results will be necessary to better understand this discrepancy.

A brief inspection of the misclassifications has led to the presumption that our best models have recognized hyperbolic or 'exaggerated' positive sentiment as a feature. We believe this occasionally causes misclassification of very positive texts as ironic. This might be because many tweets used to have an irony-related hashtag, which was indicated as essential to detect irony by human annotators. Nonetheless, confirming this would also require more thorough analysis of the data and predictions.

We consider the results of these exploratory experiments to be insightful but we have only scratched the surface. Testing has indicated both improvements (coverage and sentiment analysis of implicit sentiment of targets) and highlighted some weaknesses. The major challenge that remains is the automatic detection of 'irony targets', the topics or concepts people are ironic or sarcastic about. Hence, we will investigate this as the subject of our future research. On top of that, our implicit clash feature was only one of the 15,000 features, which might cause it to be 'undersnowed' by the many lexical features. Therefore, we will also experiment with ensemble learning to increase the weight of this feature.

In the large scope of irony or sarcasm detection, there are still many paths to pursue. One would be the incorporation of implicit sentiment features into other systems that exploit word embeddings, in the same way as Cignarella et al. (2020) used n-gram features. Another direction is to further expand the coverage of implicit sentiment of irony targets. This can be achieved by connecting related phrases or words like surgeon - doctor - dentist when there are no exact matches. Alternatively, graph knowledge bases, such as SenticNet (Cambria et al., 2020) can be leveraged for more advanced connections between concepts and already include sentiment related to a concept. Experiments with older versions of SenticNet as a sentiment lexicon, however, did provide worse results for sentiment analysis than our data-intensive tweet-based approach (Van Hee, 2017).

References

Ravinder Ahuja and SC Sharma. 2021. Transformer-based word embedding with cnn model to detect sarcasm and irony. *Arabian Journal for Science and Engineering*, pages 1–14.

Christos Baziotis, Nikos Athanasiou, Pinelopi Papalampidi, Athanasia Kolovou, Georgios Paraskevopoulos, Nikolaos Ellinas, and Alexandros Potamianos. 2018. NTUA-SLP at semeval-2018 task 3: Tracking ironic tweets using ensembles of word and character level attentive rnns. *CoRR*, abs/1804.06659.

C. Burgers. 2010. *Verbal irony: Use and effects in written discourse*. Ph.D. thesis, UB Nijmegen.

Oliver Cakebread-Andrews. 2021. Sarcasm detection and building an english language corpus in real time. In *Proceedings of the Student Research Workshop Associated with RANLP 2021*, pages 31–35.

Erik Cambria, Yang Li, Frank Z Xing, Soujanya Poria, and Kenneth Kwok. 2020. Senticnet 6: Ensemble application of symbolic and subsymbolic ai for sentiment analysis. In *Proceedings of the 29th ACM international conference on information & knowledge management*, pages 105–114.

E. Camp. 2012. Sarcasm, pretense, and the semantics/pragmatics distinction. *Nous*, 46:587–634.

Chih-Chung Chang and Chih-Jen Lin. 2011. Libsvm: a library for support vector machines. *ACM transactions on intelligent systems and technology (TIST)*, 2(3):1–27.

Somnath Basu Roy Chowdhury and Snigdha Chaturvedi. 2021. Does commonsense help in detecting sarcasm? *arXiv preprint arXiv:2109.08588*.

Alessandra Teresa Cignarella, Valerio Basile, Manuela Sanguinetti, Cristina Bosco, Paolo Rosso, and Farah Benamara. 2020. Multilingual Irony Detection with Dependency Syntax and Neural Models. In *Proceedings of the 28th International Conference on Computational Linguistics*, pages 1346–1358, Barcelona, Spain (Online). International Committee on Computational Linguistics.

Jacob Cohen. 1960. A coefficient of agreement for nominal scales. *Educational and psychological measurement*, 20(1):37–46.

Tom De Smedt and Walter Daelemans. 2012. " vreselijk mooi!"(terribly beautiful): A subjectivity lexicon for dutch adjectives. In *LREC*, pages 3568–3572.

Wietse de Vries, Andreas van Cranenburgh, Arianna Bisazza, Tommaso Caselli, Gertjan van Noord, and Malvina Nissim. 2019. Bertje: A dutch bert model. *ArXiv*, abs/1912.09582.

J. Devlin, M.-W. Chang, K. Lee, and K. Toutanova. 2019. BERT: Pre-training of deep bidirectional transformers for language understanding. In *Proceedings of the 2019 Conference of the North American Chapter of the Association for Computational Linguistics: Human Language Technologies, Volume 1 (Long and Short Papers)*, pages 4171–4186, Minneapolis, Minnesota. Association for Computational Linguistics.

Jacob Devlin, Ming-Wei Chang, Kenton Lee, and Kristina Toutanova. 2018. BERT: pre-training of deep bidirectional transformers for language understanding. *CoRR*, abs/1810.04805.

Elena Filatova. 2012. Irony and sarcasm: Corpus generation and analysis using crowdsourcing. In *Lrec*, pages 392–398. Citeseer.

H Paul Grice. 1978a. Further notes on logic and conversation. In *Pragmatics*, pages 113–127. Brill.

Herbert P Grice. 1975. Logic and conversation. In *Speech acts*, pages 41–58. Brill.

P.H. Grice. 1978b. *Further notes on logic and conversation*, volume 9, pages 113–127. P. Cole, Syntax and Semantics, New York: Academic Press.

Alexander Hogenboom, Daniella Bal, Flavius Frasincar, Malissa Bal, Franciska de Jong, and Uzay Kaymak. 2013. Exploiting emoticons in sentiment analysis. In *Proceedings of the 28th annual ACM symposium on applied computing*, pages 703–710.

Valentin Jijkoun and Katja Hofmann. 2009. Generating a non-english subjectivity lexicon: Relations that matter. In *Proceedings of the 12th Conference of the European Chapter of the ACL (EACL 2009)*, pages 398–405.

Petra Kralj Novak, Jasmina Smailović, Borut Sluban, and Igor Mozetič. 2015. Sentiment of emojis. *PloS one*, 10(12):e0144296.

Florian Kunneman, Christine Liebrecht, Margot van Mulken, and Antal van den Bosch. 2015. Signaling sarcasm: From hyperbole to hashtag. *Information Processing Management*, 51(4):500–509.

Joan Lucariello. 1994. Situational irony: A concept of events gone awry. *Journal of Experimental Psychology: General*, 123(2):129.

Tomas Mikolov, Ilya Sutskever, Kai Chen, Greg S Corrado, and Jeff Dean. 2013. Distributed representations of words and phrases and their compositionality. *Advances in neural information processing systems*, 26.

Saif M Mohammad and Peter D Turney. 2013. Nrc emotion lexicon. *National Research Council, Canada*, 2.

Rolandos Alexandros Potamias, Georgios Siolas, and Andreas-Georgios Stafylopatis. 2020. A transformer-based approach to irony and sarcasm detection. *Neural Computing and Applications*, 32(23):17309–17320.

Ellen Riloff, Ashequl Qadir, Prafulla Surve, Lalindra De Silva, Nathan Gilbert, and Ruihong Huang. 2013. Sarcasm as contrast between a positive sentiment and negative situation. In *Proceedings of the 2013 conference on empirical methods in natural language processing*, pages 704–714.

Omid Rohanian, Shiva Taslimipoor, Richard Evans, and Ruslan Mitkov. 2018. WLV at SemEval-2018 task 3: Dissecting tweets in search of irony. In *Proceedings of The 12th International Workshop on Semantic Evaluation*, pages 553–559, New Orleans, Louisiana. Association for Computational Linguistics.

Cameron Shelley. 2001. The bicoherence theory of situational irony. *Cognitive Science*, 25(5):775–818.

Grigori Sidorov, Francisco Velasquez, Efstathios Stamatatos, Alexander Gelbukh, and Liliana Chanona-Hernández. 2012. Syntactic dependency-based n-grams as classification features. In *Mexican International Conference on Artificial Intelligence*, pages 1–11. Springer.

C. Van Hee, M. Van de Kauter, O. De Clercq, E. Lefever, B. Desmet, and V. Hoste. 2017. Noise or music? investigating the usefulness of normalisation for robust sentiment analysis on social media data. *Traitement Automatique des Langues*, 58(1):63–87.

Cynthia Van Hee. 2017. *Can machines sense irony? : exploring automatic irony detection on social media*. Ph.D. thesis, Ghent University.

Cynthia Van Hee, Orphée De Clercq, and Véronique Hoste. 2021. Exploring implicit sentiment evoked by fine-grained news events. In *Workshop on Computational Approaches to Subjectivity and Sentiment Analysis (WASSA), held in conjunction with EACL 2021*, pages 138–148. Association for Computational Linguistics.

Cynthia Van Hee, Els Lefever, and Veronique Hoste. 2016a. Exploring the realization of irony in Twitter data. In *LREC 2016 - TENTH INTERNATIONAL CONFERENCE ON LANGUAGE RESOURCES AND EVALUATION*, pages 1795–1799. ELRA.

Cynthia Van Hee, Els Lefever, and Veronique Hoste. 2016b. Guidelines for Annotating Irony in Social Media Text, version 2.0.

Cynthia Van Hee, Els Lefever, and Véronique Hoste. 2018a. Exploring the fine-grained analysis and automatic detection of irony on twitter. *Language Resources and Evaluation*, 52(3):707–731.

Cynthia Van Hee, Els Lefever, and Véronique Hoste. 2018b. SemEval-2018 task 3: Irony detection in English tweets. In *Proceedings of The 12th International Workshop on Semantic Evaluation*, pages 39–50, New Orleans, Louisiana. Association for Computational Linguistics.

Ashish Vaswani, Noam Shazeer, Niki Parmar, Jakob Uszkoreit, Llion Jones, Aidan N. Gomez, Lukasz Kaiser, and Illia Polosukhin. 2017. Attention is all you need.

Chuhan Wu, Fangzhao Wu, Sixing Wu, Junxin Liu, Zhigang Yuan, and Yongfeng Huang. 2018. THU_NGN at SemEval-2018 task 3: Tweet irony detection with densely connected LSTM and multi-task learning. In *Proceedings of The 12th International Workshop on Semantic Evaluation*, pages 51–56, New Orleans, Louisiana. Association for Computational Linguistics.

Pushing on Personality Detection from Verbal Behavior: A Transformer Meets Text Contours of Psycholinguistic Features

Elma Kerz
RWTH-Aachen University
elma.kerz@ifaar.rwth-aachen.de

Yu Qiao
RWTH-Aachen University
yu.qiao@rwth-aachen.de

Sourabh Zanwar
RWTH-Aachen University
sourabh.zanwar@rwth-aachen.de

Daniel Wiechmann
University of Amsterdam
d.wiechmann@uva.nl

Abstract

Research at the intersection of personality psychology, computer science, and linguistics has recently focused increasingly on modeling and predicting personality from language use. We report two major improvements in predicting personality traits from text data: (1) to our knowledge, the most comprehensive set of theory-based psycholinguistic features and (2) hybrid models that integrate a pre-trained Transformer Language Model BERT and Bidirectional Long Short-Term Memory (BLSTM) networks trained on within-text distributions ('text contours') of psycholinguistic features. We experiment with BLSTM models (with and without Attention) and with two techniques for applying pre-trained language representations from the transformer model - 'feature-based' and 'fine-tuning'. We evaluate the performance of the models we built on two benchmark datasets that target the two dominant theoretical models of personality: the Big Five Essay dataset (Pennebaker and King, 1999) and the MBTI Kaggle dataset (Li et al., 2018). Our results are encouraging as our models outperform existing work on the same datasets. More specifically, our models achieve improvement in classification accuracy by 2.9% on the Essay dataset and 8.28% on the Kaggle MBTI dataset. In addition, we perform ablation experiments to quantify the impact of different categories of psycholinguistic features in the respective personality prediction models.

1 Introduction

Personality is broadly defined as the combination of a person's behavior, emotions, motivation, and characteristics of thought patterns (Corr and Matthews, 2020). Our personality has a major impact on our lives, influencing our life choices, well-being, health, and preferences and desires (Ozer and Benet-Martinez, 2006). Specifically, personality has been repeatedly linked to individual (e.g., happiness, physical and mental health), interpersonal (e.g., quality of relationships with peers, family, and romantic partners), and social-institutional outcomes (e.g., career choice, satisfaction and achievement, social engagement, political ideology) (Soto, 2019).

While there are several models of human personality, the predominant and widely accepted model is the Big Five or Five Factor Model (McCrae and John, 1992; McCrae, 2009). In this model, personality traits are divided into five factors: (1) Extraversion (assertive, energetic, outgoing, etc.), (2) Agreeableness (appreciative, generous, compassionate, etc.), (3) Conscientiousness (efficient, organized, responsible, etc.), (4) Neuroticism (anxious, self-pitying, worried, etc.), and (5) Openness (curious, empathetic, imaginative, etc.). These five personality traits are commonly assessed by questionnaires in which a person reflects on his or her typical patterns of thinking and behavior, such as the NEO Five Factor Inventory (Costa and McCrae, 1992), and the Big-Five Inventory (John et al., 1991); (see Matthews et al., 2009, for a comprehensive overview). The Myers–Briggs Type Indicator (MBTI) is another widely administered questionnaire, in particular in applied settings (Meyers et al., 1990). In contrast to the Big Five personality taxonomy, which conceptualizes human personality as latent trait scores, the MBTI model describes personality in terms of 16 types that result from combining binary categories into four dimensions: (a) Extraversion/Introversion (E/I) - preference for how people direct and receive their energy, based on the external or internal world, (b) Sensing/Intuition (S/N) - preference for how people take in information, through the five senses or through interpretation and meanings, (c) Thinking/Feeling (T/F) - preference for how people make decisions, relying on logic or emotion over people and partic-

Proceedings of the 12th Workshop on Computational Approaches to Subjectivity, Sentiment & Social Media Analysis, pages 182 - 194
May 26, 2022 ©2022 Association for Computational Linguistics

ular circumstances, and (d) Judgment/Perception (J/P) - how people deal with the world, by ordering it or remaining open to new information.

Given its central importance in capturing the essential aspects of human life, increasing attention is being paid to the development of models that can leverage behavioral data to automatically predict personality. Data obtained from verbal behavior is one of the key types of such data. Even in the early years of psychology, a person's use of language was seen as a distillation of his or her underlying drives, emotions, and thought patterns (see Tausczik and Pennebaker, 2010; Boyd and Pennebaker, 2017, for historical overviews). Early approaches to automatic personality prediction (APP) – also referred to as automatic personality prediction or recognition – from textual data have relied on machine learning models based on psycholinguistic features, whereas more recent approaches to APP typically draw on deep learning techniques that use pre-trained word embeddings (see Vinciarelli and Mohammadi, 2014, for an overview of the former) (see Mehta et al., 2020b, for an overview of deep learning-based APP).

In this paper, we make a valuable contribution to this dynamic area of APP research by presenting two important improvements in predicting personality traits from textual data: (1) to our knowledge, the most comprehensive set of psycholinguistic features and (2) hybrid models that integrate a pre-trained Transformer Language Model BERT and Bidirectional Long Short-Term Memory (BLSTM) networks trained on in-text distributions ('text contours') of psycholinguistic features. Since our goal is to demonstrate the utility of our modeling approach, we conduct our experiments on two widely used benchmark datasets: the Big Five Essay dataset (Pennebaker and King, 1999) and the MBTI-Kaggle dataset (Li et al., 2018), which align with the dominant personality models described above. The remainder of this paper is organized as follows: In Section 2, we briefly review recent related work on these two benchmark datasets. Then, in Section 3, we present the two benchmark datasets and the extraction of psycholinguistic features using automated text analysis based on a sliding window approach. In Section 4, we describe our modeling approach, and in Section 5, we present and discuss the results. Finally, we conclude with possible directions for future work in Section 6.

2 Related work

Majumder et al. (2017) used a convolutional neural network (CNN) feature extractor in which sentences were fed to convolution filters to obtain n-gram feature vectors. Each individual text of the Big Five Essay dataset was represented by aggregating the vectors of its sentences and the obtained vectors were concatenated with psycholinguistic (Mairesse) features (Mairesse et al., 2007). For classification, they fed the resulting document vector to a fully connected neural network with one hidden layer. Using this method, they were able to achieve an average classification accuracy of 58% for the Big Five personality traits on the Essays dataset. Kazameini et al. (2020) were the first to use a Transformer-Based Language model to extract contextualized word embeddings. Specifically, they built a Bagged-SVM classifier fed with contextualized embeddings extracted from BERT, a pre-trained language model with a Bidirectional Encoder from Transformers (Devlin et al., 2018). Their model outperformed the CNN-based model proposed by the Majumder et al. (2017) model by 1.04%. Amirhosseini and Kazemian (2020) used a Gradient Boosting Model (GBM) based on Term Frequency–Inverse-Document-Frequency features (TF-IDF) to predict personality dimensions in the Kaggle MBTI dataset. Their modeling approach achieved an average classification accuracy across all dimensions of 76.1%. Using both the Big Five Essay dataset and the Myers-Briggs' type indicator Kaggle Dataset, Mehta et al. (2020a) proposed the integration of deep learning models and psycholinguistic features with language model embeddings for APP. They extracted a total of 123 psycholinguistic features, including the Mairesse features set (Mairesse et al., 2007), SenticNet (Cambria et al., 2010), NRC-Emotion Lexicon (Mohammad and Turney, 2013), and NRC-VAD Lexicon (Mohammad, 2018). Language model features were extracted using BERT. Their experiments compared the performance of BERT-base and BERT-large in synergy with SVM or Multi-layer Perceptron (MLP) classifiers. BERT-base + MLP yielded an average score of 60.6 on the Essay dataset, while BERTlarge + MLP yielded an average score of 77.1 on the Kaggle dataset. The approach taken in Mehta et al. (2020a) outperformed the previously best-performing model by Amirhosseini and Kazemian (2020) by 1%. Zooming on classification accuracy for specific personality traits, the models in Mehta et al. (2020a) achieved the highest performance on two of the Big Five personality traits in the Essays dataset (openness, accuracy = 64.6%, and conscientiousness, accuracy = 59.2%) and on three of the four MBTI dimensions in the Kaggle MBTI dataset (Intuitive/Sensing (N/S), accuracy = 86.6%, Thinking/Feeling (T/F), accuracy = 76.1% and Perception/Judging (P/J), accuracy = 67.2%). The highest performance on the Introversion/Extraversion (I/E) MBTI dimension (79%) was obtained by the 'GBM + TFIDF' model reported in Amirhosseini and Kazemian (2020). The highest performance on the three remaining Big Five dimensions was achieved recently by Ramezani et al. (2021), which used an ensemble modeling approach (stacking) to combine linguistic and ontology-based features with deep learning-based methods based on a hierarchical attention network as a meta-model. Although the overall performance of SOTA on the Essay dataset was not superior - mainly due to relatively poor performance on the Openness trait (accuracy = 56.3%), this work has demonstrated the utility of model stacking as an effective way to boost the prediction of personality traits. For a performance overview of the models reviewed here for different data sets and personality dimensions, see Table 1 in Section 4.

3 Method

3.1 Datasets

We conducted our experiments with two widely used personality benchmark datasets: (1) The Essays Dataset (Pennebaker and King, 1999) and (2) Kaggle MBTI Dataset (Li et al., 2018). (1) Essays: This stream-of-consciousness dataset consists of 2468 essays written by students and annotated with the binary labels of the Big Five personality traits, which were obtained through a standardized self-report questionnaire. The average text length is 672 words and the total size of the dataset is approximately 1.6 million words. One of the reasons why Essays is an established benchmark dataset is the relatively large amount of continuous language use and the fact that the personality traits were obtained using a validated instrument. (2) Kaggle MBTI: This dataset was collected through the PersonalityCafe forum[1] and thus provides a diverse sample of people interacting in an informal online social environment. It consists of samples of social media interactions from 8675 users, all of whom indicated their MBTI type. The average text length is 1,288 words. The total size of the entire dataset is approximately 11.2 million words.

[1] `https://www.personalitycafe.com/`

3.2 Measurement of text contours of psycholinguistic features

The texts from both datasets (the Big Five Essay dataset and the MBTI Kaggle dataset) were automatically analyzed using an automated text analysis (ATA) system that employs a sliding window technique to compute sentence-level measurements. These measurements capture the within-text distributions of scores for a given psycholinguistic feature, referred to here as 'text contours' (for recent applications of the ATA system in the context of text classification, see (Kerz et al., 2020; Qiao et al., 2021a,b). We extracted a set of 437 theory-based psycholinguistic features that can be binned into four groups: (1) features of morpho-syntactic complexity (N=19), (2) features of lexical richness, diversity and sophistication (N=77), (3) readability features (N=14), and (4) lexicon features designed to detect sentiment, emotion and/or affect (N=326). Tokenization, sentence splitting, part-of-speech tagging, lemmatization and syntactic PCFG parsing were performed using Stanford CoreNLP (Manning et al., 2014). The group of **morpho-syntactic complexity features** includes (i) surface features related to the length of production units, such as the average length of clauses and sentences, (ii) features of the type and frequency of embeddings, such as number of dependent clauses per T-Unit or verb phrases per sentence and (iii) the frequency of particular structure types, such as the number of complex nominals per clause. This group also includes (iv) information-theoretic features of morphological and syntactic complexity based on the Deflate algorithm (Deutsch, 1996). The group of **lexical richness, diversity and sophistication features** includes six different subtypes: (i) lexical density features, such as the ratio of the number of lexical (as opposed to grammatical) words to the total number of words in a text, (ii) lexical variation, i.e. the range of vocabulary as manifested in language use, captured by text-size corrected type-token ratio, (iii) lexical sophistication, i.e. the proportion of relatively unusual or advanced words in a text, such as the number of words from the New General Service List (Browne et al., 2013), (iv) psycholinguistic norms of words, such as the average age of acquisition of the word (Kuperman et al., 2012) and two recently introduced types of features: (v) word prevalence features that capture the number of people who know the word (Brysbaert et al., 2019; Johns et al., 2020) and (vi) register-based n-gram frequency features that take into account both frequency rank and the number of word n-grams ($n \in [1,5]$). The latter were derived from the five register subcomponents of the Contemporary Corpus of American English (COCA, 560 million words, Davies, 2008): spoken, magazine, fiction, news and academic language (see Kerz et al., 2020, for details see e.g.). The group of **readability features** combines a word familiarity variable defined by a prespecified vocabulary resource to estimate semantic difficulty along with a syntactic variable, such as average sentence length. Examples of these measures include the Fry index (Fry, 1968) or the SMOG (McLaughlin, 1969). The group of **lexicon-based sentiment/emotion/affect features (SentiEmo)** was derived from a total of ten lexicons that have been successfully used in personality detection, emotion recognition and sentiment analysis research: (1) The Affective Norms for English Words (ANEW) (Bradley and Lang, 1999), (2) ANEW-Emo lexicons (Stevenson et al., 2007), (3) DepecheMood++ (Araque et al., 2019), (4) The Geneva Affect Label Coder (GALC) (Scherer, 2005), (5) The General Inquirer (Stone et al., 1966), (6) The LIWC dictionary (Pennebaker et al., 2001), (7) The NRC Word-Emotion Association Lexicon (Mohammad and Turney, 2013), (8) The NRC Valence, Arousal, and Dominance (NRC-VAD) lexicon (Mohammad, 2018), (9) SenticNet (Cambria et al., 2010), and (10) the Sentiment140 lexicon (Mohammad et al., 2013). The feature value for each subcategory in a given lexicon is the mean value of all rated/scored words in a given sentence. The informational gain of 'text contours' compared to text-averages is illustrated in Figure 1. The Figure shows the distribution of z-standardized values of three selected features for a randomly selected text from the Essay dataset. The red line represents the average feature value of the text. As can be seen from the graphs, all feature values fluctuate within the text, with high values for one feature often offset by lower values for another. The contour-based classifiers, discussed in more detail in Section 3, can take advantage of this high-resolution assessment of psycholinguistic features.

4 Modeling approach

Our models are constructed from three components: (a) a 'contour encoder' that converts a sequence of psycholinguistic features into a hidden representation vector, (b) a pre-trained transformer-based language model, BERT, that converts a sequence of tokens into a hidden representation vector, and (c) a classifier that outputs the probability of a personality feature given the hidden representation of the sample. We conduct experiments with three types of personality prediction models: (1) contour encoder + classifier, (2) hybrid models that combine the contour encoder with a transformer-based language model + classifier, and (3) a stacking model that combines ten repetitions of the best performing model. As for the contour encoder, we experiment with BLSTM and BLSTM with attention models. Attention-based models have been successfully used in a variety of tasks, including machine translation (Bahdanau et al., 2014), speech recognition (Huang and Narayanan, 2016) and relation classification (Zhou et al., 2016). In the context of personality classification, learning a scoring function gives sentence weighting to the attention mechanism and allows a model to pay more attention to the most influential sentences in a text for a personality trait. As for the hybrid models, we experiment with different strategies for applying the pre-trained language model - 'feature-based' and 'fine-tuning': In the feature-based approach, we freeze model weights during training and use the pre-trained contextualized word embeddings from BERT. In the 'fine-tuning' approach, we unfreeze all 12 layers and fine-tune towards the personality detection task (see Devlin et al., 2018).

All models are implemented using PyTorch (Paszke et al., 2019). Unless specifically stated otherwise, we use binary cross entropy as our loss function, 'AdamW' as optimizer, a fixed learning rate of 8×10^{-4} and $dropout = 0.1$, $l2 = 1 \times 10^{-4}$ as the regularization. The optimal network structures and values of hyperparameters were found by grid-search. The performance of the models is evaluated by 10-fold cross-validation (ten repetitions) to counter variability due to initialization of the weights. We report the results of the best performing models in comparison to the performance of the APP systems presented in Section 2 Table 1.

4.1 Components

Contour Encoder: The contour encoder, $\text{Encoder}_{PSYLING}(X)$, transforms a sequence of

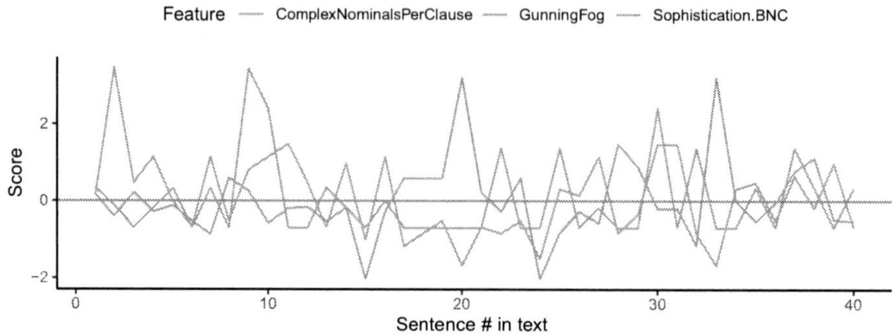

Figure 1: Text contours for three selected features of first 40 sentences of a randomly selected text from the Essays dataset (ID: 2004 499).

psycholinguistic features $X = (x_1, x_2, \ldots, x_n)$ to a hidden psycholinguistic representation vector $P_{PSYLING}$ of a given text. Here, x_i is a 436 dimensional vector for the ith sentence obtained from the APA system described in Section 3.2. In this paper, two architectures of contour encoder are applied: BLSTM and BLSTM with attention (ATTN). The BLSTM contour encoder is a L-layer BLSTM with number of hidden states of d_h. The hidden representation from this model is a $d_o = 2d_h$ dimensional vector, which is a concatenation of the last hidden states of the last layer in forward ($\overrightarrow{h_n}$) and backward direction ($\overleftarrow{h_1}$). Specifically, $X \mapsto \text{Encoder}_{BLSTM}(X) = P$:

$$[\overrightarrow{H}, \overleftarrow{H}] = BLSTM(X)$$
$$P = [\overrightarrow{h_n}^T | \overleftarrow{h_1}^T]^T$$

where $[\cdot|\cdot]$ is concatenation operator, $\overrightarrow{H} = (\overrightarrow{h}_1, \overrightarrow{h}_2, \ldots, \overrightarrow{h}_n)$ and $\overleftarrow{H} = (\overleftarrow{h}_1, \overleftarrow{h}_2, \ldots, \overleftarrow{h}_n)$ are BLSTM model's last layer hidden states in the forward and backward direction.

The ATTN contour encoder model was constructed as follows: Given a input sequence X, a sequence of weights will be computed with the help of a BLSTM model. Then the hidden representation of a given text can be obtained by computing the weighted sum of (a) concatenated hidden vectors from the last layer of the BLSTM model in forward and backward direction (b) feature vectors in X. We also experimented with (c) computing weights for each individual dimension of x_i and then taking weighted sum of X by applying this weights. Our experiments shows, that the approach (c) works best for both dataset. So in this paper, we define $X \mapsto \text{Encoder}_{ATTN}$(X)=P:

$$H = BLSTM(X)$$
$$M = \text{Tanh}(W_{att}H + b_{att})$$
$$\boldsymbol{\alpha} = \text{Softmax}(M)$$
$$V = \textstyle\sum_{i=1}^{n} \boldsymbol{\alpha_i} \odot \boldsymbol{x_i}$$
$$P = \text{Tanh}(W_{pool}V + b_{pool})$$

where $W_{att} \in \mathbb{R}^{436 \times d_o}$, $b_{att} \in \mathbb{R}^{436}$. H and d_o is defined as in BLSTM encoder description. Softmax is defined as: $\alpha_{ij} = \frac{e^{m_{ij}}}{\sum_{k=1}^{n} e^{m_{kj}}}$

BERT Language Model: We use a pre-trained BERT transformer model, 'bert-base-uncased', from Huggingface's transformers library (Wolf et al., 2019). The model consists of 12 transformer layers with a hidden size of 768 and 12 attention heads. Texts are tokenized using BERT's BPE tokenizer. We use as input to BERT language model the initial 512 tokens $T = (t_1, t_2, \ldots, t_m)$ of a given text, i.e. up to 510 word tokens plus the [cls] token at the beginning and the [sep] token at the end of a given text). Assuming the output of the l layer of BERT is $H^{(l)} = (h_1^{(1)}, h_2^{(l)}, \ldots, h_n^{(l)})$, then a hidden vector is computed by either (a) the output for the [cls]-token, i.e. i.e., $V = h_1^{(l)}$ or by (b) averaging the output at the position of the actual tokenized words, i.e., $V = \frac{1}{m-2} \sum_{i=i}^{m-2} h_i^{(l)}$. Experiments with both approaches for $l \in [1, 12]$ revealed that that (a) the latter approach consistently works better than the former and (b) that $l = 11$ works best for the Essays dataset, wheras $l = 12$ works best for the MBTI dataset. So we define $X \mapsto \text{Encoder}_{BERT}(T) = P$

$$H^{(l)} = \text{BERT}(T)$$
$$V = \frac{1}{m-2}\sum_{i=i}^{m-2} h_i^{(l)}$$
$$P = \text{Tanh}(W_{pool}V + b_{pool})$$

Classifier: We use a multi-layer feed-forward neural network as our classifier component. The input to the classifier has a dimension corresponding to the underlying encoder's output dimension. We use PReLU as the activation function. Batch normalization was applied between layers of the classifier. All hidden layers share a same hidden size.

4.2 Models

We first construct models based solely on psycholinguistic features. These models (1) serve as interpretable baselines for the hybrid prediction models and (2) allow us to determine feature importance of individual features groups in predicting personality traits. To fully utilize the information provided by the contour-based measurement of text features, the models rely on BLSTM or BLSTM with attention architecture, i.e. at position of $\text{Encoder}_{PSYLING}$, Encoder_{BLSTM} or Encoder_{ATTN} is applied.

$$P = \text{Encoder}_{PSYLING}(X)$$
$$y = \text{Classifier}(P)$$

Encoder_{BLSTM} has 3 layers with 256 hidden states. We applied a learning rate of 0.001 during training of this model. The BLSTM in Encoder_{ATTN} has 3 layers with 512 hidden states. The classifier has 3 layers with hidden size of 512.

Our hybrid architecture combines text contours of psycholinguistic features with Transformer-based language models using a late-fusion method by concatenating the hidden representations from the psycholinguistic contour encoder and BERT, specifically

$$P_{PSYLING} = \text{Encoder}_{PSYLING}(X)$$
$$P_{BERT} = \text{Encoder}_{BERT}(T)$$
$$P = [P_{PSYLING}^T | P_{BERT}^T]^T$$
$$y = \text{Classifier}(P)$$

At the position of $\text{Encoder}_{PSYLING}$, Encoder_{BLSTM} can be used, which has 3 layers with hidden states of 256, or Encoder_{ATTN}, of which BLSTM also has 3 layers with hidden states of 256 with $dropout = 0.2$. During training, parameters of BERT has a fixed learning rate of 2×10^{-5} while learning rate of 8×10^{-5} is applied to other parameters. The classifier has 3 layers with hidden size of 512.

The final model used in our experiments employed a stacking approach to ensemble our best performing models (Wolpert, 1992), which has been shown to effectively increase the accuracy of the ensembled individual models. Specifically, we employed model stacking to combine BERT+ATTN-PSYLING (FT) model instances for both dataset.

The training procedure consists of two stages: In stage one, we take the model prediction on the dev-fold of each model trained on the train-fold of a k-fold CV. These predictions are then concatenated and constitute the one dimension out of 10 of the input data in a subsequent stage (stage 2). We did the same for all 10 iterations. The final predictions of the model are derived from another logistic regression model trained on the concatenated prediction vectors from stage 1 (10-fold CV).

4.3 Feature importance

To assess the relative importance of the feature groups, we employed Submodular Pick Lime (SP-LIME; Ribeiro et al. (2016)). SPLIME is a method to construct a global explanation of a model by aggregating the weights of linear models, that locally approximate the original model. To this end, we first constructed local explanations using LIME. Analogous to super-pixels for images, we categorized our features into four groups – lexical richness, morphosyntactic complexity, readability, sentiment/emotion (see section 3.2). We used binary vectors $z \in \{0, 1\}^d$ to denote the absence and presence of feature groups in the perturbed data samples, where d is the number of feature groups. Here, 'absent' means that all values of the features in the feature group are set to 0, and 'present' means that their values are retained. For simplicity, a linear regression model was chosen as the local explanatory model. An exponential kernel function with Hamming distance and kernel width $\sigma = 0.75\sqrt{d}$ was used to assign different weights to each perturbed data sample. After constructing their local explanation for each data sample in the original dataset, the matrix $W \in \mathbb{R}^{n \times d}$ was obtained, where n is the number of data samples in the original dataset and W_{ij} is the jth coefficient of the fitted linear regression model to explain data sample x_i. The global

	Essays						MBTI Kaggle				
	O	C	E	A	N	Avg	I/E	N/S	T/F	P/J	Avg
Majumder et al. (2018)	61.1	56.7	58.1	56.7	57.3	58	-	-	-	-	-
Kazameini et al (2020)	62.1	57.8	59.3	56.5	59.4	59	-	-	-	-	-
Amirhosseini & Kazemian (2020)	-	-	-	-	-	-	79	86	74.2	65.4	76.1
Mehta et al (2020):											
Psycholinguistic + MLP	60.4	57.3	56.9	57	59.8	58.3	77.6	86.3	72	61.9	74.5
BERT-base + MLP	64.6	59.2	60	58.8	60.5	60.6	78.3	86.4	74.4	64.4	75.9
All features (base) + MLP	61.1	57.4	57.9	58.6	60.5	59.1	78.4	86.6	75.9	64.4	76.3
BERT-large + MLP	63.4	58.9	59.2	58.3	58.9	59.7	78.8	86.3	76.1	67.2	77.1
Ramezani et al. (2021)	56.30	59.18	**64.25**	60.31	61.14	60.24	-	-	-	-	-
Psycholinguistic models (ours)											
BLSTM-PSYLING	61.69	59.22	58.12	56.87	57.52	58.68	77.29	86.31	72.91	61.01	74.38
ATTN-PSYLING	63.15	59.79	59.18	58.29	59.79	60.04	77.29	86.19	73.97	63.69	75.29
Hybrid models (ours)											
BERT+BLSTM-PSYLING (FB)	64.25	60.80	60.92	59.26	60.48	61.14	78.39	86.58	74.42	64.17	75.89
BERT+ATTN-PSYLING (FB)	64.78	61.13	60.44	59.30	60.68	61.27	78.82	86.78	76.62	65.78	77.00
BERT+BLSTM-PSYLING (FT)	65.55	60.72	60.72	60.52	**62.14**	61.93	85.78	90.86	83.79	79.79	85.06
BERT+ATTN-PSYLING (FT)	66.23	60.60	61.61	**61.05**	61.65	62.28	**86.25**	90.96	84.66	79.65	85.38
BERT+PSYLING Ensemble	**71.95**	**61.38**	63.01	60.16	60.98	**63.50**	85.47	**92.27**	**85.70**	**82.58**	**86.51**

Table 1: Performance comparison (classification accuracy) of our models (bottom) with previous state-of-the-art-models (top). Best performance indicated in bold.

importance score of the SP-LIME for feature j can then be derived by: $I_j = \sqrt{\sum_{i=1}^{n} |W_{ij}|}$

5 Results and Discussion

An overview of the results of our models in comparison to those reported in the previous studies reviewed above is presented in Table 1. As Table 1 shows, we achieve state-of-the-art (SOTA) results on both benchmark personality datasets: On the Big Five Essay dataset, our best-performing model achieves a classification accuracy of 63.5%, which corresponds to an increase of 2.9% over the previous SOTA. On the MBTI Kaggle dataset, our best model improved the classification accuracy of SOTA by 8.28%. On both datasets the highest classification accuracy was achieved by the ensemble model, which combined ten iterations of a hybrid model integrating a fine-tuned BERT model with an attention-based BLSTM model trained on text contours (see BERT+PSYLING Ensemble in Table 1). Our models achieve the highest performance on four of the Big Five - all except Extraversion - and on all four MBTI dimensions, with the largest increase in performance for the Big Five on the Openness dimension (+7.35%) and for the MBTI on the T/F dimension (+9.6%). Comparing the accuracy for each personality trait from Table 1 for the hybrid models trained with the "feature-based" strategy (denoted by "FB") with the corresponding value for the models trained with the "fine-tuning" strategy (denoted by "FT"), we find that the accuracy of all traits improved when each pre-trained model was fine-tuned on the data set. Comparing the accuracy for each personality trait for the models trained with an attention mechanism (denoted by 'ATTN') to the corresponding value for the models trained without this mechanism (denoted by 'BLSTM'), we find that accuracy on all dimensions except the MBTI N/S improved when an attention mechanism was used. Our results also show that approaches grounded in interpretable features can achieve competitive performance with Transformer-based approaches: Our best-performing model trained solely on psycholinguistic features, the attention-based BLSTM model (ATT-PSYLING), achieved an average classification accuracy of 60.04%, approaching the previous SOTA model, BERT-base + MLP Mehta et al. (2020a), by only 0.54%. This is a promising finding given the need for more interpretable personality prediction models that can provide valuable insights into key psycholinguistic features to drive personality prediction and advance personality psychology research. See e.g. Rudin (2019) for more general calls for using white-box models to solve practical problems, particularly in the context of

O		C		E		A		N	
Group	I	Group	I	Group	I	Group	I	Group	I
SentiEmo	18.49	SentiEmo	21.36	SentiEmo	16.39	SentiEmo	9.28	SentiEmo	16.62
lexical	12.90	lexical	14.48	lexical	10.93	lexical	7.52	lexical	10.23
readability	9.57	readability	9.57	morph.syn	9.17	morph.syn	6.23	morph.syn	8.11
morph.syn	7.08	morph.syn	8.91	readability	7.51	readability	4.21	readability	7.06

I/E		N/S		T/F		P/J	
Group	I	Group	I	Group	I	Group	I
SentiEmo	33.73	SentiEmo	21.32	SentiEmo	45.06	SentiEmo	24.97
lexical	29.94	lexical	14.25	lexical	24.64	readability	17.21
morph.syn	20.65	readability	12.55	morph.syn	20.31	morph.syn	16.02
readability	18.33	morph.syn	10.40	readability	18.76	lexical	14.48

Table 2: Results of the feature ablation for Big Five Essays datset (top) and Kaggle MBTI dataset (bottom): Feature importance (Model: ATTN-PSYLING) macro-averaged across 100 model instances. (10×10-fold CV).

critical industries such as healthcare, criminal justice, and news. This is due to the fact that human experts in a given application domain require both accurate and understandable models (Loyola-Gonzalez, 2019).

In what follows, we present the results of the ablation experiments. Feature group importance was quantified using SP-LIME on the best performing model trained only on text contours of psycholinguistic features, the ATTN-PSYLING model. The results of the feature ablation experiment are presented in Table 2. The table shows that the prediction of personality traits was influenced by all four feature groups (all $I > 4.21$). Overall, personality traits were best predicted by the sentiment/emotion/affect (SentiEmo) feature group. The lexical richness, diversity and sophistication group consistently ranked second on all traits except the P/J MBTI dimension. This result indicates that in addition to words associated with affective-emotional categories, personality traits are also related to more general aspects of vocabulary. Morphosyntactic complexity and readability play a minor role but still achieve high I-scores compared to the highest scoring group in predicting Extraversion, Neuroticism, and Agreeableness (ratio: $I(group_j)$ / $I(SentEmo) > 0.45$). Finally, zooming in on the specific interactions between psycholinguistic cues and personality traits, we calculated the difference between the average feature scores of text samples with different labels for each personality trait. Visualizations of the most important psycholinguistic features that influence the prediction of personality traits are shown in Figures 4 and in the Appendix. Some interesting patterns emerged: For example, texts produced by extroverts tend to (a) have less complex morphosyntax than those by introverts (as indicated by the lower scores of the information-theoretic complexity measures), (b) contain a greater proportion of positive words, and (c) have a higher proportion of frequently used n-grams from the spoken language, news, and magazine registers. The language use of individuals scoring high on Neuroticism showed (a) a higher proportion of self-referencing words, (b) higher proportions of words related to sadness, anxiety and disappointment, but also (c) a higher proportion of longer n-grams from the fiction register. Highly conscientious individuals showed (a) a higher proportion of words with high prevalence, i.e. words that are known by a larger percentage of the population, (b) more words associated with affiliation (ally, friend) and (c) a higher proportions of frequently used n-grams from the academic register. These results replicate and extend previous findings reported in the literature (for overviews see, e.g., Mairesse et al., 2007; Park et al., 2015; Boyd and Schwartz, 2021).

6 Conclusion

Due to its central importance in capturing the essential aspects of human life, increasing attention is being paid to the modeling and predicting personality traits. In this work, we made valuable contributions to advance the state of the art in automatic prediction of personality traits from verbal behavior. We demonstrated that models trained with a comprehensive set of theory-based psycholinguistic features can compete with a Transformer-based model when their within-text distribution is taken into account. Moreover, we showed that hybrid models incorporating such features can improve the performance of pre-trained Transformer language models, even when the latter is based on a larger model (BERT-large). We also showed that different techniques for applying pre-trained language representations from the Transformer model have an impact on model performance. Our ablation experiments have yielded interesting insights into the interplay between theory-based psycholinguistic features and personality traits. Here, we decided to focus on the two most widely used benchmark datasets. In our future work, we intend to conduct experiments with more recent, larger personality datasets such as PANDORA (Gjurkovic et al., 2020). Since this dataset also includes metadata (gender, age, and location/region), it would be interesting to see how they contribute to modeling and predicting personality traits from language use.

References

Mohammad Hossein Amirhosseini and Hassan Kazemian. 2020. Machine learning approach to personality type prediction based on the myers–briggs type indicator®. *Multimodal Technologies and Interaction*, 4(1):9.

Oscar Araque, Lorenzo Gatti, Jacopo Staiano, and Marco Guerini. 2019. Depechemood++: a bilingual emotion lexicon built through simple yet powerful techniques. *IEEE transactions on affective computing*.

Dzmitry Bahdanau, Kyunghyun Cho, and Yoshua Bengio. 2014. Neural machine translation by jointly learning to align and translate. *arXiv preprint arXiv:1409.0473*.

Ryan L Boyd and James W Pennebaker. 2017. Language-based personality: a new approach to personality in a digital world. *Current opinion in behavioral sciences*, 18:63–68.

Ryan L Boyd and H Andrew Schwartz. 2021. Natural language analysis and the psychology of verbal behavior: The past, present, and future states of the field. *Journal of Language and Social Psychology*, 40(1):21–41.

Margaret M Bradley and Peter J Lang. 1999. Affective norms for english words (anew): Instruction manual and affective ratings. Technical report, Technical report C-1, the center for research in psychophysiology ....

Charles Browne et al. 2013. The new general service list: Celebrating 60 years of vocabulary learning. *The Language Teacher*, 37(4):13–16.

Marc Brysbaert, Paweł Mandera, Samantha F McCormick, and Emmanuel Keuleers. 2019. Word prevalence norms for 62,000 english lemmas. *Behavior research methods*, 51(2):467–479.

Erik Cambria, Robyn Speer, Catherine Havasi, and Amir Hussain. 2010. Senticnet: A publicly available semantic resource for opinion mining. In *2010 AAAI fall symposium series*.

Philip J Corr and Gerald Matthews. 2020. *The Cambridge handbook of personality psychology*. Cambridge University Press.

Paul T Costa and Robert R McCrae. 1992. *Neo personality inventory-revised (NEO PI-R)*. Psychological Assessment Resources Odessa, FL.

Mark Davies. 2008. The Corpus of Contemporary American English (COCA): 560 million words, 1990-present.

Peter Deutsch. 1996. Rfc1951: Deflate compressed data format specification version 1.3.

Jacob Devlin, Ming-Wei Chang, Kenton Lee, and Kristina Toutanova. 2018. Bert: Pre-training of deep bidirectional transformers for language understanding. *arXiv preprint arXiv:1810.04805*.

Edward Fry. 1968. A readability formula that saves time. *Journal of reading*, 11(7):513–578.

Matej Gjurkovic, Mladen Karan, Iva Vukojevic, Mihaela Bosnjak, and Jan Snajder. 2020. PANDORA talks: Personality and demographics on reddit. *CoRR*, abs/2004.04460.

Che-Wei Huang and Shrikanth S Narayanan. 2016. Attention assisted discovery of sub-utterance structure in speech emotion recognition. In *Interspeech*, pages 1387–1391.

Oliver P John, Eileen M Donahue, and Robert L Kentle. 1991. Big five inventory. *Journal of Personality and Social Psychology*.

Brendan T Johns, Melody Dye, and Michael N Jones. 2020. Estimating the prevalence and diversity of words in written language. *Quarterly Journal of Experimental Psychology*, 73(6):841–855.

Amirmohammad Kazameini, Samin Fatehi, Yash Mehta, Sauleh Eetemadi, and Erik Cambria. 2020. Personality trait detection using bagged svm over bert word embedding ensembles. *arXiv preprint arXiv:2010.01309*.

Elma Kerz, Yu Qiao, Daniel Wiechmann, and Marcus Ströbel. 2020. Becoming linguistically mature: Modeling english and german children's writing development across school grades. In *Proceedings of the Fifteenth Workshop on Innovative Use of NLP for Building Educational Applications*, pages 65–74.

Victor Kuperman, Hans Stadthagen-Gonzalez, and Marc Brysbaert. 2012. Age-of-acquisition ratings for 30,000 english words. *Behavior research methods*, 44(4):978–990.

Charles Li, Monte Hancock, Ben Bowles, Olivia Hancock, Lesley Perg, Payton Brown, Asher Burrell, Gianella Frank, Frankie Stiers, Shana Marshall, et al. 2018. Feature extraction from social media posts for psychometric typing of participants. In *International Conference on Augmented Cognition*, pages 267–286. Springer.

Octavio Loyola-Gonzalez. 2019. Black-box vs. white-box: Understanding their advantages and weaknesses from a practical point of view. *IEEE Access*, 7:154096–154113.

François Mairesse, Marilyn A Walker, Matthias R Mehl, and Roger K Moore. 2007. Using linguistic cues for the automatic recognition of personality in conversation and text. *Journal of artificial intelligence research*, 30:457–500.

Navonil Majumder, Soujanya Poria, Alexander Gelbukh, and Erik Cambria. 2017. Deep learning-based document modeling for personality detection from text. *IEEE Intelligent Systems*, 32(2):74–79.

Christopher Manning, Mihai Surdeanu, John Bauer, Jenny Finkel, Steven Bethard, and David McClosky. 2014. The stanford corenlp natural language processing toolkit. In *Proceedings of 52nd annual meeting of the association for computational linguistics: system demonstrations*, pages 55–60.

G. Matthews, I. Deary, and M. Whiteman. 2009. *Personality Traits*. Cambridge University Press.

Robert R McCrae. 2009. The five-factor model of personality traits: Consensus and controversy. *The Cambridge handbook of personality psychology*, pages 148–161.

Robert R McCrae and Oliver P John. 1992. An introduction to the five-factor model and its applications. *Journal of personality*, 60(2):175–215.

G Harry McLaughlin. 1969. Clearing the smog. *Journal of Reading*.

Yash Mehta, Samin Fatehi, Amirmohammad Kazameini, Clemens Stachl, Erik Cambria, and Sauleh Eetemadi. 2020a. Bottom-up and top-down: Predicting personality with psycholinguistic and language model features. In *2020 IEEE International Conference on Data Mining (ICDM)*, pages 1184–1189. IEEE.

Yash Mehta, Navonil Majumder, Alexander Gelbukh, and Erik Cambria. 2020b. Recent trends in deep learning based personality detection. *Artificial Intelligence Review*, 53(4):2313–2339.

Isabel Briggs Meyers, Mary H McCaulley, and Allen L Hammer. 1990. *Introduction to Type: A Description of the Theory and Applications of the Myers-Briggs Type Indicator*. Consulting Psychologists Press.

Saif Mohammad. 2018. Obtaining reliable human ratings of valence, arousal, and dominance for 20,000 english words. In *Proceedings of the 56th Annual Meeting of the Association for Computational Linguistics (Volume 1: Long Papers)*, pages 174–184.

Saif Mohammad, Svetlana Kiritchenko, and Xiaodan Zhu. 2013. Nrc-canada: Building the state-of-the-art in sentiment analysis of tweets. In *Proceedings of the seventh international workshop on Semantic Evaluation Exercises (SemEval-2013)*, Atlanta, Georgia, USA.

Saif M Mohammad and Peter D Turney. 2013. Crowdsourcing a word–emotion association lexicon. *Computational intelligence*, 29(3):436–465.

Daniel J Ozer and Veronica Benet-Martinez. 2006. Personality and the prediction of consequential outcomes. *Annu. Rev. Psychol.*, 57:401–421.

Gregory Park, H Andrew Schwartz, Johannes C Eichstaedt, Margaret L Kern, Michal Kosinski, David J Stillwell, Lyle H Ungar, and Martin EP Seligman. 2015. Automatic personality assessment through social media language. *Journal of personality and social psychology*, 108(6):934.

Adam Paszke, Sam Gross, Francisco Massa, Adam Lerer, James Bradbury, Gregory Chanan, Trevor Killeen, Zeming Lin, Natalia Gimelshein, Luca Antiga, et al. 2019. Pytorch: An imperative style, high-performance deep learning library. *Advances in neural information processing systems*, 32.

James W Pennebaker, Martha E Francis, and Roger J Booth. 2001. Linguistic inquiry and word count: Liwc 2001. *Mahway: Lawrence Erlbaum Associates*, 71(2001):2001.

James W Pennebaker and Laura A King. 1999. Linguistic styles: language use as an individual difference. *Journal of personality and social psychology*, 77(6):1296.

Yu Qiao, Xuefeng Yin, Daniel Wiechmann, and Elma Kerz. 2021a. Alzheimer's disease detection from spontaneous speech through combining linguistic complexity and (dis) fluency features with pretrained language models. *arXiv preprint arXiv:2106.08689*.

Yu Qiao, Sourabh Zanwar, Rishab Bhattacharyya, Daniel Wiechmann, Wei Zhou, Elma Kerz, and Ralf Schlüter. 2021b. Prediction of listener perception of argumentative speech in a crowdsourced data using (psycho-) linguistic and fluency features. *arXiv preprint arXiv:2111.07130*.

Majid Ramezani, Mohammad-Reza Feizi-Derakhshi, Mohammad-Ali Balafar, Meysam Asgari-Chenaghlu, Ali-Reza Feizi-Derakhshi, Narjes Nikzad-Khasmakhi, Mehrdad Ranjbar-Khadivi, Zoleikha Jahanbakhsh-Nagadeh, Elnaz Zafarani-Moattar, and Taymaz Rahkar-Farshi. 2021. Automatic personality prediction; an enhanced method using ensemble modeling. *arXiv preprint arXiv:2007.04571*.

Marco Tulio Ribeiro, Sameer Singh, and Carlos Guestrin. 2016. " why should i trust you?" explaining the predictions of any classifier. In *Proceedings of the 22nd ACM SIGKDD international conference on knowledge discovery and data mining*, pages 1135–1144.

Klaus R Scherer. 2005. What are emotions? and how can they be measured? *Social science information*, 44(4):695–729.

Christopher J Soto. 2019. How replicable are links between personality traits and consequential life outcomes? the life outcomes of personality replication project. *Psychological Science*, 30(5):711–727.

Ryan A Stevenson, Joseph A Mikels, and Thomas W James. 2007. Characterization of the affective norms for english words by discrete emotional categories. *Behavior research methods*, 39(4):1020–1024.

Philip J Stone, Dexter C Dunphy, and Marshall S Smith. 1966. The general inquirer: A computer approach to content analysis.

Yla R Tausczik and James W Pennebaker. 2010. The psychological meaning of words: Liwc and computerized text analysis methods. *Journal of language and social psychology*, 29(1):24–54.

Alessandro Vinciarelli and Gelareh Mohammadi. 2014. A survey of personality computing. *IEEE Transactions on Affective Computing*, 5(3):273–291.

Thomas Wolf, Lysandre Debut, Victor Sanh, Julien Chaumond, Clement Delangue, Anthony Moi, Pierric Cistac, Tim Rault, Rémi Louf, Morgan Funtowicz, et al. 2019. Huggingface's transformers: State-of-the-art natural language processing. *arXiv preprint arXiv:1910.03771*.

David H Wolpert. 1992. Stacked generalization. *Neural networks*, 5(2):241–259.

Peng Zhou, Wei Shi, Jun Tian, Zhenyu Qi, Bingchen Li, Hongwei Hao, and Bo Xu. 2016. Attention-based bidirectional long short-term memory networks for relation classification. In *Proceedings of the 54th annual meeting of the association for computational linguistics (volume 2: Short papers)*, pages 207–212.

A Appendices

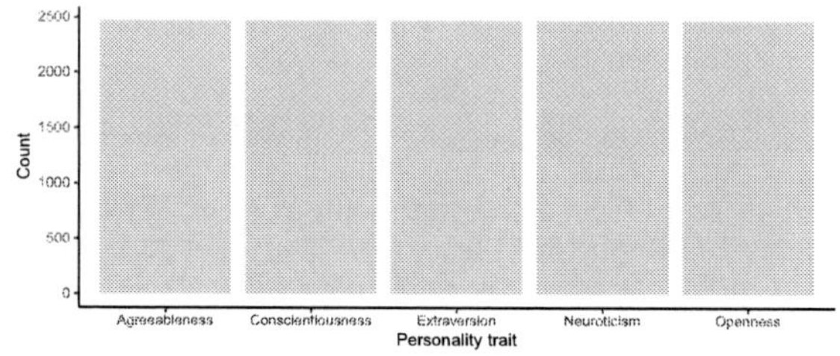

Figure 2: Distribution of labels in the Essay dataset

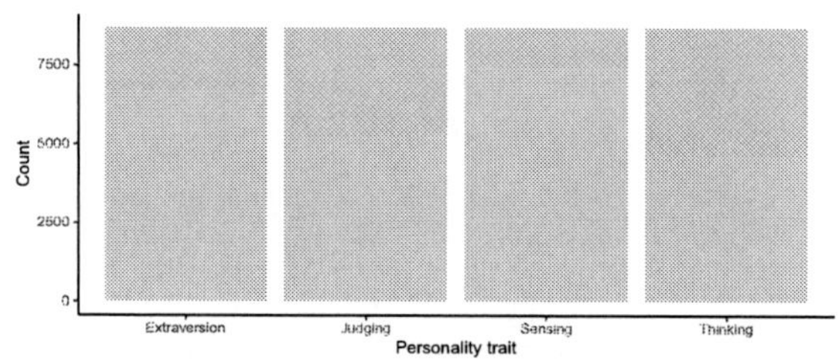

Figure 3: Distribution of labels in the Kaggle MBTI dataset

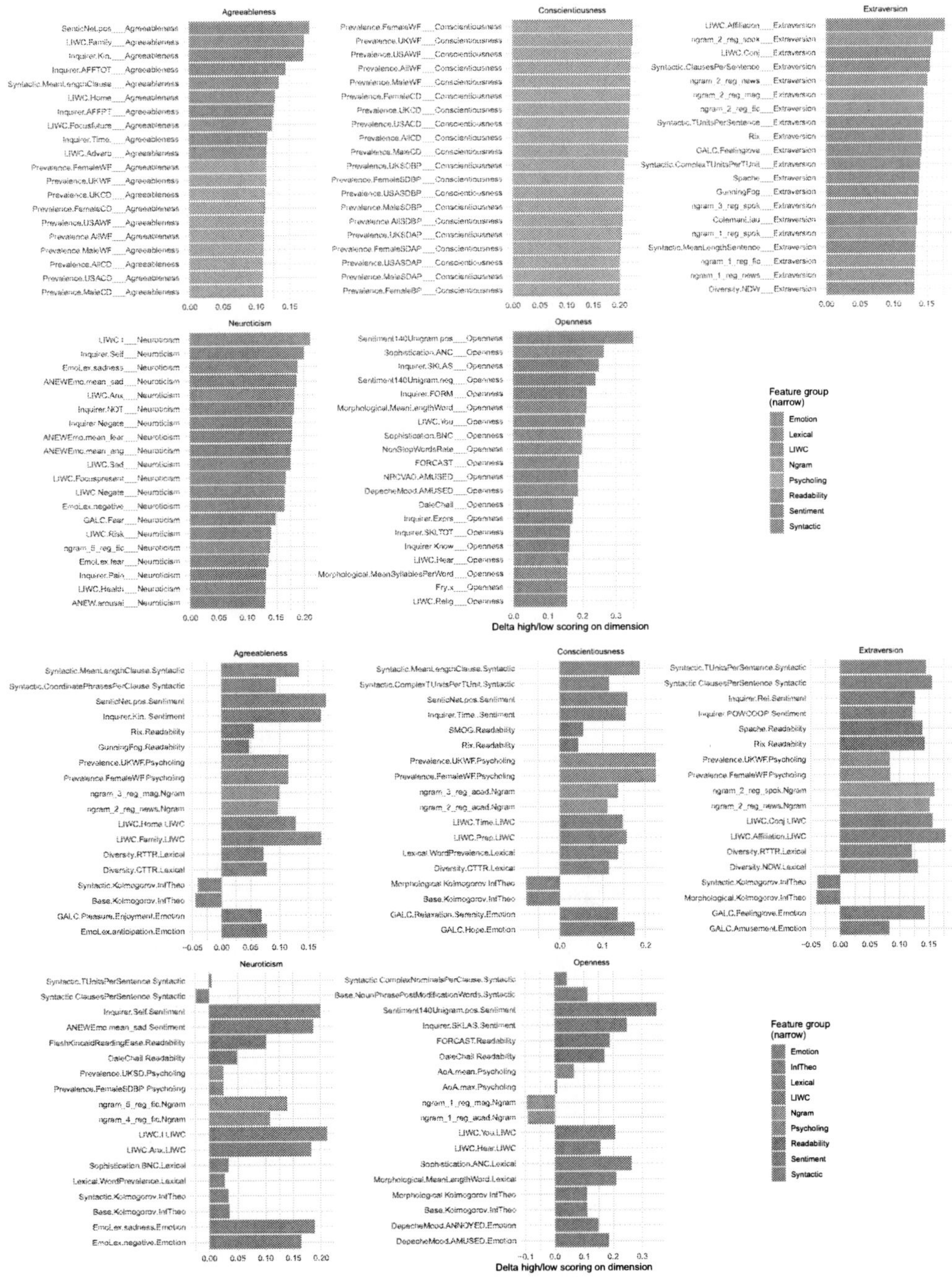

Figure 4: **Essays dataset:** Upper panel: Top 20 most characteristic features from each feature group by personality trait. Lower panel: Top 2 most characteristic features from each feature group by personality trait. Plotted scores represent the difference between the z-standardized mean scores of high- and low-scoring individuals on a given personality trait. Positive scores are characteristic of the high-scoring individuals on a given trait (e.g. individuals with high extraversion scores).

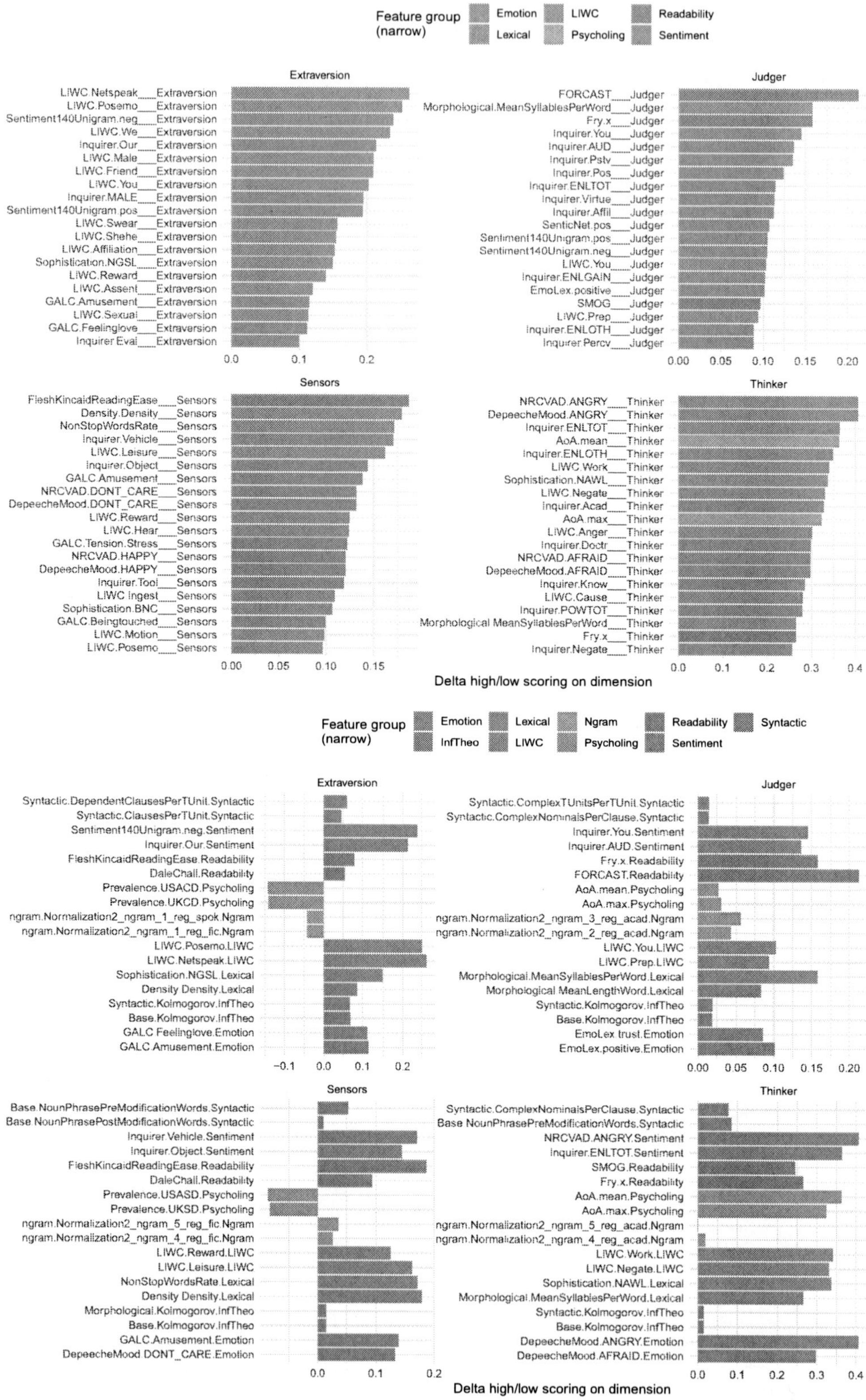

Figure 5: **MBTI Kaggle dataset:** Upper panel: Top 20 most characteristic features from each feature group by personality trait. Lower panel: Top 2 most characteristic features from each feature group by personality trait. Plotted scores represent the difference between the z-standardized mean scores of high- and low-scoring individuals on a given personality trait. Positive scores are characteristic of the high-scoring individuals on a given trait (e.g. individuals with high extraversion scores).

XLM-EMO: Multilingual Emotion Prediction in Social Media Text

Federico Bianchi
Bocconi University
Via Sarfatti 25
Milan, Italy
f.bianchi@unibocconi.it

Debora Nozza
Bocconi University
Via Sarfatti 25
Milan, Italy
debora.nozza@unibocconi.it

Dirk Hovy
Bocconi University
Via Sarfatti 25
Milan, Italy
dirk.hovy@unibocconi.it

Abstract

Detecting emotion in text allows social and computational scientists to study how people behave and react to online events. However, developing these tools for different languages requires data that is not always available. This paper collects the available emotion detection datasets across 19 languages. We train a multilingual emotion prediction model for social media data, XLM-EMO. The model shows competitive performance in a zero-shot setting, suggesting it is helpful in the context of low-resource languages. We release our model to the community so that interested researchers can directly use it.

1 Introduction

Emotion Detection is an important task for Natural Language Processing and for Affective Computing. Indeed, several resources and models have been proposed (Alm et al., 2005; Abdul-Mageed and Ungar, 2017; Nozza et al., 2017; Xia and Ding, 2019; Demszky et al., 2020, inter alia) for this task. These models can be used by social and computational scientists (Verma et al., 2020; Kleinberg et al., 2020; Huguet Cabot et al., 2020) to better understand how people react to events through the use of social media. However, these methods often require large training sets that are not always available for low-resource languages. Nonetheless, multilingual methods (Wu and Dredze, 2019) have risen across the entire field showing powerful few-shot and zero-shot capabilities (Bianchi et al., 2021b; Nozza, 2021).

In this short paper, we introduce a new resource: XLM-EMO. XLM-EMO is a model for multilingual emotion prediction on social media data. We collected datasets for emotion detection in 19 different languages and mapped the labels of each dataset to a common set *{joy, anger, fear, sadness}* that is then used to train the model. We show that XLM-EMO is capable of maintaining stable performances across languages and it is competitive against language-specific baselines in zero-shot settings.

We believe that XLM-EMO can be of help to the community as emotion prediction is becoming an interesting and relevant task in NLP; the addition of a multilingual model that can perform zero-shot emotion prediction can be of help for many low-resource languages that still do not have a dataset for emotion detection.

Contributions We release XLM-EMO which is a multilingual emotion detection model for social media text. XLM-EMO shows competitive zero-shot capabilities on unseen languages. We release the model in two versions a base and a large to adapt to different possible use-cases. We make the models[1] and the code to train it freely available under a Python package that can be directly embedded in novel data analytics pipelines.[2]

2 Data and Related Work

We surveyed the literature to understand which datasets are available in the literature and with which kinds of emotions. Details on how we operate on this data can be found in the Appendix, here we give an overview of the transformation pipeline we have adopted and which datasets have been included.

[1]Models can be found at https://huggingface.co/MilaNLProc/

[2]See https://github.com/MilaNLProc/xlm-emo, where we also release other details for replication.

Proceedings of the 12th Workshop on Computational Approaches to Subjectivity, Sentiment & Social Media Analysis, pages 195 - 203

The datasets we have collected and used in this paper are presented in Table 1 with the method of annotation and the linguistic family of the language. Figure 1 shows instead the class distribution.

We describe here the general guidelines we have used to create this dataset, readers can find details for each dataset in the Appendix. For all the datasets we removed the emotions that are not in the set *joy, anger, fear, sadness* (e.g., Cortiz et al. (2021), Vasantharajan et al. (2022), Shome (2021) used the 27 emotions from GoEmotion (Demszky et al., 2020) and we just collected the subset of our emotions). We have some exceptions to Twitter data, as the Tamil dataset Vasantharajan et al. (2022) contains YouTube comments.

Some data was impossible to reconstruct because the tweets do not exist anymore and thus only a subset is still available (e.g., Korean (Do and Choi, 2015)). For some languages, we decided to apply undersampling in order to limit the skewness of the final distribution (e.g., both Shome (2021) and Cortiz et al. (2021) provide dozens of thousands of tweets). To simplify reproducibility, we will release the exact data extraction scripts that we have used to collect our data.

There are papers that we have not included in our research: Vijay et al. (2018) introduce a Hindi dataset that contains Hindi-English code switched text. However, Hindi is Romanized and only a few of this data has been used to pre-train XLM. Sabri et al. (2021) released a collection of Persian tweets annotated with emotions, however, their data has not been evaluated in a training task and thus we decided not to include it in our training. We also found a dataset for Japanese Danielewicz-Betz et al. (2015), however, the dataset is not publicly available.

French and German are collected through the translation of Spanish (Mohammad et al., 2018) tweets using DeepL.[3] For Chinese, we use the messages found in the NLPCC dataset (Wang et al., 2018). Note that this dataset has some internal code-switching.

The most similar work to ours is the work by Lamprinidis et al. (2021). Lamprinidis et al. (2021) introduces a dataset collected through distant supervision on Facebook and covers 6 main languages for training and a set of 12 other languages that can be used for testing. We will run a comparison with this model in Section 3.3.

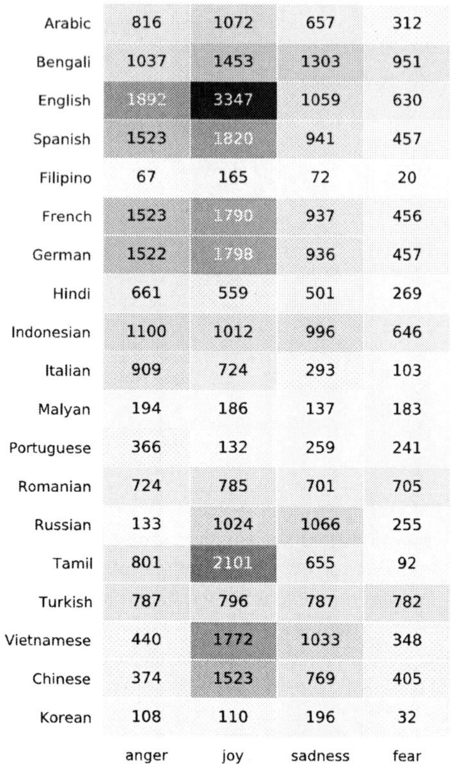

Figure 1: Label distribution. German, French have different numbers because some API translations failed.

3 Experiments

We perform three different experiments. The first one is meant to show the performance of XLM-EMO across the different languages. The second one evaluates how well XLM-EMO works on a zero-shot task in which data from one language is held out; we focus on testing three languages: English, Arabic, and Vietnamese. The third evaluation shows the performance of XLM-EMO on additional datasets different from those used for training on which we compare our model with other state-of-the-art models.

3.1 Performance on Test Set

We fine-tune 3 different models: XLM-RoBERTa-base (Conneau et al., 2020), XLM-RoBERTa-large (Conneau et al., 2020) and Twitter-XLM-RoBERTa (Barbieri et al., 2021). The first two are trained on data from 100 languages while the latter is a fine-tuned version of XLM-RoBERTa-base on Twitter data.

We use 10% for validation (we evaluate the

[3]We are aware that this process might introduce bias in the model as described by Hovy et al. (2020)

Language	Reference	Method	Family
English	Mohammad et al. (2018)	Manual Annotation	Indo-European
Spanish	Mohammad et al. (2018)	Manual Annotation	Indo-European
Arabic	Mohammad et al. (2018)	Manual Annotation	Afroasiatic
French	-	Translation	Indo-European
German	-	Translation	Indo-European
Chinese	Wang et al. (2018)	Manual Annotation	Sino-Tibetan
Korean	Do and Choi (2015)	Manual Annotation	Koreanic
Romanian	Ciobotaru and Dinu (2021)	Manual Annotation	Indo-European
Russian	Sboev et al. (2020)	Manual Annotation	Indo-European
Indonesian	Saputri et al. (2018)	Manual Annotation	Austronesian
Bengali	Iqbal et al. (2022)	Manual Annotation	Indo-European
Italian	Bianchi et al. (2021a)	Manual Annotation	Indo-European
Portuguese	Cortiz et al. (2021)	Distant Supervision	Indo-European
Turkish	Güven et al. (2020)	Distant Supervision	Turkic
Filipino	Lapitan et al. (2016)	Manual Annotation	Austronesian
Malay	Husein (2018)	Distant Supervision	Austronesian
Hindi	Shome (2021)	Translation	Indo-European
Vietnamese	Ho et al. (2019)	Manual Annotation	Austroasiatic
Tamil	Vasantharajan et al. (2022)	Manual Annotation	Dravidian

Table 1: Languages used in this work

Language	**Lang-Specific** (large)	**XLM-EMO ZeroShot** (large)	**XLM-EMO Trained** (large)
Arabic	**0.91**	0.81	0.88
English	0.83	0.82	**0.85**
Vietnamese	**0.84**	0.77	0.82

Table 2: Comparison between the language-specific models, the zero-shot XLM-EMO and an XLM-EMO that has been trained also on the additional data used for language-specific models plus all the other languages. Results are computed over the average of 5 different seeds.

Model	ME	EE-EN	EE-ES
XLM-EMO	**0.62**	**0.66**	**0.73**
LS-EMO	0.58	0.44	-
UJ-Combi	0.35	0.52	0.51

Table 3: Results on the Out of Domain test. XLM-EMO performs better than the selected baseline.

model every 50 steps and get the best checkpoint) and 5% of data for the test. Figure 2 shows the comparison between the three different models averaged on 5 runs with different seeds. These results show that the model is able to maintain a stable performance even when trained on data from 19 languages. The overall average Macro-F1s for XLM-RoBERTa-large, XLM-RoBERTa-base and XLM-Twitter-base are 0.86, 0.81 and 0.84.

The results also indicate that XLM-RoBERTa-large is the best model; however, XLM-Twitter-base performs better than XLM-RoBERTa-base and this is probably because it is a Twitter-specific model. Unfortunately, at this date, a large version of XLM-Twitter does not exist.

For all languages but Korean and Filipino, the performance is reliable. This is probably because both do not occur frequently in the training data. It should be noted that also Chinese and Tamil have a performance that is slightly above 0.6 with the large model. Considering these results, we will refer to the fine-tuned XLM-RoBERTa-large as XLM-EMO and we will use it in the rest of the paper.

3.2 Zero-shot Tests

We run 3 zero-shot comparisons to show the model performance on unseen languages. We select Arabic, English, and Vietnamese. Target language data is split into training and test (80/20). A language-specific model is trained (we again select the best model based on checkpoints on validation that is 10% of the training data). We use language-specific BERT-large for all the three languages. [4][5][6].

[4]https://huggingface.co/bert-large-uncased

[5]https://huggingface.co/aubmindlab/bert-large-arabertv02-twitter

[6]https://huggingface.co/vinai/phobert-large

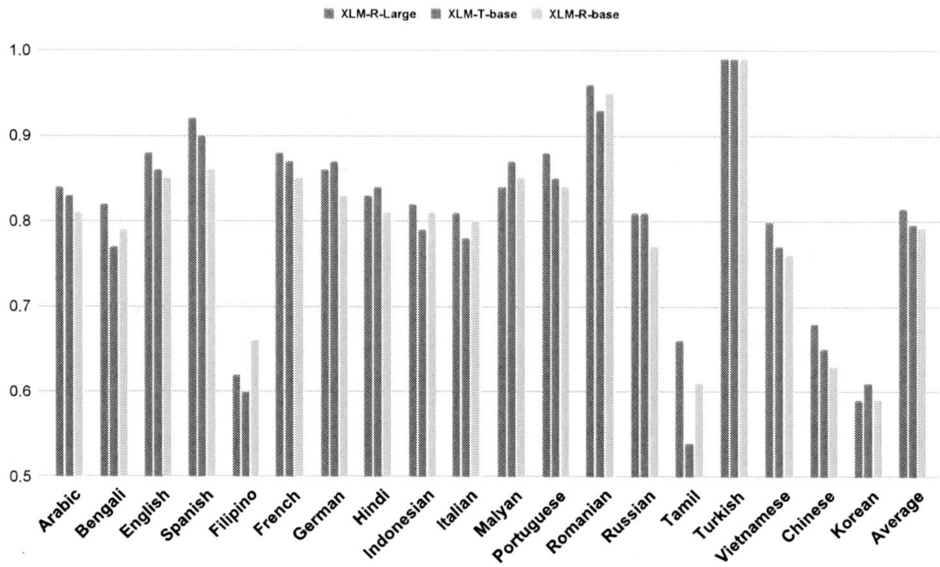

Figure 2: The performance (Macro-F1) of the three fine-tuned models across the various languages present in the test set. XLM-RoBERTa-large has the best performance. We averaged the run of 5 different seeds.

We also use an XLM-EMO trained on all the languages plus the 80% training data also used for the language-specific model.

Results in Table 2 show that XLM-EMO is competitive in the zero-shot settings. Still, language-specific models beat both the zero-shot and the model with additional training data.[7] On English data, XLM-EMO Trained seems to show better performance than the language-specific model, but this is probably because in language-specific datasets some English data might still be present.

3.3 Comparison with Available Models

We compare how XLM-EMO (large) behaves against out-of-training data to better understand if it generalizes well in other domains. In this test, we use other models to see how they perform in comparison with our XLM-EMO.

As datasets, we use the MultiEmotion Italian dataset (ME) (Sprugnoli, 2020) that contains YouTube and Facebook comments annotated with emotions (we collect only the comments with emotions that overlap with ours) and the EmoEvent dataset (EE) in English and Spanish (Plaza del Arco et al., 2020).[8] For both datasets we filtered out only the text that has been annotated with one of the labels we also use.

Respectively, as language-specific competitors (LS-EMO), we use the FEEL-IT (Bianchi et al., 2021a) as found on HuggingFace[9] and EmoNet Abdul-Mageed and Ungar (2017) as found on GitHub [10]. In addition, we also compare with the multilingual baseline Universal Joy (UJ) (Lamprinidis et al., 2021), using their *combi* model that has been trained on 6 languages (English, Spanish, Portuguese, Tagalog, Indonesian, and Chinese); note that, Italian has not been seen by the UJ model during training.

EmoNet and UJ predict additional emotions. To be as a fair as possible, we filter out the missing emotions from the predicted logits so that both models predict only *joy, anger, sadness, and fear*. The results in Table 3 show that XLM-EMO is the best performing model.

4 Limitations

Unfortunately, we have not been able to find datasets for emotions detection in any of the African Languages. Moreover, automatic translation tools do not often cover African languages or

[7] Similar conclusions have been reached by Nozza et al. (2020).

[8] We could not find another Spanish model to test against this data since the Spanish emotion recognition model (Pérez et al., 2021a,b) is trained on this data.

[9] `https://huggingface.co/MilaNLProc/feel-it-italian-emotion`

[10] `https://github.com/UBC-NLP/EmoNet`

they do not provide reliable evidence of being able to provide those translations with a certain level of quality. We reached out to members of our community to understand if there was any work that we were not aware of but we did not find any. Further iterations of this resource might want to focus on those languages.

5 Conclusion

In this short paper, we propose XLM-EMO, a novel resource for emotion detection. The model shows stable performance across 19 languages and it is competitive in a zero-shot setting, supporting its usage in low-resource contexts. We plan to enrich this model with more languages as soon as we find them so that we can continually improve these results and offer better methods to the community.

Acknowledgements

This project has partially received funding from the European Research Council (ERC) under the European Union's Horizon 2020 research and innovation program (grant agreement No. 949944, INTEGRATOR), and by Fondazione Cariplo (grant No. 2020-4288, MONICA). Federico Bianchi, Debora Nozza, and Dirk Hovy are members of the MilaNLP group, and the Data and Marketing Insights Unit of the Bocconi Institute for Data Science and Analysis.

Ethical Considerations

There is still a mismatch in the adoption of the methods we release and our understanding of them (Bianchi and Hovy, 2021). We are releasing a resource for multi-lingual emotion detection, but any list of language resources runs the risk of being (mis)interpreted as exhaustive, with languages included being regarded as more important than those that are not. We would like to emphatically state that this is not the case here: we tried to include as many languages as possible to allow for a wide comparison and provide a basis for further research. Any omission should not be read as a value judgment.

References

Muhammad Abdul-Mageed and Lyle Ungar. 2017. EmoNet: Fine-grained emotion detection with gated recurrent neural networks. In *Proceedings of the 55th Annual Meeting of the Association for Computational Linguistics (Volume 1: Long Papers)*, pages 718–728, Vancouver, Canada. Association for Computational Linguistics.

Cecilia Ovesdotter Alm, Dan Roth, and Richard Sproat. 2005. Emotions from text: Machine learning for text-based emotion prediction. In *Proceedings of Human Language Technology Conference and Conference on Empirical Methods in Natural Language Processing*, pages 579–586, Vancouver, British Columbia, Canada. Association for Computational Linguistics.

Francesco Barbieri, Luis Espinosa Anke, and Jose Camacho-Collados. 2021. XLM-T: A multilingual language model toolkit for Twitter. *arXiv preprint arXiv:2104.12250*.

Federico Bianchi and Dirk Hovy. 2021. On the gap between adoption and understanding in NLP. In *Findings of the Association for Computational Linguistics: ACL-IJCNLP 2021*, pages 3895–3901, Online. Association for Computational Linguistics.

Federico Bianchi, Debora Nozza, and Dirk Hovy. 2021a. FEEL-IT: Emotion and sentiment classification for the Italian language. In *Proceedings of the Eleventh Workshop on Computational Approaches to Subjectivity, Sentiment and Social Media Analysis*, pages 76–83, Online. Association for Computational Linguistics.

Federico Bianchi, Silvia Terragni, Dirk Hovy, Debora Nozza, and Elisabetta Fersini. 2021b. Cross-lingual contextualized topic models with zero-shot learning. In *Proceedings of the 16th Conference of the European Chapter of the Association for Computational Linguistics: Main Volume*, pages 1676–1683, Online. Association for Computational Linguistics.

Alexandra Ciobotaru and Liviu P. Dinu. 2021. RED: A novel dataset for Romanian emotion detection from tweets. In *Proceedings of the International Conference on Recent Advances in Natural Language Processing (RANLP 2021)*, pages 291–300, Held Online. INCOMA Ltd.

Alexis Conneau, Kartikay Khandelwal, Naman Goyal, Vishrav Chaudhary, Guillaume Wenzek, Francisco Guzmán, Edouard Grave, Myle Ott, Luke Zettlemoyer, and Veselin Stoyanov. 2020. Unsupervised cross-lingual representation learning at scale. In *Proceedings of the 58th Annual Meeting of the Association for Computational Linguistics*, pages 8440–8451, Online. Association for Computational Linguistics.

Diogo Cortiz, Jefferson O. Silva, Newton Calegari, Ana Luísa Freitas, Ana Angélica Soares, Carolina Botelho, Gabriel Gaudencio Rêgo, Waldir Sampaio, and Paulo Sergio Boggio. 2021. A weak supervised dataset of fine-grained emotions in Portuguese. *Symposium in Information and Human Language Technology*.

A. Danielewicz-Betz, , H. Kaneda, M. Mozgovoy, M. Purgina, , and and. 2015. Creating English and Japanese Twitter corpora for emotion analysis. *International Journal of Knowledge Engineering-IACSIT*, 1(2):120–124.

Dorottya Demszky, Dana Movshovitz-Attias, Jeongwoo Ko, Alan Cowen, Gaurav Nemade, and Sujith Ravi. 2020. GoEmotions: A dataset of fine-grained emotions. In *Proceedings of the 58th Annual Meeting of the Association for Computational Linguistics*, pages 4040–4054, Online. Association for Computational Linguistics.

Hyo Jin Do and Ho-Jin Choi. 2015. Korean Twitter emotion classification using automatically built emotion lexicons and fine-grained features. In *Proceedings of the 29th Pacific Asia Conference on Language, Information and Computation: Posters*, pages 142–150, Shanghai, China.

Zekeriya Anil Güven, Banu Diri, and Tolgahan Çakaloğlu. 2020. Comparison of n-stage latent dirichlet allocation versus other topic modeling methods for emotion analysis. *Journal of the Faculty of Engineering and Architecture of Gazi University*, 35(4):2135–2145.

Vong Anh Ho, Duong Huynh-Cong Nguyen, Danh Hoang Nguyen, Linh Thi-Van Pham, Duc-Vu Nguyen, Kiet Van Nguyen, and Ngan Luu-Thuy Nguyen. 2019. Emotion recognition for Vietnamese social media text. In *Computational Linguistics - 16th International Conference of the Pacific Association for Computational Linguistics, PACLING 2019, Hanoi, Vietnam, October 11-13, 2019*, volume 1215 of *Communications in Computer and Information Science*, pages 319–333. Springer.

Dirk Hovy, Federico Bianchi, and Tommaso Fornaciari. 2020. "You sound just like your father" commercial machine translation systems include stylistic biases. In *Proceedings of the 58th Annual Meeting of the Association for Computational Linguistics*, pages 1686–1690, Online. Association for Computational Linguistics.

Pere-Lluís Huguet Cabot, Verna Dankers, David Abadi, Agneta Fischer, and Ekaterina Shutova. 2020. The Pragmatics behind Politics: Modelling Metaphor, Framing and Emotion in Political Discourse. In *Findings of the Association for Computational Linguistics: EMNLP 2020*, pages 4479–4488, Online. Association for Computational Linguistics.

Zolkepli Husein. 2018. Malay-dataset, we gather bahasa malaysia corpus!, semi-supervised emotion dataset. `https://github.com/huseinzol05/malay-dataset/tree/master/corpus/emotion`.

MD. Asif Iqbal, Avishek Das, Omar Sharif, Mohammed Moshiul Hoque, and Iqbal H. Sarker. 2022. BEmoC: A corpus for identifying emotion in Bengali texts. *SN Computer Science*, 3(2):135.

Bennett Kleinberg, Isabelle van der Vegt, and Maximilian Mozes. 2020. Measuring Emotions in the COVID-19 Real World Worry Dataset. In *Proceedings of the 1st Workshop on NLP for COVID-19 at ACL 2020*, Online. Association for Computational Linguistics.

Sotiris Lamprinidis, Federico Bianchi, Daniel Hardt, and Dirk Hovy. 2021. Universal joy a data set and results for classifying emotions across languages. In *Proceedings of the Eleventh Workshop on Computational Approaches to Subjectivity, Sentiment and Social Media Analysis*, pages 62–75, Online. Association for Computational Linguistics.

Fermin Roberto Lapitan, Riza Theresa Batista-Navarro, and Eliezer Albacea. 2016. Crowdsourcing-based annotation of emotions in Filipino and English tweets. In *Proceedings of the 6th Workshop on South and Southeast Asian Natural Language Processing (WSSANLP2016)*, pages 74–82, Osaka, Japan. The COLING 2016 Organizing Committee.

Saif Mohammad, Felipe Bravo-Marquez, Mohammad Salameh, and Svetlana Kiritchenko. 2018. SemEval-2018 task 1: Affect in tweets. In *Proceedings of The 12th International Workshop on Semantic Evaluation*, pages 1–17, New Orleans, Louisiana. Association for Computational Linguistics.

Debora Nozza. 2021. Exposing the limits of zero-shot cross-lingual hate speech detection. In *Proceedings of the 59th Annual Meeting of the Association for Computational Linguistics and the 11th International Joint Conference on Natural Language Processing (Volume 2: Short Papers)*, pages 907–914, Online. Association for Computational Linguistics.

Debora Nozza, Federico Bianchi, and Dirk Hovy. 2020. What the [MASK]? Making sense of language-specific BERT models. *arXiv preprint arXiv:2003.02912*.

Debora Nozza, Elisabetta Fersini, and Enza Messina. 2017. A multi-view sentiment corpus. In *Proceedings of the 15th Conference of the European Chapter of the Association for Computational Linguistics: Volume 1, Long Papers*, pages 273–280, Valencia, Spain. Association for Computational Linguistics.

Flor Miriam Plaza del Arco, Carlo Strapparava, L. Alfonso Urena Lopez, and Maite Martin. 2020. EmoEvent: A multilingual emotion corpus based on different events. In *Proceedings of the 12th Language Resources and Evaluation Conference*, pages 1492–1498, Marseille, France. European Language Resources Association.

Juan Manuel Pérez, Damián A. Furman, Laura Alonso Alemany, and Franco Luque. 2021a. RoBERTuito: a pre-trained language model for social media text in Spanish. *arXiv preprint arXiv:2111.09453*.

Juan Manuel Pérez, Juan Carlos Giudici, and Franco Luque. 2021b. pysentimiento: A Python toolkit for sentiment analysis and socialnlp tasks. *arXiv preprint arXiv:2106.09462*.

Nazanin Sabri, Reyhane Akhavan, and Behnam Bahrak. 2021. EmoPars: A collection of 30K emotion-annotated Persian social media texts. In *Proceedings of the Student Research Workshop Associated with RANLP 2021*, pages 167–173, Online. INCOMA Ltd.

Mei Silviana Saputri, Rahmad Mahendra, and Mirna Adriani. 2018. Emotion classification on Indonesian Twitter dataset. In *2018 International Conference on Asian Language Processing, IALP 2018, Bandung, Indonesia, November 15-17, 2018*, pages 90–95. IEEE.

Alexander G. Sboev, Aleksandr Naumov, and Roman B. Rybka. 2020. Data-driven model for emotion detection in Russian texts. In *Proceedings of the 2020 Annual International Conference on Brain-Inspired Cognitive Architectures for Artificial Intelligence, BICA 2020*, volume 190 of *Procedia Computer Science*, pages 637–642. Elsevier.

Debaditya Shome. 2021. EmoHinD: Fine-grained multi-label emotion recognition from Hindi texts with deep learning. In *12th International Conference on Computing Communication and Networking Technologies, ICCCNT 2021*, pages 1–5. IEEE.

Rachele Sprugnoli. 2020. MultiEmotions-It: a new dataset for opinion polarity and emotion analysis for Italian. In *Proceedings of the Seventh Italian Conference on Computational Linguistics, CLiC-it 2020, Bologna, Italy, March 1-3, 2021*, volume 2769 of *CEUR Workshop Proceedings*. CEUR-WS.org.

Charangan Vasantharajan, Sean Benhur, Prasanna Kumar Kumarasen, Rahul Ponnusamy, Sathiyaraj Thangasamy, Ruba Priyadharshini, Thenmozhi Durairaj, Kanchana Sivanraju, Anbukkarasi Sampath, Bharathi Raja Chakravarthi, and John Phillip McCrae. 2022. Tamilemo: Finegrained emotion detection dataset for tamil. *arXiv preprint arXiv:2202.04725*.

Reyha Verma, Christian von der Weth, Jithin Vachery, and Mohan Kankanhalli. 2020. Identifying worry in Twitter: Beyond emotion analysis. In *Proceedings of the Fourth Workshop on Natural Language Processing and Computational Social Science*, pages 72–82, Online. Association for Computational Linguistics.

Deepanshu Vijay, Aditya Bohra, Vinay Singh, Syed Sarfaraz Akhtar, and Manish Shrivastava. 2018. Corpus creation and emotion prediction for Hindi-English code-mixed social media text. In *Proceedings of the 2018 Conference of the North American Chapter of the Association for Computational Linguistics: Student Research Workshop*, pages 128–135, New Orleans, Louisiana, USA. Association for Computational Linguistics.

Zhongqing Wang, Shoushan Li, Fan Wu, Qingying Sun, and Guodong Zhou. 2018. Overview of NLPCC 2018 shared task 1: Emotion detection in code-switching text. In *Natural Language Processing and Chinese Computing - 7th CCF International Conference, NLPCC 2018*, volume 11109 of *Lecture Notes in Computer Science*, pages 429–433. Springer.

Shijie Wu and Mark Dredze. 2019. Beto, bentz, becas: The surprising cross-lingual effectiveness of BERT. In *Proceedings of the 2019 Conference on Empirical Methods in Natural Language Processing and the 9th International Joint Conference on Natural Language Processing (EMNLP-IJCNLP)*, pages 833–844, Hong Kong, China. Association for Computational Linguistics.

Rui Xia and Zixiang Ding. 2019. Emotion-cause pair extraction: A new task to emotion analysis in texts. In *Proceedings of the 57th Annual Meeting of the Association for Computational Linguistics*, pages 1003–1012, Florence, Italy. Association for Computational Linguistics.

Param	Value
Batch Size	64
Warm Up Steps	50
Learning Rate	1e-3
Learning Epochs*	5
Optimizer	AdamW
Betas	0.9 and 0.999
Max Length	100

Table 4: The main parameters we used to run the models. *While epochs are 5, we remark that we are running a step-wise evaluation.

A Training Details

A.1 Parameters

All the models are trained with the same pipeline. We report the shared parameters in Table 4. The only difference can be found in the experiments presented in Section 3.2, the zero-shot tests. Since the language-specific datasets contain less data, we reduced the number of steps for which we run the evaluation and create a checkpoint (i.e, we evaluate every 5 steps).

The loss we use is weighted with respect to the frequency of each label.

This configuration was obtained after several grid search experiments, we found that one of the parameter that impacts the most the training of *large* configurations of the models is the batch size. Models are trained on a Nvidia GeForce RTX 2080 Ti.

A.2 Pre-processing

We align our pre-processing to the one described in (Barbieri et al., 2021), replacing user tags with

@user and links with *http*. For those datasets that had a different pre-processing (e.g., some datasets used *@username* to replace user tags) we applied a normalization procedure to align them with our pre-processing.

PhoBERT Note that the Vietnamese model requires a particular pre-processing pipeline: as suggested by the authors on their own GitHub page, for this specific model we apply segmentation on the Vietnamese text.

B Dataset Details

In general, when a message is annotated with multiple emotions we remove it from the dataset. When a dataset comes with multiple emotions that could overlap (e.g., *joy* and *enthusiasm*), we just select the emotions of our interest and we do not apply any mapping (e.g., treating *enthusiasm* messages as *joy*). This is done to avoid bias in the final collection.

We are going to release also our entire processing pipeline (that is mainly based on data transformations) so that interested researchers can re-run it. Note that all the samplings we do have been run with a fixed seed so that they are reproducible.

Arabic This data come from the Affects In Tweet dataset (Mohammad et al., 2018). We combine train, validation and test in a single dataset but we drop emotions that are not covered by our set of emotions.

Bengali This dataset contains data coming from a different source, such as youtube comments and Facebook posts. We only take the messages with emotions that are part of our set.

English This data come from the Affects In Tweet dataset (Mohammad et al., 2018). We combine train, validation and test in a single dataset but we drop emotions that are not covered by our set of emotions.

Spanish This data come from the Affects In Tweet dataset (Mohammad et al., 2018). We combine train, validation and test in a single dataset but we drop emotions that are not covered by our set of emotions.

Filipino This is one of the languages with a lower amount of data. The number of tweets in Filipino (Lapitan et al., 2016) was already low in the original work (i.e., 647) and the final number is even lower since we removed the emotions that do not overlap with ours.

French For this language, we translated the training data that comes from the Spanish subset of the Affects In Tweet dataset (Mohammad et al., 2018).

German For this language, we translated the training data that comes from the Spanish subset of the Affects In Tweet dataset (Mohammad et al., 2018).

Hindi This dataset comes from a translation of the original GoEmotion dataset (Demszky et al., 2020). We just selected the emotions we are interested in and removed the others. Since this dataset has been translated with Google API we opted for sampling only 2000 examples not to bias the representation too much.

Indonesian We collected this dataset directly from the authors work (Saputri et al., 2018), we dropped the *love* emotions and we mapped *happy* to our emotion *joy*.

Italian This dataset comes from the work of Bianchi et al. (2021a), their labels overlap with ours.

Malyan We were slightly less confident on the quality of the annotations of this dataset and we thus sampled 200 messages for each emotion.

Portuguese This dataset has been collected using a keyword search of terms related to emotions. We focus only on our target emotions and randomly sample a maximum of 1000 tweets. This is done because the keyword used for the emotions are few and we would like to avoid biasing the actual representation.

Romanian This dataset (Ciobotaru and Dinu, 2021) has been collected by scraping Twitter using specific keywords. The emotions considered are 5, where the additional one is *neutral*, which we remove. As our data, we used both the training and the validation data released by the authors.

Russian We mainly focused on Twitter data and from the Russian dataset Sboev et al. (2020) we extract only the data that comes from Twitter. We remove the tweets with *neutral* label.

Tamil The Tamil dataset contains YouTube comments and we use the training dataset described by the authors. We decided to remove the long tail of messages that have more than 30 tokens to make the dataset more consistent with the other datasets. Our labels are a subset of the labels described in the paper and we take only the messages with those labels.

Turkish The Turkish dataset contains 5 emotions, one of which is *surprise* that was removed from our datasets.

Vietnamese This dataset contains youtube comments and has been manually annotated. We drop the emotions that are not covered in our dataset.

Chinese This dataset comes from the challenge described by (Wang et al., 2018). It contains Chinese messages, some of which contain English words (it is a code-switching dataset).

Korean The Korean dataset contains tweets that we reconstructed using the Twitter API. Since the release of the dataset, most tweets have been deleted or are not available anymore for other reasons. The dataset contains the *Neutral* label that we filter out. The other labels easily map onto ours.

Evaluating Content Features and Classification Methods for Helpfulness Prediction of Online Reviews: Establishing a Benchmark for Portuguese

Rogério Figueredo de Sousa, Thiago Alexandre Salgueiro Pardo
Interinstitutional Center for Computational Linguistics (NILC)
Institute of Mathematical and Computer Sciences, University of São Paulo
Av. Trabalhador São Carlense, 400 – 13.566-590 – São Carlos – SP – Brazil
rogerfig@usp.br, taspardo@icmc.usp.br

Abstract

Over the years, the review helpfulness prediction task has been the subject of several works, but remains being a challenging issue in Natural Language Processing, as results vary a lot depending on the domain, on the adopted features and on the chosen classification strategy. This paper attempts to evaluate the impact of content features and classification methods for two different domains. In particular, we run our experiments for a low resource language – Portuguese –, trying to establish a benchmark for this language. We show that simple features and classical classification methods are powerful for the task of helpfulness prediction, but are largely outperformed by a convolutional neural network-based solution.

1 Introduction

The concern to facilitate users' decision-making is common in most e-commerce platforms. The possibility for customers to publicly provide product reviews is one of the consequences of this concern. This functionality allows future customers to read reviews from other customers and take their buying decision. Despite being useful, the amount of generated data is very large, making it impossible for a human to read them all. Moreover, a large part of this data can be considered unwanted, containing poorly written texts, vague opinions and texts of dubious quality (Kim et al., 2006), making it difficult to find relevant content.

The helpfulness voting functionality that some e-commerce platforms adopt tries to address the above problem, ranking the reviews and showing the most helpful ones to the customers. However, manual voting has some drawbacks, as new helpful reviews take time to get enough votes and gain a visible position. The solution is to automatically predict the helpfulness of reviews.

Despite the usefulness of the task of helpfulness prediction and its practical implications, literature has shown that it is a challenging open issue in Natural Language Processing (NLP). Performance results vary drastically across domains and there are several different features and classification methods in the area, as discussed in (Sousa and Pardo, 2021).

This paper aims to investigate such issues and to identify relevant features and methods for helpfulness prediction. We provide a qualitative and quantitative study of the impact of key content features in two different domains (apps and movies). By content features, we mean those that are related to the information that can be extracted directly from the review, such as the text and the "stars" given by the author. We also perform a comparative study of various classical and deep machine learning classifiers. We show that simple features and classical classification methods may be powerful for the task, but they are largely outperformed by a convolutional neural network-based approach, which reaches a f1-score of 0.90 for apps and 0.74 for movies. It is also relevant to cite that we run our experiments for a low resource language – Brazilian Portuguese –, bringing relevant contributions for NLP for Portuguese and establishing a benchmark for the task.

The rest of the paper is organized as follows. Section 2 shows the main related work. In Section 3, we describe the experimental setting adopted in this work. Section 4 reports the achieved results and Section 5 brings some final remarks.

2 Related Work

The main research line in review helpfulness prediction aims to predict the helpfulness score for a set of reviews. The helpfulness score is defined as shown in Equation 1 and can be used as the target for regression, binary classification, or ranking. The score regression aims to predict the helpfulness score $h \in [0, 1]$. For binary classification, a threshold is applied in helpfulness score (e.g., $h > 0.5$)

Proceedings of the 12th Workshop on Computational Approaches to Subjectivity, Sentiment & Social Media Analysis, pages 204 - 213
May 26, 2022

and all reviews with a helpfulness score above the threshold are classified as helpful; otherwise, they are classified as not helpful. Review ranking seeks to order the reviews by their helpfulness according to a reference ranking.

$$h = \frac{helpful\ votes}{helpful\ votes + unhelpful\ votes} \quad (1)$$

In order to understand the helpfulness of online customer reviews, researches have performed several analyses. It is worth mentioning classical works like the ones of Kim et al. (2006) and Zhang and Varadarajan (2006) that introduce many types of features for helpfulness prediction. Kim et al. (2006) split the features in 5 categories, all considered to be content features: Structural, Lexical, Syntactic, Semantic and Meta-Data Features. They build a model for a regression task and a model for a ranking task using the SVM algorithm. Using a dataset of reviews on two products (MP3 players and Digital Cameras) extracted from Amazon.com, the best results are achieved with the combination of length, unigram and number of stars features. In a similar way, Zhang and Varadarajan (2006) propose three categories of features, also for a dataset extracted from Amazon.com. Their features include Lexical Similarity (Cosine similarity over TF-IDF vectors), Shallow Syntactic Features (Proper nouns, Modal verbs, Interjection, etc.) and Lexical Subjectivity Clues (Subjective adjectives, Subjective nouns, etc.). The authors model two regressors using SVR (Support Vector Regression) and SLR (Simple Linear Regression) techniques, obtaining the best results by combining all the features.

Zeng et al. (2014), in addition to the features already used by Kim et al. (2006), propose the use of Trigrams, Comparison Expressions ("Compare to" or "ADJ + er than"), Degree of detail and Pros and Cons. Using an SVM classifier, the authors address the helpfulness prediction task as a three-class classification: Helpful positive reviews, Helpful negative reviews, and Unhelpful reviews. Furthermore, by running a series of experiments with one less feature each time, they found that the "detail" feature is the most important one, followed by length, number of stars and unigram.

More recently, researchers are using more robust methods for helpfulness prediction. It is the case of Xu et al. (2020), that use BERT (Bidirectional Encoder Representations from Transformers) (Devlin et al., 2019) along with the features of Star Rating and Product Type. With this combination, the authors model a Neural Network to predict the helpfulness score for reviews extracted from Amazom.com. Wang et al. (2020) also use BERT, but the authors add more features (Number of Words, Number of Sentences, Rating, etc.) than Xu et al. (2020) and compare the BERT-based approach to SVM and CNN models. The neural network-based classifiers achieved similar results to SVM using all features. Wu and Wang (2019) propose the use of syntactic features along with BERT sentence embeddings to helpfulness classification. The work compares some CNN models with BERT and perform an ablation study with all syntactic features. Their results showed high recall but very low precision values. In terms of f1-score, BERT achieved the best results and the main feature was Star Rating.

All these researches have in common the use of content features. The results of methods using handcrafted features were better or very close to state-of-the-art classifiers (using BERT and CNN, for instance). In such setting, this paper aims at further exploring such issues, specially for the context of Portuguese, a low resource language. We present our experiment setting in what follows.

3 Experiment Setting

3.1 Data Overview

We adopt the dataset of Sousa et al. (2019) that includes reviews written in Portuguese for two very different domains: Movies and Apps. While movie reviews are usually largely subjective and passionate, app reviews tend to be more objective and focus on technical aspects. The dataset (namely UTLCorpus) contains a total of $2,732,538$ reviews ($1,833,691$ for movies and $898,847$ for apps).

Figure 1 presents two examples of reviews extracted from the corpus (from the apps domain). The first is considered not helpful, while the second is helpful. According to the creators of the corpus, the helpfulness status is based on the number of votes the reviews received (0 and 335 helpful votes, respectively) and the posting time (more than 5 days).

As the authors report, each review includes the review text, number of stars given by its author, the number of helpfulness votes, and publication time, among some other information. As shown in Table 1, the UTLCorpus is highly unbalanced. We address the unbalancing problem using an under-

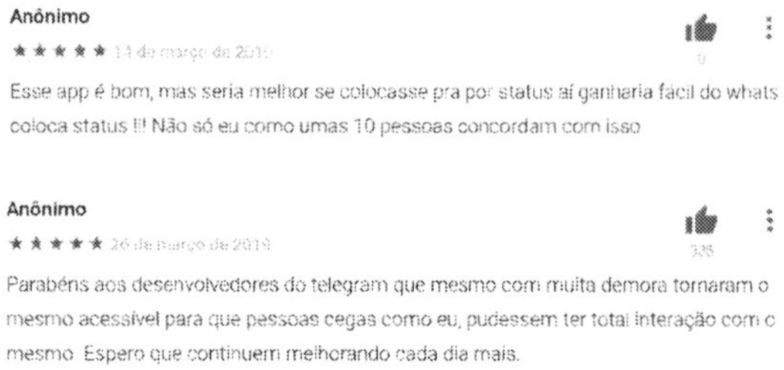

Figure 1: Examples of reviews

sampling approach, randomly removing samples of the majority class. Due to the amount of data, we decided not to carry out the oversampling strategy. Besides the class balancing information, the details of tokens and types in the table show us that the average size of movie reviews is much bigger than that of apps. This difference can make the movies' reviews more challenging than the apps' reviews. Section 4 will further elucidate this assumption.

	Movies	**Apps**
# reviews	1,833,691	898,847
# movies or apps	4,283	243
# types	1,828,647	419,713
# tokens	60,177,264	11,919,636
Avg. of Tokens p/ doc	32.7994	12.9384
Helpfulness Label	*helpful: 20%*	*helpful: 5%*

Table 1: UTLCorpus numbers. The helpfulness label refers to the percentage of reviews labeled as helpful.

For our experiments, which we report in the next section, we have randomly split our dataset in three parts: 70% for training, 20% for testing, and 10% for development.

3.2 Features

The literature on online review helpfulness explores several features. The researchers often split the features in two big groups: Content and Context features. The content features are related to the information that can be extracted directly from the review, such as the text and the "stars" given by the author. Context features are those extracted from outside the review, such as reviewer information. (Ocampo Diaz and Ng, 2018; Almutairi et al., 2019; Arif et al., 2018). Most of these features are used in domains such as products, books, hotels and so on. We desire to experiment them in apps and movies domains, which are the domains available in the dataset that we adopted in this work and that are remarkably different (which interests us in this paper).

We selected and adapted several content features to the Portuguese language. This process involved finding resources and tools that could support the use of the features in the target language. Table 2 summarizes the implemented features.

We explored the features in machine learning classification solutions. We performed a selection of the best features employing three different strategies. The first method of feature selection is the classical Information Gain (Kozachenko and Leonenko, 1987), which produces values from 0 (no information) to 1 (maximum information) for each feature. The features that contribute with more information are selected to the experiments. The second well-known method for feature selection is using the Random Forest classifier (Breiman, 2001), which is a meta estimator that uses several tree-based classifiers in various subsamples of the dataset to classify the target. Due to its characteristic of using decision trees, it can indicate the importance of features used in the classification process. The third method for feature selection consists in using the correlation values of the features with the helpfulness classes. The previous work of Sousa and Pardo (2021) presents studies of correlation among the feature values and helpfulness status using the correlation coefficients of Pearson and Spearman. Using these correlations, we order the absolute values and select the features with better values.

In addition to the previous features, we also test Term-Frequency (TF) and Term Frequency-Inverse Document Frequency (TF-IDF) techniques to generate specific text features and compare the results of the handcrafted features with these two well-known baseline features. It is important to mention that all feature values were normalized for the experimentation process. Table 3 shows an overview of all the features used in this paper.

We comment on the machine learning classifiers and report the achieved results in the next section.

4 Results

We explored the following classical classification strategies in this work: Naive Bayes (NB), Support Vector Machines (SVM), Decision Tree (DT), Random Forest (RF), Neural Network Multilayer Perceptron (NN) and a Dummy Classifier. More sophisticated (deep) strategies that we tested are a BERT-based classifier and a Convolutional Neural

Feature	Description	Portuguese Resource/Tool
Average Sentence Length (Avg-SL)	Average sentence size in terms of words (Liu et al., 2007; Lu et al., 2010)	spaCy with portuguese language model
Number of Sentences (Num-S)	Total of sentences in the review (Liu et al., 2007; Lu et al., 2010)	
Number of Words (Num-W)	Total of words in the review (Kim et al., 2006; Mudambi and Schuff, 2010)	
Star Rating (Star-R)	The review-assigned product star rating (Huang et al., 2015)	-
Readability Features (READ)	Measure how easy a text is to read and include the following features: Automated Readability Index (ARI), Coleman-Liau Index (CLI), Flesch Reading Ease (FRE), Flesch-Kincaid Grade Level (FKGL), Gunning fog index (GFI) and SMOG (Dubay, 2004; Ghose and Ipeirotis, 2011)	Readability features based on (Antunes and Lopes, 2019)
Spelling Errors (SPELL)	Number of misspelled words in review (Ghose and Ipeirotis, 2011)	Number of words not found in Wiktionary[1] and Unitex-PB lexicons (Muniz, 2004)
Dominant Terms (Dom-Terms)	Presence of important terms in reviews, considering their specificity for the domain (Tsur and Rappoport, 2009)	We use the NILC Corpus (Nunes et al., 1996) to calculate the frequencies of words that do not belong to the domains
Product Aspects (Prod-Feat)	Presence of product aspects in the reviews (Kim et al., 2006; Hong et al., 2012; Liu et al., 2007)	We manually extract the features of texts from the corpus development set.
Sentiment Words (SENT)	Number of words that express sentiments (Kim et al., 2006) according to the following categories of the LIWC dictionary (Pennebaker et al., 2001): Negate, Swear, Affect, Posemo, Negemo, Anxiety, Anger and Sad	We used a Portuguese version of LIWC dictionary (Balage Filho et al., 2013)
Sentiment Divergence (Sent-Div)	Difference between the general sentiment about the movie/app and the sentiment expressed by the author of a review (Hong et al., 2012)	Sentilex sentiment lexicon (Silva et al., 2012)
Subjectivity (SUB)	The probability of a review being subjective (Ghose and Ipeirotis, 2011)	
Morpho-Syntactic Tokens (SYN)	Number of tokens with the following Part-of-Speech tags: Noun (N), Verb (V), Adverb (ADV) and Adjective (ADJ). It also includes counting for open class words (Open) (Kim et al., 2006)	NLPNet POS-Tagger (Fonseca and Rosa, 2013)
Star Deviation (Star-Dev)	Difference between the number of stars in a review and the average star rating for the movie/app (Hong et al., 2012)	-

Table 2: List of content features

Network (CNN).

4.1 Feature Selection

As explained before, we performed feature selection using the techniques of Information Gain and Random Forest. Figures 2a and 2b show the results of feature ranking for the apps domain, while Figure 2c and 2d show the results for movies domain. We performed the classification for the top 8 features of each method of feature selection. As an alternative, we also selected the most correlated features to helpfulness status using the Pearson and Spearman values.

4.2 Classification Results

We divided the process of training classifiers in some distinct phases. In the first phase, we trained the classifiers considering the feature selection methods against the TF and TF-IDF techniques. This phase shows us the best sets of features and the best classifiers for both types of features: handcrafted and TF/TF-IDF features. In the second phase, we merged the handcrafted features with the TF/TF-IDF ones. This feature combination process

Feature category (number of features)	Description
Handcrafted Content Features (29)	The content features adapted from previous literature works.
Information Gain (8)	The handcrafted content features selected by Information Gain technique.
Random Forest (8)	The handcrafted content features selected by Random Forest Classifier.
Correlation Coefficients (8)	The handcrafted content features selected by the intersection of correlation coefficients.
Baseline TF (500)	The features selected by TF method.
Baseline TF-IDF (500)	The features selected by TF-IDF method.

Table 3: Overview of the features

consists of concatenating the vectors of each text (i.e., TF or TF-IDF vectors) with the vectors of each group of features, both with the same weight. Finally, in the third phase, we decided to use the results of the second phase to model voting-based ensemble classifiers. The classifiers with good results and fewer errors in common were selected to compose the ensembles. The chosen classifiers for the ensembles were Decision Trees and Neural Networks for apps, and Decision Trees and Random Forest for movies. Ensembles with three classifiers obtained similar results (never higher) to those with two classifiers, so we only report the results for ensembles of two classifiers[2]. Finally, in a fourth phase, we used a BERT-based classifier over a pre-trained Portuguese model (Souza et al., 2020) for both domains and a CNN using the GloVe[3] (Hartmann et al., 2017; Pennington et al., 2014) embeddings as input features.

The results referring to the first phase are shown in Figures 3a and 3b, where we show F1 scores (the best ones are written in the chart). Notice that we show in the charts the *F1-Measure* that is the average F1 score for the two classes. One may see that, for apps, the best results were 72%, which may be achieved with simple TF features with SVM and Random Forest; for movies, the best results were 63% for TF-IDF, with the same classifiers. Overall, for both domains, there were no significant performance differences for the two classes.

When we merge the two big groups of features (handcrafted and TF/IDF features), the results are better, as one may see in Figures 3c and 3d. Considering the best situation, apps classification achieved 78% with correlation-based feature selection and TF for SVM (results 8.3% better than before); movies achieved 66% with all the features and TF-IDF for SVM too (4.7% better). Again, SVM showed to be a distinctive technique, with stable classification performances for the two classes.

The results for our ensemble, the BERT-based[4] and the CNN classifiers are shown in Figure 3e. For better understanding, the X-axis in Figure 3e mentions the use of the handcrafted features along with BERT (BERT-PT+Hand). For this strategy, we appended all handcrafted features to *CLS* vector ($768 + 29$ $dimensions$), and then the method proceeds normally, using the resulting vector in the next layer to perform the classification. In the same way, for clarification, the strategy BERT-PT+CNN was modeled to merge the BERT architecture to CNN, presented before. We used the four last layers of BERT as features for CNN. The fine-tuning of BERT model was made at the same time as the CNN training. Figure 4 shows the architecture of the CNN.

Despite BERT being a new standard technique in the NLP area, it achieved results very similar to those presented by the ensemble. In the application domain, BERT shows a slight drop in performance. Further investigation is needed to find out why the

[2]We adopted a soft classification, in which the classes are weighted by their probabilities given by the classifiers; if it happens that the two classes end up with the same score, we opt for the not helpful class.

[3]http://nilc.icmc.usp.br/nilc/index.php/repositorio-de-word-embeddings-do-nilc

[4]This model was fine-tuned and the pre-trained parameters were not frozen during fine-tuning. The reviews were tokenized using the default tokenizer of Bertimbau model. We applied a single layer feed forward network in CLS output vector (768 dimensions) to classify the instances. The main hyperparameters are as follows: *epochs = 2, learning rate = 4e-5, optimizer = AdamW, train batch size = 8, max sequence length = 128.* These hyperparameters were empirically chosen.

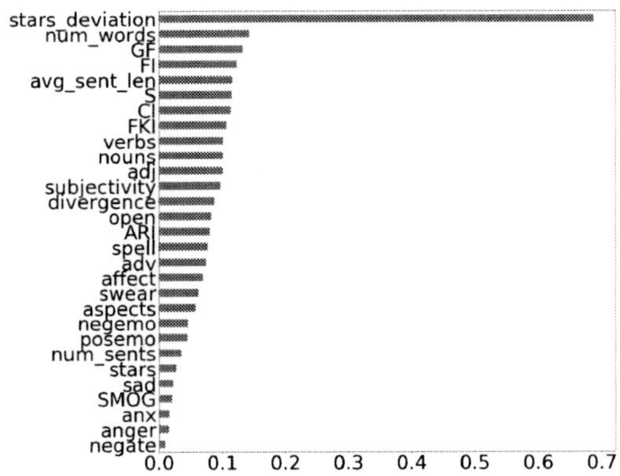

(a) Information Gain – Apps

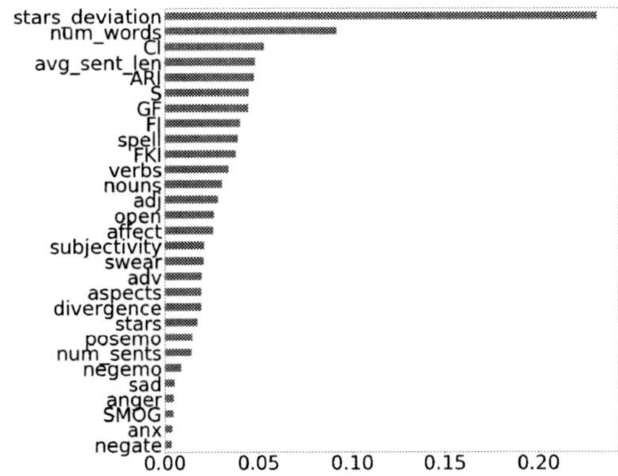

(b) Random Forest – Apps

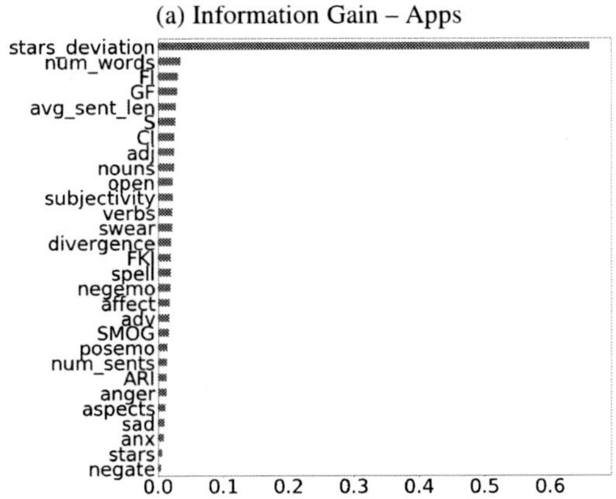

(c) Information Gain – Movies

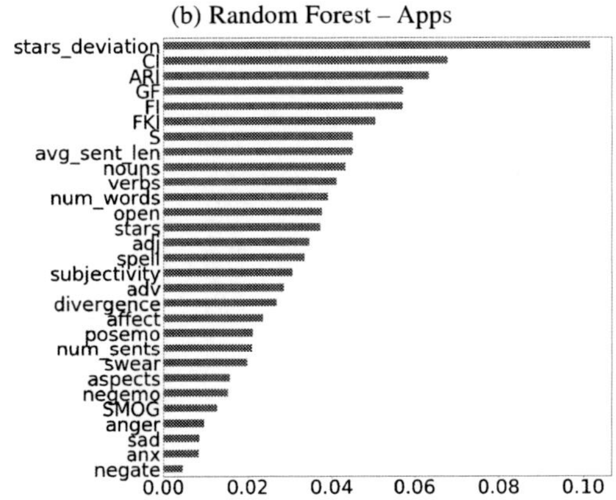

(d) Random Forest – Movies

Figure 2: Results of feature importance

results are so low for this case. Possible explanations include the more "passionate" and subjective nature of the movie reviews (while apps' reviews tend to discuss more "technical" aspects). Overall, the ensemble classification could not outperform the previous experiments, while the CNN model outperformed all classifiers.

Considering all the experiments, we have some valuable learned lessons. We may see that simple textual features such as TF and TF-IDF may be powerful features for helpfulness prediction. However, merging handcrafted content features with TF-IDF features allows us to achieve better results. Other interesting result is that traditional machine learning techniques may rival more sophisticated strategies as ensemble or BERT-based classifiers. SVM, in special, showed to be an important technique among the classical methods. Anyway, all of them were outperformed by a CNN approach.

Finally, regarding the feature selection processes, the correlation-based one was slightly better than information gain and the Random Forest-based one, but the differences appear to be insignificant. Among the best selected features, although there is some variation depending on the used correlation measure, it is possible to highlight some of them: for apps domain, we highlight average sentence length, star rating and part of speech tags; for movies domain, average sentence length, SMOG readability score, sentiment words and dominant terms.

5 Final Remarks

This paper synthesized a series of experiments on predicting review helpfulness, showing some relevant learned lessons and contributions (in particular, for Brazilian Portuguese, which is considered a low resource language). However, a lot remains to be investigated. We highlight two issues that concern us the most at this time.

Firstly, the different performances for different domains (across different classification methods) keep intriguing us. This is a known behavior in the sentiment analysis area, and we corroborate it by testing new domains in this paper. We wonder whether new methods or features should be tested,

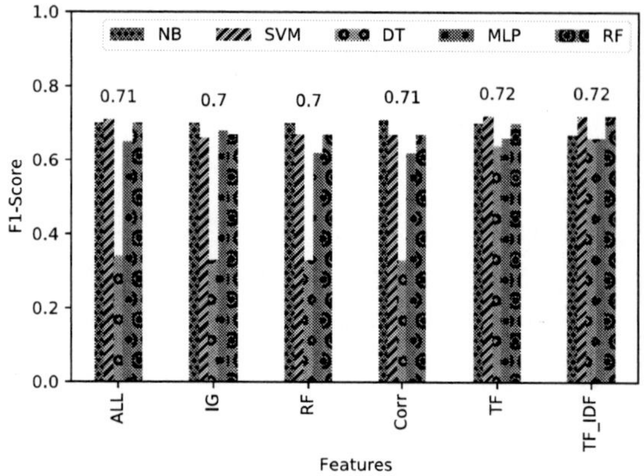

(a) Classification results for apps

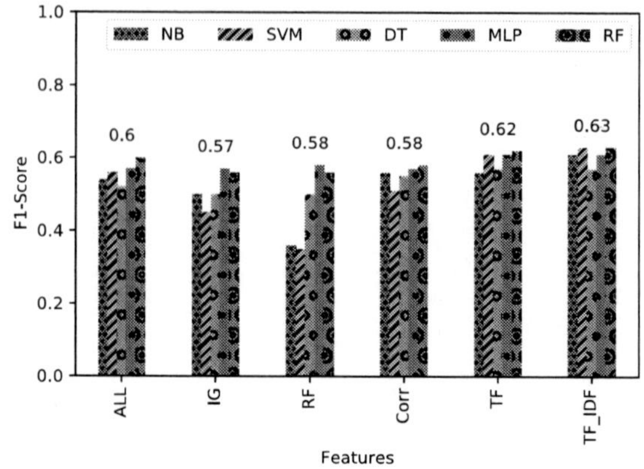

(b) Classification results for movies

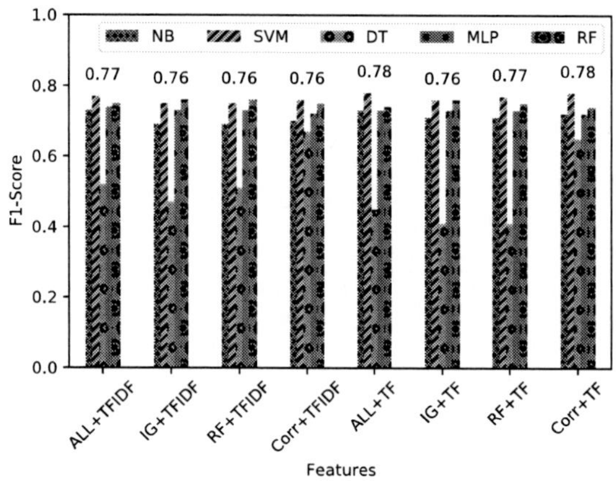

(c) Classification results with merged features for apps

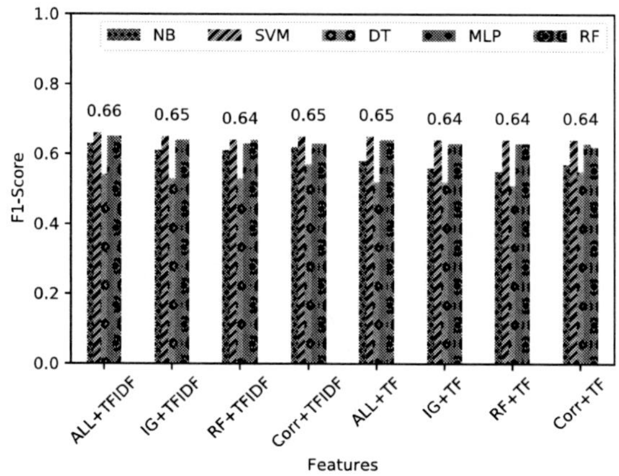

(d) Classification results with merged features for movies

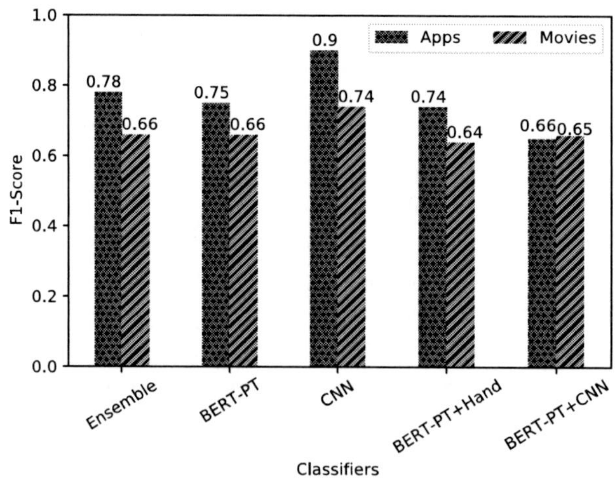

(e) Results of ensemble classification and deep models with their combinations

Figure 3: Classification Results

maybe focusing on those that are more domain independent, or whether we should "transform" our data, "eliminating" domain specific traits.

The other issue refers to the helpfulness prediction task itself. Although the literature (including us) have exhaustively tried with this task, it is a highly subjective task that (indirectly) incorporate several other tasks, as subjectivity classifi-

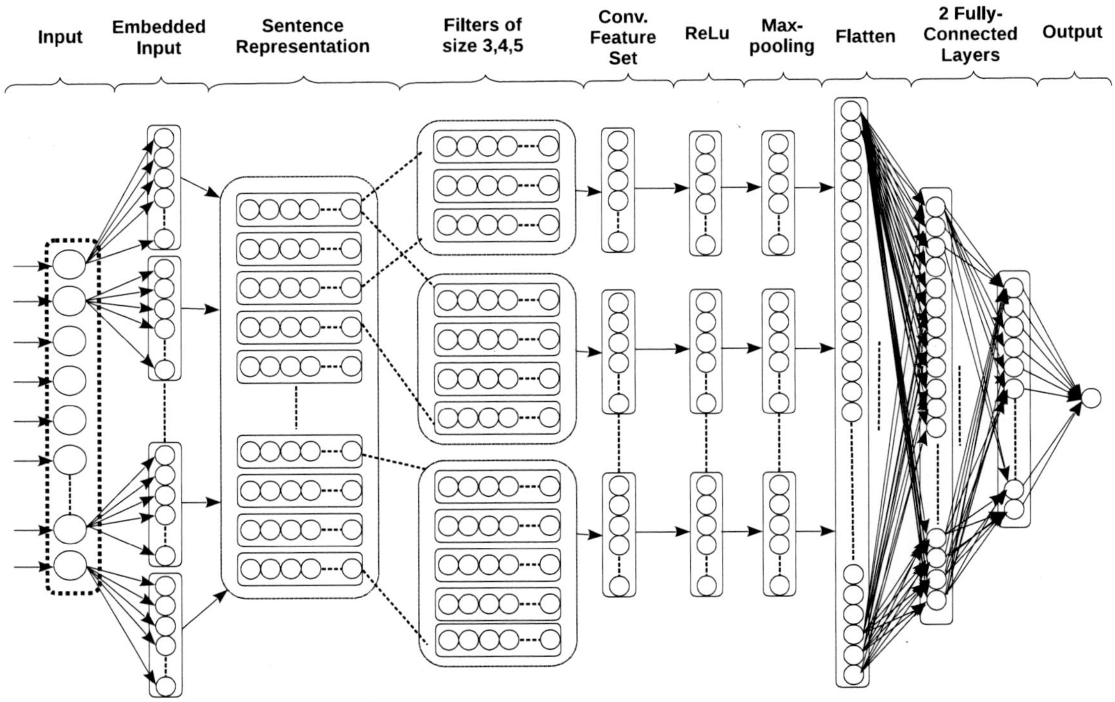

Figure 4: CNN's Architecture. We use 300-dimensional GloVe embeddings as input features. As we can see, we employ three paralels convlayers and set to 100 the size of the output channel for each convlayer. Also, the other parameters are: *epochs = 5*, *optimizer = Adam*, *batch size = 32*. Fully connected layers: input 1 = 300, output 1 = 32 and Dropout = 0.7

cation (more "personal" reviews look to be more interesting), polarity classification (more "radical" opinions call more attention), aspect identification (as reviews that directly cite some aspects look to be more useful), and detection of user information need (ultimately, a review is helpful only if it attends the information need of the user). Future efforts might explore such supporting tasks for helpfulness prediction.

The complete code for our features and models are available online at `https://github.com/RogerFig/deep-helpfulness`. The interested reader may also find more information at the POeTiSA project web portal (`https://sites.google.com/icmc.usp.br/poetisa`).

Acknowledgments

The authors are grateful to the Center for Artificial Intelligence (C4AI) of the University of São Paulo, sponsored by IBM and FAPESP (grant #2019/07665-4), and to *Instituto Federal do Piauí* (IFPI).

References

Yasamyian Almutairi, Manal Abdullah, and Dimah Alahmadi. 2019. Review helpfulness prediction: Survey. *Periodicals of Engineering and Natural Sciences*, 7(1):420–432.

Hélder Antunes and Carla Teixeira Lopes. 2019. Analyzing the adequacy of readability indicators to a non-english language. In *Proceedings of the International Conference of the Cross-Language Evaluation Forum for European Languages*, pages 149–155. Springer.

Madeha Arif, Usman Qamar, Farhan Hassan Khan, and Saba Bashir. 2018. A survey of customer review helpfulness prediction techniques. In *Proceedings of SAI Intelligent Systems Conference*, pages 215–226. Springer.

Pedro Balage Filho, Thiago Alexandre Salgueiro Pardo, and Sandra Aluísio. 2013. An evaluation of the brazilian portuguese liwc dictionary for sentiment analysis. In *Proceedings of the 9th Brazilian Symposium in Information and Human Language Technology*, pages 215–219.

Leo Breiman. 2001. Random forests. *Machine learning*, 45(1):5–32.

Jacob Devlin, Ming-Wei Chang, Kenton Lee, and Kristina Toutanova. 2019. BERT: Pre-training of deep bidirectional transformers for language understanding. In *Proceedings of the 2019 Conference of the North American Chapter of the Association for Computational Linguistics: Human Language Technologies, Volume 1 (Long and Short Papers)*, pages 4171–4186, Minneapolis, Minnesota. Association for Computational Linguistics.

William Dubay. 2004. The principles of readability. *CA*, 92627949:631–3309.

Erick Rocha Fonseca and João Luís G Rosa. 2013. Macmorpho revisited: Towards robust part-of-speech tagging. In *Proceedings of the 9th Brazilian symposium in information and human language technology*, pages 98–107.

Anindya Ghose and Panagiotis G Ipeirotis. 2011. Estimating the helpfulness and economic impact of product reviews: Mining text and reviewer characteristics. *IEEE Transactions on Knowledge and Data Engineering*, 23(10):1498–1512.

Nathan Hartmann, Erick Fonseca, Christopher Shulby, Marcos Treviso, Jéssica Silva, and Sandra Aluísio. 2017. Portuguese word embeddings: Evaluating on word analogies and natural language tasks. In *Proceedings of the 11th Brazilian Symposium in Information and Human Language Technology*, pages 122–131, Uberlândia, Brazil. Sociedade Brasileira de Computação.

Yu Hong, Jun Lu, Jianmin Yao, Qiaoming Zhu, and Guodong Zhou. 2012. What reviews are satisfactory: Novel features for automatic helpfulness voting. In *Proceedings of the 35th International ACM SIGIR Conference on Research and Development in Information Retrieval*, pages 495–504, New York, NY, USA. ACM.

Albert H Huang, Kuanchin Chen, David C Yen, and Trang P Tran. 2015. A study of factors that contribute to online review helpfulness. *Computers in Human Behavior*, 48:17–27.

Soo-Min Kim, Patrick Pantel, Tim Chklovski, and Marco Pennacchiotti. 2006. Automatically assessing review helpfulness. In *Proceedings of the 2006 Conference on Empirical Methods in Natural Language Processing*, pages 423–430, Sydney, Australia. Association for Computational Linguistics.

LF Kozachenko and Nikolai N Leonenko. 1987. Sample estimate of the entropy of a random vector. *Problemy Peredachi Informatsii*, 23(2):9–16.

Jingjing Liu, Yunbo Cao, Chin-Yew Lin, Yalou Huang, and Ming Zhou. 2007. Low-quality product review detection in opinion summarization. In *Proceedings of the 2007 Joint Conference on Empirical Methods in Natural Language Processing and Computational Natural Language Learning (EMNLP-CoNLL)*, pages 334–342, Prague, Czech Republic. Association for Computational Linguistics.

Yue Lu, Panayiotis Tsaparas, Alexandros Ntoulas, and Livia Polanyi. 2010. Exploiting social context for review quality prediction. In *Proceedings of the 19th international conference on World wide web*, pages 691–700.

Susan M Mudambi and David Schuff. 2010. Research note: What makes a helpful online review? a study of customer reviews on amazon. com. *MIS quarterly*, pages 185–200.

Marcelo Caetano Martins Muniz. 2004. *A construção de recursos lingüístico-computacionais para o português do Brasil: o projeto Unitex-PB*. Ph.D. thesis, Universidade de São Paulo.

Maria das Graças Volpe Nunes, Fabiano M Costa Vieira, Cláudia Zavaglia, Cássia RC Sossolote, and Josélia Hernandez. 1996. A construção de um léxico para o português do brasil: lições aprendidas e perspectivas. In *Anais do II Encontro para o Processamento de Português Escrito e Falado*, pages 61–70.

Gerardo Ocampo Diaz and Vincent Ng. 2018. Modeling and prediction of online product review helpfulness: A survey. In *Proceedings of the 56th Annual Meeting of the Association for Computational Linguistics (Volume 1: Long Papers)*, pages 698–708, Melbourne, Australia. Association for Computational Linguistics.

James W Pennebaker, Martha E Francis, and Roger J Booth. 2001. Linguistic inquiry and word count: Liwc 2001. *Mahway: Lawrence Erlbaum Associates*, 71.

Jeffrey Pennington, Richard Socher, and Christopher Manning. 2014. GloVe: Global vectors for word representation. In *Proceedings of the 2014 Conference on Empirical Methods in Natural Language Processing (EMNLP)*, pages 1532–1543, Doha, Qatar. Association for Computational Linguistics.

Mário J Silva, Paula Carvalho, and Luís Sarmento. 2012. Building a sentiment lexicon for social judgement mining. In *Proceedings of the International Conference on Computational Processing of the Portuguese Language*, pages 218–228. Springer.

Rogério Figueredo Sousa, Henrico Bertini Brum, and Maria das Graças Volpe Nunes. 2019. A bunch of helpfulness and sentiment corpora in brazilian portuguese. In *Proceedings of the 12th Brazilian Symposium in Information and Human Language Technology*, pages 209–218. Sociedade Brasileira de Computação.

Rogério Figueredo Sousa and Thiago Alexandre Salgueiro Pardo. 2021. The challenges of modeling and predicting online review helpfulness. In *Anais do XVIII Encontro Nacional de Inteligência Artificial e Computacional*, pages 727–738. Sociedade Brasileira de Computação.

Fábio Souza, Rodrigo Nogueira, and Roberto Lotufo. 2020. BERTimbau: pretrained BERT models for Brazilian Portuguese. In *Proceedings of the 9th*

Brazilian Conference on Intelligent Systems, pages 403–417.

Oren Tsur and Ari Rappoport. 2009. Revrank: A fully unsupervised algorithm for selecting the most helpful book reviews. In *Proceedings of the International AAAI Conference on Web and Social Media*, volume 3, pages 154–161.

Xi Wang, Iadh Ounis, and Craig Macdonald. 2020. Negative confidence-aware weakly supervised binary classification for effective review helpfulness classification. In *Proceedings of the 29th ACM International Conference on Information & Knowledge Management*, pages 1565–1574.

Shih-Hung Wu and Jun-Wei Wang. 2019. Integrating neural and syntactic features on the helpfulness analysis of the online customer reviews. In *IEEE/ACM International Conference on Advances in Social Networks Analysis and Mining*, pages 1013–1017. IEEE.

Shuzhe Xu, Salvador E Barbosa, and Don Hong. 2020. Bert feature based model for predicting the helpfulness scores of online customers reviews. In *Future of Information and Communication Conference*, pages 270–281. Springer.

Yi-Ching Zeng, Tsun Ku, Shih-Hung Wu, Liang-Pu Chen, and Gwo-Dong Chen. 2014. Modeling the helpful opinion mining of online consumer reviews as a classification problem. *International Journal of Computational Linguistics & Chinese Language Processing*, 19(2):17–32.

Zhu Zhang and Balaji Varadarajan. 2006. Utility scoring of product reviews. In *Proceedings of the 15th ACM International Conference on Information and Knowledge Management*, pages 51–57, New York, NY, USA. ACM.

WASSA 2022 Shared Task: Predicting Empathy, Emotion and Personality in Reaction to News Stories

Valentin Barriere
European Commission Joint Research Centre
Valentin.BARRIERE@ec.europa.eu

Shabnam Tafreshi
University of Maryland:ARLIS
stafresh@umd.edu

João Sedoc
New York University
jsedoc@stern.nyu.edu

Sawsan Alqahtani
Princess Nourah bint Abdulrahman University
saalqhtani@pnu.edu.sa

Abstract

This paper presents the results that were obtained from WASSA 2022 shared task on predicting empathy, emotion, and personality in reaction to news stories. Participants were given access to a dataset comprising empathic reactions to news stories where harm is done to a person, group, or other. These reactions consist of essays and Batson's empathic concern and personal distress scores. The dataset was further extended in WASSA 2021 shared task to include news articles, person-level demographic information (e.g. age, gender), personality information, and Ekman's six basic emotions at essay level Participation was encouraged in four tracks: predicting empathy and distress scores, predicting emotion categories, predicting personality and predicting interpersonal reactivity. In total, 14 teams participated in the shared task. We summarize the methods and resources used by the participating teams.

1 Introduction

Emotion and empathy prediction and analysis, in its broader perspective, has been an active research area in the last two decades, with growing volume of studies that provide insightful findings and resources. Emotion classification in natural languages has been studied over two decades and many applications successfully used emotion as their major components. Empathy utterances can be emotional, therefore, examining emotion in text-based empathy possibly has a major impact on predicting empathy. Analyzing text-based empathy and emotion have different applications; empathy is a crucial component in applications such as empathic AI agents, effective gesturing of robots, and mental health, emotion has natural language applications such as commerce, public health, and disaster management.

Despite the progress, improvements can be made to develop or further enhance the prediction and detection of emotions and psychological constructs in natural texts including empathy, distress, and personality. In this paper, we present the WASSA 2022 Shared Task: Predicting Empathy and Emotion in Reaction to News Stories. We used the same dataset provided by (Tafreshi et al., 2021) which is an extension of (Buechel et al., 2018)'s dataset that includes news articles that express harm to an entity (e.g. individual, group of people, nature). Each of these news articles is associated with essays in which authors expressed their empathy and distress in reactions to these news articles. Each assay is annotated for empathy and distress, and supplemented with personality traits and demographic information of the authors (age, gender, ethnicity, income, and education level) (Refer to Section 3 for more details).

Given this dataset as input, the shared task consists of four tracks:

1. Predicting Empathy (EMP): Participants develop models to predict, for each essay, em-

Proceedings of the 12th Workshop on Computational Approaches to Subjectivity, Sentiment & Social Media Analysis, pages 214 - 227

pathy and distress scores quantified with the Batson's empathic concern ("feeling for someone") and personal distress ("suffering with someone") (Batson et al., 1987).[1]

2. Emotion Label Prediction (EMO): Participants develop models to predict, for each essay, a categorical emotion tag from the following Ekman's six basic emotions (sadness, joy, disgust, surprise, anger, or fear) (Ekman, 1971), as well as *no-emotion* tag.

3. Personality Prediction (PER): Participants develop models to predict, for each essay, Big Five (OCEAN) personality traits (conscientiousness, openness, extraversion, agreeableness, emotional stability)(John et al., 1999)

4. Interpersonal Reactivity Index (IRI; Davis, 1980): Participants develop models to predict, for each essay, interpersonal reactivity (perspective taking, personal distress (pd), fantasy, empathic concern).

14 teams participated in this shared task: 10 teams submitted results to EMP, 14 teams to EMO, *2 teams to IRI, and 2 teams to PER* tracks. All task descriptions, datasets, and results were designed in CodaLab[2] and the teams were allowed to submit one official result during evaluation phase and several ones during the training phase. The best result for the *empathy* prediction was an average Pearson correlation of 0.541 and for distress was 0.547 and the best macro F1-score for the emotion track amounted to 69.8%. The best result for *personality* was an average Pearson correlation of 0.230 and for *IRI* was 0.255.WASSA 2022 shared task provide the second generated results for emotion and empathy (EMP and EMO tracks) and contribute with additional two new tracks (IRI and PER).

In the remainder of this paper, we first review related work (Section 2), after which we introduce the dataset used for both tracks (Section 3). The shared task is presented in Section 4 and the official results in Section 5. A discussion of the different systems participating in both tracks is presented in Section 6 and we conclude our work in Section 7.

[1]*Distress* is a self-focused and negative affective state (*suffering with someone*) while *empathy* is a warm, tender, and compassionate state (*feeling for someone*).

[2]`https://competitions.codalab.org/competitions/28713`

2 Related Work

We provide related work for each track: emotion predictions (Section 2.1), empathy and distress (Section 2.2), personality prediction, and interpersonal reactivity prediction (Section 2.3).

2.1 Emotion Prediction

Emotion classification has been studied thoroughly in terms of modeling, resources, and features as part of SemEval shared tasks for Affect computing and emotion classification (Strapparava and Mihalcea, 2007; Mohammad and Bravo-Marquez, 2017; Mohammad et al., 2018; Chatterjee et al., 2019; Sharma et al., 2020b). Emotion detection models can predict, per input, one emotion class or multi-label emotion classes for naturally co-occurring emotion classes in the same essay (Alhuzali and Ananiadou, 2021; Rajabi et al., 2020). Most emotion prediction models are learned in a supervised manner with feature engineering or continuous representation learned through pretrained language models (Peters et al., 2018; Devlin et al., 2018). Acheampong et al. (2020); Murthy and Kumar (2021); Nandwani and Verma (2021); Acheampong et al. (2021) survey state-of-the-art emotion detection techniques and resources and discuss open issues in this area.

2.2 Empathy and Distress

Prior work on modeling text-based empathy focused on the empathic concern which is to share others' emotions in the conversations (Litvak et al., 2016; Fung et al., 2016). For instance, Xiao et al. (2015, 2016); Gibson et al. (2016) modeled empathy based on the ability of a therapist to adapt to the emotions of their clients; Zhou and Jurgens (2020) quantified empathy in condolences in social media using appraisal theory; Sharma et al. (2020a) developed a model based on fine-tuning contextualized language models to predict empathy specific to mental health in text-based platforms. Guda et al. (2021) additionally utilized demographic information (e.g. education, income, age) when fine-tuning contextualized language modeling for empathy and distress prediction.

2.3 Personality and Interpersonal Reactivity Prediction

Vora et al. (2020); Beck and Jackson (2022) survey and analyze personality prediction models, theories, and techniques. Ji et al. (2020) review such models specifically to detect suicidal behavior. Developing personality detection models range from feature engineering methods (Bharadwaj et al., 2018; Tadesse et al., 2018) to deep learning techniques (Yang et al., 2021; Ren et al., 2021). Yang et al. (2021) developed a transformer based model to predict users' personality based on Myers-Briggs Type Indicator (Myers et al., 1985, MBTI;) personality trait theory given multiple posts of the user instead of predicting personality for a single post. Ren et al. (2021) utilized deep learning techniques to develop a multi-label personality prediction and sentiment analysis model based on MBTI and Big 5 datasets.

3 Data Collection and Annotation

We used the same dataset provided in WASSA 2021 shared task (Tafreshi et al., 2021). Table 1 represents the train, development, and test splits. We first briefly present how the initial/original dataset were collected and annotated in Section 3.1. We discuss the additional emotion annotation and make the dataset suitable for this shared task in Section 3.2. In Section 3.3, we discuss the annotation process and data statistics of PER and IRI tasks.

Dataset Split			
Train	Dev	Test	Total
1860	270	525	2655

Table 1: Train, dev and test set splits.

3.1 Overview of Initial Dataset

The starting point was the dataset provided by (Buechel et al., 2018) which comprises of news articles, each is associated with essays produced by several participants in reaction to reading disturbing news about a person, group of people, or situations. We used this dataset as a training dataset in this shared task.[3]

News article collection: We used the same news articles (418 total) provided by Buechel et al. (2018) in which there is major or minor harm inflicted to an individual, group of people, or other by either a person, group of people, political organization, or nature. The stories were specifically selected to evoke varying degrees of empathy among readers.

Essay collection: The corpus acquisition was set up as a crowdsourcing task on `MTurk.com` pointing to a `Qualtrics.com` questionnaire. The participants completed background measures on demographics and personality and then proceeded to the main part of the survey where they read a random selection of five of the news articles. After reading each of the articles, participants were asked to rate their level of empathy and distress before describing their thoughts and feelings about it in writing.

3.2 Data Augmentation and Enrichment

As part of the efforts made by WASSA 2021 shared task (Tafreshi et al., 2021), the dataset described in Section 3.1 was further augmented with development and testing datasets and enriched with emotion labels.

These datasets were created following the same approach described in (Buechel et al., 2018): 805 essays were written in response to the same news articles as (Buechel et al., 2018) by 161 participants and same Amazon Mechanical Turk qualifications as well as survey interface including Qualtrics.

Emotion Annotation: To extract emotion tags, WASSA 2021 shared task (Tafreshi et al., 2021) further enriched each essay with the 6 basic Ekman emotion labels in order to find out whether certain basic emotions are more correlated with empathy and distress. Emotion labels were first predicted automatically and then manually verified. For the automatic prediction, two different neural network models were applied to generate predictions at the essay level: 1) a Gated RNN with attention mechanism which is trained with multigenre corpus, i.e., news, tweets, blog posts, (Tafreshi, 2021, Thesis Chapter 5), 2) *fine-tuned* RoBERTa model (Liu et al., 2019) on the GoEmotions dataset (Demszky et al., 2020). For the manual verification another Amazon Mechanical Turk task was set up for which annotators with the Masters qualification (highest AMT quality rating) were recruited.[4]

The distribution of the emotion tags per data split split is illustrated in Table 2. As can be observed, the distribution of emotion tags is imbalanced. The majority of the essays have the emotion tag *sadness*, followed by *anger*, and subsequently an even distribution of the emotion tags *disgust, fear* and

[3]We refer the readers to the original paper (Buechel et al., 2018) for more details about the collection of news articles and essays.

[4]We refer the readers to Tafreshi et al. (2021) for more details about emotion annotation process.

surprise and lastly *joy*.[5]

3.3 PER and IRI Annotation Process

As part of the original data collection of Buechel et al. (2018) the Big 5 personality traits[6] (PER) and Interpersonal Reactivity Index (IRI) were collected at the beginning of the Qualtrics questionnaire. The train, dev, and test splits are the same as the other tasks.

4 Shared Task

We setup all four tracks in CodaLab (`https://competitions.codalab.org/competitions/28713`). We describe each task separately (objectives and metadata) in Section 4.1 and then describe dataset, resources, and evaluation metrics in Section 4.2. Note that the first two tracks are the same as offered by WASSA 2022 shared task while the last two tracks (PER and IRI) are new contributions of this shared task.

4.1 Tracks

Track 1 - Empathy Prediction (EMP): The formulation of this task is to predict, for each essay, Batson's empathic concern ("feeling for someone") and personal distress ("suffering with someone") scores (Batson et al., 1987). Participants are expected to develop models that predict the empathy score for each essay. Both empathy and distress scores are real-values between 0 and 7. Empathy score is an average of 7-point scale ratings, representing each of the following states (warm, tender, sympathetic, softhearted, moved, compassionate); distress score is an average of 7-point scale ratings, representing each of the the following states (worried, upset, troubled, perturbed, grieved, disturbed, alarmed, distressed). We made personality, demographic information, and emotion labels available for each essay and optional for use.

Track 2 - Emotion Label Prediction (EMO): The formulation of this task is to predict, for each essay, an emotion label from the following Ekman's six basic emotions (sadness, joy, disgust, surprise, anger, or fear) (Ekman, 1971), as well as *no-emotion* tag.[7] The same set of metadata that we described above were also provided for each essay in this task. Participants optionally could use this information as features to predict emotion labels.

Track 3 - Personality Prediction (PER): To code personality information, the Big 5 personality traits were provided, also known as the OCEAN model (Gosling et al., 2003b). In the OCEAN model, the theory identifies five factors (openness to experience, conscientiousness, extraversion, agreeableness and neuroticism[8]).

Track 4 - Interpersonal Reactivity Index Prediction (IRI): We use the Interpersonal Reactivity Index (Davis, 1980, IRI;). IRI is a measurement tool for the multi-dimensional assessment of empathy. The four subscales are: Perspective Taking, Fantasy, Empathic Concern and Personal Distress.

4.2 Setup

Dataset: Participants were provided the dataset described in 3. Participants were allowed to add the development set to the training set and submit systems trained on both. The test set was made available to the participants at the beginning of the evaluation period.

Resources and Systems Restrictions Participants were allowed to use any lexical resources (e.g., emotion or empathy dictionaries) of their choice, any additional training data, or any off-the-shelf emotion or empathy models. We did not put any restriction in this shared task nor did we suggest any baseline model.

Systems Evaluation: The organizers published an evaluation script that calculates Pearson correlation for the predictions of the empathy, personality and IRI prediction tasks and precision, recall, and F1 measure for each emotion class as well as the micro and macro average for the emotion label prediction task. Pearson coefficient is the linear correlations between two variables, and it produces scores from -1 (perfectly inversely correlated) to 1 (perfectly correlated). A score of 0 indicates no

[5]At first, *joy* emotion tag seems somewhat counter-intuitive given the nature of the essays. However, Tafreshi et al. (2021) explains that the position emotion that was assigned by the crowd workers could be attributed to the observation that authors of the essays were suggesting actions to *hope* to improve the situation and possibly contained political views.

[6]Buechel et al. (2018) used the Ten Item Personality Inventory (TIPI; Gosling et al., 2003a).

[7]Psychological emotion modeling suggested different categorical labeling schemes including the Ekman 6 basic emotions (Ekman, 1971), the Plutchik 8 basic emotions (Plutchik, 1984), and 4 basic emotions (Frijda, 1988). We opted for the Ekman emotions since it is well adopted in different emotion-based downstream NLP tasks and mostly suited to the dataset we aim to study in this shared task.

[8]Here the neuroticism has been reverse coded as emotional stability

	joy	sadness	disgust	fear	anger	surprise	no-emo
Train	82	647	149	194	349	164	275
Dev	14	98	12	31	76	14	25
Test	33	177	28	70	122	40	55
Total	129	922	189	295	547	218	355

Table 2: Distribution of emotion labels in the datasets.

correlation. The official competition metric for the empathy prediction task (EMP) is the average of the two Pearson correlations. The official competition metric for the emotion evaluation is the macro F1-score, which is the harmonic mean between precision and recall. The official competition metric for the personality (resp. IRI prediction) task PER (resp. IRI) is the average of the Pearson correlations of the 5 (resp. 4) variables.

5 Results and Discussion

5.1 Empathy Prediction (EMP)

Table 3 shows the main results of the track on empathy (Emp) and distress (Dis) prediction. 10 teams submitted results and the best scoring system is *bunny_gg* team (averaged r = .540). If we examine the results for the empathy and distress prediction separately, we observe that for empathy, team SINAI scored best (r = .541), whereas for distress *chenyueg* obtained the best result (r = .547).

Team	Emp	Dis	Avg
bunny_gg	0.537	0.543	**0.540**
SINAI	**0.541**	0.519	0.530
chenyueg	0.512	**0.547**	0.529
CAISA	0.524	0.521	0.523
SURREY-CTS-NLP	0.504	0.530	0.517
LingJing	0.508	0.489	0.499
PHG	0.470	0.506	0.488
IITP-AINLPML	0.479	0.488	0.483
mantis	0.484	0.453	0.468
phuonglh	0.196	0.183	0.190

Table 3: Results of the teams participating in the EMP track (Pearson correlations).

Comparison with previous results: In (Buechel et al., 2018), the best-performing system obtained r=.404 for empathy and r=.444 for distress. These results were achieved only on the training set using ten-fold cross validation experiments which is not comparable to the results in this shared task. In WASSA 2021 (Tafreshi et al., 2021), the best scoring system was *PVG* team (averaged r = .545). If we examine the results for the empathy and distress prediction separately, we observe that for empathy, team WASSA@IITK scored best (r = .558), whereas for distress *PVG* obtained the best result (r = .574).

Absolute difference between gold and predicted labels: Table 4 presents the absolute difference between the predicted and gold empathy and distress scores by the best-performing systems (*SINAI* for empathy and *chenyueg* for distress). It can be observed that the majority of predicted Batson emphatic concern and distress instances only differ in between zero or one point from the gold scores, i.e. 66% and 62%, respectively. For both labels the maximum difference amounts to 4-5 points and this in only a very few cases, no instances for empathy and 5 instance for distress.

Abs. diff	Empathy		Distress	
0-1	351	(66.85%)	329	(62.66%)
1-2	111	(21.14%)	58	(11.04%)
2-3	54	(10.28%)	70	(13.33%)
3-4	4	(1.71%)	23	(4.38%)
4-5	0	(0.00%)	5	(0.95%)

Table 4: Absolute difference in score between predicted and gold for both the empathy and distress scores of the best-performing system (expressed in number of instances and percentagewise).

5.2 Emotion Label Prediction (EMO)

Table 5 presents the results for 13 teams for emotion prediction models. The best performing system in terms of Macro F1 (69.8%) as well as accuracy (75.4%) is *LingJing* which is significantly higher than remaining emotion prediction models. To get more insight we also provide a breakdown of the macro-averaged results by emotion class in Table 6. Correlated with label frequency in the dataset, sadness and anger are predicted with the highest performance by most systems. Remaining emotion labels have reasonable performance score given its limited number of training instances. In the breakdown for all emotion labels, the emotion model submitted by team *LingJing* outperforms remaining submitted models.

Team	P	R	F1	Acc
LingJing	**0.740**	**0.679**	**0.698**	**0.754**
CAISA	0.625	0.592	0.604	0.669
himanshu.1007	0.594	0.584	0.585	0.661
chenyueg	0.599	0.555	0.572	0.646
SURREY-CTS-NLP	0.595	0.559	0.571	0.646
SINAI	0.589	0.535	0.553	0.636
mantis	0.594	0.528	0.548	0.632
blueyellow	0.571	0.531	0.544	0.623
bunny$_{gg}$	0.564	0.539	0.544	0.611
shantpat	0.552	0.532	0.534	0.623
PHG	0.557	0.529	0.531	0.611
IITP-AINLPML	0.527	0.585	0.524	0.585
PVG AI Club	0.473	0.467	0.464	0.560

Table 5: Results of the teams participating in the EMO track (macro-averaged precision (P), recall (R), F1-score (F1) and accuracy (Acc)).

5.3 Personality and Interpersonal Reactivity Prediction (PER/IRI)

The results of the tracks on personality and IRI predictions are presented in Table 7. Two teams submitted results and the best scoring system is the one of *LingJing*. For the PER task, it is interesting to note that the score of the second participant (*IITP*) is in general lower due to a negative correlation on the *agreeableness*, while the first team succeeded into performing well on this trait. They both performed similarly on *consciousness* and *extroversion*. For the IRI task, both the participants obtained good results for the *empathic concern*, nevertheless only the best performing team succeeded into performing well on *perspective taking*, *personal distress* and *fantasy*.

5.4 Error Analysis

5.4.1 Empathy prediction

We had a closer look at those instances that were predicted with a difference in score of between 4 and 5 by the best-performing system, you can find the actual essays in Appendix A.

We discuss about 3 instances: in the first one (essay 1) the gold score was 7 and the predicted one 3.65, which is actually a pretty strange error as this describes a really typical high empathy - high distress essay. This essay has mild level distress which the model has predicted very well.

For empathy there was one instance with a high discrepancy between the predicted (2.47) and gold (6) score. If we consider essay 3 we observe that there is no self-focus language at all. So a low empathy score does make sense here. Nonetheless this is not a typical low empathy response since there is some distress expressed. Same for essay 2, the difference between empathy and distress in gold label is high.

Considering essays 2 and 3 we can state that these exhibit high distress/low empathy and vice versa low distress/ mild empathy. It is possible that models have difficulty in scenarios where there is empathy with a lack of distress and vice versa.

5.4.2 Emotion label prediction

Table 8 presents the confusion matrix of the top-performing team on the test data. It can be observed that the top three occurring labels in the training data, sadness (Sa) – anger (A) – no-emotion (No) – are accurately classified most frequently and that anger and fear are most often confused with sadness, whereas the same goes for sadness being classified as anger.

Assigning an emotion label at the document level is not a trivial task as certain sentences within an essay may exhibit different emotions or sentiment. In Appendix B we present for some labels one essay which was correctly/incorrectly classified by best performer system.

Looking at the correctly classified essays, we observe that in these essays many emotional words and phrases are being used and that there is not much discrepancy of emotions between the sentences. The same cannot be said for the erroneously classified essays, there we clearly observe that often many emotions are being presented within the same essay.

In the meantime all essays have also been labeled with emotions at the sentence level using the same annotation procedure as described in Section 3, this dataset will also be made available for research purposes.

5.4.3 Personality and IRI prediction

Surprisingly, we found out that the best scoring team system was predicting at the essay-level, and not using the fact that a writer wrote 5 different essays in order to aggregate at the writer-level. Taking the average mean of *LingJing* predictions on each user allow to increase the Pearson's correlations for PER and IRI from .230 and .255 to .306

Team	Joy			Sadness			Disgust			Fear			Anger			Surprise		
	P	R	F1	P	R	F1	P	R	F1	P	R	F1	P	R	F1	P	R	F1
LingJing	**82**	61	**71**	**90**	82	**86**	**82**	**50**	**62**	64	**77**	**70**	**72**	**88**	**79**	**62**	**62**	**62**
CAISA	72	55	62	78	79	79	57	43	49	66	59	62	66	74	70	46	55	50
himanshu.1007	62	**70**	66	76	84	80	43	36	39	63	53	57	69	67	68	45	57	51
chenyueg	58	45	51	78	77	78	31	46	37	65	56	60	63	73	68	55	45	49
SURREY-CTS-NLP	73	58	64	70	**86**	77	38	36	37	62	54	58	69	62	66	48	57	52
SINAI	65	45	54	74	82	78	53	36	43	**69**	47	56	64	71	67	47	47	48
mantis	70	48	57	71	79	75	50	21	30	62	57	59	60	72	65	49	50	49
blueyellow	74	52	61	68	80	74	36	32	34	56	50	53	69	67	68	42	53	47
bunny_gg	66	58	61	69	79	74	20	36	25	65	47	55	69	61	64	55	55	55
shantpat	61	42	50	75	81	78	31	39	35	65	43	52	69	65	67	41	45	43
PHG	71	45	56	71	84	77	31	39	34	62	43	51	70	57	62	41	60	49
IITP-AINLPML	60	64	62	66	75	70	35	46	40	53	46	49	67	57	62	41	45	43
PVG AI Club	44	33	38	72	79	75	24	32	27	55	40	46	61	53	57	37	47	41

Table 6: Breakdown EMO labels (MACRO)

Team	Consc.	Open.	Extr.	Agree.	Stab.	**PER**	Persp.	Distr.	Fant.	Emp.	**IRI**
LingJing	.165	.337	.098	.246	.305	**.230**	.139	.245	.377	.257	**.255**
IITP	.134	.092	.102	-.176	.086	.047	.039	.004	.011	.252	.076
Aggreg (Org.)	.207	.506	.123	.310	.383	**.306**	.166	.29	.495	.374	**.331**

Table 7: Results of the teams participating in the PER/IRI tracks (Pearson correlations).

Gold EMO labels	Predicted EMO labels						
	A	D	F	J	No	Sa	Su
A	107	3	1	0	2	4	5
D	11	14	1	0	1	1	0
F	6	0	54	2	2	2	4
J	1	0	1	20	8	3	0
No	7	0	7	1	30	4	6
Sa	8	0	18	0	5	146	0
Su	8	0	2	0	2	3	25

Table 8: Confusion matrix best performing team on EMO for the following labels: Anger (A), Disgust (D), Fear (F), Joy (J), Sadness (Sa), Surprise (Su), no emotion (No).

and .331 (see last line Table 7).

We looked over the writers that were the most difficult to tag for the winning team system, and they were outliers for both the tasks. For the PER task, this user has a very low values on conscientiousness and openness: 1.5 and 1.5, compared to 5.6 and 5 in average. For the IRI task, it seems that there is an issue with the labels. The personal distress score of the user is 1, which is the lowest of the dataset, and does not necessarily represent how the user is reacting at every essay. We also noticed that the winning system has low standard deviation when compared to the ones from the gold standards, for this reason it struggles to predict outliers and move not far away from the mean.

6 Overview of Submitted Systems

A total of 14 teams participated in the shared tasks with 10 teams participating in both EMP and EMO and 2 participated in all tracks. In this section, we provide a summary of the machine learning models, features, resources, and lexicons that were used by the teams.

6.1 Machine Learning Architectures

All systems follow supervised machine learning models for empathy prediction and emotion classification (Table 9). Most teams built systems using pre-trained transformer language models, which were fine-tuned or from which features from different layers were extracted. CNN model were proposed by one team. Data augmentation methods and continuing to pre-training transformer model is proposed by one team. One team proposed a prompt-based architecture to integrate the metadata of the writer.

6.2 Features and Resources

Detection and classification of emotion in text is challenging because marking textual emotional cues is difficult. Emotion model performance has been always improved when lexical features (e.g., emotion, sentiment, subjectivity, etc.), emotion-specific embedding, or different emotional datasets were augmented and used (Mohammad et al., 2018) to represent an emotion. Similar to emotion, predicting text-based empathy is challenging as well, and using lexical features, and external resources have an impact on empathy model performance. As such, it is quite common to use different resources and design different features in emotion and empathy models. As part of the dataset we provided to teams, we include personality, demographic, and categorical emotions as additional features for both emotion and empathy tasks. Teams were allowed to use any external resources or design any features of their choice and use them in their models. Table 10 summarizes the features and extra resources that teams used to build their models.

6.3 Lexicons

The presence of emotion and empathic words are the first cues for a piece of text to be emotional or empathic, therefore, it is beneficial to use emotion/empathy lexicons to extract those words and create features. Table 11 summarizes the lexicons that were employed by the different teams.

6.4 Top three systems in EMP track

IUCL the team who ranked first in empathy track developed a transformer model using RoBERTa. They tuned RoBERTa model with the training set that is provided in this shared-task. They used demographic and personality features values and group them into different categories and add to each category a unique phrase. For example, the added sentence for "age of 25" is "Age is 25, young adult.", and the added sentence for "income of 150,000" is "Income is 150000, high income, rich". They represent each essay context with different input size and concatenated the context with the demographic and personality features.

SINAI The team developed Ensemble of Supervised and Zero-Shot Learning Models using Transformer Multi-output Regression and Emotion Analysis. For empathy and distress they built a Transformer multi-output regression model to predict empathy and distress and some transformer models for emotion which eventually using them both in an ensemble manner with a fine-tune RoBERTa model.

IUCL-2 the same team won the 3 place too. They used different hyperparameters while tuning RoBERTa model. They represent each sentence with higher input size and different learning rate and based on the empirical results it seems that increasing input size can impact the model performance in detecting empathy.

6.5 Team rank 1 and 3 systems in EMO track

WENGSYX the team who ranked first developed a model by continuing on fine-tuning the pre-trained DeBERTa (He et al., 2020) by an open-source dataset collected by (Öhman et al., 2020). Then they fine-tuned this model with the dataset that is provided in this study. Then they further used data augmentation methods (random and balanced) augmentation using GoEmotions: A Dataset of Fine-Grained Emotions (Demszky et al., 2020). Further they used Child-tuning Training (Xu et al., 2021) to continue fine-tuning DeBERTa. Finally, they used late fusion method (Colnerič and Demšar, 2018) with Bagging Prediction (Breiman, 1996) during prediction of emotion.

himanshu.1007 the team developed an ensemble approach. First model is fine-tuning RoBERTa on GoEmotions: A Dataset of Fine-Grained Emotions (Demszky et al., 2020), then fine-tuning BART model to get the best representation for essay-based text, then fine-tuning RoBERTa with the dataset that is provided for this shared-task. The authors empirical results suggests that all three steps in the training is necessary to reach the best performance, and how BART can capture the contextual features in multiple sentences.

6.6 PER and IRI Systems

The two approaches proposed by the participants were very different. The IITP team proposed a system that is not using at all neither the essay nor the news article texts. They employed demographic information such as gender, race, education, age, and income to train support vector machine systems. The features used as input were selected regarding the task and variable to predict. For example, only the age was used as input feature to predict *conscientiousness* and *agreeableness*.

Machine Learning Algorithms

ML Algorithm	# of team	Emp System	Emo System
RoBERTa-large	3	✓	
bert-base-go-emotion	1		✓
distil-BERT-uncased-emotion	1		✓
NLI	1	✓	✓
GPT-3	1	✓	✓
Vanilla RoBERTa	1		✓
RoBERTa	4	✓	✓
GlobalMaxPooling	1	✓	✓
BART-large	1	✓	✓
Bert-base-uncased	1	✓	✓
Longformer-base-4096	1	✓	✓
DeBERTA	1		✓

Table 9: Machine learning algorithms used by the different teams. We listed all the models that teams reported in their results.

Features and Resources

Features	# of team	Emp System	Emo System
Emotion-Enriched Word Embedding	1	✓	
Transformer embeddings	1		✓
[CLS] token from Transformer model	2	✓	✓
Affect/emotion/empathy lexicons	1		✓
Personality information	8	✓	✓
Demographic infromation	8	✓	✓
External dataset	8		✓

Table 10: Features and resources that are used by different teams. We listed all the features and resources that teams reported in their results.

The best performing system for both the tasks was the one proposed by LingJing team. They employed intensively all the meta-data available and integrated them inside a DeBERTa-v3-large model in a textual form: "A female, with fourth grade education, third race, 22 and income of 100000". They proceeded to a data augmentation technique using random punctuation, used an ensemble method using the bagging algorithm.

7 Conclusions

In this paper we presented the shared task on empathy and emotion prediction of essays that were written in response to news stories to which five teams participated. Based on the analysis of the systems we can conclude that fine-tuning a transformer language model or relying on features extracted from transformer models along with jointly learning related tasks can lead to a robust modeling of empathy, distress, and emotion. Despite the strength of these strong contextualized features, we also observed that task-specific lexical features extracted from emotion and sentiment lexicons can still create a significant impact on empathy, distress, and emotion models. Furthermore, the top-performing emotion models used external datasets to further fine-tune the language models, which indicates that data augmentation is important when modeling emotion, even if the text genre is different from the genre of the task at hand. Finally, using demographic and personality information as features revealed a significant impact on empathy, distress, and emotion models. Particularly, joint modeling of distress and empathy coupled with those features yielded the best results for most of the top-ranked systems that were developed as part of this shared task.

Empathic or Emotion Lexicons

Lexicons	# of team	Emp System	Emo System
NRC *EmoLex* (Mohammad and Turney, 2010)	1		✓

Table 11: Empathic or Emotion Lexicons that are used by different teams. We listed all the lexicons that teams reported in their results.

References

Francisca Adoma Acheampong, Henry Nunoo-Mensah, and Wenyu Chen. 2021. Transformer models for text-based emotion detection: a review of bert-based approaches. *Artificial Intelligence Review*, 54(8):5789–5829.

Francisca Adoma Acheampong, Chen Wenyu, and Henry Nunoo-Mensah. 2020. Text-based emotion detection: Advances, challenges, and opportunities. *Engineering Reports*, 2(7):e12189.

Hassan Alhuzali and Sophia Ananiadou. 2021. Spanemo: Casting multi-label emotion classification as span-prediction. *arXiv preprint arXiv:2101.10038*.

C Daniel Batson, Jim Fultz, and Patricia A Schoenrade. 1987. Distress and empathy: Two qualitatively distinct vicarious emotions with different motivational consequences. *Journal of personality*, 55(1):19–39.

Emorie D Beck and Joshua J Jackson. 2022. A mega-analysis of personality prediction: Robustness and boundary conditions. *Journal of Personality and Social Psychology*, 122(3):523.

Srilakshmi Bharadwaj, Srinidhi Sridhar, Rahul Choudhary, and Ramamoorthy Srinath. 2018. Persona traits identification based on myers-briggs type indicator (mbti)-a text classification approach. In *2018 international conference on advances in computing, communications and informatics (ICACCI)*, pages 1076–1082. IEEE.

Leo Breiman. 1996. Bagging predictors. *Machine learning*, 24(2):123–140.

Sven Buechel, Anneke Buffone, Barry Slaff, Lyle Ungar, and João Sedoc. 2018. Modeling empathy and distress in reaction to news stories. In *Proceedings of the 2018 Conference on Empirical Methods in Natural Language Processing*, pages 4758–4765.

Ankush Chatterjee, Kedhar Nath Narahari, Meghana Joshi, and Puneet Agrawal. 2019. SemEval-2019 task 3: EmoContext contextual emotion detection in text. In *Proceedings of the 13th International Workshop on Semantic Evaluation*, pages 39–48, Minneapolis, Minnesota, USA. Association for Computational Linguistics.

Niko Colnerič and Janez Demšar. 2018. Emotion recognition on twitter: Comparative study and training a unison model. *IEEE transactions on affective computing*, 11(3):433–446.

Mark H Davis. 1980. *Interpersonal Reactivity Index*. Edwin Mellen Press.

Dorottya Demszky, Dana Movshovitz-Attias, Jeongwoo Ko, Alan Cowen, Gaurav Nemade, and Sujith Ravi. 2020. Goemotions: A dataset of fine-grained emotions. *arXiv preprint arXiv:2005.00547*.

Jacob Devlin, Ming-Wei Chang, Kenton Lee, and Kristina Toutanova. 2018. Bert: Pre-training of deep bidirectional transformers for language understanding. *arXiv preprint arXiv:1810.04805*.

Paul Ekman. 1971. Universals and cultural differences in facial expressions of emotion. In *Nebraska symposium on motivation*. University of Nebraska Press.

Nico H Frijda. 1988. The laws of emotion. *American psychologist*, 43(5):349.

Pascale Fung, Dario Bertero, Yan Wan, Anik Dey, Ricky Ho Yin Chan, Farhad Bin Siddique, Yang Yang, Chien-Sheng Wu, and Ruixi Lin. 2016. Towards empathetic human-robot interactions. In *International Conference on Intelligent Text Processing and Computational Linguistics*, pages 173–193. Springer.

James Gibson, Dogan Can, Bo Xiao, Zac E Imel, David C Atkins, Panayiotis Georgiou, and Shrikanth Narayanan. 2016. A deep learning approach to modeling empathy in addiction counseling. *Commitment*, 111:21.

Samuel D Gosling, Peter J Rentfrow, and William B Swann Jr. 2003a. A very brief measure of the big-five personality domains. *Journal of Research in personality*, 37(6):504–528.

Samuel D Gosling, Peter J Rentfrow, and Williams B Swann Jr. 2003b. A very brief measure of the big-five personality domains. *Journal of Research in Personality*, 37:504–528.

Bhanu Prakash Reddy Guda, Aparna Garimella, and Niyati Chhaya. 2021. Empathbert: A bert-based framework for demographic-aware empathy prediction. *arXiv preprint arXiv:2102.00272*.

Pengcheng He, Xiaodong Liu, Jianfeng Gao, and Weizhu Chen. 2020. Deberta: Decoding-enhanced bert with disentangled attention. *arXiv preprint arXiv:2006.03654*.

Shaoxiong Ji, Shirui Pan, Xue Li, Erik Cambria, Guodong Long, and Zi Huang. 2020. Suicidal ideation detection: A review of machine learning methods and applications. *IEEE Transactions on Computational Social Systems*, 8(1):214–226.

Oliver P John, Sanjay Srivastava, et al. 1999. *The Big-Five trait taxonomy: History, measurement, and theoretical perspectives*, volume 2. University of California Berkeley.

Marina Litvak, Jahna Otterbacher, Chee Siang Ang, and David Atkins. 2016. Social and linguistic behavior and its correlation to trait empathy. In *Proceedings of the Workshop on Computational Modeling of People's Opinions, Personality, and Emotions in Social Media (PEOPLES)*, pages 128–137.

Yinhan Liu, Myle Ott, Naman Goyal, Jingfei Du, Mandar Joshi, Danqi Chen, Omer Levy, Mike Lewis, Luke Zettlemoyer, and Veselin Stoyanov. 2019. Roberta: A robustly optimized bert pretraining approach. *arXiv preprint arXiv:1907.11692*.

Saif Mohammad, Felipe Bravo-Marquez, Mohammad Salameh, and Svetlana Kiritchenko. 2018. Semeval-2018 task 1: Affect in tweets. In *Proceedings of the 12th international workshop on semantic evaluation*, pages 1–17.

Saif Mohammad and Peter Turney. 2010. Emotions evoked by common words and phrases: Using mechanical turk to create an emotion lexicon. In *Proceedings of the NAACL HLT 2010 workshop on computational approaches to analysis and generation of emotion in text*, pages 26–34.

Saif M Mohammad and Felipe Bravo-Marquez. 2017. Wassa-2017 shared task on emotion intensity. *arXiv preprint arXiv:1708.03700*.

Ashritha R Murthy and KM Anil Kumar. 2021. A review of different approaches for detecting emotion from text. In *IOP Conference Series: Materials Science and Engineering*, volume 1110, page 012009. IOP Publishing.

Isabel Briggs Myers, Mary H McCaulley, and Robert Most. 1985. *Manual, a guide to the development and use of the Myers-Briggs type indicator*. consulting psychologists press.

Pansy Nandwani and Rupali Verma. 2021. A review on sentiment analysis and emotion detection from text. *Social Network Analysis and Mining*, 11(1):1–19.

Emily Öhman, Marc Pàmies, Kaisla Kajava, and Jörg Tiedemann. 2020. Xed: A multilingual dataset for sentiment analysis and emotion detection. *arXiv preprint arXiv:2011.01612*.

Matthew E. Peters, Mark Neumann, Mohit Iyyer, Matt Gardner, Christopher Clark, Kenton Lee, and Luke Zettlemoyer. 2018. Deep contextualized word representations. In *Proc. of NAACL*.

Robert Plutchik. 1984. Emotions: A general psychoevolutionary theory. *Approaches to emotion*, 1984:197–219.

Zahra Rajabi, Amarda Shehu, and Ozlem Uzuner. 2020. A multi-channel bilstm-cnn model for multilabel emotion classification of informal text. In *2020 IEEE 14th International Conference on Semantic Computing (ICSC)*, pages 303–306. IEEE.

Zhancheng Ren, Qiang Shen, Xiaolei Diao, and Hao Xu. 2021. A sentiment-aware deep learning approach for personality detection from text. *Information Processing & Management*, 58(3):102532.

Ashish Sharma, Adam S Miner, David C Atkins, and Tim Althoff. 2020a. A computational approach to understanding empathy expressed in text-based mental health support. *arXiv preprint arXiv:2009.08441*.

Chhavi Sharma, Deepesh Bhageria, William Scott, Srinivas PYKL, Amitava Das, Tanmoy Chakraborty, Viswanath Pulabaigari, and Bjorn Gamback. 2020b. Semeval-2020 task 8: Memotion analysis–the visuo-lingual metaphor! *arXiv preprint arXiv:2008.03781*.

Carlo Strapparava and Rada Mihalcea. 2007. Semeval-2007 task 14: Affective text. In *Proceedings of the Fourth International Workshop on Semantic Evaluations (SemEval-2007)*, pages 70–74.

Michael M Tadesse, Hongfei Lin, Bo Xu, and Liang Yang. 2018. Personality predictions based on user behavior on the facebook social media platform. *IEEE Access*, 6:61959–61969.

Shabnam Tafreshi. 2021. *Cross-Genre, Cross-Lingual, and Low-Resource Emotion Classification*. Ph.D. thesis, The George Washington University.

Shabnam Tafreshi, Orphee De Clercq, Valentin Barriere, Sven Buechel, João Sedoc, and Alexandra Balahur. 2021. WASSA 2021 shared task: Predicting empathy and emotion in reaction to news stories. In *Proceedings of the Eleventh Workshop on Computational Approaches to Subjectivity, Sentiment and Social Media Analysis*, pages 92–104, Online. Association for Computational Linguistics.

Hetal Vora, Mamta Bhamare, and Dr K Ashok Kumar. 2020. Personality prediction from social media text: An overview. *Int. J. Eng. Res*, 9(05):352–357.

Bo Xiao, Chewei Huang, Zac E Imel, David C Atkins, Panayiotis Georgiou, and Shrikanth S Narayanan. 2016. A technology prototype system for rating therapist empathy from audio recordings in addiction counseling. *PeerJ Computer Science*, 2:e59.

Bo Xiao, Zac E Imel, Panayiotis G Georgiou, David C Atkins, and Shrikanth S Narayanan. 2015. " rate my therapist": automated detection of empathy in drug and alcohol counseling via speech and language processing. *PloS one*, 10(12):e0143055.

Runxin Xu, Fuli Luo, Zhiyuan Zhang, Chuanqi Tan, Baobao Chang, Songfang Huang, and Fei Huang. 2021. Raise a child in large language model: Towards effective and generalizable fine-tuning. *arXiv preprint arXiv:2109.05687*.

Feifan Yang, Xiaojun Quan, Yunyi Yang, and Jianxing Yu. 2021. Multi-document transformer for personality detection. In *Proceedings of the AAAI Conference on Artificial Intelligence*, volume 35, pages 14221–14229.

Naitian Zhou and David Jurgens. 2020. Condolence and empathy in online communities. In *Proceedings of the 2020 Conference on Empirical Methods in Natural Language Processing (EMNLP)*.

Appendices

A Examples Track I (EMP)

Below examples are shown of four essays that received an erroneous empathy or distress label by the best-performing system. This is discussed in Section 5.4.

Essay 1: even though it was a old article from the archives i still think it was horrible that those officers tortured that man like that. attacking his private parts with flashlights, arms, elbows and pretty everything else you can think of. thats horrible that we live in a world that would allow these type of actions to take place. (Gold Emp: 7, Predicted Emp: 3.65)

Essay 2: I understand that businesses need to worry about profits. But It really angers me when governments and companies throw away lives in order to protect their bottom line. When people riot and chaos breaks out, it is always for a reason. It is up to the government and our police forces to protect the everyday citizens, not take their lives to protect their own. It angers me so much, all the needless violence and lives lost for no good reason. (Gold Emp: 1, Predicted Emp: 3.67)

Essay 3: As a person who grew up around large birds and knows how temperamental they can be, I was really curious where the story was going to go. It made me laugh that the officers were able to catch the runaway so easily without any humans or birds getting hurt when I'm sure the thought of trying made them more than a little nervous. The world needs more nice stories like this and I hope the emu got a stern talking to when it got home. (Gold Emp: 6, Predicted Emp: 2.47)

B Examples Track II (EMO)

Below examples are shown of essays that received one of the seven labels and for each label we present one essay that was correctly classified by all teams (i) and one that was misclassified by most systems (ii). This is discussed in closer detail in Section 5.4.

Joy: (i) Hello friend i will like to tell you that India to ratify Paris climate deal in October — India, one of the world's largest greenhouse gas emitters, will ratify the Paris global climate agreement pact next month, Prime Minister Narendra Modi has said. CO2 emissions are believed to be the driving force behind climate change. The Paris deal is the world's first comprehensive climate agreement. It will only come into force legally after it is ratified by at least 55 countries, which between them produce 55% of global carbon emissions. (Predicted as: neutral, Gold: joy). (ii) "I like this article. It's about how the woman still gave birth to her child, even though it was a c-section. It seems as though some mothers look down upon those who have had to have c-sections because they didn't physically push the child out. Some consider it ""easier"" but the effects of a c-section and the scarring shows how difficult it is." (Predicted as: joy, Gold: joy)

Sadness: (i) I read an article about civilian causalities in Afghanistan. It is alleged that US forces struck a make shift doctors with out borders hospital. There was heavy fighting and confusion during the event. There were other civilian casualties. I feel it is unfortunate. I feel wars create much pain for non involved people. I wish people would get along and respect human life. (Predicted: sadness, Gold: Sadness). (ii) I don't get why people want to blow us up. Why people want to intentionally harm others. They don't know these people. It's hard to feel for the one blowing up people. People are just trying to live their lives and go about their business. Suddenly your whole world changes and any innocence you had left is gone. You are harmed in ways that can;t be imagined until they manifest later. I hate that people have to endure this. (Predicted: Anger, Gold: Sadness).

Disgust: (i) seems like paris is getting worse and worse every year. ever since they brought in all those refugees i believe the crime rates has risen and risen. things are getting out of control. where are the police? why is nothing being done to stop the rise in crime? even celebs are getting robbed or attacked in public. this is getting insane. it keeps getting worse also. (Predicted: anger, Gold: Disgust). (ii) Have you seen this? I am so tired of these stories! Something needs to be done about this already! How many more women will come forward with these stories before action is finally taken to get these monsters put away for good? Every single day I read about another story like this and I am sickened that this is continuing to happen. (Predicted: Disgust, Gold: Disgust).

Fear: (i) scientists have been studying the zika virus for some time now and still, don't know much about it. it is a big threat to humans everywhere though. zika is mainly carried by mosquitos and contact with an infected mosquito will give you the virus. however, you can get it from having sex with someone that has the virus even if they are not showing symptoms yet. that is horrible. (Predicted:fear, Gold: fear). (ii) April I just read a very interesting article concerning climate change. It is hard for me to believe that there are still deniers out there on climate change. Especially when 375 top scientists and 30 prize winners all state with certainty humans are the cause. If we do not take action now we are going to leave a Horrible planet for our kids, grand kids and their kids. This is something that we need to address on a daily basis. (Predicted: anger, Gold: fear).

Anger: (i) Keith is a person who is willing to save the Albatross from house mice. Those animals are getting killed because of those rodents and he is doing whatever he can in order to prolong their lives. He does not celebrate birthdays and chooses to place bait traps on the island in order to kill as many rodents that he can. (Predicted: no-emotion, Gold: anger). (ii) he horror of what we have done is beyond the comprehension of most Americans. People are being treated like animals by our own soldiers. If any one goes in innocent and good, they will come out damaged and insane or nearly so. It destroys good people with conscience (of which there are few) that work in these areas. This has been going on for decades, and the evil is off the charts. The only way that this gets fixed is if the people are identified as torturers, sought, hunted down, and burned at the stake. Psychopaths run the nation and are drawn to the military and police. As, horrible as it is, good people will have to remove these damaged individual or they WILL suffer under their boots. (Predicted: anger, Gold: anger).

Surprise: (i) I think it's silly that this is even a debate. This homeless dude hopped over a fence and attacked a security guard, the security guard defended himself despite getting stabbed. The fact that this guy hasn't already been charged with attempted murder is asinine, and I'm surprised this is even a chance he may get off. The security guard did what he should have done and defended himself and the property. (Predicted: anger, Gold: Surprise). (ii) The article is so shocking. I had heard a little about it before but I had no idea that it was so drastic. And now I am not surprised about how the weather has been so screwy for the past few years. It doesn't seem like there is anything that we can do about it though. So I feel kind of helpless about that. (Predicted: surprise, Gold: Surprise)

No-emo: (i) Hello friend I will like to let you know Leonard Cohen Died In His Sleep After A Fall, Manager Says — Songwriter and poet Leonard Cohen died in his sleep after a fall in his Los Angeles home in the middle of the night, his manager has said. "The death was sudden, unexpected, and peaceful," his manager Robert Kory said in a statement published on the Cohencentric website. Cohen, music's man of letters whose songs fused religious imagery with themes of redemption and sexual desire, died on Nov. 7, He was 82 when he died. (Predicted: no-emotion, Gold: no-emotion). (ii) What do you think, would you bring an 11 year old to a game? There's a chance of something like this happening, although I'm sure it was unintentional that it hit the kid. I guess it seems like this is a case where the one outlier makes the news, and probably the other 10000 kids at the game were completely fine, or at all the other games this same day. I'm now subject to a 1000 character limit, so even though my email is finished I have to keep typing. I don't usually write such long emails to friends, I would probably talk to them instead if it was this volume of information. Or wait maybe that's a maximum and I can just click next. (Predicted: fear, Gold: no-emotion).

C Examples Track III (PER)

Below an example of 3 essays from a user with a very low *conscientiousness* and *openness* scores.

Essay 1: The pressure we put on our entertainers is unreal. I don't know how most of them manage to make it through alive. We idolize them, and yet also criticize them so much that they are nearly pushed to their breaking. For their status we loathe them, love them, and tell them what they have to be for us. I think I would still choose to be a celebrity, if I could, but it doesn't seem as easy as people imply.

Essay 2: It's incredibly sad that this happens. While we do need to move to more environmentally sound methods of producing energy, it sucks that innocent birds are caught in the path of this progress. I hope we learn new ways to deter them from flying into them, and can better protect the world, while we try to counter our damage to it.

D Examples Track IV (IRI)

Below an example of 3 essays from a user with a very low *personal distress* score of 1/5.

Essay 1 (pd predicted: 2.79: This just totally breaks my heart. I'm not one to get emotional you know that. But reading about kids in the foster care system and how messed up they come out its just heart breaking. Kids that no one cared enough about to change their ways is what it is. It's heartbreaking. Why have kids if this is the kind of parent you are going to be? Kids didn't have a shot straight from the start.

Essay 2 (pd predicted: 2.81): We need more training for police. Police shouldn't be getting killed in the line of duty. It's not fair to their families because people are stupid and can't follow the law. People need to stop being so selfish and we need to make it less easy to obtain guns if people didn't have such easy access to them there wouldn't be so many deaths overall.

IUCL at WASSA 2022 Shared Task: A Text-Only Approach to Empathy and Emotion Detection

Yue Chen
Department of Linguistics
Indiana University
yc59@indiana.edu

Yingnan Ju
Luddy School of Informatics, Computing, and Engineering
Indiana University
yiju@indiana.edu

Sandra Kübler
Department of Linguistics
Indiana University
skuebler@indiana.edu

Abstract

Our system, IUCL, participated in the WASSA 2022 Shared Task on Empathy Detection and Emotion Classification. Our main goal in building this system is to investigate how the use of demographic attributes influences performance. Our results show that our text-only systems perform very competitively, ranking first in the empathy detection task, reaching an average Pearson correlation of 0.54, and second in the emotion classification task, reaching a Macro-F of 0.572. Our systems that use both text and demographic data are less competitive.

1 Introduction

Emotion classification has become increasingly important due to the large-scale deployment of artificial emotional intelligence. In various aspects of our lives, these systems now play a crucial role. For example, customer care solutions are now gradually shifting to a hybrid mode where an AI will try to solve the problem first, and only when it fails, will a human intervene. The WASSA 2022 Shared Task covers four different tasks on Empathy Detection, Emotion Classification, Personality Prediction, and Interpersonal Reactivity Index Prediction. We participated in task 1 on Empathy Detection and task 2 on Emotion Classification.

Most of the existing emotion classification tasks are restricted to only using signals such as video, audio, or text, but seldom using demographic data, partly because such information is often not available. However, using demographic information also raises ethical concerns. In the current shared task, additional demographic information was made available, thus implicitly inviting participants to investigate the interaction between empathy, emotion, and demographic information. In this work, we will compare two different systems, one using demographic data and one that does not.

Our text-only system performs very competitively. In the evaluation, we ranked first in the empathy detection task and second in the emotion classification task[1]. Adding demographic information to the systems makes them less competitive.

The remainder of the paper is structured as follows: In section 2, we will discuss the related work on emotion classification. In section 3, we will present our two systems and discuss their differences. We will also discuss the challenges we encountered and how we addressed them. In section 4, we will present the evaluation results of our systems and the performance of our other systems. We will also discuss the implications of these results. In section 5 we will conclude and discuss future research efforts.

2 Related Work

Though empathy detection is relatively new, a considerable amount of work has been carried out in the related areas of emotion detection (e.g. Acheampong et al., 2020; Canales and Martínez-Barco, 2014), sentiment analysis (e.g. Pestian et al., 2012; Kiritchenko et al., 2014), and stance detection (e.g. Küçük and Can, 2020; AlDayel and Magdy, 2021; Liu et al., 2016).

After initial success using SVMs (e.g. Mullen and Collier, 2004), BERT and other transformer-based models (Devlin et al., 2019; Liu et al., 2019) have become the mainstream architecture for handling these related tasks (e.g. Hoang et al., 2019; Liao et al., 2021).

While most data sets use Twitter feed, the current task uses essays as data points, which are considerably longer than tweets, and thus necessitates procedures to mitigate problems arising from the length of the input sequence. In such settings, transformer-based models have evolved to handle longer input sequences by strategic truncating (Sun et al., 2019; Ding et al., 2020), either taking the front, the end,

[1]We only consider submissions made before the shared task deadline

Proceedings of the 12th Workshop on Computational Approaches to Subjectivity, Sentiment & Social Media Analysis, pages 228 - 232
May 26, 2022

Task		Model	Seq Length	Batch size	Epoch	Learning rate	Dem. info
Task 1	Empathy	RoBERTa	128	32	25	3.00E-05	No
		RoBERTa	128	32	2	1.00E-05	Yes
Task 1	Distress	RoBERTa	128	32	25	3.00E-05	No
		RoBERTa	128	32	25	3.00E-05	Yes
Task 2	Emotion	RoBERTa	512	4	2	3.00E-05	No
		RoBERTa	512	4	12	1.00E-05	Yes

Table 1: Optimized settings for task 1 and 2

or the middle part of the text or using a sliding window method.

Additionally, packages such as the one by Gu and Budhkar (2021) provide us with methods and implementations to incorporate categorical and numerical features. Categorical and numerical features can be treated as additional tokens, or they can be treated as a different modality and handled by co-attention (Tsai et al., 2019).

3 Methodology

In this section we will describe our systems and how we approach the empathy prediction and emotion classification tasks with two different systems.

3.1 Models

We use RoBERTa large as the base model for both empathy prediction and emotion classification tasks (Liu et al., 2019). RoBERTa extends BERT by changing key hyper-parameters, such as much larger mini-batches and higher learning rates, removing the next-sentence pre-training objective, and using a byte-level Byte-Pair Encoding (BPE) (Sennrich et al., 2016)) as the tokenizer. We fine-tuned the model on the training data of the shared task, and created two different fine-tuned models, a regression model for empathy and distress detection, and a classification model for emotion classification respectively. For the regression task, the regression model consists of a transformer model topped by a fully-connected layer. A single output neuron predicts the target in the fully-connected layer.

Since empathy prediction and personal distress level are combined into the same task, we developed one unified model that addressed both tasks. The architecture of the model remains the same while different training set can be used to fine-tune the model for the two tasks. This system obtained the best performance across both tasks. Details of the configurations for the models are listed in Table 1.

3.2 BERT for Long Sequences

One of the challenges in this task is handling long sequences. Most widely used data sets in the areas of emotion detection consist of collections of tweets as data points. This data set consists of essays, which are considerably longer than tweets. The essays are between 300 and 800 characters, with an average of 450 in the training set. Because of their quadratically increasing memory and time consumption, the transformer-based models are incapable of processing long texts (Ding et al., 2020).

The results based on this strategy were higher than when using more complex hierarchical approaches that chunk the article, process the chunks, and assemble the results. However, in our task, our experiments show that cutting text (either from the beginning or the middle of the text) always results in lower scores than using the whole text. Another method of dealing with long sequences is to change the maximum sequence length that the model can receive. Our experiments for the second task show that the model with the maximum sequence length of 512 reaches the highest scores. In the empathy and distress prediction task, the best model uses 128 as the maximum sequence length.

3.3 Demographic Attributes as Features

The data set also includes person-level demographic information including age (19-71), gender (1-5), ethnicity (1-6), income (0-1,000,000), and education level (2-7)). In some of our experiments, we added this demographic information to the text. Our goal was to determine whether such information was useful for the tasks.

Since adding numerical or categorical information to a transformer-based model is a non-trivial task, we decided to follow Gu and Budhkar (2021) and group continuous values into bins and, in addition to the value, represent each bin with a unique

Team	Average	Rank	Empathy	Rank	Distress	Rank
IUCL	0.540	1	0.537	2	0.543	2
SINAI	0.530	2	0.541	1	0.519	4
IUCL-2	0.529	3	0.512	3	0.547	1
IUCL/Dem	0.124		0.295		-0.047	

Table 2: Official results (Pearson correlations) for task 1: empathy detection.

word in a plain narrative sentence. For example, the added sentence for "age of 25" is "Age is 25, young adult.", and the added sentence for "income of 150,000" is "Income is 150000, high income, rich". Since the demographic information for education level, gender, and ethnicity is represented by numbers, and no explanation was provided, we had to guess the scale for education level, assuming that a higher number corresponds to a higher level. For gender and ethnicity, we used neutral words and unique proper nouns, not related to gender or ethnicity, i.e., chemical elements for gender and planets for ethnicity. For example, the added sentences for "gender of 1 and ethnicity of 2" are "Gender is gender one, hydrogen. Ethnicity is ethnicity two, Venus.". In theory, this would allow us to test whether there are correlations between certain gender/ethnicity categories and empathy/emotion, without accessing the gender and ethnicity biases inherent in RoBERTa (Bhardwaj et al., 2021; Bartl et al., 2020) However, in practice, the small size of the training data does not allow meaningful conclusions.

3.4 Ethical Concerns

It is important to point out that predicting empathy concern, personal distress, and emotion using demographic attributes at best introduces bias into machine learning systems, and at worst raises ethical concerns (Conway and O'Connor, 2016). The demographic attributes used here are gender, education level, ethnicity, age, and income. This data set is small, so the correlation between these attributes and the prediction is not strong, but likely the model would be able to use them to make "more accurate" predictions if there were more data points available. The situation would be considerably more sensitive if actual categories had been given for the demographic information, thus allowing a transformer-based model to access the bias inherent in our society and thus in the training data for RoBERTa.

4 Results and Analysis

In this section, we discuss our results for the two tasks, empathy detection and emotion classification.

4.1 Task 1: Empathy Prediction

Table 2 shows the evaluation results for the empathy prediction task[2]. The task consists of predicting an empathy score and a distress score, both on a continuous 7 point scale.

Our system, IUCL, ranks first in this task with an averaged Pearson correlation coefficient of 0.54. We achieved Pearson correlation coefficients of 0.537 and 0.543 respectively for empathy concern and personal distress prediction. The second best system ranks first in the empathy subtask but only fourth in the distress subtask. Another system of ours, IUCL-2, is the third best system. IUCL-2 is a variant of IUCL with changes in hyper-parameter choices: we increased the sequence length to 256 and decreased the batch size to 8. While this system performs best at detecting distress, it ranks third for detecting empathy. This shows how sensitive such a model is to hyper-parameter tuning.

Although our IUCL system ranked second in both subtasks, it is the most balanced system, and according to the main evaluation metric the best performing overall system for task 1. In order to create simpler models, we also made a conscious effort to unify these two sub-tasks. This indicates that while our joint model is not optimal when only one of the subtasks is of interest, but the optimization across both subtasks results in a balanced system with reliable performance across both subtasks.

We then compared the system using only textual information with the system additionally using demographic information (IUCL/Dem). The scores for the latter system are considerably lower, even resulting in a negative correlation for distress. This shows that this information is detrimental to the

[2]These results are copied from the shared task leader board on 03/20/2022, considering only submissions made before the deadline, as no official report was released.

Team	$F1_{macro}$	R	$F1_{micro}$	R	Acc.	R	Pr_{macro}	R	Re_{macro}	R	Pr_{micro}	R	Re_{micro}	R
BEST	0.585	1	0.661	1	0.661	1	0.594	2	0.584	1	0.661	1	0.661	1
IUCL	0.572	2	0.646	2	0.646	2	0.599	1	0.555	2	0.646	2	0.646	2
SINAI	0.553	3	0.636	3	0.636	3	0.589	4	0.535	4	0.636	3	0.636	3
IUCL/Dem	0.544		0.611		0.611		0.564		0.539		0.611		0.611	

Table 3: Official results for task 2: emotion classification.

given task.

4.2 Task 2: Emotion Classification

Table 3 shows the evaluation results for the emotion classification task[3]. The task consists of predicting a categorical emotion label from one of the following: anger, disgust, fear, joy, neutral, sadness, and surprise.

Our system, IUCL, ranks second in this task with a macro-averaged F1 of 0.572. Our macro-averaged precision of 0.599 is the highest reported score, but our macro recall of 0.555 is the 2nd highest. In this task, systems are performing relatively balanced across different evaluation metrics. A further analysis of the results will have to wait until a more detailed evaluation is released.

We compared the results of a system trained only on the textual data with a system that was additionally given demographic information (IUCL/Dem). Again, we see a drop in performance, with all scores about 2-3 percent points lower than for the text-only system.

4.3 Further Analysis

We noticed that during the training phase of the emotion detection task, our model performed best when we only fine-tuned for two epochs. This is also true for the empathy task when demographic information is used, though the results for this task are not satisfactory. Overall, we experimented with the number of epochs ranging between 2 and 50. The general trend is that the optimal number of epochs is low for this task. We hypothesize that this is due to the small training set (1 861 instances). This is a small sample given that the system needs to decide between seven emotions, and each emotion can be expressed very differently in language. It is likely that with more epochs, RoBERTa is fine-tuned to overfit to our training set and loses its ability to generalize.

The optimal number of epochs is higher for the empathy task, 25. This is likely due to the higher complexity of a regression task.

As much as we believe that using demographic data raises ethical concerns, we still decided to explore using them as features to see how damaging the results may be. In both tasks, the demographic data does not increase system performance; on the contrary, results are considerably lower. For the emotion detection task, including demographic data decreased our macro F1 score from 0.585 to 0.544. For the empathy and distress task, including them was even more harmful: The Pearson correlation coefficients dropped from 0.537 to 0.295 and 0.543 to -0.047 respectively. This may again be due to the small size of the training data set.

5 Conclusion

Our system, IUCL, participated in the empathy detection and the emotion classification tasks of the WASSA 2022 shared task. Our text-only systems rank first in the empathy task and second in the emotion task. We come to the following conclusions: 1. There is a complex interaction between the size of the training data and the complexity of the task, classification for emotion detection and regression for empathy. Given a small training data set and a small set of labels, only minimal fine-tuning is required. 2. Using demographic attributes as features decreases performance given the small training set, and it may raise ethical concerns.

We plan to further investigate the biases in this data set and their implications to both the machine learning systems and society in the future.

Acknowledgments

This work is based on research partly supported by US National Science Foundation (NSF) Grant #2123618.

References

Francisca Adoma Acheampong, Chen Wenyu, and Henry Nunoo-Mensah. 2020. Text-based emotion

[3] These results are copied from the shared task leader board on 03/20/2022, considering only submissions made before the deadline, as no official report was released.

detection: Advances, challenges, and opportunities. *Engineering Reports*, 2(7):e12189.

Abeer AlDayel and Walid Magdy. 2021. Stance detection on social media: State of the art and trends. *Information Processing & Management*, 58(4):102597.

Marion Bartl, Malvina Nissim, and Albert Gatt. 2020. Unmasking contextual stereotypes: Measuring and mitigating bert's gender bias. In *Proceedings of the Second Workshop on Gender Bias in Natural Language Processing*, pages 1–16.

Rishabh Bhardwaj, Navonil Majumder, and Soujanya Poria. 2021. Investigating gender bias in BERT. *Cognitive Computation*, 13(4):1008–1018.

Lea Canales and Patricio Martínez-Barco. 2014. Emotion detection from text: A survey. In *Proceedings of the workshop on natural language processing in the 5th information systems research working days (JISIC)*, pages 37–43.

Mike Conway and Daniel O'Connor. 2016. Social media, big data, and mental health: Current advances and ethical implications. *Current Opinion in Psychology*, 9:77–82.

Jacob Devlin, Ming-Wei Chang, Kenton Lee, and Kristina Toutanova. 2019. BERT: Pre-training of deep bidirectional transformers for language understanding. In *Proceedings of the 2019 Conference of the North American Chapter of the Association for Computational Linguistics: Human Language Technologies*, pages 4171–4186, Minneapolis, Minnesota.

Ming Ding, Chang Zhou, Hongxia Yang, and Jie Tang. 2020. CogLTX: Applying BERT to long texts. *Advances in Neural Information Processing Systems*, 33:12792–12804.

Ken Gu and Akshay Budhkar. 2021. A package for learning on tabular and text data with transformers. In *Proceedings of the Third Workshop on Multimodal Artificial Intelligence*, pages 69–73, Mexico City, Mexico.

Mickel Hoang, Oskar Alija Bihorac, and Jacobo Rouces. 2019. Aspect-based sentiment analysis using BERT. In *Proceedings of the 22nd Nordic Conference on Computational Linguistics*, pages 187–196.

Svetlana Kiritchenko, Xiaodan Zhu, and Saif M Mohammad. 2014. Sentiment analysis of short informal texts. *Journal of Artificial Intelligence Research*, 50:723–762.

Dilek Küçük and Fazli Can. 2020. Stance detection: A survey. *ACM Computing Surveys (CSUR)*, 53(1):1–37.

Wenxiong Liao, Bi Zeng, Xiuwen Yin, and Pengfei Wei. 2021. An improved aspect-category sentiment analysis model for text sentiment analysis based on roBERTa. *Applied Intelligence*, 51(6):3522–3533.

Can Liu, Wen Li, Bradford Demarest, Yue Chen, Sara Couture, Daniel Dakota, Nikita Haduong, Noah Kaufman, Andrew Lamont, Manan Pancholi, Kenneth Steimel, and Sandra Kübler. 2016. IUCL: An ensemble model for stance detection in twitter. In *Proceedings of the International Workshop on Semantic Evaluation*, San Diego, CA.

Yinhan Liu, Myle Ott, Naman Goyal, Jingfei Du, Mandar Joshi, Danqi Chen, Omer Levy, Mike Lewis, Luke Zettlemoyer, and Veselin Stoyanov. 2019. RoBERTa: A robustly optimized BERT pretraining approach. *arXiv preprint arXiv:1907.11692*.

Tony Mullen and Nigel Collier. 2004. Sentiment analysis using Support Vector Machines with diverse information sources. In *Proceedings of the Conference on Empirical Methods in Natural Language Processing*, pages 412–418.

John P Pestian, Pawel Matykiewicz, Michelle Linn-Gust, Brett South, Ozlem Uzuner, Jan Wiebe, K Bretonnel Cohen, John Hurdle, and Christopher Brew. 2012. Sentiment analysis of suicide notes: A shared task. *Biomedical Informatics Insights*, 5:BII–S9042.

Rico Sennrich, Barry Haddow, and Alexandra Birch. 2016. Neural machine translation of rare words with subword units. In *Proceedings of the 54th Annual Meeting of the Association for Computational Linguistics (Volume 1: Long Papers)*, pages 1715–1725.

Chi Sun, Xipeng Qiu, Yige Xu, and Xuanjing Huang. 2019. How to fine-tune BERT for text classification? In *China National Conference on Chinese Computational Linguistics*, pages 194–206. Springer.

Yao-Hung Hubert Tsai, Shaojie Bai, Paul Pu Liang, J. Zico Kolter, Louis-Philippe Morency, and Ruslan Salakhutdinov. 2019. Multimodal transformer for unaligned multimodal language sequences. In *Proceedings of the 57th Annual Meeting of the Association for Computational Linguistics*, pages 6558–6569, Florence, Italy.

Continuing Pre-trained Model with Multiple Training Strategies for Emotional Classification

Bin Li[1]*, **Yixuan Weng**[2*], **Qiya Song**[1*], **Bin Sun**[1], **Shutao Li**[1]
[1] College of Electrical and Information Engineering, Hunan University
[2] National Laboratory of Pattern Recognition Institute of Automation, Chinese Academy Sciences, Beijing, 100190, China
{libincn, sqyunb, sunbin611, shutao_li}@hnu.edu.cn, wengsyx@gmail.com

Abstract

Emotion is the essential attribute of human beings. Perceiving and understanding emotions in a human-like manner is the most central part of developing emotional intelligence. This paper describes the contribution of the LingJing team's method to the Workshop on Computational Approaches to Subjectivity, Sentiment & Social Media Analysis (WASSA) 2022 shared task on Emotion Classification. The participants are required to predict seven emotions from empathic responses to news or stories that caused harm to individuals, groups, or others. This paper describes the continual pre-training method for the masked language model (MLM) to enhance the DeBERTa pre-trained language model. Several training strategies are designed to further improve the final downstream performance including the data augmentation with the supervised transfer, child-tuning training, and the late fusion method. Extensive experiments on the emotional classification dataset show that the proposed method outperforms other state-of-the-art methods, demonstrating our method's effectiveness. Moreover, our submission ranked Top-1 with all metrics in the evaluation phase for the Emotion Classification task.

1 Introduction

Emotion is an important component of human daily communication. However, with the growing interest in human-computer interfaces, machines still lag in possessing and perceiving emotions. Understanding human emotional states in dialogue is crucial for building natural human-machine interaction, which aims to generate appropriate responses.

Emotion classification (EMO) in the text is concentrated on projecting words, sentences, and documents to a set of emotions according to psychological models proposed by (Ekman, 1992), which is an interdisciplinary field of study that span psychology and computer science. This task has evolved from a purely research-oriented topic to play a role in various applications, including mental health assessment, intelligent agents, social media mining (Calvo et al., 2017; Rambocas and Pacheco, 2018). Therefore, emotion classification has become a hot topic in the field of natural language processing (NLP), and lots of research efforts have been devoted to its development.

With the rapid development of artificial intelligence technology, especially deep learning, researchers have made substantial progress on EMO tasks over the past few decades. Before the era of deep learning, traditional EMO methods not only ignore the order of occurrence of words in written text, but are also limited by fixed input sizes. However, obtaining contextual relations between words from the sequence texts plays a crucial role in understanding the complete meaning of sentences. With the popularity of data-driven techniques, deep learning based methods improve the shortcomings of traditional methods and achieve superior EMO performance (Ran et al., 2018; Rajabi et al., 2020; Nandwani and Verma, 2021).

More recently, the transformer self-attention architecture based (Vaswani et al., 2017) pre-trained models have been successfully applied for learning language representations by exploiting large amounts of unlabeled data. These models mainly include BERT (Devlin et al., 2018a), OpenAI GPT (Radford et al., 2018), RoBERTa (Liu et al., 2019). These architectures show superior performance when fine-tuning different downstream tasks, including machine translation (Imamura and Sumita, 2019), text classification (Sun et al., 2019), emotion classification (Luo and Wang, 2019) and question answering (Garg et al., 2020). Recent works have shown that transformer-based pre-trained methods can achieve state-of-the-art performance in EMO tasks (Acheampong et al., 2021; Luo and Wang, 2019). Motivated by this, we adopt the DeBERTa model (He et al., 2020) with continual pre-training

*These authors contribute equally to this work.

Proceedings of the 12th Workshop on Computational Approaches to Subjectivity, Sentiment & Social Media Analysis, pages 233 - 238
May 26, 2022 ©2022 Association for Computational Linguistics

method for the masked language model (MLM) (Devlin et al., 2018b) in this Track 2 to improve final downstream performance. More feasible training strategies are designed to improve the final results further. In this paper, we describe our work for Track 2 of the WASSA Shared Task 2022, addressing the issue of emotion classification.

2 Method

In this section, we will elaborate on the main methods for Track 2 of the WASSA 2022 Shared Task. More details about the training strategies are detailed at the end of this section.

2.1 Continuing Pre-training

It is a wise choice for further continual pre-training (Gururangan et al., 2020) to enhance the pre-trained model, i.e., DeBERTa model (He et al., 2020). It will be helpful to alleviate the task and domain discrepancy between the upstream and the downstream tasks (Qiu et al., 2020). As a result, we adopt the continual pre-training method for the masked language model (MLM) (Devlin et al., 2018b) in this Track 2 to directly improve final downstream performance. The available datasets are chosen from the open-source resources (Demszky et al., 2020; Öhman et al., 2020). The optimization function is written as follows

$$\max_{\theta} \log p_{\theta}(\boldsymbol{X} \mid \tilde{\boldsymbol{X}}) = \max_{\theta} \sum_{i \in \mathcal{C}} \log p_{\theta}\left(\tilde{x}_i = x_i \mid \tilde{\boldsymbol{X}}\right) \tag{1}$$

where the $\mathcal{C}$ is the index set of the masked tokens in the sequence.

We adopt the implementation of the original paper (Devlin et al., 2018b) to keep 10% of the masked tokens unchanged, another 10% replaced with randomly picked tokens and the rest replaced with the [MASK] token.

2.2 Emotion Classification with DeBERTa Model

Track 2 is a classic emotion classification task, where seven emotional labels are required to be classified. We adopt the DeBERTa-v2 (He et al., 2020) model with continuing pre-training method for processing this classification task, where the main method structure is shown in Figure 1. The given sentence is separated into tokens and then sent to the pre-trained language model (PLM) as the input. To obtain the complete meaning of the whole sentence, we take the output embedding of

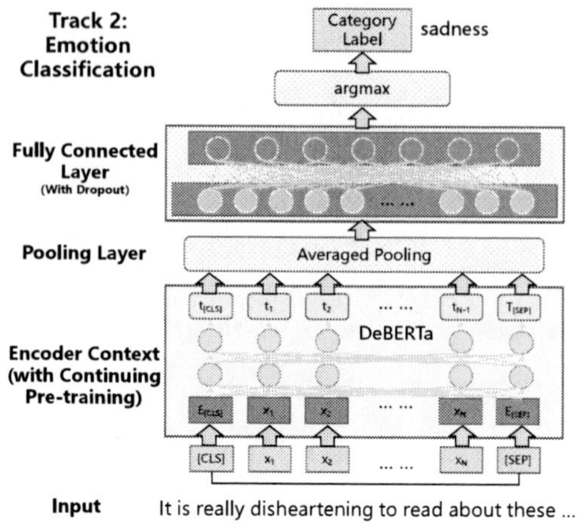

Figure 1: Main structure of the method in Track 2.

each token to be averaged by the averaged pooling layer. The seven-categories task is designed by passing the averaged encoding into the fully connected layer with dropout.

2.3 Training Strategies

We introduce some training strategies used in the Track 2 emotional classification, where the data augmentation with supervised transfer, child-tuning training, and late fusion will be introduced in detail.

2.3.1 Data Augmentation with Supervised Transfer

When fine-tuning on the English emotional classification datasets, we shall transfer the supervised knowledge into the Track 2 emotional task from the other datasets. Specifically, inspired by the work (Kulkarni et al., 2021), we adopt the data augmentation strategies with Random Augmentation (RA) and Balanced Augmentation (BA), where the GoEmotions (Demszky et al., 2020) and the XED dataset (Öhman et al., 2020) are adopted for implementation. It provides more useful knowledge transferred from the same resources to the downstream task (Durrani et al., 2021). As a result, the continuing pre-trained DeBERTa model fine-tuned on these similar datasets in English may achieve better results.

2.3.2 Child-tuning Training

The efficient Child-tuning (Xu et al., 2021) method is used for fine-tuning the DeBEATa model, where the parameters of the Child network are updated with the gradients mask. For the Track 2 task, the task-independent algorithm is used. In the phase of the fine-tuning, the gradient masks are obtained by

Bernoulli distribution (Chen and Liu, 1997) sampling from in each step of iterative update, which is equivalent to randomly dividing a part of the network parameters when updating. The equation of the above steps is shown as follows

$$\begin{aligned} w_{t+1} &= w_t - \eta \frac{\partial \mathcal{L}(w_t)}{\partial w_t} \odot M_t \\ M_t &\sim \text{ Bernoulli } (p_F) \end{aligned} \quad (2)$$

where the notation $\odot$ represents the dot production, p_F is the partial network parameter.

2.4 Late Fusion

Due to the complementary performance between different emotion prediction models (Colnerič and Demšar, 2018), we design the late fusion method with the Bagging algorithm (Breiman, 1996) to vote on the results of the various models. The Bagging algorithm is used during the prediction, which can effectively reduce the variance of the final prediction by bridging the prediction bias of different models, augmenting the overall generalization ability of the system.

3 Experimental Setting

This section will subsequently present emotion dataset, our experimental models, experimental settings, control of variables experiment.

3.1 Dataset

Computational detection and understanding of empathy is an important factor in advancing human-computer interaction (Liu, 2015). Buechel et al. (2018) presented the first publicly available gold standard for the text-based empathy prediction[1]. Two researchers collected articles from news websites. After that, they asked the participants to read the article. Moreover, participants were asked to rate their level of urgency and distress before describing their ideas and feelings about it in writing.

Each participant rating 6 items for empathy (e.g., warm,tender, moved) and 8 items for distress (e.g., trou-bled, disturbed, alarmed) using a 7-point scale for each of those. The final data set has 1860 samples in total. The author obtains their gold scores by averaging the submissions from different participants.

[1]Data and code are available at: https://github.com/wwbp/empathic_reactions

3.2 Implementation Details

We train the model using the Pytorch[2] (Paszke et al., 2019) on the NVIDIA A100 GPU and use the hugging-face[3] (Wolf et al., 2020) framework. For all uninitialized layers, We set the dimension of all the hidden layers in the model as 1024. The AdamW(Loshchilov and Hutter, 2018) optimizer which is a fixed version of Adam (Kingma and Ba, 2014) with weight decay, and set β_1 to 0.9, β_2 to 0.99 for the optimizer. We set the learning rate to 1e-6 with the warm-up (He et al., 2016). The batch size is 1. We set the maximum length of 512, and delete the excess. Linear decay of learning rate and gradient clipping is set to 1e-6. Dropout (Srivastava et al., 2014) of 0.1 is applied to prevent over-fitting. All experiments select the best parameters in the valid set. Finally, we report the score of the best model (valid set) in the test set.

We use the DeBERTa-v2-xxl (He et al., 2021) as our pre-trained model, and fine-tune the model. The DeBERTa[4] model comes with 48 layers and a hidden size of 1536. The total parameters are 1.5B, and it is trained with 160GB raw data. We spent three weeks on this continuing pre-training step.

3.3 Comparison with Baseline Methods

We compare our methods with Baseline methods on the datasets (Buechel et al., 2018). Results of comparative methods are reported on website[5]. IITK@WASSA (Mundra et al., 2021) fine-tuned the ELECTRA model with ensemble method. The [CLS] token was passed through a single linear layer to produce a vector of size 7, representing class probabilities. Moreover, they save the snapshots with the best validation scores.

Phoenix's approach(Butala et al., 2021) is primarily based on T5 Model (Raffel et al., 2020) or conditional generation of emotion labels. Hence before feeding into the network, the emotion prediction task is cast as feeding the essay text as input and training it to generate target emotion labels as text. This allows for the use of the same model, loss function, and hyper-parameters for the task of emotion prediction as is done in other Text Generation tasks.

[2]https://pytorch.org

[3]https://github.com/huggingface/transformers

[4]microsoft/deberta-v2-xxlarge

[5]https://competitions.codalab.org/competitions/28713#results

Methods	Macro F1	Micro F1	Accuracy	Macro Precison	Macro Recall	Micro Precision	Micro Recall
MTL (Fornaciari et al., 2021)	0.483	0.585	0.585	0.546	0.47	0.585	0.585
T5 (Butala et al., 2021)	0.502	0.594	0.594	0.550	0.483	0.594	0.594
ELECTRA-Ensemble (Mundra et al., 2021)	0.588	0.655	0.655	0.603	0.584	0.655	0.655
Ours	**0.698**	**0.754**	**0.754**	**0.740**	**0.679**	**0.754**	**0.754**

Table 1: Comparison with state-of-the-art methods. The best results are in bold.

Team Name	Macro F1	Micro F1	Accuracy	Macro Precison	Macro Recall	Micro Precision	Micro Recall
mantis	0.548	0.632	0.632	0.594	0.528	0.632	0.632
SURREY-CTS-NLP	0.548	0.634	0.634	0.576	0.532	0.634	0.634
SINAI	0.553	0.636	0.636	0.589	0.535	0.636	0.636
IUCL	0.572	0.646	0.646	0.599	0.555	0.646	0.646
Ours	**0.698**	**0.754**	**0.754**	**0.740**	**0.679**	**0.754**	**0.754**

Table 2: Results of the Top-5 teams participating in the EMO track for the post-evaluation. The best results are in bold.

Methods	Macro F1	Micro F1	Accuracy
Ours	**0.698**	**0.754**	**0.754**
w/o continuing pre-training	0.639	0.678	0.678
w/o supervised transfer	0.652	0.696	0.696
w/o child-tuning	0.656	0.699	0.699
w/o late fusion	0.664	0.664	0.664
w/o PLM	0.254	0.312	0.312

Table 3: Results of the ablation study.

Given the availability of further dependent variables (Fornaciari et al., 2021), create a Multi-Task Learning (MTL) model that takes the text as only input and jointly predicts emotions (classification task with categorical cross-entropy), empathy, and distress (regression task) (MTL2). They implemented a MIMTL model with text, gender, income, and IRI as input to predict emotions, empathy, and distress (MI3-MTL2).

4 Results and Discussions

The experiment results of the various methods on the evaluation dataset are displayed in Table 1. As presented in Table 1, our method achieves the best results in all evaluation metrics. Compared with the method from team IITK@WASSA that was the Top-1 last year, the adopted method gets a 0.110 increase of Macro F1, 0.137 increase of Macro Precision, 0.095 increase of Macro Recall, and 0.099 increase of Micro F1, Micro Precision, Micro Precision, and Accuracy. From this, we conclude that the proposed method outperforms the previous state-of-the-art method by an appreciable margin. It demonstrates the effectiveness of our method.

The Results of Top-5 teams participating in the EMO track for the post-evaluation are shown in Table 2. The results from our proposed method greatly exceed the second team in the different evaluation metrics. Compared with the method from the second team, our method gains a 0.126 increase of Macro F1, 0.141 increase of Macro Precision, 0.124 increase of Macro Recall, and 0.108 increase of Micro F1, Micro Precision, Micro Precision, and Accuracy. The proposed method obtains the state-of-the-art performance from the perspective of emotion classification and achieves substantial improvements over other methods.

As for the ablation study part, we implement different ablation settings to show the effectiveness of the proposed method. As shown in Table 3, the PLM model contributes a lot for the emotional classification. The continuing pre-training can further improve the emotion classification on the three metrics based on the original pre-trained language model. Other experimental results also demonstrate that the training strategies are important for better results. More concretely, the proposed supervised transfer, child-tuning, and late fusion methods help improve the final results.

5 Conclusion

This paper illustrates our contributions to the WASSA shared work on Emotion Classification. We use the DeBERTa pre-trained language model enhanced by the continual pre-training method (MLM) and some training strategies to improve the EMO performance. During the evaluation phase, our submission achieves Top-1 on all metrics for the Emotion Classification task. In the future, we will explore more efficient pre-training methods to further improve the final results.

Acknowledgement

This work is supported by the National Key R&D Program of China (2018YFB1305200), the National Natural Science Fund of China (62171183).

References

Francisca Adoma Acheampong, Henry Nunoo-Mensah, and Wenyu Chen. 2021. Transformer models for text-based emotion detection: a review of bert-based approaches. *Artificial Intelligence Review*, 54(8):5789–5829.

Leo Breiman. 1996. Bagging predictors. *Machine learning*, 24(2):123–140.

Sven Buechel, Anneke Buffone, Barry Slaff, Lyle H. Ungar, and João Sedoc. 2018. Modeling empathy and distress in reaction to news stories. *arXiv: Computation and Language*.

Yash Butala, Kanishk Singh, Adarsh Kumar, and Shrey Shrivastava. 2021. Team phoenix at wassa 2021: Emotion analysis on news stories with pre-trained language models. *arXiv: Computation and Language*.

Rafael A Calvo, David N Milne, M Sazzad Hussain, and Helen Christensen. 2017. Natural language processing in mental health applications using non-clinical texts. *Natural Language Engineering*, 23(5):649–685.

Sean X Chen and Jun S Liu. 1997. Statistical applications of the poisson-binomial and conditional bernoulli distributions. *Statistica Sinica*, pages 875–892.

Niko Colnerič and Janez Demšar. 2018. Emotion recognition on twitter: Comparative study and training a unison model. *IEEE transactions on affective computing*, 11(3):433–446.

Dorottya Demszky, Dana Movshovitz-Attias, Jeongwoo Ko, Alan Cowen, Gaurav Nemade, and Sujith Ravi. 2020. Goemotions: A dataset of fine-grained emotions. In *Proceedings of the 58th Annual Meeting of the Association for Computational Linguistics*, pages 4040–4054.

Jacob Devlin, Ming-Wei Chang, Kenton Lee, and Kristina Toutanova. 2018a. Bert: Pre-training of deep bidirectional transformers for language understanding. *arXiv preprint arXiv:1810.04805*.

Jacob Devlin, Ming-Wei Chang, Kenton Lee, and Kristina Toutanova. 2018b. Bert: Pre-training of deep bidirectional transformers for language understanding. *arXiv preprint arXiv:1810.04805*.

Nadir Durrani, Hassan Sajjad, and Fahim Dalvi. 2021. How transfer learning impacts linguistic knowledge in deep nlp models? In *Findings of the Association for Computational Linguistics: ACL-IJCNLP 2021*, pages 4947–4957.

Paul Ekman. 1992. An argument for basic emotions. *Cognition & emotion*, 6(3-4):169–200.

Tommaso Fornaciari, Federico Bianchi, Debora Nozza, and Dirk Hovy. 2021. Milanlp @ wassa: Does bert feel sad when you cry?

Siddhant Garg, Thuy Vu, and Alessandro Moschitti. 2020. Tanda: Transfer and adapt pre-trained transformer models for answer sentence selection. In *Proceedings of the AAAI Conference on Artificial Intelligence*, volume 34, pages 7780–7788.

Suchin Gururangan, Ana Marasović, Swabha Swayamdipta, Kyle Lo, Iz Beltagy, Doug Downey, and Noah A Smith. 2020. Don't stop pretraining: Adapt language models to domains and tasks. In *Proceedings of the 58th Annual Meeting of the Association for Computational Linguistics*, pages 8342–8360.

Kaiming He, Xiangyu Zhang, Shaoqing Ren, and Jian Sun. 2016. Deep residual learning for image recognition. In *2016 IEEE Conference on Computer Vision and Pattern Recognition (CVPR)*, pages 770–778.

Pengcheng He, Xiaodong Liu, Jianfeng Gao, and Weizhu Chen. 2020. Deberta: Decoding-enhanced bert with disentangled attention. *arXiv preprint arXiv:2006.03654*.

Pengcheng He, Xiaodong Liu, Jianfeng Gao, and Weizhu Chen. 2021. Deberta: Decoding-enhanced bert with disentangled attention. In *International Conference on Learning Representations*.

Kenji Imamura and Eiichiro Sumita. 2019. Recycling a pre-trained bert encoder for neural machine translation. In *Proceedings of the 3rd Workshop on Neural Generation and Translation*, pages 23–31.

Diederik P. Kingma and Jimmy Ba. 2014. Adam: A method for stochastic optimization. *arXiv: Learning*.

Atharva Kulkarni, Sunanda Somwase, Shivam Rajput, and Manisha Marathe. 2021. Pvg at wassa 2021: A multi-input, multi-task, transformer-based architecture for empathy and distress prediction. *arXiv preprint arXiv:2103.03296*.

Bing Liu. 2015. Sentiment analysis: Mining opinions, sentiments, and emotions.

Yinhan Liu, Myle Ott, Naman Goyal, Jingfei Du, Mandar Joshi, Danqi Chen, Omer Levy, Mike Lewis, Luke Zettlemoyer, and Veselin Stoyanov. 2019. Roberta: A robustly optimized bert pretraining approach. *arXiv preprint arXiv:1907.11692*.

Ilya Loshchilov and Frank Hutter. 2018. Decoupled weight decay regularization. In *International Conference on Learning Representations*.

Linkai Luo and Yue Wang. 2019. Emotionx-hsu: Adopting pre-trained bert for emotion classification. *arXiv preprint arXiv:1907.09669*.

Jay Mundra, Rohan Gupta, and Sagnik Mukherjee. 2021. Wassa@iitk at wassa 2021: Multi-task learning and transformer finetuning for emotion classification and empathy prediction. *arXiv: Computation and Language*.

Pansy Nandwani and Rupali Verma. 2021. A review on sentiment analysis and emotion detection from text. *Social Network Analysis and Mining*, 11(1):1–19.

Emily Öhman, Marc Pàmies, Kaisla Kajava, and Jörg Tiedemann. 2020. Xed: A multilingual dataset for sentiment analysis and emotion detection. In *Proceedings of the 28th International Conference on Computational Linguistics*, pages 6542–6552.

Adam Paszke, Sam Gross, Francisco Massa, Adam Lerer, James Bradbury, Gregory Chanan, Trevor Killeen, Zeming Lin, Natalia Gimelshein, Luca Antiga, Alban Desmaison, Andreas Kopf, Edward Yang, Zachary DeVito, Martin Raison, Alykhan Tejani, Sasank Chilamkurthy, Benoit Steiner, Lu Fang, Junjie Bai, and Soumith Chintala. 2019. Pytorch: An imperative style, high-performance deep learning library. In *Advances in Neural Information Processing Systems*, volume 32. Curran Associates, Inc.

Xipeng Qiu, Tianxiang Sun, Yige Xu, Yunfan Shao, Ning Dai, and Xuanjing Huang. 2020. Pre-trained models for natural language processing: A survey. *Science China Technological Sciences*, 63(10):1872–1897.

Alec Radford, Karthik Narasimhan, Tim Salimans, and Ilya Sutskever. 2018. Improving language understanding by generative pre-training.

Colin Raffel, Noam Shazeer, Adam Roberts, Katherine Lee, Sharan Narang, Michael Matena, Yanqi Zhou, Wei Li, and Peter J. Liu. 2020. Exploring the limits of transfer learning with a unified text-to-text transformer. *Journal of Machine Learning Research*, 21:1–67.

Zahra Rajabi, Amarda Shehu, and Ozlem Uzuner. 2020. A multi-channel bilstm-cnn model for multilabel emotion classification of informal text. In *2020 IEEE 14th International Conference on Semantic Computing (ICSC)*, pages 303–306. IEEE.

Meena Rambocas and Barney G Pacheco. 2018. Online sentiment analysis in marketing research: a review. *Journal of Research in Interactive Marketing*.

Li Ran, Lin Zheng, Lin Hailun, Wang Weiping, and Meng Dan. 2018. Text emotion analysis: A survey. *Journal of Computer Research and Development*, 55(1):30.

Nitish Srivastava, Geoffrey E. Hinton, Alex Krizhevsky, Ilya Sutskever, and Ruslan Salakhutdinov. 2014. Dropout: a simple way to prevent neural networks from overfitting. *Journal of Machine Learning Research*, 15:1929–1958.

Chi Sun, Xipeng Qiu, Yige Xu, and Xuanjing Huang. 2019. How to fine-tune bert for text classification? In *China national conference on Chinese computational linguistics*, pages 194–206. Springer.

Ashish Vaswani, Noam Shazeer, Niki Parmar, Jakob Uszkoreit, Llion Jones, Aidan N Gomez, Łukasz Kaiser, and Illia Polosukhin. 2017. Attention is all you need. *Advances in neural information processing systems*, 30.

Thomas Wolf, Lysandre Debut, Victor Sanh, Julien Chaumond, Clement Delangue, Anthony Moi, Pierric Cistac, Tim Rault, Rémi Louf, Morgan Funtowicz, Joe Davison, Sam Shleifer, Patrick von Platen, Clara Ma, Yacine Jernite, Julien Plu, Canwen Xu, Teven Le Scao, Sylvain Gugger, Mariama Drame, Quentin Lhoest, and Alexander M. Rush. 2020. Transformers: State-of-the-art natural language processing. In *Proceedings of the 2020 Conference on Empirical Methods in Natural Language Processing: System Demonstrations*, pages 38–45, Online. Association for Computational Linguistics.

Runxin Xu, Fuli Luo, Zhiyuan Zhang, Chuanqi Tan, Baobao Chang, Songfang Huang, and Fei Huang. 2021. Raise a child in large language model: Towards effective and generalizable fine-tuning. *arXiv preprint arXiv:2109.05687*.

Empathy and Distress Prediction using Transformer Multi-output Regression and Emotion Analysis with an Ensemble of Supervised and Zero-Shot Learning Models

Flor Miriam Plaza-del-Arco, Jaime Collado-Montañez,
L. Alfonso Ureña-López, María-Teresa Martín-Valdivia
SINAI, Computer Science Department, CEATIC, Universidad de Jaén, Spain
{fmplaza, jcollado, laurena, maite}@ujaen.es,

Abstract

This paper describes the participation of the SINAI research group at WASSA 2022 (Empathy and Personality Detection and Emotion Classification). Specifically, we participate in Track 1 (Empathy and Distress predictions) and Track 2 (Emotion classification). We conducted extensive experiments developing different machine learning solutions in line with the state of the art in Natural Language Processing. For Track 1, a Transformer multi-output regression model is proposed. For Track 2, we aim to explore recent techniques based on Zero-Shot Learning models including a Natural Language Inference model and GPT-3, using them in an ensemble manner with a fine-tune RoBERTa model. Our team ranked 2nd in the first track and 3rd in the second track.

1 Introduction

Emotion analysis is a popular and established task in natural language processing (NLP) with a large number of studies conducted during the last few years (Bostan and Klinger, 2018; Plaza-del-Arco et al., 2020). Emotion detection can be considered as the main task in this area which consists of mapping textual units to different emotion categories within a text following different psychological models such as Ekman's theory (Ekman, 1992), with six basic emotions, or Plutchik's (Plutchik, 2001) with the addition of *anticipation* and *trust*. Two inextricably related concepts to emotions that have received less attention are empathy and distress. The former is defined as the ability to sense other people's emotions, coupled with the ability to imagine what someone else might be thinking or feeling, while the latter is a self-focused, negative affective state that arises when one feels upset due to witnessing an entity's suffering or need (Batson et al., 1987; Buechel et al., 2018).

A linked task that plays an important role in the study of these concepts is personality trait detection, which is related to author profiling and is commonly defined as the task of detecting the five basic personality traits (extraversion, agreeableness, openness, conscientiousness, and neuroticism) in the text (Mehta et al., 2020). We refer the reader to a recent survey in the task (Stajner and Yenikent, 2020). All these concepts together have potential applications and play an important role in helping victims of abuse (Burleson et al., 2009; Pfetsch, 2017; SarahWoods et al., 2009), mental and physical health support (Sharma et al., 2020, 2021), and in the study of reaction to news stories (Buechel et al., 2018).

In this paper, we present our participation as SINAI team in the Shared Task on Empathy and Personality Detection and Emotion Classification (WASSA 2022). Within this shared task, four main tracks are proposed that aim to develop models that can predict empathy, distress, emotion, and personality traits in reaction to English news articles. Track 1: Empathy Prediction (EMP) consists in predicting both the empathy concern and the personal distress at the essay level. Track 2: Emotion Classification (EMO) refers to detecting the emotion at the essay level. Track 3: Personality Prediction (PER) aims to predict the Big Five personality traits, and Track 4: Interpersonal Reactivity Index Prediction (IRI) consists of predicting each dimension of assessment of empathy: perspective taking, fantasy, empathic concern. Our team SINAI has participated in the first and second tracks.

2 Data

The dataset provided by the organizers of WASSA 2022 shared task is an extension of the one presented in (Buechel et al., 2018) which is composed of posts in reactions to news articles where there is harm to a person, group, or other. Person-level demographic information (age, gender, ethnicity, income, education level) is included for each post. A set of 2,130 training documents annotated with

Proceedings of the 12th Workshop on Computational Approaches to Subjectivity, Sentiment & Social Media Analysis, pages 239 - 244
May 26, 2022 ©2022 Association for Computational Linguistics

empathy, distress, and emotions is provided (see Table 1 for the data set size). With each post, regression scores for empathy and distress that range from 1 to 7 have been associated to address track 1. For track 2, each post is annotated with seven emotions following the six Ekman's categories (*anger*, *fear*, *sadness*, *joy*, *disgust*, and *surprise*) plus the *neutral* class.

Dataset	#Instances
Training	1,860
Development	270
Test	525

Table 1: WASSA 2022 dataset splits. Training, development and test set sizes.

3 System Description

In this section, we describe the systems our team SINAI developed for Track 1 (EMP) and Track 2 (EMO) at WASSA 2022.

3.1 Track 1: Empathy Prediction

This track is a multi-output regression task in which a system has to learn to predict both empathy and distress scores from users' reaction posts to news articles. To address this task, we have focused on two main approaches: A single multi-output regression model that learns to predict both empathy and distress at once, and two separated regression models, one predicting the empathy score and the other predicting that of distress.

For each approach, three different models based on RoBERTa (Liu et al., 2020) and BERT (Devlin et al., 2019) have been tested: roberta-large, bert-base-uncased fine-tuned on the GoEmotions dataset (Demszky et al., 2020) which contains Reddit comments labeled for 27 emotion categories plus *neutral*, and a distilled version of BERT (distilbert-base-uncased) fine-tuned on the CARER dataset (Saravia et al., 2018) which contains Twitter messages labeled with six basic emotions: *anger*, *fear*, *joy*, *love*, *sadness* and *surprise*. By proposing the latter two models, we aim to observe whether sequential transfer learning models that have first fine-tuned on the emotion task help in the detection of empathy and distress, as they are inherently related tasks.

The WASSA 2022 dataset provides several numerical demographic features, namely: gender, education, race, age, and income. Two of these are actual numerical features (age and income) but the others are categorical features that have been numerically encoded. As we did not have the right labels associated with these categorical features, we tried to decode them by analyzing the training set. We noticed that all essays containing the sentence "as a woman" were labeled as 2, so we inferred gender 1 as male and gender 5, which only identifies two authors in the entire training set, as "other". The rest of the features (race and education level) have not been used in our system as we could not decode them.

We finally fine-tuned all three models with the raw essays. Then, we used both the essays and a concatenation of the three previously mentioned features (e.g. "male, 32, 20000") as two different input sentences for the tokenizer, which internally merges them with a special separator token: </s> for RoBERTa and [SEP] for BERT.

Multi-output regression model. In this approach, the prediction of both empathy and distress is learned at once by minimizing the average between the mean squared error (MSE) of each. This is accomplished by fine-tuning a single transformer model to predict two regression outputs given essays as inputs.

Separated regression models. In this case, we focused on predicting each class separately, this means, fine-tuning two different models where the former is designed to minimize the MSE loss while learning to predict the empathy's regression value while the latter does the same for that of distress.

3.2 Track 2: Emotion Classification

This task aims to predict the emotion experienced by the user at the essay level. It is a multi-class classification task where the system has to predict one of the following emotion categories: *anger*, *fear*, *sadness*, *joy*, *disgust*, *surprise* and *neutral*. In order to address this task we focused on different paradigms within the NLP area, namely supervised learning and ZSL. We aimed to compare these two approaches and evaluate how ZSL learning works in emotion classification and whether it can assist in the detection of this task. In particular, for supervised learning we followed the state-of-the-art Transformer (Vaswani et al., 2017) and, for ZSL, the natural language inference (NLI) and an autoregressive language model (GPT-3) have been tested.

Transformer fine-tuning. As a supervised model, we chose the Transformer RoBERTa, specifically roberta-base model. We fine-tuned this model on the raw essays of the corpus provided by the organizers.

NLI. One of the instances of ZSL is via NLI models, in which the inference task needs to perform abductive reasoning. The NLI model needs to decide if the hypothesis (a prompt which represents the class label) entails the premise (which corresponds to the instance to be classified) or contradict it (Yin et al., 2019). For emotion classification, we used as prompt "This person feels *emotion name*" being emotion name replaced by each emotion category (*anger*, *fear*, *sadness*, *joy*, *disgust*, *surprise*, and *neutral*). As final label, the one with highest entailment probability is picked. In our experiments, we used the DeBERTa Transformer (He et al., 2021), specifically the *microsoft/deberta-xlarge-mnli* model from Hugging Face.

GPT-3. This model aims to produce human-like text. In this case, we used the model to ask about the emotion expressed in the text. Therefore, we used as a prompt "Classify the following texts in only one of the following emotions *anger*, *fear*, *sadness*, *joy*, *disgust*, *surprise* or *neutral*." and we showed one example to the model which is "I feel so happy today: joy". We employed the OpenAI Davinci's model as it is the most capable one, often with less context.

Final Ensemble. We aim to observe how these different type of models all together perform to address the task of emotion classification. Therefore, we conducted a voting ensemble where the majority emotion is picked as the final emotion. In case of disagreement or tie, we selected the emotion given by the supervised model.

4 Experimental Setup

All the transformer based models have been fine-tuned on a single NVIDIA Ampere A100 GPU by making use of the Hugging Face's transformer library (Wolf et al., 2019). Regarding the hyperparameters used, we computed a grid search in order to find out the combination that maximized each task's metric on the development set. The batch size values tested during the optimization were 8, 16 and 32. Concerning the learning rate, the range of values we tested during the grid search was 1e-5, 2e-5, 3e-5, 4e-5 and 5e-5. We also set the maximum length of the tokenizer (the length from which the tokenizer will truncate a tokenized sequence) equal to the longest essay in the training set as tokenized by the RoBERTa's byte-pair encoding tokenizer, that is, 221. Regarding the epochs, we trained every model until an early stopping mechanism determined the model was starting to overfit on the training data, which usually happened between epochs 2 and 3, depending on the model.

5 Results

In this section, we present the results obtained by the systems we developed as part of our participation in WASSA 2022 Track 1 and Track 2. To evaluate our systems, we used the official competition metrics given by the organizers. Specifically, the average of the two Pearson correlations is computed for EMP and the macro F_1-score for EMO. Further, for the latter we report macro precision and recall scores. The experiments are conducted in two phases: the model selection phase and the evaluation phase, which are explained in the following two sections.

5.1 Model selection

In order to select the best model for each task, we trained all the systems described in Section 3 with the training set provided by the organizers and then, we evaluated them with the development one. All the results achieved by our models in this pre-evaluation phase are shown in Tables 2 and 3.

In Table 2, results obtained in the first track are shown. RoBERTa large in separated regression models (SEP) with and without features scored an averaged Pearson correlation of 0.518 and 0.503 respectively on the development set. Regarding the RoBERTa's multi-output regression models (MOR), features have proven to improve the results with respect to the baseline version (0.504 to 0.528), which is the best model we achieved and therefore, the one selected for the evaluation phase. It can also be observed that the models fine-tuned on emotions that we chose are not helpful to determine empathy nor distress on essays.

In Table 3, results obtained in the second track are presented. As can be seen, the ZSL-based models (NLI and GPT-3) obtain promising results (0.419 and 0.476 of macro-F_1) without having been tuned in the emotion task. Specifically, among these two ZSL models, the GPT-3 system obtained

Model	Emp	Dis	Avg
roberta-large (SEP)	0.523	0.512	0.518
roberta-large (SEP) + features	0.506	0.500	0.503
roberta-large (MOR)	0.496	0.513	0.504
roberta-large (MOR) + features*	**0.523**	**0.532**	**0.528**
bert-base-go-emotion (MOR)	0.299	0.425	0.362
distil-bert-uncased-emotion (MOR)	0.435	0.387	0.411

Table 2: Multi-Output Regression (MOR) and Separated Regression Models (SEP) results in Track 1 (EMP) for empathy (Emp) and distress (Dis) predictions on WASSA 2022 development set. Best results are shown in bold and selected model marked with *.

Model	P	R	F_1
RoBERTa	0.625	0.578	0.587
NLI	0.456	0.463	0.419
GPT-3	0.524	0.469	0.476
Ensemble*	**0.642**	**0.580**	**0.601**

Table 3: RoBERTa, NLI, GPT-3 and Ensemble models in Track 2 (EMO) on WASSA 2022 development set. Macro-averaged precision (P), recall (R), and F1-score (F_1). Best results are shown in bold and selected model marked with *.

the best results. The supervised model, RoBERTa, obtained an F1 of 0.587. Finally, the ensemble of these models obtained the best result for the task in this phase, a 0.602 of F_1 score and therefore, we decided to use this model for the evaluation phase.

5.2 Evaluation phase

During the evaluation phase, we trained our systems on the joint training and development sets and evaluate them on the test set. The results of the EMP track on the test set can be seen in Table 4. The multi-output regression model based on RoBERTa achieved 0.541 and 0.519 Pearson correlations on the empathy and distress predictions, respectively. This amounts to an average score of 0.53 which ranks 2nd on this track.

In Table 5 we report the results on the EMO track test set. The ensemble model achieved an accuracy of 0.636 and macro values of precision 0.589, recall 0.535, and F_1-score 0.553 which ranked 3rd in this track.

6 Conclusion

This paper presents the participation of the SINAI research group in the shared task on Empathy and Personality Detection and Emotion Classification (WASSA 2022). For the first task, we explore how different raw language models and models fine-

Model	Emp	Dis	Avg
roberta-large (MOR) + features	0.541	0.519	0.53

Table 4: Multi-Output Regression (MOR) results in Track 1 for empathy (Emp) and distress (Dis) detection on WASSA 2022 test set (SINAI Team submission). Pearson correlations.

Model	P	R	F_1	Acc
Ensemble	0.589	0.535	0.553	0.636

Table 5: Ensemble results in Track 2 for emotion detection on WASSA 2022 test set (SINAI Team submission). Macro-averaged precision (P), recall (R), F1- score (F_1) and accuracy (Acc).

tuned on emotions work for the empathy and distress prediction. For this task, we observe that the raw language model RoBERTa in a multi-output regression fashion together with the features of gender, age and income perform better than the models which contain emotion knowledge. Therefore, this shows that not all models previously fine-tuned on emotions help in the prediction of empathy and distress. Regarding the track 2, emotion detection, we have experimented with recent ZSL models including NLI and GPT-3. Results on the development set suggest that they are promising options for emotion detection when no labeled data is available. Therefore, our proposal for this task is an ensemble model that takes advantage of both supervised and ZSL models. Our final results in both Track 1 (EMP) and Track 2 (EMO) demonstrate the success of our proposal's approaches since we ranked 2nd and 3rd among all the participants, respectively. As future work, we plan to further explore ZSL models as they have shown promising results in the emotion classification task.

Acknowledgements

This work has been partially supported by the grants 1380939 (FEDER Andalucía 2014-2020), P20_00956 (PAIDI 2020) funded by the Andalusian Regional Government, LIVING-LANG project (RTI2018-094653-B-C21) funded by MCIN/AEI/10.13039/501100011033 and by ERDF A way of making Europe, and the scholarship (FPI-PRE2019-089310) from the Ministry of Science, Innovation and Universities of the Spanish Government.

References

C Daniel Batson, Jim Fultz, and Patricia A Schoenrade. 1987. Distress and empathy: Two qualitatively distinct vicarious emotions with different motivational consequences. *Journal of personality*, 55(1):19–39.

Laura-Ana-Maria Bostan and Roman Klinger. 2018. An analysis of annotated corpora for emotion classification in text. In *Proceedings of the 27th International Conference on Computational Linguistics*, pages 2104–2119, Santa Fe, New Mexico, USA. Association for Computational Linguistics.

Sven Buechel, Anneke Buffone, Barry Slaff, Lyle Ungar, and João Sedoc. 2018. Modeling empathy and distress in reaction to news stories. In *Proceedings of the 2018 Conference on Empirical Methods in Natural Language Processing*, pages 4758–4765, Brussels, Belgium. Association for Computational Linguistics.

Brant R Burleson, Lisa K Hanasono, Graham D Bodie, Amanda J Holmstrom, Jessica J Rack, Jennifer Gill Rosier, and Jennifer D McCullough. 2009. Explaining gender differences in responses to supportive messages: Two tests of a dual-process approach. *Sex Roles*, 61(3):265–280.

Dorottya Demszky, Dana Movshovitz-Attias, Jeongwoo Ko, Alan Cowen, Gaurav Nemade, and Sujith Ravi. 2020. Goemotions: A dataset of fine-grained emotions.

Jacob Devlin, Ming-Wei Chang, Kenton Lee, and Kristina Toutanova. 2019. BERT: Pre-training of deep bidirectional transformers for language understanding. In *Proceedings of the 2019 Conference of the North American Chapter of the Association for Computational Linguistics: Human Language Technologies, Volume 1 (Long and Short Papers)*, pages 4171–4186, Minneapolis, Minnesota. Association for Computational Linguistics.

Paul Ekman. 1992. An argument for basic emotions. *Cognition and Emotion*, 6(3-4):169–200.

Pengcheng He, Xiaodong Liu, Jianfeng Gao, and Weizhu Chen. 2021. DeBERTa: Decoding-enhanced BERT with Disentangled Attention. In *International Conference on Learning Representations*.

Yinhan Liu, Myle Ott, Naman Goyal, Jingfei Du, Mandar Joshi, Danqi Chen, Omer Levy, Mike Lewis, Luke Zettlemoyer, and Veselin Stoyanov. 2020. RoBERTa: A Robustly Optimized BERT Pretraining Approach.

Yash Mehta, Navonil Majumder, Alexander Gelbukh, and Erik Cambria. 2020. Recent trends in deep learning based personality detection. *Artificial Intelligence Review*, 53(4):2313–2339.

Jan S Pfetsch. 2017. Empathic skills and cyberbullying: relationship of different measures of empathy to cyberbullying in comparison to offline bullying among young adults. *The Journal of genetic psychology*, 178(1):58–72.

Flor Miriam Plaza-del-Arco, Carlo Strapparava, L. Alfonso Ureña-Lopez, and M. Teresa Martin-Valdivia. 2020. EmoEvent: A Multilingual Emotion Corpus based on different Events. In *Proceedings of the 12th Language Resources and Evaluation Conference*, pages 1492–1498, Marseille, France. European Language Resources Association.

Robert Plutchik. 2001. The Nature of Emotions: Human emotions have deep evolutionary roots, a fact that may explain their complexity and provide tools for clinical practice. *American scientist*, 89(4):344–350.

DieterWolke SarahWoods, Stephen Nowicki, and Lynne Hall. 2009. Emotion recognition abilities and empathy of victims of victims of bullying. *Development*, 75(4):987–1002.

Elvis Saravia, Hsien-Chi Toby Liu, Yen-Hao Huang, Junlin Wu, and Yi-Shin Chen. 2018. CARER: Contextualized affect representations for emotion recognition. In *Proceedings of the 2018 Conference on Empirical Methods in Natural Language Processing*, pages 3687–3697, Brussels, Belgium. Association for Computational Linguistics.

Ashish Sharma, Inna W Lin, Adam S Miner, David C Atkins, and Tim Althoff. 2021. Towards facilitating empathic conversations in online mental health support: A reinforcement learning approach. In *Proceedings of the Web Conference 2021*, pages 194–205.

Ashish Sharma, Adam Miner, David Atkins, and Tim Althoff. 2020. A computational approach to understanding empathy expressed in text-based mental health support. In *Proceedings of the 2020 Conference on Empirical Methods in Natural Language Processing (EMNLP)*, pages 5263–5276, Online. Association for Computational Linguistics.

Sanja Stajner and Seren Yenikent. 2020. A survey of automatic personality detection from texts. In *Proceedings of the 28th International Conference on Computational Linguistics*, pages 6284–6295, Barcelona, Spain (Online). International Committee on Computational Linguistics.

Ashish Vaswani, Noam Shazeer, Niki Parmar, Jakob Uszkoreit, Llion Jones, Aidan N. Gomez, Łukasz Kaiser, and Illia Polosukhin. 2017. Attention is all you need. In *Proceedings of the 31st International Conference on Neural Information Processing Systems*, NIPS'17, page 6000–6010, Red Hook, NY, USA. Curran Associates Inc.

Thomas Wolf, Lysandre Debut, Victor Sanh, Julien Chaumond, Clement Delangue, Anthony Moi, Pierric Cistac, Tim Rault, Rémi Louf, Morgan Funtowicz, Joe Davison, Sam Shleifer, Patrick von Platen, Clara Ma, Yacine Jernite, Julien Plu, Canwen Xu, Teven Le Scao, Sylvain Gugger, Mariama Drame, Quentin Lhoest, and Alexander M. Rush. 2019. HuggingFace's Transformers: State-of-the-art Natural Language Processing. *arXiv*.

Wenpeng Yin, Jamaal Hay, and Dan Roth. 2019. "Benchmarking Zero-shot Text Classification: Datasets, Evaluation and Entailment Approach". In *Proceedings of the 2019 Conference on Empirical Methods in Natural Language Processing and the 9th International Joint Conference on Natural Language Processing (EMNLP-IJCNLP)*, pages 3914–3923, Hong Kong, China. Association for Computational Linguistics.

Leveraging Emotion-specific Features to Improve Transformer Performance for Emotion Classification

Atharva Kshirsagar*[1], Shaily Desai*[1], Aditi Sidnerlikar[1], Nikhil Khodake[1] and **Manisha Marathe[2]**

[1,2]Department of Computer Engineering, PVG's COET, Affiliated to Savitribai Phule Pune University, India.

[1]{atharvakshirsagar145, shaily.desai21,
[1]sidnerlikaraditi6, nikhilkhodake2002} @gmail.com
[2]mvm_comp@pvgcoet.ac.in

Abstract

This paper describes team PVG's AI Club's approach to the Emotion Classification shared task held at WASSA 2022. This Track 2 subtask focuses on building models which can predict a multi-class emotion label based on essays from news articles where a person, group or another entity is affected. Baseline transformer models have been demonstrating good results on sequence classification tasks, and we aim to improve this performance with the help of ensembling techniques, and by leveraging two variations of emotion-specific representations. We observe better results than our baseline models and achieve an accuracy of 0.619 and a macro F1 score of 0.520 on the emotion classification task.

1 Introduction

Rapid growth in the availability of human-annotated text documents has led to an increase in methodologies for tasks such as classification, clustering and knowledge extraction. A multitude of sources have enabled public access to structured and semi-structured data comprising of news stories, written repositories, blog content, among countless other roots of information. (Bostan and Klinger, 2018) showed that the task of emotion classification has emerged from being purely research oriented to being of vital importance in fields like dialog systems, intelligent agents, and analysis and diagnosis of mental disorders.

Humans themselves sometimes find it tough to comprehend the various layers of subtlety in emotions, and hence there has been only a limited amount of prior research revolving around emotion classification. It has been noted that larger deep learning models can also find it quite challenging to fully grasp the nuances and underlying context of human emotion.

With the advent of Transformer (Vaswani et al., 2017) models, there has been an increase in performance for emotion classification of text-based models. Most transformer-based language models (Devlin et al., 2018; Raffel et al., 2019; Radford et al., 2018) are pretrained on various self-supervised objectives. Combining transformer based sentence representations with domain-specialised representations for improving performance on the specific task has been successfully used in across many NLP domains (Peinelt et al., 2020; Poerner et al., 2020; Zhang et al., 2021). Building on these foundations, we propose a similar approach to the task of Emotion classification.

In this paper, we posit a solution to the WASSA 2022 Shared Task on Empathy Detection, Emotion Classification and Personality Detection, specifically Track-2, emotion classification. We propose a hybrid model where we combine information from various entities to create a rich final representation of each datapoint, and the observed results show promise in combining the Transformer output with the emotion-specific embeddings and NRC features.

The rest of the paper is organized in the following manner: Section 2 offers an overview into the dataset on Empathetic concern in news stories, Section 3 goes in depth about our proposed methodology with subsections describing the individual constituent modules. Section 4 explains the experimental and training setup along with the baselines used; Section 5 elucidates the observed results, and Section 6 concludes this study.

2 Dataset

The dataset provided by the organizers consists of 1860 essays in the training set, 270 in the dev set and 525 in the test set. Each of these essays has been annotated for empathy and empathy scores, distress and distress scores, emotion, personality feature and interpersonal reactivity features. Since

*Equal Contribution

Proceedings of the 12th Workshop on Computational Approaches to Subjectivity, Sentiment & Social Media Analysis, pages 245 - 249
May 26, 2022

this paper describes an approach only to the Emotion classification task, we shall only describe the data for said subtask. Each essay has been assigned an emotion class similar to classes in (Ekman, 1992). Table 1 provides a description on the training, validation and testing subset, and Figure 1 shows the distribution of the training data among the various emotion classes.

Set	Essays
Training	1860
Validation	270
Testing	525
Total	2655

Table 1: Total datapoints for every set

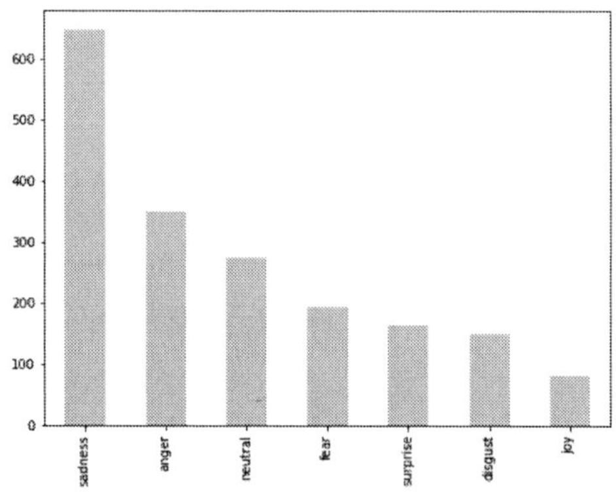

Figure 1: Distribution of the various classes among the Training Dataset

3 Methodology

3.1 RoBERTa

We make use of the pretrained RoBERTa base model (Liu et al., 2019) for this task. RoBERTa provides contextualized essay-level representations which can capture context sensitive information better than static representations. For each essay E in our corpus, we obtain a 768 dimensional representation R, encoded using the CLS token in the final hidden layer of the RoBERTa base model. We further process this representation R with Linear and Dropout layers before concatenating it with our emotion-specific representations.

$$R = RoBERTa(E) \in \mathbb{R}^{d_1} \quad (1)$$

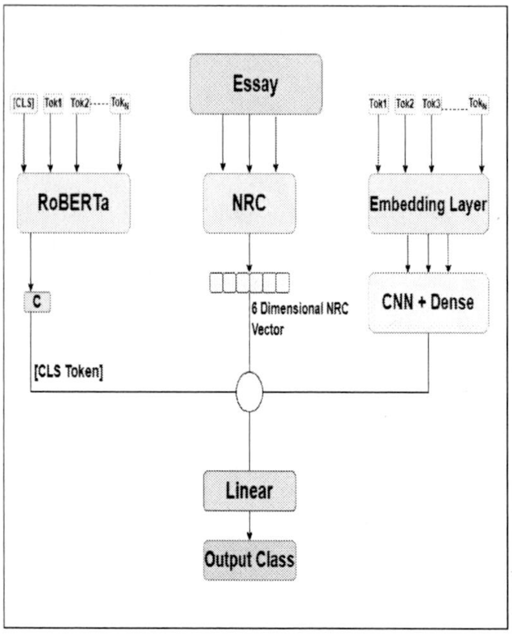

Figure 2: Model Architecture

3.2 Emotion-Enriched Word Embeddings(EWE)

(Labutov and Lipson, 2013; Bansal et al., 2014),argue that the effectiveness of word embeddings is highly task dependent. To obtain word embeddings specific for emotion classification, we used the emotion-enriched embeddings from (Agrawal et al., 2018). The weight matrix was made by mapping the vocabulary from our dataset to the 300 dimensional corresponding vector in the pre-trained embedding file. Each essay was mapped to the embedding matrix into a final representation shape of (100,300). This representation was passed through 2 Conv1d and 2 Maxpool layers to obtain a 16 dimensional feature vector $C \in \mathbb{R}^{d_2}$.

3.3 NRC Representation

The NRC emotion intensity lexicon (Mohammad, 2018) is a collection of close to 10, 000 words associated with a distinct real valued intensity score assigned for eight basic emotions. Incorporating this lexicon in classification tasks has been proven to boost performance (Kulkarni et al., 2021). Of the 8 basic emotions in the lexicon, 6 emotions-anger, joy, sadness, disgust, fear and surprise coincide with the given dataset and hence lexical features for only these features were considered. For every essay in the dataset, we calculate the value for one emotion by summing the individual scores for

Model	Accuracy		Macro-F1 Score	
	Training	Validation	Training	Validation
Vanilla RoBERTa	0.601	0.540	0.513	0.452
RoBERTa + EWE	0.684	0.608	0.561	0.499
RoBERTA + NRC + EWE	**0.693**	**0.619**	**0.618**	**0.520**

Table 2: Resulting metrics on baseline models as compared to our methodology

every word W in the essay that occurs in the NRC lexicon. We then create a six dimensional vector N corresponding to that essay which consists of the scores of the emotions in our dataset.

For a datapoint E, the six values of $S_{emotion}$ and the feature vector N was constructed in the following manner:

$$S_{emotion} = \sum W_{emotion}(W \in E) \quad (2)$$

$$N = [S_{anger}; S_{joy}; .....; S_{surprise}] \in \mathbb{R}^{d_3} \quad (3)$$

3.4 Combined Representation and Classification

The feature vectors obtained from the RoBERTa (R), Emotion-Enriched Embeddings (C) and NRC (N)were concatenated to obtain the final representation (F).

$$F = [R; C; N] \in \mathbb{R}^{d_1+d_2+d_3} \quad (4)$$

This representation is then passed through a single Linear layer with the Softmax activation. Figure 2 depicts the model architecture in detail.

4 Experimental Setup

4.1 Data Preparation

Standard text cleaning steps like removing numbers, special characters, punctuation, accidental spaces, etc. were applied to each essay in the corpus. Stopwords were removed using the `nltk` (Loper and Bird, 2002) library. Every essay was tokenized to a maximum length of 100, and essays larger than this length were truncated. No standardization was done in the case of NRC scores, as we wanted to feed our model a vector of raw emotion-intensity scores for each of the six emotions considered in our NRC representation.

4.2 Training Setup

We used the pretrained 'roberta-base' model from the Huggingface `Transformers` [1] library. All other modules used in our methodology were built using PyTorch. As observed by (Kulkarni et al., 2021), we also found that the Hyperbolic Tangent(Tanh) activation function worked better than ReLU, and hence we used the Tanh activation for all layers in our model. The model was trained using an AdamW optimizer (Loshchilov and Hutter, 2019) with a learning rate of 0.001 and beta values set to $\beta_1 = 0.9$, $\beta_2 = 0.99$ and the loss used was cross entropy loss. Additionally, early stopping was used if the validation loss does not decrease after 10 successive epochs. The batch size was set to 64 for both Baseline models as well as the proposed model. A single Nvidia P100-16GB GPU provided by Google Colab was used to train all models.

4.3 Baselines

Our goal in this work is to examine if concatenating emotional-specific features to pre-existing transformer models leads to an increase in the emotion classification performance of these models. Hence, we compare our proposed methodology to the vanilla RoBERTa model, as well as RoBERTa + Ewe for the emotion classification subtask.

5 Results and Discussion

The results for the emotion prediction task on the validation set are given in Table 2. There was no use of validation data during the training process, and the provided validation data was used as unseen testing data to benchmark the models.The official metric for Track 2 of the shared task was the macro F1 score. To ensure fair comparison, the validation set results have been averaged over 3 runs for each model. The proposed model shows a 7% increase in macro F1 scores and 8% increase in ac-

[1] `https://huggingface.co/transformers/`

curacy over the vanilla RoBERTa model. The proposed model also shows the effectiveness of adding the NRC representations described in section 3.3 as it performs slightly better than the RoBERTa + Emotion Enriched word embeddings model. We attribute this increase in performance to the task-specific representations of essays used in our system. During the training process, it was observed that the performance of all models was highly susceptible to how they were initialized, and we received a large range of results across different seeds. As a result, a true assessment of our method can only be made in comparison to baseline models with the same seed, as we have done in this study.

6 Conclusion

The goal of this study was to examine and enhance the performance of transformer models using only the Empathetic Concern in News Stories dataset that was provided to us, with the prospective of testing our method on a bigger dataset in the future. We proposed a model ensemble which combined the transformer feature vector with the emotion-intensive word embeddings along with the word-specific features obtained from the NRC lexicon. We demonstrate results that outperform the baseline vanilla RoBERTa model, and attest that combining domain-specific features can indeed improve performance on a task as involute as emotion classification.

References

Ameeta Agrawal, Aijun An, and Manos Papagelis. 2018. Learning emotion-enriched word representations. In *Proceedings of the 27th International Conference on Computational Linguistics*, pages 950–961, Santa Fe, New Mexico, USA. Association for Computational Linguistics.

Mohit Bansal, Kevin Gimpel, and Karen Livescu. 2014. Tailoring continuous word representations for dependency parsing. In *Proceedings of the 52nd Annual Meeting of the Association for Computational Linguistics (Volume 2: Short Papers)*, pages 809–815, Baltimore, Maryland. Association for Computational Linguistics.

Laura-Ana-Maria Bostan and Roman Klinger. 2018. An analysis of annotated corpora for emotion classification in text. In *Proceedings of the 27th International Conference on Computational Linguistics*, pages 2104–2119, Santa Fe, New Mexico, USA. Association for Computational Linguistics.

Jacob Devlin, Ming-Wei Chang, Kenton Lee, and Kristina Toutanova. 2018. Bert: Pre-training of deep bidirectional transformers for language understanding. *arXiv preprint arXiv:1810.04805*.

Paul Ekman. 1992. An argument for basic emotions. *Cognition and Emotion*, 6(3-4):169–200.

Atharva Kulkarni, Sunanda Somwase, Shivam Rajput, and Manisha Marathe. 2021. PVG at WASSA 2021: A multi-input, multi-task, transformer-based architecture for empathy and distress prediction. In *Proceedings of the Eleventh Workshop on Computational Approaches to Subjectivity, Sentiment and Social Media Analysis*, pages 105–111, Online. Association for Computational Linguistics.

Igor Labutov and Hod Lipson. 2013. Re-embedding words. In *Proceedings of the 51st Annual Meeting of the Association for Computational Linguistics (Volume 2: Short Papers)*, pages 489–493, Sofia, Bulgaria. Association for Computational Linguistics.

Yinhan Liu, Myle Ott, Naman Goyal, Jingfei Du, Mandar Joshi, Danqi Chen, Omer Levy, Mike Lewis, Luke Zettlemoyer, and Veselin Stoyanov. 2019. Roberta: A robustly optimized bert pretraining approach. *ArXiv*, abs/1907.11692.

Edward Loper and Steven Bird. 2002. Nltk: The natural language toolkit. In *Proceedings of the ACL-02 Workshop on Effective Tools and Methodologies for Teaching Natural Language Processing and Computational Linguistics - Volume 1*, ETMTNLP '02, page 63–70, USA. Association for Computational Linguistics.

Ilya Loshchilov and Frank Hutter. 2019. Decoupled weight decay regularization. In *International Conference on Learning Representations*.

Saif Mohammad. 2018. Word affect intensities. In *Proceedings of the Eleventh International Conference on Language Resources and Evaluation (LREC 2018)*, Miyazaki, Japan. European Language Resources Association (ELRA).

Nicole Peinelt, Dong Nguyen, and Maria Liakata. 2020. tBERT: Topic models and BERT joining forces for semantic similarity detection. In *Proceedings of the 58th Annual Meeting of the Association for Computational Linguistics*, pages 7047–7055, Online. Association for Computational Linguistics.

Nina Poerner, Ulli Waltinger, and Hinrich Schütze. 2020. E-BERT: Efficient-yet-effective entity embeddings for BERT. In *Findings of the Association for Computational Linguistics: EMNLP 2020*, pages 803–818, Online. Association for Computational Linguistics.

Alec Radford, Karthik Narasimhan, Tim Salimans, and Ilya Sutskever. 2018. Improving language understanding by generative pre-training.

Colin Raffel, Noam Shazeer, Adam Roberts, Katherine Lee, Sharan Narang, Michael Matena, Yanqi Zhou, Wei Li, and Peter J Liu. 2019. Exploring the limits of transfer learning with a unified text-to-text transformer. *arXiv preprint arXiv:1910.10683*.

Ashish Vaswani, Noam Shazeer, Niki Parmar, Jakob Uszkoreit, Llion Jones, Aidan N Gomez, Ł ukasz Kaiser, and Illia Polosukhin. 2017. Attention is all you need. In *Advances in Neural Information Processing Systems*, volume 30. Curran Associates, Inc.

Jinpeng Zhang, Baijun Ji, Nini Xiao, Xiangyu Duan, Min Zhang, Yangbin Shi, and Weihua Luo. 2021. Combining static word embeddings and contextual representations for bilingual lexicon induction. In *Findings of the Association for Computational Linguistics: ACL-IJCNLP 2021*, pages 2943–2955, Online. Association for Computational Linguistics.

Transformer based ensemble for emotion detection

Aditya Kane* and **Shantanu Patankar***
Pune Institute of Computer Technology, Pune
{adityakane1, shantanupatankar2001}@gmail.com

Sahil Khose and **Neeraja Kirtane**
Manipal Institute of Technology, Manipal
{sahilkhose18, kirtane.neeraja}@gmail.com

Abstract

Detecting emotions in languages is important to accomplish a complete interaction between humans and machines. This paper describes our contribution to the WASSA 2022 shared task which handles this crucial task of emotion detection. We have to identify the following emotions: sadness, surprise, neutral, anger, fear, disgust, joy based on a given essay text. We are using an ensemble of ELECTRA and BERT models to tackle this problem achieving an F1 score of 62.76%. Our codebase [1] and our WandB project[2] is publicly available.

1 Introduction

Even after engineering a 175B parameter language model like GPT-3 (Brown et al., 2020) we are far from artificial general intelligence. Emotion is a concept that is challenging to describe. However, as human beings, we understand the emotional effect that situations could have on other people. It is interesting to see how we can infuse this knowledge into machines. This work explores whether it is possible for machines to map emotions to situations consciously. Emotion in text has been studied for a while and has given interesting insights. The dataset that we are using is an extended version of the (Ekman, 1992) dataset. Our team, MPA_ED, participated in the WASSA 2022 Shared Task on Empathy Detection and Emotion Classification, Track 2: Emotion Classification (EMO), which consists of predicting the emotion at the essay level. This paper has the following contributions:

We propose three new datasets generated using various sampling techniques which overcome the class imbalance. We present our ensemble based solution consisting of multiple ELECTRA and BERT (Devlin et al., 2018) models to solve the emotion classification task. We provide a detailed analysis of the performance of the cluster of models and reflect on the shortcomings of the models as well as the dataset generated that affected the performance.

2 Related Work

Emotion detection and sentiment analysis has been an extensive research topic since the inception of natural language processing. It has been studied in great detail by faculties of both computer science and neurobiology (Okon-Singer et al., 2015). Murthy and Kumar (2021) presents an extensive review of the modern emotion classification techniques. The work by Alhuzali and Ananiadou (2021) remains the current state-of-the-art on emotion classification on the renowned SemEval dataset (Mohammad et al., 2018). BERT remains the best performer on the GoEmotions dataset (Demszky et al., 2020)

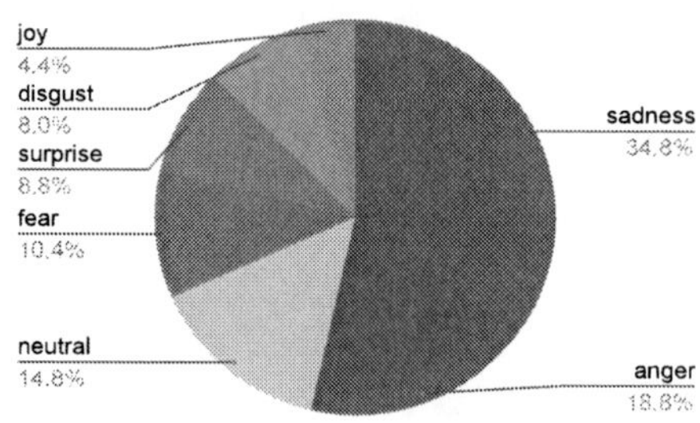

Figure 1: Class distribution in emotions

3 Data

The dataset consists of 1860 data points. Each data point has an essay and its emotion. The emotions are classified into seven types: anger, disgust, fear, joy, neutral, sadness, and surprise. The validation and test split has 270 and 525 data points respectively. The classes for the training data expresses high imbalance, as shown in Fig 1 . Here

*First authors

[1] https://bit.ly/WASSA_shared_task

[2] https://wandb.ai/acl_wassa_pictxmanipal/acl_wassa

Proceedings of the 12th Workshop on Computational Approaches to Subjectivity, Sentiment & Social Media Analysis, pages 250 - 254

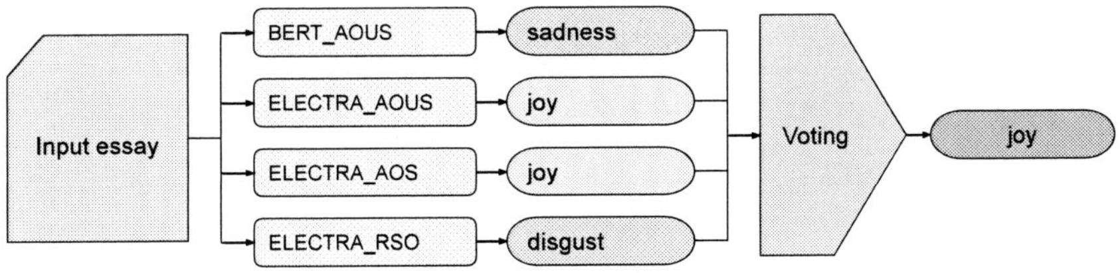

Figure 2: Ensemble pipeline

we see that the emotion "sadness" has the maximum number of data points, whereas "joy" has the least number of data points. The distribution is highly skewed and hence data augmentation is required to mitigate that. We performed basic preprocessing like removing punctuation, numbers, multiple spaces, and single line characters.

To overcome the class imbalance, GoEmotions dataset is used, which is a similar dataset with 27 emotions. We suggest three data augmentation techniques using the dataset described as follows:

- **Augmented Over-UnderSampling (AOUS)**: If X denotes the number of data points per class, in this method, if the data points in a particular class are greater than X, we undersample the data by randomly removing the essays. Otherwise, the data is oversampled by simply adding Reddit comments with maximum lengths from GoEmotions dataset (sorted by lengths) (Fig 3). As the average length of comments in GoEmotions dataset is 12 and average length of essays in WASSA dataset is 84, the comments with maximum length are chosen for oversampling. We take X as 400 in our experiments.
- **Random synthetic oversampling (RSO)**: We observe a significant difference in the average comment length of GoEmotions dataset and the average essay length in the WASSA dataset. To avoid disturbing the length distribution of the WASSA dataset after oversampling, we create synthetic essays by concatenating multiple random comments with same emotion (Fig 4). We match the distribution of lengths of the synthetically generated essays from GoEmotions dataset with the distribution of the original dataset using "Systematic Sampling." We eliminate the deficit in each class by adding synthetically generated essays.
- **Augmented Oversampling (AOS)**: X denotes the highest number of data points per class. If the number of data points is less than X, the data is oversampled by adding comments from GoEmotions dataset with the highest lengths. (Fig 3)

Model	**Dataset**	**macro F1**
BERT$_{base}$	AOUS	59.19%
ELECTRA$_{base}$	AOS	58.94%
ELECTRA$_{base}$	RSO	59.06%
ELECTRA$_{base}$	AOUS	59.67%
Ensemble	val	62.76%
	test	53.41%

Table 1: Validation metrics

The data distribution post augmentation is balanced with number of samples in AOS, RSO and AOUS datasets equal to 4528, 4828 and 2800 respectively.

4 System Description

Bidirectional Encoder Representations from Transformers (BERT) (Devlin et al., 2018) is a transformer-based (Vaswani et al., 2017) language model developed by Google.

ELECTRA (Clark et al., 2020) is a variation of BERT, having a different pre-training approach. It requires less compute time compared to BERT.

We performed ablations with many of the present well-known language models — ALBERT (Lan et al., 2019), XLNET (Yang et al., 2019), RoBERTa (Liu et al., 2019) and found BERT and ELECTRA to perform the best.

5 Ensemble Methods

We conducted extensive experimentation and observed some models to perform substantially better than others. We shortlisted the models based on the validation F1-score. We decided to ensemble these models for better performance. We shortlisted four models and used majority voting as our ensemble method: BERT with AOUS, ELECTRA with AOS, ELECTRA with RSO, ELECTRA with AOUS.

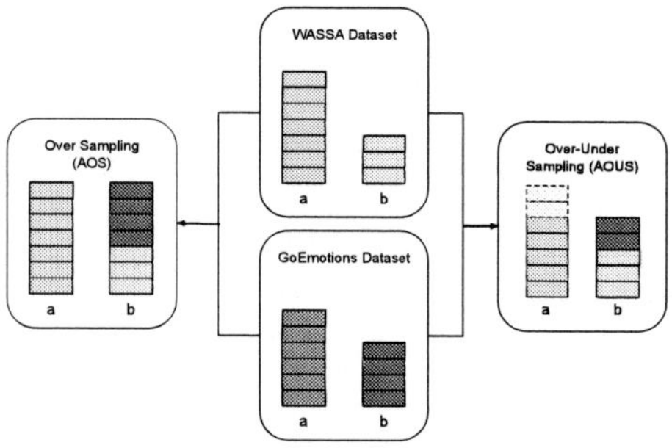

Figure 3: AOS and AOUS

We used the ensemble of the models in Table 1. The confusion matrices of each of these models are shown in Fig 5. The confusion matrix of the resultant ensemble is shown in 6. Note that all confusion matrices are normalized by the number of true samples in each class of the evaluation dataset. We deduce the following observations:

1. When the true label is "disgust," all models confuse the emotions "anger" and "disgust". All models have below average performance on "anger" and "disgust".
2. Models trained on AOUS dataset (c, d in Fig 5) are less prone to confusion in multiple close classes like "disgust", "fear" and "sadness" .
3. The emotions "anger" and "disgust" do not benefit from the ensemble, whereas "fear" suffers a bit. However we observe, the emotions "neutral", "sadness" and "surprise" experience significant gains from this process.

6 Experiments and Results

Our training setup was fairly straightforward. Language model backbone followed by fully connected layer and Softmax is used. CrossEntropy loss was used. We employed the Adam optimizer with $1e-5$ learning rate and batch size of 8. We fixed the seed for `numpy` and `torch` to 3407.

Some of the observations made during our extensive experimentation is as follows:

1. **Batch size 8 outperforms larger batch sizes**: We observed improvements across all models and datasets using a batch size of 8 over 32 or 64. We speculate this is because smaller batch size helps in generalization as the stochasticity of individual batches increase.
2. **ELECTRA fine-tuned on the AOUS dataset outperforms other models**: ELECTRA performs better than BERT for all our augmented datasets. We believe models finetuned on AOUS dataset perform better because AOUS dataset has 400 labels per class, making the dataset balanced while limiting the adulteration induced by the GoEmotions dataset.
3. **Multi-task learning has poor performance**: We experimented with multi-task learning where empathy and distress tasks (Track 1) and emotion classification task (Track 2) were trained together with a shared backbone. We observed that the training was erratic, and the training loss did not converge.
4. **Models are sensitive to data imbalance**: When trained on the original dataset with class imbalance, the model is biased towards predicting classes with more training samples. We used data augmentation techniques mentioned in Section 3 to tackle this issue. After handling the class imbalance with data augmentation, the macro F1 score of the BERT model increased from 32.19% to 59.19%.
5. **Emotion "joy" vs "surprise"**: These are the only two positive emotions in the dataset. We expected all of the models to confuse these emotions as they are semantically similar. However, to our "surprise", we observed the models performed spectacularly on these two emotions. We think this is because "surprise" and "joy" have distinct appearances in the corpus. "surprise" examples have some sort of exclamation or a questioning tone in them. This leaves us with "joy", which happens to be the only positive emotion along with "surprise" in the corpus.
6. **Randomly created synthetic essays provide little understanding**: We observed the model trained on RSO augmented data often predicts

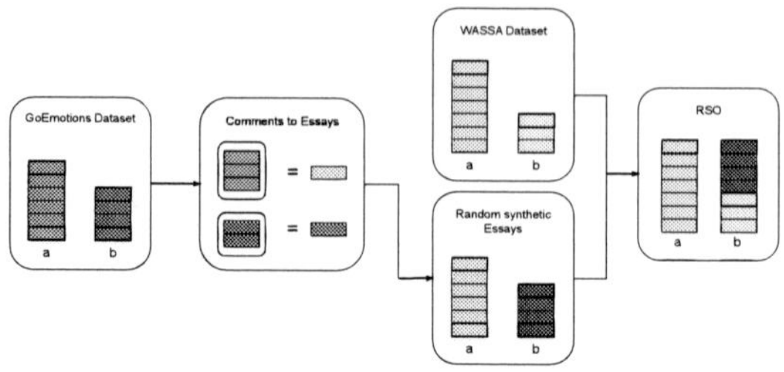

Figure 4: RSO

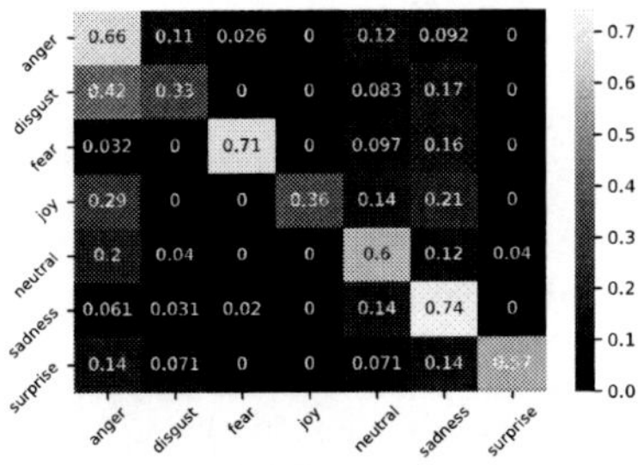

(a) ELECTRA with AOS

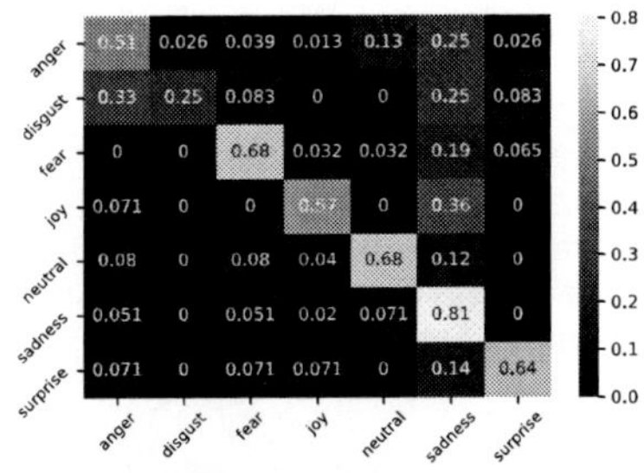

(b) ELECTRA with RSO

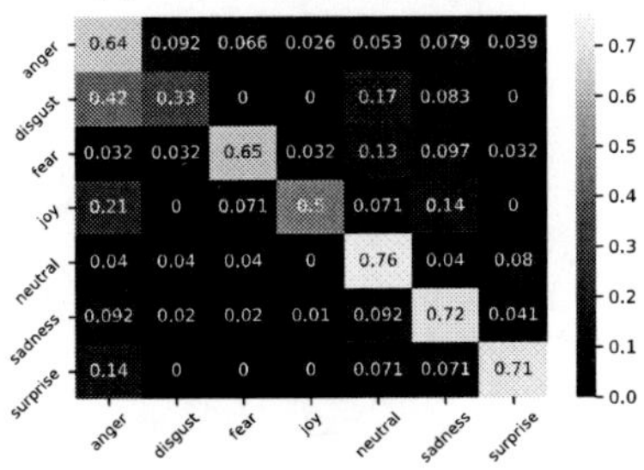

(c) ELECTRA with AOUS

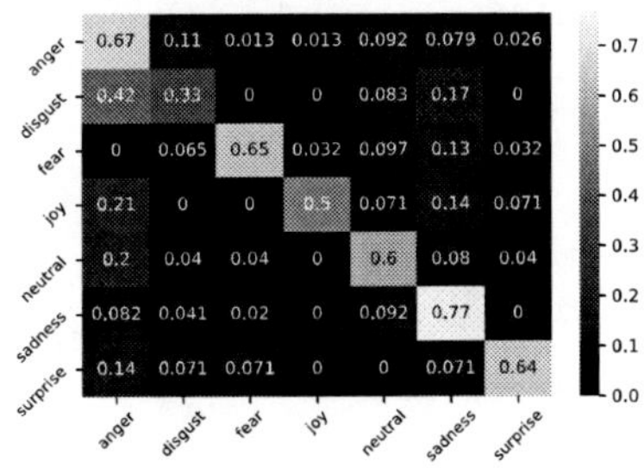

(d) BERT with AOUS

Figure 5: Confusion matrices of our models.

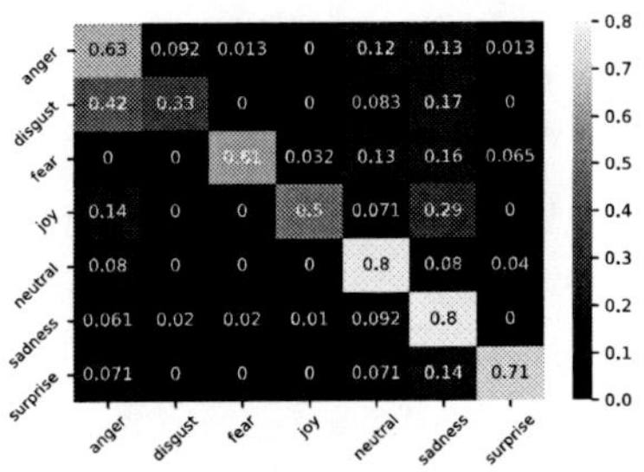

Figure 6: Confusion matrix of our final ensemble.

other emotions as "sadness" (Fig 5 (b)). We speculate this is because there was no addition of synthetically generated data for the "sadness" class as it is the largest class. We further hypothesize the synthetic data in RSO, being randomly concatenated, disrupts the context of the entire essay as a whole. However, we still use the model in our final ensemble since it performed well amongst the population. We think this occurs due to multiple factors being simultaneously at play. Further investigation is a promising future direction.

The validation confusion matrix of all the four models are displayed in Fig 5 and their results in Table 1. We present the following statistics. (True Positive (TP), standard deviation (σ), mean (μ))

1. **The highest TP** μ is for **"sadness"** and **"fear"** emotion with 76 and 67.25 values respectively. Interestingly both of these emotions also have the least TP σ with 3.92 and 2.87 values respectively.
2. **The least TP** μ is for **"disgust"** and **"joy"** emotion with 31 and 48.5 values respectively. "joy" also accounting for the highest TP σ with 8.81 value which infers that all the models are agreeing on different datapoints to classify as "joy". Whereas "disgust" has one of the least TP σ with 4.0 just following "fear" and "sadness", this suggests that all the models are able to agree on a very small sample space of the class data to be classified as "disgust".

7 Conclusion

In this work, we have explored an application of BERT and ELECTRA as a means to the task of emotion classification. Various data sampling techniques were used to overcome the large imbalance in data. In the end the best metrics were achieved by using majority voting of the 4 best models as an ensemble. We foresee multiple future directions, including multi-task learning of multiple tasks with a shared backbone, pretraining on the entire GoEmotions dataset, as well as studying and rectifying spurious behaviour of "anger" and "disgust" labels.

References

Hassan Alhuzali and Sophia Ananiadou. 2021. SpanEmo: Casting multi-label emotion classification as span-prediction. In *Proceedings of the 16th Conference of the European Chapter of the Association for Computational Linguistics: Main Volume*, pages 1573–1584, Online. Association for Computational Linguistics.

Tom Brown, Benjamin Mann, Nick Ryder, Melanie Subbiah, Jared D Kaplan, Prafulla Dhariwal, Arvind Neelakantan, Pranav Shyam, Girish Sastry, Amanda Askell, et al. 2020. Language models are few-shot learners. *Advances in neural information processing systems*, 33:1877–1901.

Kevin Clark, Minh-Thang Luong, Quoc V Le, and Christopher D Manning. 2020. Electra: Pre-training text encoders as discriminators rather than generators. *arXiv preprint arXiv:2003.10555*.

Dorottya Demszky, Dana Movshovitz-Attias, Jeongwoo Ko, Alan Cowen, Gaurav Nemade, and Sujith Ravi. 2020. Goemotions: A dataset of fine-grained emotions. *arXiv preprint arXiv:2005.00547*.

Jacob Devlin, Ming-Wei Chang, Kenton Lee, and Kristina Toutanova. 2018. BERT: pre-training of deep bidirectional transformers for language understanding. *CoRR*, abs/1810.04805.

Paul Ekman. 1992. An argument for basic emotions. *Cognition and Emotion*, 6(3-4):169–200.

Zhenzhong Lan, Mingda Chen, Sebastian Goodman, Kevin Gimpel, Piyush Sharma, and Radu Soricut. 2019. ALBERT: A lite BERT for self-supervised learning of language representations. *CoRR*, abs/1909.11942.

Yinhan Liu, Myle Ott, Naman Goyal, Jingfei Du, Mandar Joshi, Danqi Chen, Omer Levy, Mike Lewis, Luke Zettlemoyer, and Veselin Stoyanov. 2019. Roberta: A robustly optimized BERT pretraining approach. *CoRR*, abs/1907.11692.

Saif Mohammad, Felipe Bravo-Marquez, Mohammad Salameh, and Svetlana Kiritchenko. 2018. SemEval-2018 task 1: Affect in tweets. In *Proceedings of The 12th International Workshop on Semantic Evaluation*, pages 1–17, New Orleans, Louisiana. Association for Computational Linguistics.

Ashritha R Murthy and K M Anil Kumar. 2021. A review of different approaches for detecting emotion from text. *IOP Conference Series: Materials Science and Engineering*, 1110(1):012009.

Hadas Okon-Singer, Talma Hendler, Luiz Pessoa, and Alexander J. Shackman. 2015. The neurobiology of emotion–cognition interactions: fundamental questions and strategies for future research. *Frontiers in Human Neuroscience*, 9.

Ashish Vaswani, Noam Shazeer, Niki Parmar, Jakob Uszkoreit, Llion Jones, Aidan N Gomez, Łukasz Kaiser, and Illia Polosukhin. 2017. Attention is all you need. *Advances in neural information processing systems*, 30.

Zhilin Yang, Zihang Dai, Yiming Yang, Jaime G. Carbonell, Ruslan Salakhutdinov, and Quoc V. Le. 2019. Xlnet: Generalized autoregressive pretraining for language understanding. *CoRR*, abs/1906.08237.

Team IITP-AINLPML at WASSA 2022: Empathy Detection, Emotion Classification and Personality Detection

Soumitra Ghosh, Dhirendra Maurya, Asif Ekbal* and **Pushpak Bhattacharyya**
Department of Computer Science and Engineering
Indian Institute of Technology Patna, Patna, India
{ghosh.soumitra2,mauryadhirendra563,pushpakbh}@gmail.com,asif@iitp.ac.in
* : corresponding author

Abstract

Computational comprehension and identifying emotional components in language have been critical in enhancing human-computer connection in recent years. The WASSA 2022 Shared Task introduced four tracks and released a dataset of news stories: Track-1 for Empathy and Distress Prediction, Track-2 for Emotion classification, Track-3 for Personality prediction, and Track-4 for Interpersonal Reactivity Index prediction at the essay level. This paper describes our participation in the WASSA 2022 shared task on the tasks mentioned above. We developed multi-task deep learning methods to address Tracks 1 and 2 and machine learning models for Track 3 and 4. Our developed systems achieved average Pearson scores of 0.483, 0.05, and 0.08 for Track 1, 3, and 4, respectively, and a macro F1 score of 0.524 for Track 2 on the test set. We ranked 8th, 11th, 2nd and 2nd for tracks 1, 2, 3, and 4 respectively.

1 Introduction

With the growing interest in the human-computer interface, emotions are considered for listing differences between machines and living beings. Humans' inherent knowledge of these emotions is hard to pass on to machines. Hence, the introduced WASSA 2022 shared task of Empathy Detection, Emotion Classification, and Personality Detection is challenging. Although some research has been done by Gibson et al. (2015) and Khanpour et al. (2017), they have several important shortcomings, such as the simplistic definition of empathy and the lack of these corpora in the public domain.

The WASSA 2022 Shared Task consists of the following four major sub-tasks:

- Track 1: *Empathy Prediction (EMP)*: predict both the empathy concern and the personal distress scores at the essay-level
- Track 2: *Emotion Classification (EMO)*: categorize an essay into the correct emotion class
- Track 3: *Personality Prediction (PER)*: predict the personality of an author across five primary personality traits.
- Track 4: *Interpersonal Reactivity Index Prediction (IRI)*: predict the four primary aspects of empathy of an author.

In our approach, we have used a pre-trained language model to extract the features from the textual input (essay) and develop - (A). a multi-task system to predict empathic concern and personal distress score jointly (for Track 1), (B). a multi-task system that categorizes an essay into appropriate emotion class and also detects the presence or absence of empathy and distress in it. For tracks 3 and 4, we solely consider the demographic information in the dataset to predict various personality traits and interpersonal reactivity index scores.

2 Related Work

Because of language disparities across locales, empathy and distress might also vary dependent on demographics (Lin et al., 2018; Loveys et al., 2018). More recently, (Guda et al., 2021) proposed a demographic-aware empathy modeling framework based on Bidirectional Encoder Representations from Transformers (BERT) and demographic characteristics. The first publicly accessible gold-standard dataset for text-based empathy and distress prediction was introduced by Buechel et al. (2018b). Sharma et al. (2020) investigated a multi-task RoBERTa-based bi-encoder paradigm for comprehending empathy in text-based health support. Zhou and Jurgens (2020) investigated the link between distress, condolence, and empathy in online support groups using nested regression models.

Many research (Abdul-Mageed and Ungar, 2017; Nozza et al., 2017) have given various strategies for emotion recognition. The effectiveness of using transformer encoders for emotion detection was investigated by Adoma et al. (2020). The WASSA-2021 shared task (Tafreshi et al., 2021) addressed

Proceedings of the 12th Workshop on Computational Approaches to Subjectivity, Sentiment & Social Media Analysis, pages 255 - 260
May 26, 2022

Essay	Demographic Factors	Empathy	Distress	Emotion	Pers. Scores	IRI Pers. index
This person's actions were way over the top! While I may not necessarily like that Trump is in office but I still didn't get my way doesn't mean that I would act like this! This person took away from others and should be punished for what they did.	*Gen:* 2 *Edu:* 6 *Rac:* 1 *Age:* 23 *Inc:* 22000	*bin:* 0 *score:* 3.5	*bin:* 0 score: 1.375	anger	*c:* 2.5 *o:* 5 *e:* 3.5 *a:* 6 *s:* 6.5	*pt:* 4.571 *pd:* 2.857 *f:* 1.857 *ec:* 3.429
so i just read this article, a very interesting one. you all need to read it to understand what it is really about. there is a way the author puts things in a very simple way for everyone to understand. i would encourage you all to find it and read it. it will be worth your time.	*Gen:* 2 *Edu:* 6 *Rac:* 1 *Age:* 23 *Inc:* 22000	*bin:* 1 *score:* 4.333	*bin:* 0 score: 1	joy	*c:* 2.5 *o:* 3.5 *e:* 5 *a:* 5 *s:* 5.5	*pt:* 3 *pd:* 3 *f:* 3.286 *ec:* 2.857

Table 1: Sample instances from the WASSA 2022 training set.

the prediction of empathy (Track 1) and emotion (Track 2) in text. Personality detection studies (Yang et al., 2021; Ren et al., 2021) utilising computational approaches have lately gained traction, particularly language models like BERT (Devlin et al., 2019). Majority of works on this issue have employed statistical analysis (Ji et al., 2021) and feature engineering (Bharadwaj et al., 2018).

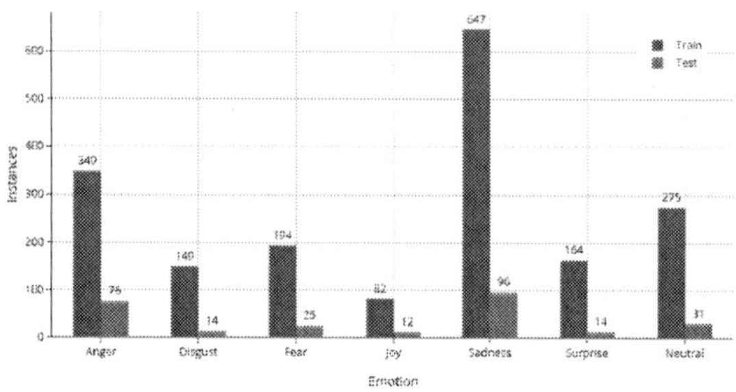

Figure 1: Data distribution over emotion classes.

3 Data

The shared task organizers made available an expanded version of the dataset from Buechel et al. (2018a). Table 1 displays a few of datapoints from the released dataset's training set. Each data instance in the train/development set consists of the following information - the essay, a binary label and a continuous score for each of the concepts of empathy and distress, an emotion class and various other demographic features[1], personality (PER) features[2] and Interpersonal Reactivity Index (IRI) features[3]. The empathy, distress and the five PER features scores are in the range (1, 7). The four IRI features scores are in the range (1, 5). Ekman's (Ekman, 1992) basic emotions plus a neutral class is considered for the annotations in the emotion classification task. The data distribution over the various emotion classes are shown in Figure 1.

Dataset	Instances
Train	1860
Development	270
Test	525

Table 2: Data distribution over various splits.

Emotion	Instances
Anger	1206
Disgust	1096
Fear	1095
Joy	8079
Sadness	6261
Surprise	2187
Neutral	8638

Table 3: Data distribution over emotion classes in the augmented dataset.

Table 2 depicts the data distribution across the train, development, and test sets. The volume of the released data was insufficient for fine-tuning large language models like BERT. We used a transfer learning-based strategy to improve overall system performance to address this. We start by compiling a collection of emotion annotated textual instances from the following three popular publicly available datasets: (A). ISEAR (Scherer and Wallbott, 1994), (B.) Crowdflower's Text Emotion dataset[4], and, (C). SemEval 2018 Task 1 English Emotion Classification dataset (Mohammad et al., 2018). Our selection of external datasets was made solely based on their accessibility and popularity. We urge the inclusion of other emotion-annotated datasets or consideration of an entirely different set of datasets. The data distribution over the emotion classes is shown in Table 3.

4 System Description

This section describes the various developed methodologies to address the different tasks in the WASSA 2022 shared task.

[1] *Gender (Gen), Education (Edu), Race (Rac), Age, Income (Inc)*

[2] conscientiousness (*c*), openness (*o*), extraversion (*e*), agreeableness (*a*), stability (*s*)

[3] perspective_taking (*pt*), personal_distress (*pd*), fantasy (*f*), empathic_concern (*ec*)

[4] `https://data.world/crowdflower/sentiment-analysis-in-text`

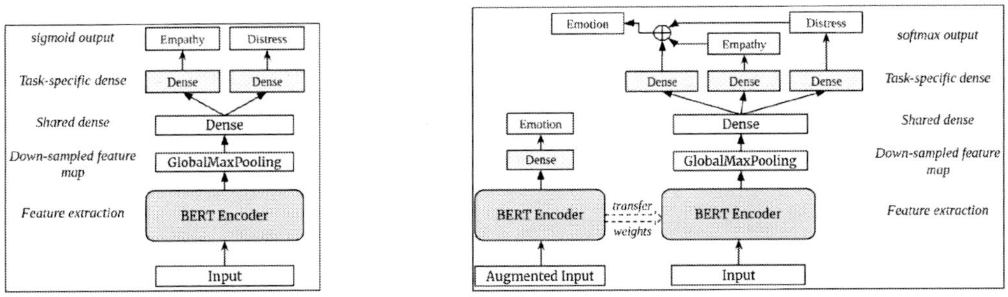

(a) Empathy prediction system.

(b) Emotion classification system.

Figure 2: Multi-task architectures for the primary tasks of Empathy-Distress prediction and Emotion classification.

4.1 Track 1: Empathy Prediction

We fine-tune the base version of the pre-trained BERT[5] encoder on the essays in the training set and extract the features from the special CLS token of the last encoder layer of BERT. A global max-pooling operation is done on the features for dimensionality reduction, after which it is passed through a shared dense layer. We add two task-specific dense layers, followed by respective output layers for the empathy and distress prediction tasks. The overall architecture is shown in Figure 2a.

4.2 Track 2: Emotion Classification

Due to the small size of the released training set of WASSA 2022, we leverage the effectiveness of transfer learning to develop an effective system for emotion classification. First, we train a BERT encoder on the augmented emotion dataset (discussed in Section 3) and transfer the weights of the BERT layers to fine-tune another BERT encoder dedicated to the emotion classification task of Track 2. This enables transferring the more general aspects of an emotion classifier. Further layers are added to the setup to capture more specific knowledge about our task's dataset. The rest of the architecture is similar to in Figure 2b, except that we make the emotion-specific features of empathy and distress aware by adding the softmax outputs for the empathy and distress detection tasks with the tasks-specific dense output for the emotion task.

4.3 Track 3 and Track 4: Personality and Interpersonal Reactivity Index Predictions

We empirically observed extremely low Pearson scores when using the essay information to predict scores for any of the tasks in PER and IRI tracks using deep learning methods. On the other hand, we obtained better scores by employing demographic information such as gender, race, education, age, and information to train support vector machine (SVM) systems for the PER and IRI tasks. Specifically, we use all the above-mentioned five demographic factors to train separate SVMs for each of the following tasks: *openness, extraversion, stability* (from PER track) and *personal distress, fantasy* (from the IRI track). We use only the age information as feature to train SVMs for predicting scores for *conscientiousness* and *agreeableness*, whereas gender feature for the tasks of *perspective taking* and *empathic concern*.

5 Results and Discussion

We discuss the hyper-parameters in our experiments, results, and analysis in this section. We report the results from our experiments considering the development set as our test dataset, as the gold standard annotations of the test are withheld in the Shared Task of WASSA-2022.

5.1 Experimental setup

We employ ReLU activation for the dense layers in Figure 2a and Figure 2b. The output layers in Figure 2a and Figure 2b use sigmoid and softmax activations respectively. The grid search approach is used to set the loss weights in Figure 2b as well as the units in the shared and dense layers in both figures. While we use 128 units in both the shared layers, we use 16 and 64 units in the task-specific dense layers for Figure 2a and Figure 2b respectively. We obtained the best results on the development set with the following hyperparameters: (A). loss weights in Figure 2b as 0.3 for the empathy and distress detection tasks and 1 for the emotion classification task; (B). sequence length of 120 and 200 in Figure 2a and Figure 2b respectively; (C). batch size = 16 (for maximum utilization of the GPU)

[5]imported from the Tensorflow Hub (`https://www.tensorflow.org/hub`) library

and learning rate = 2e-5; (D). epochs as 15 and 100 for Figure 2a and Figure 2b respectively. We use categorical cross-entropy and mean squared error loss functions for the track 1 and track 2 systems, respectively. We use Adam optimizer (Kingma and Ba, 2015) to train the above systems. A dropout (Srivastava et al., 2014) of 20% is employed after the dense layers to avoid overfitting.

5.2 Results

We observe from Table 4 and Table 5 that the multi-task (MT) systems outperform the single-task (ST) systems commendably. We show the performance of our systems on the development (D) and test sets (T) in Tables 4, 5 and 6. For Track 1, our developed MT system obtained an average Pearson score (APS) of 0.483 on the test set. The task-wise results are shown in Table 4. For the emotion classification task (track 2), our developed MT system obtained a macro-F1 score of 0.524. The transfer learning strategy proved beneficial as it helped us attain a gain of 7.4% F1-score on the development set. We empirically observed that learning the correlated tasks of empathy and distress helped elevate individual tasks' performances. Also, when the model is made aware of the empathy and distress information from the textual input in the form of essays, the performance of the emotion categorization job improves. We observe unexpected low scores on the test set compared to the development set for tracks 2, 3 and 4. We intuitively assume that the instances in the test set are drawn from a different distribution than the train or development sets. We want to investigate more on this observation in future work.

Model	$\text{Pearson}^{\text{Empathy}}$	$\text{Pearson}^{\text{Distress}}$
ST^D	0.39	0.41
MT^D	0.465	0.467
MT^T	0.479	0.488

Table 4: Track 1 results. ST: single-task; MT: multi-task; D: development set; T: test set

Model	F1 (%)	Accuracy (%)
ST^D	49.26	59.25
MT^D	59.82	66.67
MT^T	52.4	58.5

Table 5: Track 2 results.

We experimented with deep learning methods such as BERT and recurrent neural networks using the essays as input but observed extremely low scores for tracks 3 and 4. However, when demographic factors associated with an essay's author are considered features, better scores are obtained for the same. Furthermore, we observed that the age feature alone provides best results for *conscientiousness* and *agreeableness*, whereas gender feature for of *perspective taking* and *empathic concern*, indicating a significant link between them.

Track	APS^{D}	APS^{T}
PER	0.253	0.05
IRI	0.281	0.08

Table 6: Track 3 and 4 results.

The overall low scores for all four tracks are primarily due to the small size of the released training data. Additionally, for the emotion task, the available dataset suffers from severe data imbalance problems over the different emotion classes leading to biasedness in predictions towards the over-represented classes.

6 Conclusion

This paper presents our approaches to address the various tasks introduced in the WASSA 2022 shared task for empathy detection, emotion classification, and personality detection. To exploit the commonality among correlated tasks such as empathy and distress and emotion with empathy and distress, we developed multi-task systems built on pre-trained BERT models for - (A) empathy and distress detection tasks; (B). emotion classification (primary task) and empathy and distress classification (auxiliary tasks). We also presented SVM algorithms trained on various demographic features to predict personality traits and interpersonal reactivity index scores. We empirically observed how jointly learning correlated tasks such as empathy and distress, emotion with empathy and distress, helps to improve overall system performance. Our developed systems achieved average Pearson scores of 0.483, 0.05, and 0.08 for Track 1, 3 and 4, respectively, and a macro F1 score of 0.524 for Track 2 on the test set. We ranked 8th, 11th, 2nd and 2nd for the tracks 1, 2, 3 and 4 respectively.

We want to improve our multi-tasking-based systems in the future by adding lexicon features from available lexical resources alongside textual input for the EMP and EMO tasks. We also want to develop an effective technique for combining contextual information from an author's essays with demographic data to predict PER and IRI scores.

References

Muhammad Abdul-Mageed and Lyle Ungar. 2017. Emonet: Fine-grained emotion detection with gated recurrent neural networks. In *Proceedings of the 55th annual meeting of the association for computational linguistics (volume 1: Long papers)*, pages 718–728.

Acheampong Francisca Adoma, Nunoo-Mensah Henry, Wenyu Chen, and Niyongabo Rubungo Andre. 2020. Recognizing emotions from texts using a bert-based approach. In *2020 17th International Computer Conference on Wavelet Active Media Technology and Information Processing (ICCWAMTIP)*, pages 62–66. IEEE.

Srilakshmi Bharadwaj, Srinidhi Sridhar, Rahul Choudhary, and Ramamoorthy Srinath. 2018. Persona traits identification based on myers-briggs type indicator(mbti) - A text classification approach. In *2018 International Conference on Advances in Computing, Communications and Informatics, ICACCI 2018, Bangalore, India, September 19-22, 2018*, pages 1076–1082. IEEE.

Sven Buechel, Anneke Buffone, Barry Slaff, Lyle Ungar, and João Sedoc. 2018a. Modeling empathy and distress in reaction to news stories. In *Proceedings of the 2018 Conference on Empirical Methods in Natural Language Processing*, pages 4758–4765.

Sven Buechel, Anneke Buffone, Barry Slaff, Lyle H. Ungar, and João Sedoc. 2018b. Modeling empathy and distress in reaction to news stories. In *Proceedings of the 2018 Conference on Empirical Methods in Natural Language Processing, Brussels, Belgium, October 31 - November 4, 2018*, pages 4758–4765. Association for Computational Linguistics.

Jacob Devlin, Ming-Wei Chang, Kenton Lee, and Kristina Toutanova. 2019. BERT: pre-training of deep bidirectional transformers for language understanding. In *Proceedings of the 2019 Conference of the North American Chapter of the Association for Computational Linguistics: Human Language Technologies, NAACL-HLT 2019, Minneapolis, MN, USA, June 2-7, 2019, Volume 1 (Long and Short Papers)*, pages 4171–4186. Association for Computational Linguistics.

Paul Ekman. 1992. An argument for basic emotions. *Cognition & emotion*, 6(3-4):169–200.

James Gibson, Nikolaos Malandrakis, Francisco Romero, David C Atkins, and Shrikanth S Narayanan. 2015. Predicting therapist empathy in motivational interviews using language features inspired by psycholinguistic norms. In *Sixteenth annual conference of the international speech communication association.*

Bhanu Prakash Reddy Guda, Aparna Garimella, and Niyati Chhaya. 2021. Empathbert: A bert-based framework for demographic-aware empathy prediction. In *Proceedings of the 16th Conference of the European Chapter of the Association for Computational Linguistics: Main Volume, EACL 2021, Online, April 19 - 23, 2021*, pages 3072–3079. Association for Computational Linguistics.

Shaoxiong Ji, Shirui Pan, Xue Li, Erik Cambria, Guodong Long, and Zi Huang. 2021. Suicidal ideation detection: A review of machine learning methods and applications. *IEEE Trans. Comput. Soc. Syst.*, 8(1):214–226.

Hamed Khanpour, Cornelia Caragea, and Prakhar Biyani. 2017. Identifying empathetic messages in online health communities. In *Proceedings of the Eighth International Joint Conference on Natural Language Processing (Volume 2: Short Papers)*, pages 246–251.

Diederik P. Kingma and Jimmy Ba. 2015. Adam: A method for stochastic optimization. In *3rd International Conference on Learning Representations, ICLR 2015, San Diego, CA, USA, May 7-9, 2015, Conference Track Proceedings.*

Bill Y. Lin, Frank F. Xu, Kenny Q. Zhu, and Seung-won Hwang. 2018. Mining cross-cultural differences and similarities in social media. In *Proceedings of the 56th Annual Meeting of the Association for Computational Linguistics, ACL 2018, Melbourne, Australia, July 15-20, 2018, Volume 1: Long Papers*, pages 709–719. Association for Computational Linguistics.

Kate Loveys, Jonathan Torrez, Alex Fine, Glen Moriarty, and Glen Coppersmith. 2018. Cross-cultural differences in language markers of depression online. In *Proceedings of the Fifth Workshop on Computational Linguistics and Clinical Psychology: From Keyboard to Clinic, CLPsych@NAACL-HTL, New Orleans, LA, USA, June 2018*, pages 78–87. Association for Computational Linguistics.

Saif Mohammad, Felipe Bravo-Marquez, Mohammad Salameh, and Svetlana Kiritchenko. 2018. Semeval-2018 task 1: Affect in tweets. In *Proceedings of the 12th international workshop on semantic evaluation*, pages 1–17.

Debora Nozza, Elisabetta Fersini, and Enza Messina. 2017. A multi-view sentiment corpus. In *Proceedings of the 15th Conference of the European Chapter of the Association for Computational Linguistics: Volume 1, Long Papers*, pages 273–280.

Zhancheng Ren, Qiang Shen, Xiaolei Diao, and Hao Xu. 2021. A sentiment-aware deep learning approach for personality detection from text. *Information Processing & Management*, 58(3):102532.

Klaus R Scherer and Harald G Wallbott. 1994. Evidence for universality and cultural variation of differential emotion response patterning. *Journal of personality and social psychology*, 66(2):310.

Ashish Sharma, Adam S. Miner, David C. Atkins, and Tim Althoff. 2020. A computational approach to understanding empathy expressed in text-based mental health support. In *Proceedings of the 2020 Conference on Empirical Methods in Natural Language Processing, EMNLP 2020, Online, November 16-20, 2020*, pages 5263–5276. Association for Computational Linguistics.

Nitish Srivastava, Geoffrey E. Hinton, Alex Krizhevsky, Ilya Sutskever, and Ruslan Salakhutdinov. 2014. Dropout: a simple way to prevent neural networks from overfitting. *J. Mach. Learn. Res.*, 15(1):1929–1958.

Shabnam Tafreshi, Orphée De Clercq, Valentin Barriere, Sven Buechel, João Sedoc, and Alexandra Balahur. 2021. Wassa 2021 shared task: Predicting empathy and emotion in reaction to news stories. In *Proceedings of the Eleventh Workshop on Computational Approaches to Subjectivity, Sentiment and Social Media Analysis*, pages 92–104.

Feifan Yang, Xiaojun Quan, Yunyi Yang, and Jianxing Yu. 2021. Multi-document transformer for personality detection. In *Thirty-Fifth AAAI Conference on Artificial Intelligence, AAAI 2021, Thirty-Third Conference on Innovative Applications of Artificial Intelligence, IAAI 2021, The Eleventh Symposium on Educational Advances in Artificial Intelligence, EAAI 2021, Virtual Event, February 2-9, 2021*, pages 14221–14229. AAAI Press.

Naitian Zhou and David Jurgens. 2020. Condolence and empathy in online communities. In *Proceedings of the 2020 Conference on Empirical Methods in Natural Language Processing, EMNLP 2020, Online, November 16-20, 2020*, pages 609–626. Association for Computational Linguistics.

Transformer-based Architecture for Empathy Prediction and Emotion Classification

Himil Vasava **Pramegh Uikey** **Gaurav Wasnik** **Raksha Sharma**
Indian Institute of Technology Roorkee (IIT Roorkee)
{vasava_h, uikey_p, wasnik_g, raksha.sharma}@cs.iitr.ac.in

Abstract

This paper describes the contribution of team PHG to the WASSA 2022 shared task on Empathy Prediction and Emotion Classification. The broad goal of this task was to model an empathy score, a distress score, and the type of emotion associated with the person who had reacted to the essay written in response to a newspaper article. We have used the RoBERTa model for training, and on top of it, five layers are added to finetune the transformer. We also use a few machine learning techniques to augment and upsample the data. Our system achieves a Pearson Correlation Coefficient of 0.488 on Task 1 (Average of Empathy - 0.470 and Distress - 0.506) and Macro F1-score of 0.531 on Task 2.

1 Introduction

Empathy and Distress are quite important regarding human health. Emotion classification in natural languages has been studied for over two decades, and many applications successfully used emotion as their principal component. Empathy utterances can be emotional. Therefore, examining emotion in text-based empathy has a significant impact on predicting empathy. Empathic concern and personal distress are empathic responses that may result when observing someone in discomfort (Fabi et al., 2019). Some news stories are also displayed in this task, and people have reacted to them. The news is disturbing or discomforting to some people. And hence, regarding that, their empathy and distress are noted. This paper presents the WASSA 2022 Shared Task: Predicting Empathy and Emotion in Reaction to News Stories. This shared task included four individual tasks where teams developed models to predict Emotions, empathy, and personality in essays in which people expressed their empathy and distress in reaction to news articles in which an individual or a group of people were harmed. Additionally, the dataset also included the demographic information of the authors of the essays, such as age, gender, ethnicity, income, education level, and personality information. The shared task consisted of four tracks (optional):

Track 1: Empathy Prediction (EMP) task consists of predicting both the empathy concern and the personal distress. (Evaluation based on an average of Pearson correlation (Benesty et al., 2009) of empathy and distress).

Track 2: Emotion Classification (EMO) consists of predicting the emotion (sadness, joy, disgust, surprise, anger, or fear, taken from the six basic emotions (Ekman and Friesen, 1971) also including neutral) at the essay-level (Evaluation based on the macro F1-score).

Track 3: Personality Prediction (PER), which consists in predicting the personality of the essay writer, knowing all their essays and the news article from which they reacted (Evaluation based on the average of Pearson correlation over Personality values (Komarraju et al., 2011) - conscientiousness, Openness, Extraversion, Agreeableness, and Stability).

Track 4: Interpersonal Reactivity Index Prediction (IRI) consists of predicting the personality of the essay writer. (Evaluation based on an average of Pearson correlation over IRI values - fantasy, perspective taking, empathetic concern, personal distress).

We participated in only the first two tasks.

2 Related Work

Over the last few years, earnest endeavors have been made in the NLP community to analyze empathy and distress. For text-based empathy prediction, (Buechel et al., 2018) laid a firm foundation for predicting Batson's (Batson et al., 1987) empathic concern and personal distress scores in reaction to news articles. They present the first publicly available gold-standard dataset for text-based empathy and distress prediction. To annotate emotions in text, classical studies in NLP suggest categorical

Proceedings of the 12th Workshop on Computational Approaches to Subjectivity, Sentiment & Social Media Analysis, pages 261 - 264
May 26, 2022

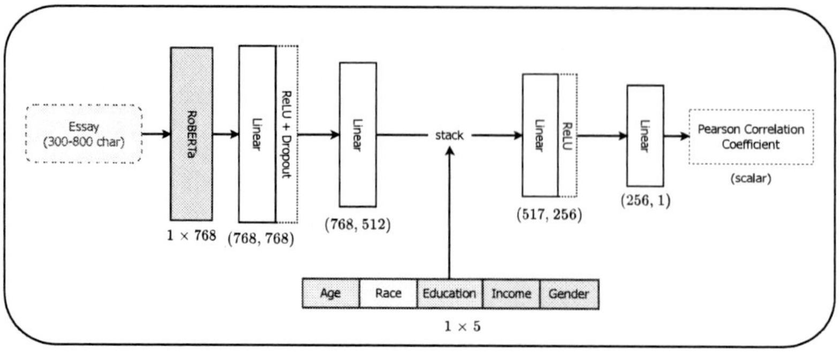

Figure 1: System Architecture

Set	Examples
Train	1860
Dev	270
Test	525

Table 1: Train-dev-test split

tagsets, and most studies are focussed on basic emotion models that psychological emotion models offer. The most popular one is the Ekman 6 basic emotions (Ekman and Friesen, 1971). The emotions presented in this dataset are the same six emotions by Ekman plus one extra emotion (neutral).

3 Dataset

The dataset is an extension to the one provided by (Buechel et al., 2018). For all the tasks, a train-dev-test split was provided. The dataset consists of essays collected from participants who had read news articles about a person, a group of people, or disturbing situations. The dataset had an essay (300-800 characters), empathy score, a distress score, emotion label, and other demographic information (age, gender, race, education, income) as well as personality information (conscientiousness, openness, extraversion, agreeableness, stability) and interpersonal reactivity index (IRI) scores (fantasy, perspective taking, empathetic concern, personal distress).

3.1 Data Augmentation

A single sentence does not always convey the information required to translate it into other languages; we sometimes need to specialize words that are ambiguous in the source languages (Sugiyama and Yoshinaga, 2019). So, we used back translation (Edunov et al., 2018) for text augmentation. The idea here was to have different sentences having the same meaning for training. Step 1: Select the essay (English).
Step 2: Select a random language and convert the essay to that language.
Step 3: Now translate that converted essay back to English.

We used Google translate API for translating essays back and forth. Every example was translated to one other language, and hence after back translation, the total number of samples was doubled (3720). Data augmentation improved the performance, as shown in the Table 2.

4 System Description

4.1 Empathy Prediction

Transformers (Vaswani et al., 2017) have outperformed recurrent neural networks (RNNs) in natural language generation (Kasai et al., 2021). For this task, we had to predict empathy and distress scores which had been done by training the same model by keeping the targets different (empathy for model 1 and distress for model 2). The approach used is based on fine-tuning RoBERta model (Liu et al., 2019) separately for empathy and distress. To take the essay as input to the RoBERTa model, initially, tokenization (Webster and Kit, 1992) was required. The input tokens were made using the Roberta Tokenizer imported from the transformer library. The loss function used was Mean Squared Error (MSE). No parameters were frozen (all of them were trainable), and on top of it, five layers were trained (to make the network deeper). Four layers were linear, while one was a dropout layer (to prevent overfitting). In the pre-final layer, five additional demographic features were taken as input.

The model was trained on both the augmented

Metric	Original	Augmented
Macro F1-Score	0.5174	0.5311
Micro Recall	0.6152	0.6114
Micro Precision	0.6152	0.6114
Micro F1-Score	0.6152	0.6114
Macro Recall	0.5054	0.5288
Macro Precision	0.5461	0.557
Accuracy	0.6152	0.6114

Table 2: Original vs Augmented on Test set

data and original data. Still, the final submission was made using the model trained on the augmented data as it resulted in a higher Pearson Correlation Coefficient.

4.2 Emotion Classification

This was a multi-classification task, i.e., to classify the emotions into seven labels. Here also, we fine-tuned RoBERTa model (Liu et al., 2019) with the same five layers, just changing the output neurons to 7 instead of 1. We had used Cross-Entropy Loss as the loss function (which already has a softmax layer). We also upsampled the dataset as it was imbalanced. Highly imbalanced data poses added difficulty, as most learners will exhibit bias towards the majority class and, in extreme cases, may ignore the minority class altogether (Johnson and Khoshgoftaar, 2019). Random over-sampling (Moreo et al., 2016) was performed using the imblearn library. The imbalanced dataset can be seen in figure 2, the minority class being the emotion labeled "joy".

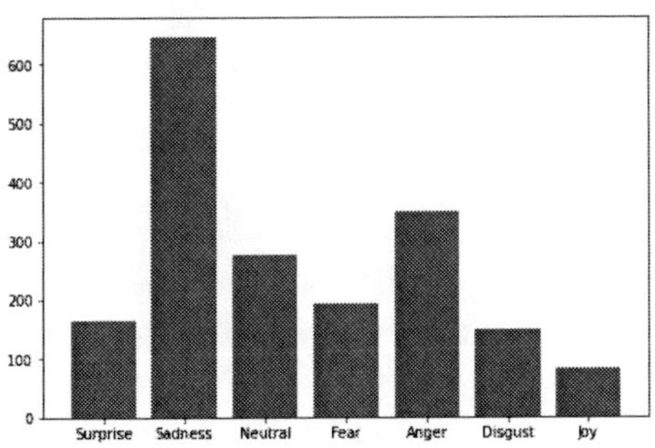

Figure 2: Imbalanced Dataset

4.3 Hyperparameters and other settings

For all the tasks, the learning rate was set to 10^{-5}, and the models were trained using Adam (Kingma and Ba, 2014) as optimizer. The parameters of Adam were Beta(0.9, 0.999) and weight decay as 0. The batch size was set to 8. The dataset was shuffled using Pytorch (Paszke et al., 2019) data loader. All the models were trained on the GPUs provided by Google Colab.

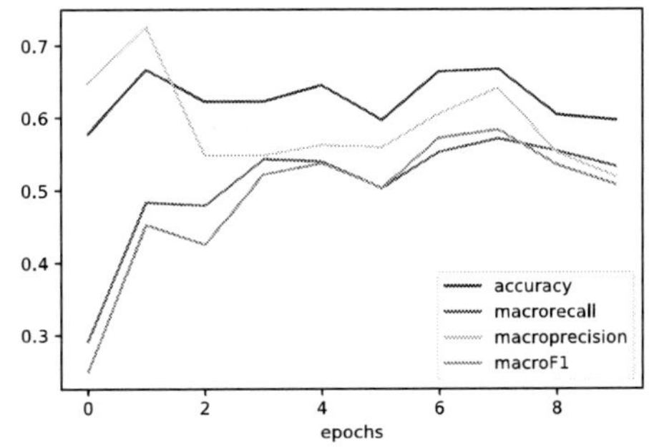

Figure 3: Metrics used for EMO task

5 Results

Our system achieved a Pearson Correlation Coefficient (Benesty et al., 2009) of 0.488 on Task 1. Empathy Pearson Correlation was 0.470, and Distress Pearson Correlation was 0.506. Hence, the average of both was taken as the final score. In the development set, the empathy score was 0.4583 (after the 8th epoch), and the distress score was 0.4415 (after the 4th epoch, as after the score was decreased due to overfitting). Although the empathy score was slightly high, it yielded less score in the test set due to overfitting. While due to early stopping, distress yielded a better score.

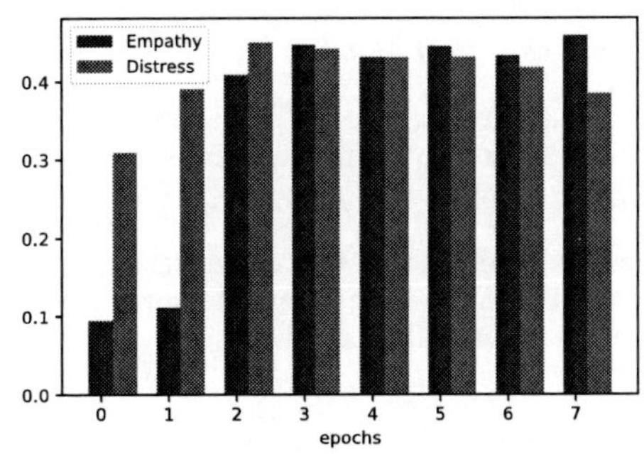

Figure 4: Empathy and Distress scores (Augmented)

We had two different submissions for the emotion classification, one with augmentation and upsampling and one without altering the data. The test scores of both submissions are mentioned in

Table 2. Also, the results of the development set are plotted in figure 4. We tested until ten epochs but decided to submit the model, trained only up to eight epochs as it was overfitting. Hence, the macro F1-score decreased on the development set despite accuracy increasing on the training set.

6 Conclusion

This paper describes our submission to the WASSA 2022 shared task, where we have used the already trained RoBERTa model on a large dataset and then used its power by just finetuning on the given dataset. By the approach we have used, it can also be deduced that text augmentation and upsampling helped in emotion classification and predicting the empathy and distress scores as most of the time, the larger amount of data helps improve the training process of a model.

References

C Daniel Batson, Jim Fultz, and Patricia A Schoenrade. 1987. Distress and empathy: Two qualitatively distinct vicarious emotions with different motivational consequences. *Journal of personality*, 55(1):19–39.

Jacob Benesty, Jingdong Chen, Yiteng Huang, and Israel Cohen. 2009. Pearson correlation coefficient. In *Noise reduction in speech processing*, pages 1–4. Springer.

Sven Buechel, Anneke Buffone, Barry Slaff, Lyle Ungar, and João Sedoc. 2018. Modeling empathy and distress in reaction to news stories. In *Proceedings of the 2018 Conference on Empirical Methods in Natural Language Processing*, pages 4758–4765, Brussels, Belgium. Association for Computational Linguistics.

Sergey Edunov, Myle Ott, Michael Auli, and David Grangier. 2018. Understanding back-translation at scale. *arXiv preprint arXiv:1808.09381*.

Paul Ekman and Wallace V Friesen. 1971. Constants across cultures in the face and emotion. *Journal of personality and social psychology*, 17(2):124.

Sarah Fabi, Lydia Anna Weber, and Hartmut Leuthold. 2019. Empathic concern and personal distress depend on situational but not dispositional factors. *PloS one*, 14(11):e0225102.

Justin M Johnson and Taghi M Khoshgoftaar. 2019. Survey on deep learning with class imbalance. *Journal of Big Data*, 6(1):1–54.

Jungo Kasai, Hao Peng, Yizhe Zhang, Dani Yogatama, Gabriel Ilharco, Nikolaos Pappas, Yi Mao, Weizhu Chen, and Noah A Smith. 2021. Finetuning pretrained transformers into rnns. *arXiv preprint arXiv:2103.13076*.

Diederik P Kingma and Jimmy Ba. 2014. Adam: A method for stochastic optimization. *arXiv preprint arXiv:1412.6980*.

Meera Komarraju, Steven J Karau, Ronald R Schmeck, and Alen Avdic. 2011. The big five personality traits, learning styles, and academic achievement. *Personality and individual differences*, 51(4):472–477.

Yinhan Liu, Myle Ott, Naman Goyal, Jingfei Du, Mandar Joshi, Danqi Chen, Omer Levy, Mike Lewis, Luke Zettlemoyer, and Veselin Stoyanov. 2019. Roberta: A robustly optimized bert pretraining approach. *arXiv preprint arXiv:1907.11692*.

Alejandro Moreo, Andrea Esuli, and Fabrizio Sebastiani. 2016. Distributional random oversampling for imbalanced text classification. In *Proceedings of the 39th International ACM SIGIR conference on Research and Development in Information Retrieval*, pages 805–808.

Adam Paszke, Sam Gross, Francisco Massa, Adam Lerer, James Bradbury, Gregory Chanan, Trevor Killeen, Zeming Lin, Natalia Gimelshein, Luca Antiga, et al. 2019. Pytorch: An imperative style, high-performance deep learning library. *Advances in neural information processing systems*, 32.

Amane Sugiyama and Naoki Yoshinaga. 2019. Data augmentation using back-translation for context-aware neural machine translation. In *Proceedings of the Fourth Workshop on Discourse in Machine Translation (DiscoMT 2019)*, pages 35–44.

Ashish Vaswani, Noam Shazeer, Niki Parmar, Jakob Uszkoreit, Llion Jones, Aidan N Gomez, Łukasz Kaiser, and Illia Polosukhin. 2017. Attention is all you need. *Advances in neural information processing systems*, 30.

Jonathan J Webster and Chunyu Kit. 1992. Tokenization as the initial phase in nlp. In *COLING 1992 Volume 4: The 14th International Conference on Computational Linguistics*.

Prompt-based Pre-trained Model for Personality and Interpersonal Reactivity Prediction

Bin Li[1]*, Yixuan Weng[2]*, Qiya Song[1]*, Fuyan Ma[1], Bin Sun[1], Shutao Li[1]
[1] College of Electrical and Information Engineering, Hunan University
[2] National Laboratory of Pattern Recognition Institute of Automation,
Chinese Academy Sciences, Beijing, 100190, China
{libincn, sqyunb, mafuyan, sunbin611, shutao_li}@hnu.edu.cn, wengsyx@gmail.com

Abstract

This paper describes the LingJing team's method to the Workshop on Computational Approaches to Subjectivity, Sentiment & Social Media Analysis (WASSA) 2022 shared task on Personality Prediction (PER) and Reactivity Index Prediction (IRI). In this paper, we adopt the prompt-based method with the pre-trained language model to accomplish these tasks. Specifically, the prompt is designed to provide knowledge of the extra personalized information for enhancing the pre-trained model. Data augmentation and model ensemble are adopted for obtaining better results. Extensive experiments are performed, which shows the effectiveness of the proposed method. On the final submission, our system achieves a Pearson Correlation Coefficient of **0.2301** and **0.2546** on Track 3 and Track 4 respectively. We ranked 1st on both sub-tasks.

1 Introduction

Personality can be defined as a set of characteristics (e.g., age, income, and hobby), which can reflect the differences of individuals in thinking, emotions, and behaviours (Vora et al., 2020). The power of personality is worth exploring and pervades human lives everywhere (Beck and Jackson, 2022). Personality prediction is an interdisciplinary field spanning from psychology to computer science. However, people's personalities can't be directly observed and measured, but are expressed in activity patterns, and thus can be inferred in that way. Humans tend to covey their personalities through language because it is the most prominent way in such an Internet society. Meanwhile, written text is one of the most important appearances of language.

Consequently, the involvement of machine-learning-based methods in predicting the personality of individuals seems necessary. Over the past 20 years, much progress has been made in natural language processing (NLP), which is faced with a revolution. Especially, with the development of deep learning and transfer learning, automatically and accurately predicting the personality is an emerging topic in NLP. Classical text representation methods and pre-trained word representation approach both make the personality prediction research area more attractive and competitive. Even though how to compute and predict someone's personality based on texts is still an open question, attracting more and more researchers to focus on it.

The approaches of personality prediction have a long research history. Early in 2008, the Personae corpus (Luyckx and Daelemans, 2008) has already been proposed for predicting the personality from the text. The corpus is used for predicting the writer's personality traits that are reflected in writing style. Input representation is one of the most components in NLP. In recent years, the novel representation method has been the pre-trained word embeddings. Therefore, we mainly focus on the personality prediction approaches with the pre-trained word embeddings. Methods with the pre-trained embeddings are firstly based on Word2Vec (Mikolov et al., 2013b,a) and GloVe (Pennington et al., 2014). Surprisingly, Poria et al. (2013) propose to extract common sense knowledge and affective information to recognize personality from text, where they represent information in a directed graph. Despite the success of early word embedding models (e.g., Word2Vec), there are still practical problems. The first one is that previously unseen words make the model get into trouble. The second one is the overwhelmingly large parameters for a model to learn. Liu et al. (2016) propose a recurrent and compositional deep-learning-based model to address these issues.

Very recently, researchers start to explore large pre-trained models for NLP (Jawahar et al., 2019; He et al., 2020; Malkin et al., 2021). Kazameini et al. (2020) use the BERT language model (Devlin

*These authors contribute equally to this work.

Proceedings of the 12th Workshop on Computational Approaches to Subjectivity, Sentiment & Social Media Analysis, pages 265 - 270
May 26, 2022 ©2022 Association for Computational Linguistics

et al., 2018) to extract contextualized word embeddings and achieve state-of-the-art performance for personality detection. Similarly, Transformer-MD (Yang et al., 2021) is proposed to put multiple posts together for representing the personality of each user. The context embeddings learned by large pre-trained models can effectively improve the performances and have theoretical advantages over traditional embedding methods. Therefore, we also adopt a pre-trained model named DeBERTa (He et al., 2020) to construct our personality prediction model. In this paper, we present our Prompt-based pre-trained network for personality prediction at Track 3 and Track 4 of WASSA-2022.

Track 3: Personality Prediction (PER), which consists in predicting the personality of the essay writer, knowing all his/her essays and the news article from which they reacted.

Track 4: Interpersonal Reactivity Index Prediction (IRI), which consists in predicting the personality of the essay writer, knowing all his/her essays and the news article from which they reacted.

2 Main Method

In this section, we will elaborate on our method in detail, including the model architecture, prompt design, regression optimization, data augmentation and model ensemble.

2.1 Model Architecture

The overall architecture of our method is shown in Figure 1, the DeBERTa pre-trained language model (He et al., 2020) is adopted as our backbone for personality and interpersonal reactivity prediction. We first input the text with a manually designed prompt to be tokenized with DeBERTa tokenizer. Then the input shall be encoded with the encoder through the self-attention (Vaswani et al., 2017) mechanism. Finally, the output is produced by the Linear layer for regression.

2.2 Prompt Design

Prompt Learning is considered to be the wise way for providing the pre-trained model with extra knowledge (Liu et al., 2021). For this reason, we manually design the prompt to extract relevant knowledge from the pre-trained model for personality prediction, which is presented as the fixed template, i.e., "A female, with fourth grade education, third race, 22 and income of 100000". Specifically, this persona information is mapped into the tokens

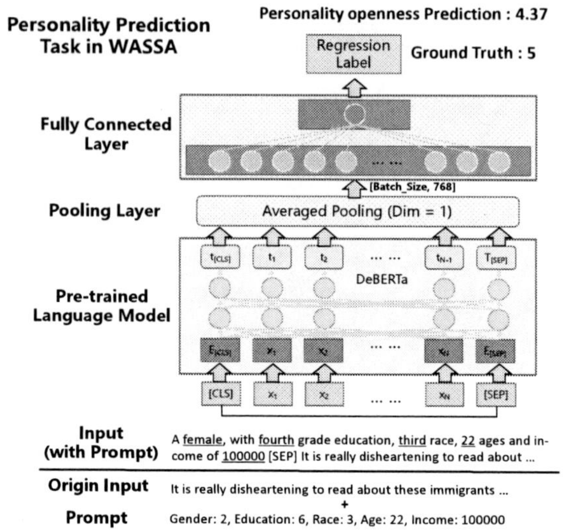

Figure 1: Overview of model architecture, where the sentence in origin input is concatenated with the prompt templates.

for providing more semantic information for the next regression task. We concatenate these fixed prompts with the origin input together for learning the joint representation in the pre-trained language model.

2.3 Regression Optimization

The personality and interpersonal reactivity prediction task is designed to regress the probable logits of different personality items. Given the training samples $D = \{(C^1, X^1), (C^2, X^2), \ldots, (C^D, X^D)\}$, where the C^i, $i = \{1, \ldots, n\}$, represents the author persona information with the corresponding stories collections X^i. The author persona information contains different other information items C, i.e., education and race, etc. We want to concatenate these texts together with the prompt learning, which aims to provide extra information for the personality prediction. The optimization function used the MSE function, which is shown as (1):

$$MSE(X, C, y) = \sum_{j=1}^{|\mathcal{D}|} \left(\text{Logits}\left(X^j, C^j\right) - y^j\right)^2 \tag{1}$$

where the Logits represents the logits output of prompt tuning from the pre-trained model, and y^j is one author's personality item, $j \in [1, D]$.

We implement the above function with the optimization of the following equation:

$$\mathcal{L} = -\sum_{k=1}^{|\mathcal{D}|} \log_\theta \left(y^k \mid X^k, C^k \right) \quad (2)$$

where the y^k represents each item personality label, and θ is the parameters of the pre-trained model.

2.4 Data Augmentation

Inspired by the work (Karimi et al., 2021), we consider the data augmentation with random punctuation marks, i.e., six punctuation marks in {".", ";", "?", ":", "!", ","}. The reason is that we want to ensure there is at least one inserted mark for more data from one author. Meanwhile, we do not want to insert too many punctuation marks as too much noise might hurt the model, especially for the personality prediction.

2.5 Model Ensemble

For different pre-trained models, the wise choice to improve the final results is to ensemble the pre-trained model (Zwanzig, 1960). As a result, we adopt the ensemble method to average the logits for the final prediction. Specifically, we implement the Bagging algorithm (Inoue and Kilian, 2008) for the personality and interpersonal reactivity prediction, which can effectively reduce the variance of the logits prediction by averaging the prediction bias produced from different models.

3 Experimental Setting

This section will subsequently present the emotion dataset, our experimental models, experimental settings, control of variables experiment.

3.1 Dataset

The shared task organizers supplied an extended dataset to participants used by (Buechel et al., 2018)[1]. The dataset includes essays between 300 and 800 characters with the Batson empathy, Personal Distress Scale, and other additional demographic and personality information. Among them, the person-level demographic information mainly contains age, gender, ethnicity, income and education level. The provided dataset of WASSA shared work contains 1860 training samples.

[1]Data and code are available at: https://github.com/wwbp/empathic_reactions

3.2 Implementation Details

In these tasks, we are mainly based on the hugging face framework[2] (Wolf et al., 2020). We add a randomly initialized linear layer after DeBERTa (He et al., 2021) to output the value of shape = [1]. We use the AdamW(Loshchilov and Hutter, 2018) optimizer and the learning rate is set to 8e-6 with the warm-up (He et al., 2016). The batch size is 12. We set the maximum length of 512, and delete the excess. Linear decay of learning rate and gradient clipping of 1e-4. Dropout (Srivastava et al., 2014) of 0.1 is applied to prevent overfitting. We implemented the code of training and reasoning based on PyTorch [3] (Paszke et al., 2019) in three NVIDIA A100 GPUs. All experiments select the best parameters in the valid set, and then report the score of the best model (valid set) in the test set.

We use the DeBERTa-v3-large[4] (He et al., 2021) as pre-trained model, and we Fine-tune the model. The DeBERTa-v3 model comes with 24 layers and a hidden size of 1036. This model uses a training framework similar to the ELECTRA (Clark et al., 2020) model, and sets up a generator and discriminator. The pre-training task of the discriminator is replaced with token detection (RTD). Finally, the RTD model is selected as the model. Compared with MLM, RTD training can bring more efficient training results.

4 Result and Discussion

This section describes our experiment results on Personality Prediction (PER) sub-task and the Interpersonal Reactivity Index Prediction (IRI) sub-task. Experiments were conducted with the development set as our test dataset, and the experimental results are shown in Table 1 and Table 2. The results of the final submissions are shown in Table 3.

4.1 Results for Track3

The results in Table 1 show the performance of our method with different components on the developments dataset. From Table 1, we can find that:

The method without ensemble component achieves 0.25788 AVG. Compared to the method without ensemble components, the combination of random punctuation and ensemble gains 0.0144

[2]https://github.com/huggingface/transformers

[3]https://pytorch.org

[4]microsoft/deberta-v3-large

Methods	conscientiousness	extraversion	openess	talking	agreeableness	AVG
Ours	**0.2225**	**0.3194**	**0.2328**	**0.3815**	**0.4044**	**0.31212**
w/o random punctuation	0.2197	0.3112	0.2246	0.3681	0.3640	0.29752
w/o prompt	0.1763	0.2841	0.2001	0.3148	0.3711	0.26928
w/o ensemble	0.1645	0.2467	0.1888	0.3201	0.3693	0.25788

Table 1: Results of the ablation study for Personality Prediction (PER). AVG represents the average of the Pearson correlations over Personality values. The best results are in bold.

Methods	concern	distress	fantasy	stability	AVG
Ours	**0.3442**	**0.2871**	**0.2744**	**0.2108**	**0.2791**
w/o random punctuation	0.3221	0.2881	0.2465	0.2049	0.2654
w/o prompt	0.3145	0.2645	0.2621	0.1893	0.2576
w/o ensemble	0.2953	0.2510	0.2346	0.1826	0.2408

Table 2: Results of the ablation study for Reactivity Index Prediction (IRI). AVG represents the average of the Pearson correlations over Personality values. The best results are in bold.

Subtask	Pearson Correlations
PER (Track3)	0.23006
IRI (Track4)	0.25460

Table 3: Results of our method on Track3 and Track4 respectively.

increase of AVG. The prompt and ensemble components are used in our method, which gains 0.02824 increase of AVG than W/o prompt. This shows that each component can improve the performance of our method. When the three components are used together, our model achieves state-of-the-art performance with 0.31212 AVG. On the final submissions shown in the Table 3, our method achieves a Pearson Correlation of 0.23006, which ranks **Top-1** in PER (Track3) sub-task.

4.2 Results for Track4

The results in Table 2 show the performance of each component for our approach on the development dataset of the Reactivity Index Prediction (IRI). From Table 2, we can find that:

Our method achieves 0.2791 AVG. Compared to the method without random punctuation, our method gains 0.0137 increase in AVG. The method without ensemble component only achieves 0.2408 AVG. These demonstrate the availability of introducing each component to our method. On the final submissions shown in the Table 3, our method achieves a Pearson Correlation of 0.25460, which ranks **TOP-1** in the IRI (Track4) sub-task.

5 Conclusion

In this paper, we describe our system to the Personality Prediction and Interpersonal Reactivity Index Prediction sub-tasks. We used the DeBERTa pre-trained language model as the backbone. The prompt is designed for providing the persona information to the pre-trained model. The data augmentation with random punctuation and model ensemble is adopted for better results. In the evaluation phase, our methods ranked **Top-1** on Track 3 and Track 4 respectively. In the future, we will focus on more effective prompt designing for performing the personality and interpersonal reactivity prediction.

Acknowledgement

This work is supported by the National Key R&D Program of China (2018YFB1305200), the National Natural Science Fund of China (62171183).

References

Emorie D Beck and Joshua J Jackson. 2022. A mega-analysis of personality prediction: Robustness and boundary conditions. *Journal of Personality and Social Psychology*, 122(3):523.

Sven Buechel, Anneke Buffone, Barry Slaff, Lyle H. Ungar, and João Sedoc. 2018. Modeling empathy and distress in reaction to news stories. *arXiv: Computation and Language*.

Kevin Clark, Minh-Thang Luong, Quoc V. Le, and Christopher D. Manning. 2020. Electra: Pre-training text encoders as discriminators rather than generators. In *International Conference on Learning Representations*.

Jacob Devlin, Ming-Wei Chang, Kenton Lee, and Kristina Toutanova. 2018. Bert: Pre-training of deep bidirectional transformers for language understanding. *arXiv preprint arXiv:1810.04805*.

Kaiming He, Xiangyu Zhang, Shaoqing Ren, and Jian Sun. 2016. Deep residual learning for image recognition. In *2016 IEEE Conference on Computer Vision and Pattern Recognition (CVPR)*, pages 770–778.

Pengcheng He, Xiaodong Liu, Jianfeng Gao, and Weizhu Chen. 2020. Deberta: Decoding-enhanced bert with disentangled attention. *arXiv preprint arXiv:2006.03654*.

Pengcheng He, Xiaodong Liu, Jianfeng Gao, and Weizhu Chen. 2021. Deberta: Decoding-enhanced bert with disentangled attention. In *International Conference on Learning Representations*.

Atsushi Inoue and Lutz Kilian. 2008. How useful is bagging in forecasting economic time series? a case study of us consumer price inflation. *Journal of the American Statistical Association*, 103(482):511–522.

Ganesh Jawahar, Benoît Sagot, and Djamé Seddah. 2019. What does bert learn about the structure of language? In *ACL 2019-57th Annual Meeting of the Association for Computational Linguistics*.

Akbar Karimi, Leonardo Rossi, and Andrea Prati. 2021. Aeda: An easier data augmentation technique for text classification. In *Findings of the Association for Computational Linguistics: EMNLP 2021*, pages 2748–2754.

Amirmohammad Kazameini, Samin Fatehi, Yash Mehta, Sauleh Eetemadi, and Erik Cambria. 2020. Personality trait detection using bagged svm over bert word embedding ensembles. *arXiv preprint arXiv:2010.01309*.

Fei Liu, Julien Perez, and Scott Nowson. 2016. A recurrent and compositional model for personality trait recognition from short texts. In *Proceedings of the Workshop on Computational Modeling of People's Opinions, Personality, and Emotions in Social Media (PEOPLES)*, pages 20–29.

Pengfei Liu, Weizhe Yuan, Jinlan Fu, Zhengbao Jiang, Hiroaki Hayashi, and Graham Neubig. 2021. Pre-train, prompt, and predict: A systematic survey of prompting methods in natural language processing. *arXiv preprint arXiv:2107.13586*.

Ilya Loshchilov and Frank Hutter. 2018. Decoupled weight decay regularization. In *International Conference on Learning Representations*.

Kim Luyckx and Walter Daelemans. 2008. Personae: a corpus for author and personality prediction from text. In *Proceedings of the Sixth International Conference on Language Resources and Evaluation (LREC'08)*.

Nikolay Malkin, Sameera Lanka, Pranav Goel, Sudha Rao, and Nebojsa Jojic. 2021. Gpt perdetry test: Generating new meanings for new words. In *Proceedings of the 2021 Conference of the North American Chapter of the Association for Computational Linguistics: Human Language Technologies*, pages 5542–5553.

Tomas Mikolov, Kai Chen, Greg Corrado, and Jeffrey Dean. 2013a. Efficient estimation of word representations in vector space. *arXiv preprint arXiv:1301.3781*.

Tomas Mikolov, Ilya Sutskever, Kai Chen, Greg S Corrado, and Jeff Dean. 2013b. Distributed representations of words and phrases and their compositionality. *Advances in neural information processing systems*, 26.

Adam Paszke, Sam Gross, Francisco Massa, Adam Lerer, James Bradbury, Gregory Chanan, Trevor Killeen, Zeming Lin, Natalia Gimelshein, Luca Antiga, Alban Desmaison, Andreas Kopf, Edward Yang, Zachary DeVito, Martin Raison, Alykhan Tejani, Sasank Chilamkurthy, Benoit Steiner, Lu Fang, Junjie Bai, and Soumith Chintala. 2019. Pytorch: An imperative style, high-performance deep learning library. In *Advances in Neural Information Processing Systems*, volume 32. Curran Associates, Inc.

Jeffrey Pennington, Richard Socher, and Christopher D Manning. 2014. Glove: Global vectors for word representation. In *Proceedings of the 2014 conference on empirical methods in natural language processing (EMNLP)*, pages 1532–1543.

Soujanya Poria, Alexandar Gelbukh, Basant Agarwal, Erik Cambria, and Newton Howard. 2013. Common sense knowledge based personality recognition from text. In *Mexican International Conference on Artificial Intelligence*, pages 484–496. Springer.

Nitish Srivastava, Geoffrey E. Hinton, Alex Krizhevsky, Ilya Sutskever, and Ruslan Salakhutdinov. 2014. Dropout: a simple way to prevent neural networks from overfitting. *Journal of Machine Learning Research*, 15:1929–1958.

Ashish Vaswani, Noam Shazeer, Niki Parmar, Jakob Uszkoreit, Llion Jones, Aidan N Gomez, Łukasz Kaiser, and Illia Polosukhin. 2017. Attention is all you need. *Advances in neural information processing systems*, 30.

Hetal Vora, Mamta Bhamare, and Dr K Ashok Kumar. 2020. Personality prediction from social media text: An overview. *Int. J. Eng. Res*, 9(05):352–357.

Thomas Wolf, Lysandre Debut, Victor Sanh, Julien Chaumond, Clement Delangue, Anthony Moi, Pierric Cistac, Tim Rault, Rémi Louf, Morgan Funtowicz, Joe Davison, Sam Shleifer, Patrick von Platen, Clara Ma, Yacine Jernite, Julien Plu, Canwen Xu, Teven Le Scao, Sylvain Gugger, Mariama Drame, Quentin Lhoest, and Alexander M. Rush. 2020. Transformers: State-of-the-art natural language processing. In

Proceedings of the 2020 Conference on Empirical Methods in Natural Language Processing: System Demonstrations, pages 38–45, Online. Association for Computational Linguistics.

Feifan Yang, Xiaojun Quan, Yunyi Yang, and Jianxing Yu. 2021. Multi-document transformer for personality detection. In *Proceedings of the AAAI Conference on Artificial Intelligence*, volume 35, pages 14221–14229.

Robert Zwanzig. 1960. Ensemble method in the theory of irreversibility. *The Journal of Chemical Physics*, 33(5):1338–1341.

SURREY-CTS-NLP at WASSA2022: An Experiment of Discourse and Sentiment Analysis for the Prediction of Empathy, Distress and Emotion

Shenbin Qian[1], Constantin Orasan[1], Diptesh Kanojia[2],
Hadeel Saadany[1] and Felix do Carmo[1]
Centre for Translation Studies[1],
Department of Computer Science[2],
University of Surrey, UK
{s.qian, c.orasan, d.kanojia, h.saadany, f.docarmo}@surrey.ac.uk

Abstract

This paper summarises the submissions our team, SURREY-CTS-NLP has made for the WASSA 2022 Shared Task for the prediction of empathy, distress and emotion. In this work, we tested different learning strategies, like ensemble learning and multi-task learning, as well as several large language models, but our primary focus was on analysing and extracting emotion-intensive features from both the essays in the training data and the news articles, to better predict empathy and distress scores from the perspective of discourse and sentiment analysis. We propose several text feature extraction schemes to compensate the small size of training examples for fine-tuning pretrained language models, including methods based on Rhetorical Structure Theory (RST) parsing, cosine similarity and sentiment score. Our best submissions achieve an average Pearson correlation score of 0.518 for the empathy prediction task and an F1 score of 0.571 for the emotion prediction task[1], indicating that using these schemes to extract emotion-intensive information can help improve model performance.

1 Introduction

Large transformer models (Vaswani et al., 2017) have shown their power in various natural language processing (NLP) downstream tasks, especially in dealing with informative text. However, for text containing human emotions, current models still need to be improved and trained on more emotion-intensive datasets. Empathy and emotion prediction has gained a lot of attention in the field of NLP with many shared tasks and challenges being proposed in recent years.

For the WASSA 2022 Shared Task, we have participated in two of their 4 tracks, which are:

Track 1: Empathy Prediction (EMP), which is a regression task to predict both the empathy and distress score at the essay-level.
Track 2: Emotion Classification (EMO), which is to classify each essay into one of seven classes of emotion.

Both tracks are supposed to use the same dataset the organisers provide, which we will discuss in the next section. In Section 2, we explore some interesting features of the dataset and show what methods and strategies we have paid closer attention to, according to the data features. Section 3 gives a detailed introduction to the schemes we use, as well as different learning strategies we adopt for analysing the dataset and for incorporating additional features to train our models. Section 4 shows results of our proposed methods, as well as future directions that would be interesting to explore. In Section 5, we present our conclusions and summarise our methods.

2 Initial Data Analysis

The original data used in this shared task were gathered for experiments to predict empathy based on Batson's Empathic Concern and Personal Distress Scale (Batson et al., 1987). Participants were given news articles to read and then wrote a short essay to describe how they feel about the news. Thereafter, they were given questions to answer, which were designed for grading their empathy and distress from level 1 to 7. The demographic and personality information of these participants were also collected for further studies on how these factors might affect their empathy and distress level. The emotion labels which annotate the data were produced semi-automatically: human annotators corrected the automatic predictions of deep learning models. More details of how this dataset was designed can be found in (Buechel et al., 2018) and

[1]The organisers have not yet released the official result and ranking on the leaderboard when this paper is written.

Proceedings of the 12th Workshop on Computational Approaches to Subjectivity, Sentiment & Social Media Analysis, pages 271 - 275
May 26, 2022 ©2022 Association for Computational Linguistics

(Tafreshi et al., 2021).

After a quick exploration of the dataset, we noticed that the training size is very small, compared to the size of the datasets used in modern transformer models, with only 2130 examples in total, including the development dataset. Due to the designing purpose of the empathy prediction task, the majority of these selected news articles are negative in nature so as to induce the annotators' empathy. However, this leads to a skewed distribution for emotion classification (see Figure 1), which might influence the prediction of the minority classes.

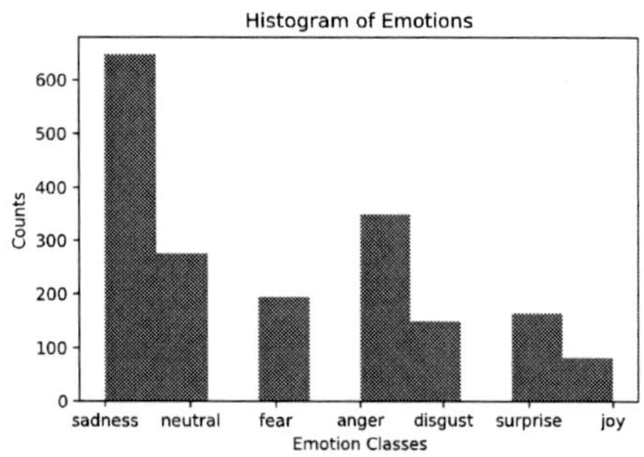

Figure 1: Distribution of Emotion Classes

Another feature in the dataset which could act as a good predictor of empathy and distress is demographic and personality information, since people from various backgrounds and with different personalities may have different views and feelings towards these news articles. We found that some variables like personality agreeableness do have a relative correlation with the empathy score (see Table 1). Therefore, we opted for incorporating this information with text as additional features.

Personality Extraversion	Personality Agreeableness
0.209025617	0.243257229

Table 1: Pearson Correlation between Empathy and Some Personality Information

From both Batson's Empathy Theory and the high Pearson correlation score (0.45) of empathy and distress, we know that the two variables are highly correlated. Therefore, multi-task learning could help us learn features from the empathy prediction task to apply to the distress prediction task.

The most important thing we learnt from this dataset, which can help supplement the lack of adequate training data, is that the essays are the responses to the news articles. We, therefore, put forward the assumption that the news article must contain features that trigger the emotion of the reader. We can regard the news article and the essay as one unified discourse, where some parts are more emotion-intensive, while others are more descriptive than emotional. Thus, we explored methods adopted for both discourse and sentiment analysis to extract emotion-intensive features from the articles to help with the prediction.

3 Methods Description

3.1 Empathy Prediction

We tried different approaches to extract features that indicate emotions from the text, namely, RST (Mann and Thompson, 1987) parsing, cosine similarity and sentiment score. We also included demographic and personality information to train a tabular transformer model to see if this information would help the prediction. Multi-task learning was also used to train one model for both the empathy and distress sub-tasks.

3.1.1 RST Parsing

Rhetorical structure theory aims to build a tree which represents the discourse structure for a sequence of text units. In such a tree structure, we know that units defined as nuclei of a rhetorical relation are more essential to the writer's purpose, while those defined as satellites would become incomprehensible if nuclei were deleted (Mann and Thompson, 1987). In our case, we assumed that in the essays there are some parts that are more emotional, carrying the intention of the writer, i.e. the annotator, whereas others are only a rephrasing of the events in the corresponding news article in a descriptive way. We also made a further assumption that nuclei should be given more weights on the text embeddings while satellites less weights during the training process.

In the experiments, we used the text-level discourse rhetorical structure (DRS) parser by Zhang et al. (2021), which uses adversarial learning to generate DRS trees from a top-down global perspective, and claims to be one the state-of-the-art parsers in this area. We gave different weights to the embeddings of nuclei and satellites and found that giving 0.3 to the nuclei and 0.7 to the entire essays for fine-tuning a RoBERTa base model (Liu et al., 2019) leads to our best performance. In the experiments, we used an AdamW optimizer (Loshchilov and Hutter, 2017) with a learning rate of 0.00002.

3.1.2 Cosine Similarity and Sentiment Score

Since these news articles are long and some of them are mixed with URLs and other noise like missing content[2], using an RST parser to get their discourse tree is not likely to produce useful information and hence not a feasible approach for feature extraction. For this reason, our goal was to extract those sentences that are highly related to the essays from the articles.

Sentence embeddings represent sentences as numerical vectors which represent the semantic information of the sentence. For this reason cosine similarities between sentence embeddings of the essays and the articles can be calculated to extract sentences in the articles that are semantically similar to those of the essays (see Equation 1, where u is the sentence embeddings for the article and v for the essay). Also, sentiment scores were used to extract sentences in the articles that contain more extreme sentiments.

$$Cosine\_similarity = 1 - \frac{u \cdot v}{||u||_2||v||_2} \quad (1)$$

To get cosine similarities between sentences, we tried two sentence-level embedders, e.g. Sentence-BERT (Reimers and Gurevych, 2019) and Universal Sentence Encoder (Cer et al., 2018). The latter was used in our final model. For the calculation of sentiment scores, we used a simple rule-based sentiment analysis tool, VADER (Hutto and Gilbert, 2014), which claims to achieve 0.96 in F1 score for sentiment classification. Cosine similarity and sentiment score can be used together or separately to extract features in the articles. We experimented different thresholds to filter sentences in the articles and concatenate them with essays. In our final model, sentences with cosine similarity higher than 0.2 and sentiment score higher than 0.6 or lower than -0.6 are kept, so that a reasonable amount of sentences which are semantically similar to the essays and sentimentally extreme can be fed into our model.

3.1.3 Tabular Models and Multi-task Learning

Demographic and personality information were used together with essays and articles to train a tabular model based on Gu and Budhkar (2021), and we got the highest Pearson correlation score (0.53) in empathy prediction during training. However, as personality information is not included in the test data, we are not able to submit the result of this approach to the Shared Task.

A weighted loss considering the homoscedastic uncertainty (Kendall et al., 2017) of our two sub-tasks was applied to our RoBERTa model (Liu et al., 2019) to predict both empathy and distress for multi-task learning. We used the same hyperparameters as in the model of RST parsing, but trained it with more epochs to minimise their shared loss.

3.2 Emotion Prediction

For the emotion classification task, we also tested those methods in empathy prediction, but the results are not as good as expected during our training process. Therefore, we adopted data augmentation and ensemble learning to improve model performance.

3.2.1 Data Augmentation with GoEmotions Dataset

As the original training data is small in size and relatively skewed in distribution, data augmentation is something that we could do to overcome the problems. The GoEmotions dataset (Demszky et al., 2020) is a manually annotated high-quality dataset with 27 emotion categories based on 58k English Reddit comments, making itself a good source for data augmentation. However, as texts in the GoEmotions dataset might have different writing styles and sequence lengths compared with our essays, we cannot simply use all the data to train our model. We selected those texts that are longer than 25 words and make sure that more joy and surprise examples are included to compensate the skewed distribution.

3.2.2 Ensemble Learning

Trying larger models or combining the results of several different models would be another way to compensate the small training size. Ensemble learning is a machine learning strategy that combines the prediction of multiple algorithms to get better performance. For this task, we fine-tuned the RoBERTa (Liu et al., 2019), ELECTRA (Clark et al., 2020) and DeBERTa (He et al., 2020) base models for majority voting to get a better predictive result.

[2]We list some of these problems in Appendix A.

	RST Parsing	Similarity & Sentiment Score	Multi-task Learning	Simple Fine-tuning
Empathy	0.431	0.501[3]	0.480	0.504
Distress	0.465	0.535	0.458	0.530

Table 2: Pearson Correlation of Predicted Empathy and Distress Scores

4 Results and Discussions

4.1 Results for Empathy Prediction

Table 2 compares the results based on RST parsing, cosine similarity and sentiment score, multi-task learning and simple fine-tuning. The Pearson correlation is calculated using the evaluation script provided by the organisers on the test dataset.

We can see that the Pearson correlation scores produced by the model using RST parser are not as high as expected, but results using extracted article sentences by cosine similarity and sentiment score are pretty high, especially the distress score. However, just fine-tuning a RoBERTa base model also achieves high scores. This indicates that there do exist features in the article that trigger the feeling of the reader but we need to better analyse and extract these features from the articles. Multi-task learning is also not bad at predicting the empathy score, but we might still need to design a better loss function to train the model.

For future directions, RST parsing or even other methods for discourse analysis is still something we can try to get useful information from the articles.

4.2 Results for Emotion Prediction

Table 3 lists the result of using the GoEmotions dataset as additional training data, the result for ensemble learning mentioned in Section 3.2, as well as the result of simply fine-tuning a RoBERTa base model.

	GoEmotions	Ensemble Learning	Simple Fine-tuning
Accuracy	0.634	0.619	0.646
F1 score	0.548	0.534	0.571
Precision	0.576	0.564	0.595
Recall	0.532	0.520	0.559

Table 3: Scores for Emotion Prediction

We see that the F1 score for the GoEmotions result is higher than the one for ensemble learning, which implicitly suggests that getting more training data is more important than using larger and more models, especially when training datasets are particularly small. However, just fine-tuning a RoBERTa base model appears to have a slightly better result than data augmentation in this task. This could be related to how we sample the dataset, since data augmentation might make the training data have a very different distribution from the test data.

For future directions, how to get and sample extra data to compensate the skewed distribution or experimenting with feature extraction techniques on existing information in the training data like the news articles or demographic information could be possible ways to improve model performance.

5 Conclusions

This paper summarises the submissions our team has made to the WASSA 2022 Shared Task for empathy, distress and emotion prediction. In this work, we tried different ways to improve model performance from the perspective of discourse and sentiment analysis, data augmentation and method optimisation like RST parsing, sentiment score and ensemble learning. We propose a reliable method to analyse and extract information from both the news articles and the essays to compensate the small training size for empathy and distress prediction, that is, using similarity and sentiment scores for feature extraction. Adding GoEmotions (Demszky et al., 2020) data to increase the training size is one way to improve emotion prediction, but attention should be paid to how much data we should sample for each category. In our best submission, we get a Pearson correlation score of 0.518 for the empathy prediction task and an F1 score of 0.571 for the emotion prediction task.

The method we used to extract emotion-intensive features is by no means perfect, future studies could explore other methods in discourse or text analysis to further improve model performance when dealing with emotion data with a small training size.

References

C Daniel Batson, Jim Fultz, and Patricia A Schoenrade. 1987. Distress and empathy: Two qualitatively dis-

[3]Only this result is based on fine-tuning a RoBERTa large model, not the base model

article_id	problem	response_id	empathy	distress	emotion
63	missing content	R_1DAmmWVuxekOzQt	4	1	surprise
36	one sentence news	R_3oZwv1aOvzgfBPT	5.5	1	sadness
142	two different articles as one	R_1rfDsNtkx9ueNuH	1	1	anger
412	mixed with URL				

Table 4: Problems of News Articles

tinct vicarious emotions with different motivational consequences. *Journal of personality*, 55(1):19–39.

Sven Buechel, Anneke Buffone, Barry Slaff, Lyle Ungar, and João Sedoc. 2018. Modeling empathy and distress in reaction to news stories. pages 4758–4765.

Daniel Cer, Yinfei Yang, Sheng yi Kong, Nan Hua, Nicole Limtiaco, Rhomni St. John, Noah Constant, Mario Guajardo-Cespedes, Steve Yuan, Chris Tar, Yun-Hsuan Sung, Brian Strope, and Ray Kurzweil. 2018. Universal sentence encoder. *arXiv preprint*.

Kevin Clark, Minh-Thang Luong, Google Brain, Quoc V Le Google Brain, and Christopher D Manning. 2020. Electra: Pre-training text encoders as discriminators rather than generators. *arXiv preprint*.

Dorottya Demszky, Dana Movshovitz-Attias, Jeongwoo Ko, Alan Cowen, Gaurav Nemade, and Sujith Ravi. 2020. Goemotions: A dataset of fine-grained emotions. *arXiv preprint*.

Ken Gu and Akshay Budhkar. 2021. Multimodal-toolkit: A package for learning on tabular and text data with transformers. pages 69–73. Association for Computational Linguistics.

Pengcheng He, Xiaodong Liu, Jianfeng Gao, and Weizhu Chen. 2020. Deberta: Decoding-enhanced bert with disentangled attention. *arXiv preprint*.

C J Hutto and Eric Gilbert. 2014. Vader: A parsimonious rule-based model for sentiment analysis of social media text. *Proceedings of the International AAAI Conference on Web and Social Media*, 8:216–225.

Alex Kendall, Yarin Gal, and Roberto Cipolla. 2017. Multi-task learning using uncertainty to weigh losses for scene geometry and semantics. *arXiv preprint*.

Yinhan Liu, Myle Ott, Naman Goyal, Jingfei Du, Mandar Joshi, Danqi Chen, Omer Levy, Mike Lewis, Luke Zettlemoyer, and Veselin Stoyanov. 2019. Roberta: A robustly optimized bert pretraining approach. *arXiv preprint*.

Ilya Loshchilov and Frank Hutter. 2017. Decoupled weight decay regularization. *arXiv preprint*.

William C. Mann and Sandra A. Thompson. 1987. Rhetorical structure theory: A framework for the analysis of texts.

Nils Reimers and Iryna Gurevych. 2019. Sentence-bert: Sentence embeddings using siamese bert-networks. *arXiv preprint*.

Shabnam Tafreshi, Orphée De Clercq, Valentin Barriere, João Sedoc, Sven Buechel, and Alexandra Balahur. 2021. Wassa 2021 shared task: Predicting empathy and emotion in reaction to news stories. pages 92–104. Association for Computational Linguistics.

Ashish Vaswani, Google Brain, Noam Shazeer, Niki Parmar, Jakob Uszkoreit, Llion Jones, Aidan N Gomez, Łukasz Kaiser, and Illia Polosukhin. 2017. Attention is all you need. *arXiv preprint*.

Longyin Zhang, Fang Kong, and Guodong Zhou. 2021. Adversarial learning for discourse rhetorical structure parsing. pages 3946–3957. Association for Computational Linguistics.

A Appendix

We randomly read some of the news articles and find several problems that might affect participants' responses and thus undermine their empathy and emotion. We list these problems in Table 4.

An Ensemble Approach to Detect Emotions at an Essay Level

Himanshu Maheshwari[1] and **Vasudeva Varma** [2]
IIIT Hyderabad
[1] himanshu.maheshwari@research.iiit.ac.in, [2] vv@iiit.ac.in

Abstract

This paper describes our system (IREL, reffered as himanshu.1007 on Codalab) for Shared Task on Empathy Detection, Emotion Classification, and Personality Detection at 12th Workshop on Computational Approaches to Subjectivity, Sentiment & Social Media Analysis at ACL 2022. We participated in track 2 for predicting emotion at the essay level. We propose an ensemble approach that leverages the linguistic knowledge of the RoBERTa, BART-large, and RoBERTa model finetuned on the GoEmotions dataset. Each brings in its unique advantage, as we discuss in the paper. Our proposed system achieved a Macro F1 score of 0.585 and ranked one out of thirteen teams (the current top team on leaderboard submitted after the deadline). The code can be found here

1 Introduction

Emotion is a concept that is challenging to describe. Nevertheless, as human beings, we understand the emotional effect situations have or could have on other people and us. In this work, we aim to transfer this knowledge of emotion detection to machines. This work aims to develop a robust system that could detect emotions at an essay level. These essays are reactions to news stories and are between 300 and 800 characters in length.

Existing literature on emotion detection mainly focuses on emotion detection at the sentence level. Different datasets consisting of sentences from social media (Mohammad (2012), Mohammad et al. (2014), Liu et al. (2017), Demszky et al. (2020)), fairytales (Alm and Sproat, 2005), dialogues (Li et al., 2017), etc. have been made available. However, the task of emotion detection at an essay level is underexplored. In essay-level emotion detection, the emotions are typically expressed by the entire narrative and not just a few words or phrases. The system must refer to the entire essay to get a more holistic view of the expressed emotion. We empirically show that systems trained on just sentence level emotion detection will not work essay level as they do not have the entire context.

We propose an ensemble approach consisting of a finetuned RoBERTa (Liu et al., 2019), finetuned BART-large (Lewis et al., 2020), and RoBERTa model first finetuned on the GoEmotions (Demszky et al., 2020) dataset and then finetuned on our dataset. RoBERTa model has shown amazing performance for various NLP tasks and thus was the default choice for the task. BART-large has shown amazing performance for summarization tasks. This suggests it is suitable for a task involving multiple sentences. The last model is a RoBERTa model that was first finetuned on the GoEmotions dataset and then finetuned on our dataset. The intuition is that since it has a good understanding of sentence-level emotions (from GoEmotions), it will combine the sentence-level knowledge into essay-level knowledge. This is especially important for cases with very strong expression of emotions in a sentence. Ablation studies show that the model performs worse in the absence of either of the three models. Another ablation study is conducted to reinforce our claim that the task can't be solved by looking at sentence level.

2 Dataset

The training dataset is a small supervised dataset consisting of various fields. However, only two fields are helpful for emotion prediction: essay and emotion; thus, we use only these fields. The dataset statistics are shown in table 1 and table 2.

The dataset is very small and heavily skewed, with anger and sadness making up ~54% of the entire dataset. This skewed dataset affects the model's performance, and it needs to be dealt with.

Usually, NLP systems deal with skewed datasets using oversampling, undersampling, augmentation, or weighted loss function. With such few data points, oversampling and undersampling are not

Proceedings of the 12th Workshop on Computational Approaches to Subjectivity, Sentiment & Social Media Analysis, pages 276 - 279
May 26, 2022

Split	Number of samples
Train	1860
Dev	270
Test	525

Table 1: Dataset statistics for different splits.

Emotion	Number of samples
Anger	349
Disgust	149
Fear	194
Joy	82
Neutral	275
Sadness	647
Surprise	164

Table 2: Emotion distribution for train set.

Emotion	Number of samples
Anger	2000
Disgust	2000
Fear	1230
Joy	2000
Neutral	2000
Sadness	2000
Surprise	2000

Table 3: Emotion distribution for train set of GoEmotions Dataset

viable. Our initial exploration with data augmentation did not help; thus, we used a weighted cross-entropy loss function to deal with data imbalance. The weights of each class were determined using the sklearn library. [1]

3 Baselines

The following section describes different approaches we tried before shifting to our proposed methodology. For each approach, grid search was used to find appropriate hyperparameters. Please note we compare different models using Macro F1 score which is the official evaluation metric.

3.1 Language Model Finetuning

The current de facto in NLP is to finetune a language model for any classification task. Our first approach was to finetune a language model and observe the results. This will serve as a baseline for other approaches. This exercise also helps us select the appropriate language model for other approaches. We experimented with the following language models:

1. Roberta Base
2. Bert-base-uncased
3. Roberta-large
4. Bart-large
5. Longformer-base-4096

Table 4 shows the results of different language models. Roberta-base is performing the best; thus, it is the suitable language model for other approaches. Roberta-large overfits and was producing the same results after each epoch. Longformer, though suitable for long sequences, did not perform well.

[1] https://scikit-learn.org/stable/modules/generated/sklearn.utils.class_weight.compute_class_weight.html

3.2 Binary Classifiers

Having a classifier doing multiclass classification is challenging. In this approach, we use a binary classifier for each emotion and take the emotion with the highest softmax classification probability. Specifically, we finetune a Roberta-base binary classifier for each emotion. The classifier aims to identify target emotion from other emotions. During inference, we take the classification probability from each classifier. The emotion with the highest classification probability from its classifier is the predicted emotion. Table 4 shows the result of this approach. The results are poor compared to finetuning a classifier; thus, a binary view of emotion is unsuitable for our use case.

3.3 Finetuning a classifier trained on GoEmotions dataset

This approach introduces an additional layer of transfer learning. We first finetune a Roberta-base model on a subset of the GoEmotions dataset. GoEmotions is a sentence-level fine-grained emotion classification dataset. We take sentences that have only one of the seven emotions of our task. This GoEmotions finetuned classifier is then further finetuned on our dataset. The idea is to finetune a classifier that has some understanding of emotions. Table 3 shows statistics of the GoEmotions dataset. Table 4 shows results for the same. The results are poor, suggesting that strong sentence-level understanding does not scale to essay-level understanding.

Model	Macro F1	Accuracy in %
Finetuning Roberta Base	0.6090	**70.000**
Finetuning Bert base uncased	0.5502	62.593
Finetuning Roberta Large	0.0760	36.296
Finetuning BART Large	0.5983	66.667
Finetuning longformer-base-4096	0.5635	66.667
Combining Binary Classifiers	0.4689	63.333
Finetuning model trained on GoEmotion Dataset	0.5568	63.333
Proposed Solution	**0.6360**	68.519
Proposed Solution	**0.6360**	68.519
Proposed Solution w/o Roberta	0.6021	67.037
Proposed Solution w/o BART	0.6067	**69.259**
Proposed Solution w/o GoEmotions Roberta	0.6248	67.778
Roberta-base with entire sequence	**0.6090**	**70.000**
Roberta-base with sentence seperated sequence	0.5812	65.185

Table 4: Results of different models on dev set.

4 Proposed Approach

We make the following observations from the baseline models:

a. Roberta-base and Bart-large perform better than the rest of the language model. Both models bring their advantage, Roberta-base is a powerful language model for NLU tasks, and Bart-large is suitable for tasks involving multiple sentences.

b. Roberta-base model that is first finetuned on GoEmotions dataset followed by finetuning on our dataset performs poorly compared to other baselines. However, it has a firm sentence-level understanding. Thus, this model is suitable for samples with very strong emotional sentences.

Based on these observations, we combine the strength of the Roberta-base, Bart-Large, and Roberta-base model that is first finetuned on the GoEmotions dataset in an ensemble fashion. More specifically, we take the linear combination of classification probability by each model and predict the emotion with the highest classification probability (or score). Thus the classification probability (or score) is given by:

$$s_{emo} = \lambda_1 P_{RB} + \lambda_2 P_{BL} + \lambda_3 P_{RBG}$$

Where s_{emo} is the classification score for a particular emotion and λ_1, λ_2, λ_3 are the weights of each model. P_{RB} is the classification probability of Roberta-base, P_{BL} is the classification probability of BART large and P_{RBG} is the classification probability of Roberta-base finetuned on GoEmotions. The emotion with the highest score is predicted. We found λ_1, λ_2, and λ_3 using grid search on the dev set. The value that gave the best result is λ_1: 0.26, λ_2: 0.26, and λ_3: 0.07. Table 4 shows the results of this approach. This approach outperforms all the baselines on the dev set, suggesting strength in using multiple language models.

5 Training

As discussed, we use grid search to find the appropriate hyperparameters. We use a batch size four and a dropout of 0.3 for Roberta-base. For Bart-Large, we use a batch size of three and a dropout of 0.4. For Roberta-base trained on the GoEmotion dataset, we use batch size eight and dropout of 0.2 for the first layer of finetuning. For the second layer of finetuning, we use a batch size four and a dropout of 0.3. The learning rate and seed were fixed to 10^{-5} and 42, respectively. The training was done on Nvidia RTX 2080 TI (11 GB) and took about one hour for each model finetuning.

6 Results

Table 4 shows the results of our dev set. We submitted the ensemble solution discussed above based on hyperparameters and results on the dev set. Table 5 shows the test set results as reported on the Codalab platform. The proposed system achieved rank two.

7 Ablation Studies

We conducted two ablation studies to better understand our proposed approach and the problem setting.

Metric	Result
Macro F1-Score	0.585
Micro F1-Score	0.661
Accuracy	0.661
Macro Precision	0.594
Macro Recall	0.584
Micro Precision	0.661
Micro Recall	0.661

Table 5: Results on test set as reported on Codalab

7.1 Role of Each Language Model

In the first ablation study, we inspect the role of each language model described in the ensemble solution. We observe the performance by removing one model at a time. Table 4 shows the results for the same. We see that removing even one language model degrades the overall performance. This builds confidence in our choice and intuition behind each language model for the ensemble solution, and each of the three language models is essential for our task.

7.2 Sentence Level Treatment of the Task

This ablation study inspects the model's performance if we treat the input at a sentence level. Specifically, instead of inputting the entire essay to the Roberta-base, we input the essay separated into individual sentences. We break the essay into sentences and separate them using a special token used in Roberta-base to separate sequences. Table 4 shows the result of this ablation study. For a fair comparison, we compare results between a Roberta-base model fed the entire sequence, and a Roberta-base model fed the sentence separated sequence. We see that a Roberta-base model that is fed the entire sequence performs better than a Roberta-base model that is fed a sentence-separated sequence. This suggests that we need to look at the entire sequence for a holistic understanding of the emotion, and we cannot just rely on sentence-level information.

8 Conclusion

In this work, we explore the task of emotion prediction at an essay level. We first explore different language models and identify Roberta-base and Bart-large suitable for the task. Next, we observe that adding an additional layer of transfer learning by finetuning on a sentence-level dataset helps identify essays with very strong emotional sentences. Building on these two hypotheses, we propose an ensemble solution that combines the linguistic knowledge of Roberta-base, Bart-large and Roberta-base finetuned on the GoEmotions dataset. Our proposed solution achieved a macro F1 score of 0.585 and was ranked one globally (the current top team on leaderboard submitted after the deadline).

References

Cecilia Ovesdotter Alm and Richard Sproat. 2005. Emotional sequencing and development in fairy tales. In *Affective Computing and Intelligent Interaction*, pages 668–674, Berlin, Heidelberg. Springer Berlin Heidelberg.

Dorottya Demszky, Dana Movshovitz-Attias, Jeongwoo Ko, Alan Cowen, Gaurav Nemade, and Sujith Ravi. 2020. GoEmotions: A Dataset of Fine-Grained Emotions. In *58th Annual Meeting of the Association for Computational Linguistics (ACL)*.

Mike Lewis, Yinhan Liu, Naman Goyal, Marjan Ghazvininejad, Abdelrahman Mohamed, Omer Levy, Veselin Stoyanov, and Luke Zettlemoyer. 2020. BART: Denoising sequence-to-sequence pre-training for natural language generation, translation, and comprehension. In *Proceedings of the 58th Annual Meeting of the Association for Computational Linguistics*, pages 7871–7880, Online. Association for Computational Linguistics.

Yanran Li, Hui Su, Xiaoyu Shen, Wenjie Li, Ziqiang Cao, and Shuzi Niu. 2017. Dailydialog: A manually labelled multi-turn dialogue dataset. *CoRR*, abs/1710.03957.

Vicki Liu, Carmen Banea, and Rada Mihalcea. 2017. Grounded emotions. pages 477–483.

Yinhan Liu, Myle Ott, Naman Goyal, Jingfei Du, Mandar Joshi, Danqi Chen, Omer Levy, Mike Lewis, Luke Zettlemoyer, and Veselin Stoyanov. 2019. Roberta: A robustly optimized BERT pretraining approach. *CoRR*, abs/1907.11692.

Saif Mohammad. 2012. #emotional tweets. In **SEM 2012: The First Joint Conference on Lexical and Computational Semantics – Volume 1: Proceedings of the main conference and the shared task, and Volume 2: Proceedings of the Sixth International Workshop on Semantic Evaluation (SemEval 2012)*, pages 246–255, Montréal, Canada. Association for Computational Linguistics.

Saif Mohammad, Xiaodan Zhu, Svetlana Kiritchenko, and Joel Martin. 2014. Sentiment, emotion, purpose, and style in electoral tweets. *Information Processing Management*, 51.

CAISA at WASSA 2022: Adapter-Tuning for Empathy Prediction

Allison Lahnala and **Charles Welch** and **Lucie Flek**
Conversational AI and Social Analytics (CAISA) Lab
Department of Mathematics and Computer Science, University of Marburg
http://caisa-lab.github.io
{allison.lahnala,welchc,lucie.flek}@uni-marburg.de

Abstract

We build a system that leverages adapters, a light weight and efficient method for leveraging large language models to perform the task Empathy and Distress prediction tasks for WASSA 2022. In our experiments, we find that stacking our empathy and distress adapters on a pre-trained emotion classification adapter performs best compared to full fine-tuning approaches and emotion feature concatenation. We make our experimental code publicly available.[1]

1 Introduction

Empathy is an important interpersonal function in communication settings from conversations between friends and family, to educational, medical, or other goal-oriented dialogues. In natural language processing research, automatic empathy recognition and generation are explored for motivations such as improved experiences with open-domain dialogue agents (Rashkin et al., 2019; Majumder et al., 2020; Lin et al., 2020), analyzing supportive interactions in online forums (Zhou and Jurgens, 2020; Sharma et al., 2020; Lahnala et al., 2021), and for the development of educational and evaluative tools for counselor training (Gibson et al., 2015; Pérez-Rosas et al., 2017; Zhong et al., 2020) in addition to other educational domains (Wambsganss et al., 2021). Yet empathy prediction is a challenge for current language technologies due to resource availability and difficulty defining a gold standard for the complex phenomenon.

The lack of proper resources for empathy modeling limits the ability of the NLP community to more widely explore it. Many studies, for instance, are on sensitive data that cannot be made public. There are some datasets that are publicly available that are built on social media platforms, or through specific data collection tasks, however, these are few and far between, and each have limitations due to inherent challenges in the collection and annotation process.

A general challenge with studying empathy is how to define the concept concretely enough to obtain consistent and relevant gold standard annotations, as there are many highly varied definitions in psychology research (Cuff et al., 2016). Furthermore, empathy datasets in NLP are almost always annotated by others rather than the person having an empathetic experience (Buechel et al., 2018) or the person on the receiving end. Such annotations thus indicate particular aspects of language identified by a removed observer, rather than provide insight into the effect that particular empathetic experiences have on language.

Toward this issue, Buechel et al. (2018) developed the EMPATHETICREACTIONS dataset, which contains empathic concern and personal distress ratings based on self-evaluations of individuals' own empathetic experiences at the time of writing the text. These reactions are short essays in which the author describes their feelings as they would to a friend after reading an article meant to evoke empathy. This data may then enable analysis into the way the empathetic experiences impact or relate to produced language. The EMPATHETICREACTIONS dataset is used for predicting empathy and distress in the WASSA 2022 Shared Task, enabling a large group of people to research empathy prediction on a standard and public set of data.

In this paper, we present our experiments for empathy and distress prediction as part of WASSA 2022. We explore adapters for the task since it is more efficient than full fine-tuning, which so far has not been explored for empathy prediction. Following work on domain transfer, we also build a system leveraging additional empathy data, as the amount of empathy data is still sparse.

[1] https://github.com/caisa-lab/wassa-empathy-adapters

Proceedings of the 12th Workshop on Computational Approaches to Subjectivity, Sentiment & Social Media Analysis, pages 280 - 285

2 Background

The ability to recognize empathy in text is important for advancing language technologies from dialogue agents to computational social science tools. As such, there is a growing body of research on automatic empathy recognition. Many studies concern highly sensitive and important scenarios such as counseling and medical dialogues (Sharma et al., 2020) or are crisis-related (Zhang et al., 2020) but such resources are protected and cannot be made public. However, there are a number of recently proposed empathy datasets available to the public, which are consolidated by means such as collecting and labeling social media (Sharma et al., 2020; Zhou and Jurgens, 2020), or through collection tasks (Rashkin et al., 2019; Buechel et al., 2018).

Annotating empathy involves a host of challenges. Most datasets are annotated by someone who did not take part in the writing or conversation, requiring them to interpret how the author felt, rather than acquiring this information from the authors directly. Also, there are various definitions of empathy across fields. Generally, NLP has considered *emotional empathy*, despite the prevalence of other components of empathy in psychology (Cuff et al., 2016). There have been valuable efforts to build resources for empathy identification, each operating upon different perspectives of empathy.

Sharma et al. (2020)'s EPITOME dataset, contains support-seeker and responder post pairs from Reddit and has multi-faceted empathy labels on the responder posts. The responder posts are annotated with the degree of three different aspects of empathy (interpretations, emotional reactions, and explorations), 0 for absent, 1 for weak, and 2 for strong. As this scheme contains distinct labels for both emotional and cognitive aspects of empathy, this dataset is a valuable resource for pursuing empathetic modeling beyond emotional aspects.

Zhou and Jurgens (2020) introduced a dataset post-response pairs from Reddit where the post contains an expression of distress and the response is a condolence. While the final dataset contained one empathy score, the annotation process was strictly guided by a multi-faceted definition of empathy, the *appraisal theory* (Lamm et al., 2007; Wondra and Ellsworth, 2015). Under this definition, the degree of empathy is how closely the responder's appraisal of another person's situation matches the person's appraisal of their own situation.

Rashkin et al. (2019)'s EMPATHETICDIALOGUES dataset contains conversations grounded in one of 32 emotions. During data collection, participants were instructed to converse with each other. Dialogues contain emotion labels but not empathy labels. Welivita and Pu (2020) further annotated empathetic intents in this dataset.

Buechel et al. (2018) built the EMPATHETICREACTIONS dataset based on Batson's Empathic Concern – Personal Distress Scale (Batson et al., 1987). Under this view, there are two aspects of empathetic reactions, the level a personal distress experienced by the reactor ("suffering with something") and the level of empathy ("feeling for someone") while maintaining self-other separation. Here, empathy involves emotional feelings such as compassion, warmth, and tenderness, whereas distress involves those such as worry, alarm, and grief.

These datasets may differ stylistically due to their different domains. Having this diversity is valuable so that we can study how empathetic communication may vary across contexts. However, as the volume of data across these datasets is still limited, it is important to understand if they can be leveraged together despite their differences.

3 Task and Dataset

This paper describes our system submitted for Track 1 of the WASSA 2022 task which concerns empathy and distress prediction in Buechel et al. (2018)'s dataset of empathic reactions to news stories. Empathetic reactions are captured in essays written by people who were asked to read an article that involves a harmful situation a write a response. Participants were asked to rate their empathy after reading an article before writing their response. These ratings were self-measured using Batson's Empathic Concern - Personal Distress Scale (Batson et al., 1987), which contains multiple items that were averaged in order to obtain the gold ratings for empathy and distress.

The task of Track 1 of WASSA 2022 was to predict the numerical values for empathy and distress on a continuous scale for the essays. Systems were evaluated by Pearson's r correlation between the predictions and the actual values in a test set. WASSA provided an extension of the dataset to include the original news articles, demographics (age, gender, ethnicity, income, education level) and personality information. The extension also included emotion labels obtained using pretrained emotion detection models.

4 System Description

Adapters offer a lightweight tuning strategy alternative to full fine-tuning (Houlsby et al., 2019). With adapter-tuning, new initialized layers are inserted at each layer of the original pretrained network, and the new weights are fine-tuned while the original network's weights remain fixed. Adapters have been shown to effectively perform at near state-of-the-art levels while drastically improving efficiency (Houlsby et al., 2019; Pfeiffer et al., 2020b, 2021).

As reported by the WASSA 2021 task (Tafreshi et al., 2021), the most robust systems for empathy and distress modeling involved fine-tuning of transformer models such as RoBERTA (Liu et al., 2019) and ELECTRA (Clark et al., 2020). In our experiments, we attempt an adapter tuning approach (Houlsby et al., 2019) motivated by their efficiency, and compare to full fine-tuning.

Furthermore, we experiment with leveraging a different empathy dataset, EPITOME (Sharma et al., 2020). This dataset contains support-seeker and responder posts on Reddit (as described in § 2).

Full fine-tuning. For our full fine-tuning approaches, we fine-tune RoBERTa using `roberta-base` from the HuggingFace library (Wolf et al., 2020) for separate models predicting the essay's empathy and distress scores. Our most basic model ROBERTA is trained only on the essay text.

The second model EMOROBERTA is fine-tuned with emotional features, by leveraging the sentence-level emotion tags provided for the shared task, particularly the labels from the transformer model. For each essay, we concatenate each sentence's emotion tag to the sentence. We define these emotion tags as special tokens when tokenizing the text (e.g., [sadness]). We also include a separator token between each sentence after the emotion tag. To obtain these labels for the test dataset, we trained an adapter for roberta-base to predict these labels. This classifier attained 83.9, 83.8, and 80.2 for accuracy, weighted F1, and macro F1 respectively on the dev dataset.

For our final full fine-tuning approach EPITOMEFT we leverage the EPITOME dataset (Sharma et al., 2020) to obtain implicit empathy features from this other domain and labeling scheme. We fine-tune roberta-base to predict the level of empathy in the emotional reactions, explorations, and interpretations defined in their labeling scheme. The model we submitted for the test set was trained on the aspects consecutively.

Adapter-tuning. For our implementation we leverage AdapterHub (Pfeiffer et al., 2020a) which is a simple framework built on HuggingFace `transformers`. For our approach we train Tasks Adapters for a RoBERTa model to predict the empathy and distress scores for an essay.

EPITOMEFUSION: First we fine-tune three separate adapters to classify the degree of each of the three aspects of empathy in the EPITOME dataset. Then, we combine these adapters using AdapterFusion composition (Pfeiffer et al., 2021). This setup allows for combining the knowledge of each of the pre-trained adapters for the EPITOME tasks in order to leverage them in the WASSA empathy and distress prediction tasks. A classification head for the WASSA tasks is added on top of the fusion layer, and then trained.

EMOTIONSTACK: Following the procedure by Poth et al. (2021) to identify a similar adapters trained on a similar dataset, we identified a pre-trained emotion adapter available on AdapterHub.[2] This adapter was trained by Poth et al. (2021) on a dataset of English tweets (Saravia et al., 2018) with Ekman's six basic emotion labels (Eckman, 1972); the same emotion labels as in EMPATHETICREACTIONS dataset. Using this adapter is an alternative to using emotions explicitly labeled for the target dataset.

To leverage the knowledge of this pretrained adapter, we use the stacked composition setup presented by Pfeiffer et al. (2020b) (see Fig. 1 [3]), by stacking our task adapter, i.e. empathy or distress prediction, on the emotion adapter. The empathetic reaction essays are first input into the emotion adapter, and its output and residual are input to the empathy task adapter. Thus, the empathy task adapter is essentially obtaining predictions of Ekman's six emotions for the essays. While training the empathy adapter, the emotion adapter remains frozen.

5 Results and Discussion

Results from our submissions to the post-evaluation phase on the test dataset are presented in Table 1. The EMOTIONSTACK outperformed all other models on the test dataset on both empathy and distress

[2]`https://huggingface.co/AdapterHub/roberta-base-pf-emotion`

[3]`https://docs.adapterhub.ml/adapter_composition.html`

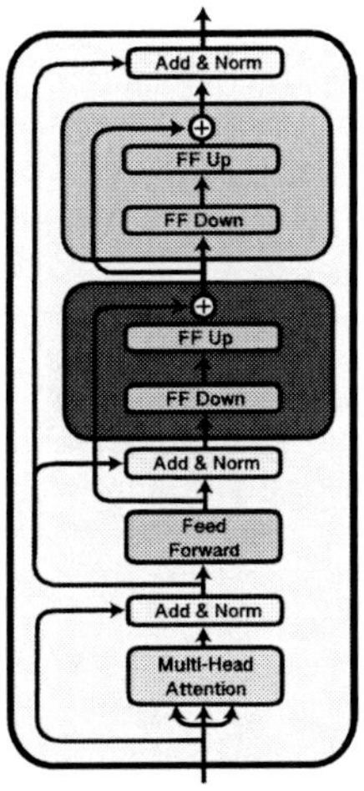

Figure 1: Stacked adapter composition.

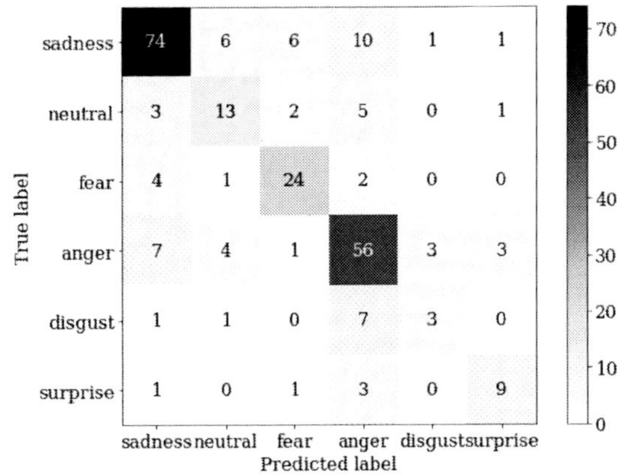

Figure 2: Confusion matrix of emotion predictions on dev dataset.

Model	Emp	Dis	Avg
EmotionStack	**0.524**	**0.521**	**0.523**
EpitomeFusion	0.472	0.496	0.484
RoBERTa	0.505	0.463	0.484
EmoRoBERTa	0.478	0.493	0.486
EpitomeFT	0.476	0.382	0.430

Table 1: Empathy and Distress prediction results on the test dataset.

detection. On average, the results of EpitomeFusion are comparable to the full fine-tuning approaches, namely RoBERTa and EmoRoBERTa, by slightly outperforming on distress detection and underperforming on empathy prediction. EpitomeFT performed worst on average due a particularly low score on distress prediction.

While we only explored the EMP track's tasks of empathy and distress prediction, the performance of the EmotionStack inspired us to submit predictions for the EMO track, predicting emotions. We used the same model, only changing the label set-up from predicting one value to predicting the six emotion categories–sadness, neutral, fear, anger, disgust, and surprise. This approach ranked highly with a macro F1-score of **0.604**. A confusion matrix for our classifier is shown in Figure 2.

The results of the adapter approach are exciting as it allievates the heaviness of full fine tuning. Adapters make it easy to leverage knowledge from other tasks learned on other datasets. In particular, we observe positive effects from using the pretrained emotion adapter on these tasks, which likely provides important emotional information relevant to empathic concern and personal distress.

However, we see no improvement from using the EPITOME data. Similarly, recent work found separate empathy types were found to have different effects on toxicity reduction (Lahnala et al., 2022). In preliminary experiments, we fine-tuned on only one of these aspects at a time, as we were interested in whether they have distinct effects and whether one or a combination of them is particularly well suited for our tasks. Further work is needed to definitively understand the effect of EPITOME and it's aspects on empathy and distress detection in the EmpatheticReactions. Given the sparsity of public empathy data, it is imperative for future work to better understand how the existing datasets can complement each other.

6 Conclusion

We presented our models for empathy and distress prediction on the EmpatheticReactions dataset for the WASSA 2022 shared task. We found that a stacked adapter composition with the WASSA task adapter stacked on a pre-trained emotion adapter (EmotionStack) outperformed other methods. This approach mitigates the costs of full fine-tuning while achieving comparable results. Furthermore, this method required no additional features beyond the empathetic reaction text. We further discussed challenges of researching empathy in natural language processing. In future work, we could explore incorporating the personal features provided for the shared task. We plan to further explore the use of different empathy datasets together for empathy prediction.

References

C Daniel Batson, Jim Fultz, and Patricia A Schoenrade. 1987. Distress and empathy: Two qualitatively distinct vicarious emotions with different motivational consequences. *Journal of personality*, 55(1):19–39.

Sven Buechel, Anneke Buffone, Barry Slaff, Lyle Ungar, and João Sedoc. 2018. Modeling empathy and distress in reaction to news stories. In *Proceedings of the 2018 Conference on Empirical Methods in Natural Language Processing*, pages 4758–4765, Brussels, Belgium. Association for Computational Linguistics.

Kevin Clark, Minh-Thang Luong, Quoc Le, and Christopher D Manning. 2020. Pre-training transformers as energy-based cloze models. In *Proceedings of the 2020 Conference on Empirical Methods in Natural Language Processing (EMNLP)*, pages 285–294.

Benjamin MP Cuff, Sarah J Brown, Laura Taylor, and Douglas J Howat. 2016. Empathy: A review of the concept. *Emotion review*, 8(2):144–153.

Paul Eckman. 1972. Universal and cultural differences in facial expression of emotion. In *Nebraska symposium on motivation*, volume 19, pages 207–284. University of Nebraska Press Lincoln.

James Gibson, Nikolaos Malandrakis, Francisco Romero, David C Atkins, and Shrikanth S Narayanan. 2015. Predicting therapist empathy in motivational interviews using language features inspired by psycholinguistic norms. In *Sixteenth annual conference of the international speech communication association*.

Neil Houlsby, Andrei Giurgiu, Stanislaw Jastrzebski, Bruna Morrone, Quentin De Laroussilhe, Andrea Gesmundo, Mona Attariyan, and Sylvain Gelly. 2019. Parameter-efficient transfer learning for nlp. In *International Conference on Machine Learning*, pages 2790–2799. PMLR.

Allison Lahnala, Charles Welch, Béla Neuendorf, and Lucie Flek. 2022. Mitigating toxic degeneration with empathetic data: Exploring the relationship between toxicity and empathy. In *Proceedings of the 2022 Conference of the North American Chapter of the Association for Computational Linguistics (Forthcoming)*.

Allison Lahnala, Yuntian Zhao, Charles Welch, Jonathan K Kummerfeld, Lawrence C An, Kenneth Resnicow, Rada Mihalcea, and Verónica Pérez-Rosas. 2021. Exploring self-identified counseling expertise in online support forums. In *Findings of the Association for Computational Linguistics: ACL-IJCNLP 2021*, pages 4467–4480.

Claus Lamm, C Daniel Batson, and Jean Decety. 2007. The neural substrate of human empathy: effects of perspective-taking and cognitive appraisal. *Journal of cognitive neuroscience*, 19(1):42–58.

Zhaojiang Lin, Peng Xu, Genta Indra Winata, Farhad Bin Siddique, Zihan Liu, Jamin Shin, and Pascale Fung. 2020. Caire: An end-to-end empathetic chatbot. In *Proceedings of the AAAI Conference on Artificial Intelligence*, volume 34, pages 13622–13623.

Yinhan Liu, Myle Ott, Naman Goyal, Jingfei Du, Mandar Joshi, Danqi Chen, Omer Levy, Mike Lewis, Luke Zettlemoyer, and Veselin Stoyanov. 2019. Roberta: A robustly optimized bert pretraining approach. *arXiv preprint arXiv:1907.11692*.

Navonil Majumder, Pengfei Hong, Shanshan Peng, Jiankun Lu, Deepanway Ghosal, Alexander Gelbukh, Rada Mihalcea, and Soujanya Poria. 2020. Mime: Mimicking emotions for empathetic response generation. In *Proceedings of the 2020 Conference on Empirical Methods in Natural Language Processing (EMNLP)*, pages 8968–8979.

Verónica Pérez-Rosas, Rada Mihalcea, Kenneth Resnicow, Satinder Singh, and Lawrence An. 2017. Understanding and predicting empathic behavior in counseling therapy. In *Proceedings of the 55th Annual Meeting of the Association for Computational Linguistics (Volume 1: Long Papers)*, pages 1426–1435.

Jonas Pfeiffer, Aishwarya Kamath, Andreas Rücklé, Kyunghyun Cho, and Iryna Gurevych. 2021. Adapterfusion: Non-destructive task composition for transfer learning. In *Proceedings of the 16th Conference of the European Chapter of the Association for Computational Linguistics: Main Volume*, pages 487–503.

Jonas Pfeiffer, Andreas Rücklé, Clifton Poth, Aishwarya Kamath, Ivan Vulić, Sebastian Ruder, Kyunghyun Cho, and Iryna Gurevych. 2020a. Adapterhub: A framework for adapting transformers. In *Proceedings of the 2020 Conference on Empirical Methods in Natural Language Processing: System Demonstrations*, pages 46–54.

Jonas Pfeiffer, Ivan Vulić, Iryna Gurevych, and Sebastian Ruder. 2020b. Mad-x: An adapter-based framework for multi-task cross-lingual transfer. In *Proceedings of the 2020 Conference on Empirical Methods in Natural Language Processing (EMNLP)*, pages 7654–7673.

Clifton Poth, Jonas Pfeiffer, Andreas Rücklé, and Iryna Gurevych. 2021. What to pre-train on? efficient intermediate task selection. In *Proceedings of the 2021 Conference on Empirical Methods in Natural Language Processing*, pages 10585–10605.

Hannah Rashkin, Eric Michael Smith, Margaret Li, and Y-Lan Boureau. 2019. Towards empathetic open-domain conversation models: A new benchmark and dataset. In *Proceedings of the 57th Annual Meeting of the Association for Computational Linguistics*, pages 5370–5381.

Elvis Saravia, Hsien-Chi Toby Liu, Yen-Hao Huang, Junlin Wu, and Yi-Shin Chen. 2018. CARER: Contextualized affect representations for emotion recognition. In *Proceedings of the 2018 Conference on Empirical Methods in Natural Language Processing*, pages 3687–3697, Brussels, Belgium. Association for Computational Linguistics.

Ashish Sharma, Adam Miner, David Atkins, and Tim Althoff. 2020. A computational approach to understanding empathy expressed in text-based mental health support. In *Proceedings of the 2020 Conference on Empirical Methods in Natural Language Processing (EMNLP)*, pages 5263–5276.

Shabnam Tafreshi, Orphée De Clercq, Valentin Barriere, Sven Buechel, João Sedoc, and Alexandra Balahur. 2021. Wassa 2021 shared task: Predicting empathy and emotion in reaction to news stories. In *Proceedings of the Eleventh Workshop on Computational Approaches to Subjectivity, Sentiment and Social Media Analysis*, pages 92–104.

Thiemo Wambsganss, Christina Niklaus, Matthias Söllner, Siegfried Handschuh, and Jan Marco Leimeister. 2021. Supporting cognitive and emotional empathic writing of students. In *Proceedings of the 59th Annual Meeting of the Association for Computational Linguistics and the 11th International Joint Conference on Natural Language Processing (Volume 1: Long Papers)*, pages 4063–4077, Online. Association for Computational Linguistics.

Anuradha Welivita and Pearl Pu. 2020. A taxonomy of empathetic response intents in human social conversations. In *Proceedings of the 28th International Conference on Computational Linguistics*, pages 4886–4899.

Thomas Wolf, Lysandre Debut, Victor Sanh, Julien Chaumond, Clement Delangue, Anthony Moi, Pierric Cistac, Tim Rault, Rémi Louf, Morgan Funtowicz, Joe Davison, Sam Shleifer, Patrick von Platen, Clara Ma, Yacine Jernite, Julien Plu, Canwen Xu, Teven Le Scao, Sylvain Gugger, Mariama Drame, Quentin Lhoest, and Alexander M. Rush. 2020. Transformers: State-of-the-art natural language processing. In *Proceedings of the 2020 Conference on Empirical Methods in Natural Language Processing: System Demonstrations*, pages 38–45, Online. Association for Computational Linguistics.

Joshua D Wondra and Phoebe C Ellsworth. 2015. An appraisal theory of empathy and other vicarious emotional experiences. *Psychological review*, 122(3):411.

Justine Zhang, Sendhil Mullainathan, and Cristian Danescu-Niculescu-Mizil. 2020. Quantifying the causal effects of conversational tendencies. *Proceedings of the ACM on Human-Computer Interaction*, 4(CSCW2):1–24.

Peixiang Zhong, Chen Zhang, Hao Wang, Yong Liu, and Chunyan Miao. 2020. Towards persona-based empathetic conversational models. In *Proceedings of the 2020 Conference on Empirical Methods in Natural Language Processing (EMNLP)*, pages 6556–6566, Online. Association for Computational Linguistics.

Naitian Zhou and David Jurgens. 2020. Condolence and empathy in online communities. In *Proceedings of the 2020 Conference on Empirical Methods in Natural Language Processing (EMNLP)*, pages 609–626.

NLPOP: a Dataset for Popularity Prediction of Promoted NLP Research on Twitter

Leo Obadić, Martin Tutek, Jan Šnajder
Text Analysis and Knowledge Engineering Lab
Faculty of Electrical Engineering and Computing, University of Zagreb
Unska 3, 10000 Zagreb, Croatia
obadic.leo@gmail.com, {martin.tutek, jan.snajder}@fer.hr

Abstract

Twitter has slowly but surely established itself as a forum for disseminating, analysing and promoting NLP research. The trend of researchers promoting work not yet peer-reviewed (*preprints*) by posting concise summaries presented itself as an opportunity to collect and combine multiple modalities of data. In scope of this paper, we (1) construct a dataset of Twitter threads in which researchers promote NLP preprints and (2) evaluate whether it is possible to predict the popularity of a thread based on the content of the Twitter thread, paper content and user metadata. We experimentally show that it is possible to predict popularity of threads promoting research based on their content, and that predictive performance depends on modelling textual input, indicating that the dataset could present value for related areas of NLP research such as citation recommendation and abstractive summarization.

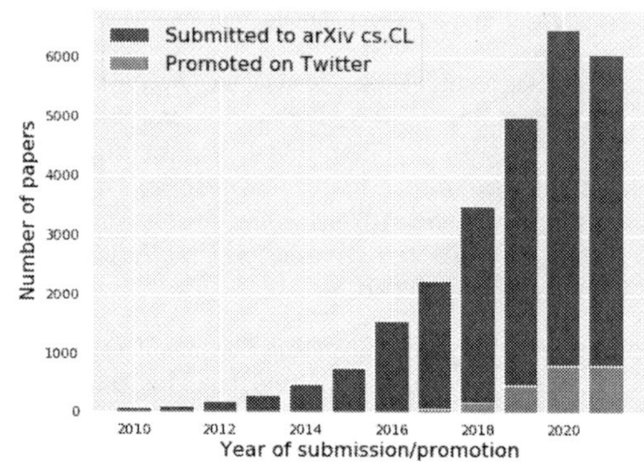

Figure 1: Distribution of the number of preprints published on arXiv under computational linguistics (cs.CL) and preprints promoted on Twitter as per the data in our dataset. Note that statistics for 2021 are incomplete.

1 Introduction

The now not-so-recent neural revolution caused a widespread increase of interest in machine learning research. Through improvements obtained across the field by applying deep neural networks, every application of machine learning became open for researchers to publish work pushing pre-neural boundaries, whether that work applied a neural architecture to a problem (Kalchbrenner and Blunsom, 2013; Sutskever et al., 2014), unveiled the black box of deep neural networks (Simonyan et al., 2014; Li et al., 2016) or coming up with a new architecture altogether (He et al., 2016; Vaswani et al., 2017). The rapid progress paved way for more researchers to enter the field, which resulted in an ever increasing volume of research work published year by year.

The large volume of work meant that it is difficult for a single person to keep up to date with relevant research. Thus, a need emerged for a platform where work can be shared, filtered and discussed on a scale larger than research labs. Twitter, a microblogging social network emerged as the chosen forum. The otherwise prohibitive 280 character limit on each post ("tweet") can in this context be viewed as a feature – it promotes succinctness and discourages lengthy academic prose. A portion of researchers accepted that promoting your academic work on Twitter is something that you do – and if done well, it is believed that your research pedigree and citation count will increase. While this statement has not yet been put to test, the increase of posts promoting research work indicates that many believe it (Figure 1).

Along with sharing a link to your paper, it is common to provide a concise summary outlining the main idea and contributions of your work in form of a post thread. In scope of this paper we aim to collect a dataset of Twitter threads promoting research work and evaluate whether the popularity of a post can be determined from the content of the thread, paper, or user information. We would like to emphasize that we do not believe that scientific work being popular implies that the work itself is good, but rather aim to analyse whether it is possi-

Proceedings of the 12th Workshop on Computational Approaches to Subjectivity, Sentiment & Social Media Analysis, pages 286 - 292
May 26, 2022 ©2022 Association for Computational Linguistics

ble to determine factors which lead to higher visibility. Researchers could then use findings from such analysis to hopefully reach a broader audience.

2 Related Work

Predicting popularity of messages is a straightforward task from the perspective of machine learning and has been framed both as a regression (Lampos et al., 2014) and classification problem (Hong et al., 2011; Jenders et al., 2013; Subramanian et al., 2018; Fiok et al., 2020), while work on information cascades (Zhao et al., 2015; Li et al., 2017; Zhou et al., 2021) focuses on modeling the entire lifetime of a post as a point process.

Work in the area of computational linguistics mainly focuses on analysing the underlying causes of popularity: Tan et al. (2014) evaluate whether wording affects popularity of posts and find a number of patterns which popular posts adhere to, Jaech et al. (2015) analyse how use of language gets people involved in online discussions, while approaches such as Karimi et al. (2016) and Zarezade et al. (2017) aim to help users reach a larger audience. Only recently has the effect of social media on collaboration between researchers been analysed (Gorska et al., 2020) although there have been indications that younger generations of scholars prefer using social media to foster collaboration (Murthy and Lewis, 2015) – which also might relate to the newly discovered phenomenon of preference for citing recent work (Bollmann and Elliott, 2020).

3 Dataset

When constructing our dataset, we limit ourselves to posts promoting academic research in the field of NLP on Twitter in English language. This choice was motivated by two reasons: (1) we believe that for a popularity prediction model to be successful, the domain should be narrow and (2) as all authors of this paper are involved in NLP research, we have a deep personal interest in whether it is possible to determine what constitutes a "good" post which promotes academic reseach on social media.

We first selected a set of NLP researcher Twitter users, which we then manually validated. We then fetched all posts of these users that contained a link which resolved on arXiv[1], and then selected a subset of these posts which formed threads containing comments from the same root user. The latter step was done to avoid bot accounts which automatically share all preprints and as an attempt to ensure that threads contain a summary of the paper referred to. Nevertheless, these simple rules are by no means exhaustive. It is likely that the dataset contains threads from users which do not summarize the paper, while it definitely contains summaries written by users that are not authors of the paper. While we considered manually validating each thread, we chose not to as doing so would make scaling the dataset in the future infeasible. For the sake of space, we omit the detailed description of dataset construction to Appendix A.

3.1 Data Feature Groups

Once finalized, our NLP preprint popularity dataset[2] (henceforth NLPOP) consists of four distinct input feature groups: (1) the preprint title and abstract text, encoded separately (PAPER), (2) the Twitter thread text (THREAD), (3) Twitter user biographical data (BIO) and (4) numeric metadata features (NUM) of the user profile and the Twitter thread. It also contains two target variables: (1) the number of likes and (2) the number of retweets.

The first three feature groups consist of textual data, but differ in style and content. The preprint title and abstract contain the academic style writeup of the research work, the thread text consists of a brief summary which elaborates the key points of the paper in a more informal manner, while the biographical data is a personal description of the researcher. The numeric features consist of various metadata which might be useful for the prediction of the model pertaining to either the user: (1) account creation timestamp, (2,3) number of followers and followings, (4) number of tweets for that user, (5) number of favourites and (6) the number of lists the user is in; or pertaining to the tweet: (7) tweet creation timestamp, and (8) the hour of day (in UTC) the tweet was posted at.

We summarize the statistics of the dataset in Table 1. We do not propose a single pre-made dataset split as multiple ways the dataset could be split exist, which we comment on in Appendix B.

4 Methodology

We will first define the notion of popularity. While some other works (Tan et al., 2014; Zhao et al., 2015) have considered only the final number of

[1] https://arxiv.org/

[2] The dataset is available at https://github.com/lobadic/nlpop

	Dataset size	2292
	Distinct users	858
Feature	Avg.	Std.
Likes	65.6	124.2
Retweets	15.3	36.6
BIO*	5.7	5.7
PAPER*	218.8	195.6
THREAD*	149.0	157.9

Table 1: Dataset statistics. For textual features (annotated with *) the average and standard deviation pertain to length in words. Statistics for the number of likes and retweets are computed on raw scores.

reshares (*retweets*) as the popularity criterion, we also consider predicting the number of *likes* a post receives (Jenders et al., 2013) as another task.

4.1 Task Formulation

As both of our target variables are numeric, a natural course of action is to approach the task as regression (Lampos et al., 2014). However, if the exact value of the target variable is not relevant, it is common to transform the problem into classification by defining thresholds for popularity categories (Fiok et al., 2020).

Regression. Treating the problem as regression (REG) preserves more information from the target variable as we avoid the lossy transformation into a categorical variable. Due to large differences in scale of the output variables, we first scale the target variable by applying the natural logarithm and use the mean squared error (MSE) as the criterion. A task trained this way is still evaluated as a classification task by performing the same transformation into discrete classes on the outputs of the regression model.

Classification. In our case, we follow (Fiok et al., 2020) and opt for the three-class approach (CLF), where the classes: "not popular", "popular" and "very popular" are determined as the lower quartile (bottom 25%), the middle 50% and the top quartile (top 25%). We compute the values for the thresholds on the training split of the dataset.

Ordinal classification. Apart from the information lost in the transformation, another downside of the classification approach is that discrete classes do not retain ordinal information. To this end, we adopt the approach from Frank and Hall (ORD; 2001) and transform the discrete classes into ordinal labels. In this approach, N classes are encoded as a binary vector of length $N - 1$, where each bit being set indicates that the target variable is greater than the treshold for that class. Thus, if a bit is set, all the less significant bits also have to be set[3]. Using this approach, the model will learn to model the order between classes – as the popularity increases, the model has to set that many more bits in the output prediction.

4.2 Preprocessing

When preprocessing text inputs, we use spaCy[4] for tokenization, filter punctuation tokens, replace hyperlinks with `<URL>` and separate posts in a thread with `<SEP>`. We consider only the 10000 most frequent word tokens for the models which do not use a pre-trained vocabulary and truncate sequences longer than 512 tokens. The numeric features are scaled to the $[0, 1]$ interval using scikit-learn's[5] `MinMaxScaler`.

We split the dataset in proportions of $0.7 : 0.1 : 0.2$ for the train, validation and test set, respectively. When splitting, we ensure that each user exists in only one of the splits to prevent information leakage via profile information. We attempt to ensure that the distribution of target variables is as similar as possible by running 10000 random splits with different seeds and choosing the one where the means and standard deviations have minimal difference between the splits.

4.3 Models

We consider three model families of text encoders with increasing complexity: an IDF-weighted averaging approach (AVG; Ramos et al., 2003), a GRU-based encoder model (RNN; Cho et al., 2014) and a pretrained RoBERTa-large model (BERT; Liu et al., 2019). For simplicity, we always use the same text encoder to encode all textual input features. In the AVG and RNN models, the word inputs are initialized to 300-dimensional GloVe embeddings (Pennington et al., 2014). Due to the small scale of the dataset, we do not fine-tine the ROBERTA encoder, but use the encodings from the last layer as-is. To obtain a fixed-size representation, we consider averaging the embeddings, pooling them using the

[3]Concretely, for our three-class approach, the vector [00] would correspond to the "not popular" class, the lowermost bit [01] would indicate that the instance is "popular", while both bits being set [11] corresponds to the "very popular" class.

[4]`https://spacy.io/`

[5]`https://scikit-learn.org/stable/`

	# Likes			# Retweets		
Feature groups	AVG	RNN	BERT	AVG	RNN	BERT
NUM	39.14			37.10		
BIO	36.90	**40.58**	40.19	35.45	34.59	37.34
PAPER	29.92	29.32	39.06	40.12	24.24	42.52
THREAD	46.65	23.17	54.43	41.19	21.96	**53.14**
NUM, BIO	40.82	37.22	42.29	35.06	**41.07**	40.11
NUM, THREAD	**49.25**	37.90	53.78	**46.59**	31.22	51.68
THREAD, PAPER	41.44	24.56	54.28	38.72	24.52	50.91
BIO, THREAD	47.82	39.36	55.93	39.28	34.53	50.85
NUM, BIO, THREAD	47.13	39.40	56.23	42.03	37.17	52.35
ALL	44.82	40.12	**58.59**	45.88	31.40	51.69

Table 2: Overall best performing models across all considered training tasks for different feature sets. Scores reported are 100×macro-F1. Best scores in each column are **boldfaced**, best scores in each row are underlined.

pretrained pooler or taking the encodings of the SEP or CLS tokens. The encoded outputs of each considered input feature group are concatenated and used as inputs to a MLP classifier. For the sake of space, we detail considered hyperparameters of all models in Appendix C.

5 Results

When reporting results, we will mainly be looking to answer the following questions: (1) do more complex text encoders improve prediction performance?; (2) which feature groups improve the performance the most?; (3) which task type suits the problem the most?; and (4) in which cases do the models make mistakes? We do not report exhaustive ablation combinations for the sake of space and as the unreported combinations perform worse.

To answer the first two questions, we perform an ablation study and report the results in Table 2. Here, we can immediately notice that BERT-based models perform the best, indicating that content does matter for popularity. Secondly, we can see that the RNN model performs the worst. We believe this is caused by the relatively small size of the dataset and the fact that the recurrent encoders need to be trained from scratch, which causes the model to frequently overfit.

Analysing the effect of feature groups, we can see that the THREAD itself performs the best in isolation for both target variables, except for RNN models – indicating that a good summary influences the popularity the most. When analysing the THREAD features in combination with other feature groups for the LIKE prediction case, the BIO offers the most improvement, with PAPER the second most important group, indicating that paper content matters for popularity. For the RETWEET case, surprisingly, adding any feature group diminishes the performance of the BERT model, emphasizing the fact that the content of the thread is the most discriminative feature for determining popularity.

	# Likes			# Retweets		
Task	AVG	RNN	BERT	AVG	RNN	BERT
REG	38.4	35.5	48.4	43.5	29.1	45.6
CLF	**49.3**	**40.6**	**58.6**	**46.6**	**34.6**	**53.1**
ORD	40.8	37.2	54.6	44.0	31.9	52.4

Table 3: Overall best performing models for different task types. Scores reported are 100×macro-F1. Best results in each column **boldfaced**, best overall underlined.

Analysing the effect of the task formulation, in Table 3 we can see that the classification task performs best overall, although ordinal classification is the close second for BERT-based models.

Finally, we aim to understand whether the models are able to understand the class boundaries. To this end, we will take a look at the confusion matrices of the best performing models for the `#likes` (Table 4) and `#retweets` (Table 5) prediction tasks. In both tables, we can immediately see that the models generally only make mistakes in neighboring classes – indicating that although some cases might be borderline, the notion of popularity can be estimated from the input features. Furthermore, we can notice that the majority of the errors made are on the boundary between the first two classes, where the distinction between classes is made for a comparatively smaller value of the target variable. We believe that the fuzzy boundary between the two classes causes issues to the model, and in future work we aim to explore whether it is possible to set a clearer boundary.

6 Conclusion

We have introduced NLPOP: a novel dataset for popularity prediction which combines Twitter thread data, academic paper content and biographical user

	$y=0$	$y=1$	$y=2$
$\hat{y}=0$	61	49	9
$\hat{y}=1$	53	171	19
$\hat{y}=2$	11	35	48

Table 4: The confusion matrix of the best performing model (BERT-CLF) on the # Likes prediction task. True classes (y) are represented in columns, predicted classes $\hat{y}$ in rows. Class 0 corresponds to "not popular", 1 to "popular" and 2 to "very popular", respectively.

	$y=0$	$y=1$	$y=2$
$\hat{y}=0$	57	68	7
$\hat{y}=1$	40	156	28
$\hat{y}=2$	5	52	43

Table 5: The confusion matrix of the best performing model (BERT-CLF) on the # Retweets prediction task. True classes (y) are represented in columns, predicted classes $\hat{y}$ in rows. Class 0 corresponds to "not popular", 1 to "popular" and 2 to "very popular", respectively.

features. After carrying out ablation studies on input feature sets we have determined that, while the thread text is the most discriminative input, the content of the academic paper is also indicative of popularity measured in the number of likes. We believe that our dataset will grow at a significant pace over time and that in the future, it could be used to augment data in citation recommendation, as well as an evaluation dataset for abstractive summarization systems.

For future work, we aim to widen the pool of considered users by automating the manual validation process and plan on ensuring that the person promoting the work is an author of the paper – which could improve the quality of the summary. In scope of the paper we focused on presenting a proof-of-concept study, aiming to determine whether it is feasible to predict popularity of Twitter posts based on content, and whether such a dataset of significant size can be collected. We believe we have sufficiently demonstrated the quality of the dataset and the feasibility of the task to indicate its value for related NLP research areas.

References

Marcel Bollmann and Desmond Elliott. 2020. On forgetting to cite older papers: An analysis of the acl anthology. In *Proceedings of the 58th Annual Meeting of the Association for Computational Linguistics*, pages 7819–7827.

Kyunghyun Cho, Bart van Merriënboer, Caglar Gulcehre, Dzmitry Bahdanau, Fethi Bougares, Holger Schwenk, and Yoshua Bengio. 2014. Learning phrase representations using rnn encoder–decoder for statistical machine translation. In *Proceedings of the 2014 Conference on Empirical Methods in Natural Language Processing (EMNLP)*, pages 1724–1734.

Krzysztof Fiok, Waldemar Karwowski, Edgar Gutierrez, and Tareq Ahram. 2020. Predicting the volume of response to tweets posted by a single twitter account. *Symmetry*, 12(6):1054.

Eibe Frank and Mark Hall. 2001. A simple approach to ordinal classification. In *European conference on machine learning*, pages 145–156. Springer.

Anna Gorska, P Korzynski, G Mazurek, and F Pucciarelli. 2020. The role of social media in scholarly collaboration: an enabler of international research team's activation? *Journal of Global Information Technology Management*, 23(4):273–291.

Kaiming He, Xiangyu Zhang, Shaoqing Ren, and Jian Sun. 2016. Deep residual learning for image recognition. In *Proceedings of the IEEE conference on computer vision and pattern recognition*, pages 770–778.

Liangjie Hong, Ovidiu Dan, and Brian D Davison. 2011. Predicting popular messages in twitter. In *Proceedings of the 20th international conference companion on World wide web*, pages 57–58.

Aaron Jaech, Victoria Zayats, Hao Fang, Mari Ostendorf, and Hannaneh Hajishirzi. 2015. Talking to the crowd: What do people react to in online discussions? In *Proceedings of the 2015 Conference on Empirical Methods in Natural Language Processing*, pages 2026–2031.

Maximilian Jenders, Gjergji Kasneci, and Felix Naumann. 2013. Analyzing and predicting viral tweets. In *Proceedings of the 22nd international conference on world wide web*, pages 657–664.

Nal Kalchbrenner and Phil Blunsom. 2013. Recurrent continuous translation models. In *Proceedings of the 2013 conference on empirical methods in natural language processing*, pages 1700–1709.

Mohammad Reza Karimi, Erfan Tavakoli, Mehrdad Farajtabar, Le Song, and Manuel Gomez Rodriguez. 2016. Smart broadcasting: Do you want to be seen? In *Proceedings of the 22nd ACM SIGKDD international conference on Knowledge discovery and data mining*, pages 1635–1644.

Vasileios Lampos, Nikolaos Aletras, Daniel Preoţiuc-Pietro, and Trevor Cohn. 2014. Predicting and characterising user impact on twitter. In *14th conference of the European chapter of the Association for Computational Linguistics 2014, EACL 2014*, pages 405–413.

Cheng Li, Jiaqi Ma, Xiaoxiao Guo, and Qiaozhu Mei. 2017. Deepcas: An end-to-end predictor of information cascades. In *Proceedings of the 26th international conference on World Wide Web*, pages 577–586.

Jiwei Li, Xinlei Chen, Eduard Hovy, and Dan Jurafsky. 2016. Visualizing and understanding neural models in NLP. In *Proceedings of the 2016 Conference of the North American Chapter of the Association for Computational Linguistics: Human Language Technologies*, pages 681–691, San Diego, California. Association for Computational Linguistics.

Yinhan Liu, Myle Ott, Naman Goyal, Jingfei Du, Mandar Joshi, Danqi Chen, Omer Levy, Mike Lewis, Luke Zettlemoyer, and Veselin Stoyanov. 2019. Roberta: A robustly optimized bert pretraining approach. *arXiv preprint arXiv:1907.11692*.

Dhiraj Murthy and Jeremiah P Lewis. 2015. Social media, collaboration, and scientific organizations. *American behavioral scientist*, 59(1):149–171.

Jeffrey Pennington, Richard Socher, and Christopher D Manning. 2014. Glove: Global vectors for word representation. In *Proceedings of the 2014 conference on empirical methods in natural language processing (EMNLP)*, pages 1532–1543.

Juan Ramos et al. 2003. Using tf-idf to determine word relevance in document queries. In *Proceedings of the first instructional conference on machine learning*, 1, pages 29–48. Citeseer.

Karen Simonyan, Andrea Vedaldi, and Andrew Zisserman. 2014. Deep inside convolutional networks: Visualising image classification models and saliency maps. In *In Workshop at International Conference on Learning Representations*. Citeseer.

Shivashankar Subramanian, Timothy Baldwin, and Trevor Cohn. 2018. Content-based popularity prediction of online petitions using a deep regression model. In *Proceedings of the 56th Annual Meeting of the Association for Computational Linguistics (Volume 2: Short Papers)*, pages 182–188.

Ilya Sutskever, Oriol Vinyals, and Quoc V Le. 2014. Sequence to sequence learning with neural networks. In *Advances in neural information processing systems*, pages 3104–3112.

Chenhao Tan, Lillian Lee, and Bo Pang. 2014. The effect of wording on message propagation: Topic- and author-controlled natural experiments on twitter. In *Proceedings of the 52nd Annual Meeting of the Association for Computational Linguistics (Volume 1: Long Papers)*, pages 175–185.

Ashish Vaswani, Noam Shazeer, Niki Parmar, Jakob Uszkoreit, Llion Jones, Aidan N Gomez, Łukasz Kaiser, and Illia Polosukhin. 2017. Attention is all you need. In *Advances in neural information processing systems*, pages 5998–6008.

Ali Zarezade, Utkarsh Upadhyay, Hamid R Rabiee, and Manuel Gomez-Rodriguez. 2017. Redqueen: An online algorithm for smart broadcasting in social networks. In *Proceedings of the Tenth ACM International Conference on Web Search and Data Mining*, pages 51–60.

Qingyuan Zhao, Murat A Erdogdu, Hera Y He, Anand Rajaraman, and Jure Leskovec. 2015. Seismic: A self-exciting point process model for predicting tweet popularity. In *Proceedings of the 21th ACM SIGKDD international conference on knowledge discovery and data mining*, pages 1513–1522.

Fan Zhou, Xovee Xu, Goce Trajcevski, and Kunpeng Zhang. 2021. A survey of information cascade analysis: Models, predictions, and recent advances. *ACM Computing Surveys (CSUR)*, 54(2):1–36.

A Dataset construction details

To start the dataset construction process, we needed to create a set of Twitter accounts which we knew belonged to NLP researchers. Our initial set of users consisted of the Twitter followings of one of the authors (175 users). We then expanded this set by fetching users whose Twitter biographies contained a NLP keyword (NLP, CL or their expansions) and a general AI keyword (ML, AI or their expansions; to ensure that we avoid neuro-linguistic programming), which yielded 608 new users. We then manually validated the collected users to ensure quality, where after removing 26 users a total of 757 remained in the initial set.

We further expanded this initial set of users by fetching all the followers and followings of each user in the initial set (yielding a pool of 1.14M users). We then applied a similar filtering procedure, but retaining users which had a NLP keyword in their Twitter biography, resulting in 7851 new candidate users. This candidate set was once more manually verified, resulting in 7079 new users and a total of 7836 accounts in the final set (USERS).

In the next step we aimed to retrieve the posts of USERS which promote research work. To do this, we fetched only the posts which contained a link leading to arXiv[6], where it is categorized in the Computation and Language (cs.CL) category, either as the primary or secondary category. From these posts, we selected only the ones that formed

[6] `https://arxiv.org/`

Name	Value(s)
Max epochs	100
Optimizer	Adam
Patience	15
Batch size	32
AVG	
Vocabulary size	10000
Learning rate	$[1e^{-4}, 5e^{-4}, 1e^{-5}, 5e^{-5}]$
Freeze embeddings	True
Classifier hidden	$[512, 256]$
RNN	
Vocabulary size	10000
Learning rate	$[1e^{-4}, 5e^{-4}]$
Max seq length	512
Freeze embeddings	[True, False]
GRU hidden	$[128, 300]$
GRU dropout	0.3
GRU layers	2
Bidirectional	True
Classifier hidden	$[300]$
BERT	
Learning rate	$[1e^{-4}, 5e^{-4}, 1e^{-5}, 5e^{-5}]$
Max seq length	512
Classifier hidden	$[512, 256]$
Freeze model	True
Pooling strategy	[AVG, POOL, CLS, SEP]

Table 6: Hyperparameters of Considered Models

a thread (had more than one comment) in order to attempt to ensure that a brief description is provided by the person posting the link, and to avoid automated accounts which merely share the links to newly submitted papers on arXiv. We selected threads as the root post and all consecutive replies by the original poster to themselves. This selection process resulted in 2292 threads written by 858 distinct users. For each of these threads, we also retrieve the title and abstract of the preprint on arXiv. We further augment the dataset with Twitter biographical user data and thread metadata retrieved via the Twitter API[7]. The dataset was last updated on the 19th of October 2021.

B Dataset Splits

When splitting the dataset, there is a number of options we considered. We started with a completely random split as an initial step to be able to determine whether more intelligent ways of splitting the dataset improve performance by reducing bias (RANDOM). Our next step was to ensure that there is no user overlap between the dataset splits, attempting to minimize information leakage and the models overfitting to user data (USERS). This procedure, however, yielded imbalanced splits with respect to the target variables. To mitigate this issue, we resorted to a random search, where we ran the same splitting procedure 10000 times with different random seeds and selected the splits with minimal difference between the mean and standard deviations of the target variables (USERS-DIST). The determined thresholds for classes are $[0, 9)$ for "not popular", $[9, 71)$ for "popular" and $[71, \infty)$ for the "very popular" class in the like prediction scenario, while the respective thresholds are $[0, 2)$, $[2, 16)$ and $[16, \infty)$ for the retweet prediction scenario.

C Model Hyperparameters

When running our models, we fix some hyperparameters using manual tuning to reduce the search space and perform an exhaustive search over the remaining combinations. The full set of hyperparameters for all models is listed in Table 6. The best hyperparameters were selected with respect to model performance on the validation split, where $F1$ was the metric for classification models and MSE for regression models. All experiments were ran on four Nvidia GTX 1080 graphics cards.

[7]`https://developer.twitter.com/en/docs/twitter-api`

Tagging Without Rewriting: A Probabilistic Model for Unpaired Sentiment and Style Transfer

Shuo Yang
yangshuo@toki.waseda.jp

Abstract

Style transfer is the task of paraphrasing text into a target-style domain while retaining the content. Unsupervised approaches mainly focus on training a generator to rewrite input sentences. In this work, we assume that text styles are determined by only a small proportion of words; therefore, rewriting sentences via generative models may be unnecessary. As an alternative, we consider style transfer as a sequence tagging task. Specifically, we use edit operations (i.e., deletion, insertion and substitution) to tag words in an input sentence. We train a classifier and a language model to score tagged sequences and build a conditional random field. Finally, the optimal path in the conditional random field is used as the output. The results of experiments comparing models indicate that our proposed model exceeds end-to-end baselines in terms of accuracy on both sentiment and style transfer tasks with comparable or better content preservation.

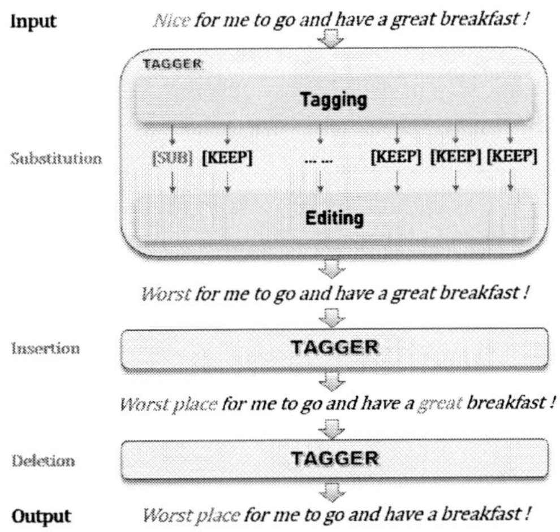

Figure 1: An example of our proposed approach.

1 Introduction

Text style refers to the attributes of text written in a particular form. Style transfer is the task of paraphrasing text into a target-style domain while retaining its content. In the domain of natural language generation, research on style transfer tasks (Li et al., 2018; Chawla and Yang, 2020) allows us to control the attributes of produced utterances.

Recently, sentiment transfer (Fu et al., 2018; Prabhumoye et al., 2018) has attracted much attention as a subtask of style transfer, an example being '*The food here is delicious*' (Positive) → '*The food here is gross*' (Negative). A style-indicative word is a word with a large contribution to style (Xu et al., 2018). In the above example, 'delicious' and 'gross' are style-indicative words.

A critical problem in sentiment transfer is the lack of available parallel data (Shen et al., 2017; Luo et al., 2019). As a result, related work has mainly focused on unsupervised learning. Among unsupervised approaches, those based on word modification have achieved state-of-the-art performance due to their ability to retain content words.

This paper mainly focuses on sentiment transfer and follows two generative models: the TAG model (Madaan et al., 2020) and LEWIS model (Reid and Zhong, 2021). The TAG model calculates term frequency-inverse document frequency scores to identify style-indicative words and trains an autoregressive model to substitute those words. The LEWIS model removes style-indicative words to extract a content template and trains a generator to perform edit operations on the template.

However, the aforementioned methods have the following drawbacks:

(1) It is unnecessary to identify style-indicative words. The fact that style-indicative words contribute more to a style does not imply that style-indicative words correspond to the optimal positions to be modified. For a negative-to-positive transfer example, the sentence '*Even great restaurants have bad days*' should be rephrased as '*Great restaurants never have bad days*' according to a human reference. Here, both the deleted word

Proceedings of the 12th Workshop on Computational Approaches to Subjectivity, Sentiment & Social Media Analysis, pages 293 - 303
May 26, 2022 ©2022 Association for Computational Linguistics

'Even' and inserted word 'never' are far away from the style-indicative word 'bad'. Furthermore, word identification may be less effective for non-descriptive text. For example, if there are no style-indicative words in a sentence, such as *'If you are into sports, this is the place for you'*(Positive), then identification will not be effective.

(2) No rationale is provided for the collocation of operations used, and models that perform different edit operations are treated as different models (Li et al., 2018; Madaan et al., 2020). However, we propose that edit operations should be used automatically in different situations. When multiple solutions exist, a basis for selecting the solution should be provided.

(3) It is redundant to rewrite style-independent words by using purely generative methods, as overlaps have been reported to be common between the input and output (Reid and Zhong, 2021). Rewriting all input words by using an end-to-end model increases the burden of the model and reduces its performance. In theory, additional learning of these words may be more likely to cause text degeneration (Holtzman et al., 2020).

To address the above-mentioned drawbacks, we propose the following:

(1) Tagging all words instead of identifying specific words. We employ edit operations to tag every word in an input sentence. To obtain a tagger without parallel data, we train a style classifier to score samples and build a conditional random field (CRF) (Lafferty et al., 2001). We use the classifier to calculate the probability distribution of tag sequences.

(2) Using a language model (LM) to select operations. If an input sentence has multiple solutions, we propose that text fluency be the basis for selection. For example, a negative sentence *'I'm not a huge fan of them'* can be rephrased as *'I'm a huge fan of them'* or *'I'm not a small fan of them'*. In this case, the former sounds more natural. To measure text fluency, we build an LM that scores sentences based on their perplexity. We use the score function as a joint feature function of the CRF.

(3) Searching in the CRF instead of rewriting the entire sentence. As mentioned above, we train a classifier and LM to build the CRF. By searching in the CRF, we generate an operation sequence. We apply the operation sequence to the input sentence to obtain the output.

In this paper, we first introduce our tagging strategy and a method we employed to implement edit operations (§ 3.1). Further, we introduce feature functions of the CRF (§ 3.2) and search strategies used (§ 3.3). We tested our model for transfer accuracy and content preservation on four data sets (§ 4) and analysed the experimental results of the automated evaluation (§ 5.1) and the experimental results of the manual evaluation (§ 5.2). In additional analysis (§ 5.3), we discussed the variances of sentence features in transformation.[1]

Our contributions are as follows:

- We propose a novel style transfer approach. To the best of our knowledge, this study is the first to apply CRFs to style transfer tasks.
- We propose a bias for selecting edit operations. The calculation of perplexity theoretically prevents generated words from conflicting with their original context.
- Experimental results show that our proposed model surpasses baselines in terms of accuracy or content retention on four data sets.

2 Related Work

2.1 Style Transfer in Latent Space

A traditional approach to style transfer is to disentangle the style and content in a latent space. For example, Shen et al. (2017) proposed a cross-aligned model that aligns samples at a shared hidden content distribution level across different corporations. In other work, Fu et al. (2018) proposed an approach that uses generative adversarial networks to extract content representations. These representations are decoded into a target-style domain as outputs. Manipulating representations in a latent space (Hu et al., 2017; Prabhumoye et al., 2018) is the main method used in the aforementioned studies. However, it has been reported that extracting style and content representations from a latent space is very difficult (Elazar and Goldberg, 2018).

2.2 Style Transfer by Modifying Words

Instead of extracting representations in a latent space, methods have recently been proposed to directly modify words (Sudhakar et al., 2019; Zhang et al., 2018). Li et al. (2018) proposed a delete-retrieve-generate pipeline that transfers samples based on the retrieval of similar sentences and performs well in sentiment transfer tasks. However, retrieval has been reported as an unnecessary

[1] Code is available on GitHub.

step (Madaan et al., 2020), and models that apply edit operations to sentences have produced superior results (Wu et al., 2019; Reid and Zhong, 2021). Malmi et al. (2020) proposed to use Masked LMs to identify tokens to modify. They replace the identified source tokens with target tokens to transform text to match the style of the target domain. However, models (Li et al., 2018; Madaan et al., 2020) based on end-to-end approaches suffer from text degeneration (Holtzman et al., 2020). Instead, we leverage intuitions about style transfer and uses smaller pieces of machine learning to build a targeted model. In this paper, we follow the second approach of fine-tuning sentences at a lexical level.

3 Methodology

Instead of training an end-to-end model, we perform a search over small edits to an input sentence, as it provides an interpretable record of the decisions the model made.

To formalize the problem, we consider sentence set $X_A = (x_A^{(1)}, ..., x_A^{(M)})$ with source style A and another sentence set $X_B = (x_B^{(1)}, ..., x_B^{(N)})$ with target style B. The sentences in these two sets are non-parallel; that is, $x_A^{(i)}$ does not correspond to $x_B^{(i)}$. The objective is to generate a new sentence set $\hat{X} = (\hat{x}^{(1)}, ..., \hat{x}^{(M)})$ in style B, where $\hat{x}^{(i)}$ is the result of transferring $x_A^{(i)}$ into style B.

3.1 Tagger

We use three basic edit operations to tag words in input sentences. Words that do not need to be modified are tagged with '[KEEP]', signifying that they will be retained in the output. Tags are presented in Table 1. We note that for words tagged with '[INS]', we will only insert words in front of them.

We introduce a terminator, denoted '<EOS>', to validate the insertion of words at the end of an input sentence. The terminator can only be tagged as '[INS]' or '[KEEP]'; that is, terminators are retained in the output. For reference, (Wu et al., 2019) regarded insertion in front of a word and behind the same word as different operations, which unnecessarily increased the burden on the tagger.

Only one word in an input sentence is modified in each iteration; that is, we introduce the constraint that only one word in each sentence cannot be tagged with '[KEEP]'. We refer to this as a one-word tagging strategy. For example, the sentence in Figure 1 is repeatedly modified three times to produce the output. The advantage of this method is that it reduces the modification of content words.

Tag	Operation
[INS]	Insert a word in front of the tagged word.
[SUB]	Substitute the tagged word with a new word.
[DEL]	Delete the tagged word.
[KEEP]	Retain the tagged word.

Table 1: Possible tags for a word and their corresponding word operations.

After a sentence is tagged, all words are subjected to the corresponding operations to generate a new sentence. We employ the Flexible Text Editing Method (Mallinson et al., 2020) to edit tagged sentences. For the input sentence in Figure 1, the first word, 'Nice', is tagged as '[SUB]' in the first iteration. We replace 'Nice' with 'Worst' and treat the modified sentence as input to the next iteration.

A difficult case is one in which multiple words must be inserted before a target word. Here, the tag of the target word is difficult to determine. In previous work (Reid and Zhong, 2021), additional models were introduced to calculate the number of inserted words, which unnecessarily increased the burden on the model. As an alternative, we use the one-word tagging strategy several times. When the modified sentence has the characteristics of the target style, we stop the modification process and output the current sentence. To generate new words, we fine-tune a Bidirectional Encoder Representations from Transformers (BERT) model (Devlin et al., 2019) on the target style corpus as an LM. Inspired by the pre-training process of BERT, we employ a mask-based training policy. For each sentence in the target corpus, we randomly replace one word with a special token, '<MASK>', and train the LM f_θ to predict it. The objective function is expressed as Equation (1):

$$\mathcal{L}_{\text{LM}}(\theta) = -\sum_j \log p(w_j^{\text{LM}} = w_j | c_j; \theta), \quad (1)$$

where c_j is the context of a masked word w_j. w_j^{LM} is the corresponding prediction of the LM.

The trained LM is used to perform substitutions and insertions. For a word tagged with '[SUB]', we substitute it with the token '<MASK>'. For a word tagged with '[INS]', we insert '<MASK>' in front of it. After this is completed, we input the masked sentence to the LM. The word predicted by the LM then replaces the mask.

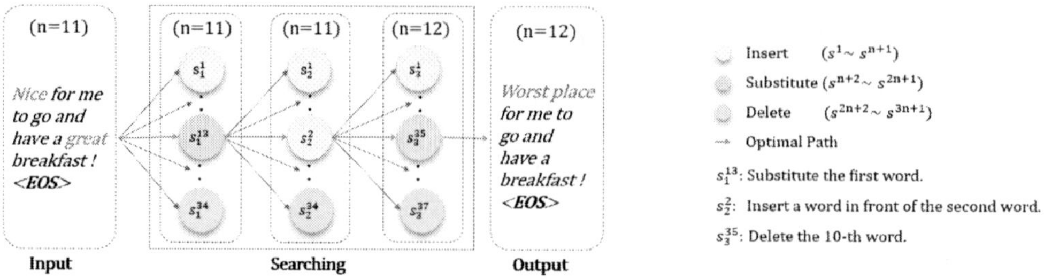

Figure 2: Proposed transfer approach with greedy search. In this example, there are three modifications between the input and output. n is the length of the sentence.

By using three edit operations on an input sentence with n words, we can generate $3n + 1$ different sentences. We note that this includes the insertion of a word at the end of the sentence. These new sentences are all at a Levenshtein distance of 1 from the previous sentence. We use $3n + 1$ different operations to modify the input sentence in each iteration. We repeatedly modify the input sentence until it is transferred into the target style domain.

The body of our method is a random process, and the sentence output in each iteration is the only input in the next iteration. We refer to these $3n + 1$ sentence-level operations as states. We consider a state set $S_1 = (s_1^1, ..., s_1^{3n+1})$, where each element represents an operation that is applied to the current sentence. Furthermore, each use of these operations represents a step of state transition. Continuous three-step transition is shown in Figure 2.

We aim at calculating the transfer probabilities between states. In this random process, a high-quality output sentence should correspond to a path of states with higher transition probability.

3.2 Conditional Random Field

As described, we use a style classifier and an LM to calculate the transfer probabilities between states. Specifically, the classifier is used to determine whether the generated sentences have the target style attributes, while the LM is used to ensure that these sentences have high fluency.

We train a multilayer perceptron (MLP) as the classifier to distinguish sentences in two style domains. The features for the MLP classifier f_ϕ is pre-trained word embedding vectors (Mikolov et al., 2013). The loss function is expressed as eq (2):

$$\mathcal{L}_{\text{CLS}}(\phi) = -\sum_j \log P(y_j|x_j; \phi) \tag{2}$$

where x_j is the j-th example in a train set and y_j is the style label for x_j.

For concerns about inference speed, we follow the standard practice (Dai et al., 2019) and train a 5-gram LM by using the KenLM library (Heafield, 2011) instead of a pre-trained neural LM to score sentences by the probabilities of their occurrence in the target corpus. The learned models are used to calculate the transfer probabilities. For sentence x_A, we consider that it passes through path $p_i = (x_A, s_1^{j_1}, ..., s_i^{j_i})$ and changes to sentence x^{p_i}. If we use state $s_{i+1}^{j_{i+1}}$ to change sentence x^{p_i} to sentence $x^{p_{i+1}}$, the classifier compute score as follows:

$$S_{\text{style}}(s_{i+1}^{j_{i+1}}, p_i) = P(B|x^{p_{i+1}}; \phi) - P(B|x^{p_i}; \phi). \tag{3}$$

Here, the score is the difference in the probabilities that x^{p_i} and $x^{p_{i+1}}$ are classified into target style B.

Similarly, the score function calculated by the LM is expressed as Equation (4):

$$S_{\text{fluency}}(s_{i+1}^{j_{i+1}}, p_i) = P(x^{p_{i+1}}|X_B) - P(x^{p_i}|X_B). \tag{4}$$

To calculate the transfer probabilities, we use the two score functions as feature functions to build a CRF (Lafferty et al., 2001). The joint score $S_{\text{Total}}(s_{i+1,j}|s_{i,t})$ is the weighted sum of the two:

$$\begin{aligned} S_{\text{Total}}(s_{i+1}^{j_{i+1}}, p_i) = \mu_1 S_{\text{style}}(s_{i+1}^{j_{i+1}}, p_i) \\ + \mu_2 S_{\text{fluency}}(s_{i+1}^{j_{i+1}}, p_i), \end{aligned} \tag{5}$$

In each iteration, we convert all the scores into probabilities using Equation (6). That is, we input these scores to a softmax layer to compute the normalised probability distribution:

$$P(p_{i+1}|p_i) = \frac{S_{\text{Total}}(s_{i+1}^{j_{i+1}}, p_i)}{\sum_{p_t} S_{\text{Total}}(s_{i+1}^{j_{i+1}}, p_t)}, \tag{6}$$

where $p_{i+1} = (x_A, s_1^{j_1}, ..., s_{i+1}^{j_{i+1}})$, and p_t is a path that contains the initial sentence x_A and i states.

The probabilities reflect the quality of the transferred sentences. Here, we transform the style transfer problem into a path search problem. For path

Category	Sentiment transfer						Formality transfer	
Data set	Amazon		Yelp		IMDb		GYAFC	
	Positive	Negative	Positive	Negative	Positive	Negative	Formal	Informal
Train set	266,041	177,218	277,228	277,769	178,869	187,597	51,967	51,967
Dev. set	2,000	2,000	985	1,015	2,000	2,000	2,247	2,788
Test set	500	500	1,000	1,000	1,000	1,000	1,019	1,332

Table 2: Statistics of the used data sets. 'Dev.' denotes 'development'. The Yelp, Amazon and IMDb data sets are used for sentiment transfer. The GYAFC data set is used for formality transfer.

$p_i = (x_A, s_1^{j_1}, ..., s_i^{j_i})$ representing consecutive i modifications, the probability of transfer from x_A to x^{p_i} is the product of all probabilities in the path:

$$P(p_i|x_A) = P(p_1|x_A) \prod_{k=2}^{i} P(p_k|p_{k-1}). \quad (7)$$

If x^{p_i} is classified into the target style domain, we stop searching and output that sentence.

3.3 Viterbi Search and Greedy Search

To find the global optimal solution, we employ the Viterbi algorithm (Viterbi, 1967). For the i-th iteration, we have $3n+1$ paths from the corresponding states. We suppose that the end of a path p_i^j is state s_i^j, where j is a variable. For path p_i^j in the set of paths $(p_i^1, ..., p_i^{3n+1})$, s_i^j may be transferred to s_{i+1}^t in the next iteration. We define a function of the transfer probability from x_A to s_{i+1}^t as follows:

$$f_{x_A \to s_{i+1}^t}(p_i^j) = P(p_{i+1}^t|p_i^j) \cdot P(p_i^j|x_A), \quad (8)$$

where t is an integer between 1 and $3n+1$.

We select the path with the highest value of $f_{x_A \to s_{i+1}^t}$ as the optimal path to state s_{i+1}^t. In other words, we retain only one path to each state:

$$p_{i+1}^t = (\text{argmax} f_{x_A \to s_{i+1}^t}(p_i^j), s_{i+1}^t). \quad (9)$$

For a modification with i steps, we find the optimal path $(x_A, s_1^{j_1}, ..., s_i^{j_i})$ from path set $\{p_i^1, ..., p_i^{3n+1}\}$. This signifies that sentence x_A is modified using the operation sequence $(s_1^{j_1}, ..., s_i^{j_i})$ and is output as the solution $\hat{x_A}$. Because we cannot confirm the sentence length during the searching, we consider all possible states, that is, the number of states is incremented by one with the number of iterative steps. Therefore, the model has a time complexity of $O(n^2)$. The time cost is $T(n) = 9kn^2 + 6kn + k$, where k is the number of iterations.

For our model to have the same time complexity as a generative model, we also use greedy search as an alternative to the Viterbi algorithm. We define the following function:

$$g_{x_A \to s_{i+1}^j}(s_{i+1}^t) = p(s_{i+1}^t|p_i), \quad (10)$$

where $p_i = (x_A, s_1^{j_1}, ..., s_i^{j_i})$.

We transfer to the state that has the highest transfer probability from the current state $s_i^{j_i}$:

$$p_{i+1} = (p_i, \text{argmax} g_{x_A \to s_{i+1}^j}(s_{i+1}^j)). \quad (11)$$

In this case, there is only one sentence as input in each iteration. Therefore, the model has linear time complexity, $O(n)$. The time cost is $T(n) = 3kn + k$, where k is the number of iterations.

4 Experiments

4.1 Data Sets Used

The statistics of the used corpora are provided in Table 2.

Yelp The Yelp data set consists of reviews from Yelp users and is provided by the Yelp Dataset Challenge. Each sample is a sentence labelled as having either positive or negative sentiment.

Amazon Similar to Yelp, the Amazon data set (He and McAuley, 2016) consists of labelled reviews from Amazon users. We used the latest version provided by (Li et al., 2018).

IMDb The IMDb Movie Review (referred to as IMDb) contains positive and negative reviews of movies. We used the latest version provided by Dai et al. (2019), which was created based on previous work (Maas et al., 2011).

GYAFC Grammarly's Yahoo Answers Formality Corpus (GYAFC) (Rao and Tetreault, 2018) is a parallel corpus of informal and formal sentences. To achieve unsupervised learning, we shuffled all of the used sentences in training.

Model	Amazon			Yelp			IMDb	
	ACC.	s-BLEU	r-BLEU	ACC.	s-BLEU	r-BLEU	ACC.	s-BLEU
DRG (Li et al., 2018)	52.2%	57.89 ± 2.19	32.47 ± 12.68	84.1%	32.18 ± 2.05	12.28 ± 1.33	55.8%	55.40 ± 1.79
StyTrans (Dai et al., 2019)	67.8%	82.07 ± 1.56	32.88 ± 2.47	92.1%	52.40 ± 2.14	19.91 ± 2.01	86.6%	66.20 ± 1.55
DGST (Li et al., 2020)	59.2%	**83.02 ± 1.25**	**42.20 ± 22.37**	88.0%	51.77 ± 2.41	19.05 ± 1.89	70.1%	**70.20** ± 1.42
TAG (Madaan et al., 2020)	**79.4%**	58.13 ± 1.46	25.95 ± 1.86	88.6%	47.14 ± 2.23	19.76 ± 1.45	N/A	N/A
DIRR (Liu et al., 2021)	62.7%	66.63 ± 2.51	32.68 ± 2.25	91.2%	56.56 ± 1.89	25.60 ± 2.33	83.5%	65.96 ± 1.12
LEWIS (Reid and Zhong, 2021)	71.8%	65.53 ± 1.44	30.61 ± 1.57	89.4%	54.67 ± 1.62	23.85 ± 1.57	N/A	N/A
Ours + Greedy Search	72.7%	53.20 ± 1.51	27.32 ± 1.91	92.1%	57.71 ± 1.80	25.26 ± 2.23	90.4%	59.97 ± 1.29
Ours + Viterbi Search	74.3%	65.30 ± 1.33	30.14 ± 1.23	**93.0%**	**59.30 ± 1.72**	**25.70 ± 2.23**	**91.1%**	63.40 ± 0.82

Table 3: The test results on 3 data sets (sentiment transfer) with 0.95 confidence level. "ACC." stands for Accuracy, "s-BLEU" stands for self-BLEU and "r-BLEU" stands for ref-BLEU. We report the results of baselines by following their official codes and outputs.

4.2 Baselines

We selected six style transfer models for sentiment transfer comparison and two additional models for formality transfer comparison. These baseline models can be broadly divided into two categories. Models in the first category transfer sentences in a latent space and include the cross-align model (Shen et al., 2017), the style-transformer model (Dai et al., 2019), the DualRL model (Luo et al., 2019), the DIRR model (Liu et al., 2021) and the DGST model (Li et al., 2020). Models in the second category are based on the substitution of words and include the DRG model (Li et al., 2018), the TAG model (Madaan et al., 2020) and the LEWIS model (Reid and Zhong, 2021).

4.3 Automated Evaluation Metric

Transfer accuracy and content preservation are currently the most important aspects in evaluating style transfer models (Huang et al., 2021; Fei et al., 2021). Following standard practise, we considered the following metrics.

Transfer Accuracy Accuracy is an important evaluation metric (Cao et al., 2020; Zhou et al., 2020) and represents the rate of successful transfer. We trained an attention-based convolutional neural network as the evaluation classifier f_ω to calculate the accuracy. For each corpus, this classifier is trained on the corresponding train set to distinguish sentences with two different styles. The accuracy is the probability that the generated sentences $\hat{X}_A$ are judged to possess the target style B. The computation of accuracy is as follows:

$$\text{Accuracy} = P(B|\hat{X}_A; \omega) \tag{12}$$

It should be noted that to avoid information leakage, the evaluation classifier is completely different from the one used in the training period (i.e. f_ϕ).

Content Preservation The Bilingual Evaluation Understudy (BLEU) score (Papineni et al., 2002) measures the similarity between two sentences at the lexical level. In recent studies (Lample et al., 2019; Sudhakar et al., 2019), two BLEU scores were computed: self-BLEU, which is the BLEU score between the input and output, and ref-BLEU, which is the BLEU score between the output and human reference sentences. We used the Natural Language Toolkit (NLTK) (Bird et al., 2009) to calculate these sentence BLEU scores.

4.4 Architecture Details

We pre-processed the input data into mini-batches with a batch size of 64. The MLP used had four layers with 768 neurons per layer. The activation function used was the hyperbolic tangent function. We added a linear layer with 768 neurons after a BERT to fine-tune it. For training, the Adam algorithm (Kingma and Ba, 2015) with a learning rate of 0.0001 was employed to update the models. All loss functions were based on cross-entropy.

5 Results and Discussion

5.1 Analysis

Table 3 presents the results of sentiment transfer on the three used data sets. On the Amazon data set, our model had an accuracy of 74.3%, a self-BLEU score of 65.30 and a ref-BLEU score of 30.14. In terms of accuracy, our model surpassed the LEWIS model, which had similar content retention to that of our model. The accuracy of our model was lower than that of the TAG model by 5%; however, the self-BLEU and ref-BLEU scores of our model were higher by 7 and 4 points, respectively. The DGST and StyleTrans models had higher BLEU scores than the scores of our model; however, examining the output sentences revealed that many were simply copied from the input to the output, which was not considered a successful transformation.

On the Yelp data set, our model achieved state-of-the-art performance in all metrics. Even the greedy search version of our model with linear time complexity outperformed the baselines. The accuracy and BLEU score of our model were approximately 1% and two points higher, respectively than those of the StyleTrans and DIRR models.

On the IMDb data set, our model achieved a high accuracy of 91.1%. In the absence of reference, only the results of the self-BLEU measurement are provided. Further, because sentences in the IMDb dataset are relatively long, a low self-BLEU score may not directly reflect semantic content retention.

Because the GYAFC data set pertains to formality transfer, it is listed in Table 4. The accuracy and self-BLEU score of our model were approximately 7% and 10 points higher, respectively, than those of the baselines. In terms of the ref-BLEU score, our proposed model and the StyleTrans model had comparable results (within 1% error). Therefore, we can conclude that our model had the highest overall performance among all compared models.

Data set	GYAFC		
	ACC.	self-BLEU	ref-BLEU
CrossAlign(Shen et al., 2017)	68.1%	3.77 ± 0.26	2.85 ± 0.20
DualRL(Luo et al., 2019)	72.6%	53.10 ± 1.86	19.27 ± 1.18
StyleTrans(Dai et al., 2019)	74.1%	65.95 ± 1.61	**22.11 ± 1.35**
DGST(Li et al., 2020)	60.5%	62.62 ± 1.21	15.72 ± 1.13
Ours + Greedy Search	80.7%	76.17 ± 0.90	20.95 ± 1.00
Ours + Viterbi Search	**81.0%**	**76.53 ± 0.90**	21.30 ± 1.03

Table 4: The test results on the GYAFC (formality transfer). The confidence level of BLEU is 0.95.

5.2 Manual Evaluation

To further evaluate the performance of our model, we randomly sampled outputs from of the most well-performed models (i.e., the TAG model and the LEWIS model) to perform a human evaluation on the Amazon and Yelp data set (the two most commonly used data sets).

Seven individuals participated in the evaluation. By following (Dai et al., 2019), for each review, we displayed one input sentence and three transferred samples to a reviewer. The reviewers were instructed to separately select the best sentence in terms of three aspects: the target style, content preservation and fluency. We also offered the option 'No preference' to allow for objectivity.

Model	Amazon			Yelp		
	Style	Content	Fluency	Style	Content	Fluency
TAG	11.4%	25.7%	22.1%	17.9%	11.4%	24.3%
LEWIS	15.0%	**35.0%**	**37.1%**	22.9%	27.1%	28.6%
Ours	**30.7%**	27.9%	30.0%	**35.0%**	**38.6%**	**31.4%**
No preference	42.9%	11.4%	10.7%	24.3%	22.9%	15.7%

Table 5: Results of human evaluation of sentences produced by three different models in terms of style, content and fluency. Following standard practice (Dai et al., 2019; Madaan et al., 2020), we randomly selected 100 sentences for evaluation.

As illustrated in Table 5, our proposed model comprehensively outperformed the baselines on the Yelp dataset. On the Amazon dataset, our method achieved the highest style transfer rate; however, the proposed model had slightly poorer performance than the LEWIS model in terms of content preservation and fluency.

5.3 Additional Analysis

Current studies focus on how to carefully design loss functions to train a generator for style transformation (Luo et al., 2019; Lee, 2020). However, they neglect to analyse the sentence features before and after the transformation. Therefore, we analyse the following questions:

1. What is the difference between transformations in two opposite directions?

2. Do the models retain semantic information?

For the first question, we counted the number of edit operations used by our model. We calculated these numbers as percentages to visually compare the differences for different transfer directions. The results are presented in Figure 3.

For sentiment transformation, we detected greater use of the '[DEL]' operation in transformations from negative-to-positive sentiment. We supposed that this was due to the presence of more negations in the negative sentences. By directly deleting negations, sentences can become positive. In contrast, positive-to-negative transitions rely more on the use of '[SUB]' operations. This signifies that replacing positive adjectives with negative adjectives is closer to natural human expression than inserting negations.

We note that the proportion of deletions was always greater than the proportion of insertions. According to the scoring rules of the statistical LM, shorter sentences had a higher probability of appearing in the target corpus. Thus, shorter sentences were more likely to score higher than longer

Figure 3: Percentage of the used three edit operations. The results are based on models with Viterbi searching.

Data set	Amazon	Yelp
TAG (Madaan et al., 2020)	53.51 ± 1.97	57.71 ± 1.94
LEWIS (Reid and Zhong, 2021)	55.32 ± 1.98	63.54 ± 1.87
Ours + Greedy Search	58.10 ± 2.00	64.37 ± 1.95
Ours + Viterbi Search	**59.46 ± 1.99**	**64.86 ± 1.89**

Table 6: SBERT scores (0.95 confidence level) between an output and the corresponding human reference.

Data set	Amazon	Yelp
TAG (Madaan et al., 2020)	87.64 ± 0.23	90.38 ± 0.32
LEWIS (Reid and Zhong, 2021)	**87.96 ± 0.24**	91.73 ± 0.32
Ours + Greedy Search	87.69 ± 0.24	91.91 ± 0.35
Ours + Viterbi Search	87.83 ± 0.23	**91.96 ± 0.35**

Table 7: BERTScores (0.95 confidence level) between an output and the corresponding human reference.

sentences. In other words, we suppose that shorter sentences were more likely to be judged as fluent than longer sentences.

For the second question, we performed analysis on the data sets that had human references (i.e. Amazon and Yelp data sets). We calculated Sentence-BERT (SBERT) scores (Reimers and Gurevych, 2019) and BERTScores (Zhang et al., 2020) to reflect the semantic content preservation. The results are presented in Table 6 and Table 7. We selected the two best performing models (i.e. TAG and LEWIS models) for comparison.

The results demonstrate that our models outperformed the baselines in terms of semantic similarity to human references. On the Amazon dataset, our model improved the SBERT score by approximately four points while obtaining similar BERTScores with the LEWIS model.

For the Yelp data set, our model improved the SBERT score by approximately one point and improved the BERTScore obtaining similar BERTScores with the LEWIS model.

6 Case Study

To further demonstrate the superiority of our model, We **randomly** sampled some positive and negative sentences from the outputs of our model and baselines for comparison, as shown in Table 8.

For the human reference outputs, although the hired workers were not asked to make minimal changes to change the sentiment of input sentences, we noticed that overlaps are commonly between inputs and human references. In other words, people naturally tend to retain content words from an input sentence when rewriting it.

An interesting thing is that, for the Amazon data set, comments with 1 or 2 stars are considered to be negative and comments with 4 or 5 stars are considered to be positive. However, looking at the data, not all low scoring reviews contain only negative sentiment, while not all high scoring reviews contain only positive sentiment. Furthermore, the human reference of the Amazon data set is not always effective. For example, a negative reference sentence "*because it might not be worth full price .*" is labelled as positive. Cases of mislabeling may be the reason why the models did not perform well on the Amazon data set.

Comparing the two different search strategies,

Yelp	Positive to negative	Negative to positive
Input	it is a cool place , with lots to see and try .	unfortunately , it is the worst .
Human	nothing to see there , not a nice place .	fortunately , it is the best .
TAG	it is a shame , not to see and try .	great food . great service and the staff is friendly .
DGST	it is a sad place , with lots to see and try .	overall , it is the best .
DIRR	it is a cold place , with no to see and try .	fortunately , it is the best .
LEWIS	it is a very busy place , with lots to see and try .	cajun food , it is the best !
Ours + GS	it is a place , with nothing to see and try .	seriously , it is the best .
Ours + VS	it is a mess , with nothing to see and try .	seriously , it is the best .
Amazon	Positive to negative	Negative to positive
Input	for my purpose this is the perfect item .	because it is definitely not worth full price .
Human	for my purpose this is the worst item.	because it might not be worth full price .
TAG	for my purpose this is the worst item .	because it is definitely not worth full price .
DGST	for my purpose this is the perfect item .	because it is definitely not worth full price .
DIRR	for my purpose this is the same thing .	because it is definitely worth full price .
LEWIS	for my purpose this is the best game ever made .	because it is definitely well made and worth full price .
Ours + GS	for my purpose this is the item .	because it is definitely well worth full price .
Ours + VS	for my purpose this is the worst item .	because it is definitely well worth full price .
IMDb	Positive to negative	Negative to positive
Input	i rate this movie 8/10 .	please , do n't see this movie .
StyTrans	i rate this movie 4/10 .	please , do also see this movie .
DGST	i rate this movie 1/10	u . do n't see this "
DIRR	i rate this movie 1/10 .	please , see this movie .
Ours + GS	i rate this movie 1/10 .	please , do n ' t miss this movie today .
Ours + VS	i rate this movie 1/10 .	please , do n ' t miss this movie .

Table 8: Sentences sampled from sentiment transfer data set. 'Human' denotes manual reference. 'GS' denotes 'Greedy Search' and 'VS' denotes 'Viterbi Search'. Red text stands for failed style transformation, brown text stands for poor content preservation and blue text stands for suitable transformation.

our model using the Viterbi search generate more fluent sentences than our model using the greedy search. However, the model using Viterbi search has a time complexity of $O(n^2)$ and the number of states linearly increased with the number of iterative steps. Further, we find that models using different search strategies have the same output in approximately half of the cases.

For the method based on transformation in latent space (i.e., DGST), it always copies sentences without transferring them into correct style domains. For this same reason, the DGST model obtained high BLEU values on all of the used data sets.

For the method based on the modification of words (i.e., TAG and LEWIS), they will retain the majority of input words. However, recognition of style-indicative words may result that part of style-indicative words are retained and content words are deleted, that is, examples listed in Table 8.

7 Conclusion

In this study, we proposed a probabilistic model for sentiment and style transfer on non-parallel data. We used a classifier and an LM to construct a CRF. Using dynamic programming search algorithms, we generated a tag sequence to modify the input sentences. The experimental results revealed that our proposed model outperformed the baselines in terms of accuracy by approximately 2%.

Our future work will focus on the simplification of the search process. By using the policy gradient (Williams, 1992) of reinforcement learning, we might be able to speed up the transfer model.

References

Steven Bird, Ewan Klein, and Edward Loper. 2009. *Natural language processing with Python: analyzing text with the natural language toolkit.* " O'Reilly Media, Inc.".

Yixin Cao, Ruihao Shui, Liangming Pan, Min-Yen Kan, Zhiyuan Liu, and Tat-Seng Chua. 2020. Expertise style transfer: A new task towards better communication between experts and laymen. In *Proceedings of the 58th Annual Meeting of the Association for Computational Linguistics*, pages 1061–1071, Online. Association for Computational Linguistics.

Kunal Chawla and Diyi Yang. 2020. Semi-supervised formality style transfer using language model discriminator and mutual information maximization. In *Findings of the Association for Computational Lin-*

guistics: EMNLP 2020, pages 2340–2354, Online. Association for Computational Linguistics.

Ning Dai, Jianze Liang, Xipeng Qiu, and Xuanjing Huang. 2019. Style transformer: Unpaired text style transfer without disentangled latent representation. In *Proceedings of the 57th Annual Meeting of the Association for Computational Linguistics*, pages 5997–6007, Florence, Italy. Association for Computational Linguistics.

Jacob Devlin, Ming-Wei Chang, Kenton Lee, and Kristina Toutanova. 2019. BERT: Pre-training of deep bidirectional transformers for language understanding. In *Proceedings of the 2019 Conference of the North American Chapter of the Association for Computational Linguistics: Human Language Technologies*, pages 4171–4186, Minneapolis, Minnesota. Association for Computational Linguistics.

Yanai Elazar and Yoav Goldberg. 2018. Adversarial removal of demographic attributes from text data. In *Proceedings of the 2018 Conference on Empirical Methods in Natural Language Processing*, pages 11–21, Brussels, Belgium. Association for Computational Linguistics.

Xiao Fei, Pang Liang, Lan Yanyan, Wang Yan, Huawei Shen, and Xueqi Cheng. 2021. Transductive learning for unsupervised text style transfer. In *Proceedings of the 2021 Conference on Empirical Methods in Natural Language Processing (EMNLP)*. Association for Computational Linguistics.

Zhenxin Fu, Xiaoye Tan, Nanyun Peng, Dongyan Zhao, and Rui Yan. 2018. Style transfer in text: Exploration and evaluation. *Proceedings of the AAAI Conference on Artificial Intelligence*, 32(1).

Ruining He and Julian McAuley. 2016. Ups and downs: Modeling the visual evolution of fashion trends with one-class collaborative filtering. In *proceedings of the 25th international conference on world wide web*, pages 507–517.

Kenneth Heafield. 2011. KenLM: Faster and smaller language model queries. In *Proceedings of the Sixth Workshop on Statistical Machine Translation*, pages 187–197, Edinburgh, Scotland. Association for Computational Linguistics.

Ari Holtzman, Jan Buys, Li Du, Maxwell Forbes, and Yejin Choi. 2020. The curious case of neural text degeneration. In *International Conference on Learning Representations*.

Zhiting Hu, Zichao Yang, Xiaodan Liang, Ruslan Salakhutdinov, and Eric P Xing. 2017. Toward controlled generation of text. In *International Conference on Machine Learning*, pages 1587–1596. PMLR.

Fei Huang, Zikai Chen, Chen Henry Wu, Qihan Guo, Xiaoyan Zhu, and Minlie Huang. 2021. NAST: A non-autoregressive generator with word alignment for unsupervised text style transfer. In *Findings of the Association for Computational Linguistics: ACL-IJCNLP 2021*, pages 1577–1590, Online. Association for Computational Linguistics.

P. Diederik Kingma and Lei Jimmy Ba. 2015. Adam: A method for stochastic optimization. *international conference on learning representations*.

John D. Lafferty, Andrew McCallum, and Fernando C. N. Pereira. 2001. Conditional random fields: Probabilistic models for segmenting and labeling sequence data. In *Proceedings of the Eighteenth International Conference on Machine Learning*, ICML '01, page 282–289, San Francisco, CA, USA. Morgan Kaufmann Publishers Inc.

Guillaume Lample, Sandeep Subramanian, Eric Smith, Ludovic Denoyer, Marc'Aurelio Ranzato, and Y-Lan Boureau. 2019. Multiple-attribute text rewriting. In *International Conference on Learning Representations*.

Joosung Lee. 2020. Stable style transformer: Delete and generate approach with encoder-decoder for text style transfer. In *Proceedings of the 13th International Conference on Natural Language Generation*, pages 195–204, Dublin, Ireland. Association for Computational Linguistics.

Juncen Li, Robin Jia, He He, and Percy Liang. 2018. Delete, retrieve, generate: a simple approach to sentiment and style transfer. In *Proceedings of the 2018 Conference of the North American Chapter of the Association for Computational Linguistics: Human Language Technologies*, pages 1865–1874, New Orleans, Louisiana. Association for Computational Linguistics.

Xiao Li, Guanyi Chen, Chenghua Lin, and Ruizhe Li. 2020. DGST: a dual-generator network for text style transfer. In *Proceedings of the 2020 Conference on Empirical Methods in Natural Language Processing (EMNLP)*, Online. Association for Computational Linguistics.

Yixin Liu, Graham Neubig, and John Wieting. 2021. On learning text style transfer with direct rewards. In *Proceedings of the 2021 Conference of the North American Chapter of the Association for Computational Linguistics: Human Language Technologies*, pages 4262–4273, Online. Association for Computational Linguistics.

Fuli Luo, Peng Li, Jie Zhou, Pengcheng Yang, Baobao Chang, Xu Sun, and Zhifang Sui. 2019. A dual reinforcement learning framework for unsupervised text style transfer. In *Proceedings of the Twenty-Eighth International Joint Conference on Artificial Intelligence, IJCAI-19*, pages 5116–5122. International Joint Conferences on Artificial Intelligence Organization.

Andrew L. Maas, Raymond E. Daly, Peter T. Pham, Dan Huang, Andrew Y. Ng, and Christopher Potts. 2011. Learning word vectors for sentiment analysis.

In *Proceedings of the 49th Annual Meeting of the Association for Computational Linguistics: Human Language Technologies*, pages 142–150, Portland, Oregon, USA. Association for Computational Linguistics.

Aman Madaan, Amrith Setlur, Tanmay Parekh, Barnabas Poczos, Graham Neubig, Yiming Yang, Ruslan Salakhutdinov, Alan W Black, and Shrimai Prabhumoye. 2020. Politeness transfer: A tag and generate approach. In *Proceedings of the 58th Annual Meeting of the Association for Computational Linguistics*, pages 1869–1881, Online. Association for Computational Linguistics.

Jonathan Mallinson, Aliaksei Severyn, Eric Malmi, and Guillermo Garrido. 2020. FELIX: Flexible text editing through tagging and insertion. In *Findings of the Association for Computational Linguistics: EMNLP 2020*, pages 1244–1255, Online. Association for Computational Linguistics.

Eric Malmi, Aliaksei Severyn, and Sascha Rothe. 2020. Unsupervised text style transfer with padded masked language models. In *Proceedings of the 2020 Conference on Empirical Methods in Natural Language Processing (EMNLP)*, pages 8671–8680, Online. Association for Computational Linguistics.

Tomas Mikolov, Ilya Sutskever, Kai Chen, Greg S Corrado, and Jeff Dean. 2013. Distributed representations of words and phrases and their compositionality. In *Advances in neural information processing systems*, pages 3111–3119.

Kishore Papineni, Salim Roukos, Todd Ward, and Wei-Jing Zhu. 2002. Bleu: a method for automatic evaluation of machine translation. In *Proceedings of the 40th annual meeting of the Association for Computational Linguistics*, pages 311–318.

Shrimai Prabhumoye, Yulia Tsvetkov, Ruslan Salakhutdinov, and Alan W Black. 2018. Style transfer through back-translation. In *Proceedings of the 56th Annual Meeting of the Association for Computational Linguistics*, pages 866–876, Melbourne, Australia. Association for Computational Linguistics.

Sudha Rao and Joel Tetreault. 2018. Dear sir or madam, may I introduce the GYAFC dataset: Corpus, benchmarks and metrics for formality style transfer. In *Proceedings of the 2018 Conference of the North American Chapter of the Association for Computational Linguistics: Human Language Technologies*, pages 129–140, New Orleans, Louisiana. Association for Computational Linguistics.

Machel Reid and Victor Zhong. 2021. Lewis: Levenshtein editing for unsupervised text style transfer. In *In Findings of the 59th Annual Meeting of the Association for Computational Linguistics*.

Nils Reimers and Iryna Gurevych. 2019. Sentence-bert: Sentence embeddings using siamese bert-networks. In *Proceedings of the 2019 Conference on Empirical Methods in Natural Language Processing*. Association for Computational Linguistics.

Tianxiao Shen, Tao Lei, Regina Barzilay, and Tommi Jaakkola. 2017. Style transfer from non-parallel text by cross-alignment. In *Advances in neural information processing systems*, pages 6830–6841.

Akhilesh Sudhakar, Bhargav Upadhyay, and Arjun Maheswaran. 2019. "transforming" delete, retrieve, generate approach for controlled text style transfer. In *Proceedings of the 2019 Conference on Empirical Methods in Natural Language Processing and the 9th International Joint Conference on Natural Language Processing (EMNLP-IJCNLP)*, pages 3269–3279, Hong Kong, China. Association for Computational Linguistics.

A. Viterbi. 1967. Error bounds for convolutional codes and an asymptotically optimum decoding algorithm. *IEEE Transactions on Information Theory*, 13(2):260–269.

Ronald J Williams. 1992. Simple statistical gradient-following algorithms for connectionist reinforcement learning. *Machine learning*, 8(3-4):229–256.

Chen Wu, Xuancheng Ren, Fuli Luo, and Xu Sun. 2019. A hierarchical reinforced sequence operation method for unsupervised text style transfer. In *Proceedings of the 57th Annual Meeting of the Association for Computational Linguistics*, pages 4873–4883, Florence, Italy. Association for Computational Linguistics.

Jingjing Xu, Xu Sun, Qi Zeng, Xiaodong Zhang, Xuancheng Ren, Houfeng Wang, and Wenjie Li. 2018. Unpaired sentiment-to-sentiment translation: A cycled reinforcement learning approach. In *Proceedings of the 56th Annual Meeting of the Association for Computational Linguistics*, pages 979–988, Melbourne, Australia. Association for Computational Linguistics.

Tianyi Zhang, Varsha Kishore, Felix Wu, Kilian Q. Weinberger, and Yoav Artzi. 2020. Bertscore: Evaluating text generation with bert. In *International Conference on Learning Representations*.

Zhirui Zhang, Shuo Ren, Shujie Liu, Jianyong Wang, Peng Chen, Mu Li, Ming Zhou, and Enhong Chen. 2018. Style transfer as unsupervised machine translation. *CoRR*, abs/1808.07894.

Chulun Zhou, Liangyu Chen, Jiachen Liu, Xinyan Xiao, Jinsong Su, Sheng Guo, and Hua Wu. 2020. Exploring contextual word-level style relevance for unsupervised style transfer. In *Proceedings of the 58th Annual Meeting of the Association for Computational Linguistics*, pages 7135–7144, Online. Association for Computational Linguistics.

Polite Task-oriented Dialog Agents: To Generate or to Rewrite?

Diogo Silva, David Semedo, João Magalhães
NOVA LINCS - Universidade NOVA de Lisboa
Lisbon, Portugal
dmgc.silva@campus.fct.unl.pt, {df.semedo, jmag}@fct.unl.pt

Abstract

For task-oriented dialog agents, the tone of voice mediates user-agent interactions, playing a central role in the flow of a conversation. Distinct from domain-agnostic politeness constructs, in specific domains such as online stores, booking platforms, and others, agents need to be capable of adopting highly specific vocabulary, with significant impact on lexical and grammatical aspects of utterances. Then, the challenge is on improving utterances' politeness while preserving the actual content, an utterly central requirement to achieve the task goal. In this paper, we conduct a novel assessment of politeness strategies for task-oriented dialog agents under a transfer learning scenario. We extend existing generative and rewriting politeness approaches, towards overcoming domain-shifting issues, and enabling the transfer of politeness patterns to a novel domain. Both automatic and human evaluation is conducted on customer-store interactions, over the fashion domain, from which contribute with insightful and experimentally supported lessons regarding the improvement of politeness in task-specific dialog agents.

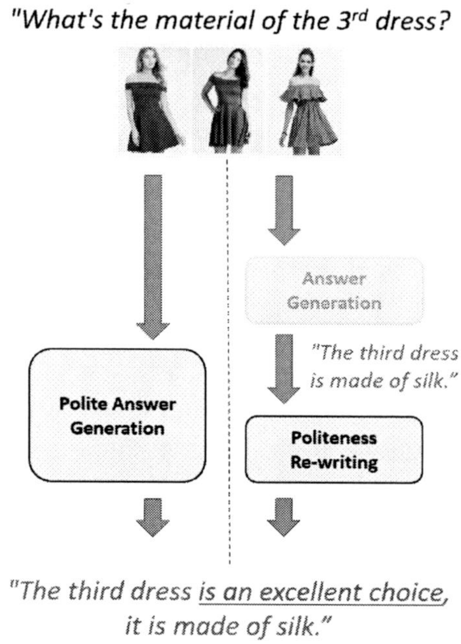

Figure 1: Politeness can be introduced either by incorporating it in the generation step or as a rewritting step. In this example the politeness strategy adopted is the use of a positive lexicon.

1 Introduction

In a conversational scenario, the tone of voice used by interlocutors is a key aspect towards achieving fruitful, engaging, and natural user-agent interactions (Brown et al., 1987; Niu and Bansal, 2018). This is deeply rooted in the fact that discoursing in a polite manner, is a social trait of human conversations, that when left unattended by dialog agents, can lead to an immediate perception of artificial discourse and lack of intelligent behavior, which in turn leads to poor engagement.

Task-oriented dialog agents require simultaneously keeping the user engaged while achieving the task goal, whether it is selling a product, booking a restaurant or simply providing assistance. This requires *informative and correct answers, embedding domain-specific language, while keeping a polite tone of voice*. Being able to accomplish this, has an impact that extrapolates isolated conversations. For example, in the fashion world, the tone and the way the customer is addressed are strongly linked to the brand culture (Sousa et al., 2021) (e.g. more eloquent vs. more casual and youthful discourse).

While politeness is a deeply seeded cultural concept and difficult to fully generalize (Meier, 1995), it has been recently approached from a computational perspective (Danescu-Niculescu-Mizil et al., 2013; Niu and Bansal, 2018; Madaan et al., 2020) under the framework of (Brown et al., 1987), which divides politeness strategies in *a) negative politeness* - where polite discourse is achieved by expressing restraint, thus avoiding being direct - and

Proceedings of the 12th Workshop on Computational Approaches to Subjectivity, Sentiment & Social Media Analysis, pages 304 - 314
May 26, 2022

b) positive politeness - where an explicit attempt of expressing solidarity, optimism and gratitude is made. Danescu-Niculescu-Mizil et al. (2013) took a pioneering approach and proposed to approximate these strategies by creating a human annotated politeness corpora, and training a classifier to capture general linguistic patterns of both negative and positive politeness. Recent works leverage on such classifier to develop either generative (Niu and Bansal, 2018; Firdaus et al., 2020) or rewriting-based (Madaan et al., 2020; Fu et al., 2020) approaches. Figure 1 contrasts these approaches, with respect to politeness strategies. While these have been applied to generic and domain-agnostic scenarios, it remains unclear how well such principles transfer to task-specific domains.

In this work, we assess under a transfer-learning scenario, the applicability of both generative and rewriting politeness approaches to a novel domain. Specifically, we use the challenging fashion domain as a use case, given its vocabulary complexity and highly specific-nature [1]. Namely, we propose to overcome the lack of labeled data by extending state-of-the-art generative (Niu and Bansal, 2018) and rewriting (Madaan et al., 2020) approaches, respectively, towards allowing each of them to overcome the domain-shift, and transferring linguistic politeness constructs to a novel (fashion) domain.

This is one of the first works to study politeness approaches for task-oriented dialog agents, contributing with:

- An adaptation of generative and rewriting politeness approaches (section 3), enabling transfer learning for specific domains.
- Comprehensive experiments (section 5), leading to valuable insights regarding how politeness approaches deal with the content-preservation vs. politeness improvement trade-off, in task-oriented dialog agents.
- A user-centered study that supports and confirms the conclusions of the automatic evaluation (section 5).
- Explored politeness on a novel domain, conversational assistants on the fashion domain (Saha et al., 2018), exposing the opportunities for improving politeness.

[1]The established politeness classifier of Danescu-Niculescu-Mizil et al. (2013) lacks $\approx$ 15k terms from the considered fashion dialog corpus.

2 Related work

The importance of politeness in social interactions and its impact in the projected self-image during social interactions has been studied for decades (Brown et al., 1978, 1987). These concepts were later reviewed and refined (Watts, 2019) with new work (Bargiela-Chiappini, 2003) proposing the label of 'polite behavior' to separate it from the theoretical and cultural baggage of the term face-work. More recently, Danescu-Niculescu-Mizil et al. (2013) introduced a labeled dataset (Stanford Politeness Corpus), along with a politeness classifier to enable further research as an NLP task. Additionally, they look into how politeness relates to the speaker's status and power within their community. Later work (Aubakirova and Bansal, 2016) introduced a new politeness classifier and several visualization techniques to gain further insight into linguistic markers of politeness. These visualization techniques reveal novel politeness strategies not considered originally, namely how punctuation affected politeness scores. The introduced politeness classifier uses a CNN and does not use politeness strategies as features while having higher accuracy.

Politeness as an NLP task has seen recent interest. Niu and Bansal (2018) uses the Stanford Politeness Corpus to investigate politeness generation models. Politeness generation here is treated as part of the answer generation task with models producing answers already in their polite form, using Reinforcement Learning and a novel politeness classifier. A Multilingual approach is taken in (Firdaus et al., 2020) where courteous responses are generated in a customer care scenario. Madaan et al. (2020) sees politeness as a style transfer task where politeness is introduced onto an utterance by rewriting it. This work uses a politeness classifier to label the Enron corpus (Klimt and Yang, 2004), and applies a transformer-based (Vaswani et al., 2017) style transfer pipeline to the utterance, using a tagger and generator approach. In a similar vein, in (Golchha et al., 2019) the authors transform neutral customer service replies into courteous ones.

Hence, we follow a similar line of work and propose to enrich fashion dialog agents with politeness. Saha et al. (2018) introduced a large-scale multimodal fashion dialog dataset (MMD) built semi-automatically, using field experts, accompanied by two RNN (Cho et al., 2014) models capable of emulating the system responses in a multimodal scenario. Due to its domain, it carries mainly neutral and polite dialog. To the best of our knowledge, there is no task-oriented conversational dataset to study politeness and we propose to fill this research gap.

3 Task-Specific Polite Dialog Agents

We consider two distinct methods of producing politeness and evaluate how each deals with domain changes: **polite answer generation** and **politeness rewriting**. We adapt each model to allow it to use transfer learning, in particular, transfer politeness patterns to a different domain, the fashion domain.

3.1 Politeness through Utterance Generation

Politeness can be improved in a generative manner, where an answer generation model learns to do so, by *merging answer generation and politeness generation in the same task*. This type of approach makes the work of the decoder two-fold: it needs to be able to accurately understand the context and produce an accurate answer, but it also needs to improve the politeness of the produced answer.

We adopted the Polite-RL generative approach (Niu and Bansal, 2018) based on a Seq2Seq model that receives the conversation history to produce a polite answer. The model is trained with Reinforcement Learning that leverages a Politeness Classifier (we will refer to as Classifier) to estimate the politeness of a sampled answer. Polite-RL uses the politeness score of a sampled utterance as a measure of politeness that acts as the Reinforcement Learning component of the loss function (see appendix A.4), to guide the generation towards a more polite output. We focused on improving the used embeddings to include a novel lexicon, given that the fashion domain (Saha et al., 2018) differs significantly from the training data (Danescu-Niculescu-Mizil et al., 2013), making out-of-vocabulary situations a major issue. Originally, this model uses embeddings initialized using a Word2Vec model trained on the Google News dataset (Mikolov et al., 2013). Despite its vocabulary size, the dataset's vocabulary can still leave out a significant portion of the terms used in the fashion-specific datasets (mainly clothes' names and attributes), due to its highly specific domain (Saha et al., 2018).

Looking at Table 7, we observe that politeness can be applied in several different ways, making it important to take into account the utterance as a whole to better understand how phrase structures affect its tone. In the Polite-RL (Niu and Bansal, 2018) model, these strategies are introduced implicitly by the politeness Classifier as the Seq2Seq model is not explicitly trained on politeness data. With this in mind, to improve the adaptability of this implementation and reduce the impact of this separation in the vocabulary, we introduce a new set of embeddings that accounts for the additional tokens from the novel domain dataset. These embeddings were obtained by training a Word2Vec (Mikolov et al., 2013) model on a concatenation of the MMD (Saha et al., 2018) - a conversational dataset on the fashion domain (see section 4.1) - and the original Politeness corpus. We will refer to these embeddings as Domain-Extended embeddings (DE).

3.2 Politeness through Utterance Rewriting

Politeness rewriting *separates the task of politeness generation from answer generation*. This enables tackling politeness individually, and avoid its dependence on the answer generation task.

For this approach, we adopt Tag-and-Generate (Madaan et al., 2020), which is composed of two main components: Tagger and Generator. The **Tagger** is responsible for extracting style makers from the utterance and adding a [TAG] token where new markers should be introduced. The style markers are defined using a TF-IDF-based approach that compares the relevance of an n-gram on the polite and rude subset of data. The **Generator** takes the tagged utterance and replaces the [TAG] token with polite style markers. This approach follows the assumption that the extracted style markers are good markers for politeness, meaning that if the model is dealing with a poor set of style markers then the results can be destructive and nonsensical.

Models such as this, apply politeness strategies in an explicit manner, Table 7. The Generator learns the best way to add each politeness strategy onto a given utterance, by observing how each style marker is used throughout the training data. For honorifics, ideally, the model learns to place them immediately before surnames.

With the Tagger architecture in mind, we focused on using Transfer Learning to better adapt the model to the fashion domain. For the rewriting part, we hypothesize that using the style markers previously learned on the original dataset (Enron) will lead to improved politeness scores. To deal with the out-of-the-domain-vocabulary problem, we propose to curate the extracted style markers, by excluding domain-specific words and terms from being classified as style markers, thus leading to more representative style markers. To assess how this affects generation quality, we define four training setups:

- **RW-Enron:** Original model trained on the Enron dataset (Klimt and Yang, 2004).
- **RW-Fashion:** Model trained on the fashion-domain dataset, using polite and rude utterances, i.e. utterances with a politeness score above 0.9 and between 0.5-0.6 respectively.
- **RW-Fashion-Clean:** Similar to the previous model, but we force the model to ignore style markers associated to product nouns. For example, "scarf" and "trousers", shouldn't be counted as a style marker of politeness.
- **RW-Mixed:** This model learns the style markers on the original domain (Enron) and is trained on the fashion dataset. This way the model circumvents the noisy style markers extracted from the fashion data. Effectively transferring knowledge learned on politeness annotated data to the fashion domain.

4 Experimental Setup

4.1 Datasets and Protocols

In our experiments, 3 datasets were considered:

Stanford Politeness Corpus (SPC) - This is the dataset used for politeness conditioning, by training the Politeness proxy classifier (Niu and Bansal, 2018). This corpus is composed of requests (Wikipedia and Stack Exchange) annotated by 5 humans. We follow (Niu and Bansal, 2018) and use the original data splits.

Enron - Collection of emails exchanged in the Enron company (Klimt and Yang, 2004) - originally used to train the Tag-and-Generate model (Madaan et al., 2020) - that we adopt as the original domain, in a domain-transfer scenario. We consider an automatically annotated subset of Enron, with 212k polite and 51k rude utterances for training, 27k polite and 5.8k rude for validation, and 26k polite and 5.8k rude utterances for testing.

MMD - This dataset comprises multi-turn dialogs for the fashion domain (Saha et al., 2018), which we use as the target domain. We first create the **MMD-R** subset, comprised by system utterances that correspond to product(s) recommendations(s) to expose the model to domain-specific product lexicon, resulting in 380k/81k/81k utterances for training/validation/testing. A second subset is created, **MMD-A**, comprising all *neutral*[2] and *polite* system utterances with more than 5 tokens, resulting in 453k/116k/116k utterances. The **MMD-A** subset generalizes **MMD-R** to include utterances from multiple dialog intents.

Please kindly refer to Appendix A.2 for more details regarding each dataset (annotation protocol, splits, and others).

4.2 Metrics

For evaluation, we will focus mainly on two aspects of the generated utterances: **a) Politeness Improvement** and **b) Content Preservation**. With **a)**, we focus on understanding if each resulting utterance is in fact more polite than the original one. For this, to automatically quantify politeness, we follow (Niu and Bansal, 2018) and compute the average Politeness Score (*Pol.*) using its politeness classifier, where 1.0 is polite, 0.5 neutral and 0.0 is rude. In **b)**, we focus on understanding whether or not the model can preserve the original content. Thus, we follow previous work (Niu and Bansal, 2018; Madaan et al., 2020) and evaluate the results using BLEU **(B)** (Papineni et al., 2002), ROUGE **(R)** (Lin, 2004), and METEOR **(M)** (Denkowski and Lavie, 2011). Given the subjective nature of the task, we complement our evaluation with human evaluation.

4.3 Model Variants and Implementation

For evaluation, we refer to politeness answer generation variants as **Gen** and rewriting variants as **RW**. For **Gen**, we use the original embeddings. The generative approach with domain extented embeddings (section 3.1) is referred as **Gen+DE**. For rewriting, the 4 proposed variants (section 3.2) are referred as **RW-Enron**, **RW-Fashion**, **RW-Fashion-C**(lean) and **RW-Mixed**.

Regarding models implementation, for RW variants we use the original hyper-parameters, and both components are trained using a 4-layer 4-

[2]Due to its nature, the number of *rude* utterances in MMD is minimal, leading to a high imbalance.

Models	B	R	M	Pol.
Gen	68.54†	85.30	48.80†	69.95
Gen+DE	66.32	85.55†	45.02	64.47
Gen+DE (β=5)	33.56	63.63	27.64	75.21
Gen+DE (β=10)	29.41	58.66	24.90	78.77†
RW-Enron	70.38	86.68	51.51	**82.24**‡
RW-Fashion	85.03	83.72	58.99	79.76
RW-Fashion-C	86.71	86.44	60.23	78.42
RW-Mixed	**87.78**‡	**87.22**‡	**60.80**‡	80.70

Table 1: Politeness generation vs. rewriting results. $\dagger$ represents the highest result among Polite-RL (Gen) variations and $\ddagger$ represents the highest results among Tag-and-Generate (RW) models.

head transformer block and 512-dimensional embeddings, for 5 epochs. For Polite-RL we also use the original hyper-parameters, but we tuned the batch size b and the β parameter, the weight of the politeness component of the computed loss. Refer to Appendix A.4 for model tuning details.

5 Results and Discussion

5.1 Politeness Generation or Rewriting?

Automatic-Evaluation. We start by comparing how the adapted generative (section 3.1) and rewriting (section 3.2) politeness approaches perform on the fashion domain, in terms of politeness and content preservation. The Gen and RW models were evaluated on the **MMD-R** and **MMD-A** datasets, respectively. Table 1 shows the evaluation results for both models and their variants. From these results, it is evident that rewriting variations (RW) outperform the generation-based ones (Gen) across all metrics, due to their need to attend to two tasks. For content preservation, the results from Gen are consistently behind its RW counterparts, with all variations of the RW model outperforming the generation-based models. Regarding politeness, the scores paint a similar picture with Gen models trailing behind and only reaching near when content preservation is significantly neglected (higher β value, the weight given to politeness in Polite-RL). Despite this, all models are able to post the politeness score on the polite spectrum (Pol. > 0.5), according to the politeness classifier.

Human-Evaluation. Automatic metrics offer a quick and reproducible way of evaluating work, however, they lack the depth needed to accurately evaluate subjective topics like politeness (Danescu-Niculescu-Mizil et al., 2013). To supplement our previous automatic analysis of the proposed changes to the RW setup, we ran a crowdsourcing experiment to assess the tone and grammar[3]of generated utterances. For this, we randomly sample 100 utterances from the **MMD-A** test set and then collect the generated utterance for each of the RW variations and Gen+DE. For each utterance, 3 annotators were asked to rate its tone on a scale of 1 to 3 (1=Rude, 2=Neutral, 3=Polite). For grammar, annotators were asked to give a binary rating, whether the utterance was grammatically correct or not (0=No, 1=Yes). Annotators were provided an example utterance for each possible value. We obtained $\approx$ 82% agreement on grammar and $\approx$ 77% for politeness. The results are show in Table 2. For a given utterance, the agreement was the measure of how many annotators labeled it the same.

Models	Politeness	Grammar
Reference	2.453	0.793
Gen+DE	2.170	0.583
RW	**2.497**	0.770
RW-Fashion	2.437	0.733
RW-Fashion-C	**2.497**	**0.790**
RW-Mixed	2.453	0.767

Table 2: Human evaluation results for Politeness and Grammar, on 100 utterances.

Regarding politeness, the Gen+DE model scored lower than the Reference, whereas all RW setups matched or improved on it. In particular, only RW-Fashion failed to improve and both RW-Fashion-C and RW were able to outscore the reference. When looking into rating distribution, we noted that of the 1800 annotations, only in 28 occasions did an annotator consider the utterance rude, and never 2 annotators agreed that an utterance was rude, showing that all models are able to keep the text neutral. For grammar, none of the models were able to score higher than the reference, and Gen+DE was rated significantly lower.

From the ratings, we note that there is a significant gap between Generative and Rewriting approaches, similar to the automatic evaluation. Additionally, Gen+DE underperforming with respect to the reference shows that generally, the model was not able to improve on the utterances' tone often leading to incoherent generations. On another note, the performance of the RW-Fashion-C shows

[3]We included grammar to understand if the models were reducing the quality of the re-written utterances.

that style marker curation can be the way forward for rewriting approaches.

5.2 Style Marker Domain Transfer

In the previous section, we observed that politeness rewriting is the top-performing approach to improve the politeness of task-oriented dialog agents. In this section, we perform a finer-grain evaluation of the rewriting model variants, i.e. the style marker-based model (**RW**), under a domain transfer setting. As this corresponds to an utterance rewriting task, we look for high content preservation paired with high politeness score.

To perform this experiment, we use the **MMD-A** subset, comprising diverse system utterances (recommendation, answering product questions, etc.). Then, we follow Madaan et al. (2020) and use the politeness classifier to split the subset into 10 buckets, corresponding to a 10-bin histogram over politeness scores.

Table 1 also depicts the results, where we compare the four RW model variations on the **MMD-A** test set. We observe that for content preservation, top performance is achieved by the RW-Mixed model, across all three content metrics. Additionally, we note that the RW-Fashion-C model is a step up on RW-Fashion, showing that excluding domain-specific words from the style attribute list helps preserve content. However, for the RW-Enron model, which is restricted to the original domain, the results were significantly lower.

Regarding Politeness scores, the RW-Enron model outperforms all the others specifically trained on **MMD-A** data. The Mixed model also performed better than its RW-Fashion and RW-Fashion-C counterparts. The success of RW-Enron in politeness score and RW-Mixed in content preservation shows that leveraging out-of-domain style markers yields positive results for neutral domains, where it is difficult to extract style markers. This also shows how models can vary in the way they add style markers. While RW-Enron does several and significant changes, thus having lower content preservation scores, RW-Mixed does less but more informed and in-domain additions.

5.2.1 Utterance Tone and Length Impact

To identify the impact of utterance tone (rude or neutral) and utterance size on the models' performance, we prepared a set of distinct scenarios covering the different aspects of utterances' tone and length. These two utterance traits were chosen due to the following reasons:

RW Model:		Enron	Fashion	Fashion-C	Mixed
BLEU	SN	83.24	88.30	**91.11**	89.45
	MN	82.31	96.22	**97.10**	96.28
	L	65.71	95.71	97.55	**97.68**
ROUGE	SN	91.04	91.32	**93.25**	92.22
	MN	89.18	94.76	**95.67**	95.40
	L	84.77	97.69	98.63	**99.05**
METEOR	SN	56.53	60.23	**64.24**	61.43
	MN	56.22	70.75	**72.07**	70.44
	L	47.98	**73.54**	70.83	72.06

Table 3: Utterance length impact in content preservation. We fix utterances tone to *neutral.*

Utterance tone - It is important to gauge models' ability to adapt to different levels of politeness. Namely, the difficulty of improving from rude to polite differs from neutral to polite. Additionally, models are trained on the neutral politeness bucket of data(to perform style transfer to polite tone), which may bias their performance towards a particular tone.

Utterance Length - During the initial experiments, we observed that the models tended to leave longer utterances untouched, and we wanted to measure the extent of that behavior for different utterance sizes.

To assess these two aspects, we evaluated our proposed four RW model variations, under a set of scenarios obtained by systematically varying the length and tone utterance properties, resulting in the following 5 scenarios:

Long (L) - Comprises of neutral[4]long utterances from the **MMD-A** test set. These correspond to recommendation of products thus being very rich in fashion-specific terms. We obtained 88 utterances.

Short & Rude (SR) - Short utterances obtained from the **MMD-A** test set. This corresponds to utterances belonging to the P_0 or P_1 buckets, i.e. utterances deemed *rude*, with less than 17 tokens. In total, we obtain 134 utterances.

Short & Neutral (SN) - Same strategy as **SR** but utterances are picked from the P_5 bucket instead - halfway of the politeness scale, meaning that utterances are deemed as *neutral.* In total we obtain 2.5k utterances.

[4]Due to the low utterance count, a long and rude test scenario was not viable.

	RW Model:	Enron	Fashion	Fashion-C	Mixed
BLEU	SR	70.22	84.28	**87.27**	86.36
	SN	83.24	88.30	**91.11**	89.45
	MR	71.35	87.62	**91.71**	90.75
	MN	82.31	96.22	**97.10**	96.28
ROUGE	SR	80.40	87.31	**88.95**	87.01
	SN	91.04	91.32	**93.25**	92.22
	MR	82.78	88.95	**91.68**	91.11
	MN	89.18	94.76	**95.67**	95.40
METEOR	SR	47.82	57.86	**60.23**	57.11
	SN	56.53	60.23	**64.24**	61.43
	MR	49.36	60.66	**63.10**	62.25
	MN	56.22	70.75	**72.07**	70.44

Table 4: Impact of tone of voice - Neutral (N) and Rude (R) - in both Short (S) and Medium (M) length utterances.

RW Model:	Enron	Fashion	Fashion-C	Mixed
Enron	+6.50	+13.15	+17.26	**+22.36**
MMD-A	**+5.76**	+3.28	+1.94	+4.22
SR	**+10.99**	+6.55	+5.34	+7.18
SN	**+8.83**	+6.49	+3.56	+6.89
MR	**+9.34**	+5.07	+3.72	+5.88
MN	**+6.11**	+1.21	+1.00	+1.96
L	**+2.45**	+1.02	+2.20	+2.43

Table 5: Relative improvement of the generated utterances over the target sentences (i.e. score=Scenario Score - Target Sentences Politeness Score), across all scenarios.

Medium & Rude (MR) - Similar to **SR** but with utterances length between 16 and 32 tokens, totaling 138 utterances.

Medium & Neutral (MN) - Similar to **SN** but with utterances length between 16 and 32 tokens, resulting in a total of 2.2k utterances.

Table 3 shows the results of each model over *neutral* utterances, but of varying lengths. The RW-Fashion-C model achieved the highest content preservation scores on the short and medium utterance scenarios. It is interesting to point that in all scenarios, models trained on **MMD-A** (all except RW-Enron), showed the same pattern: they make more changes in shorter utterances and less in longer ones, producing very few changes or even leaving utterances unaltered in the latter case. The RW-Enron model showed the opposite trend, making significant changes in longer utterances.

With respect to style changes (Table 4 and Table 5), for every model, there was a clear difference between neutral scenarios (SN and MN) and their rude counterparts (SR and MR). On average, the rude scenarios scored 7% lower on content preservation metrics than the neutral tests. This result should not lead to the conclusion that models perform better on neutral data. Actually, after inspecting the results, we observed that models obtained higher scores in neutral utterances because they are less capable of identifying what needs to be replaced or added to improve politeness. This is supported by the politeness variation, shown in Table 5. Here we observe that all models produce a higher improvement in rude utterances, but the difference in the relative improvement on neutral utterances is small, meaning that the utterance would still fall on the rude split.

Regarding Politeness scores, the models trained on the **MMD-A** (**Fashion**, **Fashion-C** and **Mixed**) show significant improvement on the Enron test. However, after a second inspection of the generated utterances, it was evident that the Politeness score increase did not translate to tone improvements given the generation being of low quality. Namely, models simply add **MMD-A** excerpts with no apparent criteria.

Overall, these models perform better in short rude utterances. When dealing with neutral text, they tend to produce a lesser amount of changes meaning that for such models to be applied as part of a pipeline of a task-oriented dialog agent, it is important to perform fine-tuning, towards overcoming domain shift issues. We also observed that, based on common politeness strategies (see section A.1), most of the politeness strategies employed were Gratitude and Positive Lexicon, as is common in a costumer-store interaction, on the fashion domain.

5.2.2 Qualitative Analysis of Style Markers

In this section, we conduct a qualitative evaluation over a set of three utterances, in order to further pinpoint each rewriting variant's characteristics.

Table 6 illustrates 2 sample output utterances, and the resulting output of each RW variant. For the first example, we have a polite-sounding utterance where the ideal behavior would be to leave the utterance untouched, given that it is already in a very polite form. For this case, the RW-Mixed model produced a slightly improved form, making the utterance less generic and more fashion-related. The utterance generated by RW-Enron and RW-Fashion-C could have been a successful case had the correct semantics been applied to the added text. In the second example, we see mixed results.

	Hi, please tell me what I can help you with?
RW-Enron	Hi, please tell me what I can help you get together with?
RW-Fashion	Hi, please tell me what I can help you with? please note
RW-Fashion-C	Hi, please tell me what I can help you show with?
RW-Mixed	Hi, please tell me what I can help fit you with?
	Hello, what I can help you with today?
RW-Enron	Hello, what I can help you get together with today?
RW-Fashion	Hello, what I can help you move with today?
RW-Fashion-C	Hello, what I can help you get ready for today?
RW-Mixed	He can go well withrit, what I can help fit fit you with today?
	Great. I think that's a great choice.
RW-Enron	Great. I think that's could be a great choice.
RW-Fashion	Great. I do not think i have a great choice but would you like something in other types.
RW-Fashion-C	Great. I think that's a great choice.
RW-Mixed	Great. I think that's a great choice thank you for shopping with us.

Table 6: Politeness rewriting output utterances analysis. Changes made by the model are highlighted with red, meaning a negative change (Grammar error or Rude tone) occurred, yellow for neutral changes, and green for positive changes. lighter green indicates a positive change but less impactful than a darker green one.

Both the RW-Enron and RW-Fashion-C models were able to improve on the utterance's sentiment by adding in-domain knowledge. The RW-Mixed model produced a bad generation, adding duplicated words and low-quality excerpts.

Overall, under the correct circumstances, we see that most of the models can successfully improve politeness. The RW-Fashion makes mostly low-quality additions, showing that there is a need for style marker curation. We also observed that the models are often more successful when improving on an already polite utterance rather than when dealing with neutral utterances. We believe this behavior is a product of the model architecture that looks for style markers to replace and said style markers are not present in neutral-sounding text.

6 Conclusion

In this work, we address the research gap regarding the development of polite task-oriented dialog agents. We demonstrate that while politeness language constructs tend not to be domain-specific, their application is, requiring politeness approaches to cope with domain-specific vocabulary. Particularly, we show that when improving politeness in task-specific utterances, rewriting approaches consistently deliver better results, given that generative alternatives need to attend to two tasks.

In summary, the key takeaways are:

- Politeness through rewriting results in the most robust approach, providing a good balance between delivering polite utterances and preserving content.
- Politeness answer generation is less stable. By definition, generation and politeness improvement need to be addressed jointly, which is too ambitious in a domain-transfer setting.
- Bringing politeness to task-oriented dialog agents, characterized by operating over highly specific domains, is achievable with the proposed model domain adaptations.

As future work, we plan to extend our work and research methods that select the best politeness strategies while accounting for the specificity of distinct conversation phases (e.g. greeting vs. product description utterances).

Acknowledgments

This work has been partially funded by the iFetch project, Ref. 45920, co-financed by ERDF, COMPETE 2020, NORTE 2020 and FCT under CMU Portugal, by the FCT Ph.D. scholarship grant Ref. PRT/BD/152810/2021, and by the FCT project NOVA LINCS Ref. (UIDB/04516/2020).

References

Malika Aubakirova and Mohit Bansal. 2016. Interpreting neural networks to improve politeness comprehension. In *Proceedings of the 2016 Conference on Empirical Methods in Natural Language Processing*, pages 2035–2041, Austin, Texas. Association for Computational Linguistics.

Francesca Bargiela-Chiappini. 2003. Face and politeness: new (insights) for old (concepts). *Journal of Pragmatics*, 35(10):1453–1469.

Penelope Brown, Stephen Levinson, and E Goody. 1978. *Universal in Language Usage: Politeness Phenomena*, volume 8, pages 56–311.

Penelope Brown, Stephen C Levinson, and Stephen C Levinson. 1987. *Politeness: Some universals in language usage*, volume 4. Cambridge university press.

Kyunghyun Cho, Bart van Merriënboer, Dzmitry Bahdanau, and Yoshua Bengio. 2014. On the properties of neural machine translation: Encoder–decoder approaches. In *Proceedings of SSST-8, Eighth Workshop on Syntax, Semantics and Structure in Statistical Translation*, pages 103–111, Doha, Qatar. Association for Computational Linguistics.

Cristian Danescu-Niculescu-Mizil, Moritz Sudhof, Dan Jurafsky, Jure Leskovec, and Christopher Potts. 2013. A computational approach to politeness with application to social factors. In *Proceedings of the 51st Annual Meeting of the Association for Computational Linguistics (Volume 1: Long Papers)*, pages 250–259, Sofia, Bulgaria. Association for Computational Linguistics.

Michael J. Denkowski and Alon Lavie. 2011. Meteor 1.3: Automatic metric for reliable optimization and evaluation of machine translation systems. In *WMT@EMNLP*.

Mauajama Firdaus, Asif Ekbal, and Pushpak Bhattacharyya. 2020. Incorporating politeness across languages in customer care responses: Towards building a multi-lingual empathetic dialogue agent. In *Proceedings of the 12th Language Resources and Evaluation Conference*, pages 4172–4182, Marseille, France. European Language Resources Association.

Liye Fu, Susan Fussell, and Cristian Danescu-Niculescu-Mizil. 2020. Facilitating the communication of politeness through fine-grained paraphrasing. In *Proceedings of the 2020 Conference on Empirical Methods in Natural Language Processing (EMNLP)*, pages 5127–5140, Online. Association for Computational Linguistics.

Hitesh Golchha, M. Firdaus, Asif Ekbal, and P. Bhattacharyya. 2019. Courteously yours: Inducing courteous behavior in customer care responses using reinforced pointer generator network. In *NAACL-HLT*.

Bryan Klimt and Yiming Yang. 2004. Introducing the enron corpus. In *CEAS*.

Chin-Yew Lin. 2004. Rouge: A package for automatic evaluation of summaries. In *ACL 2004*.

Aman Madaan, Amrith Setlur, Tanmay Parekh, Barnabas Poczos, Graham Neubig, Yiming Yang, Ruslan Salakhutdinov, Alan W Black, and Shrimai Prabhumoye. 2020. Politeness transfer: A tag and generate approach. In *Proceedings of the 58th Annual Meeting of the Association for Computational Linguistics*. Association for Computational Linguistics.

Ardith J. Meier. 1995. Defining politeness: Universality in appropriateness. *Language Sciences*, 17:345–356.

Tomas Mikolov, Kai Chen, Gregory S. Corrado, and Jeffrey Dean. 2013. Efficient estimation of word representations in vector space. In *ICLR*.

Tong Niu and Mohit Bansal. 2018. Polite dialogue generation without parallel data. *Transactions of the Association for Computational Linguistics*, 6:373–389.

Kishore Papineni, Salim Roukos, Todd Ward, and Wei-Jing Zhu. 2002. Bleu: a method for automatic evaluation of machine translation. In *ACL*.

Amrita Saha, Mitesh M. Khapra, and Karthik Sankaranarayanan. 2018. Towards building large scale multimodal domain-aware conversation systems. In *Proceedings of the Thirty-Second AAAI Conference on Artificial Intelligence, (AAAI-18), the 30th innovative Applications of Artificial Intelligence (IAAI-18), and the 8th AAAI Symposium on Educational Advances in Artificial Intelligence (EAAI-18), New Orleans, Louisiana, USA, February 2-7, 2018*, pages 696–704. AAAI Press.

Ricardo Gamelas Sousa, Pedro Miguel Ferreira, Pedro Moreira Costa, Pedro Azevedo, Joao Paulo Costeira, Carlos Santiago, Joao Magalhaes, David Semedo, Rafael Ferreira, Alexander I. Rudnicky, and Alexander Georg Hauptmann. 2021. *IFetch: Multimodal Conversational Agents for the Online Fashion Marketplace*, page 25–26. Association for Computing Machinery, New York, NY, USA.

Ashish Vaswani, Noam Shazeer, Niki Parmar, Jakob Uszkoreit, Llion Jones, Aidan N. Gomez, Łukasz Kaiser, and Illia Polosukhin. 2017. Attention is all you need. In *Proceedings of the 31st International Conference on Neural Information Processing Systems*, NIPS'17, page 6000–6010, Red Hook, NY, USA. Curran Associates Inc.

Richard J. Watts. 2019. *2. Linguistic politeness and politic verbal behaviour: Reconsidering claims for universality*, pages 43–70. De Gruyter Mouton.

Politeness Strategies
Using Honorifics: *How can I help you Ms Smith?* **Description:** Through the usage of Honorifics, the speaker conveys respect towards another person.
Gratitude: *Thank you very much for your help.* **Description:** One of the easiest ways of sounding polite is through the expression of gratitude.
Tag Questions: *Take a seat, won't you?* **Description:** Tag Questions at the end of a utterance can define the tone used, making it sound more friendly or the opposite, depending on the usage.
Positiveness: *Great choice! That's a fantastic watch.* **Description:** Using a positive lexicon keeps the utterance tone positive and conveys that same feeling to the listener.
Greeting: *Hello, welcome! Can I interest you in some ...* **Description:** A greeting can help convey a polite and respectful tone to the other interlocutor.

Table 7: Example strategies to improve utterances politeness, with style markers highlighted in blue.

A Appendix

A.1 Politeness Strategies

Table 7 shows some of the Politeness Strategies that can be identified when dealing with polite dialog.

A.2 Dataset details

Stanford Politeness Corpus (SPC) - Dataset used for politeness conditioning, by training the Politeness proxy classifier (Niu and Bansal, 2018). This corpus is composed of requests made by editors in Wikipedia and by requests made on Sack Exchange, all of which have been annotated by 5 humans. For Wikipedia and Stack Exchange requests, 4,353 out of 35,661 and 6,603 out of 373,519 were annotated, respectively. Request scores were z-score normalized and averaged. We used the data splits used originally with Polite-RL (Niu and Bansal, 2018), so we only considered the top and bottom 25% utterances for polite and rude respectively. 3808 utterances were used for training and 1056 for testing.

Enron - This dataset is a collection of emails exchanged in the Enron company (Klimt and Yang, 2004), that was originally used to train the Tag-and-Generate model (Madaan et al., 2020). We consider the subset of the Enron dataset that the authors automatically annotated using the Politeness Classifier (Niu and Bansal, 2018). This dataset is used in our work to establish an initial domain for a task-oriented dialog agent. For training, 212k polite and 51k rude sentences are considered, for validation 27k polite and 5.8k rude, and for testing 26k polite and 5.8k rude utterances.

Multimodal Dialogs Dataset (MMD) - MMD (Saha et al., 2018) comprises multi-turn multimodal dialogs for the fashion domain. MMD is used as use-case for a second domain task-oriented dialog agent, where we define two distinct (but overlapping) subsets: **MMD-R** and **MMD-A**. In **MMD-R**, based on the provided intent annotations, we only keep system utterances corresponding to product(s) recommendation(s), resulting in 380k/81k/81k utterances for training/validation/testing. The goal of this first subset is to expose the model to the domain-specific product lexicon of the fashion domain. Namely, these utterances comprise scenarios in which the system recommends and describes one or more products to the user. In **MMD-A** we keep all *neutral* and *polite* system utterances, with more than 5 tokens, totaling 39k/10k/10k and 414k/96k/96k, neutral and polite utterances, respectively, for training/validation/testing. Here we considered a style change from neutral to polite, rather than rude to polite, since the number of rude utterances is minimal (2.5k).

Model Name (b, β)	BLEU	Politeness
Reference(96, 2.0)	**66.30**	64.47
Model 1(32, 2.0)	49.64	72.40
Model 2 (128, 2.0)	63.60	60.24
Model 3 (96, 5.0)	33.56	75.21
Model 4 (96, 10.0)	29.41	**78.77**

Table 8: Experimental results of the 4 tested scenarios vs a reference model. From now on, we scale up the politeness scores into a 0 to 100 scale.

A.3 MMD Sample dialog

A sample dialog from the MMD (Saha et al., 2018) dataset can be found in Figure 2.

A.4 Polite-RL Model tuning

For the model parameter tuning, the two parameters, β and batch size (b), were tested separately, and, for each parameter, we tested 2 variations of their values. To measure the impact on the results, we use BLEU and the politeness score on the test set. As for baselines, we use a version of the model trained on the MMD data with the default values for each parameter.

$$L = L_{ML} + \beta L_{RL} \quad (1)$$

For the batch size (whose default value was 96), we tested the model with sizes 128 and 32, these values were picked to understand the model's behavior with an increase and decrease of the value. The β is an hyperparameter that dictates the weight given to the politeness reward component of the model's loss function, as shown in Equation 1 where L_{ML} is the maximum likelihood loss and L_{RL} is the politeness reward loss. For this parameter, we followed a different direction and tested with values 5 and 10, both significantly bigger than the default value of 2. This was done to understand the impact of the parameter in the politeness of the generated text and how it impacted generation quality. This is an important factor given that, for conversational agents, it is important to generate polite text but also retain high-quality question answering capabilities.

The results, shown in Table 8, are using the Classifier with custom embeddings. These results show that altering both parameters can lead to a noticeable change in the model's performance. Looking at the BLEU scores, none of the tested variations beat the base model, with only Model 2 coming close. For the two models where we changed the beta value, Model 3 and Model 4, the BLEU score took a nosedive, which was expected since by increasing the β we are changing the initial balance in the loss function making it highly favor polite generation over accurate question answering.

When looking at the inference results from both models, we see significant text degeneration on a large portion of the test sentences, with the same pattern repeating: the first dozen or so tokens are correctly predicted followed by a dozen or

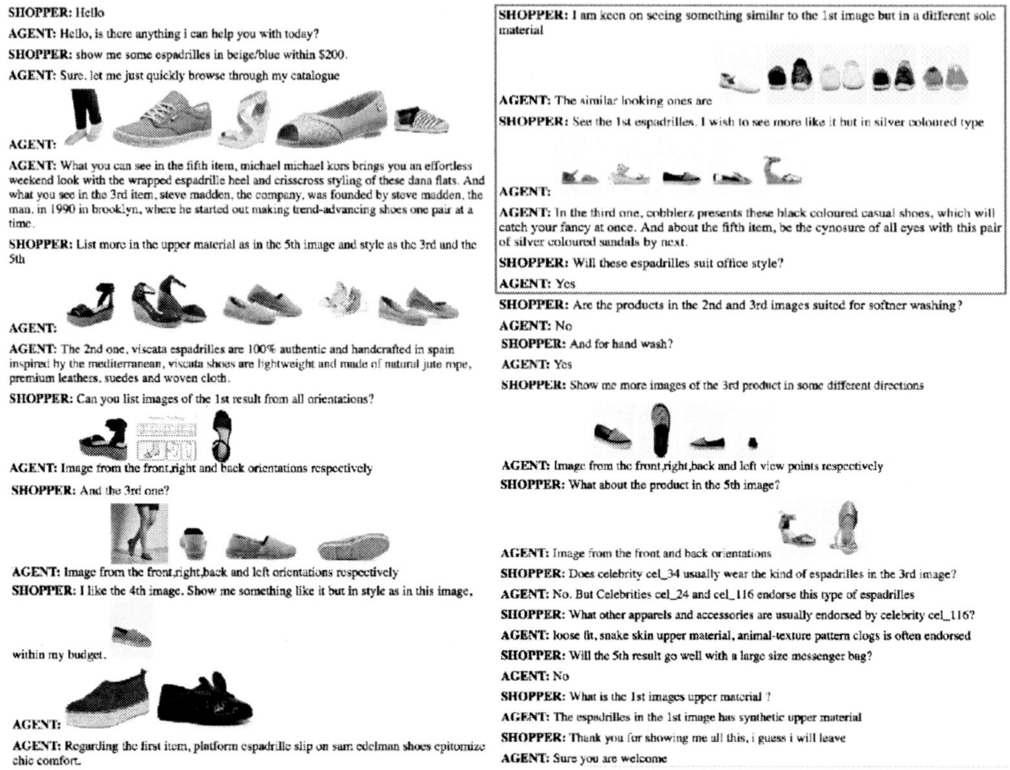

Figure 2: A sample dialog from the MMD dataset. Source: Saha et al. (2018)

more repetitions of the same token, a token favored by the politeness classifier. Still considering the BLEU scores, Model 1 presented some surprising results as we were not expecting text degeneration to also occur in this scenario, but it did, albeit not as accentuated as in the later 2 models.

When taking into account the politeness scores, we see that increasing the beta value clearly improves politeness generation, or so it would seem, as mentioned before all of the models that beat the reference in politeness generation did it by starting to generate the same token repeatedly mid-sentence.

These results showed us that when trying to encourage politeness generation, we cannot solely rely on token probability distributions, semantics need to be taken into account or, at least, vocabulary diversity at the classifier level, since any other way the model is not punished by simply outputting the classifier's favorite word, 'belt' in some cases and 'republic' in others. This means that, using the Polite-RL, the best balance that can be achieved results is a compromise in generation quality while not making the used tone polite. For conversational agents, this is important as the question answering quality needs to remain high throughout the conversation.

Items from Psychometric Tests as Training Data for Personality Profiling Models of Twitter Users

Anne Kreuter[1], **Kai Sassenberg**[2,3], and **Roman Klinger**[1]
[1]Institut für Maschinelle Sprachverarbeitung, University of Stuttgart, Germany
[2]Leibniz-Institut für Wissensmedien, Tübingen, Germany
[3]University of Tübingen, Germany
{anne.kreuter,roman.klinger}@ims.uni-stuttgart.de
k.sassenberg@iwm-tuebingen.de

Abstract

Machine-learned models for author profiling in social media often rely on data acquired via self-reporting-based psychometric tests (questionnaires) filled out by social media users. This is an expensive but accurate data collection strategy. Another, less costly alternative, which leads to potentially more noisy and biased data, is to rely on labels inferred from publicly available information in the profiles of the users, for instance self-reported diagnoses or test results. In this paper, we explore a third strategy, namely to directly use a corpus of items from validated psychometric tests as training data. Items from psychometric tests often consist of sentences from an I-perspective (*e.g.*, "I make friends easily."). Such corpora of test items constitute 'small data', but their availability for many concepts is a rich resource. We investigate this approach for personality profiling, and evaluate BERT classifiers fine-tuned on such psychometric test items for the big five personality traits (openness, conscientiousness, extraversion, agreeableness, neuroticism) and analyze various augmentation strategies regarding their potential to address the challenges coming with such a small corpus. Our evaluation on a publicly available Twitter corpus shows a comparable performance to in-domain training for 4/5 personality traits with T5-based data augmentation.

1 Introduction

The field of author profiling originally emerged from the study of stylometry (Lutoslawski, 1898) and, with the rise of social media (Bilan and Zhekova, 2016), now considers a variety of attributes, including demographic data such as age, sex, gender, nationality (Schwartz et al., 2013), personality traits (Golbeck et al., 2011), or psychological states such as emotions, or medical conditions like mental disorders (De Choudhury et al., 2013). Such automatic methods enable large-scale social media data analyses even for (combinations of) variables for which results from surveys are not available. Therefore, personality profiling in social media helps to paint a more comprehensive, complete, and timely picture for parts of a society.

State-of-the-art models reconstruct personality traits or mental health states from posts of social media users by relying on ground-truth data that links such posts to the correct annotation (Guntuku et al., 2017). The ground-truth data is typically obtained by either (1) asking participants to complete a validated survey that measures the desired variable and asking the participants to share their social media profiles, (2), by relying on self-reports of users, e.g., disclosure of a condition in the user's profile description, or (3), by having experts annotate profiles for particular properties. The quality of data obtained might therefore suffer from social-desirability bias, from being a non-representative subsample, from a lack of validated diagnoses, or from noise stemming from the challenge that annotators do not have access to the actual characteristics of users (Ernala et al., 2019).

We explore another route for which we hypothesize that it addresses these issues, but at the cost of only having access to very small data sets: We propose to leverage the existing set of high-quality, validated, and reliable psychometric instruments to measure psychological traits *directly*. Psychometric tests often come in the form of questionnaires which contain items, allowing a person to report

Variable	Cor.	Item Text
Openness	+	"Am interested in many things."
Openness	−	"Do not like art."
Extraversion	+	"Warm up quickly to others."
Extraversion	−	"Am hard to get to know."

Table 1: Example items from a psychometric test to assess personality traits (Lee and Ashton, 2018). 'Cor.' indicates if the item has been shown to correlate positively or negatively to the respective concept.

Proceedings of the 12th Workshop on Computational Approaches to Subjectivity, Sentiment & Social Media Analysis, pages 315 - 323
May 26, 2022 ©2022 Association for Computational Linguistics

about themselves. These items are sentences formulated as descriptions of the self (Table 1 shows some examples). This structure motivates our hypothesis that such psychometric tests can be used directly to induce classifiers that profile individuals in social media without the existence of designated, manually annotated in-domain training data. If indeed possible, this would lead to a straightforward route to develop a myriad of classifiers for all those concepts for which psychometric tests exist. To dampen the issue of these sets of items being comparably small, we make use of pre-trained language models (Howard and Ruder, 2018; Devlin et al., 2019; Brown et al., 2020) to transfer knowledge acquired through pretraining rich semantic representations. Some subtypes of such models can be considered few-shot learners (Brown et al., 2020; Ruder et al., 2019), however, the transfer might not be successful to data outside of the pretraining domain. Therefore, we evaluate if various data augmentation methods can further leverage the challenges coming with such small corpora.

Thus, our contributions in this paper are that we (1) assemble a corpus from publicly available psychometric tests for the 'Big Five' variables of openness, conscientiousness, extraversion, agreeableness, and neuroticism (Costa and McCrae, 1992), which have been shown to be principled factors of personality (Cattell, 1945). Based on these data, we (2) fine-tune BERT (Devlin et al., 2019) and evaluate it on an existing personality trait corpus (Rangel et al., 2015). Furthermore, (3) we evaluate three data augmentation methods, namely paraphrasing with T5 (Raffel et al., 2020), and item generation with GPT-2 (Radford et al., 2019) and synonym replacements with Easy Data Augmentation (Wei and Zou, 2019). Our results, (4), show that the models perform en par with in-domain training for 4/5 personality trait variables.

2 Related Work

Psychometric Personality Tests. A psychometric test is a standardized instrument used to measure the cognitive, behavioral, or emotional characteristics of a person. One possible form are questionnaires, which can be designed for self-reporting. For each item the information is available if it is correlated positively or negatively with the concept to be measured. Publicly available psychometric tests can be found in various online repositories.[1]

An established test for personality traits following the so-called 'big five' variables is the *International Personality Item Pool Representation* of the NEO PI-R with 300 items[2] (IPIP-NEO-300, Goldberg et al., 1999). This test is a proxy of the *Revised NEO Personality Inventory* (NEO PI-R) by Costa and McCrae (1992), which is copyrighted and can only be ordered by professionals and used with permission. We use all items of the IPIP-NEO-300 as the source of our training corpus.

Another test of personality traits would be the *HEXACO Personality Inventory-Revised* (Lee and Ashton, 2008). It measures six factors of personality (Ashton et al., 2004) with 200 items, namely Honesty-Humility, Emotionality, Extraversion, Agreeableness, Conscientiousness, and Openness to experience.

Data. Psychometric tests found application in the analysis of social media user's personality in the past. An influential study has been the work by Schwartz et al. (2014), who collected Facebook data with a dedicated application (Stillwell and Kosinski, 2004) in which users completed the 100-item IPIP-NEO-100 questionnaire (Goldberg et al., 1999). The users further shared access to their status updates. This data is not available any longer.

The data for the PAN-author-profiling shared task in 2015 has been collected in a similar way (Rangel et al., 2015).[3] It consists of Tweets of 294 English Twitter profiles (besides Spanish, Italian and Dutch Twitter profiles), which are annotated with gender, age, and the 'Big Five' personality traits. The personality traits were self-assessed by the Twitter users with the BFI-10 (Rammstedt and John, 2007), which is an economic psychometric test that allows the personality to be recorded with only 10 items. We use this corpus for evaluation.

Combining Tests and Social Media Data. An interesting combination of psychometric tests with social media posts, which is likely the one most similar to our paper, is the work by Vu et al. (2020). The authors make use of social media data of users to automatically fill the IPIP-NEO (Goldberg et al., 1999) psychometric test to predict the social media user's 'Big Five' personality traits. They do so by embedding sentences and items with BERT into the same distributional space, followed by a k-nearest-

[1] https://psychology-tools.com/, https://ipip.ori.org/, https://www.psychometrictest.org.uk/

[2] http://www.personal.psu.edu/~j5j/IPIP/

[3] https://zenodo.org/record/3745945,https://pan.webis.de/

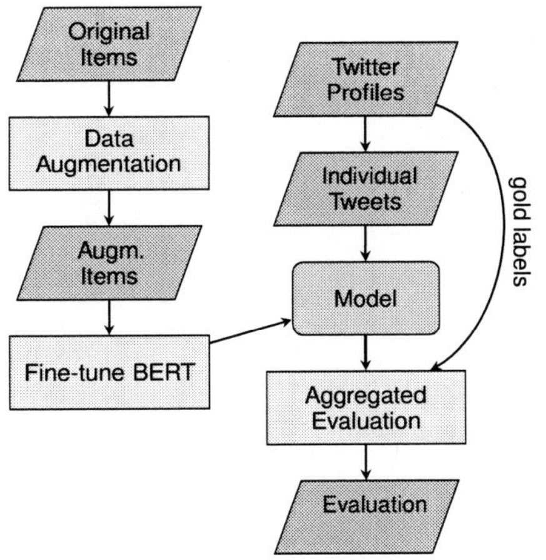

Figure 1: Workflow of our approach.

neighbor classification. This approach constitutes the opposing approach that we chose in our paper – Vu et al. (2020) use social media data to fill a psychometric test. We use psychometric tests to classify social media data.

We refer the reader to Stajner and Yenikent (2020) for a more comprehensive overview of related work.

3 Methods

3.1 Workflow

We depict the general workflow in Figure 1. The original items from the questionnaire are first augmented. The resulting augmented items inherit the labels from the respective original items. We fine-tune BERT with these items which leads to a model to make predictions for comparably short instances, like Tweets. From the labeled corpus of Twitter profiles, we obtain labels for each individual tweet with the BERT-based model and then aggregate the individual labels to obtain a label for the whole profile. In the evaluation, this predicted profile label is compared to the annotated gold label.

3.2 Corpora

We use all items of the psychometric test IPIP-NEO-300 (Goldberg et al., 1999) as training data and label each item following the evaluation guidelines accompanying the IPIP-NEO-300 (see also Table 1). These guidelines provide the information if a confirmative answer to the item indicates a positive correlation or negative correlation with the target variable, which leads to a binary label.

For evaluation, we use the English subset of the PAN-author-profiling-2015 data (Rangel et al., 2015) with annotated Twitter profiles. Table 2 summarizes the corpus statistics. Note that the distribution of the items from the test data is skewed towards positive instances – this might be a direct consequence of people with particular personality traits being more likely to share particular information on social media.

	IPIP-NEO		Profiles		Tweets	
Class.	+	−	+	−	+	−
Open.	28	32	288	3	26,743	236
Consc.	31	29	229	15	21,391	1,428
Extra.	36	24	235	21	21,686	2,000
Agree.	24	36	223	29	20,441	2,831
Neurot.	33	27	76	197	18,076	7,168

Table 2: Corpus Statistics regarding the Twitter evaluation data and the IPIP-NEO-300-based training corpus. We extracted all profiles with positive or negative scores and excluded profiles with neutral scores.

3.3 Classification Model

As our source domain, we consider a set of items $Q_C = \{(q_i, y_i)\}_{i=1}^{n}$ from a reliable psychometric test. Each of these items corresponds to one psychological concept C and consists of the item text q_i and the label $y_i \in \{\text{pos}, \text{neg}\}$ which stems from the evaluation guidelines for this test.

The task is to find a parameterized function $f_{C,\lambda}(u)$ which takes as input all posts of a user u and predicts a label for each concept C. The important aspect in our setup is that the parameters λ are only optimized on the psychometric data Q_C. This is a mismatch – we train a classifier to label short texts but need as output a prediction for a set of tweets which represents the user. Hence, to obtain a label for each user, we aggregate the labels for all their posts by accepting the majority class, for each concept separately.

To obtain the text classifier, we fine-tune BERT (Devlin et al., 2019) to approximate each function $f_{C,\lambda}$, based on *bert-base-uncased*. The sequence classification head is randomly initialized on top of the encoder.[4] For each concept C, we fine-tune a separate BERT model (no multi-task learning).

3.4 Data Augmentation

With 60 items per personality trait, our training corpora are small. To address this issue, we perform data augmentation with three different methods.

[4] https://huggingface.co/transformers/model_doc/bert.html#bertforsequenceclassification

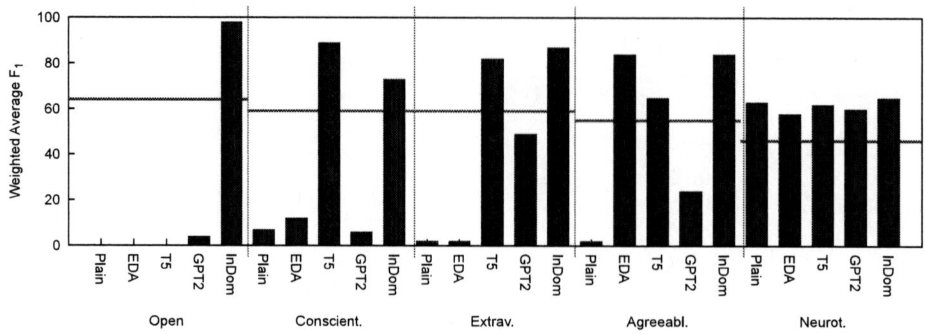

Figure 2: F_1 scores for all models and classes. Horizontal lines depict the baseline.

For every n instances $(q_i, y_i) \in Q_C$, we perform each data augmentation m times (obtaining $n \cdot m$ instances). Thus, we generate m augmented items q_i^a for each q_i. Each newly generated instance inherits the label y_i of its original instance q_i. We show examples for automatically generated items in the Appendix A.3.

Easy Data Augmentation. Easy Data Augmentation (EDA, Wei and Zou, 2019) consists of four operations on the sentence level: synonym replacement, random insertion, random deletion, and random swap. We use the default parameter of 10% of words in the sentence being changed (30% for random deletion) to perform each operation of EDA on each sentence (item) 5 times, hence generate 20 instances out of each original instance. This leads to 1,160 items for openness, 1,130 for conscientiousness, 1,080 for extraversion, 1,160 for agreeableness, and 1080 for neuroticism.

T5 item paraphrasing. We use T5 (Raffel et al., 2020) to paraphrase each item, based on the *T5ForConditionalGeneration* model provided by HuggingFace[5]. We do not perform fine-tuning to our domain, but rely on the original pre-trained parameters. For each item, we generate up to 50 paraphrases which leads to 2,285 items for openness, 2,383 for conscientiousness, 2,149 for extraversion, 2,126 for agreeableness, 2,130 for neuroticism.

GPT-2 item generation. We fine-tune GPT-2 (Radford et al., 2019) for each personality trait separately in 150 epochs, based on gpt-2-simple[6]. We generate 3000 items for each class label with a sentence length of 100 tokens and a temperature of 1.5. This leads to 6,279 items for openness, 6,177 for conscientiousness, 6,204 for extraversion, 6,271 for agreeableness, 6,242 for neuroticism.

[5]https://huggingface.co/transformers/model_doc/t5.html#t5forconditionalgeneration

[6]https://github.com/minimaxir/gpt-2-simple

4 Experiments

4.1 Experimental Settings

We split the psychometric test data to 80 % for training and use 20 % for hyperparameter optimization, while we ensure that augmented items stay in one set with their original item.[7] To avoid overfitting, we apply early stopping via observing the loss on the validation data. The maximum number of epochs is set to 200.

For a comparison to an "upper-bound" of in-domain training on Twitter, we split the corpora of social media profiles such that 50% of the Twitter profiles are in the test set. The remaining 50 % are used for training and further split into 90 % for training and 10 % for hyperparameter optimization of the in-domain model. The settings for fine-tuning the in-domain models are identical to the settings of the psychometric models.

4.2 Results

We show our main results as weighted F_1 values in Figure 2 (complete results in Table 4 in the Appendix). We compare the "plain" models without data augmentation to the augmented methods (as bar plots) and a random baseline (as horizontal line). We further show the performance of the in-domain model.

All "plain", non-data augmented models get outperformed by the random baseline, except for the personality trait neuroticism (F_1 =.63 versus F_1 =.46 random baseline). The plain psychometric models are inferior to the in-domain models for all concepts, but to various extends: Neuroticism is the only trait where the plain model shows a performance *en par* with the in-domain model.

[7]Seed set to 42 via PyTorchLighting *seed_everything*, learning rate 10^{-5}, batch size of 16, optimization with Adam (Kingma and Ba, 2014).

Regarding the augmentation methods, T5 shows considerable improvements for conscientiousness, extraversion, and agreeableness (F_1 =.89, F_1 =.82, F_1 =.65, respectively, vs. .73, .87, .84 for in-domain models). This is also the best-performing augmentation method for conscientiousness and extraversion, however, EDA shows a further improvement for agreeableness (.84). T5 does not harm the performance for neuroticism in comparison to the plain model. Therefore, we conclude that T5 augmentation is a promising choice for 4/5 traits, while the other augmentation methods appear less stable in their contribution.

In summary, we obtain a substantial model performance without the use of in-domain training data for Conscientiousness, Extraversion, Agreeableness, and Neuroticism. The transfer to or the difficulty of these concepts appears not to be the same, the performance for Conscientiousness is substantially higher than for Neuroticism. These results can only be partially compared to previous work due to the differences in the evaluation setup. However, it should be noted that the concepts that appear to be more challenging in our setup show also lower evaluation measures in related work (see for instance Table 3 in Rangel et al., 2015, note that their evaluation measure is an RSME, lower is therefore better).

4.3 Model Introspection

To provide some insights on the decision process by the classification models, we provide one example for each personality trait from the Tweet corpus with LIME explanations (Ribeiro et al., 2016) in Table 3. In the example for openness, the classifier relies on the word "love" as a positive indicator. This word can indeed be found in items from the test, namely in "Love to daydream", "Love flowers", and "Love to read challenging material". It is also a term that appears frequently in augmented data, such as in "Love problem solving" or in "Love flowers. Is it not hard to tell if you like something that's especially beautiful?". A positive indicator for conscientiousness is the word "August" and "year". This is interesting, given that these words appear not to be directly related to conscientiousness, and they do not appear in the original items of the test. However, the augmented data contains items that refer to "year", such as in "I truly love Excel and have used it for years.".

T	Tweet
O	@username What my love life will hold instore for me in the future. I'd never ask when I'm gonna die...????????
C	"@username: @username I like your profile photo. Very nice!!! You look very pretty. :)" THANK YOU! Took this photo in August this year.
E	@username Slade!!! Cool memories of my grammar school days!!
A	@username I rocked so much to their music!
N	"@username: Karma has no menu. You get served what you deserve."

Table 3: Examples of LIME explanations. Green indicates a positive contribution of the word, and red a negative contribution. The augmentation approach used in each example is the best-performing method for the respective concept. All examples are true positives.

5 Conclusion & Future Work

We outlined a novel methodology for automatic author profiling in social media users without a costly collection of annotated social media data. Instead, we directly train on items from validated psychometric tests. This data selection procedure has some advantages: items of psychometric tests are carefully validated textual instances. Such corpora of such items constitute "small data", but are available for a large number of concepts. Therefore, developing a method to induce classifiers directly from psychometric tests is also a promising avenue for future research.

For the tasks of developing models measuring the big five personality traits, we tested on Twitter data that has been collected by asking users to fill out a (different) test. The transfer appears to be achievable, we obtain results for four out of five personality traits which are *en par* with in-domain models, using T5 data augmentation (except Openness, which has very few test instances).

An important remaining research question is how models can be obtained that show consistently good results across concepts. In a real-world setup, test data from the target domain would not be available to make model selection decisions. One way to go might be to combine various augmentation methods. Another approach would be to use items as prompts in a zero-shot learning setup.

Acknowledgements

This work was supported by Deutsche Forschungsgemeinschaft (project CEAT, KL 2869/1-2).

Ethical considerations

The fact that the current research deals with the sensitive topic of personality warrants for some ethical considerations. First, the study has been conducted with anonymized publicly available data. We did not collect data ourselves and importantly the data did not allow to identify subjects. Therefore, it is neither required nor possible to request IRB approval for the current research, given that IRB is concerned with the protection of human subjects. We had no reasons to doubt that the parties, who originally collected the data got IRB approval and informed consent form the participants who provided their data.

However, we acknowledge that automatic systems for personality trait analysis can be misused. Further, the application of our proposed model creation strategy can also be used for other more sensible concepts, for instance regarding mental health. We propose that such systems are only made available in such a manner that no personalized results can be retrieved.

References

Michael C Ashton, Kibeom Lee, Marco Perugini, Piotr Szarota, Reinout E De Vries, Lisa Di Blas, Kathleen Boies, and Boele De Raad. 2004. A six-factor structure of personality-descriptive adjectives: solutions from psycholexical studies in seven languages. *Journal of personality and social psychology*, 86(2):356–366.

Ivan Bilan and Desislava Zhekova. 2016. Caps: A cross-genre author profiling system. In *CLEF (Working Notes)*, pages 824–835.

Tom Brown, Benjamin Mann, Nick Ryder, Melanie Subbiah, Jared D Kaplan, Prafulla Dhariwal, Arvind Neelakantan, Pranav Shyam, Girish Sastry, Amanda Askell, Sandhini Agarwal, Ariel Herbert-Voss, Gretchen Krueger, Tom Henighan, Rewon Child, Aditya Ramesh, Daniel Ziegler, Jeffrey Wu, Clemens Winter, Chris Hesse, Mark Chen, Eric Sigler, Mateusz Litwin, Scott Gray, Benjamin Chess, Jack Clark, Christopher Berner, Sam McCandlish, Alec Radford, Ilya Sutskever, and Dario Amodei. 2020. Language models are few-shot learners. In *Advances in Neural Information Processing Systems*, volume 33, pages 1877–1901. Curran Associates, Inc.

Raymond B Cattell. 1945. The description of personality: Principles and findings in a factor analysis. *The American journal of psychology*, 58(1):69–90.

Paul T Costa and Robert R McCrae. 1992. *Neo personality inventory-revised (NEO PI-R)*. Psychological Assessment Resources Odessa, FL.

Munmun De Choudhury, Michael Gamon, Scott Counts, and Eric Horvitz. 2013. Predicting depression via social media. In *International AAAI Conference on Web and Social Media (ICWSM)*.

Jacob Devlin, Ming-Wei Chang, Kenton Lee, and Kristina Toutanova. 2019. BERT: Pre-training of deep bidirectional transformers for language understanding. In *Proceedings of the 2019 Conference of the North American Chapter of the Association for Computational Linguistics: Human Language Technologies, Volume 1 (Long and Short Papers)*, pages 4171–4186, Minneapolis, Minnesota. Association for Computational Linguistics.

Sindhu Kiranmai Ernala, Michael L Birnbaum, Kristin A Candan, Asra F Rizvi, William A Sterling, John M Kane, and Munmun De Choudhury. 2019. Methodological gaps in predicting mental health states from social media: triangulating diagnostic signals. In *Proceedings of the 2019 CHI conference on human factors in computing systems*, pages 1–16.

Jennifer Golbeck, Cristina Robles, and Karen Turner. 2011. Predicting personality with social media. In *CHI'11 extended abstracts on human factors in computing systems*, pages 253–262.

Lewis R Goldberg et al. 1999. A broad-bandwidth, public domain, personality inventory measuring the lower-level facets of several five-factor models. *Personality psychology in Europe*, 7(1):7–28.

Sharath C Guntuku, David B Yaden, Margaret L Kern, Lyle H Ungar, and Johannes C Eichstaedt. 2017. Detecting depression and mental illness on social media: an integrative review. *Current Opinion in Behavioral Sciences*, 18:43–49. Big data in the behavioural sciences.

Jeremy Howard and Sebastian Ruder. 2018. Universal language model fine-tuning for text classification. In *Proceedings of the 56th Annual Meeting of the Association for Computational Linguistics (Volume 1: Long Papers)*, pages 328–339, Melbourne, Australia. Association for Computational Linguistics.

Diederik P Kingma and Jimmy Ba. 2014. Adam: A method for stochastic optimization. *arXiv preprint arXiv:1412.6980*.

Kibeom Lee and Michael C Ashton. 2008. The hexaco personality inventory: A short measure of the major dimensions of personality. *Journal of Personality Assessment*, 39(2):340–345.

Kibeom Lee and Michael C Ashton. 2018. Psychometric properties of the hexaco-100. *Assessment*, 25(5):543–556.

Wincenty Lutoslawski. 1898. Principes de stylométrie appliqués à la chronologie des œuvres de platon. *Revue des études grecques*, 11(41):61–81.

Alec Radford, Jeffrey Wu, Rewon Child, David Luan, Dario Amodei, and Ilya Sutskever. 2019. Language models are unsupervised multitask learners. *OpenAI blog*, 1(8):9.

Colin Raffel, Noam Shazeer, Adam Roberts, Katherine Lee, Sharan Narang, Michael Matena, Yanqi Zhou, Wei Li, and Peter J Liu. 2020. Exploring the limits of transfer learning with a unified text-to-text transformer. *Journal of Machine Learning Research*, 21(140):1–67.

Beatrice Rammstedt and Oliver P John. 2007. Measuring personality in one minute or less: A 10-item short version of the big five inventory in english and german. *Journal of research in Personality*, 41(1):203–212.

Francisco Rangel, Paolo Rosso, Martin Potthast, Benno Stein, and Walter Daelemans. 2015. Overview of the 3rd author profiling task at PAN 2015. In *CLEF*, page 2015. sn.

Marco T Ribeiro, Sameer Singh, and Carlos Guestrin. 2016. "why should i trust you?": Explaining the predictions of any classifier. In *Proceedings of the 22nd ACM SIGKDD International Conference on Knowledge Discovery and Data Mining*, KDD '16, page 1135–1144, New York, NY, USA. Association for Computing Machinery.

Sebastian Ruder, Matthew E. Peters, Swabha Swayamdipta, and Thomas Wolf. 2019. Transfer learning in natural language processing. In *Proceedings of the 2019 Conference of the North American Chapter of the Association for Computational Linguistics: Tutorials*, pages 15–18, Minneapolis, Minnesota. Association for Computational Linguistics.

H Andrew Schwartz, Johannes Eichstaedt, Margaret Kern, Gregory Park, Maarten Sap, David Stillwell, Michal Kosinski, and Lyle Ungar. 2014. Towards assessing changes in degree of depression through facebook. In *Proceedings of the workshop on computational linguistics and clinical psychology: from linguistic signal to clinical reality*, pages 118–125.

H Andrew Schwartz, Johannes C Eichstaedt, Margaret L Kern, Lukasz Dziurzynski, Stephanie M Ramones, Megha Agrawal, Achal Shah, Michal Kosinski, David Stillwell, Martin EP Seligman, et al. 2013. Personality, gender, and age in the language of social media: The open-vocabulary approach. *PloS one*, 8(9):e73791.

Sanja Stajner and Seren Yenikent. 2020. A survey of automatic personality detection from texts. In *Proceedings of the 28th International Conference on Computational Linguistics*, pages 6284–6295, Barcelona, Spain (Online). International Committee on Computational Linguistics.

David J Stillwell and Michal Kosinski. 2004. mypersonality project: Example of successful utilization of online social networks for large-scale social research. *American Psychologist*, 59(2):93–104.

Huy Vu, Suhaib Abdurahman, Sudeep Bhatia, and Lyle Ungar. 2020. Predicting responses to psychological questionnaires from participants' social media posts and question text embeddings. In *Proceedings of the 2020 Conference on Empirical Methods in Natural Language Processing: Findings*, pages 1512–1524.

Jason Wei and Kai Zou. 2019. EDA: Easy data augmentation techniques for boosting performance on text classification tasks. In *Proceedings of the 2019 Conference on Empirical Methods in Natural Language Processing and the 9th International Joint Conference on Natural Language Processing (EMNLP-IJCNLP)*, pages 6382–6388, Hong Kong, China. Association for Computational Linguistics.

A Appendix

A.1 Detailed Results per Class

	Class	*Psychometric Models* Plain P	R	F_1	EDA P	R	F_1	T5 P	R	F_1	GPT-2 P	R	F_1	*in-domain* P	R	F_1	*Baseline* P	R	F_1
Open.	−	.01	1.00	.01	.02	1.00	.04	.02	1.00	.04	**.02**	**1.00**	**.04**	.0	.0	.0	.01	.33	.03
	+	.0	.0	.0	.0	.0	.0	.0	.0	.0	**1.00**	**.02**	**.04**	.99	1.00	.99	.97	.50	.66
	AVG	.0	.50	.01	.01	.50	.02	.01	.50	.02	**.51**	**.51**	**.04**	.49	.50	.50	.49	.41	.34
	w-avg	.0	.01	.00	.0	.02	.0	.0	.02	.0	**.98**	**.04**	**.04**	.97	.99	.98	.95	.49	.64
Consc.	−	.07	.89	.13	.08	1.00	.15	**.0**	**.0**	**.0**	.08	1.00	.14	1.00	.17	.29	.05	.33	.09
	+	.80	.04	.07	1.00	.06	.12	**.93**	**.99**	**.96**	1.00	.03	.05	.96	1.00	.98	.90	.48	.63
	AVG	.43	.46	.10	.54	.53	.13	**.46**	**.50**	**.48**	.54	.51	.10	.96	.96	.94	.47	.41	.36
	w-avg	.75	.10	.07	.93	.13	.12	**.86**	**.92**	**.89**	.93	.10	.06	.78	.80	.73	.84	.47	.59
Extrav.	−	.09	1.00	.17	.09	1.00	.17	**.0**	**.0**	**.0**	.06	.42	.11	1.00	.14	.25	.08	.42	.13
	+	.0	.0	.0	.0	.0	.0	**.90**	**.92**	**.91**	.87	.38	.53	.90	1.00	.95	.89	.49	.63
	AVG	.05	.50	.08	.05	.50	.08	**.45**	**.46**	**.45**	.46	.40	.32	.95	.57	.60	.48	.45	.38
	w-avg	.01	.09	.02	.01	.09	.02	**.82**	**.83**	**.82**	.79	.38	.49	.91	.91	.87	.82	.48	.59
Agree.	−	.10	1.00	.19	**.18**	**.15**	**.17**	.08	.31	.12	.08	.62	.14	.0	.0	.0	.05	.23	.08
	+	.0	.0	.0	**.91**	**.92**	**.91**	.88	.59	.71	.77	.15	.25	.89	1.00	.94	.84	.46	.60
	AVG	.05	.50	.09	**.54**	**.54**	**.54**	.48	.45	.42	.42	.38	.19	.44	.50	.47	.44	.35	.34
	w-avg	.01	.10	.02	**.83**	**.84**	**.84**	.80	.56	.65	.70	.20	.24	.79	.89	.84	.76	.44	.55
Neur.	−	**.73**	**.93**	**.81**	.71	.78	.73	.73	.90	.80	.72	.91	.80	.73	1.00	.84	.66	.45	.53
	+	**.25**	**.06**	**.09**	.16	.10	.12	.23	.08	.12	.10	.03	.04	1.00	.12	.22	.19	.36	.25
	AVG	**.49**	**.50**	**.46**	.43	.45	.44	.47	.49	.46	.41	.47	.42	.86	.56	.53	.43	.41	.39
	w-avg	**.60**	**.70**	**.63**	.56	.60	.58	.58	.68	.62	.55	.66	.60	.81	.74	.65	.53	.43	.46

Table 4: Detailed results for *Psychometric Models* vs. *in-domain Models* vs. *Random Baseline* for psychological traits in Twitter users. The random baseline generates predictions by respecting the training sets' class distribution. The weighted average values for P, R, F_1 correspond to the average across all labels considering the proportion for each label in the data set. The bold typo highlights our best performing model w.r.t. the highest w-avg. −: scored negative, +: scored positive.

A.2 Implementation Details

We performed the experiments on 4 NVIDIA GeForce GTX 1080 Ti GPUs with Intel(R) Xeon(R) CPU E5-2650 v4 @ 2.20GH. The number of parameters is defined by the base model that we used, namely BERT base, with 110 M parameters.

We show the run-time of models (training + testing) in Table 5. The numbers do not include startup/loading times. Note that the test data is (sometimes dramatically) larger than the training data.

Concept	Model: Plain	EDA	T5	GPT-2
Depression	2460+3900	360+3900	900+3960	900+3960
Anxiety	450+2850	407+2905	921+2615	374+2584
ADHD	550+2650	380+2856	720+2100	875+2175
Openness	180+120	120+120	420+120	780+120
Conscientiousness	480+120	180+120	780+120	360+120
Extraversion	1020+120	180+120	420+120	720+120
Agreeableness	60+120	84+120	855+120	450+120
Neuroticism	474+120	85+120	400+120	650+120

Table 5: Runtime of models in seconds (train+test).

A.3 Examples for Augmentation Methods

- As an example for the EDA augmentation method, synonym replacement lead to "Love thinking about things" based on the IPIP-NEO-300 item "Enjoy thinking about things" for the trait of openness.
- As an example for the T5 augmentation method, T5-paraphrasing lead to "Have fun and be wildly inspired by wild fantasy dreams" based on the IPIP-NEO-300 item "Enjoy wild flights of fantasy" for the trait of openness.
- An example for a GPT-2 generated item measuring agreeableness is "I am an average person".

Author Index

Association for Computational Linguistics
209 N. Eighth Street
Stroudsburg, Pennsylvania 18360

ISBN 978-1-7138-6754-8